ABOUT THE AUTHORS

Patricia Casey is Professor of Clinical Psychiatry at University College Dublin and Consultant Psychiatrist in the Mater Misericordiae Hospital Dublin. She qualified as a doctor in University College Cork in 1976 and trained as a psychiatrist in Britain. She is the author of two books, *A Guide to Psychiatry in Primary Care* (Second Edition) and *Social Functioning: the Hidden Axis of Classification Exposed*. Her research interests include the epidemiology of depressive disorders, suicidal behaviour and personality disorder. She currently chairs the Fitness to Practice Committee of the Irish Medical Council.

Ciaran Craven is a Barrister, practising in Dublin. He qualified as a doctor in University College Dublin in 1983 before working for a number of years in the Defence Forces and in various clinical appointments. He read pharmacology in University College Dublin as a graduate and was a lecturer in the Medical School there for a number of years. He is the co-author (with Gerard Humphreys) of *Military Law in Ireland* and lectures on Medical Law in the Law School's LLM degree programme and in degree and diploma programmes of the Faculty of Health Sciences, Trinity College, Dublin.

PSYCHIATRY AND THE LAW

Patricia Casey
Ciaran Craven

Oak Tree Press

Dublin

Oak Tree Press
Merrion Building
Lower Merrion Street
Dublin 2, Ireland
http://www.oaktreepress.com

, 16697297

A catalogue record of this book is
available from the British Library.

ISBN 1-86076-069-4

Printed in Britain by MPG Books, Bodmin, Cornwall.

In memory of my parents
— Patricia Casey

In memory of my father
— Ciaran Craven

CONTENTS

PART FOUR: DISPOSING CAPACITY

FOREWORD

There is a growing recognition of the need for the law to have an understanding of other disciplines and for other disciplines to have an appreciation of the role they play within the law. Psychiatry is one discipline which is of direct relevance to various aspects of the law. It is important that those involved in the study and practice of the law and in the administration of justice understand the nature of psychiatry and its interaction with the law. It is equally important for psychiatry to comprehend the approach of legal practitioners to those aspects of the law that encompass consideration of mental illness, its diagnosis, study and treatment. A more informed discourse between the "medicalist" and "legalist" approaches would be invaluable to both disciplines, and this book represents a significant step in that direction.

Psychiatry and the Law provides those engaged in the practice and study of law with a very accessible insight into the field of psychiatry. It furnishes the reader with a useful and comprehensible background to the profession, while also highlighting some of the complexities and divergences within psychiatry. The authors have described the interaction, not only between psychiatry and the law, but also between psychiatry and various related disciplines, such as sociology, psychology and biology. This contextualisation is crucial in order for a person unversed in the language and theory of psychiatry to successfully appreciate and accommodate its role within a legal framework.

Part One of the book contains a highly interesting history and account of the development of psychiatry. The practice of psychiatry is described, and its relationship with other relevant disciplines considered. This section describes, in a clear and accessible manner, the approach of psychiatry to the classification, diagnosis, treatment and causation of disorders. Some of the divergences in the field of psychiatry are illustrated, such as those within the area of classification of disorders. It is crucial for a lawyer to have some comprehension of the means of classification and diagnosis of disorders, and this section of the book provides a very insightful guide in this regard.

Part Two deals with compensation for psychiatric disorders. It provides an account of how various disorders are viewed within the field of psychiatry. The authors provide a comprehensive and clear guide to how psychiatry assesses the effects of conduct such as sexual abuse and such incidents as mugging, and the possibility of treatment of these effects. The description of the legal approach towards these issues that ensues brings the contrast between the legal formulations and the psychiatric diagnoses into sharp focus.

In Part Three, the authors consider nullity of marriage, an area of the law in which the incapacity of a person frequently falls to be considered. This section describes the psychiatric analysis of personality disorder and sets out the relevant legal context. Part Four addresses the issue of disposing capacity, specifically testamentary capacity.

In Part Five, the authors consider the sphere of criminal law and its interaction with psychiatry. Particular attention is drawn to the fact that the legal label of "insanity" has long since departed from the medical lexicon. It is precisely such divergence between the two schools which both the law and psychiatry should endeavour to overcome. In this regard, the authors express the widely held view that the medical profession has a significant contribution to make in relation to the issue of criminal responsibility and the hope that the legalist school of thought will concede the role of psychiatry in this context.

The final section of this fine work concerns what the authors term "the high-water mark of the 'medicalist' approach of the law". This is the area of control of the psychiatrically disordered.

This highly interesting and informative work draws together the many contexts in which law and psychiatry interact. In considering these issues, the authors apply both legal and psychiatric analysis, rendering both accessible to the reader who may be unversed in the language of law or modern psychiatry.

The book marks an important acknowledgement of the interdependence between psychiatry and the law. Through such collation of sources and approaches, this interdependence may develop, enhancing the ability of each school of thought to understand and accommodate the other.

By means of the clear and insightful analysis of how psychiatry addresses the classification, diagnosis and treatment of various disorders, the authors have helped to demystify the field of psychiatry. This will be invaluable to those engaged in the practice of law. The various legal issues of concern have similarly been drawn together and described in a clear, comprehensible fashion. Such accessible accounts of the legal issues may contribute towards the development of a more evidence-based, scientific focus within psychiatry, which would be more easily accommodated in the law.

These developments would serve the interests of both psychiatry and the law, as well as facilitating the interaction between them. It is anticipated that this fine work will herald an enhanced discourse between the two and mark a step closer towards an informed interaction between psychiatry and the law.

Finally, I would add that, as a Judge of the Central Criminal Court, I find interesting the authors' observation that studies of the effects of sexual assaults on males are sparse. Such cases are currently increasing at an exponential rate, and I would expect an analysis of the Bills of Indictment a decade from now that will show that gender equality has been achieved.

Paul Carney
The High Court
Dublin 7

November 1998

PREFACE

The history of the interaction between law and psychiatry is characterised by a tension between the "medicalist" and the "legalist"
approaches. Evident in all areas, from the negligent infliction of
emotional suffering, through the law on testamentary capacity,
capacity for marriage, criminal "insanity", fitness to plead and
involuntary committal, the competing approaches have frequently
left a sense of bewilderment and bemusement among medical
practitioners. Legal practitioners, for their part, seem to approach
the issues raised on the basis of concepts of disease and disease
causation that often do not accurately reflect the complex clinical
constructs from which they are drawn. And, whereas the object of
clinical intervention by psychiatrists is essentially confined to the
well-being — in a fairly restricted sense — of the individual patient, the concerns of the lawyer are more diverse, ranging from
issues of property rights to individual safety and the protection of
the public interest. It is hoped that this book will be of use to legal
and medical practitioners and students and that it will illuminate
the penumbra between the two disciplines.

The text, which adopts a thematic approach, seeks to set out, in
an accessible format, a broad range of relatively specialised clinical information in a relevant legal context. It is essentially descriptive in nature. Exhaustive analytical treatment of many of
the legal issues that arise and that are available elsewhere —
particularly in the area of criminal responsibility — is beyond the
remit of this book. The legal chapters, which in all but Parts One
and Six, run in tandem with the chapters setting out the relevant
clinical information, seek to relate that information to forensic
practice in order to provide an accessible portal of entry into that
foreign country that many regard is modern psychiatry.

The book comprises six separate — but linked — parts. Part One begins by describing the nature of psychiatry as a clinical speciality and setting out its scientific research- and evidence-based approach to disease causation, classification, investigation and treatment. Memory, an issue of fundamental importance in legal proceedings, is considered in the context of its biological basis. The discussion then extends to consideration of the controversial areas of false allegations and recovered memories. Part Two goes on to consider the variety of psychiatric conditions that may accompany, or result from, personal injury and outlines the judicial concerns, fears and limitations that have emerged in the last one hundred years. It is hoped that a rigorous, scientific, evidence-based approach by psychiatrists to this contentious area of litigation will inform forensic attitudes to such claims in the future.

Part Three enters the area of nullity of marriage. Although the nullity jurisdiction of our courts has traditionally been relatively small in numerical terms — and it remains to be seen precisely what effect the introduction of divorce will have — nevertheless, it continues to be an issue of fundamental importance in any legal order. As most applications for decrees of nullity, in recent times, with the exception of those claiming duress or lack of consent, have been premised on the relational incapacity of one or both parties to the marriage sought to be annulled, this part deals extensively with the psychiatry of personality disorder, its categorisation, causation, assessment and treatment. It then proceeds to consider other conditions that may ground nullity applications, from major psychotic disorders through to sexual dysfunction and gender role disorders. Part Four deals with disposing capacity, an issue of considerable personal and social importance. Although regulated by statute insofar as the formal validity of wills is concerned, the assessment of testamentary capacity falls to be ultimately governed by case-law. As property ownership has increased — even modest family homes now command considerable sums in the marketplace — and as the population over the age of 65 is increasing dramatically, consideration of the effects of chronic organic brain disease and the dementias on disposing capacity takes on a wider importance than heretofore. Not only might chronic brain disease be problematic in this regard, but major psychotic and personality disorders must also be dealt with in this context. A classic instance of the tension between the "medicalist" and "legalist" approach to the same issue, the law on testamentary capacity has resoundingly endorsed the latter.

Part Five deals with the nub of the interaction between psychiatry and the law — criminal responsibility, an issue that is crying out for coherent statutory reform. Previous, more elegant calls for significant statutory codification have repeatedly failed to sway what appears to be the natural indolence of government on this issue. Although major psychotic disorder is a main concern of psychiatrists in this difficult area, many of the cases involve conditions that are generally not psychiatric in nature at all. They are included with such conditions in the law on criminal responsibility for reasons that have more to do with the history of the common law construct of the "mind" than with any coherent consideration of intent. In relation to fitness to plead, the obvious anomalies and inconsistencies, it is hoped, will be coherently addressed by the detailed proposals for statutory reform that have been in the public domain for over three years. Although "legalist" in nature, the indications are that law reform will adopt a more "medicalist" approach.

Part Six, on the control of those suffering from a psychiatric disability, represents the high-water mark of the "medicalist" approach of the law to psychiatry. However, in recent years, increasing judicial intervention, at the behest of patients who considered their involuntary detention in psychiatric facilities unlawful or unwarranted, has reclaimed forensic control of a system that is essentially administrative and in the hands of psychiatrists. Although substantial reform has been promised, the history of legislative revision in this area does not augur rapid repeal. Consent to treatment and research and patient confidentiality, issues of critical importance to the practice of medicine generally, assume particular importance in the field of psychiatry. These are also dealt with in this Part.

Throughout, the information — whether clinical or case-law — has been presented in as broad a context as possible. However, the treatment of certain areas is so jurisdiction-specific, especially in relation to nullity and the involuntary control of persons suffering from a psychiatric disability, that discussion and description is confined to domestic law. Extensive comparative analysis in these areas is beyond the remit of a text of this nature.

As always, completion of a work of this kind does not proceed in isolation and debt is owed to many others. Dr Art O'Connor, Consultant Psychiatrist at the Central Mental Hospital in Dundrum, provided constructive advice. The staff of the Law Library in the Four Courts in Dublin were, as always, of assistance in obtaining both the new and obscure references and thanks are due to them. Various colleagues at the Bar, perhaps unwittingly and unknowingly, helped to clarify issues that seemed shrouded in an intellectual fog, and to them — Brendan Grogan SC, Bernard Barton SC, Paul McDermott BL, Karen Fergus BL, Ann Power BL and Brendan Watchorn BL — a debt of gratitude is also owed. To Jarlath Spellman BL, who kindly read several draft chapters and made useful suggestions, and provided additional material, a special word of thanks is due. The patience of the publishers Oak Tree Press was of biblical proportions while deadlines were missed, and the excuses became more outlandish. Brian Langan, who edited the final text, is owed particular thanks. Thank you also to our colleagues, family and friends who provided the moral support and encouragement, without whom this work would never have been completed. To our long-suffering spouses and children, thank you. Finally, we would like to express our deep gratitude to the Hon. Mr Justice Paul Carney for writing the Foreword.

Where errors and omissions occur, they remain solely the responsibility of the authors, who would be grateful to receive comments and suggestions on the text. The position stated is as at 1 August 1998.

Patricia M. Casey
Ciaran D. Craven
November 1998

TABLE OF CASES

TABLE OF STATUTES

CONSTITUTION OF IRELAND, 1937

IRISH PUBLIC STATUTES

Pre-Independence British Public Statutes

Irish Statutory Instruments

BRITISH STATUTORY INSTRUMENTS

EUROPEAN CONVENTIONS AND LEGISLATION

GLOSSARY OF COMMON PSYCHIATRIC SYMPTOMS

Clang association: use of words based on similarity of sound without regard to their meaning. Seen in hypomania and mania.

Concrete thinking: the inability to think abstractly. Seen in schizophrenia.

Confabulation: a detailed description of an event which is false. May occur in antisocial personality disorder and in Korsakoff's psychosis.

Delusion: a false, fixed belief that is outside the common cultural beliefs. The content may be varied: e.g. persecution; hypochondria; reference (radio programme referring to the subject); grandeur (the subject is a film star); nihilism (the subject is dead or part of the body is missing); poverty, etc. Found in schizophrenia, severe depressive illness and organic states.

Delusional mood: the feeling that something strange is afoot. May crystallise into a specific delusion.

Depersonalisation: a feeling of being distant, detached, looking from the outside or "outside oneself". Occurs most commonly in severe anxiety or depressive illness. Can occur in any psychiatric illness and in healthy adults in association with hunger or exhaustion.

Derealisation: a feeling that nearby objects are remote or distant even though the subject knows this not to be the case. The converse of depersonalisation and occurs in similar settings.

Echo de pensée: a hallucination in which the subject hears his own thoughts spoken aloud just as he has thought them. One of Schneider's first rank symptoms of schizophrenia.

Emotional resonance: the ability to feel both sad and happy. In depressive illness, there may be loss of emotional resonance so that the patient describes an inability to feel.

Flight of ideas: the subject moves rapidly from subject to subject in conversation. There is a loose connection between the themes. Seen in hypomania and mania.

Hallucination: a perception without a stimulus (e.g. hearing a voice when there is nobody about; seeing a person when there is no person in the vicinity). Hallucination can be derived from any of the senses. They are found in a similar range of disorders to delusions, but also in non-psychiatric disorders such as epilepsy.

Illusion: an erroneous perception or a misinterpretation of a stimulus, e.g. mistaking a design on wallpaper for insects.

Mannerism: the unusual repetition of a goal-directed action or an adaptation of it, e.g. flicking back ones hair even when it is short. Seen in all psychiatric disorders as well as in normal subjects.

Made feelings: see passivity feelings.

Neologisms: new words created by the subject which have their own personal meaning. Seen in schizophrenia.

Obsessions: preoccupation with a particular theme or problem so that the subject is unable to get rid of it and its presence is associated with severe anxiety. Resistance to the preoccupation is common. Obsessions may be images, ideas, fears or impulses. Obsessional ideas are also called ruminations and consist of a preoccupation with numbers or thoughts (e.g. why is the sky blue, why is 10 plus 10 equal to 20?). Obsessional impulse may be associated with the impulse to wash the hands repeatedly. They occur most commonly in depressive illness and obsessive compulsive disorder but can occur in schizophrenia. Obsessions, which are not psychotic phenomena, must be distinguished from passivity feelings, which are psychotic in nature. The patient will describe the former as coming from his own thoughts and from within himself, whereas the latter will be felt as coming from an outside force.

Overvalued idea: a firmly held false belief which can be argued away. It represents a delusion in formation and can suddenly crystallise into a delusion.

Passivity feelings: the delusion that the subject's actions or thoughts or emotions or impulses are under the control of an outside force. It must be distinguished from the belief that one is guided by God or by parents. The feeling is specific to a particular thought, impulse, emotion or action (e.g. "When I walked into my room today my leg was lifted by an alien force."). Seen most commonly in schizophrenia and included among Schneider's first rank symptoms.

Perseveration: excessive repetition of a word or activity. Seen in schizophrenia and in organic brain disease.

Phobia: an irrational fear that is associated with anxiety on exposure to the feared object.

Pressure of speech: very rapid flow of speech so that words "tumble" out. Seen in hypomania and mania.

Primary delusion: a delusion that arises suddenly and without any underlying hallucination provoking it.

Psychomotor retardation: the slowing of physical and/or mental processes. Seen in severe depressive illness.

Resonance: see emotional resonance.

Ruminations: see obsessions.

Stereotypy: the repetition of a non-goal-directed movement (e.g. bizarre hand movements). Seen in schizophrenia.

Systematised delusions: there is a single core delusion and the remainder of the system or story is built on this error. Seen in schizophrenia.

Thought broadcasting: the delusion that one's thoughts are being aired to the world.

Thought insertion: the delusion that a specific thought(s) is being inserted by an outside force as one is thinking. One of Schneider's first rank symptoms of schizophrenia, but can be found in mania also.

Thought withdrawal: the delusion that a specific thought(s) is being taken out of one's mind as one is thinking. One of Schneider's first rank symptoms of schizophrenia but can be found in mania also.

Vorbeireden: also called "talking past the point". The answer that a subject gives indicates that he understands the question, although the answer is ridiculous (e.g. Q: what colour is grass? A: blue!). Found in schizophrenia and Ganser syndrome (hysterical pseudodementia — now believed to be a variant of schizophrenia).

Word salad: an incoherent jumble of words and phrases that lack coherence or a comprehensive meaning. Seen in schizophrenia. Could be confused with severe flight of ideas.

Part One

INTRODUCTION TO PSYCHIATRY

Chapter 1

THE ORIGINS OF PSYCHIATRY

Until the fifth century BC, the Greeks and Romans recognised only those mental disturbances which were clearly associated with physical illness. There were no institutions for the mentally ill and care was provided by the family. Those homeless insane who were seen as harmless were allowed to wander whilst those who were regarded as dangerous were either executed or exiled.[1] In the fifth century BC Hippocrates argued that mental functioning, including emotion, emanated from the brain. He viewed madness as arising from disturbances of the brain and the healthy functioning of the brain arose from the correct mixture of elements known as humours. The four humours were described as phlegmatic, choleric, sanguine and melancholic. The relative amounts led to particular personality disorders and treatment consisted of restoring the proper balance to these humours with medicines and education about diet and other environmental factors believed to be responsible.

THE PRACTICE OF PSYCHIATRY BEGINS

In 1600 the first licence to practice on "the melancholy and the mad" was issued by the Archbishop of Canterbury to John Freeman. It marked the first official recognition in England of the speciality of psychiatry, distinguishing between depression and other forms of insanity. Indeed the first prosecution for incompetence in treating the insane was recorded in 1614. At this time, mental

---

[1] J.G. Howells (1975), *World History of Psychiatry*, New York: Brunner Mazel.

illness was largely the concern of the clergy rather than the physician. However, the seventeenth century saw the clear recognition of melancholy, pseudocyesis, *folie à deux* and hypochondriasis. In addition the seventeenth century saw a growth of interest in the localisation of psychiatric disorders, stimulated particularly by the philosopher Francis Bacon who advocated investigation of the interaction between mind and body, and of the role of social factors. His interest in anatomical causes were the most popular. Bleeding became a popular treatment for mental illness, encouraged by a growth in knowledge about the circulatory system. Thomas Willis (1621–75) described dementia praecox (later called schizophrenia) and distinguished it from "passions of the heart", the latter being equivalent to depression, and also from other psychological states known today as emotional disorders.

After the Plague and the Great Fire of London, the desire to rebuild the city was paralleled by the erection of mental institutions and in 1676 the new Bethlem Hospital for the treatment of the insane was constructed. Treatments included bleeding, purging and the administration of emetics but its function was mainly custodial. Outside London, the insane who could not be cared for at home were admitted to general hospitals; Bristol's St Peter's Hospital, in 1696, was the first to provide a specific ward for the insane poor.

THE RIGHTS OF THE MENTALLY ILL ARE RECOGNISED

In the eighteenth century, private madhouses flourished in Britain and became a profitable trade. However, their reputation was so bad that the government appointed a select committee to inquire into their affairs. Daniel Defoe, the author of *Robinson Crusoe*, was among the campaigners. Jonathan Swift was equally interested in mental illness and became one of the Governors of Bethlem. He founded the first private institution for the insane in Dublin in 1746. In Ireland, the poor were provided for by St Brendan's Hospital, Grangegorman, built a few years later in 1748. During the latter half of the eighteenth century, several institutions were built in Britain, stimulated by the illness of the reigning monarch, George III. Not only did the populace at large become aware of psychiatric illness, but an Act of Parliament in 1774 emphasised that inmates of asylums were to be cured and no longer regarded as hopeless and only in need of asylum. The increasing acceptance of the necessity for humane treatments for the mentally ill resulted in an Act of Parliament in 1808 recommending the creation of asylums in every county. The opening of The Retreat in York in 1796 by the Society of Friends, at the instigation of William Tuke, with its emphasis on minimal restraint and treatment, was a landmark in the development of humane treatments.[2] The concept of criminal responsibility also emerged from this period. Two attempts on the life of George III resulted in the accused being found insane and sent to a psychiatric institution rather than to prison.[3]

Today, the compulsory treatment of the mentally ill in Britain is governed by the terms of the Mental Health Act, 1983, which specifies the criteria for such detention, the right to appeal, the duration of detention and administrative issues relating to compulsory detention. There is a separate but similar Act for Scotland. In Ireland, the Mental Treatment Act, 1945, is still operational despite its age. The diagnostic criteria for compulsory admission are not included and the Act is largely concerned with administrative issues.[4] There is little *inherent* protection for the patient; rather, this derives from common law.[5] It is anticipated that new legislation will be brought forward in the future.[6]

---

[2] See also M. Finnane (1981), *Insanity and the Insane in Post-Famine Ireland*, London: Croom Helm.

[3] *Hadfield's case* (*R* v *Hadfield* (1800) 27 St. Tr. 1281).

[4] See Chapter 18 below.

[5] See, for example, *T(R)* v *Director of the Central Mental Hospital & Others* [1995] 2 ILRM 354, High Court, Costello J; and *SC* v *Smith & Others* (Supreme Court, Unreported Judgment, 31 July 1996).

[6] In July 1995, the Department of Health published a White Paper on a New Mental Health Act.

SPECIALISATION IN PSYCHIATRY

Towards the middle of the nineteenth century, psychiatric disorders of childhood were beginning to attract attention, initially with the emphasis being on mental handicap. In the first years of this century, psychiatrists began to develop an interest in delinquency and the first child guidance/psychiatric unit, the Chicago Juvenile Psychopathic Institute, was pioneered by William Healy in 1909. This clinic used not only psychiatrists but also psychologists, social workers and pathologists.

Other specialities in psychiatry have a more recent origin. These include substance abuse and rehabilitation which developed in the 1960s and liaison psychiatry (the psychiatry of physical illness), which has only been in existence as a speciality since the 1970s. The importance of psychological aspects of physical illness has been articulated since the 1930s, particularly in the United States, when the psychosomatic school of psychiatry flourished. Although the excessive zeal of this approach, which held that specific disorders, such as ulcerative colitis and rheumatoid arthritis, had a psychological origin, has been a source of embarrassment to many in modern psychiatry, it did serve to mark the importance of factors other than organic ones in the disease process. Interestingly, the mechanisms by which psychological processes affect physical states are now being delineated using scientific methodology and include the effects of hormone release on the immune system.

THE DELINEATION OF SPECIFIC DISORDERS

The disorder which has the longest history — although not the most venerable — is hysteria. It was described by Hippocrates and was believed to be due to the wandering womb, being particularly likely to afflict virgins and widows. The theories of Hippocrates also heralded the development of the concept of personality disorder, although the terms used (e.g. sanguine) have now been eclipsed in psychiatry by other nosologies. However, these early words still remain part of everyday parlance.

The term neurosis was coined by William Cullen (1710–90), who favoured an organic cause for these conditions, although Freud later held that their origins lay in childhood sexual traumas. It would seem that the wheel has come full circle, with theorists now proposing a neurochemical basis for at least some neuroses such as obsessive-compulsive disorder and most cases of hysteria.

Generalised anxiety was identified by Hecker in 1893 and phobias by Westphal in 1871, although it is Freud's descriptions and explanations which are best remembered. Schizophrenia and manic-depressive illness were identified and distinguished from each other by Kraeplin towards the end of the nineteenth century. In 1913, his classification gained widespread recognition when the American Medico-Psychological Association (later renamed the American Psychiatric Association) incorporated it into their new nomenclature. The Kraeplinian dichotomy was based on prognosis, with schizophrenia (dementia praecox) believed to run a progressive and deteriorating course whilst manic-depression relapsed and remitted without any personality deterioration.

Other disorders such as anorexia nervosa have a long history, although they are sometimes believed to be late twentieth century conditions. Gull (1868)[7] and Lesague (1873)[8] described anorexia nervosa although the elements of the disorder had been documented prior to this. Similarly, post-traumatic stress disorder had been recognised for several centuries, although it was only after the First World War that the condition began to achieve diagnostic respectability in the form of "combat neurosis" or "shell shock". The aftermath of the Vietnam War led to a further increase in numbers diagnosed with this condition and hence to its inclusion in DSM-III, the system of psychiatric classification used in the United States, a few years later. More recent disorders to achieve

---

[7] W.W. Gull (1868), "The Address in Medicine to the Annual Meeting of the British Medical Association at Oxford", *Lancet*, 8 August, pp. 171–6.

[8] E.C. Lesague (1873), "On Hysterical Anorexia", *Medical Times Gazette*, Vol. 2, pp. 265–9.

nosological status are bulimia nervosa in 1979[9] and panic disorder in 1980 when it was included in DSM-III.

Thus, it is apparent that the recognition of disorders is evolutionary although not all of these "entities" have been validated (see Chapter 3).

PSYCHIATRY AS A PROFESSION

The first professional body for psychiatrists in Britain, the Association of Medical Officers of Hospitals for the Insane, was established in 1841. In 1971, it became the Royal College of Psychiatrists. A number of publications have emanated from this body. In 1853 it began publishing its own journal, the *Asylum Journal*, later becoming the *Journal of Mental Science*. It is now called the *British Journal of Psychiatry* and is published monthly.

The training of the psychiatrist is lengthy and begins first with a medical degree similar to that obtained by any medical consultant. After the internship year, at the end of which the doctor is now fully recognised to practice clinical medicine and is registered with the Medical Council, the aspiring psychiatrist enters a scheme of training which must be approved by the representative college of psychiatrists. In Ireland and Britain, the Royal College of Psychiatrists accredits and reviews training as well as setting the professional examinations. The initial training takes a minimum of three years, during which the trainee sits two examinations. At the end of this, the trainee enters a period of higher training which lasts up to four years, although it may be slightly shorter if the person is appointed as a consultant before that. This period of higher training is rarely less than three years. During higher training, additional skills are obtained and the doctor chooses the area of specialisation in which he or she will work (e.g. child psychiatry). Research interests are also developed during this time. Thus, from the time the decision to enter medicine

---

[9] G.F.M. Russell (1979), "Bulimia Nervosa: an Ominous Variant of Anorexia Nervosa", *Psychological Medicine*, Vol. 9, p. 429.

is made until a consultant position is obtained, a minimum of 13 years will have elapsed.

There are several specialities within psychiatry. These are adult psychiatry, child and adolescent psychiatry, old age psychiatry, rehabilitation, substance abuse, psychotherapy, mental handicap, forensic psychiatry and liaison psychiatry. Community and social psychiatry is the newest addition to the list of specialities but there is doubt as to its specificity, since almost all adult psychiatrists now work in the community setting (see below) as distinct from the long-term institutional setting.

ORGANISATION OF SERVICES

The imperative to provide psychiatric institutions on an area basis, as described above, led to the division of services by geographic area. In this way, the administration and responsibility of services evolved quite separately from that of general medical services. This geographic cover continues to the present in both Britain and Ireland and to a lesser but increasing extent in the US and continental Europe. The units of responsibility are referred to as catchment areas and these have recently been divided into smaller units called sectors.[10] Each sector has a consultant psychiatrist and other professionals known collectively as the multidisciplinary team. This includes psychiatrists in training, community nurses, nurse therapists, psychologists and social workers. Each sector service has access to acute in-patient beds in a designated hospital, increasingly being based in a general hospital, as well as access to hostel accommodation for those requiring longer term care and day hospital facilities. A catchment area is made up of several sectors and this unit of service in turn is headed administratively by a clinical director (previously called a resident medical superintendent).[11] This organisational structure

---

[10] Department of Health (1984), *The Psychiatric Services: Planning for the Future*.

[11] Mental Treatment Act, 1945, s. 94. A health board is obliged to appoint a resident medical superintendent in respect of each psychiatric hospital under its functional control. Although it is proposed to formally replace the post

has been in operation in Britain since the early 1980s and is still developing in Ireland. It is defined by law in Britain although only *de facto* in Ireland because of the age of the Mental Treatment Act, 1945. In spite of this, the development of sector services is part of government policy, outlined in *Planning for the Future*, which it is anticipated will be enshrined in proposed new mental health legislation.[12]

Community Psychiatry

The concept of community psychiatry is not a new one; it has been in operation in Britain since the 1960s. In the past decade, it has been boosted in Ireland and Britain by government policy. Community psychiatry involves both the early discharge of patients from in-patient treatment and the holding of out-patient clinics in convenient locations such as health centres and general practitioners' surgeries. The community psychiatrist would treat most patients as out-patients, as in general medical practice, where necessary referring the patient to a day hospital or more rarely for brief in-patient treatment. The shift in approach from asylum to treatment is the direct result of the dramatic progress that has been made in understanding the aetiology of psychiatric disorders as well as the great strides that have been made in treatment.

A further and more high profile aspect of community psychiatry has been the transfer of long-stay patients from institutions into smaller more compact units "in the community" including high, medium and low support hostels as well as into independent accommodation. In many instances, these hostels are identical to hospital wards in terms of nursing and medical input except that they are outside the traditional institution, and their patients are known as the "old long-stay" group. However, "new long-stay" patients, who have repeated admissions and have difficulty func-

---

with that of clinical director under the proposals for the implementation of a new Mental Health Act, as suggested by the White Paper on a New Mental Health Act, para. 11.8, the practice has, in fact, commenced.

[12] Department of Health (1995), White Paper on a New Mental Health Act, para. 1.8.

tioning outside an institutional setting, are accumulating at a rate of about 1/100,000 of the population and these are now being admitted for long-term care to high or medium support hostels but with a view to achieving greater independence after rehabilitation, where possible.

Recent trends in acute hospital stay demonstrate that 45 per cent of patients are discharged within two weeks of admission, 65 per cent within one month and only 8 per cent remain in hospital for longer than three months.[13] (The figures add up to more than 100 per cent because of readmissions during the study period.) Moreover, the diagnostic profile of patients has shifted from psychotic disorders such as schizophrenia or manic-depressive illness to less serious illnesses such as depressive illness, eating disorders, alcohol abuse and stress related conditions. This shift is not because those suffering from schizophrenia or manic-depression are no longer referred to psychiatrists, but because more patients overall are being referred, as psychiatry becomes less stigmatised, more scientific and overwhelmingly moves away from asylum into the arena of treatment.

PSYCHOLOGY AND PSYCHIATRY

It is impossible to provide an all-inclusive definition of psychology and psychiatry, but to use a simple one, psychology can be defined as the study and treatment of abnormal behaviour, whilst psychiatry is the study and treatment of mental illness. As both have evolved, there is considerable overlap, since many psychologists use their skills of assessment in the measurement and treatment of illness, whilst psychiatrists include a range of behavioural disorders and phobias within their clinical ambit.

Since the middle of the nineteenth century, psychology had been concerned with the assessment of intelligence, reaction time and motor skills. The first incursion of clinical psychology into therapy was in the United States with the establishment of a

---

[13] R. Moran and D. Walsh (1993), *Activities of Irish Psychiatric Hospitals and Units 1991*, Dublin: Health Research Board.

child guidance clinic in Chicago in 1909 under the aegis of William Healy. Nevertheless, until the Second World War their role was largely one of assessment and measurement of psychological disorders and functioning. During the war they were increasingly utilised in the assessment of army and ancillary personnel and because of the scarcity of psychiatrists and army medical doctors to treat and rehabilitate war casualties, clinical psychologists increasingly found a role in this area. Initially, the work was individual and based largely on Freudian psychodynamics. In the 1960s, the theories and writings of researchers like Skinner[14] led to the development of behaviour therapy and proved to be a natural focus for the attention of clinical psychologists, increasingly disenchanted with the time-consuming approaches in use up to that time. Thus the 1970s saw a further expansion of the role of psychologists as therapists, a role often castigated by psychiatrists and viewed as a threat by them.

Training in Clinical Psychology

Academic psychology is studied in universities, usually as part of the arts faculty but in some institutions under the umbrella of the science faculty. The training of clinical psychologists is approved by their professional body and membership of this body thus confers evidence of appropriate training and standards. The training for a clinical psychologist consists of a primary degree in psychology, at honours standard. Thereafter, the aspiring clinical psychologist has to obtain a place in an accredited training course, located in a university. This normally takes two years during which time the trainee treats patients under supervision and writes a dissertation based on his research.

Friction

Not only have psychiatrists and psychologists often been adversaries in relation to their clinical roles, but in the past 15 years the training and establishment of nurses as behaviour, and

---

[14] B.F. Skinner (1963), "Behaviourism at Fifty", *Science*, Vol. 140, pp. 951–8.

cognitive therapists[15] has led to another layer of friction between clinical psychologists and nurse therapists. The latter are seen as potentially usurping the role of the clinical psychologist, although this attitude is certainly not universal. Economic forces have also come to the fore in this issue, since administrators/employers regard nurse therapists as less costly to employ than clinical psychologists and therefore more cost-effective. Others argue that nurse therapists have a limited theoretical base, being trained as practitioners rather than theoreticians, and are therefore less flexible in their interventions than are clinical psychologists.

CONCLUSION

Psychiatry is now a recognised part of medicine with a scientific pedigree. The contribution of other disciplines has led to an eclectic approach to understanding and treating psychiatric disorders in settings similar to those used by other medical professionals. The rights of the mentally ill are clearly recognised and these have been incorporated into legislation throughout Europe. Further legislation is awaited in Ireland.

---

[15] D. Ginsberg, I. Marks and H. Waters (1984), "Cost-Benefit Analysis of a Controlled Trial of Nurse Therapy for Neurosis in Primary Care", *Psychological Medicine*, Vol. 14, pp. 683–90.

Chapter 2

THE SCIENTIFIC BASIS OF PSYCHIATRY

WHAT IS DISEASE?

Among physicians, as among the lay public, there is no concept more fundamental yet more elusive than that of disease or illness. Implicit in its use is the belief that there is a single, unambiguous, all-embracing definition of illness. On further reflection, however, it is apparent that this is not the case, no less in psychiatry than in surgery or any other branch of medicine. Is the common cold an illness? Is a fracture a disease? Is pregnancy an illness and if not why do doctors become involved? Within psychiatry, debate has raged about the disease status of alcoholism, homosexuality and personality disorder; some on the fringes of psychiatry even challenge the disease concept of schizophrenia. Despite the sometimes acrimonious and politicised nature of these controversies, they have not led to a concise definition of disease and illness. Interestingly, the uncertainty about disease and its definition is not confined to psychiatry. For example, doctors regard disorders due to infections as diseases, whilst those due to the effects of chemical or physical agents are less likely to be so defined, although this varies with the branch of medicine. Moreover, lay people have different and narrower concepts of illness.[1]

---

[1] E.J.M. Campbell, J.G. Scadding and R.S. Roberts (1979), "The Concept of Disease", *British Medical Journal*, Vol. 2, pp. 757–62. Distinctions also appear to arise from judicial dicta, especially in the area of nullity. Thus, in *JSJ* v *RSJ* [1982] ILRM 263, the issue was an "illness"; in *D* v *C* [1984] ILRM 175 (Costello J), it was "psychiatric disability"; in *UF (orse C)* v *JC*

Even consideration of any dictionary meaning of disease is unhelpful, describing it in terms such as "any impairment of normal physiological function affecting an organism, especially a change caused by infection, stress etc. producing characteristic symptoms". This does not take account of asymptomatic disorders and focuses on physiological function rather than anatomical or psychological function. Moreover, it fails to delineate the limits of "normality" which shift with changes in medical knowledge.

Disease is what Doctors Treat

A number of approaches have been adopted in an attempt to clarify the issue. The most basic definition is to describe disease as that which doctors treat. This introduces the element of therapeutic concern.[2] However, a broad definition such as this would include even those who did not require treatment but believed they did, such as those with hypochondriasis. Moreover, it would exclude those who had no knowledge of or insight into their illness as well as those who deny illness — a problem particularly pertinent to psychiatry. This would also lead to the politicisation of the medical profession, as in the Nazi concentration camps where doctors decided which lives were "unworthy of life", or as in the psychiatric practice of the USSR where, until recently, psychiatric disorder was defined circularly as that which required treatment. This included political dissent. Defining disease as that which doctors treat or as that which doctors say requires treatment is so nebulous as to be dangerous.

Disease is a Lesion

Developments in anatomy and histology led to the knowledge that disease was frequently accompanied by structural changes at a

---

[1991] 2 IR 330, it was an "inherent quality or characteristic"; and in *S* v *K* [1993] 1 FamLJ 18, it was an "inherent psychiatric disorder". Given the thrust of *UF (orse C)* v *JC*, however, the distinctions previously apparent in the written judgments seem illusory.

[2] K. Taylor (1979), *The Concept of Illness, Disease and Morbus*, Cambridge: Cambridge University Press.

macroscopic or even a microscopic level. Subsequent developments in biochemistry and physiology led to an expansion of the concept to include changes in these areas as constituting diseases also. Thus the presence of a lesion — anatomical, biochemical or physiological — led to a definition of the lesion as the illness or disease. In psychiatry this would cause problems, for example in relation to phobias where no lesion is visible. Even in general medicine, this would pose problems in relation to minor anatomical abnormalities such as harelip or short-sightedness which, according to this view, should be regarded as diseases. It was the belief that lesions were necessary for disease which led Thomas Szasz[3] of the anti-psychiatry school to suggest that since no definable lesion was present in schizophrenia, it could not be regarded as an illness. History has of course proved him wrong, but his position illustrates the limitations of this approach.

Disease is a Plan of Action

This is the pragmatic approach[4] which asks the question: "Is it appropriate that this person should be under medical care?" Underpinning this is the belief that medical intervention is likely to be helpful. This poses special problems in relation to the personality disorders for which, as yet, there is no effective treatment, but where other guiding principles obtain, i.e. should this person be held responsible for his actions? In the context of the courts, this question replaces the question of whether the sufferer would benefit from treatment. In arguing for the pragmatic approach, it is recognised that there is no unifying definition of illness and that it is defined only by the availability of treatment and ability to treat. This would exclude certain disorders currently classified as belonging within the body of psychiatry (i.e. personality disorders) but would also exclude medical disorders which are as yet

---

[3] T. Szasz (1960), "The Myth of Mental Illness", *American Psychologist*, Vol. 15, pp. 113–18.

[4] R. Linder (1965), "Diagnosis: Description or Prescription? A Case Study in the Psychology of Diagnosis", *Perceptual and Motor Skill*, Vol. 20, pp. 1081–92.

untreatable (e.g. muscular dystrophy). Clearly, a definition of disease which is tied to therapeutic availability is unsatisfactory.

Disease is Statistical Abnormality

This definition holds that changes from the statistical norm (e.g. blood pressure) constitute the basis for illness. This has limitations, since it does not distinguish those statistical deviations which are harmful (e.g. high blood sugar), those which are neutral (e.g. height), and those which are advantageous (e.g. high IQ). Scadding[5] expanded this definition and suggested that the abnormal feature must place the individual at a biological disadvantage.

Disease is Biological Disadvantage

The definition of disease offered by Scadding has found favour with many doctors.[6] It states that a disease is

> the sum total of the abnormal phenomena displayed by a group of living organisms in association with a specified common characteristic or set of characteristics by which they differ from the norm of their species in such a way as to place them at a biological disadvantage.

Inherent in the definition is deviation from the statistical norm, thus requiring an arbitrary boundary between health and sickness. Another problem arises in relation to the question of biological disadvantage — whose disadvantage? A disadvantage to the individual may be an advantage to the population as a whole. For example, certain genetic disorders confer benefits on the population who carries that particular trait; e.g. carriers of the gene for sickle cell anaemia are protected against malaria.

---

[5] J.G. Scadding (1967), "Diagnosis: The Clinician and the Computer", *Lancet*, Vol. 2, pp. 877–82.

[6] R.E. Kendell (1975), *The Role of Diagnosis in Psychiatry*, Oxford: Blackwell Scientific Publications.

It is apparent that there is no single unifying definition of disease and that the approach offered by Scadding is the best available, notwithstanding its limitations.

THE CONTRIBUTION OF PSYCHOLOGY TO UNDERSTANDING PSYCHIATRIC DISORDER

Psychology in its pure form is the study of the psychological or inner processes which lead to emotional disturbances. Over time it has broadened to include the more visible behavioural and biological causes of these disorders. Freud is regarded as the founder of psychology. He postulated that emotional traumas in childhood, mainly but not exclusively sexual, led to the appearance in adulthood of symptoms which later became known as the neuroses. He also believed that defence mechanisms were used by the psyche to protect it from overwhelming trauma; these were elaborated further by other psychoanalysts such as Melanie Klein. Although Freud is now less important in psychiatry than at any time in its history, and his theories on the origins of the neuroses have largely been jettisoned, some of his insights are relevant in clinical practice. For example, the role of unconscious mechanisms in hysteria (widely and mistakenly believed to be the same as malingering) and in abnormal illness behaviour is helpful in understanding the delay in recovery from accidents. Denial is the best-known defence mechanism and explains why patients, when told of a diagnosis, particularly one which is serious, claim subsequently that they were never informed.

Behavioural Psychology

Behavioural psychology, invoking learning theory, has attempted to explain the development of phobias and of some abnormal behaviours such as aggression. In the former, the effects of an adverse stimulus, such as tension, sweating, etc., lead to measures to avoid it which, by bringing about symptomatic relief, reinforces the avoidance. Thus the patient who is attacked or has an accident in a particular place comes to associate this location with the incident and avoids it to reduce the anxiety which its recollection engenders. The explanation for the repetition of violence from generation to generation within a family has been postulated as deriving from the role models to which the subject is exposed. By a process of learning and imitation, a behaviour is adopted.

Developmental Psychology

Developmental psychology, in particular Bowlby's attachment theory,[7] has contributed to our understanding of some personality traits such as dependence, self-esteem and assertiveness. His view is that the early relationship between mother and infant provides a safe environment in which to explore the outer world and develop independence. However, many of those with personality difficulties related to dependence and self-esteem also have a secure and stable background as described above — these contributions are therefore speculative rather than substantive.

Cognitive Psychology

Cognitive psychology, or the way in which the day-to-day world is viewed, has been cited by some, particularly Beck[8], as leading to depressive illness. The depressive perspective on the world, self and the future (known as the cognitive triad) is believed to lead to negative assumptions about all aspects of life and hence to depressive disorders. The focus of treatment, using Beck's approach, should be on challenging these assumptions. He has also offered theories relating to the causes of and treatment for personality disorders.

THE CONTRIBUTION OF SOCIOLOGY TO UNDERSTANDING PSYCHIATRIC DISORDER

Sociology is the study of man in his social environment and the interaction between both. The sociologist who has had the

---

[7] J. Bowlby (1984), *Attachment and Loss, Vol. 1: Attachment*, 2nd edition, Harmondsworth: Penguin.

[8] A.T. Beck, A. Freeman et al. (1992), *Cognitive Therapy for Personality Disorders*, New York: Guildford Press.

greatest impact on psychiatric thought is undoubtedly Émile Durkheim. His classic work on suicide[9] suggested the sociological roots of suicide emanating from three perspectives. The first or altruistic suicide occurs when the individual in society is subservient to the community and suicide is committed for the sake of the community as a whole. Included in this category are hunger strikers, Kamikaze pilots, car bombers. Mental illness is generally absent in this group, although there is a poor sense of self-identity. The second or egoistic suicide occurs when the individual is isolated from his group in society; this view has been suggested as an explanation for the high suicide rates among migrants, among the elderly and among the divorced when compared to the married. In modern jargon, this is called social isolation and is a recognised factor in also leading to chronicity of depressive illness. The third aspect of suicide is the state of anomie, in which the normative values of society no longer influence or govern the behaviour of the individual. Thus, at a time of crisis in an anomic society, the person will not be constrained by society's condemnation of suicide. Anomie occurs when society is no longer tightly knit and when values are shifting. This has been used as an explanation for the decline in suicide during war when individuals feel a sense of purpose and belonging, as well as an explanation for the rise that is currently taking place in Europe as traditional values are changing. Periods of economic depression are also associated with anomie and suicide rates have been shown to rise during these periods.

At first glance, it may seem that this sociological perspective is contrary to the psychiatric view that most people who commit suicide are suffering from a psychiatric disorder. However, these social backdrops have also been shown to be associated with psychiatric disorder, especially depressive illness. Rather than excluding the psychiatric basis for suicide, it adds an additional

---

[9] E. Durkheim (1951), *Suicide: a Study in Sociology*, Translated by J. Spaulding and G. Simpson, New York: Free Press.

dimension to our understanding, particularly in relation to trends over time.

The work of a modern sociologist, George Brown, brings into *bas relief* the association between sociology and psychiatry[10] in his work on depressive illness in urban and rural settings. He has shown that the absence of confiding relationships, the presence of unemployment, loss of a mother in childhood and young children in the home are associated with an increased risk of depressive illness. Moreover, when he investigated the vulnerability factors for depressive illness on a Scottish island, he found that the same risk factors pertained, but the lower prevalence found there was a result of the protective effects of religious beliefs. Finally, he demonstrated that stressful events could trigger a depressive illness and listed these in order of decreasing risk. The greatest stressor was going to prison, followed by marital breakup and moving house. He thus distinguished between vulnerability factors and causative factors. In clinical practice, the distinction between predisposing, precipitating and prolonging factors is important when considering both treatment and prognosis.

THE CONTRIBUTION OF THE BIOLOGICAL SCIENCES TO UNDERSTANDING PSYCHIATRIC DISORDERS

The contribution of the neurosciences in particular has led to major advances in our understanding of the causes of some common psychiatric disorders such as schizophrenia, manic-depression and depressive illness, as well as anxiety and obsessional disorders. These have led to what some critics dub the medical model of psychiatric disorders.

Neurochemistry and Genetics

Neurochemical theories relate to the increase or decrease in certain neurotransmitters in brain tissue, such as dopamine, serotonin, adrenaline, nor-adrenaline, acetylcholine, gamma-amino-

---

[10] G.W. Brown, and T. Harris (1978), *Social Origins of Depression*, London: Tavistock.

butyric acid and others. These are receiving extensive attention at present and will be described in greater detail in the sections dealing with specific disorders. Genetic studies are also illuminating our knowledge of the inheritance of some disorders, such as schizophrenia, manic-depression, alcoholism and panic disorder. However, there is no consensus on the exact mode of transmission. In clinical practice, no biological markers or measures have as yet been identified to distinguish patients from those who are well or to make diagnostic distinctions between the various diagnostic groups. In spite of the pace of study in the biological aspects of psychiatry, it remains almost exclusively a clinical speciality.

Radiology

Advances in radiological investigation have been the most remarkable aspect of the scientific developments of recent years. These advances could eventually lead to a reappraisal of the defences used in criminal proceedings. For example, if it were possible to demonstrate consistent abnormalities of brain structure in schizophrenia, then these patients who commit serious crimes could be regarded as suffering from diseases of the brain rather than of the mind, perhaps with a consequent redefinition of the insanity defence.[11] Similarly if abnormalities of receptor function could be shown to be abnormal in patients with antisocial personality disorder, extending the range of possible dispositions might

---

[11] Oxford's Case (*R* v *Oxford*) (1840) 4 St. Tr. (ns) 497, 9 C&P 526; and M'Naghten's Case (*R* v *M'Naghten*) (1843) 4 St. Tr (ns) 87, 1843 10 Cl. & F. 200 are the *loci classici* that demonstrate an accused suffering from a delusional state, evidence of a psychosis, probably paranoid schizophrenia. Insofar as evidence of abnormality may possibly be detectable — whether on computerised tomography (CT scanning), magnetic resonance imaging (MRI), positron emission tomography (PET scanning) or neurochemically at pre- or post-receptor level (see below) — the issue of criminal responsibility remains a matter of law; see *R* v *Kemp* [1957] 1 QB 399 at 408, 40 Cr. App. R. 121 at 127, Assizes, per Devlin J; and *R* v *Sullivan* [1983] 3 All ER 673, [1983] 3 WLR 123 HL, per Diplock LJ at 677.

be desirable.[12] Caution must be exercised in using radiological approaches to understanding disorders for forensic purposes since the whole area is still embryonic. Moreover the proportion of false positive or false negative findings associated with such investigations has yet to be established.

Computerised Axial Tomography

Computerised Axial Tomography (CAT) scanning is the most commonly used radiological tool to assess macroscopic (visible) brain damage. However, it does not show changes in the early stages of dementia. In patients with schizophrenia, a consistent finding has been enlargement of the lateral and third ventricles of the brain — these are channels in the brain tissue through which cerebro-spinal fluid circulates. The temporal lobes, lying at each side of the brain and concerned with perception and to a lesser extent language, have also been shown to be abnormal. However, the changes are relatively small and unhelpful in making the diagnosis in the absence of other features. Patients with anorexia nervosa have, in some studies, been found to have pseudo-atrophy or transient shrinkage of the brain, which returns to normal when weight is gained. A more consistent finding has been the presence of brain atrophy in alcoholic patients. This may improve with abstinence although not infrequently it persists and is indicative of alcoholic dementia. No consistent changes have been found using CAT scanning in those with mood disorders, personality disorders or obsessive-compulsive disorder.

Magnetic Resonance Imaging

Magnetic Resonance Imaging (MRI) has become more widely available in Ireland recently, although it is still only carried out at

---

[12] P. Fenwick (1993), "Brain, Mind and Behaviour: Some Medico-Legal Aspects", *British Journal of Psychiatry*, Vol. 163, pp. 565–73. Although in Britain, the Homicide Act, 1957, where diminished responsibility is pleaded, permits a range of options insofar as disposition is concerned, in Irish law there is no such defence at common law or in statute. Accordingly, raising personality disorder as a defence raises the issue of insanity simpliciter.

a few hospitals. It is considerably more expensive also than CAT scanning. MRI provides information about brain tissue not available using CAT scanning. Attempts to match the degree of tissue damage to the memory and spatial (cognitive) deficits seen in the dementias is as yet experimental. Among patients with schizophrenia, changes to the temporal lobes and to the ventricles have been demonstrated. The diagnostic usefulness of these features has to be clarified. Early studies in patients with mood disorders have yielded uncertain results. In cases of eating disorders and alcohol abuse changes similar to those found with CAT scanning have been found.

Positron Emission Tomography

Positron Emission Tomography (PET) scanning is a technique which measures brain function, such as oxygen consumption, rather than structure. It is expensive and not available in Ireland. Single Photon Emission Computed Tomography (SPECT) is somewhat less expensive. Changes in brain metabolism and the sites of these changes have been identified and appear to be related to the cognitive deficits found in dementias. Patients with schizophrenia have been shown to have reduced activity in certain brain areas, although attempts to relate psychotic symptoms to PET abnormalities have yielded inconsistent findings. Areas which receive nervous impulse on being stimulated by neurochemicals are known as receptors and PET techniques have been used to map changes to these in various parts of the brain in patients with a range of psychiatric disorders. These mapping studies, especially those directed at dopamine receptors, have shown higher density receptors in certain areas of the brain in untreated patients with schizophrenia. No consistent findings have been reported in mood disorders, but anxiety disorders have yielded increased activity in the anterior temporal lobes, whilst obsessive compulsive disorders are associated with elevated metabolism in the caudate nucleus, an area deep in brain tissue, and in the frontal cortex. Other disorders, such as substance misuse, personality disorders, etc., have not been extensively investigated. An excellent review of the current status of PET, the most powerful neuro-radiological technique, is provided by Bench et al.[13]

Electro-diagnostic Techniques

These techniques are older than the radiological methods described above. They are also more useful in the clinical management of patients. The most common tool is the electro-encephalogram (EEG), a measure of brain activity first discovered in 1875. EEG changes are common in the dementias such as Alzheimer's and Pick's disease, and in delirium (acute confusion), EEG changes are found which help distinguish it from the confusion sometimes seen in depression. Some patients with antisocial personality disorders also have abnormal EEGs but the significance of this is little understood.

Evoked Potentials

Evoked potentials are the responses that are seen in the EEG when a sensory stimulus is applied. Thus, auditory, visual and somatosensory (tactile and painful) stimuli may be tested. These have been used both in neurology and in psychiatry to examine impairment in the sensory cortex, that part of the brain concerned with receiving sensory input. In schizophrenic patients, some abnormalities of auditory evoked potentials have been demonstrated. These have been associated with CAT scan changes and with positive symptoms such as hallucinations in some reports, although inconsistencies remain and evoked potentials are not yet used routinely in clinical practice.

Electro-Dermal Activity

Measures of electro-dermal activity include calculating changes in the electrical resistance of the skin. This is part of the assessment carried out by polygraph methods, especially in the United States.

---

[13] C.J. Bench, R.J. Dolan, K.J. Friston and R.S.J. Frackowiak (1990), "Positron Emission Tomography in the Study of Brain Metabolism in Psychiatric and Neuropsychiatric Disorders", *British Journal of Psychiatry*, Vol. 157 (suppl. 9), pp. 82–95.

In addition, heart rate and respiratory rate are also measured. Changes to the sympathetic nervous system, that component of the nervous system, that component of the nervous system which controls these functions, are believed to occur when a person is lying and it is in this context that the polygraph has found use. However, these measures are influenced by a number of factors, including skin thickness, medication and ambient temperature, and are unreliable for forensic purposes.

THE DIAGNOSTIC PROCESS

In considering whether a particular disorder exists or not, two aspects require consideration. The first is that the cluster of features measured must distinguish those who possess them from those who possess other features and also from those who have none at all, i.e. the healthy population. This is known as validity. In addition, it must be possible to demonstrate that the features are consistent when measured by two people or at two time intervals. This is known as reliability. Although reliability is relatively simple to measure, validity, an essential component of any diagnostic label, is much more complex. For this reason, studies of validity are less common than are those measuring reliability.

VALIDITY OF PSYCHIATRIC DISORDERS

The approach to current psychiatric classification has its roots in the approach of the clinician Kraeplin. He developed a classification (1913) which has remained largely unchanged, based on symptom clusters (syndromes) and on their course. This tradition has continued to the present. However, were the list of disorders confined exclusively to those originally described by Kraeplin, they would be few in number. With each edition of the DSM or ICD classifications (see Chapter 3), disorders are added or removed on the basis of their perceived relevance to clinical practice. The addition of borderline personality disorder to ICD-10 is an example of this although there is little evidence for the existence of this as a distinct disease entity. It is commonly assumed by the general public and indeed by members of the medical profession, even psychiatrists, that the syndromes defined in the ICD and DSM systems have been shown to be valid — in other words, that the clusters of symptoms so defined individually have a known aetiology, response to treatment, natural history, epidemiology and stability over time, as well as being clearly distinguished from other syndromes. The process of validation is relatively primitive in psychiatry, with few of the syndromes being validated in respect of the above variables. There is controversy also over the validity of such commonly cited disorders as post traumatic stress disorder, schizo-affective psychosis and panic disorder. The most commonly diagnosed disorder, depressive illness, has been clearly validated, as have schizophrenia and manic-depressive illness, phobias and generalised anxiety disorders. In the court situation, this uncertainty about the validity or existence of some disorders, such as post-traumatic stress disorder, may explain why some psychiatrists make certain diagnoses sparingly. Others take the pragmatic view and diagnose on the basis of the ICD or DSM system, irrespective of the scientific evidence for the validity of the specific disorder.

RELIABILITY OF DIAGNOSIS

This is the extent to which a diagnosis is repeated when assessment is made independently by two assessors or by one assessor at two points in time. It is generally not relevant in clinical practice, but in court, when interview schedules and questionnaires (psychometric instruments) such as those commonly used by psychologists are cited, it is important to ensure that they have been properly tested for reliability during their development. Many schedules, particularly those used to assess personality, have poor reliability and validity.

CLINICAL ASPECTS OF DIAGNOSIS

In psychiatric practice, diagnosis is made both on the basis of current symptoms and on the longitudinal history of the disorder.

Both should usually be the same but at times a discrepancy may occur. For example, those with schizophrenia may at times develop a depressive illness and exhibit the latter as the major symptom pattern in the short term; sufferers with anorexia nervosa frequently develop a depressive disorder during treatment of the former. In both of these examples, the treatment for the primary disorders would be maintained whilst appropriate treatment for the secondary disorder would also be instituted. Indeed, most psychiatric disorders can lead to secondary disorders, albeit briefly, which require their own treatment. Diagnosis is therefore both longitudinal and cross-sectional. In the case of a disorder being treated for the first time, the diagnosis will inevitably be cross-sectional only.

Additional problems arise in relation to disorders which have a prodromal phase before the fully fledged symptoms are manifest. For example, schizophrenia at the outset may begin with the symptoms of lack of interest, lack of motivation, despondency and social withdrawal, symptoms that at first assessment may appear to indicate depressive illness until the disorder is fully crystallised and the patient describes hallucinations and delusions. For this reason, there may appear to be a diagnostic discrepancy between the initial presentation and the later diagnosis. For the purposes of the law, it is important to establish at which point in the course of the disorder the patient was assessed, as this may explain what appear to be gross differences in diagnosis between two psychiatrists.

In view of the absence of any reliable biological markers, diagnosis is made on the basis of symptoms and behaviour. However, the role of behaviour in itself is limited since behaviour disturbance may be caused by many psychiatric disorders and indeed may even occur when there is none — thus psychiatrists concentrate largely on the assessment of current symptoms to reach a diagnosis. For this reason, much attention is given to the interview itself and to the techniques that are employed to obtain information. Since insight may be limited by the presence of psychiatric illness, considerable attention is paid to the collateral history which is usually obtained from a close relative. Interestingly, little scientific attention has been directed to establishing the reliability of informants or to identifying those informants who are most reliable. Moreover, ICD-10 recommends the use of informants, particularly when assessing personality, whilst DSM-III-R makes no such suggestion. Psychiatrists operating with either system may thus arrive at different diagnostic conclusions, particularly where the more nebulous disorders such as personality disorder are being considered.

The process of arriving at a particular diagnosis has been studied in some detail and been shown to be more reliable than the earlier literature would suggest. Firstly, the current symptoms as described by patient and informant are noted and direct the diagnostic possibilities in a broad direction. Then the behaviour or "body language" observed by the psychiatrist will be noted and used to validate or call into question the preliminary opinions. In the context of an in-patient ward, the assessment of behaviour will be ongoing but will always be governed by the caveat that the behaviour may be modified by factors independent of illness such as the attitudes of staff and the ward environment.[14]

The relevance of life events in the causation of psychiatric disorder is well recognised, although in any individual it is impossible to say with certainty that the particular event led directly to the disorder. The most that can be claimed is that on the balance of probability the event did or did not lead to the disorder. For example, a patient with a past history of depressive illness which has been successfully treated is then involved in a serious accident and develops symptoms of depressive illness six months later. The question likely to be posed is whether the illness would have recurred if the patient had not had the accident. In such situations, it is impossible to say with certainty and the approach to answering this question would include assessment of the

---

[14] This is a critical issue in interpreting psychiatric reports, especially in criminal matters.

number of previous episodes, their precipitant, if any, and the patient's style of coping when well.[15]

Some psychiatrists also use questionnaires/structured interview schedules to supplement the available clinical data, although this is not widespread. These, however, are only as useful as the information available and will not access material unobtainable by ordinary clinical interview. Structured interviews or measuring schedules, whilst allowing quantification of the severity of the disorder, are based on clinical interview and have no magical ability to obtain hidden or covert symptoms.

THE PSYCHIATRIC INTERVIEW

This usually takes place in a medical setting but occasionally in the patient's home. The patient is seated, as is the psychiatrist. The psychiatrist's couch is now largely a myth, except for the very few who practice classical Freudian psychoanalysis. Informants are interviewed separately except in unusual circumstances such as a confused patient who is unable to give an accurate history or one who is very disturbed and likely to be violent. Ordinarily consent to interview an informant would be obtained from the patient.[16]

The psychiatrist allows the patient to describe the symptoms and background in their own words and will later hone in on specific areas by using "closed" questions. These are questions which require a specific answer (e.g. "do you wake early in the

---

[15] In effect, upon an assessment of the plaintiff's special characteristics or vulnerability, i.e. whether or not he or she is a psychological "egg-shell skull" plaintiff.

[16] However, this is a problematic area. If a patient is disturbed, his capacity to consent may be significantly impaired. Insofar as it may be appropriate to obtain consent in the ordinary course of events, where such consent is not forthcoming, or the patient lacks the capacity to give the appropriate consent, proceeding without such consent must be defensible on the grounds of clinical necessity. That said, the legal or ethical contours of this issue remain to be shaped. Where allegations have been made by the patient against the person who would normally be the appropriate informant, the exercise of clinical discretion and the maintenance of patient confidentiality might dispense with the requirement to obtain certain collateral histories.

morning?"), and are distinct from open questions which allow the patient latitude to expand answers (e.g. "tell me about your sleep"). To maximise rapport and information gathering, it is recommended that the interview should begin with open questions and conclude with closed questions. Again, there are exceptions to this, as in dealing with an acutely disturbed patient.

The history is obtained under the following headings and documented, generally, in the following order:

1. *History of presenting complaint* will contain information about the patient's symptoms, their duration and severity. Details about perceived precipitants will also be outlined.

2. *Family history* will provide details of siblings and parents, their ages, marital status, closeness of the relationship to the patient and information about their psychiatric and medical history. Information about the extended family may also be sought if it is considered relevant.

3. The *personal history* is often the most difficult for the patient to provide, since it may evoke painful memories or unearth areas of difficulty currently concealed. The stages of development are delineated chronologically, beginning with the early years and ending with current life circumstances. Many provide information, obtained from others, about their developmental milestones, such as walking, talking, etc. Common difficulties experienced in childhood include bed-wetting, nail-biting and short-term school refusal. The relationship between parents and the patient (in childhood) will be included in this section, as will more serious traumas such as serious illness, parental absences and physical or sexual abuse. Details relating to schooling and third level education, both academic and social, will assist in painting a picture of the world of the developing child and adolescent. Employment history will include details of previous jobs, reasons for leaving, promotions obtained, relationship with peers and authority figures and future ambitions. For those not working outside the home, such

as the unemployed or housewives, attitudes to their status and their ambitions will be obtained.

Sexual history will include details of sex education, menstrual history in women, sexual orientation, relationships including sexual activity and problems of a sexual nature. Details about current sexual activity, whether married or single, along with the support obtained from the partner provide important information which may impact on the response to treatment. Data about children, the patient's relationship with them and any previous miscarriages, induced abortions or stillbirths complete this very intimate portion. Finally, the present housing arrangements, details of and current or previous trouble with the law and current friendships and personal supports conclude the personal history. The breadth of inquiry, outlined above, suggests that herein may lie some clues as to risk factors or precipitants (if any) for the disorder or information affecting the level of emotional support the patient may expect during treatment. The latter has been shown to affect the duration and response to treatment in some patients. It is obvious that this part of the interview requires sensitivity and may need to be deferred until the therapeutic relationship between doctor and patient has been solidified.

4. *Past medical and psychiatric history* is useful in providing a longitudinal perspective on the patient's disorder. Information relating to contacts with the psychiatric services, with related professionals such as counsellors as well as admissions to hospital and duration of stay augment the understanding of the patient. The patient's medical history may offer an explanation for the current psychiatric disorder. Previous case notes are frequently sought from other doctors, provided the patient gives written permission.[17]

---

[17] A requirement for written permission is a counsel of perfection and caution. However, the handing over of clinical notes or clinical information from one treating medical practitioner to another — even without express patient consent — does not constitute a breach of patient confidentiality. Insofar as

5. *Drug history* includes information on both licit and illicit drugs. Past medication for psychiatric disorders including dosage, duration and response often provides an invaluable guide to treatments for the current episode of illness. Medications for other conditions, especially those which have a known impact on psychological functioning, such as steroids, or those which might interact with the psychiatrist's treatment, are also identified.[18]

6. *Pre-morbid personality* refers to the pre-illness traits of the patient. In particular, those attributes which lead to problems in dealing with others will assist in arriving at a diagnosis of personality disorder, if it is present (see Chapter 9 for further details). Details of religious beliefs and practices provide valuable insights into the patient's support systems, as does information about hobbies and friends. Finally, inquiry is made about cigarette smoking and alcohol consumption prior to the current episode.

7. The *mental state assessment* is the final section in the formal description of the patient's status. It is the psychological equivalent of the physical examination and systematically outlines the symptoms elicited on examination. The study of these symptoms is known as descriptive psychopathology. Mental state is assessed under a number of headings.[19]

---

such information may well be of critical importance — both in terms of understanding more fully the extent of previous investigations and treatments — and may well inform the next appropriate step, a failure to seek or consult such notes, if readily available, may ground an action in negligence. See, for example, *Armstrong* v *Eastern Health Board* (High Court, Unreported Judgment, Egan J, 5 October 1990). The refusal of consent, if sought, may itself be of significance and arguably should suggest caution.

[18] It is in this area that past clinical notes may be of critical importance, especially if the patient is not in a position to provide a complete treatment or drug history.

[19] *Speech* — spontaneity, speed, etc. *Behaviour* — agitation, obsessional behaviour, psychomotor retardation, etc. *Mood* — appropriateness, sad, tearful, elated, flat, etc. *Perception* — illusions, hallucinations and their modality (auditory, visual, etc.) *Thought content* — overvalued ideas or delusions and

The initial interview takes about 50 minutes. Several assessment interviews may be required, depending on the complexity of the case and especially in those relating to personality disorder. There is a distinction between the assessment interview and the therapeutic interview, with the former being more interrogative than the latter, where explanation, interpretation and direction are offered.

Finally, a diagnosis is made which includes the main working diagnosis and differential or alternative diagnoses. Increasingly, the diagnosis is made using the multi-axial system[20] with mental state diagnoses being considered separately from personality disorder diagnoses. Some psychiatrists may also provide a diagnostic formulation — this is an attempt to explain the occurrence of the patient's disorder in the context of his/her life at present as well as delineating predisposing, precipitating and maintaining factors.

All interviews, whether for assessment or therapy, are recorded in the patient's case notes, along with data from informants. When the history, mental state examination and working diagnosis are committed to paper under the headings outlined above, letters are sent to general practitioners or other referring parties and notes are generally also made of telephone conversations.

HIERARCHY

Where the patient has symptoms that meet the criteria for two disorders, then the convention common to all branches of medicine applies and a composite diagnosis is reached. To achieve this, a hierarchical approach is used with some symptoms always superseding others. Symptoms indicative of organic disorders supersede

---

their content, primary or secondary, ruminations, suicidal ideas, passivity feelings, etc. *Concentration and memory* — short- and long-term memory, serial 7 test. *Orientation* — time, place, person. *Insight* — knowledge about illness, attitude to it. *Motivation for change* if substance abuser, marital problems, etc.

[20] See Chapter 3.

psychotic symptoms of hallucinations and delusions, whilst in turn they supersede symptoms of depression, followed by anxiety. The effect in practice is that a single diagnosis is made and treatment offered usually for the condition highest in the hierarchy, since treatment of this will result in relief from other symptoms lower in the hierarchy also. If, for example, a patient has clinical evidence of organic brain damage following an accident and also has anxiety, a diagnosis of organic brain damage will be made and the anxiety is regarded as secondary. Thus, the secondary symptoms are regarded as symptomatic of the primary condition. The diagnostic hierarchy applies to axis 1 disorders only and personality is assessed separately on axis 2.[21]

PSYCHOLOGICAL ASSESSMENT

The use of psychological tools to supplement psychiatric assessment is a common practice, particularly in the context of medicolegal cases. In particular, assessments of personality by clinical psychologists are frequently requested by psychiatrists. However, the same caveats apply in this context as apply in the general clinical setting outlined in the preceding paragraph — the schedules supplement rather than supplant the information which is available and their usefulness is determined by the information available directly from the patient or an informant. The ability of these schedules to divine hidden or "unconscious" material is apocryphal.[22]

These caveats, however, do not apply to the schedules which are available for testing cognitive function, i.e. the assessment of brain damage or intelligence. Whilst they have their own limitation, they do provide valuable information about brain structure and function even before structural change is visible radiologically, as in early dementia.

In the court setting, it is thus important to place the psychological assessment in the context of the overall clinical assessment

---

[21] See Chapter 3.

[22] See Chapters 4 and 5 for further information on psychological assessment.

and to obtain information on the benefits and limitations of each test that has been applied.

PROVING CAUSATION

It is often assumed that because an event occurred in close juxtaposition to a psychological disorder the former must have caused the latter. Indeed, it is also incorrectly assumed that some stressor in the distant past must be responsible for the present emotional difficulties experienced by the patient, particularly when there is no obvious current precipitant, and often leads to demands for "counselling". Regrettably, it is this assumption which has led to the burgeoning of recovered memory techniques[23] with their attendant problems. The search for an understanding of the symptoms and illness is inherent in human nature and "effort after meaning" is particularly common in psychiatry. However, caution must be exercised in ascribing causality to events either in the remote or recent past.[24]

To demonstrate a causative role for an event, it must be shown that it occurs with greater than chance frequency in the group under study when compared to the general population and that the disorder would not have occurred without the stressor. Whilst this type of study can be conducted with large samples, problems arise in relation to individual patients, since it is impossible to conduct a scientific study to prove the hypothesis.

Several explanations may underpin the association between an event and an illness. It must be remembered also that association does not necessarily imply causation. For example, there is an association between childhood emotional deprivation and depressive illness, but deprivation does not necessarily cause depression (although this is one possibility). A second explanation for the association between deprivation and depressive illness is that the former increases the risk — hence not everybody who is poor

---

[23] See Chapter 5.

[24] This is of particular relevance in the context of cases involving the negligent infliction of emotional suffering; see Chapter 8.

becomes depressed and not all depressed persons were poor as children. This is referred to as a vulnerability or predisposing factor.[25]

Suppose a patient diagnosed as suffering from a depressive illness described recent job loss. One possibility is that the loss directly precipitated the illness but a second possibility might be that this merely brought forward the onset of the illness which would have occurred anyway. This is referred to as "brought forward time" and has been invoked in explaining the role of life events in precipitating schizophrenia.[26] Thirdly, it may be that the event and the illness had some other common factor underlying them both, giving a spurious impression of causality.[27] For example, the presence of alcohol abuse might lead to depressive illness and to job loss. Fourthly, the event (e.g. job loss) might be an early sign of depressive illness (e.g. due to an inability to concentrate). Finally, both might be coincidental.

With careful study design, many of these issues can be addressed when examining large samples, but for individual patients treated in the context of their specific life histories, caution is indicated in assuming simple cause-and-effect relationships between events and illness.

SUMMARY

The scientific basis for psychiatry is rapidly becoming apparent as a result of strides in neurochemistry and the biological sciences. Sociology and psychology enrich this understanding, leading to a truly eclectic appreciation of all facets of psychiatric disorder.

---

[25] The equivalent of the "eggshell skull" principle.

[26] It is worth noting that if it is established the event produced that (otherwise inevitable, but later) result at that time, liability may be imposed. See, for example, *Smith* v *Leavy* (Supreme Court, Unreported Judgment, 7 November 1960) — a fatal injuries case — cited in B. McMahon and W. Binchy (1990), *Irish Law of Torts*, Second Edition, Dublin: Butterworths (Ireland), p. 43.

[27] See, for example, *Wilsher* v *Essex Area Health Authority* [1988] 1 All ER 871, [1988] AC 1074.

Diagnosis remains a clinical exercise relying on accurate and detailed history-taking. Psychiatrists work with a combination of models and not just exclusively with the so-called "medical model". Whilst some of these approaches are well developed, others, such as the newer neuroradiological techniques, are still embryonic.

Chapter 3

CLASSIFICATION OF DISORDERS

GENERAL

The inclusion of a chapter on classification may seem unnecessary to members of the legal profession, who are likely to be more focused on the application of law to various psychiatric disorders.[1] Such a chapter is required in order to answer the common criticisms from the legal profession that psychiatric diagnoses are unreliable[2] and that, in a court setting, agreement between psychiatrists is difficult to achieve.[3] Moreover, it may explain the use of particular diagnoses and terminology by some psychiatrists which are rejected or held to be non-existent by others. For example, the word "neurosis" is often used by psychiatrists to describe a particular constellation of symptoms that includes phobias, anxiety, depression, tension, etc., whilst others contend that this

---

[1] That said, in the areas of "nervous shock" and nullity in particular, the actual diagnosis, as much as the functional impact of the condition on the individual, appears to be of concern to the courts; see Chapters 8 and 11. See the comments of Geoghegan J in the Divisional High Court in *Gallagher* v *Director of the Central Mental Hospital & Others* (High Court, Unreported Judgment, 9 July 1996) in relation to the distinction between mental "illness" and mental "disorder".

[2] A.T. Beck (1962), "Reliability of Psychiatric Diagnoses: A Critique of Systematic Studies", *American Journal of Psychiatry*, Vol. 119, pp. 210–16.

[3] See, for example, the evidence of the psychiatrists in *RSJ* v *JSJ* [1982] ILRM 263.

term has no meaning, is pejorative and consequently avoid mention of this word in court.[4]

A Simple Classification

In court, some psychiatrists speak of disorders being psychotic, organic, neurotic or related to personality. These terms are derived from a simple classification which forms the basis of the modern system of classification and which was in general use until recently.

Using this older system of classification, the most severe disorders are those in which there is loss of touch with reality yet no physical cause is identified. These are called the functional (no physical cause) psychoses (loss of touch with reality) and include manic-depression and schizophrenia.

Those disorders that have a physical basis, such as an infection or a dementia, are associated with disorientation and confusion and are termed the organic psychoses. They are divided between those of acute onset (delirium or acute confusional state) and those of long standing (dementia). The patient with delirium invariably makes a complete recovery. Common causes include infections, anaesthesia, head injury and alcohol withdrawal, also called delirium tremens. The elderly and those with pre-existing dementia are particularly susceptible to delirium. In the dementias, the onset is insidious, and forgetfulness and confusion are prominent. These are progressive until death.

The third group of disorders recognised in this simple classification are the neuroses, including phobias, anxiety states, hysteria, depressive illness and obsessive-compulsive disorder. These were believed by Freud to arise from childhood conflicts and later were believed to be associated with personality problems. The term neurotic became associated with personality disorder and for

---

[4] See, for example, the discussion of "immaturity" in the context of personality disorder (Chapter 9) in the High Court in *O'M(M)* v *O'C(B)* (High Court, Unreported Judgment, Kinlen J, 5 May 1994; a finding not upset in the Supreme Court appeal, reported as *O'M(M)* v *O'C(B)* [1996] IR 208).

this reason psychiatrists in court have sometimes used the terms neurosis and personality disorder interchangeably. Many psychiatrists reject this, since it creates confusion and misunderstanding.

The fourth group comprises personality disorders, defined as enduring traits and behaviours which impinge negatively upon the patient and upon society. Included are the psychopathic or antisocial personality, the obsessional personality disorder and others.[5] Older textbooks of psychiatry also talked of immature and inadequate personality disorder and these terms are still used by some psychiatrists.

The fifth category of disorder comprises drug and alcohol abuse. These are believed to be associated with personality disorder. Thus, when a diagnosis of substance abuse is made, a diagnosis of personality disorder is frequently implied.

This classification is used in the older textbooks and continues to be used by some psychiatrists. It has the merit of being simple and easily understood but suffers the disadvantage of leading to misunderstanding (e.g. the belief in the overlap between the neuroses and personality disorder) and of not being based on a modern understanding of psychiatry. Criticism of the poor level of agreement between psychiatrists in making a diagnosis is indeed a valid one in the context of this simple system of classification. Moreover, terms such as "inadequate" and "immature" when applied to personality are judgmental rather than clinical.

A newer system of describing and classifying disorders has been developed in response to these problems.

DEVELOPING A MODERN CLASSIFICATION

Since one of the criticisms is the low level of diagnostic agreement between psychiatrists, the profession has set about clearly specifying the symptoms and their duration in order to make a particular diagnosis. These are referred to as operational definitions and their use in clinical practice, although procrustean, has greatly enhanced the level of agreement between psychiatrists.

---

[5] See Chapter 9.

Thus, a psychiatrist may say in court that a patient did or did not meet the criteria or operational definition for a specific disorder.

Clearly defining each disorder is only the first step, since listing a group of symptoms and specifying their duration does not prove that the disorder exists as a diagnostic entity. For example, it is possible to say that a disorder called "barristeritis" exists and is operationally defined as affecting men in their fifties with grey hair, who take snuff, play the cello and have an interest in astronomy! This condition is mainly found in urban areas and tends to improve with increasing age. However, such a "disorder" is meaningless, since, even though some people could be found to meet the criteria, such people may be found in other diagnostic categories also or in those with no psychiatric disorder. In order to prove that "barristeritis" is a disorder, and not just a group of features plucked from the imagination, it is necessary to demonstrate that the features described do in fact co-occur, that is has a specific course, response to treatment and causation and that those with this constellation of features are different from other diagnostic groups and from those with no diagnosis. This is called validating the disorder. Unfortunately, many of the diagnostic labels used in clinical practice have not been investigated with this rigour and cannot be said to have been validated. It is for this reason that uncertainty and disagreement still exists between psychiatrists about some categories. In particular, the categories of personality disorder, post-traumatic stress disorder and panic disorder have been the butt of debate in relation to their validity. Thus, in court some psychiatrists may speak of post-traumatic stress disorder whilst others will hold that the same symptoms are indicative of, say, depressive illness precipitated by the trauma.

Older textbooks of psychiatry and also hospital case-notes recorded no more than one diagnosis for the patient. The use of a single diagnostic label is now generally regarded as being overly narrow and as failing to convey the fact that a patient may have more than one diagnosis and may have a complex social background relevant to the diagnosis which is not captured in a simple label (see the case vignette in the next section). In response to this, a system of diagnostic labelling has been developed called the multi-axial system of classification.

THE MULTI-AXIAL SYSTEM OF CLASSIFICATION

An axis refers to an aspect of the patient's diagnosis. Five specific axes are considered to be of importance in diagnosis and this is termed the multi-axial system of classification. The axes, along with their explanations, are listed in Table 3.1.

TABLE 3.1: AXES IN THE MULTI-AXIAL SYSTEM OF CLASSIFICATION

Axis 1	Diagnosis excluding personality disorder
Axis 2	Personality disorder, if present
Axis 3	Physical illness
Axis 4	Stressors contributing to or causing the disorder
Axis 5	Social functioning, i.e. the patient's current level of functioning in day-to-day roles such as work, parenting, friendships.

Only axes 1 (current mental state) and 2 (pre-illness or pre-morbid personality) are in common clinical use. For the lawyer, the importance of the multi-axial system lies in the fact that psychiatrists, when providing reports, may use this approach and provide a diagnosis on two (axis 1 and 2) but sometimes more axes. Thus a report may read that a patient suffered from agoraphobia following an accident but also had a personality disorder (by definition, personality disorder exists throughout adult life). It would then be necessary to ascertain if the presence of personality disorder increased the vulnerability to agoraphobia or if the abnormal personality adversely affected the long-term prognosis.

The multi-axial approach and the use of operational definitions are now incorporated into the two systems of classification in world-wide use. The system used in Europe and developed by the World Health Organisation is called the International Classification of Diseases, 10th edition (ICD-10)[6] and in the United States, the American Psychiatric Association has developed the Diagnostic and Statistical Manual, 4th edition (DSM-IV).[7]

The broad categories into which disorders are grouped in ICD-10 are listed in Table 3.2.

TABLE 3.2: CATEGORIES OF DISORDER IN ICD-10

Organic disorders
Mental and behavioural disorders due to psychoactive drug use
Schizophrenia, schizotypal and delusional disorders
Mood (affective) disorders
Neurotic, stress-related and somatoform disorders
Behavioural syndromes associated with physiological disturbances and physical factors
Disorders of adult personality and behaviour
Mental retardation
Disorders of psychological development
Behavioural and emotional disorders with onset usually occurring in childhood and adolescence
Unspecified mental disorder

The following case vignette illustrates how a diagnosis is reported using the multi-axial system of ICD-10.

> Mrs A, a 58-year-old woman, was involved in an accident in which she was knocked down by a motorcyclist. She was not unconscious but suffered a fracture in her right leg. The fracture healed but she developed pain in her right leg which required pain-killers to bring about relief. This kept her awake at night and she woke early in the morning also.

---

[6] World Health Organisation (1992), *International Classification of Diseases*, Tenth Edition, Geneva: World Health Organisation.

[7] American Psychiatric Association (1994), *Diagnostic and Statistical Manual*, Fourth edition, Washington, DC: American Psychiatric Association.

In the 12-month period following the accident, she began to complain of poor concentration and of anxiety when she was in the area where the accident occurred. She felt panic frequently, even when she was alone at home and at the time of referral was getting a panic attack every day. She was unable to do the shopping because of this and had lost interest in going out to visit her sister and a friend to whom she was close. Neither would she go out socially with her husband, fearing a panic attack and not feeling interested. She cried almost every day. She gradually lost interest in her appearance and in her children. In her personality she was very house-proud, had a rigid routine of housework for each day and found change difficult. She liked to plan everything in advance and her family often complained that she would not agree to spontaneous outings and she always became anxious if visitors called unannounced. Her family life was happy in spite of this, as a result of the adjustments they made.

The Axis 1 diagnosis (current diagnosis) in this lady is of a depressive episode of moderate severity. Axis 2 diagnosis (pre-illness personality) is that of obsessional (anankastic) personality disorder. Axis 3 (physical illness) diagnosis is post-traumatic pain. The Axis 4 stressor is the accident. Axis 5 (social functioning) shows impairment in functioning.

CURRENT CLASSIFICATION IN PRACTICE — DIFFERENCES IN APPROACH

Psychiatrists trained in the United States use DSM whilst Europeans use both systems because of the delay in developing ICD into a satisfactory system of classification. Although both ICD and DSM provide operational definitions and are multi-axial, there are some differences between them, particularly in the specific disorders described. In court, this may lead to discrepant diagnoses and even to differences in approaching diagnosis if psychiatrists are using different systems.

Differences that are relevant to the legal profession centre on some of the diagnoses used. For example, schizotypy (a disorder characterised by eccentric behaviour and beliefs)[8] is believed by some to be a personality disorder and is classified as such in DSM, whilst others believe that it is a variant of schizophrenia, requiring the treatment for this disorder. Hence, in ICD it is included with schizophrenia. DSM also includes some categories of personality disorder (e.g. passive-aggressive and narcissistic) which are not mentioned in ICD.[9]

An important difference between ICD and DSM lies in the tendency to give a single diagnosis on Axis 1 for all the symptoms using ICD, whilst DSM allows for several. For example, the patient described in the vignette above would be diagnosed in the ICD system as having depressive disorder, since symptoms of anxiety, panic and tension would be viewed as symptomatic of depression. In other words, a hierarchy of diagnoses is constructed in which anxiety, panic, etc., would be subsumed by the symptoms of depression, which come higher in the hierarchy. DSM does not operate a hierarchy and this patient would be given a diagnosis of major depression and panic disorder. Similarly, a patient with hallucinations, delusions, depression and irritability would be diagnosed in the ICD system as having schizophrenia but in the DSM system as having both schizophrenia and major depression. The presence of two disorders simultaneously is referred to as comorbidity; this concept has also been the subject of controversy in the psychiatric world. Thus, a psychiatrist trained in the US may give the impression of a greater number of disorders in the patient and by implication of greater incapacity than one trained in the European system.

---

[8] The accused in *R* v *Oxford* (1840) 4 St. Tr. (ns) 497, 9 C&P 526 might readily have been so classified, as might also the testator in *Dew* v *Clark* 5 Russ 166. For a historically and socially revealing categorisation of beliefs as the product of an abnormal value system that would probably be unsustainable today, see *Doyle* v *Wicklow County Council* [1974] IR 55.

[9] See also, for example, *C(P)* v *M(C) (orse C(C))* (High Court, Unreported Judgment, Laffoy J, 11 January 1996), on the differences in approach to personality disorders between ICD-10 and DSM-IV.

A further difference between the two systems of classification is that ICD recommends using all sources of information, especially information from family and friends, whilst no such requirement is stipulated in DSM. This in particular has implications for making a diagnosis of personality disorder, which is made more readily using DSM than ICD because of these differing requirements.[10]

DIFFERENCES BETWEEN THE OLD AND NEW CLASSIFICATIONS

Some of the differences that exist between the old and the newer (ICD and DSM) systems have been outlined already. These include the provision of operational definitions in the newer classifications, as well as the use of multi-axial diagnoses in contrast to the single label provided by the old system.

Differences in terminology also exist and this may cause problems in court. For example, the word "neurotic" is seldom used in the new classifications, whilst it is an important concept in the older one. The reason for its relegation lies in the association with personality disorder, which had developed over time. Also, it implied a particular causation for the disorders arising in childhood. This is now believed to be an over-simplification and without scientific foundation. The word "functional" is not used either, since it implies a non-physical cause for the disorder. However, modern techniques for assessing brain tissue have shown that there are changes at a microscopic level, even in the "functional" psychoses. The word is therefore redundant. The old system of classification did not recognise "stress reactions" and doctors using this system will not diagnose conditions such as adjustment reaction and acute stress reaction.[11]

---

[10] The differing approaches are rehearsed in the evidence of the psychiatrists and psychologists and set out in the judgment in *T(S) (orse T(B))*v *J(B)* (High Court, Unreported Judgment, O'Hanlon J, 2 September 1993).

[11] As, for example, classically occurs in "nervous shock" type claims that fail to meet the threshold damage requirement for recovery. These conditions are those that the law does not recognise for the purposes of compensation. See Chapter 8.

IMPLICATIONS

It is essential to establish (a) that the psychiatrist is using a modern system of classification, and if he is, (b) whether it is ICD-10 or DSM-IV. In court, two psychiatrists, one adhering to the old and the other to the new system, may appear superficially to be differing in diagnosis. Differences between psychiatrists will also become apparent if both of the newer classifications are being used simultaneously. In the interests of simplicity, only one of the modern systems should be used.

Chapter 4

BIOLOGICAL AND PSYCHOLOGICAL INVESTIGATIONS

This chapter considers the biological and psychological investigations commonly performed on accident victims and persons presenting for psychiatric assessment. "Biological investigations" in this context refer to medical investigations which do not have a specific psychiatric dimension, such as X-rays, urinalysis and electrocardiography. Psychological investigations include tests of cognitive function (brain function) and tests for the measurement of psychiatric disorder, including personality disorder. It should be noted, however, that psychiatry is largely a clinical specialty and that the function of these tests is limited and supplementary to clinical assessment. In a legal setting, their use may give a spurious sense of certainty.

BIOLOGICAL INVESTIGATIONS

Biological investigations include radiological examination (X-ray), electrocardiography (a measure of heart activity), electroencephalography (a measure of brain activity), urinalysis (urine tests) and haematological (blood) investigations. Haematological investigations are commonplace among both outpatients and inpatients and are useful in excluding a number of physical disorders which present with psychological symptoms. Some investigations are also carried out prior to commencing treatment with drugs of potential toxicity, such as lithium, and thereafter to monitor blood levels of certain drugs.

Haematological Investigations

Patients with depression often complain of tiredness and lack of energy. These are common symptoms in anaemia, which can be excluded by taking a sample of blood and measuring haemoglobin (a constituent of red blood cells) and full blood count. The latter measures the number of red cells, which carry oxygen to the body tissues, white cells, whose function is to fight infection, and platelets, which facilitate blood clotting.

In patients who abuse alcohol, the mean cell volume, a measure of red cell size, is increased. This is probably due to the direct toxic effects of alcohol on bone marrow, where red cells are produced. Liver function tests are also routinely carried out on alcohol abusers and abnormalities may be reversible in the early stages of the abuse. Persistent changes indicate ongoing liver damage. The most sensitive indicator of liver damage, often being found before other liver function tests indicate damage, is the level of the enzyme, gamma-glutamyltransferase. Serum alcohol levels are also sometimes requested, particularly when an in-patient denies drinking during in-patient treatment. One unit of alcohol, consumed by a 72kg man, will produce a maximum blood alcohol level after about half an hour and will take half an hour to be metabolised.

Depression is a common symptom of hypothyroidism (under-functioning of the thyroid gland) and should be excluded in patients with depression, particularly when it is unresponsive to anti-depressant treatment. However, other symptoms of hypothyroidism will also usually be present, such as weight gain, slowed reflexes and cold intolerance.[1] Even with treatment of the hypothyroidism, the depression is frequently resistant to single anti-depressants and combinations may have to be used whilst monitoring thyroid function regularly. Over-activity of the thyroid gland or hyperthyroidism is associated with anxiety, palpitations and sweating, which respond to treatment of the underlying physical disorder. It may be necessary to check thyroid function in

---

[1] However, it is a diagnosis that is notoriously missed.

the presence of anxiety symptoms that appear to be unrelated to stress and to be associated with weight loss and heat intolerance.

The dexamethasone suppression test is a blood test which is used by some psychiatrists to confirm the diagnosis of a depressive illness. In healthy persons, secretion of the hormone cortisol is suppressed by injected dexamethasone. This does not occur in those with depressive illness. One of the problems with this test is that it is positive in only 50 per cent of depressed patients and false positive results have been found in a range of other psychiatric disorders. It should be regarded as no more than an adjunct in confirming the diagnosis and pointing to the necessity for biological treatments.

Hypo-pituitarism or under-functioning of the pituitary gland, situated near the base of the skull, is associated with disorders of menstruation — a feature of anorexia nervosa also. As a result, many sufferers with anorexia nervosa are initially referred to an endocrinologist for investigations. Those with hypo-pituitarism do not have the pervasive fear of food or fatness seen in anorexia nervosa. In order to rule out hypo-pituitarism, a radiological scan of the pituitary gland will often be requested, as will hormone assays.

Because of starvation and vomiting, a number of abnormalities are found in the laboratory investigations carried out in those with anorexia nervosa.[2] These are particularly important when weight loss is life threatening and close monitoring of blood electrolytes (e.g. sodium, potassium, during in-patient medical treatment) is essential. Patients with anorexia nervosa are treated in a psychiatric ward, although when the disorder becomes life threatening, emergency medical treatment may necessitate transfer to a medical ward.

---

[2] Low luteinizing and follicle-stimulating hormone and oestradiol levels; low T3 and T4; raised growth hormone and cortisol levels. Luteinizing hormone release shows immature pattern. Neutropenia; normocytic, normocromic anaemia; low ESR. Hypercholesterolaemia, increased serum beta-carotene, hypoglycaemia and electrolyte abnormalities.

The patient presenting in a manic state, particularly if the onset is very sudden (e.g. over a few hours), should have a blood sugar test, since hypoglycaemia (low blood sugar), a complication of the treatment of diabetes mellitus, can mimic mania. However, the hypoglycaemic patient will also be disoriented, whilst the manic patient rarely is.[3]

Patients who are prescribed lithium, most commonly for manic-depression, should have serum lithium checked every week in the early stages of prescribing, but every three months once the level has stabilised. If the levels fluctuate, then more frequent tests are required. Estimation of levels of this drug are essential if the optimum effective blood level is to be established. If levels are too low, it is ineffective, and if they are too high, serious side effects can develop and in rare cases lead to death. Before commencing lithium, the functioning of the thyroid gland as well as renal and cardiac function should be checked and thereafter annually, since lithium is known to be toxic to these organs in some patients. Carbamazepine and sodium valproate are drugs for which there are similar indications to those of lithium and levels should be checked regularly if toxicity is to be avoided. Unlike lithium, there is no necessity for checks prior to commencing the drug.

Urinalysis

Urine samples are easily obtained by requesting the patient to urinate into a container. They have the disadvantage that they can easily be tampered with, a problem particularly prominent among drug abusers.

Urine tests are most commonly sought when a patient develops confusion and infection is suspected of causing this. Urine tests are also carried out when abuse of amphetamines is suspected. Amphetamine intoxication produces symptoms similar to schizophrenia and its abuse must be ruled out in any patient presenting for the first time with symptoms of acute schizophrenia. Opiates

---

[3] See, for example, in a criminal context, *R* v *Quick* [1973] QB 910, 57 Cr App R 722, CA; see Chapter 16, pp. 400–1.

and benzodiazepines may also be detected in urine, although the speed of their metabolism and excretion makes this less useful than for amphetamine detection. Blood levels of all drugs or their breakdown products are also available, although the usefulness of this is limited because of the necessity for immediate sampling and the delays in obtaining an accurate result.

Electrocardiography

The electrocardiograph (ECG) provides a measure of the electrical activity of heart muscle. In medical practice, it can show irregularities in the heart rate and indicate the part of the heart at which the abnormality is located. It is carried out by placing leads on the chest area overlying the heart and takes a few minutes to complete. Sometimes it may be necessary to monitor heart activity over several hours or days, and for this the patient wears a special monitor, known as a Holter Monitor. This does not preclude the patient from carrying out normal day-to-day activities, since it is small and relatively inconspicuous.

An ECG should routinely be requested when a patient is having electro-convulsive (electrical) treatment. Cardiac monitoring is essential if doses over 250 mgs of amitryptiline or its equivalent are being prescribed for the treatment of refractory depression. Once it has been established after a week that no irregularities in heart rate are occurring, then monitoring can be discontinued. Patients with panic attacks will sometimes request an ECG to rule out a cardiac basis for their symptoms of palpitation. In clinical practice, however, it is not difficult to distinguish an irregular heart rate from a panic attack.

Electroencephalography

The electroencephalograph (EEG) is a method for measuring electrical activity in the brain. Its most common application is in the diagnosis of epilepsy. In psychiatry, its greatest use is in assessing disorders of the brain which have a physical basis, such as dementia or head injury.[4] It is a non-invasive and safe procedure. It is not useful in diagnosing disorders such as depressive illness, schizophrenia or mania.

Some patients with temporal lobe epilepsy may have symptoms identical to those found in schizophrenia — an EEG is helpful in distinguishing one from the other. Caution must be exercised in relation to the findings in the EEG, since normal tracings are found in up to 40 per cent of patients with physical abnormalities in the brain. However, an abnormal result is confirmatory of an organic disorder such as dementia. The EEG is therefore an adjunct to other investigations. Drugs used in treating psychiatric disorders can cause EEG changes and this investigation should not be carried out within six weeks of concluding a course of ECT (electro-convulsive therapy), since this treatment distorts the reading.

EEGs are sometimes helpful in distinguishing true dementia from pseudo dementia[5] — a disorder of memory which resembles dementia but is caused by depressive illness and is therefore treatable. Whilst a normal record will be of little help in making this important distinction, an abnormal record will confirm the presence of an organic cause.

Patients with severe personality disorder,[6] such as the anti-social type, sometimes show EEG abnormalities indicative of delayed brain maturation, although in clinical practice this group derive only limited benefit from the use of anti-epileptic drugs. The EEG is therefore of little clinical benefit in those with anti-social behaviour and its main contribution is to rule out epilepsy. It is not helpful in diagnosing depressive or anxiety disorders or in distinguishing mania from schizophrenia.

EEG investigations are commonly used to help distinguish various types of dementia from each other. These include such disorders as Alzheimer's disease (pre-senile and senile type),

---

[4] See Chapter 12.

[5] See Chapter 12.

[6] See Chapter 9.

Huntington's Chorea and Creutzfeldt-Jakob disease, which are themselves associated with distinctive abnormalities. When dementia is of the multi-infarct type, due to narrowing of the blood vessels supplying the brain, the EEG may show localised changes. Space-occupying lesions such as tumours can sometimes be diagnosed using an EEG.

Radiological Tests

Diagnostic radiology is the medical speciality concerned with minimally invasive imaging. The images produced vary according to which modality is used — X-ray, sonography, radionuclides, CAT scanning or magnetic resonance imaging (MRI).

A chest X-ray will usually be sought in those over the age of 45 who are admitted for in-patient treatment.[7] This is essential in those receiving ECT.

A CAT scan of the brain is the most commonly sought after radiological investigation by psychiatrists. It is helpful in identifying whether dementia is present or not, especially if the diagnosis is uncertain. It will also aid in ruling out space-occupying lesions, particularly when symptoms are treatment-resistant. As described already, changes to the ventricles of those with schizophrenia have been consistently found in those with negative symptoms of schizophrenia.[8] However, this is unhelpful in clinical practice, since the changes are small and are sometimes found in the general population.

A more sensitive but more expensive form of imaging is magnetic resonance imaging (MRI). In psychiatric practice, MRI scanning is seldom sought as yet, except to confirm or refute a negative finding on a CAT scan where a dementing process is clinically diagnosed or when small degrees of brain damage from

---

[7] However, this practice will have to be evaluated when the provisions of the *Medical Exposures Directive* (MED) [97-43 EURATOM of 30/6/1997] (No. L 180/22 *Official Journal of the European Communities*, 9 July 1997) is implemented into domestic law, as it must by 13 May 2000 under the provisions of Article 15.

[8] See p. 25.

trauma are suspected. The superiority of MRI over CAT scanning lies in the greater clarity of visualisation of brain tissue and of certain parts in the brain such as the temporal lobe. Positron emission tomography or PET scanning, which identifies changes to blood flow, metabolism and activity in the brain, is not yet used in clinical psychiatry, although it is finding a role in research.

PSYCHOLOGICAL TESTING

Cognitive Function

Tests of cognitive function measure brain function using verbal assessments, rather than applying radiological or biological techniques. They show abnormality earlier than radiological investigations but require repetition over time to prove change.

When organic brain damage is suspected, a number of tests are available to quantify and aid in localisation of the lesions. Varying degrees of specialisation are required to conduct these.

The Mini-Mental State[9] is the most commonly used test in a clinical setting and only takes five to ten minutes to administer. It is a pointer to deficits in memory and can be affected by poor co-operation, dementia or depression. Five aspects of function are assessed using ten questions and scored out of a maximum of 30 points. Deficits in the score point to the necessity for detailed cognitive assessment, using measures such as the WAIS (see below), or for radiological investigations such as a CAT scan of the brain. Its principal use is in the elderly and it can be carried out routinely.

The Wechsler Adult Intelligence Scale (WAIS)[10] is an extensively used measure of intelligence, giving scores for both performance and verbal abilities. The verbal component has six subtests (information, comprehension, arithmetic, similarities, digit

---

[9] M.F. Folstein, S.E. Folstein and P.R. McHugh (1975), "'Mini-Mental State': a Practical Method for Grading the Cognitive State of Patients for the Clinician", *Journal of Psychiatric Research*, Vol. 12, pp. 189–98.

[10] D. Wechsler (1958), *The Measurement and Appraisal of Adult Intelligence*, Baltimore, MD: Williams and Wilkins.

span and vocabulary) whilst the performance component has five (digit symbol, picture completion, block design, picture arrangement and object assembly). An overall score is obtained and deviations from the established population norms indicate learning disability. A discrepancy between the verbal and performance scores indicates brain damage, with scores in the performance sub-scale being lower than verbal scores following tissue damage such as head injury or dementia. Sub-test scores aid in identifying the location of the lesions, although this has to be confirmed by radiological assessment for brain damage, since the WAIS scores are not reliable enough in isolation. Moreover, psychiatric disorders such as depression can affect the overall score due to motivational and concentration factors. This is a lengthy scale to administer and interpretation by a psychologist trained in its use is essential.

Other Psychological Tests

These are tests other than the cognitive tests already described. They are divided into three major groups — diagnostic, screening and symptom measures. Their main application is in research, but they may occasionally be used to provide objective measures for the courts. In particular, measures of personality are used extensively by those giving evidence in relation to civil annulments on the grounds of personality disorder.[11] Only a few examples of each category are outlined here.[12] Measurements for a host of disorders and difficulties are available, ranging from depression, anxiety and obsessions to sexual behaviour, social function and suicidal ideation.

---

[11] See Chapters 9 and 11. This does not appear on the face of the written judgments.

[12] For further information, see, D.F. Peck and C.M. Shapiro (1990), *Measuring Human Problems: A Practical Guide*, Chichester: John Wiley and Sons.

Diagnostic Instruments

Diagnostic instruments are not generally used in clinical practice; their main application is in research. They provide a diagnosis on the basis of symptoms elicited. They are usually time-consuming and require complex computer programs to arrive at a diagnosis. Intensive training in their use is essential.

The best known tool in European psychiatry is the Present State Examination (PSE).[13] This instrument takes between 30 and 90 minutes to administer by a trained interviewer. The training itself is time-consuming and a special computer program is required to collate the scores for each of the 140 items measured. It covers symptoms over the previous month and these are clearly defined, as well as prescribing the exact wording of the questions for each symptom. A recently expanded version (termed SCAN) also covers lifetime diagnosis, as well as episode-based symptoms. This revision has further increased the complexity and comprehensiveness of the instrument.

In the United States, several diagnostic instruments exist and these are even more lengthy than the PSE. The Schedule for Affective Disorders and Schizophrenia (SADS)[14] is one of the oldest. The interview takes one to two hours and has been designed for use with hospital patients. It has probably been superseded in research by the Diagnostic Interview Schedule (DIS),[15] which is highly structured and takes over one hour to complete.

Screening Instruments

Screening instruments are used mainly in research to identify those who may be suffering from a psychiatric disorder. They are

---

[13] J.K. Wing, J.E. Cooper and N. Sartorius (1974), *The Measurement and Classification of Psychiatric Symptoms*, London: Cambridge University Press.

[14] J. Endicott and R.L. Spitzer (1978), "A Diagnostic Review: the Schedule for Affective Disorders and Schizophrenia", *Archives of General Psychiatry*, Vol. 35, pp. 837–44.

[15] L.N. Robins, J.E. Helzer, J. Croughan and K.S. Ratcliff (1981), "National Institute of Mental Health Diagnostic Interview Schedule", *Archives of General Psychiatry*, Vol. 38, pp. 381–9.

easily administered and do not take more than a few minutes to complete. A supplementary assessment is required to confirm or refute the possibility of disorder, using a diagnostic instrument such as SCAN.

The General Health Questionnaire (GHQ)[16] is the best known and simplest screening test available. It has found extensive use although it has many drawbacks including the tendency to underestimate the prevalence of psychiatric disorder in those with chronic physical illnesses. It also has to be followed by a diagnostic interview. The questionnaire consists of 60 items, although shorter versions are also available. Each item is rated on a four-point scale. Its popularity lies in the speed with which it can be completed — about ten minutes. A patient scoring above a certain score known as the "threshold" score is deemed a "case" and further diagnostic assessment is required. The GHQ is sometimes erroneously used as a diagnostic instrument.

The PSE also includes a screening version and has found extensive use in World Health Organisation studies, as well as myriads of other studies throughout the psychiatric world.

Symptom Measures

Symptom measures are used to quantify the severity of the disorder in a patient already diagnosed clinically as suffering from a particular disorder. They are not appropriate to use in arriving at a diagnosis, although this is a common error. Their main use lies in measuring symptom changes during treatment, particularly in drug trials.[17]

The Brief Psychiatric Rating Scale (BPRS)[18] measures 11 items on an eight-point scale and the assessment takes about twenty minutes. Its use is with psychiatric in-patients, either acute or

---

[16] D.P. Goldberg (1972), *The Detection of Psychiatric Illness by Questionnaire*, Oxford: Oxford University Press.

[17] See Chapter 19.

[18] J.E. Overall and D.R. Gorsham (1962), "The Brief Psychological Rating Scale", *Psychological Reports*, Vol. 10, pp. 799–812.

long-stay and is unsuitable for those with less serious psychiatric disorders.

The Hamilton Rating Scale for Depression[19] is used to quantify the severity of depressive symptoms. Its most common application is in clinical drug trials where the symptom score is an indication of severity (and therefore of suitability for the study) and progress is monitored by changes in total score. It is designed to be completed at the end of a clinical interview. It contains 17 items rated on a three- or five-point scale and detailed instructions are available to explain the criteria for each score. It should only be used on those already diagnosed as having a depressive illness, since it is not a diagnostic instrument.

The Beck Depression Inventory[20] is a scale completed by the patient consisting of 21 items and, like the Hamilton scale, it is not a diagnostic instrument and its uses are also similar. Statements for each item, which describe the patient's current state, are read aloud and the patient selects the statement of best fit. It takes about 30 minutes to administer.

The Eating Attitude Test (EAT)[21] was developed to measure symptoms of anorexia nervosa and can be completed in a few minutes. A 40-item and a 26-item form exist and scores obtained above a cut-off of 30 and 20 respectively indicate anorexia nervosa. It is not suitable as a diagnostic tool since people in the general population who have abnormal eating habits score positive also.

---

[19] M. Hamilton (1967), "Development of a Rating Scale for Primary Depressive Illness", *British Journal of Social and Clinical Psychology*, Vol. 6, pp. 278–96.

[20] A.T. Beck, C.H. Ward, M. Mendelson, J. Mock and J. Erbaugh (1961), "An Inventory for Measuring Depression", *Archives of General Psychiatry*, Vol. 4, pp. 561–71.

[21] D.M. Garner and P.E. Garfinkel (1979), "The Eating Attitudes Test: an Index of Symptoms of Anorexia Nervosa", *Psychological Medicine*, Vol. 9, pp. 273–9.

Psychosocial Adjustment to Illness Scale (PAIS)[22] was designed to assess adjustment to physical illness. Forty-six items are rated on a three-point scale. It is rated by the interviewer.

Personality tests are described in detail in Chapter 9.

SUMMARY

A number of biological and psychological tests are used in psychiatry. These are generally ancillary to the clinical assessment of the patient and must be taken in conjunction with the clinical findings.

---

[22] L.R. Derogatis (1986), "The Psychosocial Adjustment to Illness Scale (PAIS)", *Journal of Psychosomatic Research*, Vol. 30, pp. 77–91.

Chapter 5

MEMORY

ASSESSING THE VERACITY OF STATEMENTS

Central to decisions in law, especially in the courts, is the veracity, or otherwise, of statements and evidence that is given. This is a judgement made on a daily basis and the approach is rarely explicit but is based on impression. How do we assess the truthfulness of evidence? Are there behavioural or verbal cues that assist in this? Regrettably, the strategies employed by adults, when examined in an experimental setting, suggest that accuracy assessment is very poor and just exceeds chance. Adults ascribe far too much significance to facial and bodily indicators and too little to verbal queues such as speech hesitation, voice pitch and speech errors.[1]

Statement Validity Analysis[2] is a technique that has evolved within the inquisitorial system of Europe as a means of objectively assessing the veracity of children's statements in relation to allegations of sexual abuse. Each statement is assessed on 19 different points which in turn are grouped into five major categories such as the detail, the spontaneity, the level of knowledge of the crime and a host of other items. The importance of this approach, still in its infancy, is the potential for extension to adult statements. Should this technique evolve further, it is clear that the

[1] B. De Paulo, J. Stone and G. Lassiter (1985), "Deceiving and Detecting Deceit" in B. Schlenker (ed.), *The Self and Social Life*, New York: McGraw-Hill.

[2] M. Steller and G. Koenken (1989), "Criteria-based Statement Analysis" in D.C. Raskin (ed.), *Psychological Methods in Criminal Investigation and Evidence*, New York: Springer, pp. 217–45.

subjective impression of evidence presented in court may, at some time in the future, no longer be acceptable.

TYPES OF MEMORY

Memory is of three types: sensory, short-term and long-term memory. The function of sensory memory is to allow the rapid processing of incoming stimuli so that comparisons can be made with material which is already stored in long-term memory. There are separate registers for each of the senses and they give coherence and continuity to the world. For example, as a sentence is read, the first few words are read and identified. At the same time subsequent words are scanned and put into visual sensory memory until they are also processed. Sensory memories fade quickly unless further processing takes place, leading to storage in short-term memory. This process is facilitated by selective attention, which sifts the relevant material for storage in short-term memory, since it would be impossible to deal with all the sensory stimuli impinging on the individual at one time. Short-term or working memory, as it is called, allows for the storage of memories for much longer than the few seconds available to sensory memory. This aids the constant updating of surroundings — short-term memories can be thought about and organised in a way that is impossible with sensory memory. For example, if you see a man walking his dog, and a few seconds later you hear a dog bark, you would not be startled because you would recognise the source of the sound from the visual memory, which had been encoded in working memory.

Long-term memory is what is usually meant by "memory" in general parlance and it is believed to have a limitless capacity. The placing of information into long-term memory is termed encoding and can occur for the specific stimulus or for the general meaning conveyed by the image. For example, seeing an advertisement for a 50 per cent reduction in the price of dresses in shop X as a result of a fire might be recorded exactly in memory word for word (visual coding) or might be recalled as an advertisement for shop X (semantic coding). Semantic coding, or storage of the general meaning of the stimulus, is the most common method of encoding material in long-term memory. People with automatic vivid and detailed imagery of what they have seen are said to have photographic memory — also called eidetic imagery — although this is virtually absent in adults and present in only about 5 per cent of children.

Memory is also affected by stress — this is mediated by the effect on attention.[3] In general, attention cannot be divided unless both tasks tap into different aspects of attentional resources. This allows a skilled pianist to read music and press the keys simultaneously, but prevents the accurate perception and storage of, for example, a vast array of dials/monitors and the facial details of people nearby simultaneously. When stress is present, such as anxiety, panic or depression, attention is even narrower. This has implications for areas as diverse as aviation psychology and eyewitness evidence in court.

REMEMBERING

Remembering requires that the item be correctly stored and then brought to consciousness (retrieved/recalled). For storage to occur, the item must be rehearsed or the memory decreases consistently over about 20 seconds and can never be retrieved — this decay is one reason for a failure to recall. The second reason is interference from related material. In proactive interference, old memories interfere with new learning and hence with recall, whilst in retroactive interference, new memories impair retrieval of old ones. For example, proactive interference would explain why learning Spanish this year will make it more difficult to learn French next year. Retroactive interference helps explain why learning German this year makes it more difficult to recall the Spanish learnt last year.

In general, recall is better when it takes place in the same physical environment as that in which the event was initially stored in memory, since surrounding features will also be encoded

---

[3] See also sensory memory, above, p. 66.

and will act as retrieval cues — hence the use of actors to re-enact crimes as a stimulus to public recall. This importance of the physical environment in recollection is termed context-dependent retrieval. As well as the physical environment, the proximity between the emotional environment at the time of encoding and retrieval will also facilitate accurate recall — this is termed state-dependent retrieval. Material learned when the subject is under the influence of alcohol or is anxious will be recalled better if this occurs under similar influences. Moreover, negative events are best recalled when people are in a negative or depressed mood, whilst positive events are best recalled when happy.

Memories are not just the exact reconstruction of an event or item but are influenced by the subject's existing knowledge, which is used to fill in gaps in encoding and retrieval. Memories are constructed in this way, a process termed "constructive memory". Needless to say, this can influence recall and may lead to distortions. An example of the use of constructive memory comes from the experiment in which undergraduate students were asked to wait in the office of a graduate student. When asked to recall everything that was in the office, most mistakenly described books, even though there were none. The existing knowledge that graduate students read many books influenced their recall. Another example derives from the study in which subjects were asked to read a long passage about a dictator. For one group of subjects, he was a fictitious character named Gerald Martin and for the other Adolf Hitler. Later the subjects were asked if the passage contained the sentence "He hated Jews particularly and so persecuted them." The statement was not in the passage and the Gerald Martin group answered correctly whilst the Adolf Hitler group "remembered" reading the statement. These and other studies[4] suggest that people can believe their imaginings.

---

[4] M. Garry, C.G. Manning, E.L. Loftus and S.J. Sherman (1996), "Imagination Inflation: Imagining a Childhood Event Inflates Confidence that it Occurred", *Psychonomic Bulletin Review*, Vol. 3, pp. 208–14; M.S. Zaragoza and K.L. Mitchell (1996), "Repeated Exposure to Suggestion in the Creation of False Memories", *Psychological Science*, Vol. 7, pp. 294–305.

THE BIOLOGICAL BASIS OF MEMORY

The biological basis of memory is evident from the effects that some procedures and drugs have on recall. Damage to an area of the brain called the hippocampus often results in loss of memory for events after the injury (anterograde amnesia) although memories for earlier events are intact, as is procedural memory (the ability to perform learned tasks such as combing hair). This is due to failure to transfer information from short-term to long-term memory. Retrograde amnesia is the loss of memory for events prior to the injury. This may be extensive or cover just the moments before the accident. Other areas involved in the storage of memories include the cortex, the amygdala, and the thalamus. As knowledge of memory and of the brain increases, it is clear that short- and long-term memory are separate processes and that the formation and storage of memories involve distinct areas. In addition, different aspects of memory (e.g. sight and sound for an event) are stored in different parts of the brain. Overall, it is apparent that no single brain structure is responsible for all types of memory and several neurotransmitters are implicated.

When memories are formed and stored, communication between existing nerve endings (synapses) improves and additional synapses also develop, with neurotransmitters passing across these synapses. Research has generally focused on the neurotransmitters acetylcholine and glutamate, rather than on the synapses, in relation to the common disorders of memory such as Alzheimer's disease, and this is the basis on which memory-enhancing (nootropic) drugs are being developed.

FALSE ALLEGATIONS

Increasingly, there are accusations of child sexual abuse directed at those who have committed no such crime.[5] This may occur in the context of a psychotic illness where the sufferer becomes

---

[5] In respect of the corroboration of the unsworn statements of minors, and those under a mental disability, see, generally, Children's Act, 1908, s. 30, as amended by the Criminal Evidence Act, 1992, s. 28.

deluded that he or she has been the victim of sexual abuse by another. The presence of accompanying psychotic symptoms, either
delusions or hallucinations, give a clue to the basis for the allegations. These delusions remit when treatment with neuroleptic
medication is instituted.

This scenario is uncommon and by far the commonest situation
in which accusations of sexual abuse are made is in the context of
marital breakdown. Here, the accusation is made in an attempt to
influence decisions relating to custody and access.[6] As with many
charges, proving the negative is difficult, especially when the
truth is based on one word against another.

RECOVERED MEMORIES

Those working with survivors of traumatic events have sometimes
noted the existence of amnesia and the subsequent recovery of
these memories during treatment. This has sparked controversy
regarding sexual abuse which comes to light during treatment for
some other disorder and has resulted in claims that these are not
true memories but arise as a result of suggestion by powerful
therapists on vulnerable patients — hence the term "false memory
syndrome". The counterclaim is that recall of these events has
been repressed during the traumatic event as a way of protecting
the psyche and that therapy facilitates recollection.

What is Repression?

Repression is an unconscious but active inhibitory mechanism,
first described by Freud, in order to keep memories out of consciousness and protect the psyche. This is distinct from trying not
to think about the events, or putting them "to the back of the
mind". It must be distinguished from denying the abuse because
of embarrassment or from some conscious motivation such as extending the statute of limitations. Repression is also different

---

[6] E. Mikkelson, T. Gutheil and M. Emens (1992), "Sexual Abuse Allegations
by Children and Adolescents: Contextual Factors and Clinical Subtypes",
American Journal of Psychotherapy, Vol. 46, pp. 556–70.

from normal forgetfulness and a satisfactory test of repression must demonstrate amnesia for abuse sufficiently traumatic that no person could reasonably forget it. Biological causes of amnesia must also be excluded and this includes amnesia due to fits, intoxication or head injury. A further biological cause of amnesia is the immaturity of the central nervous system in the young child. Children under the age of three have nearly complete amnesia and those under the age of six have substantial amnesia for earlier events. Attempts to find a biological substrate for repression such as encephalographic (EEG) and other measures have so far proved fruitless.[7] An elegant review of the literature on repression is provided by Pope and Hudson.[8]

Corroboration of Memories[9]

An essential requirement in examining the veracity of "recovered memories" is to seek corroboration regarding the events described. One study reported that of 129 women taken into care as children having been diagnosed as being sexually abused, 12 per cent reported no abuse experience at all when assessed 17 years later,[10] suggesting that extremely traumatic events can be forgotten and/or repressed. However, some researchers point to the necessity for stringent evidence of the authenticity of the recovered memory — this would include written information from childhood

---

[7] T.P. Zahn, R. Moraga and W.J. Ray (1996), "Psycho-physiological Assessment of Dissociative Disorders" in L.K. Michelson and W.J. Ray (eds.), *Handbook of Dissociation: Theoretical, Empirical and Clinical Perspectives*, New York: Plenum, pp. 269–87.

[8] H.G. Pope Jr. and J.I. Hudson (1995), "Can Memories of Childhood Sexual Abuse be Repressed?", *Psychological Medicine*, Vol. 25, pp. 121–6.

9 See, generally, the requirements for a warning in relation to corroboration of visual identification and recognition evidence in *People (A-G)* v *Casey (No. 2)* [1963] IR 33; *R* v *Turnbull* [1977] QB 224; *Arthurs* v *Attorney General for Northern Ireland* (1971) 55 Crim App Rep 161; *People (DPP)* v *Strafford* [1983] IR 165; *People (DPP)* v *Fagan* (Court of Criminal Appeal, Unreported Judgment, 13 May 1974). See, generally, C. Fennell (1992), *The Law of Evidence in Ireland*, Dublin, Butterworths (Ireland) Ltd., pp. 126–33.

[10] L.M. Williams (1994), "Recall of Childhood Trauma: a Prospective Study of Women's Memories of Child Sexual Abuse", *Journal of Consulting and Clinical Psychology*, Vol. 62, pp. 1167–76.

records, evidence of conviction for an offence, etc. — and have concluded that, to date, this is lacking[11] in corroborative studies.

Some researchers[12] have identified women who denied abuse in spite of written confirmation that abuse did occur but later, during a "clarification interview", confirmed the events as described, and admitted withholding the information for a variety of reasons, such as a wish to forget or to spare the perpetrator who had since attempted to make amends.

A recent report from the Royal College of Psychiatrists in London has been scathing of the concept of repression and of recovery techniques.[13] Moreover, it is sceptical of the view that memories can be recovered after years of apparent amnesia and cites evidence that they can be distorted. It states: "There is no means of determining the factual truth or falsity of a recovered memory except through external evidence, difficult though this is to obtain." Guidelines for good clinical practice are offered.

A pertinent question is whether memories are recovered in situations other than therapy or if recovery applies to traumas other than sexual abuse. There is at least one study[14] which has found that memories other than those relating to sexual abuse can be retrieved from total amnesia and also that memories can be recollected before entering therapy. The method used in this study can, however, be criticised, since the data was derived from the 27 per cent of respondents, all chartered psychologists, who replied to a questionnaire about their own patients. It can therefore be said to be based on opinion rather than being a hypothesis-testing investigation and its reliance on memory of specific cases is a further drawback.

---

[11] Pope and Hudson (1995), op. cit.

[12] D.D. Femina, C.A. Yeager and D.O. Lewis (1990), "Child Abuse: Adolescent Records vs. Adult Recall", *Child Abuse and Neglect*, Vol. 145, pp. 227–31.

[13] S. Brandon, J. Boakes, D. Glaser and R. Green (1998), "Recovered Memories of Childhood Sexual Abuse: Implications for Clinical Practice", *British Journal of Psychiatry*, Vol. 172, pp. 296–307.

[14] B. Andrews, J. Morton, D. Bekerian et al. (1995), "The Recovery of Memories in Clinical Practice", *The Psychologist*, Vol. 8, pp. 209–14.

MULTIPLE PERSONALITY DISORDER AND RECOVERED MEMORIES

Multiple personality disorder (MPD) is a controversial diagnosis which has gained popularity since its popularisation in the book *Sybil*.[15] This very entertaining book describes in detail the numerous personalities of a woman who in childhood had been sexually abused by her mother. Beginning in 1899, only 200 cases were reported worldwide until 1980, but a marked growth in the number of reported cases followed its inclusion in DSM-III in 1982 and several investigators claimed that up to 5 per cent of college students in Canada were afflicted with MPD. As well as an increase in the number of cases diagnosed, the number of personalities has also increased, with some claiming hundreds of "alters". The diagnosis is confined to the United States and Canada and is rarely made in Europe. ICD-10 is circumspect about the diagnosis and suggests that, if it exists at all, it should be categorised under dissociative disorders. DSM-IV has renamed MPD as dissociative identity disorder, although this text will continue with the term MPD.

Much of the interest in MPD arises from the belief that it arises as a result of sexual abuse, and that when memories of abuse are lacking, they have been repressed in childhood. Sceptics claim that the burgeoning number of cases is due to the frequent use of the label by a few psychiatrists and psychologists offering "recovered memory" therapy for sexual abuse, that it is largely an iatrogenic disorder and point to the absence of criteria for distinguishing false from true memories.[16] The counterclaim is that numbers are increasing due to a greater understanding of the disorder. Scientific investigation of MPD and recovered memory seems to be moving away from these concepts, however, and increasingly there is concern about the ethical aspects of "recovered memory" therapy, centring around the potential harm that an in-

---

[15] F.R. Schreiber (1973), *Sybil*, Chicago: Henry Regnery.

[16] H. Merskey (1996), "Ethical Issues in Search of Repressed Memories", *American Journal of Psychotherapy*, Vol. 50, pp. 323–35.

correct diagnosis can do to the patient's family and the dependence of the patient on the therapist which ensues.[17]

MEMORY AND THE COURT

It is assumed that, in the courtroom setting, witnesses can accurately recall information, that jurors can encode, store and retrieve this information accurately and that a just decision can
then be reached by the jurors on the basis of legal instruction from
the judge. The courtroom is the place where memory plays a vital
role and where deficiencies in recall can have tragic consequences.

There are many reasons to believe that witnesses and jurors do
not accurately recall everything that is presented to them. Jurors
have to remember the instructions that are given to them even
before any evidence is presented at all. There is some evidence
that they are poor at this and have particular problems with the
use of legal jargon that they do not understand.[18] There is further
evidence that specific instructions relating to the charges which
have to be proven and the criteria for each are also not compre-
hended.[19]

The most interesting aspect of trials concerns witness memory.
Only that which has been attended to and perceived can be recalled. However, eyewitnesses make mistakes and even the manner in which a question is posed by counsel can lead to alterations
in memory. For example, asking the question "How fast was the
blue car travelling when it slammed into the truck?" is likely to
evoke a faster speed than the question "How fast was the blue car

---

[17] H.G. Pope Jr. and J.I. Hudson (1996), "'Recovered Memory' Therapy for
Eating Disorders: Implications of the Ramona Verdict", *International Journal of Eating Disorders*, Vol. 19, pp. 139–45; S.L. McElroy and P.E. Keck Jr.
(1995), "Recovered Memory Therapy: False Memory Syndrome and Other
Complications", *Psychiatric Annual*, Vol. 25, pp. 731–5.

[18] N. Younstrom (1991), "Legal Terms may Elude Jurors in Capital Cases".
American Psychological Association Monitor, October.

[19] L. Deutsch (1992), "Bias, Confusion, Emotion Led to Verdict, Responses
Show", *Champaign-Urbana News Gazette*, May. However, the process of jury
selection seeks to ensure at the very least a minimum standard of competence. See Juries Act, 1976.

travelling when it hit the truck?". Moreover, there is evidence that when an object is mentioned after an event, it is often mistakenly remembered as having been there in the first place.[20] Uncertainty exists as to whether the witnesses are actually aware that they did not see the objects, whilst some suggest that mentioning the new object creates retroactive interference, making it difficult to retrieve the original memory reliably.

The credibility of witnesses in the eyes of jurors is as likely to be based on how the witness presents as much as on the content of the evidence. Many jurors are impressed by large amounts of detail and believe that the witness paid close attention to the crime or has a particularly accurate memory and is therefore highly credible. However, the ability to divide attention is limited, particularly under stressful conditions, and recall of unimportant detail at the scene of an incident may be associated with less accurate recall of other important aspects (e.g. facial features).

The confidence of witnesses about the accuracy of their testimony is not a reliable guide either. In several experiments, crimes have been staged for subjects who then report on details of the event and how confident they are about their accuracy. Witness confidence ratings tend to be much higher than the accuracy of their reports and some studies have demonstrated that witness confidence is unrelated to accuracy.[21]

SUMMARY

Memory is a complex process which has a biological basis although influenced by environmental and psychological factors. This limits the accuracy of recall and has implications for the

---

[20] C. Dodson and D. Reisberg (1991), "Indirect Testing of Eyewitness Memory: the (Non-) Effect of Misinformation", *Bulletin of the Psychonomic Society*, Vol. 29, pp. 333–6; R.H. Ryan and R.E. Geiselman (1991), "Effects of Biased Information on the Relationship between Eyewitness Confidence and Accuracy", *Bulletin of the Psychonomic Society*, Vol. 29, pp. 7–9.

[21] S.M. Kassin, S. Rigby and S. Castillo (1991), "The Accuracy–Confidence Correlation in Eyewitness Testimony: Limits and Extensions of the Retrospective Self-awareness Effect", *Journal of Personality and Social Psychology*, Vol. 61, pp. 698–707.

giving and interpretation of evidence in court. False memory syndrome has recently been described and, although still under scientific investigation, research is casting serious doubt on the ability to recover memories of previously forgotten material from the distant past.

Part Two

COMPENSATION FOR PSYCHIATRIC DISORDERS

Chapter 6

EMOTIONAL DISORDERS FOLLOWING PERSONAL INJURY

The whole range of psychiatric disorders, from depressive illness to phobias, can be provoked by personal injury. Post-traumatic stress disorder is the most frequently cited in the legal and psychiatric literature.

POST-TRAUMATIC STRESS DISORDER

The recognition that combat could lead to emotional suffering, long after the war had ceased, came about in the early twentieth century. The terms "shell shock", "battle fatigue", "combat fatigue" and "post-traumatic stress disorder" (PTSD) were applied; the latter is the official term used now in both ICD-10[1] and DSM-IV.[2] Initially, it was believed that the symptoms occurred as a result of brain damage due to carbon monoxide, but it was later recognised that the effects were due to the shocking emotional experiences of the veterans. It also became recognised that war was not the only cause of PTSD; it could also result from other experiences outside the realms of "normal" experience, including mass disasters and personal injury.[3] A death in the family due to illness would be within the boundaries of "normal" experience, whilst the death of a family member in a car driven and witnessed by the person

---

[1] World Health Organisation (1993), *International Classification of Diseases*, Tenth edition, Geneva: World Health Organisation.

[2] American Psychiatric Association (1994), *Diagnostic and Statistical Manual*, Fourth edition, Washington, DC: American Psychiatric Association.

[3] See Chapter 7.

would be outside this boundary and could lead to PTSD. Increasingly, accidents of a less serious nature have been shown to cause a similar constellation of symptoms and it is for this reason that controversy has arisen about the prevalence of the disorder, about the role of the stressor in its causation and also about the nature of the disorder itself. Studies have demonstrated that between 0 and 70 per cent of those subjected to severe stress develop the disorder,[4] and no satisfactory explanation for this variability has been offered — although it is likely that the inclusion of those subjected to a variety of traumas from traffic accidents to crime might at least provide part of the explanation. A well-designed study by Mayou et al.[5] demonstrated that 18 per cent of victims of road traffic accidents suffered acute distress in the immediate aftermath and this figure rose to 25 per cent twelve months later. They were diagnosed as suffering from mood disorders (depressive syndromes and anxiety), post-traumatic stress disorder and travel phobia. This outcome was not related to the extent or severity of physical injury and was as common in those with whiplash as with multiple injuries. This study points to the danger of overlooking likely emotional disturbance following seemingly "trivial" accidents.

Miller's View

The term "compensation neurosis" was first used in 1879 to describe the emotional damage caused by a railway accident without any obvious physical pathology.[6] In succeeding years, psychiatrists elaborated further upon the term by suggesting that the emotional disability following accidents was motivated by greed

---

[4] D.H. Barlow (1988), Anxiety and its Disorders: The Nature and Treatment of Panic, New York: Guildford Press.

[5] R. Mayou, B. Bryant and R. Duthie (1993), "Psychiatric Consequences of Road Traffic Accidents", *British Medical Journal*, Vol. 307, pp. 647–51.

[6] See, for example, the early "nervous shock" cases, which always seemed to involve railways, e.g. *Byrne* v *Southern and Western Railway Co.* (Irish Court of Appeal, Unreported Judgment, February 1884); *Bell* v *Great Northern Railway Co.*, 26 LR Ir 428 (Exchequer Division); *Victorian Railway Commissioners* v *Coultas* (1888) 13 App Cas 222 (Privy Council).

and avarice and tantamount to malingering. Miller[7] reinforced this view in his study of 45 patients whom he examined in his work as a neurologist with an insurance company. His view was that patients with unexplained physical symptoms or with psychological symptoms were deliberately deceiving the doctor and exaggerating their symptoms in order to maximise compensation. Unfortunately, this research was methodologically flawed, since he selected for the study only 45 of a much larger sample of 200 patients whom he was assessing. They cannot therefore be considered to be representative of the generality of patients who suffer emotional consequences following accidents. However, his findings were highly regarded by the legal profession for many years and frequently cited in court by those wishing to discredit evidence for emotional disorder following accidents.

Most studies since then have refuted his findings, in particular those which have followed up the victims of personal injury (see below). The psychological consequences of these injuries are similar in jurisdictions where there is no possibility of litigation (e.g. Spain) to the effects seen where legal proceedings are relatively common.[8] This finding has been replicated by a study of women injured in motor accidents, with no significant difference in the prevalence of emotional problems between the 50 involved in litigation and the 17 who were not.[9]

Does PTSD Exist?

While there is little doubt that events which are stressful lead to emotional disorders, there is debate about the label which should be attached to these. Although the term "post-traumatic stress disorder" (PTSD) has been in common usage since the early

---

[7] H. Miller (1961), "Accident Neurosis", *British Medical Journal*, Vol. 1, pp. 992–8.

[8] G. Mendelson (1984), "Follow-up Studies of Personal Injury Litigants", *International Journal of Law and Psychiatry*, Vol. 7, pp. 179–88.

[9] C.H. Shutt and F.C. Dohan (1968), "Neck Injuries to Women in Auto Accidents: a Metropolitan Plague", *Journal of the American Medical Association*, Vol. 206, pp. 2689–92.

1980s, there has been controversy about the exact nature of PTSD and the factors associated with its causation.[10] Implicit in the concept is the specific nature of the traumatic event. In other words, without the stressful event the disorder would not have arisen. By specifying the necessity for an overwhelming stressful event to cause the disorder, there is also an implicit assumption that this disorder is distinct from other disorders such as depressive illness or phobias, which can also be precipitated by stressful events, although of lesser magnitude than those causing PTSD. The counter-argument is that extreme stressors do not form a discrete class in terms of the probability of psychiatric sequelae, nor is the psychopathology (symptom pattern) distinctive. Indeed, symptoms of PTSD have been shown to occur following other lesser stresses such as house-moving, job loss and relationship problems, suggesting that the symptoms are not specific to PTSD.[11] The importance of personal vulnerability over that of the nature of the stressor has been emphasised by some.[12] A further problem is that many patients given the label of PTSD meet the criteria for other diagnostic labels also, most commonly substance abuse, anxiety disorders and depressive illness.[13] The danger that the label of PTSD would obscure the associated disorders and thereby reduce the probability of specific treatments being offered must be borne in mind.

---

[10] Post-traumatic stress disorder amounting to criminal "insanity" arose in the Court of Criminal Appeal in *People (DPP)* v *Courtney* (Court of Criminal Appeal, Unreported Judgment, 21 July 1994) (see Chapter 16, pp. 383–4). It was also the label expressly affixed to the plaintiff's condition in *Kelly* v *Hennessy* [1995] 3 IR 253.

[11] S.D. Solomon and G.J. Canino (1990), "Appropriateness of DSM-III-R Criteria for Post-Traumatic Stress Disorder", *Contemporary Psychiatry*, Vol. 31, 227–37.

[12] A.C. McFarlane (1988), "The Aetiology of Post Traumatic Stress Disorders Following a Natural Disaster", *British Journal of Psychiatry*, Vol. 152, pp. 116–21. However, the law is not always quite so sympathetic to vulnerable bystanders; see Chapter 8, pp. 196–8.

[13] F.S. Sierles, Jang-June Chen, R.E. McFarland and M.A. Taylor (1983), "Post-Traumatic Stress Disorder and Concurrent Psychiatric Illness: a Preliminary Report", *American Journal of Psychiatry*, Vol. 140, pp. 1177–9.

Further questions about the assumptions underlying PTSD are raised by recent studies demonstrating that trauma, such as combat, may not be required and that even peacekeeping soldiers can develop symptoms of PTSD.[14] Moreover, recollections of combat trauma have been found to be inconsistent among returned veterans from the Gulf War with more memories being recalled at two-year follow-up when compared with those reported one month after return. Memory amplification was also associated with greater levels of symptomatology.[15] These findings call into question the retrospective methodology traditionally used to demonstrate a link between severity of combat exposure and the subsequent development of PTSD, and also challenge the view of trauma being a requirement.

In relation to judicial decisions, the debate about vulnerability is not imperative, since the "eggshell" principle operates in relation to individual claims, irrespective of the psychiatric label which is used.[16] The controversy about the status of PTSD is sometimes reflected in court reports, with clinicians variously diagnosing PTSD when a specific constellation of symptoms is present and others labeling the same symptoms as depressive illness or phobia, etc., precipitated by the traumatic event. Thus, the former implies that the disorder is distinct from all others, with a specific course and response to treatment, and that the disorder is specific to that trauma, whilst the latter approach implies that the disorder could also have been precipitated by other traumas, even less serious than the current one, and that the course and response to treatment is as for the specific diagnostic condition.

---

[14] B.T. Litz, S.M. Orsillo, M. Freidman, P. Ehlict and A. Batres (1997), "Post-Traumatic Stress Disorder Associated with Peace Keeping Duty in Somalia for US Military Personnel", *American Journal of Psychiatry*, Vol. 154, No. 2, pp. 178–84. Although there were other factors involved, this was the basic point contended for in *People (DPP)* v *Courtney* (Court of Criminal Appeal, Unreported Judgment, 21 July 1994); see Chapter 15, pp. 327–8.

[15] S.M. Southwick, C.A. Morgan, A.L. Nicolaou and D.S. Charney (1997), "Consistency of Memory for Combat Related Traumatic Events in Operation Desert Storm", *American Journal of Psychiatry*, Vol. 154, No. 2, pp. 173–7.

[16] However, see Chapter 8.

In legal texts, the concept of "nervous shock" is frequently invoked, a notion which is unrecognised in clinical practice,[17] although it is accepted that many events — ranging from bereavement, to slipping on the floor, to being raped — can provoke an emotional reaction with overlapping symptoms. It is the practice of some psychiatrists[18] to label all such disorders by the symptom pattern (e.g. depressive illness), irrespective of the precipitating stressor, whilst others offer the label PTSD when the symptoms have arisen in the context of an accident.

The Biological Basis of PTSD

Animal models of the role of physiological mechanisms in causing psychiatric disorders such as PTSD have contributed to our understanding of this difficult area. At present, there exist some explanations but our knowledge is still incomplete. The current model suggests that, when a stress occurs, there is activation of a number of transmitters as well as of hormones, especially corticosteroids, within the brain. These in turn stimulate areas of the brain concerned with memory recording and retrieval. Thereafter, exposure to situations or memories resembling the original trauma results in recall of the event and, by a reciprocal interaction, the surge in neurotransmitter and hormone release produces symptoms.[19] Changes to the sleep/dream cycle have also been described in PTSD sufferers. The realisation that PTSD is not a universal occurrence in those exposed to severe stress has led to the suggestion that only those who are physiologically vulnerable will succumb to PTSD.

Studies of hormone release in brain structures, referred to as neuroendocrine studies, have focused on alterations in the brain's own opioids and on abnormal cortisol and catecholamine excretion (substances secreted in the "flight and fight" reaction), but

---

[17] See Chapter 8.

[18] Including the psychiatrist author of this text.

[19] D.S. Charney, A.Y. Deutch, J.H. Krystal, S.M. Southwick and M. Davis (1993), "Psychobiological Mechanisms of Post-Traumatic Stress Disorder", *Archives of General Psychiatry*, Vol. 50, pp. 294-305.

findings have been inconsistent due to the large co-existence of other disorders, particularly anxiety and depressive illness. Moreover, attempts to relate underlying neurochemical abnormalities to behaviour have been unsuccessful.

Clinical Features of PTSD

The stressor must be an event that would cause distress to most people and includes such traumas as natural disasters (earthquakes, hurricanes), serious human stressors such as hostage taking, concentration camp imprisonment, torture and severe accidents,[20] as in major road or air disasters.[21] Some occupational groups are also at risk for PTSD, including fire fighters, body handlers, ambulance personnel.[22] Those involving the handling of children are particularly at risk.[23] However, it is also recognised that the actual seriousness of the trauma is a less important determinant of risk to the disorder than is the perceived threat.[24] For this reason, even relatively minor incidents such as non-serious traffic accidents can lead to PTSD. The theme that

---

[20] As in, for example, *McLoughlin* v *O'Brian* [1983] AC 410; *Jaensch* v *Coffey* [1984] 54 ALR 417, 155 CLR 549 (High Court of Australia); *Mullally* v *Bus Éireann* [1992] ILRM 722 (HC); *Alcock* v *Chief Constable of South Yorkshire Police* [1992] 1 AC 310, [1991] 3 WLR 1057, [1991] 4 All ER 907; *Kelly* v *Hennessy* [1995] 3 IR 253 (SC).

[21] Those which relate to crime are described in detail in Chapter 7.

[22] As a parallel, psychological disability may also arise out of the conditions in which a person has to work; see *Walker* v *Northumberland County Council* [1995] 1 All ER 737 (QBD); *Gillespie* v *Commonwealth of Australia* (1991) 104 ACTR 1; *Petch* v *Customs and Excise Commissioners* [1993] ICR 789.

[23] C. Fullerton, J. McCarroll, R.J. Ursano and K. Wright (1992), "Psychological Responses of Rescue Workers: Fire-fighters and Trauma", *Journal of Orthopsychiatry*, Vol. 62, pp. 371–8. See, for example, cases of psychological injury to parents where their children have been killed or injured close by: *Chester* v *Waverley Corp.* (1939) 62 CLR 1 and *King* v *Phillips* [1953] 1 QB 429 (recovery denied); and *Boardman* v *Sanderson* (1961) [1964] 1 WLR 1317 (CA); *Dillon* v *Legge* (1968) 69 Cal. Rep. 72, 80, 441 P.2d 912, 920; *McLoughlin* v *O'Brian* [1983] AC 410, where recovery was allowed. See Chapter 8.

[24] However, where psychological injury occurs to a person within the zone of physical danger, the law may not be overly sympathetic, even if the perceived threat is non-minor, unless the perception of the perceived threat is reasonable. See Chapter 8, pp. 144–59.

underpins all these events is the threat, real or perceived, to life. Up to 70 per cent of the victims of serious accidents/disasters will develop post-traumatic stress disorder and this is more common following manmade than natural disasters.

The following clusters of symptoms have been shown to occur in the disorder:

• Recollection phenomena such as flashbacks, dreams.

• Emotional changes including detachment, anxiety, depression, unresponsiveness to surroundings.

• Avoidance of situations, events or memories associated with the trauma or likely to provoke recollections of it.

• Numbing, leading to the inability to feel any emotion or to fully appreciate the significance of the event that has occurred.

• Hyper-arousal, an enhanced startle reaction and insomnia.

• Alcohol and other substance misuse may be a complication of the above symptoms.

However some researchers question the usefulness of some of the symptoms, especially recollection of the events and avoidance, since these may be part of the normal response to any trauma.[25] Numbing has also been shown to occur in other disorders, particularly depressive illness.

The latency period between the occurrence of the trauma and the onset of symptoms varies from a few hours to a few months, and generally is not in excess of six months.[26]

Sometimes after overwhelming stress, such as torture or prolonged captivity with the possibility of imminent death, there may not initially be any evidence of emotional trauma. However, many months or years after the experience, permanent changes to

---

[25] A. MacFarlane (1992), "Commentary: PTSD among Injured Survivors of a Terrorist Attack", *Journal of Nervous and Mental Diseases*, Vol. 180, pp. 505–9.

[26] See also Chapter 7.

personality may occur, in the absence of any previous personality difficulties or of brain damage. The features include a hostile attitude to the world, social withdrawal, feelings of emptiness or hopelessness, chronic anxiety and feelings of detachment and estrangement from the world. The prognosis for these personality changes is poor.

Treatment of PTSD

Psychological debriefing (also called critical incident stress debriefing) was introduced in 1983 to treat ambulance personnel. Since then, the use of this technique following the release of hostages has received much attention. It consists of a brief, two-hour process designed to facilitate the release of emotions and the gradual return to day-to-day living. Typically, the session takes place a few days after the trauma, or after the release of the victims. The rationale for its use is one of prevention of major emotional disturbance. However, because it is a new treatment, studies are sparse and suffer from flaws, such as failure to include a control group, absence of random allocation to treatment and failure to take account of other factors likely to affect outcome, such as prior history. The results therefore vary, with some indicating a good outcome whilst others demonstrate no benefit. For this reason, it is premature to suggest that debriefing is essential or that failure to provide it is negligent. The issues relating to the current status of this intervention are reviewed by Bisson and Deahl.[27]

Since the seminal work of Lindemann[28] following the Coconut Grove Fire in the US, there has been a recognition of the benefit of accepting in consciousness the event which has occurred. Although distressing, the necessity of recalling the trauma and of venting the emotions associated with it is acknowledged. This bringing to consciousness and acceptance is referred to as

---

[27] J.I. Bisson and M.P. Deahl (1994), "Psychological Debriefing and Prevention of Post-Traumatic Stress Disorder: More Research is Needed", *British Journal of Psychiatry*, Vol. 165, pp. 717–20.

[28] E. Lindemann (1944), "Symptomatology and Management of Acute Grief", *American Journal of Psychiatry*, Vol. 101, pp. 141–8.

"working through". However, failure to undergo this process, either by denial or repression (themselves controversial defence mechanisms), leads to major difficulties in emotional adjustment and adaptation. Since avoidance both of memories and of places associated with the trauma is common in PTSD, it is likely that exposure would be a helpful component in treatment. It is surprising that this has not been investigated with any rigour, although it is recommended by some workers.

On the basis of assumptions relating to the neurochemical basis for this disorder,[29] antidepressants have been prescribed with mixed success.[30] Caution has to be exercised when using benzodiazepine tranquillisers (e.g. diazepam) in this group of patients, since some can lead to a retrograde amnesia (i.e. amnesia for prior events) and impede the recovery process by facilitating the mental mechanism of denial.[31]

Follow-up Studies

Studies of outcome following litigation generally use return to work as the benchmark for improvement. Several studies have shown that a proportion, varying between 30 and 49 per cent, return to work before settlement is reached. Moreover, a proportion who are unemployed at the time of settlement do not return to work thereafter, for a prolonged period. The most optimistic figure was described by Encel and Johnson[32] who found that 35 per cent were unemployed three years after settlement. Of those who had returned to work, most did not regain their pre-accident status, and many were in positions with less responsibility. Higher unemployment figures were described by other workers, who found

[29] See above, p. 84.

[30] J.B. Frank, T.R. Kosten, E.L. Giller et al. (1988), "A Randomised Clinical Trial of Phenelzine and Imipramine for Post-Traumatic Stress Disorder", *American Journal of Psychiatry*, Vol. 145, pp. 1289–91.

[31] P. Tyrer (1989), "Choice of Treatment in Anxiety" in P. Tyrer (ed.), *Psychopharmacology of Anxiety*, pp. 255–82, Oxford: Oxford University Press.

[32] S. Encel and C.E. Johnson (1978), *Compensation and Rehabilitation: A Survey of Worker's Compensation Involving Back Injuries and Lump Sum Payments*, Sydney: New South Wales University Press.

that two-thirds of sufferers were unemployed for 16 months to 7 years.[33] It is apparent from these figures that return to work is the exception rather than the rule, and even when settlement has been completed, those who do return to work seldom regain their previous status. The poor emotional outcome following settlement has also been clearly described,[34] with over 85 per cent continuing to have significant emotional disturbance after settlement.

Delays in the legal process have been described[35] as contributing to the adverse prognosis. Other factors affecting the outcome include pre-morbid personality and a previous history of emotional disturbance.

OTHER DISORDERS

Phobias

A phobia is a persistent fear of a specific object or situation so that it is avoided and if exposure occurs a panic attack ensues. The primary fear is of the situation rather than of the panic attack *per se*. Thus, there are two components: the feared object and avoidance. In the context of the law, the most frequent phobias are fear of driving a car or being a passenger in one, following an accident; fear of social interactions because of facial scarring; fear of going outside in case of being hit by a car or being mugged again. Any situation of exposure to an accident or a crime can provoke a phobia. The phobia may also be symptomatic of post-traumatic stress disorder.

---

[33] J.L. Balla and S. Moraitis (1970), "Knights in Shining Armour — a Follow-up Study of Injuries after Legal Settlement", *Medical Journal of Australia*, Vol. 2, pp. 355–61; J.N. Morgan, M. Snider and M.G. Sobol (1984), "Lump Sum Redemption Settlements and Rehabilitation" in G. Mendelson, "Follow-up Studies of Personal Injury Litigants", *International Journal of Law and Psychiatry*, Vol. 7, pp. 179–88; M.J. Tarsh and C. Royston (1985), "A Follow-up Study of Accident Neurosis", *British Journal of Psychiatry*, Vol. 146, pp. 18–25.

[34] G.N. Thompson (1965), "Post-Traumatic Psychoneurosis — a Statistical Survey", *American Journal of Psychiatry*, Vol. 121, pp. 1043–8.

[35] R. Kelly and B.N. Smith (1981), "Post-Traumatic Syndrome: Another Myth Discredited", *Journal of Royal Society of Medicine*, Vol. 74, pp. 274–7.

The aetiology of a phobia is understood in terms of learning theory, which explains the generalisation of the fear from a specific stimulus to more generalised and extensive stimuli (e.g. a phobia of dogs generalising to all furry creatures). Although genetic factors do not play a part, personality vulnerability is more significant in predisposing to phobias, especially to agoraphobia and social phobias.

Phobias are grouped into four major categories — agoraphobia, animal phobias, social phobias and miscellaneous phobias. A fifth group is labeled by some as illness phobias and by others as obsessional illness. Agoraphobia, or "fear of the market place", presents with a fear of leaving home. Claustrophobia is regarded as a variant of agoraphobia. Social phobia is defined as fear of social interaction such as speaking in public, answering the telephone, standing in a queue, etc., and may be confused with agoraphobia. Animal phobias are associated with fear of dogs, cats, etc., whilst the miscellaneous group includes fear of thunder, of blood, of flying, etc.

There is no information on the proportion of people developing phobias following accidents or violent crime, although avoidance of situations associated with the trauma is a feature of PTSD. Social phobias in particular are sometimes complicated by alcohol abuse,[36] due to its anxiety-lowering and confidence-enhancing properties.

Treatment is with behaviour therapy, although this may be combined with pharmacotherapy (drug treatment) and cognitive therapy. Behaviour therapy is time-consuming and consists of exposing the patient to the feared object/situation in a graded manner, beginning with the least anxiety-provoking and progressing, at the patient's pace, through a hierarchy to the most stressful. There is some evidence that volunteers can be successfully trained to deliver behaviour therapy under supervision. Medication in the form of minor tranquillisers, such as diazepam, or of beta-blockers, which slow the heart rate, are sometimes used as an aid

---

[36] See Chapter 10.

in the early stages of behaviour therapy, although they are not the primary treatment and the risk of dependence is a problem with the former. Cognitive therapy can help where the fear persists despite exposure, by examining the way in which the thought processes contribute to maintaining the fear. Like behaviour therapy, this is also time-consuming. The outcome is good and follow-up studies for phobias in general show that about 50 per cent of patients overcome the phobia. Those with poor premorbid adjustment, manifesting as high base levels of anxiety or excessive dependence on others, have a poorer prognosis, as do those whose phobia is long-standing, whose motivation is low or who have little emotional support. In addition, patients whose phobias are reinforced by others also have a poorer response to treatment (e.g. a woman with agoraphobia whose family does the weekly shopping for her). Thus, being over-supportive can also lead to a poor prognosis.

Generalised Anxiety

Generalised anxiety consists of feelings of tension for which there is no cause or which are disproportionate to the seriousness of any underlying stressor. Symptoms are both emotional (tension, worry, hyper-vigilance, etc.) and physical (headaches, palpitations, sweating, gastrointestinal disturbances, etc.). Unlike phobias, the anxiety is not directed at any particular object or situation and is felt even when at rest. Anxiety is most commonly a symptom of another disorder, especially depressive illness, and may be mistaken for the latter. Generalised anxiety rarely occurs for the first time in those over the age of 35.

There may be genetic vulnerability to the disorder in some, since there is a higher concordance for the disorder in monozygotic (identical) than in dizygotic (non-identical) twins. Learning theory and Freudian theories of loss have each been invoked as causing anxiety. The actual chemical changes which occur both in the brain and peripherally have also been studied, but with inconclusive results.

Treatment is with a combination of cognitive and pharmaco-therapy. Benzodiazepine tranquillisers were used extensively and with dramatic effect in the 1960s and 1970s to treat this disorder. However the problems of dependence have made their use now more restricted.[37] Symptomatic treatment with beta-blockers reduces the physical symptoms but not the psychic distress. There is evidence that tricyclic antidepressants are even more effective than benzodiazepines for primary anxiety. Those with the poorest prognosis are those who have high base levels of anxiety in association with anxious personality disorder. In the context of personal injury, generalised anxiety is most likely to develop in relation to the impending court case rather than to the injury itself. When anxiety is symptomatic of some other disorder, such as depressive illness, the treatment is of the primary condition.

Panic Disorder

This is one of the newly identified disorders and may be considered to have been serendipitously discovered. The realisation in 1962 that imipramine, an antidepressant, relieved panic attacks independent of the level of background anxiety suggested to some that it had a specific anti-panic action. Hence the concept of panic disorder evolved. However, many have been critical of the strategy of identifying a disorder having first found the cure.[38] Thus a debate exists about the validity of the diagnosis[39] with protagonists variously contending that it is a more serious manifestation of anxiety, a variant of depressive illness or a disorder in its own right.

Since first described, numerous studies have investigated an array of predisposing and precipitating factors. Genetic predisposition has been considered by some investigators and a risk of 17.4

---

[37] See Chapter 10, p. 232.

[38] P. Casey (1994), "Panic Disorder", *Irish Medical Journal*, Vol. 4, No. 9.

[39] See Chapter 2.

per cent for this disorder in first degree relatives has been found.[40] There is no excess risk for other disorders such as generalised anxiety, alcoholism or depressive illness among these relatives, suggesting that it is distinct from them. In spite of many neuro-chemical changes, involving serotonin, adrenaline, melatonin, as well as changes to blood flow and right-sided brain abnormalities on PET scanning,[41] no conclusive neuro-biological pattern has yet emerged.

There is an excess of women among sufferers and the disorder predominates in the under-45 age group, although there is no relationship to social class. The six-month prevalence lies between 0.6 and 1 per cent of the adult population. Panic attacks are a common feature of depressive illness.

This patient group are heavy users of benzodiazepines and although they have been successfully used in treatment, they carry the risk of dependence. Various antidepressants have been shown to be effective in treatment and the anti-panic effects are independent of the degree of depression at the outset. Cognitive therapy is also effective in helping the patient re-interpret the bodily sensations which lead to anxiety and to a spiral into panic. Simpler techniques such as breathing exercises are helpful in some patients and re-breathing from a *paper* bag can also terminate an acute panic attack.[42]

Follow-up studies have shown that the diagnosis of panic disorder is not a stable one and many develop alcohol misuse, agoraphobia and depressive illness, suggesting that it may not be a disorder in its own right.

---

[40] R.R. Crowe, R. Noyes, D.L. Paul and D. Slymen (1983), "A Family Study of Panic Disorders", *Archives of General Psychiatry*, Vol. 40, pp. 1065–9.

[41] See Chapter 2.

[42] Where the panic attack involves hyperventilation.

SOMATIC PRESENTATION OF PSYCHIATRIC ILLNESS

Many who have psychiatric disorders present with physical (somatic) rather than emotional symptoms.[43] These patients are termed somatisers. It is often wrongfully assumed that such symptoms "are all in the mind"; this is inaccurate, since the sensations are present but have a psychiatric rather than a physical basis. An example is the occurrence of chest pain during a panic attack, which the patient may mistake for a heart attack.

The disorder which most commonly manifests itself with physical symptoms is depressive illness presenting with anxiety symptoms. These include palpitations, sweating, tremors, dizziness, diarrhoea, urinary frequency, nausea, breathing difficulties and headache. Other common physical symptoms of this disorder are anorexia and weight loss, pain and fatigue. Many patients seen especially by physicians find it difficult to accept that the failure to find a physical cause for the symptoms is linked to their causation by depressive disorder. This is compounded by the mistaken belief, often among family members, that these are deriving from the imagination.

Apart from depressive illness, there are a number of other syndromes, which, although less common, are nevertheless seen regularly in clinical practice. These will be described below.

Malingering

This consists of the deliberate production of false or exaggerated symptoms in order to obtain some external benefit such as avoiding conscription or gaining better housing or compensation. It includes not only the feigning of symptoms but also falsely and consciously imputing causes that have no relationship to the symptoms. In the court setting, there is often confusion with hysteria; both are quite different disorders and have a different aetiology.

---

[43] This is not the equivalent of the requirement that persons suffering "nervous shock" had to have physical "injury"; see Chapter 8, pp. 135–40.

Miller's work[44] suggested that most patients with emotional difficulties following accidents were malingerers, although this has now been discredited. Psychiatrists are reluctant to diagnose malingering, as it is rare and there are no objective measures of symptoms other than those described by the patient. Moreover, the doctor–patient relationship is founded on honesty and the possibility of this being in question is at variance with the philosophy of trust inculcated throughout medical training.

However, a number of features suggest that an individual patient may be falsifying symptoms. These include:

- A marked discrepancy between symptoms and functioning

- Defensiveness in describing past or personal history

- Failure to comply with treatment, including missed appointments

- Lack of co-operation in the assessment process, e.g. refusing permission to obtain a collateral history.

It is imperative only to make this diagnosis after several assessments and it should never be made on the basis of a single outpatient interview.

Unlike the patient with hysteria, whose symptoms develop in the context of emotional conflict, no such background is evident in the malingerer. The symptoms themselves are often described as being noticed from the time of the accident, present constantly, of unchanging severity irrespective of treatment, yet with obvious discrepancies between the alleged severity and the impact on day-to-day behaviour.[45]

---

[44] See above, p. 80–1.

[45] K.M. Quinn (1985), "Meet the Malingerer: Clinical Presentation and Detection", *Audio-Digest Psychiatry*, Vol. 14, p. 24. This phenomenon is not unknown to personal injury practitioners.

Factitious Disorder

This condition is sometimes confused with malingering, since in both, the symptoms are feigned. However, the incentives from factitious disorder are internal rather than external. Examples of internal gains are the fulfillment of dependency or masochistic needs, avoidance of responsibility, attention-seeking. When this disorder presents with physical symptoms, it may be associated with multiple hospitalisations and surgical interventions known as Munchausen's Syndrome. An array of psychological symptoms may also be described. A disorder called the Ganser Syndrome, first described during the First World War, was viewed as a variant of factitious disorder or malingering. It consisted of hallucinations and answering past the point, so that the answer, although ridiculous, indicates that the meaning was understood (e.g. "Q: How many legs does a horse have? A: Three"). It is now recognised that it is indicative of schizophrenia or organic brain disease. Risk factors for factitious disorder include a previous history of true physical illness and dependent personality disorder.[46] Of course, some develop the disorder without any risk factors.

Hysteria

This condition, recognised even by Hippocrates, came to prominence in the writings of Freud. It is a recognised but rare disorder in which psychic difficulties are converted into physical symptoms, most commonly paralysis or anaesthesia. The manifestation of symptoms in this way is referred to as conversion hysteria. Dissociation hysteria manifests itself as amnesia for an event or a set of events.[47] The symptoms are often focused on organs which have been injured or damaged previously or have symbolic significance. For example, a singer who has marital problems may lose her voice due to serious marital problems which centre on her professional career.

---

[46] See Chapter 9.

[47] See *People (AG)* v *O'Brien* [1936] IR 263; *Rabey* v *R* (1977) 37 CCC (2d) 461, affirming (1980) SCR 513, 54 CCC (2d) 1; and Chapter 16, pp. 406–7.

Hysteria is not, as many mistakenly believe, produced intentionally — this is malingering or factitious disorder, depending on whether the gain is external or internal. Rather, the symptoms are produced unknowingly by the patient. As well as the confusion about the unconscious nature of the symptoms, the term hysteria has judgmental connotations and in the past has frequently been used as a term of opprobrium (as in "that hysterical woman!"). Two further problems arise with the concept — one is that hysteria may augur serious physical pathology, especially incipient multiple sclerosis, or is frequently symptomatic of severe psychiatric disorder, such as depressive illness or early dementia. The second problem is that the prognosis for hysteria is poor and the symptoms may not resolve even after the underlying stress is removed. It is therefore a diagnosis which is rarely made in modern psychiatry and then only after physical illness and other psychiatric disorders have been out-ruled completely. Moreover, the diagnosis cannot be made unless specific conflicts and psychological (secondary) gain accruing from the symptoms are identified. Sometimes it is suggested that patients in whom no organic cause for their symptoms is found are suffering from hysteria. In view of the restricted criteria for making the diagnosis, it is apparent that, of itself, the absence of an organic cause for symptoms is not a basis on which to make this diagnosis.

Treatment initially consists of physiotherapy directed at the affected organ. This allows the patient a channel for symptomatic improvement. Later the conflicts leading to the symptoms need to be explored. Abreaction, or the exploration of conflicts when the patient is relaxed using intravenous medication, is also used if symptoms do not improve rapidly. Whilst in this state, the therapist explores the possible underlying conflicts that may have been kept from consciousness through the patient's defences. The unearthing of these conflicts may then lead to symptom resolution. Above all, the patient should not be told that "this is in your mind" or that pretence is suspected, since this is erroneous. In the setting of the legal process, there is a temptation to suggest that the symptoms are due to malingering, especially since physical findings are negative. To do so would be cruel and has no empirical basis.

Hysteria as a symptom of depressive illness should be treated as for the underlying disorder.

Somatoform Disorders

This is a group of disorders in which the patient presents with physical symptoms in the absence of physical cause and with persistent requests for medical investigations. The preoccupation may be with one or multiple organs and this is called somatization disorder or Briquet's syndrome. Included in this group are disorders such as hypochondriasis, a belief that some serious illness is present despite negative investigations, persistent somatoform pain disorder and dysmorphophobia. The latter is a belief that parts of the body, such as the nose, ears, etc., are disfigured and is associated with demands for cosmetic surgery. Meeting the patient's requests for repeated investigation or for cosmetic surgery does not result in improvement and symptom substitution is common. The beliefs and preoccupations about disease and disfigurement are not of delusional intensity, but should this occur, they are referred to as persistent delusional disorder (also called monosymptomatic delusional psychosis or MDP) and treated with major tranquillisers. Those who suffer from these disorders are often hostile to doctors, since they perceive that the medical profession has no interest in them. The potential for allegations of negligence to be made by the patient against the doctor is enormous.

The aetiology of somatoform disorders is not understood, although vulnerability factors include a family or childhood history of serious or prolonged physical illness. The realisation that some people do not possess a language to describe emotional suffering is also believed to be important in causing physical rather than emotional manifestations of distress. This lack of vocabulary is termed alexithymia. Precipitants to actual symptoms include physical traumas such as accidents or injuries, personal stresses such as bereavements or other losses, and the disorders may be perpetuated by relationships in which the attention of the partner serves to meet needs such as dependence, punishment or responsibility avoidance. In this regard it resembles factitious disorder although unlike the latter, the symptoms are not produced consciously and if the patient is confronted with them will react with anger, hostility and denial. The most common perpetuating factor in the context of personal injury is the manner in which the initial injury/accident was dealt with by the defendant. This may be compounded by delays in proceeding to court hearings. There is little to be gained from being confrontational with the patient about perpetuating factors such as these, since they are not deliberately contrived, as in malingering or factitious disorder.

Treatment is difficult and the doctor should avoid the pitfalls of repeated intensive investigations or of referral for cosmetic surgery. Neither should benzodiazepine tranquillisers be prescribed, since there is no evidence for their efficacy in somatoform disorders and there is a serious risk of dependence in view of the chronicity of the disorder. Cognitive therapy has been used with some success in some patients. Overall, these tend to be chronic disorders which incapacitate the sufferer and impact gravely upon the family.

DEPRESSIVE ILLNESS

This is a confusing area since many regard "depression" as part of everyday life. Indeed, it is and depression as a symptom afflicts everybody at some point. However, depressive illness is quite different to unhappiness and is best described as an altered mood state with a particular constellation of associated symptoms and although it may have been provoked initially by some stressor, the severity and momentum of the symptoms render it independent of that stressor. Implicit in this definition is the observation that the symptoms are excessive and that the removal of the stressor (if this were possible) would have no effect on the symptoms. In this regard, it is different from unhappiness or from adjustment disorder where the symptoms are understandable and removal of the precipitant leads to symptomatic improvement. The distinction between endogenous and neurotic depression, so prominent in older classifications, has been replaced in ICD-10 by the single term "depressive illness".

Prevalence

This is the most common disorder in psychiatric practice and is a common sequel to road traffic accidents, either on its own or as part of PTSD. The debate surrounding the concept of PTSD and the use of the term "depressive illness" in preference to "PTSD" has already been described. Studies of prevalence in the general population in western cultures (epidemiological studies) suggest that between 10 and 15 per cent of the general adult population suffer from a depressive illness at any point in time and the life-time risk is about 40 per cent. It is more common in women than in men and peaks in the 35–45 age group. However, severity increases with increasing age, as does treatment resistance. There is no association with the menopause, contrary to popular belief.

Chemical Basis for Depressive Illness

Several neurochemicals have become implicated as being of aetiological significance in this disorder, especially serotonin (5-hydroxytryptamine) and nor-adrenaline. It is believed that the availability of these at the junctions (synapses) between nerve endings is diminished or that the receptors to which they attach themselves are abnormal and the rationale for giving pharmacological treatments is to increase the availability of these transmitters. The onset of depressive illness following a stressful event is believed to be related to the increase in corticosteroid production, which in turn alters the metabolism of these neurotransmitters, leading to symptoms.

Predisposing Factors

A number of features which render the individual vulnerable to developing depressive illness have been identified. These are sociological in origin and include the absence of a confiding relationship, the presence of more than three young children in the home, the loss of a mother in childhood and not working outside the home.[48] The protective effects of religious beliefs have also been described by the same author. These variables, therefore, do not cause depressive illness but place the individual at increased risk in the face of stressful events such as bereavement. It is also true that a significant minority who develop depressive illness do not possess any risk factor.

Some studies have shown a genetic basis for depressive illness, but this is more common in manic-depressive illness. The exact mode of inheritance has not yet been established. Vulnerability deriving from personality is described anecdotally, but there is little empirical evidence for this. Individual patients may, however, exhibit a pattern of difficulty relating to loss or to change which leads to depressive illness. Other workers suggest that the individual's schema or view of the world renders some people vulnerable to depressive illness; cognitive therapy, which aims to change these distorted attitudes, has been successful in preventing relapse in some with depressive illness. There is no evidence to suggest that the primary prevention of depressive illness is feasible using this approach.

Precipitating Factors

In psychiatric practice, depressive illness sometimes does not have a precipitant and this is often a source of concern and indeed guilt to many patients as they try to seek a cause. Following an accident, the role of what may seem like a relatively minor stress in causing a disorder is a puzzle. It is important to realise that it is the perceived rather than the real magnitude which is important in determining causation[49] and this may explain why some relatively minor accidents are associated with major emotional upheaval.

---

[48] G.W. Brown and T. Harris (1978), *Social Origins of Depression*, London: Tavistock Publications.

[49] That is, in determining causation of the depressive illness, not in establishing legal causation.

For example, a patient developed a depressive illness of moderate severity after a car accident in which the car she and her young grandson were in was hit from behind. There was no physical injury and the second party admitted liability. Her illness seemed inexplicable until she disclosed that a relative had earlier that year been killed in a road traffic accident.

Amongst the events significantly associated with the risk of developing depressive illness are going to prison, losing a job, bereavement and childbirth. Thus, even positive events are associated with the risk of developing psychiatric disorder in some people.

Interestingly, the treatment and prognosis does not seem to be affected by the presence or absence of a precipitant and some who develop a depressive illness in response to an event subsequently have episodes of illness occurring spontaneously.

It is important to recognise that the symptoms lead to a marked deterioration in functioning, but they do not necessarily parallel each other. Indeed, symptomatic recovery precedes social recovery and this can delay return to work or return to full social activity for months after symptoms have reduced. This may lead to a false suspicion that the patient is malingering. The common symptoms are listed in Table 6.1.

Severe depressive illness is also called psychotic depression and may sometimes be described in the court setting when a person with delusions of catastrophe murders a family member in order to spare them from suffering. At such times, a person may also commit suicide.[50]

The defendant who appears in court on charges of shoplifting may also be suffering from depressive illness. Shoplifting, without motivation, in any person of otherwise impeccable character,

---

[50] So-called dyadic murders. See M. Bolster, F. O'Garabhan and J. Harbison (1995), "Dyadic Deaths in Ireland", *Medico-Legal Journal of Ireland*, Vol. 91. See also Chapter 15, p. 354.

TABLE 6.1: COMMON FEATURES OF DEPRESSIVE ILLNESS

Mild/Moderate Illness	Severe Illness
Gloom/tearfulness	Inability to cry
Irritability	Inability to feel
Anorexia or overeating	Delusions of guilt
Anxiety: free-floating/phobic	Delusions of persecution
Agitation or retardation	Delusions of reference
Insomnia: early, middle or late	Auditory hallucinations, 2nd person critical
Hypersomnia	Nihilistic delusions
Aches or pains	Hypochondriacal delusions
Depersonalisation	
Reduced concentration	
Lack of confidence	
Inability to cope	
Over-valued ideas of guilt, reference, hypochondriasis	
Obsessional rituals or ruminations	

should alert the solicitor to seek a psychiatric assessment, as the client may be harbouring a masked depressive illness.[51] Middle-aged women who take inexpensive items should raise a high index of suspicion that a psychiatric illness underlies the crime. The explanation for the shoplifting may simply lie in the poor concentration which sufferers with depressive illness have.[52] However, amongst those whose shoplifting is a symptom of depressive illness, recall of the event is often present and it has been suggested that the taking of the item may be for comfort or even a way of seeking help.[53] Although depressive illness is the most common

---

[51] As to criminal "insanity" that this suggests, see Chapter 16.

[52] However, momentary inattention, in itself, does not amount to a defect of reason caused by a disease of the mind. See *R* v *Clarke* [1972] 1 All ER 219, 56 Cr App R 225, CA and Chapter 16, pp. 388–9.

[53] Such activity amounting to an irresistible impulse has not yet arisen for decision; see Chapter 16, pp. 380–2.

psychiatric disorder associated with shoplifting in those of good character, the possibility of an organic brain disease such as senile or pre-senile dementia should also be considered.[54] In these disorders, there is progressive damage to the frontal lobe of the brain, resulting in loss of inhibitions. The diagnosis can usually be confirmed by performing a CAT scan of the brain.

The treatment of depressive illness is with antidepressants and if the illness is severe, electroconvulsive therapy may be required. This treatment is particularly useful and indeed necessary when psychotic symptoms of depression are present. There is no evidence that ECT is associated with brain damage, in spite of anecdotal claims. In all patients, even those who require ECT, anti-depressants will also be prescribed and at present the recommended minimum period of treatment is for nine months, although in clinical practice it may be much longer than this. The small proportion of patients who have recurrent episodes of depressive illness benefit from prophylaxis with long-term antidepressants. There is no evidence that the older antidepressants are physically addictive, although some uncertainty exists about some of the newer drugs, i.e. the specific serotonin re-uptake inhibitors (SSRIs). Recently, two further groups of antidepressants have become available. These are known as the selective nor-adrenergic re-uptake inhibitors (SNRIs) and the nor-adrenergic serotonin antagonists (NaSAs). Their exact place in treating depressive illness remains to be evaluated, although the SNRIs are reported to be particularly effective in improving social function by their effect on nor-adrenaline, which is the transmitter driving motivation.

ABNORMAL GRIEF REACTIONS

Grief can be divided into normal and pathological reactions. During the course of a normal reaction, the patient will variously describe emotions such as numbing, denial, anger, sadness and

---

[54] See Chapters 12 and 16 and *R* v *Kemp* [1957] 1 QB 399.

guilt.[55] The hallmark of this reaction is that the sufferer passes through some or all of these phases until finally resolution is reached.[56] Abnormal reactions are divided into two major groups — inhibited and prolonged — although recent research has questioned the existence of the former. In this, the sufferer remains "stuck" at any point in the grieving process. For example, the person may feel perpetually numbed and thus be unable to cry or may continue to deny the death and behave as if the lost relative were still alive, setting a place at table, refusing to discard clothes, etc. The treatment of this form of abnormal grief reaction is by "forced mourning" in which the sufferer is shown pictures of the deceased, is taken to the graveside and is actively encouraged to express emotion.

The second form of abnormal reaction, prolonged grief reaction, manifests itself with continuing sadness and tearfulness, along with a refusal to be reminded of the deceased by looking at reminders. This form of reaction is more correctly called a depressive illness[57] and whilst psychotherapy in the form of visits to the grave and discussion around feelings such as guilt and anger are helpful, antidepressants are also required if a successful outcome is to occur. Although bereavements follow the loss of any loved person or object (e.g. pets), in the context of the courts this is most likely to arise in the context of a fatal injuries claim. Factors affecting the response to such loss are the suddenness of the death, the closeness of the relationship to the deceased and the person-

---

[55] However, see *Lynch v Knight* (1861) 9 HCL 577 at 598, 11 ER 854, *per* Wensleyale LJ: "Mental pain or anxiety, the law cannot value, and does not pretend to redress, when the unlawful act causes that alone".

[56] Also, the hallmark of the law is that grief is something that comes to everyone, hence the non-recovery, but for statutory provision, for limited damages for *solatium* — as distinct from special damages — upon the deaths of certain relatives caused by the wrongful acts of others. See Civil Liability Act (1961), s. 47 as amended by the Civil Liability (Amendment) Act (1996), s. 2. See, generally, J.P. White (1989), *Irish Law of Damages for Personal Injuries and Death*, Dublin: Butterworths, Part III; E. Veitch (1972), *Solatium — A Debt Repaid* (1972) Ir Jur (ns) 77–95. See also Chapter 8.

[57] See p. 99.

ality of the survivor. In addition, the use of sedatives after an accident is contraindicated, since the grieving process may be inhibited. Other factors affecting the reactions to death are the age of the deceased and aspects relating to the funeral.

In ICD-10 and DSM-IV, abnormal grief reactions are subsumed under the heading of depressive disorders.

PSYCHOTIC DISORDERS

All forms of schizophrenia, as well as paranoid psychosis,[58] have been reported after head injuries and the incidence in those with a history of head injury is higher than in the general population.[59] Schizophrenia is the most common of the functional psychoses to be reported following head injury. Although some patients have a predisposition to the disease, the evidence to date is that head injury is of direct aetiological significance and not just a precipitant in a vulnerable individual. The onset of the disorder may be a few hours after the injury or a latent period may elapse. There is a suggestion that the onset after a latent period is associated with a poor prognosis. To date, there is no definitive link with any particular site of damage, although rapid onset is associated with severe diffuse damage and possibly with temporal lobe damage also.[60] Paranoid psychosis has also been reported after head injury and is unrelated to the site or severity of the injury. The onset may be delayed and is most common in middle age. Paranoid symptoms are often associated with organic personality change following head injury.[61]

---

[58] See Chapter 15.

[59] Thus, for example, see, *R* v *Hadfield* (1800) 27 St. Tr. 1281 and Chapter 16, p. 372.

[60] K. Davison, and C.R. Bagley (1969), "Schizophrenia-like Psychosis Associated with Organic Disorders of the Central Nervous System: a Review of the Literature" in R.N. Herrington (ed.), *Current Problems in Neuropsychiatry, British Journal of Psychiatry Special Publication No. 4*, Ashford, Kent: Headley Brothers.

[61] See below, p. 107.

Manic-depressive psychosis[62] may occur after relatively minor trauma. Unlike schizophrenia, it is believed that the illness is precipitated in a predisposed individual. Suicide is increased in head-injured patients and often occurs in the context of personal difficulties such as financial hardship or marital conflict. The rate increases with the passage of time.[63] In one series, 41 per cent of suicides had occurred during an episode of depressive psychosis.[64] Some early studies point to lesions in the temporal and frontal lobes of the brain, although the subsequent evidence is conflicting. Further detailed studies are reviewed by Lishman.[65]

PERSONALITY CHANGE

Personality change may occur with or without brain tissue injury. Gross brain damage, such as occurs with frontal lobe lesions, leads to dramatic changes to personality such as coarsening, explosive outbursts, loss of motivation, withdrawal, disinhibition, etc. This scenario is most likely with frontal lobe damage, but is also found in those with temporal lobe trauma. Personality change has been reported without brain damage and frequently represents an intensification of pre-existing abnormal traits. This may be secondary to minor degrees of cognitive impairment and is associated with persistent anxiety and irritability, possibly due to the presence of insight into the deficits.

HEAD INJURY

The severity of the head injury is an important guide to the long-term outcome, although there are some age differences and the

---

[62] See Chapter 15.

[63] See, for example, *Pigney* v *Pointers Transport Services Ltd.* [1957] 2 All ER 807.

[64] K.A. Achte, E. Hillbom and V. Aalberg (1967), *Post-Traumatic Psychosis Following War Brain Injuries*, Report from The Rehabilitation Institute for Brain-Injured Veterans in Finland, Vol. 1, Helsinki.

[65] W.A. Lishman (1987), Organic Psychiatry: The Psychological Consequences of Cerebral Disorder, Oxford: Blackwell Scientific Publications.

elderly are more vulnerable to the effects of head injury than the young. A further guide to the likely outcome is the period of post-traumatic amnesia (PTA) — the time lag between the moment of injury and the restoration of memory for everyday events (see Table 6.2).

TABLE 6.2: AMNESIA AND INJURY

Duration of PTA	Severity of Injury
< 10 minutes	Very mild injury
10–60 minutes	Mild injury
1–24 hours	Moderate injury
1–7 days	Severe injury
> 7 days	Very severe injury

The duration of the coma is also a guide to prognosis and has greater predictive power in relation to cognitive than to behavioural changes. Most cognitive recovery occurs during the first six months after injury. Improvement to mood and behaviour occur over a more protracted time-scale, even over several years.

Several aspects of function are assessed as a measure of impairment. These include intelligence, memory, language, motor skills and perceptual changes.[66] Personality changes are also associated with head injury.[67]

Head injury will not only affect the capacity of the person to work following rehabilitation; it will also impinge upon the quality of life of the sufferer and his/her family. Moreover, there may be implications for testamentary capacity.[68]

---

[66] The tests in common use are described in Chapter 4.

[67] See above, p. 93.

[68] See Chapters 12 and 14.

Deficits Associated with Specific Sites of Head Injury?

There is no convincing evidence linking specific sites of damage to specific disorders, with some notable exceptions. Organic changes to the frontal lobes of the brain are most commonly associated with behavioural changes such as disinhibition, apathy, withdrawal, etc. This constellation is known as the frontal lobe syndrome and is described above.[69] Injuries to the temporal lobe are associated with personality change, as well as schizophrenia-like symptoms, known as schizophreniform psychosis. These symptoms may also be associated with post-traumatic epilepsy and may respond to treatment of the epilepsy. Injuries to the basal part of the brain such as the mid-brain and hypothalamus lead to apathy, sudden outbursts of anger and changes to the instinctual drives such as thirst, appetite, sleep and sexual function. Apart from the association between schizophreniform psychosis and temporal lobe pathology, there is no specific connection between other psychiatric disorders and the site of a brain injury. However, injuries to the left hemisphere have a greater propensity to cause psychiatric disorder overall.[70]

SUICIDE

In the context of law, suicide is important in relation to its predictability, its prevention and the potential for negligence claims to be taken against a doctor in the event of a completed suicide.[71]

---

[69] See above, p. 107.

[70] W.A. Lishman (1968), "Brain Damage in Relation to Psychiatric Disability after Head Injury", *British Journal of Psychiatry*, Vol. 114, pp. 373–410.

[71] See, for example, *Kelly v St. Laurence's Hospital* [1989] ILRM 437 (SC) (failure to observe patient with temporal lobe epilepsy); *Armstrong v Eastern Health Board* (High Court, Unreported Judgment, Egan J, 5 October 1990) (suicide attempt following failure to read clinical notes that might have led to hospital admission); *Healy v North Western Health Board* (High Court, Unreported Judgment, Flood J, 31 January 1996) (successful suicide following discharge of patient without proper examination); and *Pigney v Pointers Transport Services Ltd.* [1957] 2 All ER 807. The issue also arises in relation to inquests: see *McKeown v Scully* [1986] ILRM 133; *Greene v McLoughlin* (Supreme Court, Unreported Judgment, Blayney J (for the Court), 26 January 1995); and the Criminal Law (Suicide) Act 1993.

Vulnerable Groups

The suicide rate in Ireland is currently 13.5 per 100,000, being more common among men than among women. Men under 35 and the elderly of both sexes are the most vulnerable groups. Those who are single, widowed or separated also have an increased risk. The question of what causes suicide is impossible to answer, since many variables are associated with it. Using psychological autopsy techniques (PAT), it has been shown that the most powerful association is with psychiatric illness and up to 95 per cent of victims have a psychiatric disorder — thus, it can be seen that very few occur in the context of an existential, rational, decision to end one's life. However, the PAT method has its critics, as it depends on obtaining information from all sources and arriving retrospectively at a diagnosis. The potential for inaccuracy and particularly for "effort after meaning" in making a diagnosis is immense.

Depressive illness is the disorder most associated with suicide and those depressed patients who are in the early stage of recovery following discharge from hospital[72] or who have just achieved an antidepressant response, such that motivation has improved but hopelessness is still present, are particularly at risk. This is by way of contrast with alcohol abuse, the second most common disorder found among suicide victims, when the period of greatest risk is in the late stages of alcoholism and often linked to the termination of a relationship. Those with schizophrenia are also at risk, especially young, chronically ill patients, although the suicide is often committed during a period of wellbeing and may be unexpectedly violent. Some suggest that, in these circumstances, it is related to insight about the illness. Up to 15 per cent of those with severe untreated depressive illness, 15 per cent of alcoholics and 10 per cent of those with schizophrenia commit suicide. More recent studies have focused on the presence of low levels of serotonin in the brains of suicide victims, thereby raising the spectre

---

[72] As, on one reading, appears to have been the case in *Healy* v *North Western Health Board* (High Court, Unreported Judgment, Flood J, 31 January 1996).

of biological markers for this behaviour. This very interesting work is still embryonic.

Trends over Time

Suicide rates throughout Europe are rising and the reasons for this have been speculated upon. One possibility, given the connection between psychiatric illness and suicide, is that the former is rising and elevating the rate. However, there is no evidence for this. Another explanation is that the change is due to more accurate reporting. However, the changes in suicide are observed across cultures where widely different methods of calculating suicide rates are employed. In Ireland, studies of the number of accidental or undetermined deaths, the categories to which suicides incorrectly recorded would have been assigned, have not diminished in parallel with the changes in the suicide rate. It is apparent that the increase in suicide is a true increase.

The weight of opinion now is that these changes are a reflection of social change in Europe and the concept of *anomie* or normlessness is central to this. During periods of social change, such as occurred during the great depression or more recently with changes to family and personal life, the uncertainty generated as society reaches a new equilibrium leads those who are suicidally ambivalent to contemplate and at times indulge in this behaviour. Thus, there is an interaction between psychiatric illness and social values influencing decisions about suicide. In addition, the copycat or "Werther" effect may be important, especially in small communities, and lead to similar methods being employed by those of a similar age and gender to the index case. The influence of these social changes and of the "copycat" effect makes the reduction of suicide very difficult and underlines the importance of careful reporting of suicide when it does occur.

Parasuicide

This is often referred to as deliberate self-harm. The term "attempted suicide" is inaccurate, since many who resort to self-destructive behaviour may not be attempting suicide but be manipulating another or seeking help using behavioural rather than verbal methods (the "cry for help" theory). However, in every patient presenting with such behaviour, the assessment of suicidality is essential to sift out those who are truly "attempting suicide" (assessment of suicide intent) from the other groups who may need help in various ways. For example, the clinically depressed person who has been untreated may be attempting suicide or alternatively crying for help — the motivation and context of the act will direct the help that is offered. Thus, the distinction must be made between those who have low and high suicide intent.[73]

The parasuicide rate is difficult to calculate, since many do not consult their doctor but sleep off the overdose at home. Figures from Britain suggest a rate of 250/100,000. It is therefore much more common than completed suicide. One per cent of this group per year go on to kill themselves and much effort has been invested in trying to predict this group with a view to reducing the suicide rate. This has proved impossible.[74] Women outnumber men by two to one in this behaviour and, unlike suicide, which peaks in spring and summer, there is no such peak in parasuicide. Neither is there an association with depressive illness or schizophrenia, but up to 60 per cent meet the criteria for personality disorder.[75] Rates are highest in the 25–35 age group and in socioeconomic groups IV and V.

Suicide Risk Assessment

Although effecting a reduction in suicide is very difficult and is more likely to be a socio-political and religious issue than a medical one, intervention to prevent *individual* suicides are imperative and occur on a daily basis in hospitals throughout the country.

---

[73] As an example of a suicide threat that culminated in an actual attempt (although it is difficult to assess, on the judgment, whether it was a genuine attempt or otherwise), see *Armstrong* v *Eastern Health Board* (High Court, Unreported Judgment, Egan J, 5 October 1990).

[74] See below, p. 113.

[75] See Chapter 9.

Assessment of Suicidal Ideation

Every person with a psychiatric illness must be asked about death wishes. About three per cent of the general population have these thoughts, but they are generally fleeting. The persistence, pervasiveness and strength of these are the most important guide to their significance, rather than their presence *per se*. Death wishes may be passive (e.g. wanting to go to sleep and not wake up) or active (e.g. wanting to take steps to end one's life). The latter must be examined further in order to assess the degree of suicide intent.[76] In addition to suicide intent, hopelessness has been shown to be a very useful measure of suicide risk and direct questions about this are an essential component of the assessment procedure.[77] Despair is a common manifestation. When the patient can describe such thoughts and provide the details of plans to end one's life in a cold and unemotional manner, then the risk of suicide is very high and admission to hospital, compulsorily if necessary, is essential for further assessment and possible treatment. Obtaining collateral information is also important, as some who are planning suicide may distort the information provided to reduce the possibility of detection. Further clinical risk factors are pathological guilt, brittleness of mood and agitation. The patient who promises not to commit suicide so as to please the doctor should also be regarded with caution.

Assessment of Suicide Intent

Once one has made an attempt on one's own life by overdose or some other method such as wrist-cutting, then details of the attempt must be obtained, including efforts to avoid discovery, the presence of a suicide note and the patient's concept of medical lethality. This latter is important, since many people have no

---

[76] See below, and *Armstrong* v *Eastern Health Board* (High Court, Unreported Judgment, Egan J, 5 October 1990); and *Healy* v *North Western Health Board* (High Court, Unreported Judgment, Flood J, 31 January 1996).

[77] For competing views as to how formalised this should be, see the evidence recited in the judgment in *Healy* v *North Western Health Board* (High Court, Unreported Judgment, Flood J, 31 January 1996).

knowledge of the likely effects of particular drugs in overdose. In general, the more violent the method (e.g. jumping off a bridge), the higher the intent. Those who have not tried to harm themselves but are threatening should be asked direct questions about the method being considered, and details about the time and place of the intended act.

Prediction of Suicide

Due to the very powerful association between psychiatric illness and suicide, it might seem that the potential for the prevention of suicide exists with the vigorous treatment of these disorders. One of the problems faced by psychiatrists is that compliance with treatment is poor and up to 60 per cent of patients do not take drugs in the dosage or for the duration prescribed. In addition, retrospective studies of suicide victims confirm their low consultation rates.

Even more difficult is the prediction of suicide in an individual patient or in particular groups of patients. Numerous studies have tried to predict suicide in high-risk groups, such as those indulging in deliberate self-harm (DSH). Up to one per cent per year go on to kill themselves following such an episode; by identifying the variables which distinguish the two groups, predictive scales have been devised. Because suicide is such a rare event, the problems of prediction are manifold and lead to excessively high false positive rates (i.e. those who would be predicted to commit suicide but who in fact do not). If an intervention were tailored to prevent suicide in this high-risk group, then the input would far exceed the necessity and would be unmanageable and unresourceable. Using clinical criteria, as distinct from statistical prediction, similar problems arise and are illustrated by the study of Pokorny[78] in which 4,800 in-patients were examined. Using the best possible clinical predictors, e.g. having been on an in-patient suicide risk list, etc. 35 of the 65 who took their lives were

---

[78] A.D. Pokorny (1983), "Prediction of Suicide in Psychiatric Patients: Report of a Prospective Study", *Archives of General Psychiatry*, Vol. 40, pp. 249–57.

correctly identified. This, however, was offset by wrongly predicting that 1,206 cases would kill themselves. In summary, for every
100 cases predicted, the forecast was wrong 97 times.

Recent studies have examined those who commit suicide during or immediately after a period of in-patient psychiatric treatment and confirm the absence of any "suspicious" features to alert
the clinician to this possibility, since improvement had been
shown to be sustained during the in-patient period. The only factor identified as distinguishing the suicide from the non-suicide
patient was a return following discharge to ongoing social and interpersonal problems — features which are difficult to change
even with intensive therapy.

Even greater problems with prediction arise in relation to
threats of suicide. Since almost all those who threaten suicide do
not actually carry it out, predicting future behaviour on this basis
is impossible. Moreover, when suicide is threatened, if suicide intent is high then treatment of the underlying cause, whether it be
a depressive illness or a personal crisis, is offered.[79] Suicide intent
diminishes very quickly thereafter.[80]

Antidepressants and Suicide

Attention has focused on two aspects of this debate within psychiatry. The first is the potential role of some antidepressants in
causing suicidal behaviour. In the United States, there has been
litigation and investigation by the Food and Drugs Administration
into the link between fluoxetine and aggression. These cases have
been unsuccessful.

The second aspect to this debate concerns the older antidepressants and their potentially toxic effects when taken in overdose.
In particular, they have an effect on the heart which can be fatal
in overdose. Some have suggested that these drugs are in part
responsible for the increase in suicide in recent years. As evidence

---

[79] See *Armstrong* v *Eastern Health Board* (High Court, Unreported Judgment, Egan J, 5 October 1990).

[80] M. Kelleher (1994), "The Prediction of Suicide and the Law on Abortion",
Irish Journal of Psychological Medicine, Vol. 11, No. 2., pp. 55–6.

to substantiate these claims, the "Fatal Toxicity Index" has been calculated — this is a measure of the number of suicide deaths from overdosing on a particular drug per 100,000 prescriptions. This has been shown to be highest for some of the older antidepressants and has lead to suggestions that the use of these should be curtailed. Against that, however, others draw attention to "The Suicide Index" — a measure of the suicide risk by any method — and show that this is highest for at least one of the newer antidepressants. Moreover, the proportion of suicide deaths from antidepressant overdose alone is less than four per cent. These issues have been aired in recent publications.[81] It is essential to remember that the speed of onset and efficacy of the older and newer antidepressants are similar, both taking a minimum of two weeks for the onset of antidepressant effect. The patient who is suicidal as a result of a depressive illness should be treated in hospital if suicide is to be avoided.

SUMMARY

A range of psychiatric disorders can follow upon personal injury. There is no evidence for the view that many such people are malingering and that once litigation is over the symptoms spontaneously disappear. In fact, the evidence points to a poor functional outcome for such disorders. The specificity of PTSD is open to question, although it is now incorporated into the current systems of classification. Suicide is particularly associated with depressive illness, schizophrenia and alcohol misuse. Its accurate prediction is impossible due to the rarity of the event.

---

[81] B. Leonard (1996), "Litigation and the Toxicity of Psychotropic Drugs", *Irish Journal of Psychological Medicine*, Vol. 13, No. 3, pp. 89–90; Reply by P. Casey (1996), "Litigation and the Toxicity of Psychotropic Drugs", *Irish Journal of Psychological Medicine*, Vol. 13, No. 3, pp. 89–90.

Chapter 7

VICTIMS OF DISASTER AND CRIME[1]

BACKGROUND

The study of victims began with the descriptions given by concentration camps survivors of their experiences. In the 1960s, war veterans, particularly those from the United States, provided further data. However, the scientific investigation of the victims of crime and disasters has until recently been largely neglected. Some suggest that serious emotional sequelae to disasters are a Western phenomenon due to the relative lack of exposure of the developed world to death. Recent studies from the developing world refute this and show that adverse effects are as common and as severe as those found in Western populations.

There is recognition that the onset of symptoms can be delayed, particularly when physical injury is present. In these circumstances, there is initially greater preoccupation with this than with the psychological symptoms. The presence of strong social supports can also delay the onset of symptoms. In some reports, the latency can be of several years' duration, with symptoms emerging only in the face of some stress. However, delayed onset post-traumatic stress disorder (PTSD) is the exception rather than the rule.

---

[1] This chapter will concentrate on the victims of crime, disasters and war but should be read in conjunction with Chapter 8, which deals with victims of accidents.

EPIDEMIOLOGY

In general, man-made disasters appear to produce higher rates of post-traumatic stress disorder than natural disasters — the likelihood of major emotional problems after a crime are therefore greater than after an earthquake, a forest fire or a hurricane. Among civilians, crime is a much more potent provoking agent than non-crime trauma. Thus, a mugging or a rape is more likely to result in emotional disorder than being caught in a riot.

- *War Veterans*: Low estimates of disorder have been found in a recent study, probably due to the schedule used for screening. A prevalence of just over 2 per cent was found in a study of 2,400 male Vietnam veterans covering the month prior to the assessment, whilst the life-time risk of 15 per cent must also be considered low.[2] A more recent study using a different screening instrument[3] found that the current rates for PTSD among men and women were 15 and 8 per cent respectively, whilst the lifetime rates were 30.6 per cent and 26.9 per cent respectively.

- *Victims of terrorism*: In a study of Northern Irish adults claiming compensation for violence directed at them personally or for witnessing violence, 23 per cent were found to be suffering from PTSD.

- *Crime*: studies of the prevalence of PTSD following crime found that the rate is about 18 per cent following physical assault and about 12 per cent following rape. Lifetime rates are much higher at 39 per cent and 32 per cent respectively.

---

[2] F. Stefano and The Centres for Disease Control, Vietnam Experience Study (1988), "Health Status of Vietnam Veterans — 1: Psychosocial Characteristics", *Journal of the American Medical Association*, Vol. 259, pp. 2701–7.

[3] T.M. Keane, J.M. Caddell and K.L. Taylor (1988), "Mississippi Scale for Combat-Related Post-Traumatic Stress Disorder: Three Studies in Reliability and Validity", *Journal of Consulting and Clinical Psychology*, Vol. 56, pp. 85–90.

VULNERABILITY AND RISK FACTORS

There are many studies which demonstrate that the risk of developing PTSD is greatest in those who have pre-morbid vulnerability either in terms of a previous psychiatric disorder, a family history of same or personality dysfunction. Moreover, those who have a history of negative life events immediately prior to the trauma are at increased risk when compared with those who have no such prior stresses. Also at increased risk are those who have emerging symptoms at the time of the trauma.[4] Indeed, the presence of pre-existing symptoms has been shown to be a better predictor of disorder than the trauma itself. In the group most widely studied (i.e. war veterans), pre-military factors interact with war-related variables in determining the risk of PTSD. Thus, poor social supports, low educational status, a history of pre-military diagnosis along with severity of combat exposure and exposure to grotesque death have been identified as increasing vulnerability.[5]

Interestingly, these findings were refuted in a study of Northern Irish adults claiming compensation following attempted assassination, sexual violence or witnessing violence[6] and neither severity of the incident, personal, family or past history predicted subsequent development of PTSD.

Among victims of violent crime, risk factors for the development of PTSD are greatest if a threat to life is perceived during the attack and if physical injury occurs. These effects are additive, but there is uncertainty if co-occurring rape increases the risk further.

---

[4] G. Canino, M. Bravo, M. Rubio-Stipec and M. Woodbury (1990), "The Impact of Disasters on Mental Health: Prospective and Retrospective Analyses", *International Journal of Mental Health*, Vol. 19, pp. 51–69.

[5] B.L. Green, M.C. Grace, J.D. Lindy, G.C. Gleser and A. Leonard (1990), "Risk Factors for PTSD and Other Diagnoses in a General Sample of Vietnam Veterans", *American Journal of Psychiatry*, Vol. 147, No. 6, pp. 729–33.

[6] P. Bell, M. Kee, G.C. Loughrey, P.S. Curran and R.J. Roddy (1988), "Post-Traumatic Stress in Northern Ireland", *Acta Psychiatrica Scandinavica*, Vol. 77, pp. 166–9.

The specific coping mechanisms, such as identification of an external locus of control (i.e. believing that control of events lies outside oneself), emotion rather than problem-focused coping (i.e. ventilating emotion rather than seeking practical solutions), and distancing, also predisposed to PTSD in a combat situation.[7] It is unclear if these psychological risk factors can be generalised to other situations associated with PTSD.

An overview of these theories is presented by Boehnlein,[8] which postulates that PTSD arises from a number of factors including genetically determined neurophysiological vulnerability, as well as cognitive, environmental and cultural factors. Much more research is essential to unravel the relative magnitude of each and to clarify the present confusion.

DOES THE NATURE OF THE TRAUMA AFFECT THE MANIFESTATION OF THE DISORDER?

General Features

There is some evidence to suggest that Vietnam veterans are amongst the most incapacitated by PTSD. The complications of alcohol abuse, marital breakdown and employment instability were more common in this group when compared with road accident victims.[9] Symptoms such as vivid flashbacks and dissociative episodes (loss of memory for long periods) were almost exclusively reported in veterans when compared with survivors of violence in

---

[7] Z. Solomon, M. Mikulincer and E. Avitzur (1988), "Coping, Locus of Control, Social Support and Combat-Related Post-Traumatic Stress Disorder: a Prospective Study", *Journal of Personality and Social Psychology*, Vol. 55, pp. 279–85.

[8] J.K. Boehnlein (1989), "The Process of Research in Post Traumatic Stress Disorder", *Perspectives in Biological Medicine*, Vol. 32, pp. 455–65.

[9] A. Burnstein, P.E. Ciccone, R.A. Greenstein, N. Daniels, K. Olsen, A. Malarek and N. Johnson (1988), "Chronic Vietnam PTSD and Acute Civilian PTSD: A Comparison Of Treatment Experiences", *General Hospital Psychiatry*, Vol. 10, pp. 245–9.

Northern Ireland.[10] Some of the classic symptoms described in the literature are uncommon in survivors of Northern Ireland violence including survivor guilt, estrangement from others, dissociative states and emotional numbing. Depression was prominent in this group, however, and develops in most groups. Fire fighters also do not exhibit survivor guilt or estrangement and by contrast feel a greater sense of community identity.[11] Dissociation is a particularly common symptom in the victims of child sexual abuse,[12] as is hypochondriasis (preoccupation with possible illness). Male victims are at risk for gender-identity problems[13] and both sexes have difficulties with sex. Following rape, guilt is a common feature. Among torture victims, particularly political activists, depression and anxiety are common, but substance misuse and impulse control uncommon, unlike war veterans, where these features are to the fore. There is some evidence that chronic and repeated trauma, such as that associated with sexual abuse, leads predominantly to depression and anxiety, dissociation and somatic symptoms, as well as more profound problems of self- and sexual-identity.[14] In general those who have suffered from PTSD have a higher incidence of unexplained physical symptoms, even several years after the disaster.

---

[10] G.C. Loughrey, P. Bell, M. Kee, R.J. Roddy and P.S. Curran (1988), "Post-Traumatic Stress Disorder and Civil Violence in Northern Ireland", *British Journal of Psychiatry*, Vol. 153, pp. 544–60.

[11] A.C. McFarlane (1988), "The Phenomenology of Post-Traumatic Stress Disorder Following a Natural Disaster", *Journal of Nervous and Mental Diseases*, Vol. 176, pp. 22–9.

[12] M.R. Nash, T.L. Hulsey, M.C. Sexton, T.L. Harralson and W. Lambert (1993), "Long-term Sequelae of Childhood Sexual Abuse: Perceived Family Environment, Psychopathology and Dissociation", *Journal of Consulting and Clinical Psychology*, Vol. 61, pp. 276–83.

[13] See Chapter 15.

[14] J.L. Herman (1992), "Complex PTSD: a Syndrome in Survivors of Prolonged and Repeated Trauma", *Journal of Traumatic Stress*, Vol. 5, pp. 377–91.

Victims of Violent Crime

Mugging

The effects of violent crime can be persistent and severe. The fact
that the crime was perpetrated by another person impinges upon
the victim's capacity to trust others. This lack of trust, combined
with feelings of shame and failure, leads to difficulties in confiding
with family members or friends, thereby depriving the victim of
the usual sources of support at times of stress.[15] Avoidance of the
area in which the attack occurred is common in all victims and
may lead to agoraphobia. The victim may feel that he or she contributed to the crime and may obsessively contemplate how the
attack could have been avoided.

Rape

Depressive illness and anxiety are common symptoms following
rape. The duration of the depressive symptoms is uncertain;
studies report variously that they diminish rapidly within three
months,[16] whilst others point to almost half of the victims describing symptoms several years after the attack.[17] However,
anxiety tends to persist for much longer and to progress to avoidance and general fears of being attacked. A consistent finding has
been the chronicity of sexual dysfunction, particularly sexual satisfaction, and whilst the frequency of sexual activity is reduced
initially, this returns to pre-rape levels usually within one year of
the assault.[18]

---

[15] M. Bard and D. Sangrey (1986), *The Crime Victim's Book*, 2nd edition, New
York: Brunner Mazel.

[16] G. Steketee and E.B. Foa (1987), "Rape Victims: Post-Traumatic Stress
Responses and their Treatment — a Review of the Literature", *Journal of
Anxiety Disorders*, Vol. 1, pp. 69–86.

[17] C.C. Nadelson, M.T. Notman, H. Zackson and J. Gornick (1982), "A Follow-
up Study of Rape Victims", *American Journal of Psychiatry*, Vol. 139, pp.
1266–70.

[18] K.S. Calhoun, B.M. Atkeson and P.A. Resick (1982), "A Longitudinal Examination of Fear Reactions in Victims of Rape", *Journal of Counselling Psychology*, Vol. 29, pp. 655–61.

Studies of the effects of sexual assault on males are sparse, although anecdotal reports suggest that coerced sexual intercourse is as harmful to men as it is to women.

The common emotions described by the victims of rape include numbness or the absence of any feelings about the crime and the perpetrator. This may give way to anger and also to depression. Feelings of guilt are common, as is the feeling of dirt and contamination. Although the victims of crime rarely develop psychosis, the use of alcohol and benzodiazepines by victims to provide symptomatic relief from anxiety and depression may subsequently lead to substance misuse if the suffering of the victim is unrecognised or untreated.

There is no evidence that other sexual crimes, such as witnessing genital exposure, have a permanent effect on psychological wellbeing, except in the very vulnerable,[19] although it may cause transient distress.

Victims of Child Sexual Abuse — Long-term Effects

Prevalence

The exact figure for sexual abuse is unknown, largely due to the acknowledged variations in definition and the population under study. Patients attending a psychiatric outpatient clinic have higher rates than those attending a general practice surgery. A recent study of sexual abuse beginning in those under 13 found that sexual intercourse occurred in 6.1 per cent of adult female outpatient attenders and the corresponding figure for general practice attenders was 0.8 per cent; the figures for intercourse occurring between the ages of 13 and 16 were 12.2 per cent and 4.2 per cent. For all types of sexual contact (e.g. fondling, oral contact, sexual kissing/hugging, intercourse), the figures for the under-13 groups were 33 per cent and 22.5 per cent, whilst for the over-13 group, the figures were 30.4 per cent and 10.8 per cent respec-

---

[19] N.L. Gittleson, S.E. Eacott and B.M. Metha (1978), "Victims of Indecent Sexual Exposure", *British Journal of Psychiatry*, Vol. 132, pp. 61–5.

tively.[20] A recent review of the epidemiology of sexual abuse outside North America found a prevalence ranging from 3–29 per
cent in men and 7–36 per cent in women. Interfamilial abuse was
higher among women.[21]

Emotional Complications

It is now acknowledged that many victims of childhood abuse suffer very serious emotional sequelae. Three problems present
themselves in studying this relationship. The first relates to
whether sexual abuse *per se* or other co-occurring social depriva-
tions are responsible for these emotional problems. The second
relates to whether the abuse directly causes the emotional consequences or whether it acts as a risk factor. The third issue for consideration is the association between specific psychiatric disorders
and a history of sexual abuse.

1. Mullen[22] attempted to disentangle the effects of abuse from
    deprivation. He demonstrated that the effects of abuse were
    independent of these other disadvantages, but commented:
    "the overlap between the possible effects of the matrix of dis-
    advantage from which it so often emerges were, however, so
    considerable as to raise doubts about how often, in practice, it
    operates as an independent causal element". He found that
    reported emotional disturbance was linked to the severity of
    abuse but also demonstrated that many victims do not exhibit
    any emotional damage. These findings were largely replicated

---

[20] R.L. Palmer, L. Coleman, R. Chaloner, R. Oppenhimer and J. Smith (1993),
"Childhood Sexual Experiences with Adults: a Comparison of Reports by
Women Psychiatric Patients and General Practice Attenders", *British Jour-
nal of Psychiatry*, Vol. 163, pp. 499–504.

[21] D. Finkelhor (1994), "The International Epidemiology of Child Sexual
Abuse", *Child Abuse and Neglect*, Vol. 18, pp. 409–17.

[22] P.E. Mullen, J. Martin, J.C. Anderson, S.E. Romans and G.P. Herbison
(1994), "The Effects of Child Sexual Abuse on Social, Interpersonal and Sexual Function in Adult Life", *British Journal of Psychiatry*, Vol. 165, pp. 35–
47.

by Nash,[23] who described the effects of sexual abuse on self-esteem.

2. Whilst it is recognised that there is an association between childhood sexual abuse and later psychiatric disorder, there is uncertainty about the nature of the relationship. Some contend that sexual abuse directly causes later emotional disturbance, whilst others contend that the former increases vulnerability, which only leads to dysfunction in the presence of some other stressor. Research in this area has been hampered by inadequately designed studies. In scientific investigation, the distinction between vulnerability and causation of a disorder is of vital importance, although often ignored by the courts, which adhere to a simple cause-and-effect model.[24] For example, there is an association between being male and committing suicide, although being a man is not in itself the cause of suicide. Being male increases the vulnerability and other factors are required to cause the suicide. A similar distinction between vulnerability and direct causation exists in relation to the issue of childhood sexual abuse and the study by Mullen already cited attempted to disentangle this complicated issue.

3. An association between abuse and a number of disorders has been demonstrated. Patients with alcohol abuse, eating disorders,[25] dissociation disorder and borderline personality have comparatively higher frequencies of sexual abuse in their past histories than do comparison groups chosen from the non-patient population. Attempts to relate specific disorders to sexual abuse have foundered and suggest a generally

---

[23] Nash et al. (1993), op. cit.

[24] See Chapter 2.

[25] See below and S.L. Welch and C.G. Fairburn (1994), "Sexual Abuse and Bulimia Nervosa: Three Integrated Case Control Comparisons", *American Journal of Psychiatry*, Vol. 151, pp. 402–7.

increased risk of all disorders.[26] Sexual abuse has been shown
to be associated with sexual dysfunction in adult life, in particular vaginismus and frigidity.[27] Whilst many women relate
well to men emotionally, it is only when a sexual aspect enters
the relationship that flashbacks to the earlier trauma occur,
leading to dysfunction. There are also reports of early sexual
activity in victims of abuse as well as promiscuity, increased
masturbation and a preoccupation with sexual matters.[28] In
their personality, victims are often found to have low self-
esteem and to continue to describe isolation and feelings of
stigmatisation. Episodes of self-harm are common after disclosure of the trauma[29] and during treatment.

Sexual Abuse — Other Aspects

The importance of a supportive mother in ameliorating or reducing the effects of abuse have been clearly described, as has a
strong parental relationship.[30]

The suggestion of an intergenerational transfer of sexual or
physical abuse has entered the general vocabulary with little empirical research to sustain it. A recent attempt to assess this found
some supportive evidence and demonstrated that one third of
child victims grow up to be continuously abusive, another third do
not and the final third remain vulnerable to becoming abusive at
times of major stress.[31]

---

[26] G.R. Brown and B. Anderson (1991), "Psychiatric Morbidity in Adult Inpatients with Childhood Histories of Sexual and Physical Abuse", *American
Journal of Psychiatry*, Vol. 148, pp. 55–61.

[27] See Chapter 10.

[28] C. Sheldrick (1991), "Adult Sequelae of Child Sexual Abuse", *British Journal of Psychiatry*, Vol. 158 (suppl. 10), pp. 55–62.

[29] Sheldrick (1991), op. cit.

[30] S.E. Romans, J.L. Martin, J.C. Anderson, M.L. O'Shea and P.E. Mullen
(1995), "Factors that Mediate between Child Sexual Abuse and Adult Psychological Outcome", *Psychological Medicine*, Vol. 25, pp. 127–42.

[31] H.E. Oliver (1993), "Intergenerational Transmission of Child Abuse: Rates,
Research and Clinical Implications", *American Journal of Psychiatry*, Vol.
150, pp. 1315–24.

See Chapter 15 for discussion of the abuser.

Eating Disorders

Although the majority of sufferers with anorexia and bulimia nervosa have no history of sexual abuse, a significant minority do; for this reason, it is appropriate to consider eating disorders in this chapter. Anorexia nervosa was first described in 1868 and even then its psychological origin was recognised. The average age of onset among girls is 16, but in boys, in whom it is less common but increasing, it is much younger at 12. It predominates in higher socio-economic groups. The core symptom is not anorexia (loss of appetite), but a distorted attitude to food and body shape. Other features include loss of 25 per cent of body weight, an intense desire for thinness and amenorrhoea (cessation of menstrual bleeding), whilst among males there is loss of libido.

Normally anorexia nervosa begins with dieting which is pursued relentlessly and leads to purging, vomiting, excessive exercise and a distortion in body image, so that body shape and weight are overestimated. As weight loss increases, body image becomes increasingly distorted. Some also steal food and indulge in food rituals such as preparing elaborate meals for others while refusing any themselves. The prevalence is about 250/100,000 in those over the age of 16 and is more common in certain groups such as ballet dancers, fashion models and other groups in whom bodily appearance and shape are important. Milder forms of the condition may occur in 1–2 per cent of university students.

The causes are speculative and various theories have been proposed, including social attitudes to food and body shape, the use of diet and food control as a symbolic way of establishing independence from parental control, a primary abnormality of the hypothalamus, fear of adulthood and changes to brain neurochemicals, especially those such as beta-endorphins, which stimulate feeding behaviour.

The treatment of anorexia nervosa is difficult and time-consuming, partly because the patient is frequently reluctant to accept the diagnosis and denies the illness. Management of anorexia nervosa focuses first on achieving weight gain and reducing the risk of death from malnutrition. This may require hospitalisation and even compulsory treatment if there is an imminent risk of death. Indeed, anorexia nervosa has a mortality rate of 5 per cent. The second aspect of treatment is aimed at reducing relapse and involves both behaviour and cognitive therapy. Medication has little role, except when depressive illness supervenes, a common occurrence during the early phases of treatment. In spite of intense treatment, the prognosis is not good; up to two-thirds of patients remain preoccupied with food and diet. While two-thirds regain weight in the short term, relapses are common and social and sexual difficulties lead to isolation and loneliness.

Bulimia nervosa was first described in 1979 and defined as an intractable urge to overeat, followed by vomiting and purging. In spite of this, weight is usually normal or even high and menstruation is normal. During a binge, there is a feeling of loss of control followed by guilt and shame. The cause is unknown and the frequency is uncertain, depending on the definition. Up to 80 per cent of college students in the US admit to excessive eating and guilt but only 4 per cent describe induced vomiting. Treatment is psychotherapeutic and, unlike those with anorexia nervosa, sufferers are generally keen to be helped. Both cognitive and behaviour therapy seem to be helpful but outcome studies are lacking. The use of medication such as fluoxetine, an antidepressant, in high doses to stabilise appetite is a useful addition to current strategies. Some who develop bulimia nervosa have a prior history of anorexia nervosa and therefore a poorer prognosis than those without this history. Electrolyte disturbances from vomiting may be life threatening. Bulimia nervosa may be confused with psychogenic vomiting in which spontaneous vomiting occurs but overeating does not proceed this. Obesity is occasionally associated with emotional factors as, for instance, when excessive eating is used to ward off depression, anxiety or unhappiness. So far, drugs to induce loss of appetite have little effect and treatment should focus on the abnormal mood states and social reinforcers which induce overeating.

PHYSICAL ABUSE IN THE FAMILY

The effects upon children of witnessing violence in the home has been clearly documented and can be divided into the immediate effects and the delayed effects. The former include high anxiety and behaviour disorders. Acting-out in the form aggressive behaviour or school truancy may occur. These problems in the child and adolescent will be compounded by the stressors associated with family violence such as alcohol abuse, unemployment, frequent moves and separations from the mother. Many children feel responsible for the violence and harbour persistent guilt that impacts upon their functioning as adults. These children are vulnerable in later life to depression, anxiety, low self-esteem and, as a result of exposure, to becoming violent themselves, especially male victims, although this is not inevitable[32] and violence may occur in those not exposed to any neglect or aggression in childhood.[33] The consequences of violence directed to the child are similar to effects of witnessing violence.

WAR-RELATED TRAUMA AND
CONCENTRATION CAMP SURVIVORS

Veterans are the most widely studied group of victims of PTSD. In particular, data gathered from Vietnam veterans points to a high prevalence for alcohol abuse and personality change among this group of veterans, a picture quiet different from the anxiety and depression reported among the World War II soldiers. Other people involved in war, other than those in combat, are also at risk. Body handlers were studied during the Gulf War and it was found that up to 50 per cent developed PTSD.

---

[32] C.S. Widom (1984), "Child Abuse, Neglect and Adult Behaviour: Research Design and Findings on Criminality, Violence and Child Abuse", *American Journal of Orthopsychiatry*, Vol. 59, pp. 355–67.

[33] B.K. Luntz (1994), "Antisocial Personality Disorder in Abused and Neglected Children Grown Up", *American Journal of Psychiatry*, Vol. 151, pp. 670–4.

The psychological sequelae to being a prisoner of war are different from the effects of being a war veteran. The latter have a sense of purpose and of comradeship with other soldiers and are to some extent in control of their destinies. Unlike these, concentration camp survivors and prisoners of war are deprived of any power over their own lives, they are subjected to torture and degradation and witness brutality meted out to others. The effects may persist for decades afterwards and, as well as depression, nightmares, anxiety, depersonalisation and flashbacks, there is a pervasive passivity, loss of trust and restriction in social life. Often, a sense of overwhelming guilt develops at what had to be done to survive. The impact upon the family is striking and is associated with poor relationships with children and spouses, as well as the avoidance of expressions or displays of emotion.

Among female torture victims, sexual violence and head injury are common. Therefore it is essential to conduct a thorough neurological examination. Some reports of seizures following rape or combat trauma have focused attention on the role of these in generating flashbacks. The addition of an anti-epileptic drug such as carbamazepine eliminates this symptom.[34]

There is some evidence that commitment to a cause, preparedness and strong social supports serve to modify the effects of torture and imprisonment among political activists.

OTHER TRAUMAS

Mass shootings, such as that which occurred in Hungerford, are also associated with the development of PTSD in a significant minority of those who witness the episode. Survivors of earthquakes, of air crashes or of any disaster are also at risk.

Recently, the effects of stalking have been investigated[35] and confirm that almost all victims make major life changes such as

---

[34] A.E. Goldfield, R.F. Mollica, B.H. Pesavento and S.V. Farone (1988), "The Physical and Psychological Sequelae of Torture: Symptomatology and Diagnosis", *Journal of the American Medical Association*, Vol. 259, pp. 2725–9.

[35] M. Pathe and P.E. Mullen (1997), "The Impact of Stalkers on their Victims", *British Journal of Psychiatry*, Vol. 170, pp. 12–17.

changing job and moving house. Nightmares, depressed mood and appetite disturbance are also described in a large proportion and 24 per cent admit to suicidal ideation. Moreover, the study confirms that many (34 per cent) are later physically or sexually assaulted. Caution has to be exercised in generalising the findings of this study to the general population, since it focused on patients attending a unit with a special interest in this problem.

Those working with the victims of disasters may themselves suffer adverse sequelae to the events. Included in this group are body handlers, fire fighters or other rescuers. For example, 25 per cent of a group of oil rig disaster rescuers themselves reported poor mental health nine months later. Whilst training helped cope initially, it did not prevent disturbance at follow-up.[36]

PREVENTION, TREATMENT AND OUTCOME

There is little evidence to suggest that PTSD can be prevented[37] and specific interventions such as psychological debriefing have not been shown to be effective at reducing psychiatric morbidity, in spite of intuitive experience. Pre-disaster preparation has also failed to prevent the development of disorder in the long term, at least among oil rig rescuers.[38] Attempts to prevent sexual abuse or to aid in the early detection of abuse have been underway for a few years. These focus of "good and bad touches", on saying no and on confiding the abuse to a person in authority. These have not been evaluated scientifically, either in terms of their success at leading to disclosure or at preventing unwanted sexual advances.

There is little hard data on the treatment of PTSD. Antidepressants, either tricyclics or MAOIs, have a role to play where depressive symptoms are to the fore in the early stages of the

---

[36] S. Ersland, L. Weisaeth and A. Sund (1989), "The Stress upon Rescuers Involved in an Oil Rig Disaster, 'Alexander L. Kielland', 1980", *Acta Psychiatrica Scandinavica* (supplement 355), Vol. 80, pp. 131–7.

[37] *Lancet* (1989), "Psychiatric Intervention after Disaster", Editorial, *Lancet*, Vol. ii, p. 138.

[38] Ersland et al. (1983), op. cit.

disorder.[39] In addition, other complications such as alcohol or drug misuse must be treated symptomatically. Thereafter pharmacological interventions have little effect. There is some evidence to support the use of exposure to feared memories to reduce symptoms. Cognitive therapy also has its proponents, although further studies are required. The use of counselling techniques to aid in recovery from abuse, sexual or physical, is well established although little researched. Treatment generally focuses on the specific disorders which present in the victims and in the absence of systematic studies of talking therapies, practitioners rely on therapeutic intuition. A good review of the diversity of therapies for adult survivors of sexual abuse is provided by Crowe and Dare.[40]

Once PTSD is established, there is little evidence that treatment, either pharmacological or psychological, is effective and some studies have found the converse, i.e. that psychotherapeutic intervention leads to symptomatic deterioration. However, following acute post-traumatic stress disorder, symptoms improve with the passage of time and the role of treatment in effecting this is questionable. There is little information on the proportion of the total sufferers who continue to be symptomatic in the long term. Some research suggests that settlement of the lawsuit, following a disaster, leads to resolution of symptoms; however, non-litigants also improve, suggesting that it is the general level of community preoccupation engendered by litigation following a major disaster which leads to the change, rather than the settlement itself.[41]

---

[39] J. Davidson (1992), "Pharmacological Treatments in PTSD", *British Journal of Psychiatry*, Vol. 160, pp. 309–14.

[40] M. Crowe and C. Dare (1998), "Survivors of Childhood Sexual Abuse: Approaches to Therapy", *Advances in Psychiatric Treatment*, Vol. 4, No. 2, pp. 96–100.

[41] B.L. Green, J.D. Lindy, M.C. Grace, G.C. Glesser, A.C. Leonard, M. Korol and C. Winget (1990), "Buffalo-Creek Survivors in the Second Decade: Stability of Stress Symptoms", *American Journal of Orthopsychiatry*, Vol. 60, pp. 43–54.

SUMMARY

Post-traumatic stress disorder has received considerable attention during the last 25 years, stimulated initially by the emotional casualties of the Vietnam War and more recently by the increased awareness of sexual abuse. In spite of this, few strides have been made in prevention or treatment.

Chapter 8

NEGLIGENT INFLICTION OF EMOTIONAL SUFFERING

INTRODUCTION[1]

An individual's response to any given event may range from finding it agreeable, through indifference, to finding it objectionable
and/or upsetting. The strength of the "negative reaction" induced
may thus extend from simple intellectual through intuitive objection, emotional upset, disturbance and distress.[2] Whether these
latter "negative reactions" are characterised as "mental" or "emotional" seems hardly to create a difference. They clearly represent
non-physical reactions.[3] To characterise such reactions as upset,
disturbance or distress at best suggests no more than differing

---

[1] See, generally, W.P. Keeton, D.B. Dobbs, R.E. Keeton and D.G. Owen
(1984), *Prosser and Keeton on the Law of Torts*, 5th edition, St Paul MN:
West Publishing Company, pp. 359–66; J.G. Fleming (1987), *The Law of
Torts*, 7th edition, Sydney: The Law Book Company, pp. 144–52; R.F.V.
Heuston and R.A. Buckley (1992), *Salmond and Heuston on the Law of Torts*,
20th edition, London: Sweet and Maxwell, pp. 219–23; and B. McMahon and
W. Binchy (1990), *Irish Law of Torts*, 2nd edition, Dublin: Butterworth (Ire-
land), Chapter 17.

[2] According to Prosser, emotional distress "includes all highly unpleasant
mental reactions, such as fright, horror, grief, shame, humiliation, anger,
embarrassment, chagrin, disappointment, worry and nausea (*sic*)"; 44 Calif.
L. Rev. 40, 43, cited in Salmond and Heuston (1992), op. cit., p. 220. Although
nausea may be emotionally distressing, and significantly impair function, it
hardly follows that the converse is also automatically true.

[3] Similarly, a reflexive physical reaction in response to a noxious stimulus,
mediated through well-defined and evolved neural pathways could be classified as non-physical reaction.

degrees of responses. As with many subjective symptoms,[4] they may also be accompanied by observable manifestations. However, the assertion that:

> . . . medical science has recognised long since that not only fright and shock, but also grief, anxiety, rage and shame, are in themselves "physical" injuries, in the sense that they produce well marked changes in the body, and symptoms that are readily visible to the professional eye. . . .[5]

not alone misunderstands the critical clinical difference between symptoms (subjective elements) and signs (objective elements), but overstates the understanding of the physiological — or pathophysiological — mechanisms and the observability of the "physical" signs involved.[6]

As such reactions are an intrinsic part of everyday existence, the common law has refused to compensate mere mental or emotional upset that is negligently inflicted. As Lord Bridge stated in *McLoughlin* v *O'Brian*:[7]

> The common law gives no damages for the emotional distress which any normal person experiences when someone he loves is killed or injured. Anxiety and depression[8] are normal human emotions. Yet an anxiety neurosis or a reactive depression may be recognisable psychiatric illnesses, with or without psychosomatic symptoms. So, the first

---

[4] In contradistinction to signs, which are objectively observable.

[5] Prosser and Keeton (1984), op. cit., p. 56, referring, *inter alia*, to Goodrich (1922), "Emotional Disturbance as Legal Damage", 20 Mich. L. Rev. 497, listing, upon medical authority (*sic*), a variety of physical symptoms, from accelerated pulse to pyorrhoea! Whatever about the validity of a finding in relation to an accelerated pulse, any claim of a causal connection to pyorrhoea is untenable.

[6] That said, however, given improved understanding of the neurobiological nature of psychiatric disease, such a proposition may not be too far off verification; see Chapter 2. Nevertheless, this and similar assertions are still cited with approval in academic writings.

[7] [1983] AC 410.

[8] Presumably this means low spirits, as distinct from a clinical depression.

hurdle which a plaintiff claiming damages . . . must sur-
mount is to establish that he is suffering, not merely grief,[9]
distress or any other normal emotion, but a positive psychiatric illness.[10]

Nevertheless, in two special groups of cases, the American courts
have allowed recovery for emotional or mental disturbance, not
amounting to, or causing, such psychiatric "injury". Thus, compensation has been allowed for the negligent transmission of tele-
graphs, especially ones announcing death[11] and for the negligent
handling of corpses. Although, traditionally, negligence alone was
insufficient — aggravating circumstances were also required —
this no longer appears to be the case. The underlying policy consideration seems to be that the circumstances of such cases guarantee the genuineness of the claims.[12] That other similar examples
also exist seems beyond doubt, although it has been asserted that:

---

[9] Although the common law denies recovery for such injuries, damages for
the emotional upset and grief caused by a negligently caused death are specifically provided for by statute; see Civil Liability Act, 1961, s. 49, as
amended by the Courts Act, 1981, s. 28(1), and the Civil Liability (Amendment) Act, 1996, s. 2; and (in Britain) the Fatal Accidents Act, 1976, s. 1A,
substituted by the Administration of Justice Act, 1982, s. 3. See also Veitch
(1972), "Solatium — A Debt Repaid?", *Irish Jurist*, Vol. V11, pp. 77–95.

[10] [1983] AC 410 at 431. See also *Alcock v Chief Constable of South Yorkshire
Police* [1992] 1 AC 310 at 416 *per* Lord Oliver: "Grief, sorrow, deprivation and
the necessity of caring for loved ones who have suffered injury or misfortune
must . . . be considered as ordinary and inevitable incidents of life which,
regardless of individual susceptibilities, must be sustained without compensation. It would be inaccurate and hurtful to suggest that grief is made any
the less real or deprivation more tolerable by a more gradual realisation, but
to extend liability to cover injury in such cases would be to extend the law in
a direction for which there is no pressing policy need and in which there is no
logical stopping point."

[11] Although, with the increased availability of facsimile and electronic mail
communications, telegrams are rarely used nowadays, there is no reason,
either in logic or principle, why the same considerations should not also apply to these forms of communication — although the sender may be more
difficult to identify and may not be a "mark" for damages.

[12] Prosser and Keeton (1984), op. cit., p. 362.

> . . . cases will obviously be infrequent in which "mental dis-
> tress", not so severe as to cause physical harm, will clearly
> be a serious wrong worthy of redress and sufficiently at-
> tested by the circumstances of the case.[13]

However, recognised psychiatric or "mental" illness, which the law clearly recognises and compensates, arguably represents no more than a stage beyond the mere upset, distress or disturbance. Indeed, diagnosis of the presence or absence of a recognised psychiatric illness (e.g. depressive illness) depends on assessment of not alone the intensity of the sadness, or low spirits, but also on its duration. The diagnosis of a recognised psychiatric illness, at least in part, is dependent on assessment of the particular mental or emotional response or symptom, on a time–intensity continuum. Although the characterisation of that response or symptom as "upset", or "distress" or "disturbance", as distinct from a "positive psychiatric illness", implies an important distinction as far as the common law is concerned, it is a linguistic difference that may be without significant clinical relevance.[14]

The common law's recognition of the compensability of "mental" injury has evolved through a tortuous and lengthy evolution of judicial precedent.[15] Given the antiquity of some of the decisions — and the limited development of the understanding of disease-causing mechanisms up to relatively recent times — it is hardly surprising that there was a requirement for "bodily" or "physical" injury as a consequence of the "nervous" or "emotional" insult. Thus, the requirement for bodily injury was effectively used as an

---

[13] Prosser and Keeton (1984), op. cit., p. 362. See also *Kelly* v *Crowley* [1985] IR 212; *Phelan Holdings (Kilkenny) Ltd.* v *Hogan*, High Court, Unreported, 15 October 1996, Barron J.

[14] At least from the perspective of the treating or reporting psychiatrist. This view may also be reinforced by advances in the understanding of neurobiology.

[15] In *McLoughlin* v *O'Brian* [1983] AC 410, Lord Bridge (at 431) observed that the whole area was in urgent need of review. Legislation governing aspects of recovery in this area, advocated by Lord Scarman in that case, was introduced in New South Wales and the Australian Capital Territory — as far back as 1944 in the case of the former jurisdiction.

evidentiary control device.[16] However, in tandem with rapid advances in psychiatry, the requirement for evidence of such injury — limited enough in the early cases — was quickly abandoned. In the aftermath of the First World War, Atkin LJ (as he then was) in *Hambrook* v *Stokes Brothers*[17] could state with confidence:

> . . . at one time the theory was held that damage at law could not be proved in respect of personal injuries, unless there was some injury which was variously called "bodily" or "physical", but which necessarily excluded an injury which was only "mental". There can be no doubt at the present day that this theory is wrong. It is perhaps irrelevant to discuss at length how it arose. It may be due partly to a false analogy between the action of negligence and the action of trespass to the person involving some sort of impact with the person; and in part to the law following a belated psychology which falsely removed mental phenomena from the world of physical phenomena.[18]

Other cases from the late nineteenth century onwards reflect a similar approach. In more recent times, the House of Lords, in only the second case of its type to reach that court in a century, *McLoughlin* v *O'Brian*,[19] set out the nature of the injury or harm to be compensated. Lord Wilberforce stated:

> Although we continue to use the hallowed expression "nervous shock," [the] law, and common understanding, have moved some distance since recognition was given to this symptom as a basis for liability. Whatever is unknown about the mind–body relationship (and the area of

---

[16] It seems that the "nervous shock" which the Victorian common law judges had within their contemplation refers to the presence of objective responses to a horrific event and which they interpreted as consequential to an assault on the nervous system. Thus, they logically concluded that this was capable of amounting to a "physical injury" for which compensation would lie.

[17] [1925] 1 KB 141.

[18] [1925] 1 KB 141 at 153–154.

[19] [1983] AC 410.

ignorance seems to expand with that of knowledge), it is now accepted by medical science that recognisable and severe physical damage to the human body and system may be caused by the impact, through the senses, of external events on the mind. There may thus be produced what is as identifiable as any that may be caused by direct physical contact. It is safe to say that this, in general terms, is understood by the ordinary man or woman who is hypothesised by the courts in situations where claims for negligence are made.[20]

Such negligently inflicted non-physical injury[21] may occur in one of two basic situations. Firstly, it may occur with physical injury, either contemporaneously, or as a consequence. Secondly, it may be suffered by a person who, while not actually physically injured, is fearful for his own safety or that of another. Thus, in this second category, the person may have been within the zone of physical danger, feared for his own safety and apprehended that he was about to be physically injured,[22] while escaping without any actual physical injury. Or, not having been within the zone of physical danger and not having feared for his own safety, the person may have apprehended imminent or actual harm or injury to another, or to his own property. Each will be considered in turn.

NON-PHYSICAL INJURY ASSOCIATED WITH PHYSICAL INJURY

Where non-physical injury is accompanied by physical injury, the courts will readily compensate the victim for both types of damage, although the award is not invariably expressed as such. Thus, the "pain and suffering" component of compensation for physical injury is non-physical. Being consequential in nature,

---

[20] [1983] AC 410 at 418.

[21] Where it is recognised and accepted that it is possible to sustain an injury that is not physical — in the sense of not being physically manifest as bodily injury — and that it may legitimately be compensated in certain circumstances, "non-physical injury" is, arguably, a preferable term for describing the appropriate head of damages.

[22] Sometimes presented as alternatives. See Fleming (1987), op. cit., p. 148.

"pain and suffering" is merely expressed, and frequently conceptualised, as being in respect of the physical injury alone. However,
compensation for the purely non-physical element of the damage
suffered (e.g. fright at the time of the injury), apprehension as to
its effects — in general terms now classifiable as an acute stress
reaction[23] — and nervousness or humiliation at disfigurement has
also been awarded.[24]

When a cause of action has been established by the physical
injury sustained, it seems reasonable to conclude that the risk of
the non-physical injury being feigned is remote. In such cases, recovery for the non-physical injuries is essentially "parasitic" on
the physical injuries, and the "eggshell" plaintiff rule applies.[25]

Not infrequently, however, the trauma occasioning a physical
injury also causes a non-physical injury as, for example, where the
victim ruminates excessively on the circumstances causing the
physical injury and on the moment of impact, to such an extent
that a depressive illness — or a post-traumatic stress disorder —
develops.[26] Even if the accompanying physical injuries are relatively minor in nature, recovery for the non-physical injury will
not, on that account alone, be barred.

Non-physical injury may also result from a physical injury, not
accompanied by the kind of ruminations referred to. Thus, in addition to suffering mere apprehension and ordinary "pain and suffering", a person sustaining incapacitating injuries may become

---

[23] See Chapter 6.

[24] There is, objectively observable, a range of expected and predictable reactions to noxious stimuli. Individual variations are not necessarily amenable
to rationalisation on the basis of apparently objective criteria. Undoubtedly,
this represents no more than the current limitations of medical science to
similarly explain a wide range of readily observable differences in individual
responses to a wide variety of events, both physical and non-physical. It is
unclear as to why some individuals display graphic signs of acute stress
while others appear to bear the same stimulus with equanimity. See Chapter
6, p. 80, and, generally, J.P. White (1989), *Irish Law of Damages for Personal
Injuries and Death*, Dublin: Butterworth (Ireland), Chapter 30.

[25] See, generally, Prosser and Keeton (1984), op. cit., p. 363.

[26] See Chapter 6, pp. 79–89.

depressed — because of incapacity, the slowness of recovery, the degree of dependency and frequent hospitalisations — to such an extent that it amounts to a recognised psychiatric illness, requiring appropriate treatment.[27] In such cases, also, recovery for the non-physical injuries is also "parasitic" on the other injuries.

All of these sub-categories may also co-exist in any combination. Insofar as the compensability of such injuries is concerned, the law is relatively unproblematic.[28]

NON-PHYSICAL INJURY WITHOUT PHYSICAL INJURY

This is the category of non-physical injury that comprises the cases on "nervous shock". However, "nervous shock" is not a clinically recognised entity. It is legal shorthand for a species of personal injury — non-physical injury — suffered by persons as a consequence of the negligence of others.[29] Although the concept is of relatively recent origin, it can be a source of both confusion and bemusement to clinicians who have difficulty comprehending what it is meant to connote. The confusion is apt to arise because of the manner in which it is represented in standard legal texts. Bemusement results from the nature of the early cases where causation was accepted as having been established in circumstances that defy a modern understanding of disease-causing

---

[27] See Chapter 6, pp. 99–104.

[28] See, generally, White (1989), op. cit., Chapter 30.

[29] Nervous shock is "the 'hallowed expression' by which 'lawyers quaintly persist in calling psychiatric illness'. Psychiatric damage is now the preferred term." Salmond and Heuston, op. cit., p. 219, quoting *McLoughlin* v *O'Brien* [1983] AC 410 at 418 *per* Wilberforce LJ, and at 432 *per* Bridge LJ, and *Attia* v *British Gas* [1987] 3 All ER 255, [1988] QB 304 at 317 (although the English courts also appear to have lapsed into the "traditional terminology"). It has also been referred to, in *Kelly* v *Hennessy*, as a "term . . . used to describe any recognisable psychiatric illness" [1995] 3 IR 253 at 258 *per* Hamilton CJ; "a legal term used to connote a mental as opposed to physical injury in a person . . . [It] is a mental injury, being a recognisable and distinct psychiatric illness" *Kelly* v *Hennessy* [1995] 3 IR 253, at 269 *per* Denham J (SC), also relying on *Hinz* v *Berry* [1970] 2 QB 40; or "recognised legal terminology for a medically recognised psychiatric illness resulting from shock" [1995] 3 IR 253, at 274 *per* Denham J.

mechanisms. That said, judicial pronouncements on the issue have been modest and restrained in nature and scope. Such bemusement as might arise is attributable more to the primitive nature of the evidence adduced in the early cases than to any particular judicial misconceptions about the compensability of non-physical injury. Whereas policy limitations are effectively imposed in respect of the latter,[30] the reluctance of the earlier authorities in this regard is noteworthy.

THE CATEGORIES

In *Alcock* v *Chief Constable of South Yorkshire Police*[31] two categories of persons who suffered nervous shock through fear of injury were identified. Firstly, there were those involved mediately or immediately as participants in the event who feared injury to themselves; and secondly, those who were no more than passive and unwilling witnesses of injury caused to others.[32] In the Court of Appeal in *McFarlane* v *EE Caledonia Ltd.*,[33] Stuart-Smith LJ enumerated three situations in which a person could be regarded as falling into the first category, i.e. as a participant who sustains psychiatric injury through fear of physical injury to himself.

> Firstly, where he is in the actual area of danger created by the event but escapes physical injury by chance or good fortune. . . . Secondly, where the plaintiff is not actually in danger but because of the sudden and unexpected nature of the event he reasonably thinks that he is . . . Thirdly, the situation may arise where the plaintiff who is not originally within the area of danger comes into it later. In the ordi-

---

[30] See *McLoughlin* v *O'Brien* [1983] AC 410 and *Alcock* v *Chief Constable of South Yorkshire Police* [1992] 1 AC 310, [1991] 3 WLR 1057, [1991] 4 All ER 907 (the Hillsborough Stadium disaster).

[31] [1991] 4 All ER 907, [1991] 3 WLR 1057, [1991] 4 All ER 907 (the Hillsborough Stadium disaster).

[32] [1991] 4 All ER 907 at 923, [1992] 1 AC 310 at 407 *per* Lord Oliver.

[33] [1994] 2 All ER 1 (the Piper Alpha disaster). Leave to appeal to the House of Lords was refused.

> nary way, such a person, who is a volunteer, cannot recover
> if he has freely and voluntarily entered the area of danger.
> ... However, if he comes as a rescuer, he can recover.[34]

Consideration of the two principal categories described in *Alcock* and the first of the sub-categories of participant set out in *McFarlane* is of immediate relevance.[35] The law in relation to rescuers — where there is a clear primary duty to the rescuer and recovery is permissible — is beyond the scope of the present discussion.[36] Review of the evolution of the judicial approach to recovery for injury sustained by persons who did not also suffer physical injury most readily informs an understanding of the current limitations the law now imposes in this area.

Non-Physical Injury Sustained by a Person within the Zone of Physical Danger

Initially, the law categorically refused to compensate persons suffering purely non-physical injury. Thus, in *Allsop* v *Allsop*[37] it was held that mere mental suffering or sickness would not be special damage to support an action in defamation in respect of the speaking of words not actionable in themselves. In *Lynch* v *Knight*[38] Wensleydale LJ was of the view that:

---

[34] [1994] 2 All ER 1 at 10.

[35] In relation to the second of these subcategories, see *Dulieu* v *White & Sons* [1901] 2 KB 669 at 685, quoting from *Spade* v *Lynn and Boston Rail Road Company* (1897) 60 Am St Rep 393 at 395. See also the later Scottish decision, *Cooper* v *Caledonian Railway Company* (1902) 4 F 880, where recovery was dependent upon whether or not the fright resulting from the negligence might reasonably arise in a mind of average intelligence and strength, and in the other cases cited in *Hay (or Bourhill)* v *Young* [1943] AC 92 at 119–120 *per* Lord Porter.

[36] See, for example, Chapter 7, and *Haynes* v *Harwood* [1935] 1 KB 146 and *Chadwick* v *British Transport Commission* [1967] 2 All ER 945, [1967] 1 WLR 912 (the Lewisham rail disaster in 1957 in which 90 people were killed — where the plaintiff subsequently suffered a "psychoneurotic condition", or an "acute anxiety neurosis" for which he required inpatient hospital treatment for over six months).

[37] 5 Hurl & Nor 534.

[38] (1861) 9 HLC 577, 11 ER 854.

Mental pain or anxiety the law cannot value, and does not pretend to redress, when the unlawful act complained of causes that alone; though where a material damage occurs, and is connected with it, it is impossible that a jury, in estimating it, should altogether overlook the feelings of the party interested.[39]

Although arising in the context of a slander that resulted in the defendant's expulsion of his wife from the family home and her return to her father's house, the court was clear that lacerated feelings, unaccompanied by material damage of some description, were insufficient to amount to compensable damage.

Byrne — *Impact not Necessary*

In *Byrne* v *Great Southern and Western Railway Company*[40] the first of the "modern" "nervous shock" cases came to be considered by the superior courts in this jurisdiction. On 7 December 1881, through some railway points having been negligently left open, a train entered a siding, broke down the permanent buffer at the end and crashed into the wall of the telegraph office at the Limerick Junction station of the defendant's railway. The plaintiff, who was the superintendent of the telegraph office, claimed that by hearing the noise, and seeing the wall falling, he sustained a "nervous shock" that resulted in certain (unspecified) injuries to his health. In evidence, he stated:

A hair of my head was not touched; I swear I received no physical injury; I got a great fright and shock; I do not mean a physical shake; it was the crash and falling in of the office, and shouts of the clerks saying that they were killed; I saw part of the office falling in; I believed it was all falling in.[41]

---

[39] (1861) 9 HLC 577, at 598, 11 ER 854.

[40] Irish Court of Appeal, Unreported Judgment, February 1884.

[41] Recited in *Bell* v *Great Northern Railway Company of Ireland* (1890) 26 LR Ir 428 at 442 *per* Palles CB. See also McMahon and Binchy (1990), op. cit., p. 306.

The verdict in favour of the plaintiff was upheld on appeal, there being a clear recognition that a person could suffer compensable injury even in the absence of direct physical contact or impact.[42]

Coultas — *Damage Too Remote*

However, four years later in *Victorian Railway Commissioners* v *Coultas*[43] the Privy Council, on an appeal from the Supreme Court of Victoria, denied recovery in a situation essentially on all fours with *Byrne*. Mary Coultas, who was a passenger in a buggy driven by her husband, through the negligence of the Railway Commissioners' servant, was allowed to enter a level crossing while a train was approaching. The buggy cleared the line, the train passing close to the back of, but not touching, it. As the train approached, Mary Coultas fainted and fell forward. According to her evidence, she suffered fright as a result of seeing the train approaching, and thinking they were going to be killed. The medical evidence:

> shewed that she received a severe nervous shock from the fright, and that the illness from which she afterwards suffered[44] was the consequence of the fright. One of the plaintiff's witnesses said she was suffering from profound impression on the nervous system, nervous shock, and the shock from which she suffered would be a natural consequence of the fright. Another said he was unable to detect

---

[42] Given his experience, the plaintiff, at this remove, might readily be considered to have suffered, at the very least, an acute stress reaction, with, perhaps, other sequelae with or without physical manifestations, as set out in Chapter 6. Given the clinical understanding and relatively limited therapeutic interventions available at the time, this could readily — then as now — have resulted in moderate, observable disability or "injuries to his health".

[43] (1888) 13 App Cas 222 (Privy Council).

[44] In subsequent cases, e.g. *Bell* v *Great Northern Railway Company of Ireland* (1890) 26 LR Ir 428 (Exchequer Division), citing the then standard text on negligence (*Beven on Negligence*), it was noted that she had suffered a miscarriage. Mechanistically, this might now be difficult to establish as a matter of causation.

any physical damage; he put down her symptoms to nervous shock.[45]

The Privy Council allowed the Railway Commissioners' appeal
against the award of £400 in damages.

> Damages arising from mere sudden terror unaccompanied
> by any actual physical injury, but occasioning a nervous or
> mental shock, cannot under such circumstances . . . be con-
> sidered a consequence which, in the ordinary course of
> things, would flow from the negligence of the gate-keeper.[46]

Applying the then rule of English law in relation to the recovery of
damages in negligence,[47] the appeal was allowed. Although ostensibly deciding the appeal on the question of remoteness of damage, however, the underlying policy reasons are instructive. Sir
Richard Crouch, for the court, was concerned that to hold otherwise would be extending liability much further than it had been to
date. He continued:

> Not only in such a case as the present, but in every case
> where an accident caused by negligence had given a person
> a serious nervous shock, there might be a claim for dam-
> ages on account of mental injury. The difficulty which now
> often exists in cases of alleged physical injuries of deter-
> mining whether they were caused by the negligent act
> would be greatly increased, and a wide field opened for
> imaginary claims.[48]

This, the first glimmer of concern over opening the "floodgates" to
wild and imaginary claims, was effectively to bedevil significant
elements of the subsequent case-law, culminating in *Alcock* v

---

[45] (1888) 13 App Cas 222 at 224.

[46] (1888) 13 App Cas 222 at 225.

[47] *The Notting Hill* 9 PD 105. But now, see *Overseas Tankship (UK) Ltd* v
Morts Dock & Engineering Co. Ltd. (The Wagon Mound, No. 1) [1961] AC
388, [1961] 1 All ER 404, [1961] 2 WLR 126 (Privy Council).

[48] (1888) 13 App Cas 222 at 225–226.

Chief Constable of South Yorkshire Police.[49] Noting that no precedent had been produced in support of the proposition that damages were recoverable in a situation such as this,[50] the Privy Council refused to establish such a precedent. However, having decided that the injuries were too remote a consequence of the negligence, the court expressly declined to express a view as to whether or not "impact" of some description was necessary and the question was left open.

Bell — *Damage Not Too Remote*

This early conflict between *Byrne* and *Coultas* was effectively settled in yet another case involving a railway company, *Bell* v *Great Northern Railway Company of Ireland.*[51] Here, the defendant railway company's train, on account of its weight, was unable to negotiate an incline. Having uncoupled some carriages, the engine reversed at speed down the incline, with a number of other carriages still attached. The female plaintiff, who was in one of these carriages, gave evidence that she heard the rattling of chains, and heard cries of "Jump out; jump out: you'll all be killed". The carriage doors were locked and some passengers jumped out through the windows, notwithstanding that there was a steep embankment at one side. The train, having come to a curve, pulled up suddenly and the plaintiff, who was then standing up, was thrown down, as all the passengers were thrown about. The evidence of her injuries, as recited in the report, appears to suggest a severe acute anxiety or PTSD.[52] Having been awarded damages in the sum of £300, the defendant appealed. The defendant's argument was summarised thus:

---

[49] [1992] 1 AC 310, [1991] 3 WLR 1057, [1991] 4 All ER 907.

[50] The non-reporting of *Byrne* v *Great Southern and Western Railway Company* was criticised by Palles CB in *Bell* v *Great Northern Railway Company of Ireland* (1890) 26 LR Ir 428 at 441.

[51] (1890) 26 LR Ir 428 (Exchequer Division).

[52] See Chapter 6.

. . . damages for such injury [to health, which is bodily or physical injury] are not recoverable, if two circumstances occur: (1) if the only connection between the negligence and this bodily injury is that the former caused fright, which caused nervous or mental shock,[53] which shock caused the bodily injury complained of; and (2) that this so-called bodily injury did not accompany the fright, which I suppose means that the injury, although in fact occasioned by the fright, assumed the character of bodily injury subsequently to, and not at, the time of the negligence or fright.[54]

Noting that, in *Coultas*, the Privy Council seemed to suggest that "injuries, other than mental, cannot result from nervous shock; and . . . that injuries resulting from such a shock cannot be 'palpable'",[55] Palles CB refused to follow the reasoning insofar as the first proposition (remoteness of damage) was concerned. He was further critical of the court's finding against the verdict of the jury in relation to fright having caused physical injuries, a finding he was not prepared to make in the instant case. However, his principal criticism of *Coultas* was that:

. . . the judgment assumes, as a matter of law, that nervous shock is something which affects merely the mental functions, and is not in itself a peculiar physical state of the body. This error pervades the entire judgment. Mr Beven states, in his recent work on negligence, and I entirely concur with him, that "the starting-point of the reasoning there

---

[53] Although the terms "mental" and "nervous" shock were used apparently interchangeably in *Coultas*, Palles CB in *Bell* v *Great Northern Railway Company of Ireland* (1890) 26 LR Ir 428, while raising the question as to whether or not there was a distinction between the two, considered that introduction "of the word 'mental' may cause obscurity, by involving matter of a wholly different nature. . . ." (1890) 26 LR Ir 428 at 437–438. See also *Dulieu* v *White & Sons* [1901] 2 KB 669 at 673 *per* Kennedy J.

[54] (1890) 26 LR Ir 428 at 437 *per* Palles CB.

[55] (1890) 26 LR Ir 428 at 440.

is that nervous shock and mental shock are identical; and
that they are opposed to actual physical injury".[56]

Insofar as the second proposition was concerned, i.e. that where
negligence caused fright, and the fright contemporaneously
caused physical injury, only then the damage would not, as a matter of law, be too remote,[57] Palles CB was of the view that it was
the equivalent of maintaining that:

> . . . a death caused by poison is not to be attributed to the
> person who administered it because the mortal effect is not
> produced contemporaneously with its administration.[58]

Concluding in favour of the plaintiff, he was of the opinion that:

> . . . as the relation between fright and injury to the nerve
> and brain structures of the body is a matter which depends
> entirely upon scientific and medical testimony,[59] it is impos-
> sible for any court to lay down, *as a matter of law*, that if
> negligence causes fright, and such fright, in its turn, so af-
> fects such structures as to cause injury to health, such in-
> jury cannot be "a consequence which, in the ordinary course
> of things would flow from the negligence, unless such injury
> accompany such negligence in point of time".[60] (*emphasis
> added*)

---

[56] (1890) 26 LR Ir 428 at 441.

[57] This may still be relevant in some US jurisdictions. See Prosser and Keeton (1984), op. cit., pp. 364–5.

[58] (1890) 26 LR Ir 428 at 439.

[59] Although an evidentiary prospect — given the terms in which it is expressed — not likely to be eagerly embraced by modern physicians, this central requirement remains true in modern times.

[60] (1890) 26 LR Ir 428 at 442. Although it is impossible to ascertain what conceptual framework, or theory of injury or causation, was being applied, the
central thesis — especially in the light of modern neurobiology (see Chapter
2) — seems eminently defensible. That said, in each of the cases, *Byrne*,
Coultas and *Bell*, the non-physical injury that was apparently suffered by the
injured parties is virtually indistinguishable, in terms of either biological
causation or effect, from the acute stress reaction suffered by persons who

For Murphy J, the categorisation or mechanism of the "injuries" was irrelevant. Advancing Palles CB's proposition, for his part, he was of the view that it was:

> . . . immaterial whether the injuries may be called nervous shock, brain disturbance, mental shock or injury. The only questions to be considered . . . are: was the health or capacity of the plaintiff for the discharge of her duties and enjoyment of life affected by what occurred to her. . . .[61]

Although ultimately decided by following *Byrne*, Palles CB was clear that *Byrne* went further than was necessary to sustain the conclusion in *Bell*. It could certainly be distinguished from both *Byrne* and *Coultas* where neither injured party was being carried on the defendant railways. Furthermore, the evidence adduced in *Bell* — although not specifically referred to in the judgment — clearly suggests an impact of some description, albeit not one that caused actual physical injury to the plaintiff. However, the approval of *Byrne* — impact not necessary — set the scene for subsequent judicial developments. The rejection of *Coultas* — damages for injury sustained as a consequence of "nervous shock" were not too remote — effectively resolved the central legal issue, at least in the type of case described. The question of individual vulnerability — a consideration that Palles CB *obiter* regarded as irrelevant to recovery[62] — also fell to be decided in later cases.[63]

---

also sustain physical injuries. Similarly, the subsequent development of depression or a post-traumatic stress disorder is indistinguishable. Miscarriage, in the case of *Coultas*, however, must be considered an outcome that would be problematic given the modern understanding of the pathophysiology of pregnancy loss.

[61] (1890) 26 LR Ir 428 at 433. This conceptualisation, which does not depend on notions of disease or shock, in effect reduces issues to consequences and causation; it is not concerned with either the pathophysiological mechanisms or definitions of injury in structural or functional terms. See Chapters 2, 3 and 4.

[62] (1890) 26 LR Ir 428 at 438.

[63] See, in particular, *Hay (or Bourhill)* v *Young* [1943] AC 92 at 110 *per* Lord Wright.

Dulieu — *No Floodgates*

Thus, the rapid retreat from *Coultas* and the application of *Bell* continued with the judgment of Kennedy J in *Dulieu* v *White & Sons*[64] where the central issue again was whether or not the non-physical injury suffered by the plaintiff was too remote a consequence of negligence on the part of the defendant's servants. The facts of the case were straightforward. As a result of the allegedly negligent driving by the defendant's servant of a pair-horse van into a public house, the plaintiff, who at the time was working behind the bar, "sustained a severe shock and was seriously ill".[65] It was further alleged that, as a result, some nine weeks later she gave premature birth to a child.[66]

For Kennedy J, the question of the existence of a duty of care on the part of the defendants' servant, in driving the pair-horse van, was self-evident.[67] The only question was, as he succinctly put it, whether there was an actionable breach of that duty if the person "is made ill in body by [its] negligent driving as does not break his ribs but shocks his nerves".[68] For the purposes of

---

[64] [1901] 2 KB 669.

[65] [1901] 2 KB 669 at 670.

[66] As in *Coultas*, reservations might be expressed as to the causation of the premature birth. However, it was also alleged that "in consequence of the shock sustained by the plaintiff the said child was an idiot". This latter element of the claim was treated as untenable and not pursued [1901] 2 KB 669 at 670–671. On any analysis, however, some sort of physical manifestation of the "nervous shock" was evident.

[67] [1901] 2 KB 669 at 671–672. For Phillimore J, the other member of the Divisional Court, however, the primary difficulty was in determining whether or not there was a duty of care, not in establishing that the damage was not too remote. He was of the view: "It is not certain that as between people travelling on highways, there is a duty so carefully to conduct yourself or your vehicle as not to frighten others. It is a duty so carefully to conduct yourself or your vehicle as not to cause collision or some other form of direct physical damage." [1901] 2 KB 669 at 684. Furthermore, it seems that for him, the question of individual vulnerability also arose for consideration in establishing whether or not a duty of care existed (*ibid*). The question of *volens* he reserved. The issue of a duty of care is revisited in all of the judgments of the House of Lords in *Hay (or Bourhill)* v *Young* [1943] AC 92.

[68] [1901] 2 KB 669 at 671.

argument,[69] it was assumed that the plaintiff suffered a nervous or mental shock[70] by her reasonable apprehension of immediate bodily hurt, and that causation of subsequent damage had been established.

Again, the notion of fright was of central importance.[71] Thus the first issue was whether or not fright, caused by negligence, could give rise to any cause of action.[72] Kennedy J, noting that, in the earlier cases, proof of physical impact was not necessary to ground a cause of action for damages, observed:

> . . . if . . . the fear is proved to have naturally and directly produced physical effects, so that the ill results of the negligence which caused the fear are as measurable in damages as the same results would be if they arose from an actual impact, why should not an action for those damages lie just as well as it lies where there has been an actual impact?[73]

---

[69] The divisional High Court was called upon to decide whether or not, as a matter of law, a cause of action existed and, if so, whether the damages sought to be recovered were too remote. Thus, the facts were presumed to be proven for the purposes of argument.

[70] Kennedy J used these words interchangeably, as did Palles CB in *Bell*, following on *Coultas*. However, it was considered that "'nervous' is probably the more correct epithet where terror operates through parts of the physical organism to produce bodily illness. . . . The use of the epithet "mental" requires caution, in view of the undoubted rule that merely mental pain unaccompanied by any injury to the person cannot sustain an action of this kind [i.e. where damage requires to be proved before a cause of action is established]." [1901] 2 KB 669 at 673. See also *Lynch* v *Knight* (1861) 9 HLC 577, 11 ER 854.

[71] Fear and fright appear to be used interchangeably.

[72] In the New York case of *Mitchell* v *Rochester Railway Company* (1896) 151 NY 107 at 109–110, which was referred to in *Dulieu* v *White & Sons* [1901] 2 KB 669 at 673, it was held: "That the result [of fright] may be nervous disease, blindness, insanity, or even a miscarriage, in no way changes the principle. These results merely shew the degree of fright or the extent of damages. The right of action must still depend upon the question whether a recovery may be had for fright."

[73] [1901] 2 KB 669 at 675. That recovery was also possible under the intentional torts heavily influenced this conclusion. See, *Wilkinson* v *Downton* [1897] 2 QB 57 and the cases cited therein at 61. However, the case did not support the limitation subsequently imposed by Kennedy J.

The approach adopted resiled from *Coultas* and endorsed the reasoning in *Bell*.[74] However, it was clear that further concerns of
opening the floodgates to a wide range of claims required that
some restriction be placed on the right to recover damages. Kennedy J, in a formulation that was to be revisited[75] because of the
narrowness of its approach, articulated the limitation as follows:

> It is not, however, to be taken that in my view every nerv-
> ous shock occasioned by negligence and producing physical
> injury to the sufferer gives a cause of action. There is, I am
> inclined to think, at least one limitation. The shock, where
> it operates through the mind, must be a shock which arises
> from a reasonable fear of immediate personal injury to one-
> self. A has, I conceive, no legal duty not to shock B's nerves
> by the exhibition of negligence towards C, or towards the
> property of B or C. . . . I should not be prepared in the pres-
> ent case to hold that the plaintiff was entitled to maintain
> this action if the nervous shock was produced, not by the
> fear of bodily injury to herself, by the horror or vexation
> arising from the sight of mischief being threatened or done
> either to some other person, or to her own or her husband's
> property, by the intrusion of the defendants' van and
> horses.[76]

---

[74] Although Phillimore J was satisfied ([1901] 2 KB 669 at 683) that the
authorities established that ". . . terror wrongfully induced and inducing
physical mischief gives a cause of action" even though the medium through
which it had been inflicted was the mind (impact implicitly not necessary) he
was considerably less critical of *Coultas* than his brother judge.

[75] See, *Hambrook* v *Stokes Brothers Limited* [1925] 1 KB 141.

[76] [1901] 2 KB 669 at 675–676. Here, the issue here was confined to an absence of a duty of care. This went further than the authority cited, *Smith* v
Johnson & Company, an unreported decision referred to in *Wilkinson* v
Downton (1897) 2 QB 57, where the harm to a bystander, solely from the
shock of seeing another killed by the negligence of the defendant — there
being no fear of harm to himself — was considered too remote a consequence.
But *Wilkinson* v *Downton* itself was hardly authority for Kennedy J's limitation. However, Phillimore J, the other member of the Divisional Court ([1901]
2 KB 669 at 682–683), implicitly did not insist upon such a strict limitation
— a matter averred to in *Hay (or Bourhill)* v *Young* [1943] AC 92 at 111 and
114 *per* Lord Wright and Lord Porter, respectively.

Thus, ill effects brought about through fear of injury to a third party, or to one's property or that of another, were beyond the limits of compensability — there being no duty in this regard.[77] A duty having been established, however, it then fell to be determined whether or not the consequences of a breach of duty were too remote to be compensated. Insofar as *Coultas* required that there be actual physical injury, Kennedy J asked why such injury was essential.[78] In suggesting his approach to the answer, he implicitly endorsed the approach of Palles CB in *Bell*, holding:

> . . . I should not like to assume it to be scientifically true that a nervous shock which causes serious bodily illness is not actually accompanied by physical injury, although it may be impossible, or at least difficult, to detect the injury at the time in the living subject. I should not be surprised if the surgeon or the physiologist told us that nervous shock is or may be in itself an injurious affection of the physical organism.[79]

Insofar as it might be argued that "physical injury . . . upon proper and sufficient medical evidence that it *follows* the shock as its direct and natural effect"[80] (*emphasis added*) was too remote, the approach of Palles CB in *Bell* was expressly adopted.[81]

---

[77] Now, however, see *Attia* v *British Gas plc* [1987] 3 All ER 255 (CA), [1988] QB 304.

[78] In *Dulieu*, the plaintiff actually argued that she was entitled to be compensated only if she proved physical injury.

[79] [1901] 2 KB 669 at 677. No model of disease causation is attempted here. Nevertheless, the approach has a modern resonance, and may well ultimately be verified by advances in neurobiology. See Chapter 2, pp. 22–7.

[80] [1901] 2 KB 669 at 677.

[81] However, for the avoidance of doubt, Kennedy J continued: "As a matter of experience, I should say that the injury to health which forms the main ground of damages in actions of negligence . . . frequently is proved, not as a concomitant of the occurrence, but as one of the sequelae." [1901] 2 KB 669 at 678. His comments in relation to remoteness as a legal ground for the exclusion of damages, not meaning severance at a point in time, did not survive *Alcock* v *Chief Constable of South Yorkshire Police* [1992] 1 AC 310, [1991] 3 WLR 1057, [1991] 4 All ER 907, albeit expressed in a duty context, although

As in *Bell*, therefore, proof of injury was to be considered a matter of expert evidence. But proof of some injury or damage is essential to succeed in any action in negligence. Kennedy J observed:

> If . . . negligence has caused . . . neither injury to property nor physical mischief, but only an unpleasant emotion of more or less transient duration an essential constituent of a right of action for negligence is lacking. "Fear . . . taken alone falls short of being actual damage not because it is a remote or unlikely consequence, but because it can be proved and measured only by physical effects" (Sir Frederick Pollock: *The Law of Torts*). It may . . . be . . . that . . . direct bodily impact is, without resulting damage, as insufficient a ground of legal claim as the infliction of fright.[82]

It was apparent that there might be evidentiary difficulties. In *Dulieu*, whereas Kennedy J imposed some limitations on recovery, he was not prepared to impose a policy limitation as *Coultas* suggested. Phillimore J, however, although implicitly not imposing a limitation as stringent as Kennedy J's, seemed to accept the policy limitations of *Coultas*. Considering whether the floodgates might be opened, Kennedy J alone was relatively unconcerned, stating:

> I should be sorry to adopt a rule which would bar all such claims on grounds of policy alone, and in order to prevent the possible success of unrighteous or groundless actions. Such a course involves the denial of redress in meritorious cases, and it necessarily implies a certain degree of distrust, which I do not share, in the capacity of legal tribunals to get at the truth in this class of claim. My experience gives me no reason to suppose that a jury would really have more difficulty in weighing the medical evidence as to the effects of nervous shock through fright, than in weighing the like evidence as to the effects of nervous shock through

---

his damning criticism of the findings of the Privy Council in *Coultas* was a fatal blow to the further acceptability of that decision.

[82] [1901] 2 KB 669 at 673.

a railway collision or a carriage accident, where, as so often happens, no palpable injury, or very slight palpable injury, has been occasioned at the time.[83]

Difficulties of proof, at least for Kennedy J, would not be dressed up as legal principle. If mere fright — without proof of damage — was to disentitle a plaintiff from recovery, this was no different from any other case involving physical impact without damage. Nor would vulnerable plaintiffs be barred from recovery. In a restatement of the eggshell skull plaintiff rule, Kennedy J pointed out:

> If a man is negligently run over or otherwise negligently injured in his body, it is no answer to the sufferer's claim for damages that he would have suffered less injury, or no injury at all, if he had not had an unusually thin skull or an unusually weak heart.[84]

Phillimore J, on the other hand, in endorsing the approach taken in the United States, considered that the ordinary conduct of

---

[83] [1901] 2 KB 669 at 681. This approach was endorsed by Atkin LJ in *Hambrook* v *Stokes Bros.* [1925] 1 KB 141 at 158. However, in *Spade* v *Lynn and Boston Rail Road Company* (1897) 60 Am St Rep 393, 168 Mass 285 the Supreme Judicature Court of Massachusetts had effectively endorsed *Coultas* and was accepted by Phillimore J, with some reservations. That case went further than was necessary to decide *Dulieu*. It conceded that if damages for physical injury caused by fright were not too remote, it was difficult to hold, on principle, why there should not also be recovery for negligently inflicted mental suffering not accompanied by any perceptible physical effects. But, the remoteness issue having been disposed of, the court continued: ". . . the real reason for refusing damages sustained from mere fright must be something different, and it probably rests on the ground that in practice it is impossible satisfactorily to administer any other rule." Refusal was to be based on public policy, ". . . the hardship of holding persons bound to anticipate and guard against anything but the probable consequences to ordinary people . . . and the risk of opening 'a wide door for unjust claims which could not successfully be met'." [1901] 2 KB 669 at 680–681.

[84] [1901] 2 KB 669 at 679. It must be presumed, from the context, that bodily injury, here, includes injury as a consequence of fright. Psychological eggshell skull plaintiffs were not to be excluded. This, however, should be contrasted with the approach of the House of Lords in *Hay (or Bourhill)* v *Young* [1943] AC 92 at 110 and 117 *per* Lord Wright and Lord Porter, respectively.

human affairs "must be done on the assumption that persons who are liable to be affected thereby are not peculiarly sensitive, and are of ordinary physical and mental strength".[85] As a general rule, in his view, a person was not bound to anticipate or to guard against an injurious result that would only happen to a person of peculiar sensitivities.[86]

Following *Dulieu*, at least certain issues were clear. Thus, physical impact was not necessary in order to recover for non-physical damage. Also, proof of damage was to be a matter for expert evidence — specific damage-causing mechanisms did not necessarily have to be invoked. But two major issues remained clouded because of the differing approaches of the two judges. Firstly, the applicability of the limitation that, in order to recover, the damage complained of had to be caused by fright induced by fear for one's own safety, was uncertain. Secondly, the effect of an individual's peculiar vulnerabilities on his right to recover remained to be defined. In short, *Dulieu* established a right to recover for fright — non-physical injury — and proof of physical impact was unnecessary. Beyond that, the law was no more certain than following *Coultas*. These matters fell to be determined in the next category of cases — where non-physical injury was caused to persons not within the zone of physical danger.

---

[85] [1901] 2 KB 669 at 685, quoting from *Spade* v *Lynn and Boston Rail Road Company* (1897) 60 Am St Rep 393 at 395. This is also reflected in a later Scottish decision, *Cooper* v *Caledonian Railway Company* (1902) 4 F 880 where recovery was dependent upon whether or not the fright resulting from the negligence might reasonably arise in a mind of average intelligence and strength, and in the other cases cited in *Hay (or Bourhill)* v *Young* [1943] AC 92 at 119–120 *per* Lord Porter.

[86] This previews the approach of Lord Wright and Lord Porter in *Hay (or Bourhill)* v *Young* [1943] AC 92 at 110 and 117 respectively, in terms of establishing whether or not a duty of care existed, as distinct from assessing individual vulnerability as an aspect of remoteness of damage. For Phillimore J, it also seems central to establishing that a duty of care, in fact, exists.

In the United States, however, recovery was denied unless the person had been subjected to an "impact" of some description.[87] Whereas there is no absolute bar to recovery for pure "non-physical" injury, many US jurisdictions retain a requirement that physical harm be established before recovery is allowed. However, unlike those cases involving compensation for non-physical injury being parasitic on recovery for the physical injury sustained, where recovery for pure non-physical injury is allowed, an objective standard is applied. Psychological "eggshell skull" plaintiffs, with particular vulnerabilities which cause them further harm, carry no advantages.[88]

Non-Physical Injury Sustained by a Person Not within the Zone of Physical Danger

Hambrook — *a Question of Duty*

The questions the courts were required to address in this vexed area were essentially twofold. Could a bystander who witnessed *peril* or *injury* to another, and was fearful for that person's safety, recover damages for injury caused by "shock"? Or, could a bystander, who witnessed *injury that had occurred* to another, similarly recover damages? The evolution of the case law is tortuous but instructive in comprehending the current state of the law in this area. The first question was answered in the affirmative by

---

[87] Ostensibly the conclusions in such cases were predicated on notions of causation of the subsequent physical harm. However, the real, and underlying policy, consideration appears to have been that requirement of proof of "impact" guaranteed that the non-physical injury sustained was genuine. That said, "impact" was imputed in many cases of minor contacts with plaintiffs, which were utterly irrelevant from the point of view of causation of the non-physical injury; see Prosser and Keeton (1984), op. cit., pp. 363–4. Examples cited include electric shock, a trivial jolt or jar, dust in the eye, inhalation of smoke, falling following a faint after a collision, wrenching a shoulder in reaction to a fright, and the evacuation of a horse's bowels into the lap of a plaintiff at a circus. Similar policy considerations arise also in cases of pure emotional or mental distress.

[88] Prosser and Keeton (1984), op. cit., pp. 364–5; also discussed, in a related context, in Fleming (1987), op. cit., p. 147.

a majority of the Court of Appeal in *Hambrook* v *Stokes Bros.*,[89] which raised a question as to how the second might be answered. However, later cases reserved the question of the correctness of the approach of the Court of Appeal and inconsistent results followed. An affirmative response to the second question awaited the late 1960s.

In *Hambrook*, which was a fatal injuries action, the plaintiff's wife had died some ten weeks after an accident in which one of her children had been seriously, though not gravely injured. The facts were relatively straightforward. A lorry, with its engine running, had been left unattended and not properly secured by the defendants' servant at the top of a hill in Folkstone. It careered down the hill, out of control, along a narrow street that was in places only six feet wide, swaying from side to side and ricocheting from one side of the road to the other. Mrs Hambrook, just before the lorry came crashing along, had just taken her two children — two boys and a girl — across the road on their way to school. They had just walked a short distance up the street and out of her sight, around a bend in the road, when the lorry dashed into the children and then shot across the road, coming to a halt against a shop on Mrs Hambrook's side of the road, some fifteen to twenty feet away. The progress of the lorry would be heard by those around the bend, including Mrs Hambrook. She immediately became frantic and was found tearing her hair and inquiring as to the safety of her daughter. She was pregnant at the time — although there was some dispute about the stage — and suffered a severe haemorrhage some two days later. Having partially recovered, she deteriorated about eight weeks later. After a further fortnight, having undergone an operation when a dead child — stated to have died a month previously — was removed, she died.[90]

---

[89] [1925] 1 KB 141.

[90] A dispute also arose as to causation. Suffice it to say, as in the other "miscarriage" cases, causation might be more difficult to establish in more modern times.

The plaintiff's case was that his children, having regard to the time at which they started, would presumably be where the lorry might strike them, the street being so narrow. He further contended that the shock to his deceased wife was due either to a reasonable fear of immediate personal injury to herself,[91] or alternatively, of injury to her children, and that her death was the result of the shock. The jury was directed in accordance with *Dulieu* — i.e., that if Mrs Hambrook's death was caused by fear for her children's safety, as distinct from fear for her own, the plaintiff could not recover. Accordingly, they returned a verdict for the defendants and the plaintiff appealed on the ground that there had been a misdirection to the jury.[92]

The majority of the Court of Appeal[93] were not inclined to apply the limitation imposed by *Dulieu*. Even though the existence of a duty of care to Mrs Hambrook had been admitted by the defendants,[94] both Bankes and Atkin LJJ set about an excursus on the duty issue. Bankes LJ was of the view that:

> It may well be that the duty of a person to take care does not extend to a person in the position of the plaintiff in *Smith* v *Johnson & Company*,[95] or to the person indicated

---

[91] Atkin LJ was satisfied, given the verdict of the jury, that this was not the case, and Sarjant LJ considered that the evidence did not support it and the verdict of the jury negatived any such view ([1925] 1 KB 141 at 153, 160 and 165 respectively).

[92] The plaintiff also appealed on the ground that there had been a misdirection in relation to causation; this is not, in the circumstances, central to the determination of the appeal.

[93] Bankes and Atkins LJJ, Sarjant LJ dissenting. Sarjant LJ solidly endorsed the reasoning of *Dulieu* insofar as the non-requirement of impact was concerned. Indeed, he noted that the American cases were to the contrary ([1925] 1 KB 141 at 161–162).

[94] Subsequently, in *Hay (or Bourhill)* v *Young* [1943] AC 92 the fact that duty had been admitted in *Hambrook* was used to distinguish it from the facts of that case, where the existence of a duty of care fell to be determined. Accordingly, *Bourhill* could be decided without expressly over-ruling *Hambrook*; see [1943] AC 92 at 103 *per* Lord Russell.

[95] (1897) Unreported decision cited in *Wilkinson* v *Downton* [1897] 2 QB 57 at 61.

as B in Kennedy J's illustration, and yet may extend to a person in the position of the plaintiff's wife.[96]

He quaintly illustrated the absurdity of an uncritical application of the proposition by the following example.

> Assume two mothers crossing this street at the same time when this lorry comes thundering down, each holding a small child by the hand. One mother is courageous and devoted to her child. She is terrified, but thinks only of the damage to the child, and not at all about herself. The other woman is timid and lacking in the motherly instinct. She also is terrified, but thinks only of the damage to herself and not at all about her child. The health of both mothers is seriously affected by the mental shock occasioned by the fright. Can any real distinction be drawn between the two cases? Will the law recognise a cause of action in the case of the less deserving mother, and none in the case of the more deserving one? Does the law say that the defendant ought reasonably to have anticipated the non-natural feeling of the timid mother, and not the natural feeling of the courageous mother? I think not. In my opinion . . . the dictum of Kennedy J, laid down in quite general terms in that case, cannot be accepted as good law applicable in every case.[97]

---

[96] [1925] 1 KB 141 at 150. In testing the limitation imposed by Kennedy J, Bankes LJ relied on Phillimore J's slightly different formulation in *Dulieu* and the then authorities in relation to the imposition of a duty of care. Atkin LJ was more harshly critical. He stated: "I can find no principle to support the self-imposed restriction. . . . It appears to me inconsistent with [the authorities] in [none] of which cases was the shock the result of the apprehension of the injury to the plaintiff." [1925] 1 KB 141 at 157. However, the cases relied upon were considered as not in point by Sargent LJ ([1925] 1 KB 141 at 164).

[97] [1925] 1 KB 141 at 151. This analogy was also applied by Atkin LJ who was of the opinion that: ". . . such distinctions would be discreditable to any system of jurisprudence in which they formed part." [1925] 1 KB 141 at 157. Sarjant LJ, in his dissent ([1925] 1 KB 141 at 164), considered that no assistance was rendered by the consideration of such possible cases. As far as he was concerned, there was no risk of confusion as to the origin of the mother's apprehension in the instant case.

Atkin LJ, having endorsed this approach, however, went further. He could see no reason

> . . . for excluding the bystander in the highway who receives injury in the same way from apprehension of or the actual sight of injury to a third party. There may well be cases where the sight of suffering will directly and immediately physically shock the most indurate heart;[98] and if the suffering of another be the result of an act *wrongful to the spectator*, I do not see why the wrongdoer should escape.[99] (*emphasis added*)

In a passage reminiscent of Kennedy J's statement in *Dulieu* of the duty of care of those who use the highway, for him, the duty of the defendants — and the breach of that duty[100] — was obvious. Once the breach of duty had been established, then recovery for all damage, whether foreseeable or not, followed.[101] Although not

---

[98] This reference to emotional normality or resilience was to become central to the determination of whether or not bystanders could recover in cases from *Hay (or Bourhill)* v *Young* [1943] AC 92 to *McFarlane* v *EE Caledonia Ltd* [1994] 2 All ER 1.

[99] [1925] 1 KB 141 at 150, 158. The reasoning of Atkin LJ was endorsed by Singleton LJ in *King* v *Phillips* [1953] 1 QB 429 at 436. Opening of the floodgates did not concern Atkin LJ as he adopted the approach of Kennedy J in *Dulieu* to the same issue.

[100] However, Sarjant LJ ([1925] 1 KB 141 at 163) considered the extension of a duty of care of road users to avoid damage, through nervous shock of bystanders, by the sight or apprehension of injury to a third party to be "unwarranted". No reason is given and the assertion seems to be purely policy-based.

[101] [1925] 1 KB 141 at 157 and 158, on the authority of *In re Polemis and Furness, Withy & Company* [1921] 3 KB 560, which he endorsed. This is in contrast to the later decisions of Lord Thankerton and Lord MacMillan in the House of Lords in *Hay (or Bourhill)* v *Young* [1943] AC 92. Now, however, see, *Overseas Tankship (UK) Ltd* v *Morts Dock & Engineering Co. Ltd (The Wagon Mound, No. 1)* [1961] AC 388, [1961] 1 All ER 404, [1961] 2 WLR 126 (Privy Council). However, Atkin LJ's analysis was distinguished in *King* v *Phillips* [1953] 1 QB 429.

strictly necessary for disposing of the issue, Atkin LJ[102] was prepared to accept the view that the defendants' duty of care extended to avoiding:

> . . . threatening personal injury to a child in such circum-
> stances as to cause damage by shock to a parent or guard-
> ian then present, and that the duty was owed to the parent
> or guardian. . . .[103]

Thus, there had also to be a duty to the bystander before recovery
was possible. But herein lay a problem. Assuming the correctness
of such an approach, why should the duty be confined to the parents or guardians of children and not extend also to other relationships? Sarjant LJ raised the question of defining the degrees
of relationship and the extent of the extra liability involved.[104]
Hambrook did not resolve this issue. That fell to be determined in
later cases.[105]

Notwithstanding the imposition of a duty of care, however,
Bankes LJ confined the decision narrowly to situations similar to
this where shock resulted from what the plaintiff's wife:

---

[102] Atkin LJ's excursus on the duty issue was considered "too wide" by Lord
Thankerton in *Bourhill* [1943] AC 92 at 100, a point repeated by Hodson LJ
in *King* v *Phillips* [1953] 1 QB 429 at 444.

[103] [1925] 1 KB 141 at 158. In this, Atkin LJ was going further. He contemplated recovery for apprehension of, and witnessing injury to, another. He
did not, however, address the question of recovery for "shock" caused by
coming upon the scene of the accident after the event, or by being told of it,
on which point the evidence was considered somewhat unclear.

[104] [1925] 1 KB 141 at 163. He also (at 164) raised the question as to whether
or not recovery ought to be allowed where the apprehended danger takes
place out of the sight of a plaintiff (as in *Hambrook*) but the person whose
safety was in question had, for whatever reason, never been in imminent
danger at all. This may have informed his approach to the issue of whether
or not part (or all) of the injury sustained by Mrs Hambrook had been caused
by what she had been told, rather than by what she had apprehended with
her own senses.

[105] See *Alcock* v *Chief Constable of South Yorkshire Police* [1992] 1 AC 301,
[1991] 3 WLR 1057, [1991] 4 All ER 907; *Jaensch* v *Coffey* [1984] 54 ALR 417,
155 CLR 549.

... either saw or realised by her own unaided senses, and
not from something which some one told her, and that the
shock was due to a reasonable fear of immediate personal
injury to herself or to her children.[106]

The net effect, therefore, was that recovery by some bystanders
was now possible, but only where there was a breach of a duty of
care to them and then, only in relation to what they had directly
apprehended. Reports of calamity to another were insufficient to
ground recovery. The limitation imposed by *Dulieu* did not necessarily always apply.

Owens — *A Questionable Duty*

A unanimous Court of Appeal[107] similarly found in favour of the
mourner-plaintiffs in *Owens* v *Liverpool Corporation*.[108] They were
travelling in a carriage directly behind the hearse containing the
body of a near relative when the hearse was negligently struck by
a tramcar driven by the defendants' servant. The coffin was overturned such that, as was alleged, there was a danger of its falling

---

[106] [1925] 1 KB 141 at 152. On this point, Atkin LJ was of the view that the
evidence was not to the effect that the shock to Mrs Hambrook had been
caused by what she had been told ([1925] 1 KB 141 at 159), although Sarjant
LJ, in his dissent, considered that there was strong ground for such a view
([1925] 1 KB 141 at 160). In fact, he read the judgments of the majority as
confining recovery only to those situations where the shock was caused by
the sight or sound of the accident or the apprehension of danger to the children ([1925] 1 KB 141 at 165). This seems the correct view of the majority
judgments. This particular limitation, which was to be revisited later on
many occasions, arose primarily because it was unclear on the evidence
whether the shock suffered by the deceased was caused by her realisation of
what had happened or because of what she had been told by bystanders
about the injured child matching the description of her daughter. No question was asked of the jury on that point — nor in relation to her going to the
school and finding her daughter missing or going to the hospital and finding
her seriously injured there. This, however, was central to *McLoughlin* v
O'Brian [1983] AC 410.

[107] MacKinnon, Goddard and du Parcq LJJ.

[108] [1939] 1 KB 394. This decision did not consider the issue of the defendants'
duty of care and was roundly criticised in *Hay (or Bourhill)* v *Young* [1943]
AC 92. However, in *King* v *Phillips* [1953] 1 QB 429, Denning LJ (at 439)
appeared to consider that the duty issue was clear.

out onto the road. Only one plaintiff saw the collision, the rest saw its immediate effects. They claimed that they were horrified by the accident and by what they saw and suffered severe shock as a consequence.[109] Although, at first instance, the trial judge was satisfied that causation had been established,[110] he nevertheless denied recovery on the grounds that it was only permissible when there was an apprehension of injury, or actual sight of injury to a human being. On the plaintiffs' appeal, the court held that, on principle, the right to recover damages for "mental shock"[111] was not limited to cases in which apprehension as to human safety was involved (as in *Dulieu* or *Hambrook*). Having so found, the court was not concerned with opening floodgates to unmeritorious claims, relying on the dictum of Kennedy J in *Dulieu*. Thus, they held:

> That alleged shock results from apprehension as to a less important matter may well be material in considering whether the allegation be proved. But fear that unfounded claims may be put forward, and may result in erroneous conclusions of fact, ought not to influence us to impose legal limitations as to the nature of the facts that it is permissible to prove.[112]

---

[109] The nature of the "shock" is not set out in the judgment.

[110] Although the appeal judges expressed a reservation as to whether or not they were satisfied that the injuries alleged, or their extent, had been proved, they did not upset this finding on appeal for procedural reasons [1939] 1 KB 394 at 398 and 400.

[111] [1939] 1 KB 394 at 400 *per* MacKinnon LJ for the court. This was used interchangeably with "mental or nervous injury, unaccompanied by any physical damage to the plaintiff" or "the form of ill health which is known as shock" ([1939] 1 KB 394 at 398 and 400 respectively), the physical damage in this case presumably being physical damage caused by impact — as distinct from shock. The court were satisfied ([1939] 1 KB 394 at 400) that there was no distinction between mental or nervous shock and physical damage although it was "less obvious to the layman, but nowadays equally ascertainable by the physician."

[112] [1939] 1 KB 394 at 400.

Nor were they concerned about individual sensitivities, applying the eggshell skull principle. While doubting that an ordinary person might have been affected as the plaintiffs were found to have been, the court considered that:

> It may be that [they] are of that class which is peculiarly susceptible to the luxury of woe at a funeral and may be disastrously disturbed by an untoward accident to the trappings of mourning.[113]

Bourhill — *No Duty*

Although *Hambrook* and *Owens* extended the range of liability beyond that expressly limited by Kennedy J in *Dulieu*, the evolution of the case-law in respect of injury suffered by persons not within the zone of physical danger was far from complete, and the correctness of those decisions remained uncertain. Furthermore, the role of individual vulnerability in permitting recovery had not been finalised. In *Hay (or Bourhill)* v *Young*[114] where a fishwife sought damages from the estate of the deceased defendant motorcyclist, the nexus between the plaintiff and the danger could, on one level, be regarded as fairly remote. The plaintiff had just alighted from a tram when the motorcyclist passed and collided with a car on the road junction some 45 to 50 feet away. It was found as a fact that the motorcycle had been travelling at an excessive speed. The plaintiff saw and heard nothing of the motorcyclist until the noise of the impact, at which time she had her back turned to the area of collision. The motorcyclist, having been thrown onto the street, died as a result of his injuries. When his body had been removed, the plaintiff approached and saw the blood left on the roadway. She alleged that as an immediate result of the collision and the extreme shock of the occurrence, she "wrenched and injured her back and was thrown into a state of

---

[113] [1939] 1 KB 394 at 400. Such an approach, arguably, would not find favour in the US courts.

[114] [1943] AC 92.

terror and sustained a very severe shock to her nervous system".[115] She further alleged that her child, who was born at term approximately one month later, was stillborn on account of the terror she had suffered. It was further accepted that her terror had not involved any element of reasonable fear of bodily injury to herself.[116] At first instance, it was found that the plaintiff had sustained "nervous shock" as the result of hearing the noise of the collision — which disabled her from carrying on her business for some time. But she failed to prove that either the stillbirth or the injury to her back resulted from the shock or her immediate reaction to the fright of the event. She appealed to the House of Lords who unanimously refused the appeal.

For all five Law Lords,[117] the duty of the motorcyclist was clear. In a succinct statement of that duty, with echoes of *Donoghue* v *Stevenson*[118] Lord Thankerton held that it was to drive

> with such reasonable care as [would] avoid the risk of *injury* to such persons as he can reasonably foresee might be injured by failure to exercise such reasonable care. *It is now*

---

[115] [1943] AC 92 at 94.

[116] Although, on this point, there was some inconsistency between the evidence and the pleadings, the subsequent appeal proceeded on this basis.

[117] Lord MacMillan expressly declined to express a view on whether the approach of Kennedy J in *Dulieu* v *White & Sons* [1901] 2 KB 669 at 682 or the Court of Appeal in *Hambrook* v *Stokes Brothers* [1925] 1 KB 141 was correct, other than evincing a certain concern in relation to *Owens* v *Liverpool Corporation* [1939] 1 KB 394 — a concern shared by Lord Thankerton and, more robustly, by Lord Wright and Lord Porter. Lord Russell, for his part, ([1943] AC 92 at 103) appeared to doubt the correctness of *Hambrook*. On the other hand, Lord Wright ([1943] AC 92 at 111) preferred *Hambrook* to *Dulieu*. Neither Lord Thankerton nor Lord MacMillan would express a view as to the correct approach to the issue of remoteness of damage, although Lord Russell ([1943] AC 92 at 101) suggested that the appropriate test was that of reasonable foreseeability, whereas Lord Wright seemed to endorse the approach of *In re Polemis and Furness, Withy & Company Limited* [1921] 3 KB 560. Having quoted from all the authorities, Lord Porter expressed no view on the correctness of any (with the exception of *Owens*), although he appeared not to confine himself to Kennedy J's limitation in *Dulieu* and to accept the correctness of *Hambrook*.

[118] [1932] AC 562, on which Lords Russell, Wright and Porter relied.

> *settled that such injury includes injury by shock, although no direct physical impact or lesion occurs.*[119] *(emphasis added)*

However, on the facts, he found that "the shock resulting to the [plaintiff], situated as she was, was not within the area of potential danger which the cyclist should reasonably have had in view".[120] The other Law Lords agreed that the plaintiff was not reasonably foreseeable and, accordingly, no duty was owed. No duty, no liability.

On the authority of *Bourhill*, a person's duty in respect of "nervous shock" was to avoid causing injury by shock — as distinct from causing "shock" — that was reasonably foreseeable.[121]

---

[119] [1943] AC 92 at 98. The use of the phrase "lesion" (see Chapter 2) is curious and seems to suggest that a physical manifestation of the "shock" is unnecessary. This was echoed by Lord MacMillan ([1943] AC 92 at 103) who was equally robust in setting out the non-requirement for an impact: "It is no longer necessary to consider whether the infliction of what is called mental shock may constitute an actionable wrong. The crude view that the law should take cognisance only of physical injury resulting from actual impact has been discarded, and it is now well recognised that an action will lie for injury by shock sustained through the medium of the eye or the ear without direct contact." For Lord Wright ([1943] AC 92 at 106) it was also equally clear ". . . that damage by mental shock may give rise to a cause of action is now well established. . . ." He continued (at 108–109): "There may indeed be no one injured in a particular case by actual impact, but still a wrong may be committed to anyone who suffers nervous shock . . . The man who [acts] negligently . . . is committing a breach of duty towards every person who comes within the range of foreseeable danger, whether by impact or shock. . . ." Lord Porter ([1943] AC 92 at 112), however, refers to "emotional injury . . . at any rate if that emotion results in physical illness. . . ." Later (at 117) he describes the plaintiff thus: "[She] was never herself in any bodily danger nor reasonably in fear of danger either to herself or others. She was merely a person who, as a result of the action, was emotionally disturbed and rendered physically ill by that emotional disturbance. The question whether emotional disturbance or shock, which a defend[ant] ought reasonably to have anticipated as likely to follow from his reckless driving, can ever form the basis of a claim is not in issue." Thus, "emotional" is substituted for "nervous" — a formulation that probably has a happier resonance for modern practitioners.

[120] [1943] AC 92 at 99.

[121] Although Lord MacMillan ([1943] AC 92 at 104) applied the standard of what was "reasonable *and probable*" *(emphasis added)*. For Lord Porter ([1943] AC 92 at 119), however, the issue was the reasonable foreseeability of *emotional injury*.

However, the distinction might be regarded as somewhat academic. Discarding any putative difference between "nervous" and "mental" shock,[122] Lord Macmillan was unconcerned about the definition of "injury". He held:

> The distinction between mental shock and bodily injury was never a scientific one, for mental shock is presumably in all cases the result of, or at least accompanied by, some physical disturbance in the sufferer's system.[123]

As to whether or not a plaintiff's individual susceptibilities[124] should be taken into account in determining the existence of a duty,[125] Lord Wright had this to say:

> . . . the question of liability . . . must generally depend on a normal standard of susceptibility. It is . . . a question of what the hypothetical reasonable man . . . would say it was proper to foresee. What danger of particular infirmity that would include must depend on all the circumstances, but generally, I think, a reasonably normal condition, if medical evidence is capable of defining it, would be the standard. The test of the plaintiff's extraordinary susceptibility, if unknown to the defendant, would in effect make him an

---

[122] See *Victorian Railway Commissioners* v *Coultas* (1888) 13 App Cas 222 and *Dulieu* v *White & Sons* [1901] 2 KB 669.

[123] [1943] AC 92 at 103. This articulation seems perceptively correct and conceptually ahead of its time in terms of neurobiology. If it represents a concept of an interference with normal activities, such that it amounts to a global dysfunction, without apparent structural anomaly, it could be readily identified with clinically. At the same time, one could conceptualise purely functional disturbance, without any "physical" manifestations. On the issue of physical injury caused by nervous shock, which Lord Wright considered required to be established, he noted: "Modern medical science may, perhaps, show that the nervous shock is not necessarily associated with any particular mental ideas. The worst nervous shock may for the moment at least paralyse the mind. . . ." [1943] AC 92 at 112. Fortunately, before confusing matters further by imputing any causal mechanisms, he drew his musings to an abrupt end.

[124] However, these comments, not being central to the ultimate dismissal of the appeal, are, strictly speaking, *obiter*.

[125] As distinct from determining the question of damages.

insurer. The law likes to draw fixed and definite lines and is apt to ask where the thing is to stop. I should reply it should stop where in the particular case the good sense of the jury or of the judge decides.[126]

Amounting to a further control device, dressed up in terms of duty that was to determine the outcome of subsequent cases, this approach contrasted sharply with the earlier approach taken by Palles CB in *Bell*.[127] In effect, entitlement to recover depended not on the individual response, but on the nature of the incident that had occurred. In other words, the "shock" is not referable to the individual, but to an objective standard — the critical question being whether or not an ordinary person would normally have the capacity to withstand it.[128] This is not a case of the defendant taking the plaintiff as he finds him. Questions of vulnerability or subjective responses are irrelevant. Objective criteria are determinative of the outcome.[129]

The message from *Bourhill*, such as it is, is reasonably clear. Recovery may be had where "shock" induces physical injury — although the precise mechanism is relatively unimportant. But the test of liability is breach of a duty to avoid reasonably foresee-

---

[126] [1943] AC 92 at 110. Lord Wright continued that he was of the view that it should have stopped short of judgment for the plaintiffs in *Owens*. "The particular susceptibility there was to my mind beyond any range of normal expectancy or of reasonable foresight." Lord Porter ([1943] AC 92 at 116) agreed, and (at 117) continued: "It is not every emotional disturbance or every shock which should have been foreseen. The driver of a . . . vehicle, even though careless, is entitled to assume that the ordinary frequenter of the streets has sufficient fortitude to endure such incidents as may from time to time be expected to occur in them, including the noise of a collision and the sight of injury to others, and is not to be considered negligent towards one who does not possess the customary phlegm."

[127] However, the question of susceptibility was not central to the ultimate determination in *Bell*. In fact, the plaintiff in *Bell* was quite normal, in all respects.

[128] Another view is that "shock" is the control device designed to limit recovery.

[129] See, for example, in a criminal context, *Rabey* v *R* (1977) 37 CCC (2d) 461, affirming (1980) 2 SCR 513, 54 CCC (2d) 1; see Chapter 16, pp. 406–7.

able injury by "shock". Limitations — whether recovery could only be had for "shock" induced by fear for one's own safety (*Dulieu*) rather than by fear for the safety of others (*Hambrook*) — remained to be determined on another occasion. Only Lord Porter had no doubt that shock ". . . occasioned by reasonable apprehension of injury to oneself or others, at any rate, if those others are closely connected with the claimant . . ."[130] afforded a valid ground of claim. A related limitation — insofar as the duty of care was concerned — was the exclusion of the unduly sensitive. A concern first raised in *Coultas*, this remains essentially determinative of cases in more modern times.[131] However, *Bourhill* was decided on the basis that a duty of care did not arise. Could illness, caused by reasonably foreseeable shock as a result of witnessing injury that *had* occurred to others, form the basis of a successful claim? This after all, was what arose in *Bourhill*. On this, no view was expressed and it was left to later cases to resolve.[132]

Dead Children — Still no Duty

If a plaintiff was not reasonably foreseeable — essentially being neither physically injured, nor in the zone of physical danger — recovery for "shock" was well nigh impossible. A few years before *Bourhill*, in the Australian case of *Chester* v *Waverley Corporation*,[133] recovery was denied for the "shock" suffered by a mother on seeing her dead child recovered from a water-filled trench, which had been left inadequately fenced by the defendant

---

[130] *Hay (or Bourhill)* v *Young* [1943] AC 92 at 120.

[131] See *McFarlane* v *EE Caledonia Limited* [1994] 2 All ER 1 (CA).

[132] This matter was raised by Lord Porter in *Hay (or Bourhill)* v *Young* [1943] AC 92 at 120. However, such recovery was regarded as too remote in *Smith* v *Johnson & Company* (1897) cited in *Wilkinson* v *Downton* [1897] 2 QB 57, and in relation to which Kennedy J in *Dulieu* v *White & Sons* [1901] 2 KB 669 at 675–676 considered that there was no duty of care. It appears that at least some evolution and further development was possible.

[133] (1939) 62 CLR 1 (High Court of Australia), cited in *Hay (or Bourhill)* v *Young* [1943] AC 92; *King* v *Phillips* [1953] 1 QB 429 at 441 *per* Denning LJ; and *McLoughlin* v *O'Brian* [1983] AC 410 at 438 *per* Lord Bridge. See also Fleming (1987), op. cit., p. 146.

corporation. The child, who was seven years old, had failed to return home from playing when expected. Following a search that lasted for several hours, the body was recovered in the presence of the mother. By a majority,[134] the High Court of Australia considered that no duty was owed to the plaintiff mother, as her injury was not reasonably foreseeable.[135] Recovery was also denied by the Court of Appeal in a not dissimilar case, *King* v *Phillips*.[136] Here, the plaintiff mother's small son was playing outside on his tricycle. While she was at an upstairs window in her house, she heard a scream and, on looking down the road, she saw a taxi reversing onto the child's tricycle, the tricycle under the vehicle; but she could not see her son. Having run out into the street, she met the boy running towards her and took him inside. Although he had been slightly hurt, he gathered himself together and ran towards his house. As a result of what she had seen and heard, she suffered what might now be regarded as an acute stress reaction[137] and apparently remained unwell for a number of months. At first instance, it was held that the defendant taxi driver was not liable in respect of the mother's claim, and she appealed.

A unanimous Court of Appeal[138] dismissed the appeal. Lord Singleton, having cited *Bourhill* extensively, in a passage that lacks any modern resonance, explained why the mother could not recover. No duty was owed to her, as she could not be regarded as someone who might reasonably foreseeably be affected by the

---

[134] Latham CJ, Rich and Starke JJ, Evatt J dissenting.

[135] However, the floodgates argument also appeared to feature prominently, especially for Latham CJ. See *McLoughlin* v *O'Brian* [1983] AC 410 at 438. The dissent by Evatt J was preferred by Lord Bridge in *McLoughlin* v *O'Brian* [1983] AC 410 at 439.

[136] [1953] 1 QB 429. In *McLoughlin* v *O'Brian* [1983] AC 410 at 437, Lord Bridge was of the view that the case would have been decided differently in 1983, as was Lord Oliver in *Alcock* v *Chief Constable of South Yorkshire Police* [1992] 1 AC 310 at 412.

[137] See Chapter 6.

[138] Lords Singleton, Denning and Hodson.

defendant's act (which was undoubtedly negligent towards the injured boy). It was, in his view, in accord with common sense.[139]

> Can it be said that the driver (or any driver in the world) could reasonably or probably[140] anticipate that injury — either physical or from shock — would be caused to the mother [in her house some 70 or 80 yards away up a side street] . . . when he caused his taxicab to move backwards a short distance . . . without looking to see if anyone was immediately behind? There can surely be only one answer to that question. The driver owed a duty to the boy, but he knew nothing of the mother; she was not on the highway; he could not know that she was at the window, nor was there any reason why he should anticipate that she would see his cab at all; . . . I cannot see that the fact that she saw the tricycle under the cab distinguishes this case from *Bourhill*.[141]

He held that no damage[142] to the mother was, in the circumstances, foreseeable. Lord Denning also considered that recovery should be denied. However, his reasoning departed from that on the imposition of duty that stretched back to *Dulieu*. He could see no difference between *Hambrook* and the instant case where the

---

[139] This conclusion specifically endorses the approach of the trial judge, McNair J. Hodson LJ ([1953] 1 QB 429 at 443) was reluctant to disturb the trial judge's determination. Indeed, Hodson LJ considered that it was doubtful on the authorities whether liability could lie for negligence causing shock where there was no fear of personal injury to the plaintiff.

[140] The introduction of "probable" follows from the dictum of Lord MacMillan in *Hay (or Bourhill)* v *Young* [1943] AC 92 at 104.

[141] [1953] 1 QB 429 at 435–436.

[142] [1953] 1 QB 429 at 437. In this regard, Singleton LJ was unconcerned about the actual classification of the damage caused. He continued: "I find it difficult to draw a distinction between damage from physical injury and damage from shock; *prima facie*, one would think that, if a driver should have foreseen either, and damage resulted from the one or from the other, the plaintiff would be entitled to succeed". He did not consider it necessary, however, to pursue this "somewhat academic point" further. This is a "direct consequences" approach; see *In re Polemis and Furness, Withy and Company Limited* [1921] 3 KB 560.

mother was actually closer to the site of the accident to her child.[143] That she was in a house rather than on the street did not make any difference. In his view, the duty of the defendant to the child's mother was clear,[144] but the damage was too remote, i.e. the damage was not reasonably foreseeable.[145] As to where the line should be drawn on the issue, he considered that Lord Wright's finding in *Bourhill* that it should be wherever "in the particular case the good sense of the judge decides"[146] was correct.

Denning LJ was clear that certain cases were plain enough. He considered that a wife or mother who suffered "shock" on being told of an accident to a loved one could not recover. Nor could a bystander who suffered "shock" by witnessing an accident from a safe distance — although a mother in the position of Mrs Hambrook might be able to.[147] Irrespective of how a restriction on recovery for "shock" is articulated, however, since *Bourhill*, the test

---

[143] Although Hodson LJ also found it difficult to draw a valid distinction on the facts between *King* and *Hambrook*, he considered it appropriate to prefer the approach of the House of Lords in *Bourhill* to that of the Court of Appeal in *Hambrook*, given the approach of the House of Lords to the latter.

[144] "If [a driver] drives negligently with the result that a bystander is injured, then his breach of duty is the same, no matter whether the injury is a wound or is emotional shock. Only the damage is different. . . . If you . . . refuse a bystander to recover for shock, it is not because there was no duty owed to him, nor because it was not caused by the negligence of the driver, but simply because it was too remote to be admitted as a head of damage." [1953] 1 QB 429 at 439–440. In this, Denning LJ, as Lord Porter ([1943] AC 92 at 117) did in *Bourhill*, refers to "emotional" rather than "nervous" shock.

[145] [1953] 1 QB 429 at 442. Although Denning LJ appeared to endorse *In re Polemis and Furness and Withy Company Limited* [1921] 3 KB 560, his test of remoteness here is in line with *Overseas Tankship (UK) Ltd* v *Morts Dock & Engineering Co. Ltd (The Wagon Mound, No. 1)* [1961] AC 388, [1961] 1 All ER 404, [1961] 2 WLR 126 (Privy Council) following which reasonable foreseeability is now considered the test both of duty and remoteness. As such, his articulation of the relevant principles is most consonant with their modern application.

[146] [1943] AC 92 at 110. However, in that case, Lord Wright was considering where the line should be drawn in imposing a duty of care. This approach had been adopted by McNair J at first instance in *King* and approved by Singleton LJ ([1953] 1 QB 429 at 437).

[147] [1953] 1 QB 429 at 441.

of liability for shock is the foreseeability of injury by shock.[148] However, it has been claimed that the "fragmentation of injury into bodily and psychic for the purpose of the risk criterion is a deliberate and crucial control device".[149] Although the foreseeability of "shock" should be categorised in the same manner as physical injury, nevertheless whether mere foreseeability of some "shock" is sufficient is controversial. Such an approach has been described as "too liberal and generalised. Despite protestations that foreseeability is just a question of fact, it really remains a matter of policy how to define the foreseeable risk."[150]

In any event, if a duty to a mother, in a situation like *King*, requires that she herself must be in some foreseeable danger (through "shock"), then, when a child is endangered, it is not wholly unforeseeable that the mother will be somewhere nearby, and may thus suffer that "shock".[151] By the 1960s, recovery was allowed for "nervous shock" by parents who directly perceived[152] accidents to their children. Such a case was *Boardman* v *Sanderson*,[153] where a unanimous Court of Appeal[154] found a defendant liable for causing "slight shock"[155] to the plaintiff father, arising

---

[148] [1953] 1 QB 429 at 441 cited in *Overseas Tankship (UK) Ltd.* v *Morts Dock & Engineering Co. Ltd. (The Wagon Mound, No. 1)* [1961] AC 388, [1961] 1 All ER 404, [1961] 2 WLR 126 (Privy Council).

[149] Fleming (1987), op. cit., p. 147.

[150] Fleming (1987), op. cit., p. 147, a view reflected in Prosser and Keeton (1984), op. cit., p. 366: "[I]f recovery is to be permitted . . . it is also clear that there must be some limitation." These policy impositions are capable of producing bizarre and inconsistent results. See Fleming (1987), op. cit., p. 148.

[151] Prosser and Keeton (1984), op. cit., p. 366, which statement was cited with approval in *Dillon* v *Legge* (1968) 29 ALR 3d 1316 at 1326–1327, 69 Cal. Rep. 72, 80, 441 P. 2d 912 920. Prosser and Keeton (at page 366) go on to state: "[It] is surely no great triumph of logic in a rule which permits recovery for distress over an unborn being, where the mother miscarries, yet which denies it once the child is born."

[152] Whether by hearing or vision.

[153] (1961) [1964] 1 WLR 1317.

[154] Ormerod, Devlin and Danckwerts LJJ.

[155] (1961) [1964] 1 WLR 1317 at 1320. The father was awarded £75.

out of injury to his eight-year old son. The defendant had negligently reversed his car out of a garage and over the infant's foot, thereby trapping it, actually knowing that the father was elsewhere in the garage and within hearing of the infant's screams. Having heard the screams, the father had come rushing out and helped to free his son. He later developed psychological symptoms.[156] The court considered that a duty was owed not alone to the injured infant but also to his near relatives who were, as the defendant knew, within earshot and likely to come upon the scene if any injury occurred to the infant — the father was a clearly foreseeable plaintiff.[157] Also, they refused to limit liability only to cases where the accident was actually witnessed.[158]

Recovery by bystanders, outside the zone of physical danger and in positions of complete safety, for "nervous shock" caused by fear for the safety of another was possible since *Hambrook*, notwithstanding *Bourhill* and *King*. Now, also, recovery was possible for "nervous shock" caused by injury to another — even if the perception of the injury having occurred was acoustic and the bystander came upon the scene after the event.[159] But, for a bystander to be owed a duty of care, he had to be reasonably foreseeable. At least those in a close degree of relationship to the injured person could be considered to fall into this category.[160] Nevertheless, the restriction on recovery for "shock" at being told

---

[156] These were not specified in the report of the judgment.

[157] However, the mother in *King*, who had actually witnessed at least part of the accident, was not fortunate enough to be so classified. This probably merely represents development of the concept of reasonable foreseeability.

[158] (1961) [1964] 1 WLR 1317 at 1321. For Danckwerts LJ, it is clear that he considered the test of reasonable foreseeability of injury by shock set out in *Bourhill* to go to the issue of remoteness, as Denning LJ had suggested in *King*, cited in *Overseas Tankship (UK) Ltd.* v *Morts Dock & Engineering Co. Ltd. (The Wagon Mound, No. 1)* [1961] AC 388, [1961] 1 All ER 404, [1961] 2 WLR 126 (Privy Council).

[159] This was the matter reserved for later decision by Lord Porter in *Bourhill* [1943] AC 92 at 120.

[160] In this regard, the decision in *Boardman* is not necessarily in conflict with *Bourhill* — although it makes the decision in *King* seem incorrect.

of a calamity that had befallen a loved one, and set out by Lord Denning in *King*, remained.

Injured and Dead Spouses and Children — Duty in the Aftermath

The question of determining who was, or was not, a reasonably foreseeable plaintiff, however, remained problematic. Recovery was allowed in the cases of close relatives, such as spouses,[161] and, in certain circumstances, fellow-workers.[162] However, it is to *Dillon* v *Legg*,[163] a decision of the Supreme Court of California, that the "bystander proximity rule"[164] is attributed. Here, a mother who saw her infant daughter run over and killed as she crossed the road was allowed to recover for the emotional trauma caused. But, under the formulation, which set out to be a proposition of general applicability, certain factors were to be taken into account in determining whether or not a plaintiff was owed a duty of care. Tobriner J, for the majority, stated that such factors as the following ought to be taken into account:

> (1) Whether plaintiff was located near the scene of the accident as contrasted with one who was a distance away from it. (2) Whether the shock resulted from a direct emotional

---

[161] See, for example, *Marshall* v *Lionel Enterprises Inc.* [1972] 2 OR 177, (1971) 25 DLR (3d) 141 (Ontario Court of Appeal) where the wife was held not to be disentitled, as a matter of law, to recover damages for the "nervous shock" she suffered, having come upon her badly injured husband shortly after an accident caused by defective machinery. In *Benson* v *Lee* [1972] VR 879 (Supreme Court of Victoria) the plaintiff mother rushed to the scene of an accident (100 yards away) where her child had been injured, and accompanied him in the ambulance to hospital where he died. She was held to be entitled to damages for "nervous shock", notwithstanding evidence that she was prone to mental illness from stress. Both cases are cited in *McLoughlin* v *O'Brian* [1983] AC 410 at 418–419 and 438, *per* Lord Wilberforce and Lord Bridge, respectively.

[162] See *Dooley* v *Cammell Laird & Company Limited* [1951] 1 Lloyd's Rep 271 (crane operator) and Salmond and Heuston (1992), op. cit., p. 221. Rescuers fall into a category of their own; see *Chadwick* v *British Railways Board* [1967] 2 All ER 945, [1967] 1 WLR 912. However, in each of these cases, the plaintiffs could properly be described as participants.

[163] (1968) 29 ALR 3d 1316, 69 Cal. Rep. 72, 441 P. 2d 912.

[164] Prosser and Keeton (1984), op. cit., p. 366.

impact upon plaintiff from the sensory and contemporaneous observance of the accident, as contrasted with learning of the accident from others after its occurrence. (3) Whether plaintiff and the victim were closely related, as contrasted with an absence of any relationship or the presence of only a distant relationship.[165]

Noting that all these elements shade into each other, the court was of the view that the fixing of obligation was intimately tied into the facts and depended upon each case. In light of these factors the court was to determine whether the accident and harm were reasonably foreseeable.

In effect, therefore, a bystander could only recover if he:

a) was near the site of the accident (physical proximity), and

b) observed the accident (temporal proximity), and

c) was closely related to the (primary) victim (relationship proximity).

Reasonable Foreseeability and Proximity — Limitations on the Duty of Care

Dillon came to be considered by the House of Lords in *McLoughlin v O'Brian*.[166] Here, the plaintiff wife/mother mother was at home two miles away, when a road traffic accident, caused by the

---

[165] (1968) 29 ALR 3d 1316 at 1326–1327, 69 Cal. Rep. 72, 80, 441 P. 2d 912 920.

[166] [1983] AC 410. As already noted, this was only the second "nervous shock" case to come to the House of Lords since the first reported decision in such a case, that of the Privy Council in *Coultas* in 1888. *Byrne* had not been reported and only came to prominence in *Bell*. However, much of the law was settled. Thus, in *Hinz v Berry* [1970] 2 QB 40, which proceeded to the Court of Appeal on an assessment only, the plaintiff mother had witnessed, from one side of the road, a terrible accident to her family picnicking on the other side of the road. There was no dispute as to the liability for the psychiatric illness that she consequently suffered from. Lord Denning MR stated: "The law at one time said that there could not be damages for nervous shock: but for these last 25 years, it has been settled that damages can be given for nervous shock caused by the sight of an accident, at any rate to a close relative." [1970] 2 QB 40 at 42.

defendant's negligence, resulted in serious injuries to her husband and two of her children. A third child had died almost immediately at the scene. An hour or so after the accident, the driver of the following car, which was not involved in the accident, told her what had happened, and that he thought her son was dying. A fourth child, who had been travelling in his car, was unharmed. The motorist brought the plaintiff to the hospital where she saw what had happened to her family and their distress and disarray. Lord Wilberforce described the scene she encountered as "distressing in the extreme and . . . capable of producing an effect going well beyond that of grief and sorrow".[167] As a result, the plaintiff suffered what was summarised as "severe shock, organic depression and a change of personality".[168] At first instance, the plaintiff failed to recover, the trial judge holding on the authorities that, as she was not a reasonably foreseeable plaintiff, no duty was owed to her. The Court of Appeal, however, having found that a duty of care was owed to her,[169] denied her recovery on policy grounds.[170] A unanimous House of Lords allowed the plaintiff's appeal on the grounds that as she was a reasonably foreseeable plaintiff, she was owed a duty of care. Recovery was permitted, notwithstanding that there had been neither visual nor acoustic perception of the event in question, but merely an experiencing of its near immediate aftermath.

All were satisfied that policy arguments were insufficient to deny recovery in this case. Although not impressed with the floodgates arguments,[171] Lord Wilberforce was of the opinion that as

---

[167] [1983] AC 410 at 417.

[168] [1983] AC 410 at 417.

[169] Stephenson and Cumming-Bruce LJJ.

[170] Griffiths LJ, although holding that the plaintiff's injuries were *readily* foreseeable, held that she was owed no duty, as this, in his view, in line with the earlier authorities, was limited to those on the road nearby. The opening of the floodgates to claims of this type prompted the Court of Appeal to deny recovery.

[171] These are succinctly summarised and criticised at [1983] AC 410 at 421 and 425 *per* Lord Wilberforce and Lord Edmund-Davies, respectively. Kennedy J's dictum on the issue in *Dulieu* was further approved. Lord

"shock" in its nature was capable of affecting so wide a range of people, it was necessary for the law to place some limitation on the extent of admissible claims.[172] This, in itself, however, almost seems a resurrection of the floodgates argument.[173] Reflecting the approach of the Supreme Court of California in *Dillon*, he continued:

> It is necessary to consider three elements inherent in any claim: the class of persons whose claims should be recognised; the proximity of such persons to the accident; and the means by which the shock is caused. . . . Subject only to these qualifications . . . a strict test of proximity by sight or hearing should be applied. . . .[174]

The first of these considerations is the equivalent of the proximity of relationship set out in *Dillon*. Both the tie of actual relationship and also the tie of care were considered relevant here, although without strict categorisation.[175] However, this had to be viewed in the light of the second consideration — spatial and temporal

---

Russell and Lord Bridge (with whom Lord Scarman agreed) were similarly unimpressed with the floodgates argument, although Lord Scarman nevertheless considered that legislation in relation to policy limitations might be necessary.

[172] He was also of the view that reasonable foreseeability alone did not determine the existence of a duty of care.

[173] This seems implicit in the judgment of Lord Jauncey in *Alcock* v *Chief Constable of South Yorkshire Police* [1992] 1 AC 310 at 419.

[174] [1983] AC 410 at 422. In the context of the floodgates argument, any attempt to advance solutions or guidelines, in hypothetical cases, Lord Russell ([1983] AC 410 at 429) considered might well "do more harm than good". The same criticism might be made of Lord Wilberforce's approach, especially given that it was not essential to the disposal of the appeal. Lord Wilberforce's comments were regarded as *obiter* by Lord Oliver in *Alcock* v *Chief Constable of South Yorkshire Police* [1992] 1 AC 310 at 415.

[175] Mere bystanders who are strangers — in the literal sense — are denied recovery under this formulation for one of two basic policy reasons: either on the basis that strangers must be assumed to be "possessed of fortitude sufficient to enable them to endure the calamities of modern life or on the basis that defendants cannot be expected to compensate the world at large". [1983] AC 410 at 422. This approach is reflected in judgments as far back as *Coultas*. See pp. 196–8 below.

proximity to the accident, also required by *Dillon*.[176] By analogy
with the duty owed to rescuers, a defendant should foresee that
close relations might be at, or soon come upon, the scene of an accident, or its immediate aftermath.[177] Finally, the "shock" had to
be brought about by sight or hearing of the event or of its immediate aftermath. Mere communication to a plaintiff by a third party
that a disaster had befallen a loved one was to be insufficient.[178]
However, whether or not the equivalent — simultaneous television broadcast — would be sufficient, was reserved for another
occasion.[179]

Lord Edmund-Davies, for his part, was not satisfied that reasonable foreseeability was the sole ground for determining liability in cases of this type and that it was permissible to invoke
public policy to deny recovery — even if a duty was owed and

---

[176] The "aftermath" doctrine may be defensible, as was stated in *Benson* v *Lee*
[1972] VR 879 at 880 as "direct perception of some of the events which go to
make up the accident as an entire event . . . includes . . . the immediate aftermath. . . .", quoted with approval in *McLoughlin* v *O'Brian* [1983] AC 410 at
422 per Lord Wilberforce. In this regard, Lord Wilberforce seems to have regarded *Chester* v *Waverley Corporation* (1939) 62 CLR 1 as correctly decided.
See also *Mullally* v *Bus Éireann* [1992] ILRM 722 (HC).

[177] As to what constitutes "immediate" is not precisely defined, but appears,
from the authorities, at least to be up to eight hours and certainly includes
coming upon the hospital afterwards. This limit of eight hours falling outside
the definition of "immediate" was relied on by Lord Ackner in *Alcock* v *Chief
Constable of South Yorkshire Police* [1992] 1 AC 310 at 405.

[178] As seemed clear from *Hambrook*, with which conclusion Lord Wilberforce
([1983] AC 410 at 423) expressly agreed. In *Abramzik* v *Brenner* (1967) 65
DLR (2d) 651 (cited at [1983] AC 410 at 423 and 438) the Saskatchewan
Court of Appeal denied recovery to a mother who suffered "nervous shock" on
being informed by her husband that two of her children had been killed in a
road accident. The decisions of the Queen's Bench in *Hevican* v *Ruane* [1991]
3 All ER 65 and *Ravenscroft* v *Rederiaktiebolaget* [1991] 3 All ER 73 where
the effective cause of the plaintiffs' psychiatric illness was the fact of a son's
death and the news of it were seriously doubted in *Alcock* v *Chief Constable
of South Yorkshire Police* [1992] 1 AC 310, [1991] 3 WLR 1057, [1991] 4 All
ER 907. However, *Kelly* v *Hennessy* [1995] 3 IR 253 (Supreme Court) suggests that a slightly different approach might be taken in this jurisdiction.

[179] See *Alcock* v *Chief Constable of South Yorkshire Police* [1992] 1 AC 310,
[1991] 3 WLR 1057, [1991] 4 All ER 907 (the Hillsborough Stadium disaster).

damage was reasonably foreseeable.[180] But, on the facts, he was satisfied that the plaintiff was owed a duty of care and that it had been wrong to reject her claim on policy grounds. Lord Russell did not differ in his approach. For Lord Scarman, reasonable foreseeability was the sole test of liability and, if policy considerations were to be invoked, as he considered they should, he was of the view that that was a matter for legislation and not for the courts. He considered that the factors set out by Lord Wilberforce ought to be weighed, but that they were not legal limitations in the application of the test of reasonable foreseeability. Lord Bridge differed sharply from Lord Edmund-Davies. He was of the view that the test of liability for nervous shock was that of reasonable foreseeability *simpliciter*. While recognising the importance of the factors set out in *Dillon* as bearing on the degree of foreseeability[181] of the plaintiff's psychiatric illness, Lord Bridge considered that to draw a line by reference to any of those criteria would be to impose a largely arbitrary limit of liability.[182] He was happy to judge each case on its own facts and was reluctant to predetermine a defendant's obligations in every situation.[183]

---

[180] In this he was criticised by Lord Bridge ([1983] AC 410 at 443) for not specifying what those policy considerations might be, especially as he (Lord Edmund-Davies) expressed himself unimpressed with the floodgates argument.

[181] i.e. in determining, on the facts, whether or not the plaintiff was reasonably foreseeable, as distinct from determining the existence of a duty of care in the first instance, as *Dillon* suggested.

[182] [1983] AC 410 at 442. In support of his contention he gave two examples — communication of death of, or injury to, a loved where it was not possible to visit the scene and rescuers. However, the law in relation to rescuers generally appears not to be affected by the law on "nervous shock" — primarily because rescuers are nearly always foreseeable. His extension of this example, of a bystander at the scene of a disaster — if he were a participant — would have been covered by the principles laid down in *Bell* and *Hambrook*.

[183] He was of the view that the line should be drawn, in the words of Lord Wright in *Hay (or Bourhill)* v *Young* ([1943] AC 92 at 110) as modified by Stephenson LJ in *McLoughlin* in the Court of Appeal ([1981] QB 599 at 612) "where, in the particular case the good sense of the judge, enlightened by progressive awareness of mental illness, decides". In this regard, and as Lord Wilberforce pointed out ([1983] AC 410 at 420), the concept of duty is, in

Although for Lord Bridge, proximity of space, time and degree of relationship were important in bearing on the degree of foreseeability of the plaintiff's condition, rather than being criteria determinative of the limit of liability,[184] the standard by which foreseeability was to be judged was important. He observed that, as a matter of history ". . . psychiatric medicine is far from being an exact science. The opinions of its practitioners may differ widely"[185] and that "[F]or too long, earlier generations of judges have regarded psychiatry and psychiatrists with suspicion, if not with hostility. Now . . . that attitude has disappeared".[186] Nevertheless, he was satisfied that:

> . . . the consensus of informed judicial opinion is probably the best yardstick available to determine whether, in any given circumstances, the emotional trauma resulting from the death or injury of third parties, or indeed the threat of such death or injury,[187] *ex hypothesi* attributable to the defendant's negligence, was a foreseeable cause in law, as well as the actual cause in fact, of the plaintiff's psychiatric or psychosomatic illness.[188]

---

itself, a control device, into the determination of which policy questions have entered.

[184] See, generally, McMahon and Binchy (1990) op. cit., p. 309–10.

[185] [1983] AC 410 at 432.

[186] [1983] AC 410 at 433.

[187] In this regard, Lord Bridge ([1983] AC 410 at 431) also noted that the instant case involved death or injury to a third party. Indeed, none of the reported cases deal with a situation where "nervous shock" was caused by apprehended injury to a third party that did not, in fact, eventuate — a matter averred to by Sarjant LJ in *Hambrook* v *Stokes Brothers* [1925] 1 KB 141 at 164. Problems of proof, in such a situation, might well be formidable. However, in *Alcock* v *Chief Constable of South Yorkshire Police* [1992] 1 AC 310 at 412, Lord Oliver considered that psychiatric or physical injury in such a situation was "readily conceivable" and that, had the child in *Hambrook* escaped injury, the outcome to that case would have been no different. Thus, for all practical purposes, the issue only arises in respect of *actual* death or injury.

[188] [1983] AC 410 at 432. This, in his view, was in line with the authorities, in all of which, it has to be admitted, the judges assumed competence to decide

In common with judges as for back as Palles CB in *Bell*, Lord Bridge was of the view that proof of a causal link between the death or injury of a third party and the plaintiff's psychiatric illness. But he considered that to treat the question of foreseeable causation — and thus the scope of a defendant's duty — as a question of fact to be determined in the light of the expert evidence adduced in each case would be going too far. This might represent no more than a healthy disregard for expert opinions on matters within the provenance of ordinary human experience also seen in other areas of the law.[189]

After *McLoughlin* it remained unclear as to whether or not reasonable foreseeability was the sole criterion by which liability for psychiatric disability caused by death or injury to a third party was to be tested.[190] To invoke certain unspecified policy considerations was deemed appropriate by the majority of the House of Lords. An apparent limitation on recovery for psychiatric injury brought about by communication of bad news by a third party, or medium, rather than by some other direct sensory perception, of the events in question remained.[191] Also, questions relating to a plaintiff's individual vulnerability and whether or not the negligence of the third party who was injured or killed should be taken into consideration in determining a plaintiff's right to recover also remained unanswered.[192] Limitations on the mode of perception or

---

whether or not a plaintiff's psychiatric disability was reasonably foreseeable. This approach was endorsed by Hamilton CJ in *Kelly* v *Hennessy* [1995] 3 IR 253 at 260.

[189] See, for example, in criminal matters, *People (DPP)* v *Kehoe* [1992] ILRM 481 (CCA). See also *R* v *Weightman* [1991] Crim LR 204, 92 Cr App Rep 291 and *R* v *Stockwell* (1993) 97 Cr App R 260 (CA).

[190] In *Attia* v *British Gas plc* [1987] 3 All ER 255, [1988] QB 304, the Court of Appeal contemplated that psychiatric illness resulting from the "shock" of seeing one's property destroyed through the defendant's negligence would not be too remote. See, however, McMahon and Binchy (1990), op. cit., p. 313.

[191] Notwithstanding Lord Bridge's specific dissent on this very point.

[192] In *Jaensch* v *Coffey* [1984] 54 ALR 417, 155 CLR 549, Deane J was of the view that no claim could be entertained, as a matter of law, in a case where the primary victim is the negligent defendant himself and the "shock" to the plaintiff arises from witnessing the victim's self-inflicted injury. In *Alcock* v

injury to a third party seem only directed at "floodgates" concerns.[193] It can scarcely be deemed to have any regard to the real
evidentiary difficulties that have to be overcome before such an
action could succeed. It almost seems that the rationale underlying the US approach to cases where recovery is sought by persons
within the zone of physical danger (i.e. an "impact" requirement)
is being applied. Thus, the fact of having come upon the scene of
an accident, or its immediate aftermath, is such that it is likely
that the psychiatric injury is not feigned. Arguably, however, this
conflicts both with the common experience and the clinical reality
that there may be no real or significant difference between the
distress caused whether a plaintiff has direct perception of an
event, or its aftermath, or is merely told, and ruminates about it
later.[194] If there is a difference in degree, then, it seems, that is
more correctly matter for evidence, and may ultimately go to proof
of damage and, accordingly, liability. Also, if previous authorities
are to be applied and are correct in holding that the mode of perception of injury is not strictly limited to visual perception,[195] then

---

Chief Constable of South Yorkshire Police [1992] 1 AC 310 at 401, Lord
Ackner noted that there was no authority on the point, apart from an *obiter
dictum* of Lord Robertson, the Lord Ordinary in *Bourhill* v *Young* (1941) SC
395 at 399. However, he seemed of the view that there must be "a limit at
some reasonable point to the extent of the duty of care owed to third parties
which rests upon everyone in all his actions". Lord Oliver [1992] 1 AC 310 at
418, thought that English law would take the same view as Deane J in
Jaensch v *Coffey*, although he conceded that in logic such a position was inde-
fensible and would be particularly problematic where the injured party was
guilty of a significant degree of contributory negligence. In his view, such a
limitation could only be based on policy grounds, which should be dealt with
by way of legislation. In this, he echoes the approach of Lord Scarman in
McLoughlin v *O'Brian* [1983] AC 410 at 430–431. However, in claims for loss
of consortium, the contributory negligence of the injured party is not a factor
to be taken into account in assessing damages. See *Coppinger* v *Waterford
County Council* [1996] 2 ILRM 427. This cause of action was abolished in
Britain by the Administration of Justice Act, 1982.

[193] This is obliquely averred to by Lord Wilberforce [1983] AC 410 at 422. See
the criticisms in McMahon and Binchy (1990), op. cit., pp. 311 to 313.

[194] The reality of this proposition is averred to in *Alcock* v *Chief Constable of
South Yorkshire Police* [1992] 1 AC 310 at 411 *per* Lord Oliver.

[195] As in *Hambrook* and *King*.

there can be no principled objection to perception by reporting by a third party or medium. That the perception of the aftermath of an accident (for example in a hospital emergency department) is not alone visual, but also auditory, olfactory and tactile, must indicate that, on principle, the mode of perception is irrelevant.[196]

The Australian View

Similar issues faced the High Court of Australia in *Jaensch v Coffey*[197] where the plaintiff wife saw her injured husband at the hospital to which he had been taken in severe pain — following a road traffic accident — before and between his undergoing a series of emergency operations. The following day she stayed with him in the intensive care unit and thought he was going to die. She was held to be entitled to recover for the psychiatric illness she suffered as a result. The majority of the Court[198] imposed a barrier of policy (proximity criteria) suggested in *McLoughlin v O'Brian*[199] in addition to a simple test of reasonable foreseeability of injury, although the determinants of liability were not imposed as rigidly as contemplated by Lord Wilberforce.[200] However, here,

---

[196] In a related context, Fleming (1987), op. cit., p. 148 notes that the concept of recovery being dependant on fear for one's own safety "derives some support from a reputable medical view that *lasting* damage to the nervous system can ordinarily only result for fear to oneself" (*emphasis added*) footnoted to Havard (1956), "Reasonable Foresight of Nervous Shock" 19 Mod L Rev 1956, p. 478 (also cited in McMahon and Binchy (1990), op. cit., p. 307 in support of Palles CB's position in *Bell v Great Northern Railway Company of Ireland* (1890) 26 LR Ir 428). This approach should be contrasted with that in *Jaensch v Coffey* [1984] 54 ALR 417, 155 CLR 549 (High Court of Australia). In *Alcock v Chief Constable of South Yorkshire Police* [1992] 1 AC 310 at 405, Lord Ackner (agreeing with Nolan LJ in the Court of Appeal) agreed that simultaneous broadcasts of a disaster could, in some circumstances, be regarded as the equivalent of the actual sight or hearing of an event or its immediate aftermath.

[197] [1984] 54 ALR 417, 155 CLR 549 (High Court of Australia).

[198] Gibbs CJ, Deane and Murphy JJ.

[199] [1983] AC 410.

[200] [1983] AC 410 at 422. See *Jaensch v Coffey* [1984] 54 ALR 417, 155 CLR 549 at 583 *per* Deane J. The wooliness of the approach is criticised by McMahon and Binchy (1990), op. cit., p. 311.

at least, the court was prepared to contemplate recovery where a plaintiff, so devastated by being told of an accident involving family members, that he was unable to attend at the scene or at the hospital, an eminently sensible extension of a logical approach to the issue.[201]

The Irish View

The position in Irish law of *McLoughlin* had been expressly reserved by the Supreme Court in *State (Keegan and Lysaght)* v *Stardust Victims' Compensation Tribunal*.[202] It first fell to be considered in yet another case involving a wife and mother who suffered non-physical injury as a consequence of a serious accident to her husband and children. In *Mullally* v *Bus Éireann*,[203] the plaintiff was informed that her husband and three young sons[204] had been seriously injured in a road traffic accident, subsequently attributed to the negligence of the defendants. Having gone[205] to the hospitals where they had been brought, she came upon scenes that were described looking "like a hospital out of a war film, like a field hospital".[206] Some days after the accident, the plaintiff

---

[201] See McMahon and Binchy (1990), op. cit., pp. 310–11. In Australia, legislative intervention in New South Wales and the Capital Territory has effectively dispensed with the "bystander proximity" criteria.

[202] [1987] ILRM 202 at 212 *per* Finlay CJ.

[203] [1992] ILRM 722.

[204] One of the sons subsequently died, approximately eight months after the accident. Although the plaintiff also appeared to have a prolonged grief reaction (see Chapter 6, pp. 104–6) in respect of this death, this was expressly excluded from the reckoning. As to whether or not this must always be the case, such that the only head under which compensation might be claimed is under the provisions of the Civil Liability Act, 1961, s. 49, as amended by the Courts Act, 1981, s. 28(1), and the Civil Liability (Amendment) Act, 1996, s. 2, remains to be determined.

[205] The plaintiff became physically ill on a number of occasions *en route* to the hospitals, a factor which appears to have been implicitly regarded as relevant in the ultimate determination of the case. A similar response by the plaintiff in *Kelly* v *Hennessy* [1995] 3 IR 253 was expressly considered to be evidence of "shock".

[206] [1992] ILRM 722 at 724.

evidenced signs of a profound psychological disturbance that persisted to the date of the trial.[207] Although there was a clear proximity of relationship between the plaintiff and the primary
victims of the defendants' negligence, it is clear that the plaintiff
did not happen upon the scene of the accident and, indeed, came
upon the aftermath in the different hospitals many hours later.[208]
However, Denham J was not concerned with issues of proximity.
For her, the test of liability was — with an advancing awareness
of medical knowledge of mental illness — simply that of reasonable foreseeability.[209] Also, the scenes of the aftermath of the accident having been caused by the defendants,[210] the plaintiff was
entitled to succeed as it was, in Denham J's view "readily foreseeable"[211] that a mother exposed to that experience would suffer illness, as the plaintiff did. Considerations of judicial policy-making
and the fear of opening the floodgates that had so occupied the
House of Lords in *McLoughlin* were irrelevant. Denham J considered that:

> . . . there is no bar in law, or under the Constitution, to this
> determination. If it causes commercial concern then that is

---

[207] Denham J was satisfied on the evidence that the plaintiff fulfilled the
criteria for a post-traumatic stress disorder as set out in DSM-III-R, the fore-
runner of DSM-IV (see Chapter 3, and Chapter 6, pp. 79–89).

[208] The exact duration is unclear from the report but it was certainly longer
than in *McLoughlin*, although perhaps not as long as in *Alcock*. Nevertheless,
Denham J was satisfied ([1992] ILRM 722 at 731) that the plaintiff fell
within the parameters of proximity set by Lord Wilberforce in *McLoughlin*.

[209] Denham J expressly acknowledged ([1992] ILRM 722 at 731) that she was
"guided more by Lord Bridge [in *McLoughlin*]".

[210] Denham J stated ([1992] ILRM 722 at 731): "It would be unjust, and contrary to the fundamental doctrine of negligence, not to find that there is a
legal nexus between the actions of the defendants causing the accident, and
the resultant aftermath of the accident in the scenes in the hospitals. . . ." In
coming to her ultimate conclusions, she relied on both *Byrne v Great Southern and Western Railway Company* and *Bell v Great Northern Railway Company of Ireland* (1890) 26 LR Ir 428.

[211] [1992] ILRM 722 at 730.

a matter for another place, where a policy can be established in the law.[212]

Thus, reasonable foreseeability *simpliciter* of psychiatric damage
by "shock" — as in *Bourhill* — was endorsed as the test of liability
for "nervous" shock in Irish law. Also, the question of temporal
proximity was deftly disposed of. As the aftermath of the accident,
even in hospital — and the injuries to the primary victims — was
directly attributable to the defendants' negligence,[213] and as it was
reasonably (or "readily") foreseeable that a wife and mother would
come upon such a scene, it did not appear to matter that some
considerable time might have elapsed.[214]

---

[212] [1992] ILRM 722 at 731. This reflects, at least in part, the view expressed
by Lord Wilberforce in *McLoughlin* [1983] AC 410 at 431.

[213] However, in this case, the accident had resulted in 3 deaths and 49 serious
injuries, overwhelming the emergency services for several hours. It remains
to be seen if the same considerations would apply where there were only a
few victims who were rapidly dealt with in hospital (unlike in *McLoughlin*).
On Denham J's formulation, this, arguably, is irrelevant — insofar as serious
personal injuries obvious in the aftermath of an accident are invariably (bar-
ring negligence on the part of the injured party or a *novus actus interveniens*)
caused by the defendants' negligence and are reasonably foreseeable. Non-
physical damage (not necessarily a post-traumatic stress disorder) could still
ensue, even if the hospital does not look like a battlefield. However, it has
been held that ". . . the aftermath of [an] accident extend[s] to the hospital to
which the injured person was taken and persisted for so long as he remained
in the state produced by the accident up to and including immediate post-
accident treatment". *Jaensch* v *Coffey* [1984] 54 ALR 417, 155 CLR 549 at
608 *per* Deane J, cited in *Alcock* v *Chief Constable of South Yorkshire Police*
[1992] 1 AC 310 at 397–398 *per* Lord Keith. Such a formulation might well
act to negative a wider-ranging proposition on temporal proximity.

[214] The issue of the length of time that had elapsed between the accident to
the primary victims and the coming upon the scene by the plaintiffs was
critical in the assessment of the House of Lords in *Alcock* v *Chief Constable of
South Yorkshire Police* [1992] 1 AC 310, [1991] 3 WLR 1057, [1991] 4 All ER
907. However, as Hamilton CJ observed in *Kelly* v *Hennessy* [1995] 3 IR 253
at 262, quoting *Jaensch* v *Coffey* [1984] 54 ALR 417, 155 CLR 549 *per*
Brennan J, "Liability cannot rationally depend on a race between a spouse
and an ambulance."

The English View Revisited

However, in England the House of Lords was to revisit the duty issue in "nervous" shock cases. In *Alcock & others* v *Chief Constable of South Yorkshire Police*[215] the defendant was sued as the person responsible for the policing of the football match at Hillsborough Stadium in which 95 people died and over 400 suffered crush injuries. At first instance, the High Court[216] did not find it necessary to consider the scope of the "aftermath" doctrine. Having found that it was reasonably foreseeable that the relatives of those killed and injured in the football stadium might suffer reasonably foreseeable psychiatric illness upon seeing the events live on television, the court then went on to consider whether or not sufficient proximity had been established. Proximity of relationship was considered first, followed by examination of the sufficiency of proximity in space and time. In relation to the latter, it was found that all of those plaintiffs who saw the events live on television were sufficiently proximate in space and time in order to recover, once the appropriate degree of proximity of relationship had been established. Ten plaintiffs succeeded in the High court, six were unsuccessful. A unanimous Court of Appeal[217] allowed an appeal against nine of the ten successful plaintiffs and dismissed an appeal against the six who were unsuccessful.

The appeal of ten plaintiffs — who were in various degrees of relationship to persons killed in the disaster and who came about it in a variety of ways, e.g. from being in or near the football stadium, through live television broadcasts and radio news reports — was dismissed by a unanimous House of Lords.[218] The approach of Lord Wilberforce in *McLoughlin* v *O'Brian*[219] was applied. Thus, it was held that in order to recover for psychiatric injury caused by "shock", not alone was it necessary to show that such injury was

---

[215] [1992] 1 AC 310, [1991] 3 WLR 1057, [1991] 4 All ER 907.

[216] Hidden J.

[217] Parker, Stocker and Nolan LJJ.

[218] Lord Keith, Lord Ackner, Lord Oliver, Lord Jauncey and Lord Lowry.

[219] [1983] AC 410 at 422.

reasonably foreseeable, but also that the relationship between the plaintiff and the person killed or injured was sufficiently close. In this regard, it was held that the class of persons to whom a duty was owed was not limited by reference to particular relationships, (e.g. parents, spouses, etc), but was based on ties of love and affection. Accordingly, in each case, the closeness of the relationship fell to be proved, although in certain circumstances, it might be presumed.[220] In addition, proximity (or propinquity) of space and time to the accident, or its aftermath, also had to be proved. In effect, reasonable foreseeability *simpliciter* was insufficient to ground recovery.

In relation to the important issue of the mode of perception of peril or injury befalling another, in *Alcock* it was accepted that it was reasonably foreseeable that the pictures of football fans being crushed would be televised live and that relatives and friends of those who were in difficulty would view those pictures. However, the defendant also knew of the broadcasting code of ethics[221] that the television companies could have been expected to follow, namely that they would not show pictures of suffering by recognisable individuals.[222] This, in the unanimous view of the House of Lords, could not be regarded as being within sight or sound of the event or its immediate aftermath.[223] *A fortiori* a person who

---

[220] "The quality of brother love is well known to differ widely — from Cain and Abel to David and Jonathan." [1992] 1 AC 310 at 406 *per* Lord Ackner.

[221] It was accepted that breach of this code would have constituted a *novus actus interveniens*, breaking the chain of causation.

[222] *Alcock* v *Chief Constable of South Yorkshire Police* [1992] 1 AC 310 at 398, 405, 417 and 423 *per* Lords Keith, Ackner, Oliver and Jauncey respectively. In the case of the two plaintiffs who were actually in the football ground, Lord Keith and Lord Ackner were not satisfied that there was evidence of particularly close ties of love and affection between them and the deceased, in respect of whose deaths claims were made for psychiatric illness. Lord Ackner also held that there was not sufficient proximity in time and space to the accident — even in the case of one of the plaintiffs who was in the football ground, identification of the deceased not having taken place for at least eight hours.

[223] "A psychiatric illness induced by mere knowledge of a distressing fact is not compensable; perception by the plaintiff of the distressing phenomenon is essential." *Jaensch* v *Coffey* [1984] 54 ALR 417, 155 CLR 549 at 567 *per*

listened to a radio broadcast or saw a subsequent television recording fell even further short of the requirement.[224]

A Modified Irish View?

The circumstances in *Kelly* v *Hennessy*[225] were nearly identical to those in *Mullally* v *Bus Éireann*.[226] The plaintiff having recovered in the High Court, the defendant appealed. Hamilton CJ (with whom Egan J agreed), in refusing the appeal, endorsed reasonable foreseeability of injury by "shock" as the test of liability.[227] Holding both that the defendant owed a duty of care[228] to the plaintiff and that the damage she suffered was reasonably foreseeable,[229] he refused to interfere with the trial judge's findings that she had suffered immediate "shock"[230] as a result of a telephone call informing her of the accident to her family, and that that was gravely aggravated by what she subsequently saw in the

---

Brennan J, cited in *Alcock* v *Chief Constable of South Yorkshire Police* [1992] 1 AC 310 at 401 *per* Lord Ackner.

[224] *Alcock* v *Chief Constable of South Yorkshire Police* [1992] 1 AC 310 at 423 *per* Lord Jauncey. Lord Wilberforce in *McLoughlin* v *O'Brian* [1983] AC 410 at 422 had also held that a "strict test of proximity or hearing should be applied. . . ."

[225] [1995] 3 IR 253.

[226] [1992] ILRM 722 (HC).

[227] Relying on *Jaensch* v *Coffey* [1984] 54 ALR 417, 155 CLR 549 (High Court of Australia). However, in *Kelly*, "shock" here is used in two contexts. Firstly, it is used to denote any recognisable psychiatric illness, and secondly to denote the sudden manner in which it is induced ([1995] 3 IR 253 at 258). *Jaensch* suggests that the shock must also be reasonably foreseeable. Insofar as the requirement seems to be for a "recognisable psychiatric illness" before recovery is allowed, the dictum of Murphy J in *Bell* v *Great Northern Railway Company of Ireland* (1890) 26 LR Ir 428 (see p. 148 above) seems preferable. This should not, however, as a matter of practical reality, serve to bar claims, although the characterisation of a post-traumatic stress disorder was disputed by the defendant in *Kelly* (see [1995] 3 IR 253 at 275 to 276).

[228] Citing *Donoghue* v *Stevenson* [1932] AC 562 at 580 *per* Lord Atkin — the classic "neighbourhood" formulation considered at length in *McLoughlin* and *Alcock*.

[229] However, the issue of foreseeability did not arise on the appeal.

[230] As in *Mullally*, the plaintiff became physically ill after she had received the news of the accident.

hospital.[231] This appears to extend beyond what the House of Lords was prepared to admit in *Alcock*. However, Hamilton CJ superimposed on this finding a requirement for proximity of relationship, time and space that *Alcock* required.[232] Denham J, having cited the authorities, considered that it was not necessary, in the instant case, to choose between either the "general or more restricted approach in common law".[233] As questions of proximity of relationship, space and time did not have to be decided in *Kelly* for the determination of the appeal, the conclusions of Hamilton CJ could be regarded, strictly speaking, as *obiter*. In those circumstances, it remains unclear whether or not the proximity requirement, in addition to reasonable foreseeability, now determines the existence of a duty of care in this area of Irish law.[234]

However, somewhat more complex considerations arose for analysis in *Kelly*. The primary victims of the accident, two of whom were severely injured and permanently brain-damaged, recovered compensation for their injuries, including sums for their future needs. However, upon their ultimate discharge from hospital, the plaintiff refused to admit or accept professional help for their ongoing care and continued to look after her injured

---

[231] ". . . she saw her family, each of [whom was] in an appalling condition and one of [whom] she . . . described as looking like mince meat." [1995] 3 IR 253 at 266 *per* Denham J, setting out the trial judge's findings.

[232] Although proximity was also of importance to Denham J's (see [1995] 3 IR 253 at 269) disposal of the appeal, she noted that neither proximity of relationship nor spatial proximity were in issue. However, she uses temporal proximity in the sense not of the plaintiff coming upon the scene of the injuries to her family but in relation to the temporal relationship between the onset of her illness and the accident. In this regard, she agreed with Hamilton CJ and accepted the evidence of the trial judge that the plaintiff was immediately affected. The specific issue of a delayed onset of damage is expressly considered by Palles CB in *Bell* v *Great Northern Railway Company of Ireland* (1890) 26 LR Ir 428.

[233] [1995] 3 IR 253 at 274, i.e. between the approach of Lord Bridge or Lord Wilberforce in *McLoughlin*.

[234] Especially as Denham J, as trial judge in *Mullally*, had expressly favoured Lord Bridge's approach in *McLoughlin* and appeared to implicitly dispose of any problems in relation to a requirement for temporal proximity of the plaintiff to the accident.

husband and child herself. It was contended by the defendant that the plaintiff's illness was not related to her being told of the accident, or coming upon its immediate aftermath. Rather it was alleged that it was caused by the grief and worry caused by the serious injuries sustained by her family, the constant visits to hospital and the strain imposed by caring for her injured family after their discharge. It was submitted that an illness caused in such circumstances did not come within the proximity rule and that public policy required that the plaintiff's claim be excluded. In *Jaensch* v *Coffey*[235] the High Court of Australia had noted:

> A plaintiff may recover only if the psychiatric illness is the result of physical injury inflicted on him by the defendant or if it is induced by shock. Psychiatric illness caused in other ways attracts no damages, though it is reasonably foreseeable that psychiatric illness might be a consequence of the defendant's carelessness.[236]

The Supreme Court refused to interfere with the trial judge's findings on causation, and Hamilton CJ dismissed the public policy argument in summary fashion, thus:

> There is no public policy that the plaintiff's claim, if substantiated, should be excluded.[237]

Nevertheless, it seems that even if policy will not disentitle a plaintiff from recovery in such a situation, the control device

---

[235] (1984) 155 CLR 549.

[236] (1984) 155 CLR 549 *per* Brennan J, cited with approval by Hamilton CJ in *Kelly* v *Hennessy* [1995] 3 IR 253 at 258, a view that is echoed in *Alcock* v *Chief Constable of the South Yorkshire Police* [1992] 1 AC 310 at 387 and 396 *per* Nolan LJ in the Court of Appeal and Lord Keith in the House of Lords, respectively. Also, "'Shock', in the context of this cause of action, involves the sudden appreciation by sight or sound of a horrifying event, which violently agitates the mind." *Alcock* v *Chief Constable of South Yorkshire Police* [1992] 1 AC 310 at 401 *per* Lord Ackner.

[237] [1995] 3 IR 253 at 262. In this, Hamilton CJ seemed reluctant to lay down general propositions, citing Lord Russell in *McLoughlin* v *O'Brian* [1983] AC 410 at 429.

requiring that non-physical injury must result from "shock" may well debar recovery. This must await determination on another occasion.

Insofar as failing to accept professional help to look after her injured family aggravated her condition, the Supreme Court refused to interfere with the trial judge's conclusion that, as this was consistent with her condition, it did not amount to a failure to mitigate her own loss. Accordingly, there was no finding of contributory negligence.

Although a claim for loss of parental consortium was rejected by the High Court in *Hosford* v *Murphy*,[238] such a head of claim is arguably capable of addressing the foreseeable mischief that arises in situations such as *Kelly* — as is a claim for loss of spousal consortium.[239]

BYSTANDERS NEED NOT APPLY

With the exception of *Bourhill* v *Young*[240] some element of proximity of relationship can be discerned in all of the cases — even if the plaintiffs failed to recover in *Alcock* v *Chief Constable of South Yorkshire Police*.[241] What of the bystander, the stranger who happens upon the scene but who is not a rescuer? Although such circumstances might be difficult to envisage, nevertheless, from *Hambrook* v *Stokes Brothers*[242] to *Alcock* v *Chief Constable of South Yorkshire Police*[243] the position of such a person has been considered *obiter*. Thus, in the latter case, Lord Ackner was not prepared to rule out a successful claim by a passer-by so shocked

---

[238] [1988] ILRM 300 (High Court).

[239] *Spaight* v *Dundon* [1961] IR 201; *McKinley* v *Minister for Defence* [1992] 2 IR 335 (and High Court, Unreported Judgment, 12 June 1997, Carney J); and *Coppinger* v *Waterford County Council* [1996] 2 ILRM 427. However, see McMahon and Binchy (1990), op. cit., pp. 312–13.

[240] [1943] AC 92.

[241] [1992] 1 AC 310.

[242] [1925] 1 KB 141.

[243] [1992] 1 AC 310, [1991] 3 WLR 1057, [1991] 4 All ER 907.

by a petrol tanker careering out of control into a school in session and bursting into flames.[244] However, for such a person to recover, the "the circumstances of a catastrophe occurring very close to him [would have to be] particularly horrific"[245] and the "shock" would have to be foreseeable to a person of "normal fortitude",[246] or to a "reasonably strong-nerved person".[247] But, in *McFarlane* v *EE Caledonia Limited*[248] Stuart-Smith LJ, for the unanimous Court of Appeal,[249] identified

> . . . great practical problems. . . . Reactions to horrific events are entirely subjective; who is to say that it is more horrific to see a petrol tanker advancing out of control on a school, when perhaps unknown to the plaintiff none of the children are in the building but are somewhere safe, than to see a child or group of children run over on a pedestrian crossing. There must be few scenes more harrowing than seeing women and children trapped at the window of a blazing building, yet many people gather to witness these calamities.[250]

This, however, while admitting of practical difficulties, seems to ignore the very real evidentiary hurdles that must be overcome before any such claim could succeed — irrespective of any policy barriers that might be interposed.[251] Also, it is reminiscent of the

---

[244] [1992] 1 AC 310 at 403.

[245] [1992] 1 AC 310 at 397 *per* Lord Keith.

[246] *Jaensch* v *Coffey* [1984] 54 ALR 417, 155 CLR 549.

[247] [1992] 1 AC 310 at 403 *per* Lord Ackner. This is merely a latter-day formulation of the concerns expressed in relation to a little old lady being frightened by the traffic at Charing Cross, see *Dulieu* v *White & Sons* [1901] 2 KB 669 at 684 *per* Phillimore J.

[248] [1994] 2 All ER 1 (CA) (the Piper Alpha disaster).

[249] McCowan and Ralph Gibson LJJ concurring.

[250] [1994] 2 All ER 1 at 14.

[251] The Court of Appeal, both as a matter of principle and policy, was not inclined to extend the duty of care to mere bystanders or witnesses of horrific events unless the proximity criteria set out in *Alcock* v *Chief Constable of*

argument — difficulty of proof — that was rejected as far back as Kennedy J's approach in *Dulieu* v *White & Sons*.[252] Insofar as this would exclude hypersensitive and psychological "eggshell skull" plaintiffs, with particular vulnerabilities which could cause them further harm, it has been regarded as a "desirable safeguard against unduly interfering with otherwise tolerable conduct".[253] This reflects no more than an underlying policy consideration that it would be unreasonably burdensome on human activity if, having endangered one person, a defendant was then "compelled to pay for the lacerated feelings of every other person disturbed by reason of it. . . ."[254] In effect, it is the floodgates argument — rejected in *McLoughlin* v *O'Brian*[255] — writ large.

South Yorkshire Police [1992] 1 AC 310, [1991] 3 WLR 1057, [1991] 4 All ER 907 were satisfied.

[252] [1901] 2 KB 669 at 681.

[253] Fleming (1987), op. cit., p. 148. In *McFarlane* v *EE Caledonia Limited* [1994] 2 All ER 1, the Court of Appeal was satisfied that there was no evidence to suggest that a person of "ordinary fortitude and phlegm" would have been reasonably foreseeably affected as the plaintiff had been and, indeed, that there was evidence to suggest that he was not such a person. In the circumstances, having failed on the proximity issue, he would also have failed on this element of the case.

[254] Prosser and Keeton (1984), op. cit., p. 366.

[255] [1983] AC 410.

Part Three

MATRIMONIAL REMEDIES

Chapter 9

PERSONALITY DISORDERS AND CIVIL ANNULMENT

People with personality disorder may come in contact with the law for a number of reasons, including criminal behaviour[1] and/or substance misuse,[2] associated with antisocial personality disorder. Since marital disharmony may also be associated with personality disorder,[3] it is pertinent to consider it in some detail, as requests for civil annulment may ensue.[4] Whilst all classes of abnormal personality may potentially lead to marital disharmony and applications for civil annulment, it is the paranoid and antisocial types which most frequently are associated with this issue.

Personality disorders are the most nebulous and under-researched syndromes in psychiatry. A number of reasons for this exist. Firstly, the diagnosis is difficult to make and indeed is often made on the basis of value judgements rather than on specific diagnostic criteria. Secondly, until recently the tools for quantifying

---

[1] Thus, the accused in *People (DPP)* v *Gallagher* [1991] ILRM 339 (SC), who was the applicant in *Gallagher* v *Director of the Central Mental Hospital & Others* (High Court, Unreported Judgment, 9 July 1996) (Divisional High Court), who was found "guilty but insane" of murder was suffering from a personality disorder involving "extreme egocentricity, extreme immaturity and impetuousness".

[2] See Chapter 10, pp. 223–36.

[3] Its manifestations could be sufficient for the granting of a decree of judicial separation pursuant to the provisions of section 1 of the Family Law Reform and Judicial Separation Act, 1989, or for the granting of a decree of divorce pursuant to Part II of the Family Law (Divorce) Act, 1996.

[4] However, a rigorously defined personality disorder — according to the schema set out in this chapter — rarely arises on the written judgments of the superior courts; see Chapter 11, pp. 260–2 and the footnotes thereto.

the severity of the disorder were limited and flawed.[5] Thirdly, with the exception of those with antisocial personality disorder, patients rarely presented with the primary problem arising from their personality; thus, personality disorder and antisocial personality became synonymous. These deficiencies have now been largely rectified with the advent of operational definitions.[6] Moreover, several new reliable schedules for assessing personality have emerged.[7] These developments have improved the rigour with which the diagnosis is made.

DEFINITION

The ICD-10 definition of personality disorders states that they are deeply ingrained maladaptive patterns of behaviour, generally recognisable by adolescence or earlier and continuing throughout most of adult life. They are referred to as axis 2 disorders.[8] The behaviour is abnormal, not just in response to stress, but also in the absence of stressful events, and is noticeable to others, even to those outside the person's immediate family. Where the behavioural abnormality is apparent only to those close to the patient, it is unlikely to be severe enough to meet the criteria for a disorder of personality. Since the distinction between normal and abnormal behaviour is arbitrary, the negative effect on others is the criterion that is applied. The categories of personality disorder used in ICD-10 are described below. "Immature" and "inadequate" are sometimes used in clinical practice, although these should be avoided since they are terms of opprobrium.[9]

---

[5] See below, pp. 213.

[6] See Chapter 3.

[7] See below, p. 215.

[8] See Chapter 3.

[9] See, for example, *C(P) (orse O'B)* v *O'B(D)* (High Court, Unreported Judgment, Carroll J, 2 October 1985) and *O'M(M)* v *O'C(B)* [1996] IR 208, reversing Kinlen J (High Court, Unreported Judgment, 5 May 1994). However, emotional or psychological "immaturity" — if severe — may ground a nullity decree; see Chapter 11, pp. 260–2. Whether or not a party to nullity proceedings falls within one of the relevant diagnostic categories is less

Short-term changes to personality can occur in a patient with depressive illness,[10] or indeed in any acute psychiatric illness. This change is a symptom of the illness rather than an enduring abnormality and resolves when the primary disorder is treated. These short-term changes are not regarded as personality disorders.

Persistent personality change can occur in schizophrenia[11] and is termed residual schizophrenia. The change is part of the process of schizophrenia and is not labelled as a personality disorder.

Permanent changes to personality following brain damage or trauma are not regarded as personality disorders.[12] Permanent alterations to personality following psychiatric illness (excluding schizophrenia) in those with no previous personality disorder are classified in the section of ICD-10 dealing with personality disorder. They are uncommon and the inclusion of personality change due to illness in this section of the classification is confusing and arguably unwarranted, since it is symptomatic of severe illness rather than conforming to what is ordinarily regarded as personality disorder.

Problems and Controversies

In spite of the development of operational definitions to improve the accuracy of diagnosis, little is known about the specific categories of personality disorder. In particular, there is little information on the course throughout the patient's life, the response to treatment and the association with other psychiatric illnesses.[13] It is best to regard the categories in common usage (e.g. anxious personality, obsessional personality, etc.) as no more than ways of

---

important than the court's assessment of the issues; see *C(P)* v *M(C) (orse (C))* (High Court, Unreported Judgment, Laffoy J, 11 January 1996).

[10] See Chapter 6, p. 99.

[11] See Chapter 13, p. 291, and Chapter 15, p. 337.

[12] See Chapter 6, p. 107.

[13] However, this does not affect the robustness of the evidence adduced by psychiatrists on behalf of parties in nullity proceedings; see Chapter 11, p. 261 and the cases cited in the footnotes therein.

identifying the predominant abnormal traits. In practice, there is considerable overlap between the categories and although court reports may mention specific disorders, there is no scientific justification for most of the individual categories. The exception is the antisocial personality disorder, which has been demonstrated to be a valid category, and use of this term is therefore justified. Borderline personality has also been subject to much investigation but interpretation about the validity of this category is divided.

Given the uncertainties about the existence of specific categories, some suggest that these labels be abandoned and instead a profile on each patient be provided, irrespective of the presence or absence of a personality disorder — this is known as the dimensional approach. Whilst this may be intuitively appealing, it has not found widespread clinical support, since this system would not identify those with personality disorders and communication about individual patients would be cumbersome. Consider a description of a patient as having a high score on the anxiety dimension, a low impulsivity score and a low self-esteem score. When compared with a simple statement that the patient has an anxious personality disorder, the appeal of the latter, categorical approach is obvious, notwithstanding its limitations.

The importance of this debate for the lawyer lies in the fact that many of the personality inventories in common use measure dimensions, not categories, and when used in court, unless properly understood and interpreted, can be credited with providing more information than is actually the case. The categorical and dimensional approaches represent very different ways of conceptualising patients and their personalities and a proper understanding of the theoretical framework being used by the professional medical witnesses is essential if muddle and obfuscation is not to manifest itself during examination and cross-examination. In clinical practice, the use of categories is commonplace, whilst the instruments commonly used by psychologists in assessing personality adopt a dimensional approach.

CATEGORIES OF PERSONALITY DISORDER

The number of categories recognised in clinical practice has increased recently and they are listed in Table 9.1. Some differences exist between ICD-10 and DSM-IV.[14] Each will be described below.

TABLE 9.1: CATEGORIES OF PERSONALITY DISORDER IN ICD-10 AND DSM-IV

ICD-10	DSM-IV
Paranoid	Paranoid
Schizoid	Schizoid
No equivalent	Schizotypal
Anankastic/obsessional	Anankastic/obsessional
Histrionic	Histrionic
Dependent	Dependent
Antisocial	Antisocial
No equivalent	Narcissistic
Anxious/avoidant	Anxious/avoidant
Impulsive/borderline	Impulsive/borderline

Antisocial Personality Disorder

This is the most extensively researched category and has been shown to manifest itself in early adolescence and sometimes even in childhood. The features are truancy, suspension from school, cruelty to animals, leading later to aggressive behaviour, lack of guilt, failure to plan ahead and work-related problems, often leading to dismissal. Deliberate self-harm may be a feature in some patients, as may alcohol abuse or dependence. Difficulties with the law may also arise. Because of their callousness, such people do not form loving relationships and may have many short-

---

[14] See, for example, *C(P)* v *M(C) (orse (C))* (High Court, Unreported Judgment, Laffoy J, 11 January 1996).

term liaisons.[15] There is some evidence that these features attenuate with increasing age.

Anankastic or Obsessional Personality Disorder

This disorder may be under-diagnosed, since many of the features are deemed socially desirable. However, it is the presence of these to excess that distinguishes the responsible, mature person from the personality disordered patient. The salient feature of these people is their rigidity and attention to detail. They set themselves high standards and failure to achieve these objectives leads to subjective distress. The standards are not necessarily of major import, such as professional success, but rather focus on minutiae such as dress, time-tabling and organisation. Sufferers will describe being hide-bound by routine and any deviation from this leads to anxiety and feelings of insecurity. Because of their rigidity, they are difficult to live and work with. Others notice their constant desire for order and predictability and describe them as unimaginative and lacking spontaneity. There was a view in the older psychiatric literature that obsessional personality was associated with depressive illness. This has since been shown to be erroneous. The relationship to obsessive-compulsive disorder[16] (OCD) is more complex — those who develop OCD have a higher than chance frequency of obsessional personality disorder. Conversely, the majority of those with obsessional personality do not develop OCD. These conditions should not be confused.[17]

Anxious or Avoidant Personality Disorder

This is characterised by persistent self-consciousness, shyness and fear of rejection. Risks are exaggerated and so there is avoidance of many day-to-day situations. The sufferer will describe having

---

[15] This appears to be the appropriate category into which the respondent husband fell in *M(A)* v *M(T)* (High Court, Unreported Judgment, O'Hanlon J, 11 February 1993). See also *W(C)* v *C* [1989] IR 696 (Barron J).

[16] As was alleged in *T(S)* v *J(B) (orse T(B))* (High Court, Unreported Judgment, O'Hanlon J, 2 September 1993) (nullity decree refused).

[17] See Chapter 13, pp. 294–6.

few friends in spite of a desire to form relationships. It is difficult to distinguish this disorder from social phobia or from chronic generalised anxiety disorder. It is one of the newest categories to be introduced into psychiatric classification and has yet to prove its clinical and heuristic value.[18]

Histrionic or Hysterical Personality Disorder

This is one of the most abused and inappropriately used categories of personality disorder.[19] Too often, it is a term of opprobrium used to describe women who are perceived to be difficult and demanding. The core features of histrionic personality disorder are self-dramatisation and self-centredness. The mood is shallow and labile, being subject to rapid changes in response to minor environmental changes. Sexual provocativeness and theatricality, along with an insatiable need for approval and praise, make sustaining a relationship difficult. There was an erroneous belief that such personalities were at an increased risk of developing hysteria.[20] This disorder should not be confused with hysteria.

Dependent Personality Disorder

The dependent personality is characterised by excessive dependence on others, inability to make decisions, inability to accept responsibility, submissive behaviour, such that the sufferer is taken advantage of, and a constant fear of rejection or abandonment. There is considerable overlap clinically with the anxious personality.[21] This disorder subsumes the "inadequate" personality, a term now abandoned because of its judgmental and pejorative connotations.

---

[18] The authors have never made this diagnosis in any patient.

[19] D.J. Thompson and D. Goldberg (1987), "Hysterical Personality Disorder: the Process of Diagnosis in Clinical and Experimental Settings", *British Journal of Psychiatry*, Vol. 150, pp. 241–5.

[20] See Chapter 6, p. 96.

[21] See above, p. 206.

Impulsive or Borderline Personality Disorder

Although extensively investigated, especially in the United States, there is still disagreement on the existence of this disorder. The features include a pattern of intense but unstable personal relationships, with initial idealisation of the partner followed by feelings of rejection. Gender identity problems and body image distortions leading to eating disorders also occur and a variety of mood changes are described including depression, anger, chronic boredom and emptiness. Suicidal threats and repeated episodes of deliberate self-harm are frequent. Some patients have brief psychotic episodes. Many patients so diagnosed have a history of sexual abuse, although the exact role the abuse plays in the genesis of the disorder is uncertain. However, since borderline personality is described almost exclusively in young women, is rare in those over the age of 40 and seems to overlap with other personality disorders, particularly the antisocial and histrionic categories, many do not subscribe to its existence and therefore do not make the diagnosis. This may lead to disagreement between professional medical witnesses in the courtroom setting.

Schizoid Personality Disorder

The patient with a schizoid personality disorder is characterised by extreme aloofness, a desire to remain apart from other people and disinterest in relationships. In consequence, such people appear cold and even callous, since they are unable to sympathise with the suffering of other people. The features of aloofness and failure to form relationships seen in the schizoid patient must be contrasted with the shyness of the anxious personality. In the former, there is no desire to become close to others, whilst in the latter there is an intense desire to make relationships but it is timidity which prevents this. The older literature suggested an association between schizoid personality disorder and schizophrenia. This now appears to be erroneous and the schizoid features found in those with schizophrenia are in fact early symptoms of the disease rather than pre-morbid personality traits.[22]

Paranoid Personality Disorder

Excessive litigiousness, suspiciousness and a tendency to bear grudges are the hallmarks of this disorder. The patient is sensitive to setbacks and rebuffs and conspiracy will be found in innocent events. In relationships, such people may be possessive and jealous. In the early stages of a relationship, this is often accepted as flattery, concern and love but major marital difficulties arise when the sufferer requires constant reassurance of fidelity. The sufferer can be temporarily reassured about these uncertainties, only for the doubting to return rapidly. Such marriages are often violent and separation is indicated to prevent physical harm to the spouse, as this disorder is untreatable. There is an association with alcohol abuse and with paranoid psychosis in many patients.[23] This is the disorder most commonly associated with annulment.

Schizotypal Personality Disorder

This is not regarded as a personality disorder in ICD-10 but is held to be a variant of schizophrenia and is treated as such with major tranquillisers.[24] In DSM-IV, however, it is regarded as a personality disorder characterised by eccentricity, odd speech and mannerisms leading to difficulties relating to others at even a most basic conversational level.

Narcissistic Personality Disorder

This category is included in DSM-IV only. Such patients would be diagnosed under ICD-10 as having a histrionic personality

---

[22] See Chapter 15, p. 341.

[23] See Chapter 10, p. 223 and *K(P)* v *N(MB) (orse K)* (Supreme Court, Unreported Judgment, 3 April 1995, affirming High Court, Unreported Judgment, Costello J, 27 November 1992).

[24] See Chapter 15, p. 341.

disorder. The hallmarks of the disorder are self-importance, the need for admiration and emotional coldness, with difficulties empathising with others.

Passive-Aggressive Personality Disorder

This term is still sometimes used in clinical practice, although it is not recognised by ICD-10 and is only included in the appendix of DSM-IV for further investigation.[25] One of the problems with this category is that the diagnosis is made not on the basis of behaviours or traits but on inference and the interpretation that is made in relation to some behaviour patterns. At its core is passive resistance, exemplified by sulking, procrastination, obstruction and slowness in relation to unwelcome requests.

CAUSATION OF PERSONALITY DISORDERS

Because of the paucity of research in this area, theories of causation are necessarily vague and unsatisfactory. Freud held that personality development was related to the very early relationship between child and mother. He did not, however, postulate a cause for personality disorder, rather a charting of personality development. Bowlby, in describing attachment theory, held that personality had its roots in the early years of life[26] and in particular believed that the bond with the mother paved the way for the security that was necessary to the developing child. He did not speculate on the specific causes of personality disorder.

---

[25] Disorders are relegated to the appendix when there is controversy about the utility of a specific disorder. In subsequent editions of DSM-IV, the category will either achieve full recognition or be excluded.

[26] However, background is sometimes advanced as an explanation for the disorder from which a party to nullity proceedings is allegedly suffering; see, for example, *W(K)* v *W(M)* (High Court, Unreported Judgment, Lynch J, 19 July 1994); and *T(S)* v *J(B) (orse T(B))* (High Court, Unreported Judgment, O'Hanlon J, 2 September 1993), where decrees were refused.

Is There a Genetic Basis for Personality Disorder?

Much of the research into the genetics of personality has focused on the inheritance of individual traits rather than the inheritance of the categories of disorder. The genetic factors in antisocial personality have been measured by studying the single trait of criminality, whilst the genetic contribution to the anxious personality has been measured using social avoidance as the manifestation of the disorder. In view of this narrowness of investigation, the findings are limited. In order to demonstrate the inheritance of personality disorders, clear differences should emerge on examining both monozygotic (MZ) (identical) and dizygotic (DZ) (non-identical) twins. An important study in 1980[27] identified patients who themselves were twins with a diagnosis of personality disorder. A structured measure of personality[28] was then administered to both the patients and their co-twins. No MZ/DZ differences were demonstrated for the individual categories, but traits were clearly different between both groups of twins. This suggests that it is the underlying personality dimension that is genetically determined and that other influences impinge upon the template to cause personality disorder. Some researchers are also attempting to relate the genetic vulnerability to personality disorder to abnormal neurotransmitter activity governing impulse control, mood stability, perception and anxiety. In particular, the role of serotonin in governing impulse control is the focus of continuing research.

What are the Environmental Influences Leading to Personality Disorder?

Psychological Risk Factors

Psychological risk factors which might impinge upon the inherent personality structure include abnormal social learning, which

---

[27] S. Torgersen (1980), "The Oral, Obsessive and Hysterical Personality Syndromes: a Study of Heredity and Environmental Factors by Means of the Twin Method", *Archives of General Psychiatry*, Vol. 37, pp. 1272–7.

[28] See Chapter 4, pp. 58–63, and pp. 215–18 below.

plays an important part in shaping behaviour in the young child. For example, a child with an extrovert temperament reared in a violent family may later develop violent tendencies but a shy child in the same environment might become timid. By contrast, over-protective parenting may lead to later dependent patterns. Negative childhood experiences, especially repeated trauma of a physical or sexual nature, have been implicated especially in borderline personality disorder. However, these risk factors are non-specific and are present in many other psychiatric disorders and indeed may also be absent in many with a diagnosis of personality disorder. The aetiological significance of childhood abuse therefore remains unclear.[29] Similar limitations are apparent in relation to the effects of separation from or loss of parents in childhood, although both seem to influence later self-esteem.[30]

Social Risk Factors

Social risk factors become apparent when studies of the prevalence of personality disorder show changes over time. In particular, there is evidence that antisocial personality disorder is increasing, as is borderline personality. The nature of these social risk factors are speculative but relate to changes in "social integration" as manifested by marital breakdown, poverty, secularisation, absence of a "sense of community", and mobility. Waning social integration fails to provide social containment for those with abnormal traits. The individuals who function during periods of social stability, even at a minimal level, become malfunctional when their society undergoes rapid social change.[31]

---

[29] See, for example, the allegations raised in *B(A)* v *B(E)* [1997] 1 IR 305 (Budd J). See also *K(D)* v *H(T)* (High Court, Unreported Judgment, O'Higgins J, 25 February 1998).

[30] See, for example, the allegations raised in *W(K)* v *W(M)* (High Court, Unreported Judgment, Lynch J, 19 July 1994); and *T(S)* v *J(B) (orse T(B))* (High Court, Unreported Judgment, O'Hanlon J, 2 September 1993).

[31] T. Millon (1993), "Borderline Personality Disorder: A Psychosocial Epidemic", in J. Paris (ed.), *Borderline Personality Disorder*, Washington, DC: American Psychiatric Press. See also Chapter 6, p. 109, in relation to suicide.

This complex bio-psycho-social model, although speculative at present, is probably the most parsimonious explanation for the cause of personality disorders.[32] Moreover, it fits with the current empirical evidence, although, as the tentacles of biology spread, alternative organic models may emerge. What is apparent at present is that no single cause is likely to be found to explain the aetiology of personality disorder, and evidence suggesting otherwise must be regarded as simplistic.

THE CLINICAL ASSESSMENT OF PERSONALITY

Methods

The most common method of assessing personality is by standard clinical interview, in which questions are asked about pre-morbid functioning and behaviour. Ideally, collateral information is sought from an informant who has long-standing knowledge of the patient, to clarify, refute or confirm the history.[33] On the basis of the abnormal traits described and the extent to which the patient meets the criteria for an ICD-10 or DSM-IV diagnosis of personality disorder, the patient will be diagnosed as having a normal personality or a personality disorder of specific type. DSM-IV and ICD-10 allow for the diagnosis of more than one personality disorder concurrently in the patient. Where a discrepancy exists between the information obtained from patient and informant, a clinical decision must be made as to which constitutes the more reliable source. Generally, informants are regarded as more reliable, particularly if the subject is ill at the time of interview.

---

[32] J. Paris (1993), "Personality Disorders: A Biopsychosocial Model", *Journal of Personality Disorders*, Vol. 7, No. 3, pp. 255–64.

[33] In the context of any marital proceedings, caution must be exercised in relying on a collateral history obtained from one spouse in respect of the other. See Chapter 18, p. 458, and the footnotes thereto, in relation to proceedings under the Mental Treatment Act, 1945, s. 260.

Problems

Two problem areas present themselves when making a clinical assessment of personality: the first set of difficulties is patient-related, the second clinician-related.

Patient-related

The greatest problem in making this assessment lies in the likelihood that the patient has an axis 1 diagnosis[34] such as depressive illness, distorting the patient's view of pre-illness traits and behaviours. A related difficulty is the problem of insight, since many, even without illness, do not have a detached view of their personality and may fail to identify weaknesses or conversely underplay attributes. A third problem stems from the chance of a patient confusing long-standing traits with current symptoms. For example, a patient who has a depressive illness may describe the accompanying anxiety as a personality attribute rather than as a symptom. In making the assessment, the distinction between traits and symptoms must be clarified if the final assessment is to be accurate.

Clinician-related

The second aspect to assessing personality in the clinical setting is related to the clinician and his acumen as well as bias. Studies conducted in the 1970s suggest that the overall agreement for psychiatrists when making the diagnosis of personality disorder was low and of the order of 30 per cent. This, however, has improved dramatically due to the application of strict criteria, such as those incorporated in DSM-IV or ICD-10. Another source of poor reliability is the bias of psychiatrists who themselves have been shown to make the diagnosis of personality disorder on insufficient grounds[35] and to make judgements about personality on

---

[34] See Chapters 3 and 4.

[35] D.J. Thompson and D. Goldberg (1987), "Hysterical Personality Disorder. The Process of Diagnosis in Clinical and Experimental Settings", *British Journal of Psychiatry*, Vol. 150, pp. 241–5.

the basis of information gleaned during episodes of illness only. Moreover, there is sometimes a failure to gather information from sources other than the patient, leading to inaccurate patient profiles.[36] This is important since informants achieve a higher reliability than do subjects. In the context of court, these issues must be borne in mind when assessing the value of information about personality contained in the court report and also in cross-examination.

There is no advantage to using a personality schedule to assess personality in preference to the properly conducted clinical interview, since interview schedules themselves have pitfalls.

PSYCHOMETRIC ASSESSMENT OF PERSONALITY

This refers to the assessment of personality using interview schedules and questionnaires.[37]

Methods

A more structured approach than the clinical assessment of personality involves the use of specifically designed interview schedules to make the assessment. By prescribing the content as well as the style of questions, it is believed that a more reliable and valid assessment is made. However, the use of a schedule is no guarantee of reliability and indeed its use may lull the unwary into over-generalisations. These issues will be discussed in greater detail below.

Problems

There is a belief articulated by popular magazines that the questionnaires provide a truer insight into the patient's personality than does simple clinical inquiry. This view is largely mistaken, since the information gathered by such a method is only as

---

[36] See, for example, the arguments set out in the judgment in *T(S)* v *J(B) (orse T(B))* (High Court, Unreported Judgment, O'Hanlon J, 2 September 1993).

[37] See also Chapter 4, p. 58.

accurate and reliable as its source. The use of structured schedules does, however, avoid the pitfalls alluded to above in relation to interviewer bias.

Firstly, one of the difficulties in using schedules is that some of those in common use do not actually measure personality disorder but instead provide a dimensional profile of the patient's personality. In the judicial context, this can be confusing and misleading. This is a limitation in relation to the MMPI and the EPI,[38] both of which are still in use. Secondly, some schedules, including the MMPI and the EPI, are contaminated by the mental state of the patient. The person who is depressed, anxious or psychotic may accentuate their abnormal traits and conversely the person with antisocial or impulsive personality disorder may minimise their negative features in favour of social desirability. Unless a specific distinction is made between state and trait features in the schedule, many patients will describe as traits, symptoms which are state-dependent. Thirdly, there is a belief that personality schedules can predict and diagnose behaviours such as sexual abuse and serious violence. The use of personality schedules for such purposes is untenable, since they were not designed for this (the development of scales which have adequate predictive validity is in its infancy) and indeed criticism has been meted out to one specific schedule, the MMPI, in this regard. Fourthly, two categories of schedules are available — the first is a self-report questionnaire which the subject completes himself, the second is a detailed schedule in which the questions are prescribed and the interview is administered by an interviewer trained in that schedule's usage. The former is convenient but generates excessively high prevalence rates for personality disorder. The latter is time-consuming and requires a high degree of skill.[39]

---

[38] See p. 217.

[39] For a comprehensive guide to personality assessment using clinical methods as well as structured interview (psychometric) schedules, see P.R. Casey (1997), "Clinical Assessment of Personality", *Advances in Psychiatric Treatment*, Vol. 3, pp. 182–7.

Schedules in Common Use

The schedules most commonly used in proceedings before the courts in Britain and Ireland are the Eysenck Personality Inventory (EPI)[40] and the Minnesota Multiphasic Personality Inventory (MMPI).[41] There has been a proliferation of instruments to assess personality in recent years, but their use is largely confined to research.

The Eysenck Personality Inventory (EPI) is a questionnaire comprising 108 questions, which provides a dimensional profile of the patient using the dimensions neuroticism, psychoticism and extroversion. The scores obtained bear little relationship to the personality disorders seen in practice, although attempts have been made to marry the two. The response to questions has been shown to be heavily distorted by the current mental state of the patient and the scores obtained are likely to change with repeated use.[42]

The Minnesota Multiphasic Personality Inventory (MMPI) is a questionnaire of 566 questions in which replies are based on a forced choice "yes/no" basis. It was developed to distinguish between different clinical groups. It has since been used inappropriately in vocational selection and even to identify sexual abusers, the latter drawing serious criticism.[43] Such uses are totally inappropriate, since the schedule has not been designed for these purposes. Moreover, when used in the legal setting, it must be remembered that, like the EPI, the MMPI does not provide a measure of personality disorder but rather uses a dimensional

[40] H.J. Eysenck and S.B.G. Eysenck (1964), *Manual of the Eysenck Personality Inventory*, London: University of London Press.

[41] S.R. Hathaway and J.C. McKinley (1940), "A Multiphasic Personality Schedule (Minnesota): 1. Construction of the Schedule", *Journal of Psychology*, Vol. 10, pp. 249–54.

[42] R.E. Kendell and W.J. DiScipio (1968), "Eysenck Personality Inventory Scores of Patients with Depressive Illness", *British Journal of Psychiatry*, Vol. 114, pp. 767–70.

[43] S.M. Levin and L. Stava (1987), "Personality Characteristics of Sex Offenders: a Review", *Archives of Sexual Behaviour*, Vol. 16, No. 1, pp. 57–79.

approach as described earlier. In addition, it is unstable due to the contaminating effects of mood, anxiety, etc.

An indirect approach to personality assessment involves the use of "projective tests" such as the Rorschach test in which the patient is presented with a number of inkblots and asked to describe the image that is conveyed. These responses are then interpreted by a person trained in its use. This test suffers from the major flaw of relying on individual interpretation without any standardisation. Since this schedule does not have any normative data and since the patient response may be contaminated by other disorders such as schizophrenia, it cannot be considered a reliable measure of personality.

The Personality Assessment Schedule[44] is an interview which must be administered by a trained interviewer. It assesses 24 personality traits using information from both the subject and an informant. It generates both dimensional measures for each subject as well as giving an ICD or DSM diagnosis when personality disorder is present. It takes about 30 minutes each for the subject and informant to complete. Its use has mainly been in research.

HOW DOES PERSONALITY DISORDER LEAD TO NULLITY?

Most people with personality disorders can sustain a marriage, although the spouse may describe problems within the relationship. Indeed at times the presence of a personality disorder in one may complement a personality disorder in the other partner. For example, a woman with an obsessional personality disorder may be able to form a successful relationship with a man who has a dependent personality disorder, since the abnormal traits found in the obsessional (e.g. orderliness, control, etc.) may be the mirror of those found in the dependent partner (e.g. indecisiveness, an excessive need for security). Conversely, such a woman married to an antisocial partner would almost certainly be unable to tolerate the chaos, unpredictability and lack of scruple found in such a

---

[44] P. Tyrer and J. Alexander (1979), "Classification of Personality Disorders", *British Journal of Psychiatry*, Vol. 135, pp. 163–7.

person. Thus, it is the interaction between partners rather than the presence of personality disorder *per se* which constitute the grounds for voiding the marriage.[45]

Since civil annulment is concerned with the capacity of the individual not alone to give full and free consent, but also to undertake the normal responsibilities of married life, it is apparent that some categories are more likely to fail in this regard than others.[46] For example, the person with a dependent personality disorder may be easily coerced by a partner who is antisocial or assertive. However, a relationship with a similarly dependent person may not be associated with coercion, once again underpinning the importance of context rather than of personality disorder *per se*. The category most likely to have difficulties with responsibility in marriage is the antisocial personality or the person with borderline personality disorder, where impulse control is poor and, especially in the latter, there is a tendency initially to idealise and then to reject those with whom one has relationships. Understanding the obligations of marriage may also be impaired in these groups.

---

[45] In this regard, based on the analogy with impotence, this is a species of relational incapacity *quoad hunc quoad hanc*. See Chapter 11, p. 256 and for example (in the context of paranoid schizophrenia), *C(D) (orse W(D)) v W(D)* [1987] ILRM 58. See also *S v K* (High Court, Unreported Judgment, Denham J, 2 July 1992); *C(P) v C(V)* [1990] 2 IR 91 (O'Hanlon J); *T(R) v P(V) (orse T(V))* (High Court, Unreported Judgment, Lardner J, 30 July 1989); *T(K) v T(D)* (Supreme Court, Unreported Judgment, 12 October 1995) affirming refusal of the High Court (Murphy J) to grant a decree of nullity reported at [1992] 2 IR 11; and *C(P) v C(V)* [1990] 2 IR 91.

[46] See, for example, *O'M(M) v O'C(B)* [1996] IR 208 (SC), reversing the refusal of the High Court (High Court, Unreported Judgment, Kinlen J, 5 May 1994) to grant a decree of nullity on the ground that the husband had not disclosed that he had received treatment from a psychiatrist prior to his marriage for an unspecified disorder. However, as to whether the disorder, however it is characterised, goes to relational incapacity or duress, may be difficult to determine; see *O'R v B* [1995] ILRM 57 (HC) (Kinlen J). See also *W v P* (High Court, Unreported Judgment, Barrington J, 7 June 1984).

TREATMENT

When considering the likely effects of personality disorder on the long-term relationship and in the context of sentencing for crime,[47] it is pertinent to inquire if personality disorders can be treated.[48] At present, the treatability of personality disorders is seriously in doubt, at least within the limitations of the health service and on the basis of current research. Although there are volumes written on the psychoanalysis of those with borderline personality disorder and on the effectiveness of "therapeutic communities" for repeated offenders, there is no clear evidence from controlled trials of such interventions that they are effective. Indeed most of the evidence derives from individual case reports or from using very small sample sizes. Moreover, since psychoanalysis is outside the bounds of everyday clinical practice, both in terms of cost and time, such claims for success must be greeted with the utmost caution. Some recent investigation suggests that cognitive therapy may be helpful in the treatment of personality disorders[49] and this is currently being evaluated scientifically.

It is pertinent to realise that those who suffer from dual axis 1 and axis 2 diagnoses (e.g. depressive illness and personality disorder)[50] are less responsive to treatment, utilise the psychiatric services more and probably have a poorer long-term prognosis than their counterparts who suffer only from a single axis diagnosis (e.g. depressive illness).

---

[47] See, for example, *Gallagher* v *Director of the Central Mental Hospital & Others* (High Court, Unreported Judgment, 9 July 1996) (Divisional High Court).

[48] In this regard, *C(S)* v *D(P) (orse C(P))* (High Court, Unreported Judgment, McCracken J, 14 March 1996) should be noted; see Chapter 11, p. 263.

[49] A.T. Beck, A. Freeman et al. (1992), *Cognitive Therapy for Personality Disorders*, New York: Guildford Press.

[50] As appears might have been the case in *M(C)* v *L(E) (orse M(E))* (High Court, Unreported Judgment, Barr J, 27 July 1994), although the evidence as recited is insufficient to make such an assertion definitively.

SUMMARY

Personality disorder is difficult to assess and the results may be unreliable as a result of contamination from symptoms. Clinical and psychometric methods are used. The categories of personality disorder, whilst having intuitive appeal, have not been validated. It is the interaction between personality disorder in one partner and the personality of the spouse that may lead to nullity, rather than presence of a personality disorder *per se*.

Chapter 10

OTHER DISORDERS AND CIVIL ANNULMENT

In theory, any disorder can lead to marital difficulties and subsequent breakdown. However, these disorders are only occasionally implicated in, and successfully ground, applications for decrees of nullity. Of particular importance is alcohol misuse and its associated psychiatric and social consequences.

ALCOHOL MISUSE AND DEPENDENCE[1]

Alcohol dependence refers to physical dependence on alcohol with withdrawal symptoms on discontinuing and is a more severe form of alcohol misuse, the descriptive term for those who abuse alcohol without exhibiting withdrawal symptoms. Many who abuse alcohol do not wish to be called alcoholic, a term which conjures up an image of skid-row. In this chapter, the term alcoholic will be

---

[1] Although alcohol misuse and dependence may contribute to marital disharmony and breakdown, such that one or more grounds for the granting of a decree of judicial separation, set out in section 1 of the Family Law Reform and Judicial Separation Act, 1989, or for the granting of a decree of divorce pursuant to Part II of the Family Law (Divorce) Act, 1996, may be established, its role in nullity must be regarded as relatively minor. Nevertheless, the issue did arise for consideration in *McG(R)* v *K(N)* (High Court, Unreported Judgment, Morris J, 23 May 1995) reported as *RMcG* v *KMcG* [1995] 3 Fam LJ. Here, the petitioner husband had a long pre- and post-marital history of alcohol abuse and dependence, for which he had received in-patient hospital treatment. It was suggested that he had been intoxicated at the time of the marriage ceremony and may have suffered an alcohol "blackout" in respect of it. However, on the evidence, the trial judge refused to grant a decree of nullity on this ground. Such incapacity would go to the issue of consent and, if established, render a marriage void. See also, for example, *Sullivan* v *Sullivan* (1818) 161 ER 728.

reserved for the person who is chemically dependent on alcohol and who therefore displays withdrawal symptoms.

Prevalence

The exact frequency of alcohol abuse in the general population is almost impossible to assess, since its definition changes. Some workers investigate the physical consequences only, others include social problems also and others measure the amounts consumed. The arguments relating to each are frequently articulated in the psychiatric literature.

Admissions to psychiatric hospitals in Ireland for alcohol abuse constitute almost 25 per cent of all acute admissions,[2] by comparison with only 10 per cent in England and Wales. This is almost certainly not due to a higher prevalence in Ireland but to differing admission policies.

Psychological Complications

Depression

Alcohol abuse is associated with feelings of gloom, despondency and dysphoria. The relationship between alcohol abuse and depressed mood is a complex one. The mood change tends to be transient and a direct consequence of the central effects of alcohol. In addition, many heavy drinkers have family, financial and marital problems making them unhappy. This may be mistaken for depressive illness. Depressive illness occurs in less than 10 per cent[3] and the diagnosis cannot be made with certainty until the patient is alcohol-free. Antidepressants are only effective in the latter group and may be dangerous in those who are depressed due to the direct effects of alcohol itself, since interactions with alcohol may occur. In general, women are more prone to depressive illness

---

[2] R. Moran and D. Walsh (1992), "Activities of Irish Psychiatric Hospitals and Units 1991", Dublin: Health Research Board.

[3] S.A. Brown and M.A. Schuckit (1988), "Changes in Depression among Abstinent Alcoholics", *Journal of Studies in Alcohol*, Vol. 49, pp. 412–17.

following detoxification than are men and in some a pre-existing depressive disorder is often present.

Anxiety Disorders

Panic attacks frequently occur during periods of relative abstinence. These are overwhelming feelings of fear associated with palpitations, sweating, dizziness and are of acute onset, lasting for variable periods of time. They usually disappear or subside when total abstinence has been established. However, the pathological fear of social encounters such as talking with others or eating in public, termed social phobia, often manifests itself following detoxification and is usually a manifestation of a pre-existing social phobia for which alcohol may have been used to bring about relief.

Other Drug Abuse

Many alcoholics abuse other drugs in addition to alcohol; in particular benzodiazepine tranquillisers or chlormethiazole, both prescribed to relieve withdrawal symptoms, are common drugs of abuse following detoxification. It is advisable to be circumspect when prescribing to alcoholics and medication such as these should never be prescribed on a long-term basis.

Marital and Sexual Problems

These are a common accompaniment to alcohol abuse. The violence, poverty and unemployment which are associated with alcohol misuse are common sources of conflict. Unless the patient becomes abstinent, there is little point in pursuing marital therapy, since any attempts at resolving the conflicts will be sabotaged during periods of drinking. Sexual difficulties, especially impotence, are common complications and alcohol increases the desire but reduces the ability to perform sexually. Unless abstinence from alcohol is achieved, treatment of the sexual problem is doomed to failure.

Pathological Jealousy and Paranoid Psychosis

These are common complications of alcohol misuse but can occasionally occur in those who are abstinent.[4] Of particular importance is pathological jealousy (the Othello Syndrome). In this condition, the sufferer believes his spouse is indulging in illicit affairs and will seek to prove this by examining clothing, letters, etc. When confronted by the distress caused to the partner by these allegations, the falsity of the beliefs will be accepted, although this insight is only short-lived and further allegations follow.[5] A more extreme form, called paranoid psychosis,[6] is based on the absolute belief that infidelity is occurring and is not amenable to reasoned argument to the contrary. Impotence, if present, compounds the jealousy. Those with paranoid psychosis may elude diagnosis for a long time, since the delusions are circumscribed

---

[4] See Chapter 13, pp. 292–3.

[5] Although this may be a problem during marriage, there are no written judgments of the Superior Courts in nullity applications where the issue has specifically arisen.

[6] A group of disorders, termed persistent delusional disorders, have encapsulated delusions, but no hallucinations or personality deterioration. Thus, for example, in *K(P)* v *N(MB) (orse K)* (High Court, Unreported Judgment, Costello J, 27 November 1992, affirmed Supreme Court, Unreported Judgment, 3 April 1995), a decree of nullity was granted on the basis of the respondent wife's paranoid psychosis that appeared to focus only on her husband and his mother and brothers. Although the first sign was only manifested on the honeymoon, the court was satisfied, on the basis of the psychiatrists' evidence, that the condition was likely to have been present at the time of the marriage and that the wife's capacity to sustain a normal marital relationship was impaired. The non-medical evidence from the wife's work colleagues was to the effect that she was quite normal outwardly. Her personality and general capacities appeared otherwise fairly intact. On appeal, the Supreme Court was satisfied that the High Court judge was entitled to rely on and accept the evidence of the psychiatrists in respect of the wife's condition and refused her appeal against the declaration of nullity. More detail as to the wife's paranoia does not appear on the face of the judgment.

However, included also in this group is paranoid psychosis, with delusions of infidelity, of persecution or of reference (where the patient believes that the television, radio, etc., is referring specifically to him). Alternatively, the patient may think that others believe he emits a smell. Also included is monosymptomatic hypochondriacal psychosis, a psychotic disorder in which the patient holds the conviction that his body is misshapen or dysfunctional, leading often to cosmetic surgery with which the patient is dissatisfied.

and the listener may fail to grasp the falsity of the allegations initially. The fact that other aspects of behaviour and functioning are intact and only one pocket of thinking is affected contributes to this delay.[7] Both of these disorders are frequently associated with paranoid pre-morbid personality.[8]

Unfortunately, the history obtained from the spouse confirms the long-standing nature of the jealousy. Many describe initially being flattered by the possessiveness only to become increasingly bewildered by behaviour such as allegations of infidelity, escalating intrusiveness leading to the hiring of private detectives, searching of underwear and increasing fear of violence. Attempts at reassurance and at allaying the jealousy are commonplace initially, only to be met with temporary acceptance and finally total disbelief.

While paranoid psychosis sometimes responds to major tranquillisers, paranoid personality disorder and pathological jealousy are largely untreatable. Some improvement may, however, be noticed when alcohol is discontinued. Since violence may occur as a result of the beliefs about infidelity, and in view of the intractability of the disorders in most sufferers, separation is frequently advised.

Delirium Tremens[9]

This is the acute confusional state which occurs during withdrawal from alcohol. It lasts up to four days and is accompanied by agitation, visual hallucinations and intense fear. Mortality is high due to the chemical (electrolyte) disturbances which accompany the condition. Emergency treatment with major tranquillisers, correction of the electrolyte imbalance and intravenous

---

[7] As in *K(P)* v *N(MB)* *(orse K)* (High Court, Unreported Judgment, Costello J, 27 November 1992, affirmed Supreme Court, Unreported Judgment, 3 April 1995), above.

[8] See Chapter 3, p. 45.

[9] Not to be confused with acute alcohol intoxication. See, for example, *Legeyt* v *O'Brien* (1834) Milw Rep 325; the allegation that the husband was suffering from *delirium tremens* at the time of the marriage failed on the evidence.

vitamin supplements are essential. This latter is to prevent the development of Korsakoff's psychosis (see below).

Brain Damage

Brain damage is a common complication of alcohol dependence.[10] The most exotic is termed the amnestic syndrome or Korsakoff's psychosis, and is caused by thiamine (vitamin B1) deficiency. Korsakoff's psychosis is associated with a profound impairment of recent memory, disorientation in time, apathy and confabulation. It may be preceded by Wernicke's encephalopathy — an acute neurological condition caused by bleeding into the mid-brain due to thiamine deficiency.

Korsakoff's psychosis must be distinguished from the generalised impairment of intellect or *alcoholic dementia*, which is more common and presents with symptoms similar to those occurring in dementia from any other cause. CT scans show generalised atrophy. Female alcoholics are particularly vulnerable.

More rarely, *focal changes* occur such as frontal lobe damage, cerebellar (the area of the brain concerned with balance) degeneration, and temporal lobe lesions may develop. These organic brain disorders may lead to legal difficulties in relation to wills, trusts and financial matters generally.[11]

Personality Deterioration

This is frequently described in alcoholics who often appear to become coarse and aggressive. The debate about whether this is the cause or the result of excessive drinking has aroused much controversy. While it is recognised that personality deterioration can occur both due to the social consequences and due to frontal lobe

---

[10] Evidence that the petitioner had probably suffered brain damage as a consequence of his chronic alcohol abuse prior to his marriage was given by one psychiatrist in *McG(R)* v *K(N)* (High Court, Morris J, 23 May 1995) reported as *RMcG* v *KMcG* [1995] 3 Fam LJ. If established as going to the issue of his capacity to consent to contracting a marriage, it would render the marriage void.

[11] And, if present at the time of marriage, may be of sufficient severity to ground a decree of nullity.

damage, recent work on personality suggests that antisocial personality is a common prodrome of alcohol abuse and tends to be the cause of the alcohol abuse rather than vice versa.

Suicide

Suicide is a common outcome, particularly in chronic, middle-aged alcoholics. It tends to be associated with concurrent depressive symptoms and is often precipitated by interpersonal loss or conflict. Long-term studies have demonstrated that between 7 and 21 per cent commit suicide. Moreover, among the parasuicide (deliberate self-harm) population, alcohol abuse has been shown to be a major problem with up to 50 per cent of men showing evidence of dependence. In addition, alcohol is frequently taken prior to such an attempt.[12]

Treatment

Treatment involves detoxification either as an outpatient or as an inpatient. Judicious use of benzodiazepine tranquillisers, such as chlordiazepoxide or alprazolam, is necessary to prevent delirium tremens. Detoxification is usually completed after 14 days or may even be more rapid. The addition of vitamins prevents Korsakoff's psychosis. Following detoxification, benzodiazepines should be discontinued and long-term counselling can be instituted, as well as antibuse. This drug affects the metabolism of alcohol such that, if it is consumed with this medication, nausea and vomiting ensues. In this way, it acts as a prop against the impulsive reinstatement of drinking. Recently, a drug to reduce craving has become available. Acamprosate acts on the central nervous system transmitters which stimulate craving. It is not useful in detoxifi-

---

[12] A threat of suicide, although not in an alcohol-related context, was pleaded as amounting to duress to induce a marriage in *W v P* (High Court, Unreported Judgment, Barrington J, 7 June 1984) although the decree of nullity was ultimately granted on other grounds. In *W(P) v O'C(A) (orse W)* [1993] 1 IR 324, a decree was granted on this ground, being deemed sufficient to vitiate the petitioner husband's consent in the circumstances.

cation and must be combined with psychotherapy to address the factors underlying the need for alcohol in the individual patient.

OTHER DRUGS OF ABUSE/DEPENDENCE[13]

Although uncommon in absolute numbers when compared to alcohol abusers, the potential for marital disharmony associated with some drugs of abuse is considerable. In particular, those substances that lead to high expenditure to sustain the habit, or those that engender spouse-directed violence in the abuser, are likely to be associated with marital conflict.

In clinical practice, a distinction is made between drugs of abuse and drugs of dependence. The importance of this is that drugs of dependence lead to physical withdrawal symptoms, which require physical treatment.[14] They are also associated with a tendency to increase the dose over time in order to achieve the same effect (known as tolerance). Drugs of abuse are associated with psychological but not physical dependence and can thus be stopped abruptly without the risk of developing withdrawal symptoms. Tolerance is not a feature of drugs of abuse. All drugs, even those which do not require a prescription such as paracetamol,

---

[13] Abuse of drugs, unless either accompanied by acute intoxication at the time of the marriage ceremony (see, for example, *Sullivan* v *Sullivan* [1818] 161 ER 728) or amounting to an addiction such that the addict lacked the capacity to enter into and sustain a normal marital relationship, as with alcohol abuse, is more likely to be a factor in marital breakdown leading to judicial separation or divorce than in nullity. Although in *D* v *C* [1984] ILRM 173, there was evidence of substance abuse, the decree of nullity was granted on the basis of the husband's underlying psychiatric disorder, which existed in association with his addiction. Also, in *C(P)* *(orse O'B)* v *O'B(D)* (High Court, Unreported Judgment, Carroll J, 2 October 1985), the petitioner wife had problems with drug abuse prior to her marriage. However, nullity was refused as, on the whole of the evidence, the court was satisfied that she had sufficient capacity to enter into and sustain a normal marital relationship. Drug use by the petitioner was one factor considered in the overall context of relational incapacity in *K(D)* v *H(T)* (High Court, Unreported Judgment, O'Higgins J, 25 February 1998).

[14] By analogy with *delirium tremens*, a marriage contracted during the phase of acute withdrawal from a drug of dependence to which a person is addicted is probably invalid.

have the potential for abuse, whilst only a limited number are associated with physical dependence. In spite of this distinction, the potential for destructive behaviour exists with the use of preparations from both classes. Regrettably, both ICD-10 and DSM-IV have abandoned the distinction between abuse and dependence, resulting in tea being now regarded as a drug of addiction.

Drugs of Dependence

Opiates

Opiates are drugs of both physical and psychological dependence. Heroin is the most widely abused opiate, although the prescribed drug methadone is also widely available. The rationale for prescribing the latter is that the feelings of euphoria are less than with other opiates. Its function is therefore to limit recourse to the "black market", while also minimising the pleasurable effects. Opiates are used orally, nasally or most commonly intravenously. Dependence develops rapidly and the abrupt cessation is associated with an unpleasant, but non-life-threatening, withdrawal syndrome. Colloquially known as "cold turkey", it is associated with abdominal cramps, goose-flesh, lacrimation (watery eyes), rhinorrhoea (runny nose), nausea, yawning and sleeplessness. Opiate abuse is not associated with any long-term psychiatric disorder such as occurs with amphetamines or cocaine. Death can occur due to infections from contaminated needles or from sudden increases in intake which cause respiratory arrest. This is particularly a problem after detention in prison, during which tolerance should have decreased. After release, injection with a quantity similar to that which was used prior to imprisonment can be fatal.

The treatment of withdrawal consists of inpatient detoxification using reducing doses of an opiate, usually methadone. Some patients can be successfully detoxified using clonidine, a drug normally used to treat migraine. The practice of using major tranquillisers such as chlorpromazine for this purpose is without any medical basis and does not reduce the discomfort of withdrawal, although it does induce drowsiness. The cost involved in sustaining the drug habit can lead to marital difficulties, particularly if the spouse is a non-abuser. Moreover, crime, especially shoplifting or more serious theft, is common, also placing an obvious burden on the marriage.

Benzodiazepines

The benzodiazepine group of tranquillisers, such as diazepam, is also associated with physical dependence. The withdrawal symptoms are identical to the symptoms of anxiety itself, for which they may have been originally prescribed. About 5 per cent of patients have withdrawal fits and there are also case reports of psychotic reactions occurring. About 50 per cent of patients on regular treatment develop physical dependence, and this is most likely with the short-acting compounds. There is evidence that dependence on benzodiazepines is associated with dependent personality disorder, at least in some patients. The careful management of benzodiazepine withdrawal is essential. This usually necessitates a change to a long-acting compound such as diazepam and a gradual reduction thereafter. Some "cover" the withdrawal period with a sedative antidepressant such as dothiepin, although this is not essential. Some discomfort is almost inevitable during withdrawal, which can take several months since it must occur at the patient's pace. Unlike the opiates, which are associated with craving, this is generally not the case with benzodiazepine abuse and the drugs are taken in order to prevent withdrawal symptoms, rather than to induce euphoria. The Royal College of Psychiatrists recommends that dependence can be minimised by using flexible rather than fixed doses and that short-acting compounds be avoided where possible. If a fixed dose is required, it should not be used for longer than six weeks. There is little concrete information about the long-term consequences of dependence in those who do not or cannot discontinue benzodiazepines. The effects on marriage are minimal and may relate more to the underlying personality of the patient than to the drugs themselves. A further complication of benzodiazepine use is the potential for some to release aggression, in some patients at least.

Barbiturates

Barbiturates were once common drugs of abuse, but this is no longer the case. They were associated with dangerous withdrawal symptoms such as fits and depression. Their use has plummeted in the past 30 years and they have been replaced by the benzodiazepines.

Drugs of Abuse

These are the most readily available drugs on the black market and although not associated with physical dependence, they are widely abused due to their mood-enhancing properties and are also associated with serious psychiatric disturbance in many abusers.

Cocaine

Cocaine is one of the most dangerous drugs available due to its association with psychosis, particularly the paranoid variety. As well as paranoid delusions, it also leads to hallucinations, especially of the tactile variety with a sensation of insects crawling under the skin — known as formication or "the cocaine bug". The delusions of persecution may lead to violent and unpredictable behaviour. Excitement, confusion and respiratory arrest are among some of the other acute effects. Cocaine is usually snorted or may be injected intravenously. A rapidly acting derivative is known as "crack" and if smoked gives an immediate effect. It is believed to be one of the most stimulating drugs available and is associated with profound depression once the effects have worn off. Intense craving to alleviate this effect is believed to be responsible for the violent crimes associated with the use of cocaine.

Amphetamines

Amphetamines are used in a manner similar to cocaine. A derivative of amphetamines known as "ecstasy" has both stimulant and hallucinogenic (see LSD) properties. Amphetamines have an energising effect but may also lead to psychotic symptoms similar to those occurring with cocaine use. However, symptoms may persist after cessation, leading to a schizophrenia-like syndrome.[15] It is unclear if this occurs in those at risk of schizophrenia or if amphetamines actually induce the disorder. Psychotic episodes are treated in the usual manner with major tranquillisers and if symptoms persist, long-term treatment with depot injections may be required as in schizophrenia.

Both amphetamines and cocaine can be discontinued without any physical withdrawal symptoms, although during the period of detoxification from cocaine there may be a risk of suicide due to transient but severe depression. For this reason, inpatient observation is required. Antidepressants may be required in some cocaine abusers during withdrawal and there is a suggestion that prophylactic tricyclics, particularly desimipramine, may be effective at reducing the risk of depression.

In relation to marital disharmony, the paranoid delusions which supervene with cocaine abuse may place a spouse or family members at risk, as may the persistent psychotic symptoms which sometimes occur in amphetamine abusers. Moreover, the negative symptoms which are part of poor prognosis schizophrenia[16] may also develop in amphetamine psychosis, leading to similar interpersonal difficulties.[17]

Hallucinogens

Included in the drugs of abuse are the hallucinogens — so called because of their tendency to cause hallucinations — of which lysergic acid diethylamide (LSD) is the best known. There is seasonal use of psilocybine (magic mushrooms) in the autumn. Although not associated with physical dependence, there is a risk of distressing psychotic experiences or "bad trips". These are

---

[15] See Chapter 15, p. 348.

[16] See Chapter 15, pp. 341 and 348.

[17] Should such problems be present prior to the time of marriage, they could be sufficient to ground a decree of nullity, although the dictum of Finlay CJ in *F(U) (orse C(U))* v *C(J)* [1991] 2 IR 330, [1991] ILRM 65, in relation to voluntary or self-induced inherent qualities or characteristics of an individual's nature or personality could, on one analysis, present evidential difficulties.

characterised by visual hallucinations and delusions. Flashbacks are a further complication and these may occur long after abuse has ceased. They too are associated with intense fear. A patient may seek treatment during such an episode. Marital disharmony arises from drug-seeking behaviour.[18]

Cannabis

Cannabis is the most widely abused illicit drug and smoking is the most common method of intake. Expectations play a major part on the effects, which may be pleasant if taken in a positive ambience or negative if the environment is hostile. The most common feeling is one of relaxation and wellbeing. Anxiety and panic attacks may occur in novice users and brief psychotic episodes have also been reported. It is unclear if all abusers are equally at risk. There is speculation that long-term abuse may lead to a psychotic disorder, although the evidence is inconclusive. Moreover, suggestions that a persistent amotivational syndrome, with apathy, withdrawal and reduced ambition, may develop with long-term use persist but remain unproven. It is known, however, that abuse of cannabis can provoke relapses in patients with schizophrenia or manic-depressive illness. The main impact of cannabis abuse on marriage is related to the relapses which it induces in some patients with major mental illness and the effects of euphoria and secondary apathy which are associated with heavy persistent use.[19]

Unlike alcohol, most drugs of abuse and dependence are only indirectly associated with marital disharmony as described above.[20] In particular, the financial hardship associated with the

---

[18] As to whether prior exposure to hallucinogens of these categories would be sufficient to ground the granting of a decree of nullity is a question yet to be resolved in our courts.

[19] As with hallucinogens, whether heavy and prolonged use of cannabinoids producing such effects would be sufficient to ground the granting of a decree of nullity is also a question that has yet to be addressed by our courts.

[20] And they have yet to be implicated in nullity applications, except in *C(P) (orse O'B) v O'B(D)* (High Court, Unreported Judgment, Carroll J, 2 October 1985).

purchase of these substances puts a major strain on a non-abusing spouse. Other likely sources of disharmony are violence and the occurrence of psychotic disorders with some. However, the under-lying personality of the patient is likely to be the greatest source of conflict, particularly since studies have demonstrated a link between substance misuse and personality disorder, although the magnitude of this has yet to be clarified. Many of the perceived personality abnormalities are secondary to drug misuse and do not constitute personality disorder as defined.[21]

PSYCHOTIC DISORDERS

Manic-depressive Illness[22]

Manic-depressive illness[23] is usually well controlled with mood-stabilising drugs.[24] In a small proportion of patients, however, the illness is unstable and episodes of mania or depression recur on a regular basis. In some cases, this is due to the inherent nature of the illness, whilst in others, it arises from poor compliance with medication. In particular, those manic-depressives who also suffer from a personality disorder may fall into the latter category. The unpredictability of behaviour and moods, the indiscretion result-ing from mania (e.g. debt, pregnancy, infidelity) and the stress of

---

[21] See Chapter 9.

[22] See Chapter 15, pp. 348–53.

[23] See, for example, *D* v *C* [1984] ILRM 173, where a decree of nullity was granted; and *C(S)* v *D(P) (orse C(P))* (High Court, Unreported Judgment, McCracken J, 14 March 1996), where it was refused.

[24] In *C(S)* v *D(P) (orse C(P))* (High Court, Unreported Judgment, McCracken J, 14 March 1996), the respondent wife was ultimately successfully main-tained with lithium. Although McCracken J held that her condition was "la-tent" at the time of her marriage, it did not render her incapable of entering into the relationship and, while a normal marital relationship was not main-tained, she was not incapable of sustaining it. The effect of medication in limiting her episodes of illness appears to have been a factor critical to his determination.

regular depressive[25] episodes, especially if associated with suicidal ideation, inevitably place a strain on marriage.[26]

During episodes of mania, judgement is impaired as a result of elation or delusions. Decisions such as those relating to marriage, sale of property, etc., may be made and executed without fully understanding their gravity and may provide grounds for the annulment of marriage. However, when controlled with medication, the person with manic-depressive illness is capable of leading a fulfilling and happy life.[27]

Schizophrenia

Schizophrenia[28] may also affect the stability of a marriage as well as the capacity to enter into and to sustain such a relationship,[29]

---

[25] In *M(G) (orse G(G))* v *G(T)* (High Court, Unreported Judgment, Lavan J, 22 November 1991), a decree of nullity was granted where the evidence indicated that the respondent husband was suffering from a severe psychotic depression (although not apparently in the context of a bipolar affective disorder) at the time of the marriage, such that he lacked the requisite capacity. He had previously been treated for depression, but had been off treatment for some time prior to the marriage. Although there was also a question of a background emotional immaturity, this was not determinative of the outcome. In the light of the later decision in *C(S)* v *D(P) (orse C(P))* (High Court, Unreported Judgment, McCracken J, 14 March 1996), above, and the relative success of modern antidepressant treatment, arguably the outcome would have been different had the respondent been adequately or successfully treated for his underlying depression prior to his marriage.

[26] Such that it may ground a finding that there was inability to enter into and sustain a normal marital relationship, as in *D* v *C* [1984] ILRM 173.

[27] See, for example *C(S)* v *D(P) (orse C(P))* (High Court, Unreported Judgment, McCracken J, 14 March 1996); the comments of Barrington J in *RSJ* v *JSJ* [1982] ILRM 263 at 264–265; and, in the context of schizophrenia, *R* v *R* (High Court, Unreported Judgment, Costello J, 21 December 1984), below.

[28] See Chapter 15, pp. 332–45.

[29] See *R* v *R* (High Court, Unreported Judgment, Costello J, 21 December 1984) where the husband had been diagnosed as suffering from paranoid schizophrenia for five years prior to the marriage, of which fact the wife was unaware. Although, on the facts, a decree of nullity was granted, Costello J (as he then was) was careful to point out that not all cases involving a spouse suffering from schizophrenia would necessarily succeed. Also, in *E(CM)* v *E(A) (orse W)* [1987] IR 147 (O'Hanlon J), paranoid shcizophrenia of the husband petitioner at the time of the marriage was sufficient, on the facts, to void his consent to the marriage. In *C(D) (orse W(D))* v *W(D)* [1987] ILRM 73,

particularly if the marriage takes place whilst the patient is acutely ill. Judgement may be altered and decisions may be made on the basis of delusions or hallucination.[30]

Two other aspects of schizophrenia, however, are more likely to have an adverse effect on capacity for marriage or a person's relational capacity than is acute schizophrenia. The first of these relates to the chronicity of symptoms.[31] Even with treatment, delusions may sometimes persist in those with schizophrenia or with paranoid psychosis. The content of delusions, when related to fidelity or to persecution, may place an unbearable strain on a marriage, being associated as they sometimes are with searching of clothes, accusation of telephones being bugged and vigilance for "signals" from imagined lovers. The converse delusion — that another person is in love with the sufferer (erotomania) — can also place an excessive burden on the healthy partner. In either case,

---

the fact that the wife petitioner, at the time of the marriage, suffered from paranoid schizophrenia, which had also been present for five years prior to the marriage, was sufficient for a decree of nullity to be granted on the grounds that, at that time, she lacked the capacity to enter into and sustain a normal marital relationship — even though she subsequently had a successful stable relationship with another man. The respondent wife's paranoid schizophrenia was sufficient for decree of nullity in *K(W)* v *C(M) (orse K)* (High Court, Unreported Judgment, Lavan J, 31 July 1992).

[30] Acute psychotic illness may be present, and detectable, at the time of the marriage ceremony, in which case establishing that the marriage is invalid may be relatively straightforward from an evidential perspective — probably on consent grounds. However, even in the absence of acute symptoms at that time, the nature of the disease may be such as to render the marriage voidable notwithstanding apparent normality at the time of the marriage ceremony. See the cases noted in the previous footnote.

[31] The presence, or potential development, of such symptoms may be central to the finding that an individual lacked the capacity to enter into and sustain a normal marital relationship, where the disease was present at the time of the marriage ceremony, even if not diagnosed at that time. However, in this regard, the findings in *C(S)* v *D(P) (orse C(P))* (High Court, Unreported Judgment, McCracken J, 14 March 1996) are apposite. For a review of the potential philosophical difficulties involved, see R. Byrne and W. Binchy (1997), *Annual Review of Irish Law 1996*, Dublin: Round Hall Sweet & Maxwell, pp. 383–4. The potential for relapse of the petitioner wife's symptoms of paranoid schizophrenia was also averred to in *C(D) (orse W(D))* v *W(D)* [1987] ILRM 73 and seems to have been relevant to the ultimate determination.

attempts to convince the ill person of the falsity of the beliefs is likely to lead to arguments and, at times, violence.

The second aspect of schizophrenia which may place a strain on marriage relates to the development of negative symptoms.[32] The negative symptoms include lack of motivation, poor hygiene, flattening of personality and withdrawal and might be assumed to be due to laziness, rather than being an inherent part of the illness. Until recently, these negative symptoms have been untreatable, as they represented an inexorable aspect of the illness, in some patients at least. Recent research has led to the development of new drugs targeting these symptoms. Their role in alleviating or preventing negative symptoms in the generality of patients with schizophrenia remains to be evaluated. However, since only a proportion of sufferers with schizophrenia develop negative symptoms, the consequence of marital breakdown is not inevitable on that basis alone.[33]

SEXUAL DYSFUNCTION

Non-consummation[34] of marriage was one of the traditional bases on which marriages were annulled. This springs from sexual dysfunction, which can be classified into two broad categories:

---

[32] See Chapter 15, p. 341.

[33] The issue of negative symptoms in schizophrenia has not arisen in the written judgments of the Superior Courts in nullity cases. Nevertheless, even in the absence of development of negative symptoms, the courts have found that the nature of the underlying disease is such that there never was sufficient capacity to enter into and sustain a normal marital relationship. With the development and availability of effective treatment, however, the finding in *C(S)* v *D(P) (orse C(P))* (High Court, Unreported Judgment, McCracken J, 14 March 1996); and the dictum of Costello J in *R* v *R* (High Court, Unreported Judgment, Costello J, 21 December 1984); coupled with the observations of Barrington J in *RSJ* v *JSJ* [1982] ILRM 263 at 264–265, are apposite.

[34] The essence of non-consummation is failure of penetration. Emission or insemination — and thus, ejaculatory disorders or sterility — are irrelevant. Accordingly, a decree of nullity was refused in *M(M) (orse G)* v *M(P)* [1986] ILRM 515 (McMahon J), where penetration had been achieved, but there was no emission. In law, the marriage had been consummated.

primary, in which dysfunction has always been present; and secondary, in which the disturbance follows a period of normal function. The causes of primary dysfunction are varied and are related
to physical illness, to social, cultural or religious factors, to
trauma in childhood and adolescence and at times to medication.
Secondary dysfunction, however, is often related to an associated
psychiatric disorder such as depressive illness, to marital disharmony or infidelity, to excessive alcohol consumption or to physical
illness.

Treatment for sexual dysfunction, by and large, is modelled on
the techniques devised by Masters and Johnson,[35] termed "sensate
focus". This is based on behaviour therapy in which there is
graded exposure from kissing through touching to genital contact
and finally intercourse. Masters and Johnson claimed that there
was a remarkably low dropout rate and the five-year relapse rate
was only 5.1 per cent. Since then, results have been more circumspect and it is believed their results were a reflection of the selection procedure.

Prevalence

Although there are no reliable figures on the epidemiology of sexual dysfunction, up to 15 per cent of married women report orgasmic failure. Men are less likely to admit dysfunction.
Impotence and premature ejaculation are the most common difficulties found in men, while lack of enjoyment and vaginismus
predominate among women. Sexual problems are found in both
partners in about one-third of those attending sex therapy clinics.

In the following sections, the common sexual dysfunction disorders will be discussed, along with the common causes.

Vaginismus

Vaginismus is the most common disorder of sexual function seen
in females and is the involuntary spasm of vaginal muscles,

---

[35] W.H. Masters and V.E. Johnson (1970), *Human Sexual Inadequacy*,
Boston: Little Brown.

making intercourse difficult or impossible.[36] It may develop in the context of fear of pregnancy, anxiety and inhibition about sexuality or following trauma such as sexual abuse. Secondary causes include pelvic inflammatory disease and a number of other physical disorders. The outcome with treatment is excellent[37] although when it occurs against a background of sexual trauma[38] the prognosis is less good.[39]

---

[36] As, for example, in *O'H(A) (orse F)* v *F* [1986] ILRM 489 (Barron J), where no physical cause was found, but it ultimately resolved. See also *C* v *C* (High Court, Unreported Judgment, Lynch J, 18 November 1985); and *C(E) (orse M(E))* v *M(A)* [1991] 2 IR 192; the wife, in each case, had no difficulty consummating a (later) sexual relationship with men other than their respective husbands, so-called impotence *quoad hunc*.

[37] K. Hawton and J. Catalan (1990), "Sex Therapy for Vaginismus: Characteristics of Couples and Treatment Outcome", *Sexual and Marital Therapy*, Vol. 5, pp. 39–48. However, in cases where there is a delay in treatment, it seems, secondary impotence in the husband may occur. Thus, in *O'H(A) (orse F)* v *F* [1986] ILRM 489 (Barron J) where the husband appeared to have become secondarily impotent, and remained so even after resolution of the wife's vaginismus, a decree of nullity was granted on that ground. In *C* v *C* (High Court, Unreported Judgment, Lynch J, 18 November 1985), the question of possible secondary impotence of the husband was not relevant. Secondary — in this context — means secondary to the primary impotence of the wife. It is a matter of settled law that, where the condition is capable of being remedied without the necessity of subjecting oneself to a dangerous procedure, failure to avail of such treatment as is available will debar the granting of a decree of nullity on this ground.

[38] In *B(A)* v *B(E)* [1997] 1 IR 305 (affirmed on appeal, Supreme Court, Unreported Judgment, 31 July 1995), Budd J refused to grant a decree of nullity where the wife did not suffer from vaginismus (indeed the marriage was consummated and there were four children of the marriage within five years) and the petitioner husband maintained that as a result of his wife's having been allegedly sexually abused as a child, she had an abhorrence of sexual intercourse, avoided being left alone with her husband and was incapable of a sexual relationship involving a reasonable degree of frequency of intercourse. The wife, for her part, gave evidence of having no memory of previous sexual abuse. It was a factor considered in the overall context of relational incapacity in *K(D)* v *H(T)* (High Court, Unreported Judgment, O'Higgins J, 25 February 1998).

[39] See Chapter 7, p. 123.

Orgasmic Dysfunction

Orgasmic dysfunction[40] may arise as a primary dysfunction following sexual trauma or as a reflection of sexual inhibitions. Secondary causes include poor relationships, poor sexual technique in
the spouse or inability to relax. In general, those who receive
treatment early in the relationship have a good outcome, as do
those with primary rather than secondary anorgasmia.[41] Orgasmic
difficulties arising in the context of a poor relationship do not
have a good outcome, unless the basis for the latter can be overcome (e.g. alcohol abuse).

Inhibited Sexual Desire

Inhibited sexual desire may be related to relationship difficulties,[42] substance misuse, especially opiate abuse, lack of privacy,
disfigurement,[43] prolonged abstinence or psychiatric disorder such
as depressive illness. Indeed, loss of libido is regarded as one of
the core symptoms in depressive illness. Increasing age is also associated with reduced desire, as is tiredness associated with
having young children. Primary causes include sexual inhibition
secondary to cultural attitudes and inability to relax and

---

[40] Given the conclusions in *B(A)* v *B(E)* [1997] 1 IR 305, and that it may be
difficult to establish evidentially that this condition existed at the time of the
marriage, it seems unlikely that anorgasmia would ground a successful nullity petition.

[41] L.G. Barbach and M. Flaherty (1980), "Group Therapy in Situationally
Orgasmic Women", *Journal of Sex and Marital Therapy*, Vol. 6, pp. 19–29.

[42] These appear to have been relevant in *B(A)* v *B(E)* [1997] 1 IR 305, where
the court refused the petition. Here, the court-appointed psychiatrist indicated that the respondent probably suffered from a degree of sexual inhibition, which, in his view, could affect up to 30 per cent of couples.

[43] Disfigurement of the respondent wife, producing a psychological repugnance, was sufficient in *M(BJ)* v *M(C)* (High Court, Unreported Judgment,
Flood J, 31 July 1996) for a decree of nullity — although the precise basis for
the decision is somewhat unclear. A number of children had been born of the
marriage and the petitioner husband generally made the sexual advances.

fantasise. Treatment outcome is determined by the quality and stability of the relationship.[44]

Premature Ejaculation

Premature ejaculation[45] is the most common dysfunction found in men and is associated with prolonged abstinence. Secondary causes include anxiety, depression, relationship problems, some drug treatments and disorders affecting the genito-urinary tract. The outcome following treatment is excellent for the primary condition. Delayed ejaculation occurs with the use of certain medications, especially antidepressants.

Impotence

Impotence may be partial or total.[46] In some, it may occur only when intercourse is attempted and in others it may effect both masturbation as well as intercourse. It can be due to a number of factors, both psychological and physical, including medication such as antidepressants, alcohol misuse, depressive illness or anxiety and neurological disorders such as multiple sclerosis.

In legal practice, primary disorders of sexual dysfunction may lead to applications for annulment because of the persistence of the difficulty. However, in view of the good outcome for these with treatment, especially if the relationship is strong and motivation is high, every attempt should be made to ensure that a course of sex therapy by a trained therapist has been availed of.

---

[44] This complex determinant of outcome may effectively render some marriages voidable if assistance is not sought sufficiently early. See, for example, the evidence of the psychiatrist in *B(A)* v *B(E)* [1997] 1 IR 305 at 316; and, in the case of impotence, *C(E) (orse M(E))* v *M(K)* [1991] 2 IR 192 (Barr J).

[45] There are no written judgments in nullity applications in the Superior Courts that deal specifically with this issue, although it might arise in the context of a relational incapacity that might otherwise successfully ground a nullity petition.

[46] As in *N(AM)* v *C(JP)* [1988] ILRM 170; or *O'H(A) (orse F)* v *F* [1986] ILRM 489.

HOMOSEXUALITY

Although no longer regarded as a psychiatric disorder, sexual dysfunction is likely to be present in marriages where one partner is homosexual.[47] Often fear or naivete will have prevented the homosexual partner from disclosing[48] or even considering their orientation, although most will describe same-sex attraction from adolescence. However, many adolescents have fleeting homosexual relationships[49] and it is only the small minority with persistent homosexual desires who should be regarded as truly homosexual. There is no evidence that therapy aimed at changing sexual orientation is effective.

GENDER ROLE DISORDERS

Transsexualism[50]

Transsexualism is a disorder of gender identity characterised by the belief that the true gender is determined not by the anatomical but by the psychological gender. This leads to requests for sex change surgery and hormone replacement therapy to make psychological and anatomic sex congruent. Cross-dressing is common as a way of approximating to the chosen gender. There is no treatment to change the attitude to gender and sex change operations are sometimes indicated. Assessment for gender reassign-

---

[47] And it may be sufficient grounds for a successful nullity petition. See, for example, *F(U) (orse C(U))* v *C(J)* [1991] 2 IR 330, [1991] ILRM 65 (Supreme Court reversing the High Court's refusal (Keane J) to grant a decree of nullity) and *F* v *F* [1990] 1 IR 348 (Barron J) (although here it also appeared that the husband may also have had a severe psychological disturbance). However, in *McD(MF)* v *O'R(W)* (High Court, Unreported Judgment, Hamilton J, 26 January 1984), evidence of a single previous homosexual encounter alone was not sufficient to establish a relational incapacity and the petition was refused.

[48] In *F* v *F* [1990] 1 IR 348, there was deliberate non-disclosure, which effectively vitiated the wife's consent to the marriage.

[49] As, for example, appeared in *McD(MF)* v *O'R(W)* (High Court, Unreported Judgment, Hamilton J, 26 January 1984).

[50] A marriage contracted with by a person with a transsexual of the same genetic sex is void.

ment is painstaking and requires the patient to live exclusively in the chosen gender for two years prior to surgery and even then, many do not meet the criteria. Transsexualism is rare, affecting 1/35,000 males and 1/100,000 females. Most transsexuals do not regard themselves as homosexual and regard their sexual orientation as heterosexual.

Transvestism

This is defined as the repeated dressing in clothes of the opposite sex. It should not be confused with transsexualism, since there is no gender identity problem and the transvestite feels entirely male or female according to gender. Homosexuality may be associated with transvestism but is not inevitable, being more common among female than among male cross-dressers. The cause and frequency are unknown.[51]

PARAPHILIAS

These are defined as disorders of sexual preference excluding problems of sexual orientation.[52]

Fetishism is the use of inanimate objects to achieve sexual arousal. Often, they are extensions of the human body, such as articles of clothing or footwear. Sometimes the fetish is related to texture such as rubber or plastic. *Voyeurism* is defined as sexual arousal obtained chiefly by observing the sexual activity of others. *Exhibitionism* is the recurrent tendency to expose genitalia to strangers or to people in public places without inviting closer contact. Sexual excitement at the time is common and may be followed by masturbation. *Sadomasochism* is a preference for sexual activity involving the infliction of pain or humiliation. *Paedophilia* is a sexual preference for children and may be homosexual or

---

[51] If causative, or a manifestation, of a relational incapacity, transvestism could, arguably, on principle, void a marriage.

[52] Although not yet an issue that has fallen to be determined by our courts, depending on the type and severity of the paraphilia, it could be grounds, on principle, for voiding a marriage. See Chapter 11.

heterosexual. It is rare in women and invariably indicative of severe mental illness such as schizophrenia. Some paedophiles are involved in adult heterosexual relationships also, while others have a preference for adult partners but, being perpetually frustrated in achieving these, turn to children instead. Other less common paraphilias include activities such as making obscene telephone calls, sexual activity with animals, sexual arousal achieved through rubbing against other people in crowded places, the use of strangulation to enhance sexual excitement, and a range of others.

Since paraphilias are longstanding and difficult to treat, if not untreatable. Their presence in a marriage is likely to lead to serious marital problems. Of course, many will not be married at all and will lead isolated, socially poor lives.

SUMMARY

Civil annulment may be sought for problems relating to alcohol abuse which was present prior to and subsisting during marriage. Although other substance misuse is also associated with marital disharmony, many such abusers are not married. Some of the paraphilias, as well as transsexualism, might also constitute grounds for considering marriage annulment. Primary sexual dysfunction disorders should first be treated before annulment is considered, since the outcome with treatment is potentially good.

Chapter 11

NULLITY OF MARRIAGE[1]

INTRODUCTION

The role of psychiatric disorder in the law of nullity, important from a practical and conceptual perspective, has increased in significance over the past quarter century or so. In Britain and Ireland, nullity represents only a relatively small area of practical concern in relation to marriage and family law. In Britain, in particular, since the extension of divorce legislation in 1969,[2] the number of decrees of nullity granted, both in absolute terms and when compared with the number of divorce decrees is tiny, amounting to only a few hundred cases annually.[3] In Ireland, again, the absolute number annually rarely exceeded a handful, a tiny figure when compared with the number of separation agreements and orders granted under the Family Law Reform and Judicial Separation Act, 1989. How even this small number might be affected by the passing of the constitutional amendment in November 1995 which allowed for the introduction of divorce

---

[1] See, generally, W.R. Duncan and P.E. Scully (1990), *Marriage Breakdown in Ireland*, Dublin: Butterworths (Ireland) Ltd, Chapter 2; A. Shatter (1997), *Shatter's Family Law*, 4th Edition, Dublin: Butterworths, Chapter 5; W. Binchy (1984), *A Casebook on Irish Family Law*, Dublin: Professional Books; S.M. Cretney and J.M. Masson (1997), *Principles of Family Law*, 6th edition, London: Sweet & Maxwell, Chapter 2; and P.M. Bramley and N.V. Lowe (1992), *Bromley's Family Law*, 8th edition, Butterworths, Chapters 2 and 3.

[2] Family Law (Reform) Act, 1969.

[3] In 1988, for instance, there were only 389 decrees of nullity and 154,788 divorce decrees in Britain (*Civil Judicial Statistics 1988*). See Cretney and Masson (1997), op. cit., Chapter 2.

legislation[4] remains to be seen. The law of nullity is simply concerned with and determines the validity of a marriage in the first instance and determines not alone who may marry whom, but also when.

GROUNDS FOR INVALIDITY

A marriage may be invalid for a number of reasons; for example, if the formal requirements of law have not been complied with (e.g. the requisite notice may not have been given). Also, the marriage of a person under the age of 18 years[5] (or in Britain, 16 years[6]) who has not previously obtained the consent to marry from the President of the High Court, is invalid. Similarly, "marriage" between two persons who are not respectively male and female, or between persons, one of whom is already lawfully married and whose spouse is still alive and where the marriage has not been dissolved or annulled, or between persons of certain defined degrees of relationship, whether based on consanguinity or affinity of relationship, are invalid. A marriage entered into under duress,[7] mistake, fraud, or where one party is suffering a psychiatric disability,[8] may also be invalid. Psychiatrists are primarily concerned with this last area, although they may also have input into treatment of the consequences of marital breakdown.

---

[4] Family Law (Divorce) Act, 1996.

[5] Family Law Act, 1995, s. 31.

[6] Nullity of Marriage Act, 1971, s. 1, consolidated as the Matrimonial Causes Act, 1973, s. 11, reproduced as amended by the Marriage Act, 1983, s. 2(4). The legislation applies only in respect of marriages taking place after 31 July 1971. Prior to that date, the common law rules must be relied upon (see below).

[7] The fact that a party to a marriage is suffering from a psychiatric disability at the time of the marriage may be peripherally relevant also to the issue of duress. See, for example, *E(CM)* v *E(A) (orse W)* [1987] IR 147; *C(A) (orse J)* v *J(P)* (High Court, Unreported Judgment, Barron J, 23 February 1995); and *O'M(M) (orse O'C(M))* v *O'C(B)* [1996] 1 IR 208.

[8] See Chapters 9 and 10.

VOID OR VOIDABLE MARRIAGE — THE CANON LAW AND HISTORICAL CONTEXT

Historically,[9] the nullity jurisdiction, until recently vested solely in the High Court[10] was a function solely of the ecclesiastical courts, which determined whether a marriage was valid or void. Any canonical impediment (e.g. prior subsisting marriage, impotence) rendered a marriage invalid, notwithstanding that the parties had been through a ceremony of "marriage" and had lived together for many years thereafter as man and wife. At the beginning of the seventeenth century, however, the civil courts, concerned with the ease with which marriages could be set aside by the ecclesiastical courts by the extension of the grounds upon which a decree of nullity could be granted *inter alia* restricted the available grounds.

Thus, impediments were categorised as either "civil" or "canonical". A marriage could be impugned after the death of either party only where the disability was "civil", e.g. where one party was, at the time of the marriage impeached, lawfully married to a third person. Such marriages remained void *ab initio*. Where the disability was "canonical" (e.g. impotence), the marriage was merely voidable, i.e. the marriage was valid until the challenge to its validity was proven and the decree of nullity granted, the right to such challenge being confined solely to the parties to the marriage. Accordingly, any offspring of such a union remained legitimate unless and until the annulment of the marriage.

CIVIL NULLITY JURISDICTION

The nullity jurisdiction remained exercisable only by the courts of the established church until 1857 in Britain, when it was transferred to the Divorce and Matrimonial Court where the principles to be applied were to be those of the ecclesiastical courts, unless

---

[9] Cretney and Masson (1997), op cit., pp. 31–33 and the footnotes thereto.

[10] See Family Law Act, 1995, s. 38, conferring a concurrent jurisdiction on the Circuit Court, subject to certain conditions.

and until modified by statute.[11] Statutory reform was effected by
the Nullity of Marriage Act, 1971,[12] which codified English internal law[13] on the subject.

In Ireland, upon the dis-establishment of the Church of
Ireland in 1870, the nullity jurisdiction was transferred to the
civil courts where the principles to be applied were those

> which, in the opinion of the . . . Court, shall be as nearly as
> may be conformable to the principles and rules upon which
> the Ecclesiastical Courts of Ireland have heretofore acted
> and given relief.[14]

Despite many recommendations[15] in relation to reform and extension of the civil nullity jurisdiction, no significant statutory reform
took place.[16] However, in 1976 it was held that:

> Section 13 of the Act of 1870 did not have the effect of fos-
> silising the law in its state in that year. That law is, to
> some extent at least, judge-made, and courts must recog-
> nise that great advances made in psychological medicine
> since 1870 make it necessary to frame new rules which re-
> flect these.[17]

---

[11] Matrimonial Causes Act, 1857, s. 22.

[12] Which only applies to marriages taking lace after 31 July 1971. Now consolidated in the Matrimonial Causes Act, 1973.

[13] As distinct from issues arising from the recognition of a decree of nullity
granted in a foreign jurisdiction under the "rules" of private international
law.

[14] Matrimonial Causes and Marriage Law (Ireland) Amendment Act, 1870, s.
13.

[15] Including a discussion paper *The Law of Nullity in Ireland* published in
1976 by the office of the Attorney General. The then Attorney General was
Mr Declan Costello SC, later President of the High Court.

[16] Certain procedural modifications were effected by the Family Law Act,
1995, ss. 39 and 47.

[17] *S* v *S* (Supreme Court, Unreported Judgment, 1 July 1976, Kenny J) applied in *RSJ* v *JSJ* [1982] ILRM 263 *per* Barrington J; *D* v *C* [1984] ILRM
173 (Costello J); and *MFMcD (orse MO'R)* v *WO'R* (High Court, Unreported
Judgment, 24 January 1984, Hamilton J).

Accordingly, the law was subsequently extended to take account of developments in psychiatry and psychology over the previous century. That said, the post-Reformation categorisation of marriages as void (*ab initio*) or voidable remains.

Void marriages — those that are impermissible on grounds of social and public policy (as, for example, marriages involving minority, affinity or consanguinity, or bigamy at the date of the marriage) — and in which policy considerations take precedence over the wishes of the parties to the marriage, are not of particular concern to psychiatrists.[18] Certain conditions, which might not be ascertainable until after the parties have married, might make a marriage voidable (e.g. impotence).[19]

Once a voidable marriage has been annulled, however, it is unclear as to whether capacity to marry again (in the absence of consideration of compliance with statutory formalities) is a prerequisite, or if such capacity is to be always presumed unless and until the contrary is established. Even if established, there is no guidance as to whether or not a persisting lack of capacity, whether on account of psychiatric disability or otherwise, is sufficient ground for prohibiting a person suffering such an impediment from contracting a marriage after the annulment of a previous union. Whether or not consideration of the common good is relevant has yet to be considered.[20] Such a restriction might

---

[18] *A* v *B* LR 1 P&D 559, especially at 561–2, cited in *D* v *C* [1984] ILRM 173 (Costello J); and *Re Roberts dec'd* [1978] 1 WLR 653 at 656.

[19] Impotence, although a canonical impediment that renders a marriage void, merely makes a marriage voidable in civil law. Furthermore, the impotence, interestingly, need not be total but may be peculiar to the partner of the person affected, so called impotence *quoad hunc* (towards him) or *quoad hanc* (towards her). Although this work is not concerned with all the factors which might make a marriage void or voidable, given the analogy drawn between impotence and psychiatric disability in the cases (see below) suffice it to say that a person may suffer a repugnance to his or her partner which renders him or her unable to consummate the marriage, notwithstanding that if one or the other had sexual intercourse with another person, no such impediment would arise. Whether or not this amounts to, or results from, a psychiatric disability will, of course, be determined by the facts (which is not to say that the condition of *vaginismus* always results from a psychiatric disability).

[20] See Binchy (1984), op. cit., p. 17.

well, in any event, fall foul of the provisions of Article 12 of the European Convention on Human Rights, which expressly recognises the right to marry and found a family.[21]

GROUNDS FOR NULLITY[22]

At common law, marriages vitiated by mental incapacity and an intention not to consummate the marriage are voidable, as are marriages where one party is impotent.[23] In England, statutory reform has extended the grounds upon which a marriage might be found voidable to a wilful refusal of the respondent to consummate it. Whereas, in Ireland, the view has been that lack of consent renders a marriage void,[24] the question has arisen as to whether or not such marriages are merely voidable.[25] In England, lack of consent of either party, whether in consequence of duress, mistake, unsoundness of mind or otherwise, renders a marriage voidable. Similarly, mental disorder within the meaning of the Mental Health Act, 1983,[26] of such a kind or to such an extent, and suffered by either party at the time of the marriage, that, although capable of giving a valid consent, as to be unfitted for marriage, also renders a marriage voidable. Other conditions rendering a marriage voidable under statute include venereal disease in a communicable form in the respondent at the time of the

---

[21] In *F v Switzerland*, Series A, No. 128 (1988) 10 EHRR 41, the European Court of Human Rights held that a temporary restriction imposed by the Swiss Civil Code on F's right to re-marry because F had been held to be primarily responsible for the dissolution of an earlier marriage, violated the provisions of Article 12. See J.M. Kelly (1994), *The Irish Constitution,* 3rd Edition, G. Hogan and G. Whyte (eds.), Dublin: Butterworths, pp. 996–7 and the footnotes thereto.

[22] The discussion will be confined to those issues arising from the capacity of parties to a marriage insofar as the other grounds arising are largely self-explanatory. The analogy with the canonical impediment of impotence is important in this regard; see below.

[23] See *S v S* (Supreme Court, Unreported Judgment, 1 July 1976, Kenny J).

[24] See Shatter (1997), op. cit., para 5.05.

[25] See Binchy (1984), op. cit., p. 17.

[26] Schedule 4, para. 34.

marriage and pregnancy in the respondent at the time of the marriage by some person other than the petitioner.[27]

CAPACITY FOR MARRIAGE

In order for a marriage to be valid, it is axiomatic that the parties to that marriage have the capacity to marry. Traditionally, this has involved consideration of a person's understanding of the nature of marriage (whether as a contract or otherwise) and the commitments that it entails. Over the past twenty-five years or so, the capacity of a person to enter into and to sustain a normal marital relationship,[28] or his or her "fitness for marriage"[29] has become a further important factor to be considered in this assessment. Apart from the bars to marriage arising from policy grounds (e.g. age, consanguinity and affinity), there are neither statutory nor common law requirements as to the definition of the capacity to marry.[30] Although not expressed in such terms, it is as if there is, subject to certain public policy exceptions, a legal presumption of capacity to marry unless and until the contrary is shown, much as "sanity",[31] testamentary capacity[32] and the capacity of adults to consent to diagnostic or therapeutic interventions is presumed.

It has been asserted that marriage is a very simple contract that does not require a high degree of intelligence to understand.[33] Beyond this, however, there is no express guidance as to how ca-

---

[27] Nullity of Marriage Act, 1971, s. 2, consolidated as the Matrimonial Causes Act, 1973, s. 12.

[28] See below.

[29] See below.

[30] The provisions of the Nullity of Marriage Act, 1971, in England notwithstanding.

[31] See Chapter 16.

[32] See Chapter 14.

[33] *Re Park* [1954] P 112 at 136, where, although it was held that that the deceased lacked testamentary capacity, he nevertheless had sufficient capacity to consent to marriage a few hours earlier.

pacity to marry is to be assessed. Whether or not a decree of nullity will or will not be granted in any particular instance, depends on the nature and the reliability of the evidence adduced and cases turn largely on their own facts.

An inability, howsoever arising, to understand the nature of marriage and the attendant commitments at the time of marriage, amounts to a lack of capacity to marry. A person lacking such a capacity, accordingly, cannot validly give consent. Similar considerations arise in the law of "ordinary" contract. At common law, lack of capacity vitiating consent at the time of the marriage was generally regarded as rendering a marriage void. In Ireland, in the light of decisions involving the annulment of marriages where the issue of capacity to enter into and sustain a normal marital relationship arose, some such marriages are probably classifiable as voidable.[34] In England, statutory provision is now to this effect.[35]

Psychiatric Disorder at the Time of the Marriage Ceremony[36]

However, the fact that one or other party to a marriage is suffering from a psychiatric disorder at the time of the marriage is not in the common law approach, of itself, sufficient proof of a lack of capacity. Thus, it has been held that for the consent to a marriage to be invalid, the person's lack of capacity for the requisite understanding at the time of the marriage must result from the psychiatric disorder.[37] The presence or otherwise of psychiatric disorder, on a plain

---

[34] See Binchy (1984), op. cit., p. 17.

[35] Nullity of Marriage Act, 1971, s. 2, consolidated as the Matrimonial Causes Act, 1973, s. 12.

[36] Under the Marriage of Lunatics Act, 1811, the marriage of a certified "lunatic" or "a lunatic or person under a frenzy" (*sic*) whose person (and estate) has been committed to the care and custody of trustees is void, even if it occurred in a "lucid interval", until (s)he has been declared "sane"; see Shatter (1997), op. cit., para. 5.19.

[37] See: *Re Park* [1954] P 112, *Hill* v *Hill* [1959] 1 WLR 127. However, in *O'M(M) (orse O'C(M))* v *O'C(B)* [1996] 1 IR 208, the Supreme Court held that non-disclosure by the respondent husband of previous treatment by a psychiatrist, voided the marriage on the basis that there was no fully in-

construction of the English Nullity of Marriage Act, 1971,[38] is merely one factor to be taken into account in such an assessment. Irish case law is to the same effect.[39] Such marriages are voidable.

Although the existence of psychiatric disorder prior or subsequent to, but not obviously at, the marriage ceremony, may provide powerful supporting evidence as to the probability of its existence at the relevant time, evidentially this may be difficult to establish and will require the availability of expert opinion in that regard.[40] Furthermore, in the absence of such a condition at the time of marriage, supervening psychiatric disorder after the marriage ceremony is insufficient to successfully ground an application for nullity.[41]

INTOXICATION

Intoxication — which should be distinguished from the sequelae of chronic intoxication or the abuse of intoxicants[42] — at the time of the marriage ceremony may render a marriage invalid, whether

---

formed consent to the marriage by the petitioner wife. This was followed in *J(S)* v *J(M)* (High Court, Unreported Judgment, Lavan J, 10 December 1997).

[38] Section 2, now consolidated as the Matrimonial Causes Act, 1973, s. 12.

[39] Given the probability of the presence of a psychiatric disorder at the time of the marriage, it may be difficult to ascertain precisely the grounds upon which the decree of nullity is granted, whether on the basis of absence of consent or relational incapacity. See, for example, *E(CM)* v *E(A)* [1987] IR 147 (High Court, O'Hanlon J) (paranoid schizophrenia in the husband), *M(G) (orse G(G))* v *G(T)* (High Court, Unreported Judgment, Lavan J, 22 November 1991) (husband's severe psychotic depression).

[40] As to the deference that will be given to such evidence, particularly in cases of relational incapacity, see below.

[41] In this regard, *C(S)* v *D(P)* (High Court, Unreported Judgment, McCracken J, 14 March 1996) again in the context of relational incapacity, where the disease (manic depressive psychosis) was characterised as being "latent" at the time of the marriage and was ultimately successfully treated, is apposite. See also *T(S)* v *J(B) (orse T(B))* (High Court, Unreported Judgment, O'Hanlon J, 2 September 1993).

[42] See Chapter 9. In *Legeyt* v *O'Brien* (1834) Milw Rep 325, the allegation that the husband was suffering from *delirium tremens* at the time of the marriage ceremony failed on the evidence.

at common law[43] or by statute.[44] In England, the fact that one party was voluntarily intoxicated at the time of the marriage ceremony does not debar the annulment of the marriage and his being relieved of the usual attendant consequences.[45]

Capacity to Enter into and Sustain a Normal Marital Relationship

The capacity to marry of one or other party at the time of the marriage ceremony may be difficult to determine evidentially,[46] save in the most obvious case. Given those difficulties, a global aspect of capacity — the question of the person's "fitness to marry" — arose for consideration. Statutory reform in Britain, initially in 1937[47] provided for the annulment of a marriage where one party, on account of mental illness, was "unfit to marry". In its modern formulation, a marriage is merely voidable where the party is, at the time of the marriage, suffering, whether continuously or intermittently, from a mental disorder within the meaning of the Mental Health Act, 1983,[48] of such a kind or to such an extent as to be unfitted for marriage, notwithstanding that he or she is capable of giving a valid consent in the context ordinarily understood, i.e. as to the nature of marriage and the rights and

---

[43] See *Sullivan* v *Sullivan* [1818] 161 ER 728. Such an allegation failed in the High Court in *McG(R)* v *K(N)* (High Court, Unreported Judgment, Morris J, 23 May 1995) reported as *RMcG* v *KMcG* [1995] 3 Fam LJ.

[44] Nullity of Marriage Act, 1971, s. 2 (ground (c)), now consolidated as the Matrimonial Causes Act, 1973, s. 12.

[45] As to whether or not voluntary intoxication *simpliciter*, i.e. not associated with substance dependence (see Chapter 10) would also ground a successful nullity petition in Ireland has yet to be decided.

[46] For an illustration of the difficulties involved, see: *Re Park* [1954] P 112.

[47] Matrimonial Causes Act, 1937, s. 5.

[48] Section 1(2). Whereas previously the fact that a person was subject to recurrent attacks of epilepsy could ground an application for a decree of nullity, a reflection of a primitive understanding of, and attitude towards, those suffering from epilepsy (not without its bizarre parallels in the criminal law; see Chapters 15 and 16) this provision was repealed by later mental health legislation.

responsibilities involved.[49] A person is unfit for marriage if his/her mental disorder makes him incapable of carrying on a normal married life.[50]

In Ireland, the courts expressly addressed themselves to the capacity of a party to a marriage to enter into and to sustain a normal marital relationship, the apparent "valid" consent to the marriage notwithstanding. In the first such case to come before the courts, *RSJ* v *JSJ*[51] Barrington J was of the opinion that

> the illness of one of the parties, they both being in other respects capable of contracting a valid marriage, could not under any circumstances make a marriage void provided both parties knew of the illness and wished to get married. To hold otherwise would be an unwarranted interference with the right to marry. People have entered into a contract of marriage for all sorts of reasons, and their motives have not always been of the highest. The motive for the marriage may have been policy, convenience, or self-interest. In these circumstances, it appears to me that one could not say that a marriage is void merely because one party did not love or had not the capacity to love the other.

Nevertheless, he was satisfied that a ground upon which a decree of nullity might be granted would exist

> if it could be shown that, at the date of the marriage, the petitioner, through illness, lacked the capacity to form a caring or considerate relationship with his wife.

Relying on the analogy of impotence as a ground for avoiding a marriage, the court was satisfied that the new ground put

---

[49] Nullity of Marriage Act, 1971, s. 2, consolidated as the Matrimonial Causes Act, 1973, s. 12.

[50] See, for example, *Bennett* v *Bennett* [1969] 1 WLR 430. The normative element introduced here may present particular difficulties. The facts of *B(A)* v *B(E)* [1997] 1 IR 305 illustrate the possible problems.

[51] [1982] ILRM 263.

forward was a much more serious impediment to marriage. Barrington J continued:

> No doubt there have been happy marriages where one of the parties was impotent. But it is impossible to imagine any form of meaningful marriage where one of the parties lacks the capacity of entering into a caring, or even a considerate, relationship with the other.

A further analogy with impotence was drawn in that, under Irish law, impotence makes a marriage merely voidable, and an impotent spouse can rely upon his own impotence[52] to avoid the marriage only if the other party has previously repudiated the marriage.[53] On the facts, however, the court was not satisfied that the ground had been made out.[54]

In the next such case to come before the courts, *D v C*[55] the approach adopted in *RSJ v JSJ*[56] was followed. Costello J (as he then was) stated:

> [M]arriage is by our common law (strengthened and reinforced by our constitutional law) a lifelong union, and it seems to me to be perfectly reasonable that the law should recognise (a) the obvious fact that there is more to marriage than its physical consummation and (b) that the lifelong union which the law enjoins requires for its maintenance the creation of an emotional and psychological relationship between the spouses. The law should have regard to this relationship just as it does to the physical one . . . [I]t is

---

[52] Under the Nullity of Marriage Act, 1971, s. 2, consolidated as the Matrimonial Causes Act, 1973, s. 12, a petitioner may petition for a decree of nullity on the basis of his own mental disorder.

[53] *McM v McM* [1936] IR 177, *A v A (sued as B)* 19 LR Ir 403.

[54] The evidence established that the petitioner was suffering from some form of psychiatric disorder, although the precise diagnosis appeared to be in some doubt (see Chapter 3). However, the respondent wife had not repudiated the marriage.

[55] [1984] ILRM 173 (Costello J).

[56] [1982] ILRM 263.

> now possible to identify psychiatric illness . . . which in
> some cases may be so severe as to make it impossible for
> one of the partners to the marriage to enter into and sus-
> tain the relationship which should exist between married
> couples if a lifelong union is to be possible . . . [I]f the law
> declares to be null a marriage on the grounds that one
> spouse is through physical disability incapable of the physi-
> cal relationship required by marriage it should do likewise
> where one spouse is through psychiatric disability unable
> to enter into and sustain the normal interpersonal relation-
> ship which marriage also requires.

Applying the analogy of impotence, it was held that such marriages are voidable and on the facts,[57] the petitioner made out her
case and was granted a decree of nullity.

In *RSJ*, the emphasis was on "illness", whereas in *D* v *C*, "psychiatric illness" and "psychiatric disability" appeared to be used
almost interchangeably. In *W* v *P*,[58] Barrington J granted a decree
on nullity based upon severe "psychiatric and emotional disability". In *B* v *M*,[59] in the context of the emotional immaturity of the
respondent, he noted:

> I do not know if M's condition can be described as an ill-
> ness. It is apparently a "disorder". . . . But whether it is an
> illness or a disorder it is equally incapacitating so far as the
> formation of a marital relationship is concerned . . . com-
> pounded by the fact that B was quite unable to cope with
> the problems which M's immaturity created.

The decree of nullity was granted on the basis of the respondent's
emotional immaturity and "because of the respective states of
mind and mental conditions of the petitioner and the respondent".
Moving further away from the restrictions that consideration of

---

[57] The respondent was suffering from a manic-depressive disorder; see
Chapter 10.

[58] High Court, Unreported Judgment, Barrington J, 7 June 1984.

[59] High Court, Unreported Judgment, Barrington J, 27 March 1987.

notions of "disease" or "disorder" involve,[60] Lardner J, in refusing a decree in *T(R)* v *P(V)*[61] noted that:

> One cannot say there may never be exceptions where the incapacity is shown . . . to exist without serious mental illness or serious personality disorder.

A unanimous Supreme Court, in *F(U) (orse C(U))* v *C(J)*,[62] having reviewed *RSJ* and *D* v *C*, was of the view that:

> . . . the analogy . . . between . . . impotence and the incapacity to enter into and sustain a proper marital relationship would appear to be valid not only in cases where that incapacity arose from psychiatric or mental illness so recognised or defined but also in cases where it arose from some other inherent quality or characteristic of an individual's nature or personality which would not be said to be voluntary or self-induced.[63]

Following *RSJ* and its progeny, decrees of nullity were granted on the basis that one or other of the parties was, at the date of the marriage, suffering from paranoid schizophrenia,[64] paranoid

---

[60] See Chapter 2.

[61] High Court, Unreported Judgment, Lardner J, 30 July 1989.

[62] [1991] 2 IR 330.

[63] See also Chapter 10. In the instant case, it was held that an inherent and unalterable homosexual nature in one party to a marriage could form a proper legal ground for annulling the marriage at the instance of the other party to the marriage in the case, at least, where that party had no knowledge of the existence of the homosexual nature. Previously, in *F* v *F* [1990] 1 IR 348 (Barron J) (although here it also appeared that the husband may also have had a severe psychological disturbance) a similar decree was also granted. However, in *McD(MF)* v *O'R(W)* (High Court, Unreported Judgment, Hamilton J, 26 January 1984), the petition failed on the evidence.

[64] See Chapters 10 and 15 and *R* v *R* (High Court, Unreported Judgment, Costello J, 21 December 1984) (husband); *E(CM)* v *E(A) (orse W)* [1987] IR 147 (wife); *C(D) (orse W(D)* v *W(D)* [1987] ILRM 58 (Blayney J) (wife); and *K(W)* v *C(M)* (High Court, Unreported Judgment, Lavan J, 31 July 1992) (wife).

psychosis,[65] schizo-affective disorder,[66] psychotic depression,[67] "gross" personality disorder,[68] immaturity,[69] other personality disorders[70] or disfigurement[71] and, accordingly, unable to enter into

---

[65] See also Chapter 10 and *K(P)* v *N(MB) (orse K)* (Supreme Court, Unreported Judgment, 3 April 1995), affirming Costello J (High Court, Unreported Judgment, 27 November 1992).

[66] See Chapter 15 and *S* v *K* (High Court, Unreported Judgment, Denham J, 2 July 1992) (wife); this case also involved consideration of the immaturity of both parties.

[67] See Chapters 6 and 10; *M(G) (orse G(G))* v *G(T)* (High Court, Unreported Judgment, Lavan J, 22 November 1991) (husband).

[68] See Chapter 9 and *W(C)* v *C* [1989] IR 696 (Barron J), where the evidence recited in the judgment is suggestive of a sociopathic personality disorder.

[69] See Chapter 9 and *W* v *P* (High Court, Unreported Judgment, Barrington J, 7 June 1984); *C(P)* v *C(V)* [1990] 2 IR 91 (O'Hanlon J) (immaturity on both sides); *S* v *K* (High Court, Unreported Judgment, Denham J, 2 July 1992); and *O'R* v *B* [1995] 2 ILRM 57 (Kinlen J). Similarly grounded applications were refused in *C(P) (orse O'B)* v *O'B(D)* (High Court, Unreported Judgment, Carroll J, 2 October 1985); *H(H)* v *S(J)* (Supreme Court, Unreported Judgment, 3 April 1992) affirming (O'Flaherty and Egan JJ *diss*) the High Court's refusal (Carroll J) (High Court, Unreported Judgment, 19 December 1990); *O'D(M)* v *O'D(C)* (High Court, Unreported Judgment, O'Hanlon J, 8 May 1992); *T(K)* v *T(D)* (Supreme Court, Unreported Judgment, 12 October 1995) affirming the High Court's refusal [1992] 2 IR 11 (Murphy J); *C(P)* v *M(C) (orse C(C))* (High Court, Unreported Judgment, Laffoy J, 11 January 1996); and *H(JW)* v *W(G)* (High Court, Unreported Judgment, O'Higgins J, 25 February 1998). A decree of nullity based on the husband's emotional and psychological development was refused in *W(K)* v *W(M)* (High Court, Unreported Judgment, Lynch J, 19 July 1994).

[70] See Chapter 9 and *M(C)* v *L(E) (orse M(E))* (High Court, Unreported Judgment, Barr J, 27 July 1994), where the personality disorder in the wife was unspecified but appears to have been depressive in nature. A decree was refused in *T(S)* v *J(B) (orse T(B))* (High Court, Unreported Judgment, O'Hanlon J, 2 September 1993), where it was alleged that the husband suffered from an obsessive-compulsive personality disorder. In *M(A)* v *M(T)* (High Court, Unreported Judgment, O'Hanlon J, 11 February 1993), although decided on other grounds, the evidence recited in the judgment suggests a sociopathic personality disorder in the husband. Incompatibility of personalities was insufficient to ground a decree of nullity in *T(R)* v *P(V) (orse T(V))* (High Court, Unreported Judgment, Lardner J, 30 July 1989). The finding of Kinlen J in the High Court that the respondent did not suffer from a personality disorder was not upset on appeal to the Supreme Court in *O'M(M) (orse O'C(M))* v *O'C(B)* [1996] 1 IR 208.

[71] *M(B)* v *M(C)* (High Court, Unreported Judgment, Flood J, 31 July 1996).

and sustain a normal marriage relationship. However, a decree was refused on the basis of alleged sexual inhibition of the wife.[72] Post *F(U)*, however, the presence of a precisely diagnosed psychiatric disease or disorder (frequently used clinically as synonyms) is not essential. In *K(D)* v *H(T)*[73] the cumulative effect of the petitioner's background circumstances (including sexual and drug abuse) was sufficient to void a marriage.

Thus, in *S* v *K*[74] a decree of nullity was granted on the grounds that, not alone did the respondent suffer from an "inherent psychiatric disorder"[75] that was stress-activated, but also that both parties were immature when they decided to, and went through the ceremony of marriage. However, immaturity *per se* is an insufficient ground.[76] Thus, in *S(H)* v *S(J)*[77] Finlay CJ stated:

> . . . neither immaturity in a general sense nor irresponsibility can of itself and to a general degree only, constitute a ground for nullity, though in particular cases personality disorders, including immaturity or irresponsibility arising from psychiatric or personality disorder may affect true consent or may affect the capacity of a person to maintain a lasting marriage relationship.

Accordingly, the effect of the disability may be a matter of degree. In this regard, however, although it is highly dependent on the

---

[72] *B(A)* v *B(E)* [1997] 1 IR 305 (Budd J).

[73] High Court, Unreported Judgment, O'Higgins J, 25 February 1998.

[74] High Court, 2 July 1992, reported at [1993] 1 FamLJ 18.

[75] Although this appears to have ultimately attracted the label schizoaffective disorder. See Chapters 3 and 15.

[76] Thus, for example, in *C(P)* *(orse O'B)* v *O'B(D)* (High Court, Unreported Judgment, Carroll J, 2 October 1985); *S(H)* v *S(J)* (Supreme Court, Unreported Judgment, 3 April 1992) affirming (O'Flaherty and Egan JJ *diss*) the High Court's refusal (Carroll J) (High Court, Unreported Judgment, 19 December 1990), reported at *HS* v *JS* [1992] 2 FamLJ 33; and *C(P)* v *M(C)* *(orse C(C))* (High Court, Unreported Judgment, Laffoy J, 11 January 1996) the evidence in relation to the severity of the condition was insufficient to ground a grant of a decree of nullity.

[77] *S(H)* v *S(J)* (see fn 76 above).

available evidence, it is ultimately a matter for the trial judge, and not for psychiatrists, to determine.[78]

As noted, the disability must be present at the time of the marriage.[79] Thus, as in the case of the husband in *D* v *C*,[80] in *C(S)* v *D(P) (orse C(P))*[81] the respondent wife suffered from a bipolar affective disorder. Although her behaviour on her wedding day was somewhat bizarre and she cried and laughed inappropriately, it was only upon her subsequent pregnancies that she manifested the symptoms of her ultimate diagnosis. On the evidence, McCracken J held that the incidents prior to, and at, her wedding were not manifestations of her illness. Rather, he held that her condition was "latent" at the time of her marriage, and it did not affect her ability to have a normal marital relationship, unless triggered by some event; in this case, her pregnancies. In the final analysis, the illness having been triggered by later events (pregnancies) it did not impair her capacity to form a normal marital relationship. With proper management, he was also satisfied that she was capable of sustaining that relationship. That said, the characterisation of her condition as having been latent at the time of her marriage, given the nature of the diagnosis, must be a questionable proposition.[82] Furthermore, as noted in *C(E) (orse*

---

[78] Thus, for example, see *T(K)* v *T(D)* [1992] 2 IR 11 (Supreme Court, affirming the High Court's refusal (Murphy J) to grant a decree of nullity). In the High Court, Murphy J, notwithstanding the expert evidence adduced in relation to the wife's incapacity, refused to be bound by that evidence and assessed the matter on the totality of the evidence. In not yielding to the views of the psychiatrists in the case, Egan J in the Supreme Court approved. See also below.

[79] See also the conclusion of O'Hanlon J in *T(S)* v *J(B) (orse T(B))* (High Court, Unreported Judgment, O'Hanlon J, 2 September 1993).

[80] [1984] ILRM 173.

[81] High Court, Unreported Judgment, McCracken J, 14 March 1996.

[82] See also Chapters 9 and 15. It is unclear what "latent" means in this context. If it means present but undiagnosed, then, arguably, it represents a fundamental defect present *ab initio*. The analogy of the condition with epilepsy or a brain tumour seems hardly *ad rem*. For further brief discussion, see R. Byrne and W. Binchy (1997), *Annual Review of Irish Law 1996*, Dublin: Round Hall Sweet & Maxwell, pp. 382–4.

M(E) v *M(K)*,[83] in the case of alleged impotence, if the analogy with relational incapacity is to be further applied, the court must be satisfied that the disability is incurable; and, in determining the issue of nullity, the court should consider the willingness of the party suffering the disability to co-operate with appropriate medical treatment, the nature and strength of the marital relationship, and the co-operation of the other party in demonstrating the appropriate response to the problem. When applied to a case of psychiatric disability going to relational incapacity — as distinct from sexual impotence arising from such a problem — an unwillingness to co-operate with treatment may be no more than a manifestation of the underlying disorder. Strictly speaking, this may be involuntary, and given a lack of insight,[84] is arguably not a proper matter to be weighed as it might be in the case of impotence.

Sexual Dysfunction

Issues of sexual dysfunction, from impotence to the paraphilias are considered in the previous chapter.[85] The law of nullity in relation to impotence — whether male or female — is settled.[86] Frequently caused by psychological rather than physical causes, female impotence in the form of vaginismus leading to secondary impotence in the husband has been considered by the courts. Such a situation arose in *O'H(A) (orse F)* v *F*[87] where a decree was granted. Impotence of a wife *quoad hunc*, for example, grounded a decree in *C* v *C*[88] and *C(E) (orse M(E))* v *M(K)*[89] and impotence of a

---

[83] [1991] 2 IR 192 (Barr J).

[84] See Chapter 2, pp. 31–5.

[85] See Chapter 10, pp. 239–46.

[86] For example, *McM* v *McM* [1936] IR 177, and *M(M) (orse G)* v *M(P)* [1986] ILRM 515 (McMahon J).

[87] [1986] ILRM 489 (Barron J)

[88] High Court, Unreported Judgment, Lynch J, 18 November 1985.

[89] [1991] 2 IR 192 (Barr J).

husband, in *N(AM)* v *C(JP)*.[90] However, as noted, sexual inhibition of one party is not a sufficient ground,[91] although repugnance caused by physical disfigurement may be.[92]

Whereas issues relating to orgasmic dysfunction and the paraphilias have yet to be considered by our courts in a nullity context,[93] it seems clear that ejaculatory disorders, however they might be moulded into the contours of *RSJ*, might not be sufficient to ground a decree of nullity.[94] However, an inherent and unalterable homosexual nature in one party may be sufficient.[95]

PROOF

What Proof?

Because of the nature of the subject matter before the courts in nullity matters, it may be difficult to establish the facts objectively. Only in rare cases is there evidence from psychiatrists who have treated one of the parties a short time before the marriage.[96] On occasions, the petition is uncontested. Thus, it has always been held that there is a heavy burden of proof resting on a person who seeks to impeach a marriage that is *prima facie* and presumed to be valid.[97] In *McM* v *McM* and *McK* v *McK*[98] it was held

---

[90] [1988] ILRM 170 (Barron J).

[91] *B(A)* v *B(E)* [1997] 1 IR 305 (Budd J).

[92] *M(B)* v *M(C)* (High Court, Unreported Judgment, Flood J, 31 July 1996).

[93] See Chapter 10, pp. 239–46.

[94] Arising from consideration of *M(M)* *(orse G)* v *M(P)* [1986] ILRM 515 (McMahon J) (penetration, no emission); *B(A)* v *B(E)* [1997] 1 IR 305 (Budd J) (alleged inadequacy of the sexual intercourse); and *C(E)* *(orse M(E))* v *M(K)* [1991] 2 IR 192 (Barr J) (willingness to undergo treatment).

[95] *F(U)* *(orse C(U))* v *C(J)* [1991] 2 IR 330; and *F* v *F* [1990] 1 IR 348 (Barron J). See also in *McD(MF)* v *O'R(W)* (High Court, Unreported Judgment, Hamilton J, 26 January 1984), where the application failed.

[96] For example, *C(D)* *(orse W(D))* v *W(D)* [1987] ILRM 58 (Blayney J); *M(G)* *(orse G(G))* v *G(T)* (High Court, Unreported Judgment, Lavan J, 22 November 1991); and *McG(R)* v *K(N)* (High Court, Unreported Judgment, Morris J, 23 May 1995) reported as *RMcG* v *KMcG* [1995] 3 Fam LJ.

[97] See *Griffith* v *Griffith* [1944] IR 35, *per* Haugh J.

that petitions based on impotence were to be established "clearly, unequivocally and beyond reasonable doubt . . . "[99] Thus, the evidence put forward by a petitioner in a nullity suit is generally regarded with some caution and there is a disinclination merely to rely on the petitioner's uncorroborated version of events.[100] However, in *N (orse K) v K*[101] McCarthy J noted that:

> A petitioner must establish the case upon the balance of probabilities standard, but this must take into account the frequent absence of opposition, the possibility of collusion, and so forth.[102]

In *F(U)* the Supreme Court expressly declined to consider the standard of proof required[103] and Denham J in *S v K*[104] considered that there was a "severe and heavy burden on the petitioner, of a quasi-criminal trial nature". In *C(S) v D(P) (orse C(P))*,[105] McCracken J asserted that the civil standard was applicable.[106]

In order that the court might benefit from a professional assessment before determining the issues, the Master of the High Court has jurisdiction to order one or both parties to a nullity suit to attend a psychiatric examination and assessment.[107] It has been held that the court will not lightly order an examination that is unpleasant, painful or potentially dangerous, although a psychiatric examination does not necessarily constitute an

---

[98] [1936] IR 177.

[99] [1936] IR 177 at 187 *per* Hanna J.

[100] See *RSJ v JSJ* [1982] ILRM 263.

[101] [1985] IR 733, [1986] ILRM 75.

[102] [1985] IR 733 at 755, [1986] ILRM 75 at 94.

[103] The issue is considered at length in *B(A) v B(E)* [1997] 1 IR 305 at 324 to 330 *per* Budd J.

[104] High Court, Unreported Judgment, 2 July 1992.

[105] High Court, Unreported Judgment, McCracken J, 14 March 1996.

[106] As did Kinlen J in *O'R v B* [1995] 2 ILRM 57 and as Lynch J applied in *W(K) v W(M)* (High Court, Unreported Judgment, Lynch J, 19 July 1994).

[107] RSC Order 70 Rule 32.

interference with a right to bodily integrity. Furthermore, it has been held that the ordering of such an "inspection" does not constitute a breach of marital privacy (especially if it is contended that there was no valid marriage in the first instance) or interfere with the privilege against self-incrimination.[108] That said, it also appears that the party so ordered is not obliged to attend.[109]

As to who has the final say on the issue, the preponderance of the written judgments firmly assert that it is the courts. Thus, the expert psychiatric evidence is weighed with the other available evidence, but is not determinative of the outcome. Indeed, there is only infrequently clear, objective, expert psychiatric evidence relating to the relevant time, i.e. the time of marriage, the rest of the professional evidence being in the nature of opinion rather than objective fact, and opinion frequently based on hearsay rather than primary knowledge. The difficulties are neatly illustrated by the first two principal cases on relational incapacity to come before the courts, although they are also reflected in more recent decisions.

In *RSJ* v *JSJ*[110] the court found the petitioner's evidence unsatisfactory. However, he had been examined and treated by three different consultant psychiatrists, although none of these had seen the petitioner either immediately before or after his wedding. Although the psychiatric evidence might seem inconsistent, the opinions expressed by the psychiatrists involved could also be regarded as representing no more than different "snapshots" of a relatively severe and global psychiatric disorder.[111]

Thus, one psychiatrist who was of the view that the petitioner was eccentric, a hypochondriac, introverted and schizoid[112]

---

[108] *S(J)* v *S(C) (orse T(C))* [1997] 2 IR 506 (Budd J).

[109] *S(J)* v *S(C) (orse T(C))* [1997] 2 IR 506 at 522, although failure to comply might result in adverse judicial comment at trial. See also Family Law Act, 1995, s. 47, and Shatter (1997), op. cit., para. 5.88.

[110] [1982] ILRM 263.

[111] See Chapter 3.

[112] See Chapter 9, pp. 208–9.

considered that his capacity for emotional relationships was impaired, but declined to express a view as to whether or not he was incapable of having a successful marriage. The second psychiatrist who saw the petitioner some two months after he had last been seen by the first psychiatrist, and approximately one year after his wedding, considered that the petitioner was suffering from a schizo-affective or schizophreniform[113] illness and that he would have great difficulty in marriage or in maintaining a relationship with anyone, and that he would find it hard to love anyone on a continuous basis. When seen approximately a year after the wedding, the petitioner seemed more depressed than previously and the psychiatrist was also of the view that it would be reasonable to assume that the petitioner had continued in this or in some similar condition throughout the period during which he had been seen, including, therefore, the date of his marriage. The third psychiatrist who saw the petitioner some four months after his wedding was of the opinion that he was suffering from endogenous depression[114] and a schizophreniform illness, that he would find it difficult to relate to people or to get close to them, that he would not be able to have a meaningful relationship with another person and that he lacked the capacity for empathy. Having considered all the evidence, the court concluded that both before and after his marriage, the petitioner "suffered from some form of personality defect or illness similar to schizophrenia (*sic*)" and that this made it difficult for him to have a successful marriage. Notwithstanding this finding, however, considering all the evidence, including that of the petitioner and his sisters and the respondent, the court was not satisfied that that the petitioner had proven that on the date of his wedding he was so incapacitated as to make the marriage void or voidable.[115]

---

[113] See Chapter 15, pp. 347–8.

[114] See Chapter 6, pp. 99–104.

[115] In any event, as the petitioner was relying on his own incapacity and the respondent's evidence was to the effect that she had not repudiated the marriage, the application could not have succeeded.

In *D* v *C*,[116] in contrast, there was no evidence from a psychiatrist who had examined or treated the respondent before the date of his marriage. Nevertheless, the court accepted the evidence of a consultant psychiatrist called to give evidence by the petitioner-wife as to the psychiatric disorder suffered by her respondent-husband, notwithstanding that he (the psychiatrist) had not had an opportunity to examine the respondent (as the respondent had refused a request for such an examination). This evidence was accepted, as the trial judge was satisfied as to the veracity of the petitioner's evidence and insofar as the professional opinion and diagnosis of the respondent by the psychiatrist was based on this, the court was satisfied that the psychiatrist was fully entitled to rely on it. The psychiatrist who had treated the respondent after his marriage, who was mainly concerned with the treatment of the respondent's drug addiction, did not reach any conclusions as to his pre-marriage psychiatric state and declined to make any comment about his mental health at the time of his marriage, as he considered that it was not possible to make a retrospective diagnosis in the case. On the basis of the petitioner's history, the post-marital history insofar as it was relevant in throwing light on his pre-marital psychiatric health, and the opinion expressed on reliance of that history by the psychiatrist called on her behalf, and who had never seen or examined the respondent, the court concluded that the petitioner was suffering from a manic-depressive psychosis[117] before, at the time of, and after his marriage, which condition was sufficiently severe at the time of his marriage, as to incapacitate him from entering into and sustaining a viable marriage relationship (a conclusion which the psychiatrist called on behalf of the respondent did not deny as a general proposition). The evidence of other witnesses who indicated that they had seen nothing untoward in the respondent's behaviour was deemed not to be sufficient to displace the conclusions to be drawn from what was regarded as the more direct and

---

[116] [1984] ILRM 173 (Costello J).

[117] See Chapter 10, pp. 236–7, and Chapter 15, p. 348.

convincing evidence in the case. However, such medical evidence, from a psychiatrist who had never seen or examined the respondent may be dismissed as hearsay.[118]

Thus, for example, in *C(P) (orse O'B)* v *O'B(D)*,[119] *T(K)* v *T(D)*,[120] *S(H)* v *S(J)*,[121] the court decided the issue of relational incapacity notwithstanding the psychiatric evidence adduced to that effect. In *McG(R)* v *K(N)*[122] the court decided the issue of the effects of chronic alcohol abuse on the petitioner's capacity to consent to marriage on the date of his wedding, despite the evidence of a consultant psychiatrist to the effect that it was not unlikely that he had an alcoholic blackout in relation to it. However, the psychiatric evidence adduced in the High Court in *K(P)* v *N(MB) (orse K)*[123] was sufficient for the rejection of the appeal by the respondent against the granting of a decree of nullity in the High Court. Similarly, the Supreme Court did not upset the findings of the High Court in respect of the respondent's relational incapacity in *O'M(M) (orse O'C(M))* v *O'C(B)*.[124] Although it was questionable as to whether the presence of a diagnosable psychiatric disorder is the determining factor (the classification of a clinical state as a "disease", "disorder" or "condition", in this context, compounding the forensic difficulties) the matter has now been settled by *F(U) (orseC(U))* v *C(J)*.[125] In this regard, the approach of Laffoy J in

---

[118] See, for example, *T(R)* v *P(V) (orse T(V))* [1990] 2 IR 545 (Lardner J).

[119] High Court, Unreported Judgment, Carroll J, 2 October 1985.

[120] [1992] 2 IR 11 (Supreme Court), affirming the High Court's refusal (Murphy J).

[121] Supreme Court, Unreported Judgment, 3 April 1992, affirming the High Court's refusal (High Court, Unreported Judgment, Carroll J, 19 December 1990).

[122] High Court, Unreported Judgment, Morris J, 23 May 1995.

[123] *K(P)* v *N(MB) (orse K)* (Supreme Court, Unreported Judgment, 3 April 1995), affirming Costello J (High Court, Unreported Judgment, 27 November 1992).

[124] [1996] 1 IR 208.

[125] [1991] 2 IR 330.

C(P) v *M(C)* *(orse C(C))*[126] is instructive. She considered that once the psychiatric evidence had established that there was no question of mental "illness" involved (and, in this case there was a dispute between the psychiatrists about whether or not the respondent suffered from a personality disorder properly so-called) that it was for the court to decide whether or not the petitioner had established that the respondent

> . . . was incapable of entering into and sustaining a proper marital relationship by reason of incapacity attributable to some inherent quality or characteristic . . .

This approach is not dissimilar to that taken by the courts in relation to the role of the evidence of a psychiatrist where the defence of provocation is raised in response to a charge of murder.[127]

---

[126] High Court, Unreported Judgment, 11 January 1996.

[127] See Chapter 16, pp. 409–11, and *People (DPP)* v *Kehoe* [1992] ILRM 481 (CCA).

Part Four

DISPOSING CAPACITY

Chapter 12

ORGANIC DISORDERS AFFECTING
TESTAMENTARY CAPACITY

Testamentary capacity is most likely to be affected by those psychiatric disorders which have a permanent effect on understanding and is particularly associated with the dementias (disorders in which macroscopic damage to the brain tissue occurs). Other disorders also affect understanding, including acute confusional states, most commonly due to infections, and sometimes depressive illness, but the treatability of these makes their impact temporary.[1] The severity of the dementia is the factor most likely to impinge upon testamentary capacity[2] and decisions about this are made clinically and are not related to the amount of radiological change as measured by brain scanning.

However other factors such as intelligence[3] may also impinge and a patient with early dementia whose pre-existing IQ was low will show greater problems with understanding than one whose dementia is more severe but is of normal intelligence.

When asked to give advice on testamentary capacity, it is advisable to assess the patient on at least two occasions, particularly if dementia is suspected or diagnosed, in order that discrepancies

---

[1] Producing "lucid intervals". See Chapter 14.

[2] There is no empirical reason not to correlate clinical severity of a dementia with testamentary incapacity.

[3] See Chapter 14, pp. 304–7; and T. Jarman (1951), *A Treatise on Wills*, R. Jennings and J.C. Harper (eds.), 8th edition, London: Sweet & Maxwell, Vol. 1, at p. 50 and the footnotes thereto: "The will of an idiot is, of course, void."

over time in the patient's understanding of the issues involved can be fully documented.[4]

Three aspects need to be assessed:

1. Does he understand the implications of making or changing a will?

2. Does he appreciate the size of his estate?

3. Does he appreciate which people may expect to benefit from his estate?[5]

CAUSES OF CHRONIC ORGANIC BRAIN DISEASE

The common causes of organic brain damage are listed below.[6] Other causes of organic brain disease are symptomatic of a primary disorder and are generally reversible once the primary disorder has been treated.[7] This chapter will focus almost exclusively on the primary organic brain diseases with the exception of those induced by alcohol or head injury.

The dementias are a group of disorders in which death of brain cells leads to progressive deterioration in intellect, personality and behaviour. The process is generally inexorable and no treatment as yet is available to reverse or halt the deterioration. The dementias are classified into two groups — pre-senile and senile, affecting those

---

[4] See also Chapter 14.

[5] See *Sefton* v *Hopwood* 1 Fos&F 578 *per* Cresswell J; *Harwood* v *Baker* (1840) 3 Moo PC 282; *Banks* v *Goodfellow* [1870] LR 5 (1870) QB 549; *Boughton* v *Knight* (1873) 3 P&D 64; *Battan Singh* v *Amirchand* [1948] AC 161.

[6] Common causes of chronic organic brain disease are as follows. *Primary Degenerative*: Alzheimer's disease/senile dementia; Atherosclerotic dementia; Normal pressure hydrocephalus; Pick's disease; Huntington's chorea; Creutzfeldt-Jakob disease; Multiple sclerosis; Parkinson's disease; Lewy Body dementia. *Symptomatic Disease:* Cerebral tumours; Subdural haematoma; Cerebral infection (e.g. HIV); Collagen diseases (e.g. SLE); Poisoning from alcohol, lead or other metals; Anoxia; Vitamin deficiency (e.g. thiamine); Endocrine disorders (e.g. hypoglycaemia, hypothyroidism); Head injury.

[7] Unless the primary disorder is fatal. See, for example, *Duffy* v *Duffy* (High Court, Unreported Judgment, O'Hanlon J, 10 August 1994), where the testator, who was terminally ill, died four days after executing his will in hospital.

under and over the age of 65 respectively. However, there is overlap between the pre-senile and senile categories, particularly with the most common types (i.e. Alzheimer's disease and multi-infarct dementia).

Pre-Senile Dementia

Alzheimer's disease is the most common pre-senile dementia. In the under-65 group, it is called Alzheimer's type 2, to distinguish it from type 1 found in the over-65 age category.

Inheritance

There is a genetic component to the disorder and this is higher in type 2, the magnitude of the inheritance being of the order of 50 per cent. However, in about 35 per cent of cases, there is no family history[8] and the concordance for the disease in monozygotic twins (genetically identical) is less than 50 per cent, suggesting that environmental as well as genetic factors are important in the aetiology. There is an increased incidence of Alzheimer's disease in those with Down's syndrome, suggesting that chromosome 21, the abnormal gene in Down's syndrome, might also be involved in the transmission of Alzheimer's disease. Studies have suggested that several genes are probably involved in its transmission (genetic heterogeneity).

Pathology

There is loss of up to 50 per cent of neurones (brain cells) in post-mortem specimens. In the late onset variety, the loss is somewhat less at about 25 per cent. This results in shrinkage in brain size. Senile plaques, which are found in normal ageing, occur to excess in both senile and pre-senile Alzheimer's disease. Aluminium may be involved in plaque formation, although results to date are conflicting. Neurofibrillary tangles are found in both early and late onset types of the disease, although they are more common in the former.

---

[8] H.C. Chui, E.L. Teng and V.W. Henderson (1985), "Clinical Subtypes of Dementia of Alzheimer Type", *Neurology*, Vol. 35, pp. 1544–50.

Neurotransmitter Changes

A reduction in the quantity of a neurotransmitter known as acetylcholine may be associated with the cognitive changes found in sufferers.[9] Other transmitter changes occur later in the course of the disease and are not believed to be involved in causation. These include a reduction in serotonin, nor-adrenaline and GABA (gamma-amino butyric acid).

Symptoms

The initial symptom is likely to be difficulty in recent memory, impaired concentration, agitation and word-finding problems. In the early phase, Alzheimer's disease may resemble depressive illness and care must be taken to exclude the latter, since it can be treated effectively (see depressive pseudo-dementia). The disease progresses gradually until all memory is grossly impaired with an inability to recall remote as well as recent events. Misidentification of people occurs, as well as misidentification of the patient himself, termed "the mirror sign".[10] Disorientation in time, place and person is almost universal and up to 15 per cent of patients develop hallucinations and delusions.[11] Terminally, there is double incontinence, wandering, muscle rigidity and grossly impaired speech. Muscle contractures and emaciation finally set in.

Because of the insidiously progressive nature of the memory impairment, insight is retained for some time. This leads to frustration and outbursts of agitation and tearfulness when

---

[9] E.K. Perry, B.E. Tomlinson, G. Blessed, K. Begmann, P.H. Gibson and R.H. Perry (1978), "Correlation of Cholinergic Abnormalities with Senile Plaques and Mental Test Scores in Senile Dementia", *British Medical Journal*, Vol. ii, pp. 1457–9.

[10] Such severe disability in a testator at the time of execution of a will or codicil would clearly render any disposition void, by virtue of *Banks* v *Goodfellow* [1870] LR 5 (1870) QB 549.

[11] See Chapter 2, p. 34, and Chapter 13, p. 291.

confronted with a challenge (e.g. doing simple arithmetic). This is known as a catastrophic reaction.[12]

Investigations

In many patients, there is little CAT scan evidence of change until the disease is well established. MRI scan is superior, although more expensive. EEG changes are present but non-specific. Thus, the diagnosis is largely a clinical one and can be present in the absence of any radiological changes. If the disease is confirmed radiologically, serial CAT scans, perhaps every 6 to 12 months, are carried out to confirm the progress of the disease. Since there is no association between the clinical stage of the disease and the extent of CAT scan abnormalities, this is but a crude measure of progression.

In addition to these radiological investigations, clinicians apply a number of psychological tests to quantify and measure the progress of the disease. The Mini-Mental State Examination[13] is easily administered by the clinician and is the most frequently used measure. Others include the Weschler Adult Intelligence Scale,[14] Camdex[15] and Camcog (the computerised version of Camdex), the Crichton Behaviour Rating Scale,[16] and the Clifton Assessment Procedure for the Elderly (CAPE).[17] Abnormalities are often detected by these tests in advance of radiological change. Again,

---

[12] Depending on the stage of progression of the disorder (see investigation and assessment below), a testament executed during the insightful phase of deterioration could be valid.

[13] M.F. Folstein, S.E. Folstein and P.R. McHugh (1975), "Mini-mental State", *Journal of Psychiatric Research*, Vol. 12, pp. 189–98.

[14] See Chapter 4, p. 58.

[15] M. Roth, E. Tym and C.Q. Mountjoy (1986), "CAMDEX: a Standardised Instrument for the Diagnosis of Mental Disorders in the Elderly with Special Reference to Early Detection of Dementia", *British Journal of Psychiatry*, Vol. 149, pp. 698–709.

[16] R.A. Robinson (1975), "The Assessment Centre" in G. Howells (ed.), *Modern Perspectives in the Psychiatry of Old Age*, Edinburgh: Churchill Livingstone.

[17] A.H. Pattie and C.J. Gilleard (1976), "The Clifton Assessment Schedule: Further Validation of a Psychiatric Assessment Schedule", *British Journal of Psychiatry*, Vol. 129, pp. 68–72.

repeated testing, usually separated by several months, will assist in tracking the course of the disease.

Treatment

There is no known treatment for this disorder. A recent addition to the market has been the drug tacrine, which slows down the process of degeneration in some patients. More recently, donepezil, an inhibitor of the neurotransmitter acetylcholine, has been recommended for those with mild to moderate disease but is only effective in 40 per cent of sufferers.[18] Symptomatic treatment is required for paranoid symptoms, for agitation or depression.[19] Death is inevitable, although the time period from initial diagnosis until this occurs varies and can take up to ten years.[20]

Differential Diagnosis[21]

a) Depressive illness, especially in the elderly, may sometimes be associated with confusion. This is known as depressive pseudodementia and may be mistaken for dementia. Excluding depressive illness is therefore essential and, if uncertain, a course of antidepressant treatment or even ECT may be required to establish the diagnosis. None of the psychological tests delineated above assist in distinguishing between pseudodementia and true dementia, since they are all affected by mood disturbance. It has been suggested that up to 10 per cent of those in long-term care are in fact suffering from a depressive illness misdiagnosed as dementia.

---

[18] Depending on the efficacy of the agent, testamentary capacity could theoretically be maintained or restored.

[19] For the effects of delusions on testaments, see Chapter 13, pp. 253–8.

[20] It is this relatively long interval between onset and death, coupled with the age distribution of the disease, that makes it a particularly relevant consideration in testamentary capacity.

[21] The issue of correct diagnosis is critical to subsequent forensic assessment; see Chapter 14, pp. 321–3.

b) Since some patients develop paranoid symptoms during the illness, it may be confused with paranoid psychosis, especially in the early stages before memory impairment becomes marked. The longitudinal course of the disease will confirm the diagnosis.[22]

c) Focal lesions such as tumours can present with memory impairment and it is essential to rule these out, since they may be treated surgically. Other organic disorders such as normal pressure hydrocephalus should also be eliminated.[23]

d) Other dementias (see below) should also be considered, although there is little by way of treatment available.

e) Non-cerebral causes of confusion and memory impairment[24] such as thyroid disease must be considered, since these are treatable by treating the underlying condition.[25]

Alcohol-induced Brain Disease

Two types of brain damage are associated with alcohol abuse — Korsakoff's psychosis and alcoholic dementia.[26]

Korsakoff's Psychosis

Korsakoff's psychosis is a complication of thiamine deficiency, a vitamin lacking in alcohol abusers. It is sometimes preceded by Wernicke's encephalopathy, which develops in the course of

---

[22] Nevertheless, paranoid symptoms may invalidate a will. See for example: *Dew* v *Clark* (1826) 3 Add 79, 5 Russ 166; *Banks* v *Goodfellow* [1870] LR 5 (1870) QB 549; and Chapter 14, pp. 311–15.

[23] See below, p. 289.

[24] See above.

[25] Thus, underactivity of the thyroid (myxoedema) — which can be, and is, readily and successfully treated — may present as a depressive or dementing illness.

[26] Alcohol intoxication at the time of execution of a will may invalidate the will, see *Legeyt* v *O'Brien* Milw 337, although chronic alcohol abuse may not; see Chapter 14, p. 326 and, for example *Handley* v *Stacey* (1858) 1 F&F 574.

delirium tremens.[27] This is a condition in which nystagmus (sideways movements of the eyes), ataxia (staggering gait), peripheral neuropathy (damage to the nerves supplying the muscles and skin) and confusion occur, leading to profound impairment of recent memory, confabulation and apathy. Total recovery from Korsakoff's psychosis, even with abstinence from alcohol and thiamine supplements, is rare, but improvement may occur.[28] On post-mortem examination, there is evidence of small haemorrhages in the mamillary bodies of the brain.

Alcoholic Dementia

Alcoholic dementia is largely due to the direct toxic effect of alcohol on brain tissue, leading to a reduction in the white matter, although vitamin deficiencies and repeated trauma to the head also contribute.[29] Women are most at risk and it develops earlier in the course of alcohol dependence in them as compared to men. Memory and skills are impaired and there is difficulty learning new material. CAT scan of the brain reveals generalised shrinkage of tissue, but in some this may be confined to specific areas such as the frontal lobe or the cerebellum (the area concerned with balance), presenting with personality change or abnormalities of gait respectively. There is some correlation between the degree of atrophy and impairment of function. Improvement occurs in the early stages, provided the patient remains abstinent.

Pick's Disease

This is a rare form of pre-senile dementia. Unlike Alzheimer's disease, which affects all areas of the brain, the atrophy in Pick's disease is limited to the frontal and temporal lobes. The micro-

---

[27] See for example, *Brunt v Brunt* (1873) LR 3 P&D 37 (tearing up of a will in a "fit" of *delirium tremens* did not amount to revocation).

[28] Recovery could be sufficient to preserve testamentary capacity.

[29] If a sufficiently lucid interval occurs, this may be sufficient to establish testamentary capacity; see, for example, *Wheeler and Barsford v Alderson* (1831) 3 Hag Ecc 574.

scopic pathology is different from Alzheimer's disease. There is a small genetic contribution.

Clinical Features

The patient presents with changes to personality and to social behaviour. As the disease progresses, speech becomes impaired with nominal aphasia (difficulties naming objects) predominating and later progressing to echolalia (repetition of words) and finally mutism. Memory is impaired, but catastrophic reactions do not occur. Everyday activities are not affected until late in the disease and the patient may therefore be able to cook and even travel alone. Orientation also remains intact. Agitation is much less common than in Alzheimer's disease and hyperalgesis (an increased awareness of pain), prominent in the middle stage of the disease, disappears later.[30]

Investigations

Non-specific EEG changes occur and up to 50 per cent of patients show no abnormality. CAT and MRI scans show atrophy of the frontal and temporal lobes.

Treatment

There is no treatment for the disease.

Creutzfeldt-Jakob Disease

This uncommon disease, first described in the 1920s, has come to public attention recently, being associated with bovine spongiform encephalopathy (BSE).[31] Some cases are familial and inherited by dominant transmission. The majority are either due to infection or are sporadic.

---

[30] E.E. Robertson, A. Le Roux and J.H. Brown (1958), "The Classical Differentiation of Pick's Disease", *Journal of Mental Science*, Vol. 104, pp. 1000–24.

[31] Given the apparent increase in incidence of new variant Creutzfeldt-Jakob Disease (nv-CJD), and the fact that the victims are relatively young, this may, in the future, present problems of testamentary incapacity in an age group in which it is not particularly recognised as an issue of forensic concern.

Pathology

There is loss of nerve cells, although cerebral atrophy is minimal. Plaques, distinguishable from those seen in Alzheimer's disease, accumulate and astrocytes[32] proliferate in the grey matter of the brain. There are spaces dotted throughout the grey matter, giving the brain a spongy appearance.

Clinical Features

Creutzfeldt-Jakob disease is rapidly progressive and leads to death within two years. There may be a fleeting prodromal phase of anxiety, depression and psychotic symptoms, although this is not universal. Intellectual deterioration is rapid and profound and associated with spasticity and wasting of muscles. Tremors of the limbs, choreoform (writhing) movements, ataxia (unsteadiness when walking) and fits also occur. Blindness is a terminal feature.

Treatment

There is none.

Huntington's Disease

This slowly progressive disease was first described by Huntington in 1872. It is uncommon, affecting people with an incidence of 5/100,000. It is transmitted by autosomal dominant gene; therefore 50 per cent of offspring will be affected, although the offspring of unaffected children are not at risk. Men and women are equally affected. Occasionally, sporadic cases occur in which there is no family history. The age of onset is slightly later when inheritance is maternal.[33]

---

[32] Supporting cells of the central nervous system, so-called because they are star-shaped. They function in support, protection and nutrition of the nerve cells.

[33] J.B. Martin and J.F. Gusella (1986), "Huntington's Disease: Pathogenesis and Management", *New England Journal of Medicine*, Vol. 315, pp. 1267–76.

Pathology

There is generalised cortical atrophy, although atrophy is particularly prominent over the frontal lobe and in the caudate nucleus and putamen,[34] areas which lie deep in brain tissue.

Neurochemistry

There is a deficiency of gamma-amino-butyric acid (GABA), a neurotransmitter in the brain. Somatostatin, which stimulates dopamine activity, is increased, whilst choline acetyltransferase is reduced. Nor-adrenaline and adrenaline levels are not diminished.

Clinical Features

The onset is insidious. It may initially appear to be nothing more than fidgetiness. Spontaneous movements and grimaces are first noticed in the face and upper limbs. These are jerky and choreiform and gradually extend to all parts of the body, affecting movement, speech and respiration. Since insight is present in the early stages, depression and irritability may occur. Suicide is also a risk, not just in sufferers but also in non-afflicted relatives. Dementia develops as the disease progresses, although in some patients it may be a presenting feature. A state of complete apathy may obscure the extent of intellectual impairment.

Emotional disturbances such as depression and fleeting paranoid ideation may precede the physical symptoms. Other more nebulous difficulties, such as refusal to work, cruelty to others, and petty crime are also prominent. Schizophrenia occurs in a proportion and predates the onset of overt symptoms by several years.

Investigations

The EEG is flat, although this may occur in some normal adults also. CAT scan of the brain will demonstrate atrophy of the

---

[34] Parts of the basal ganglia of the brain that are concerned with providing a stable dynamic and automatic platform upon which ordinary voluntary movement can be executed.

caudate nucleus. PET scanning, which measures glucose utilisation in the caudate nucleus, will confirm the diagnosis even before the clinical features are evident.

Treatment

There is no treatment to halt the underlying disease process and death is inevitable. Symptomatic control of the choreiform movements may be achieved by using phenothiazines (major tranquillisers normally used in schizophrenia and mania) which reduce dopamine. Other drugs such as thiopropazate or tetrabenazine are also useful. Depression or paranoid symptoms are treated symptomatically. There is also a focus on genetic counselling — informing at-risk families of the likelihood of transmission of the disease in order that decisions about childbearing can be made in advance of pregnancy.

Differential Diagnosis

a) In the early stages, the disease may resemble any other psychiatric disorder, although a family history should alert the clinician to the likely diagnosis.

b) Chorea is an uncommon neurological disease, which is milder and not associated with a family history.

c) Tardive dyskinesia is a complication of the phenothiazine group of drugs, but it is not progressive and is not associated with dementia.

Prognosis

This is a slowly progressive disease that leads to inevitable death. The average duration is 10–15 years.[35]

---

[35] Given the protean manifestations of the condition, and the interval from onset to death, this condition is clearly capable of presenting particular problems of testamentary capacity; see Chapter 14.

Senile Dementia

Senile dementia affects 10 per cent of those over the age of 65, and 20 per cent over the age of 80.

Alzheimer's Disease

In those over the age of 65, this is referred to as Alzheimer's disease, type 1. There was a view that senile dementia was nothing more than an accelerated form of normal ageing, since post-mortem examination of the brains of the non-demented elderly showed similar pathology.[36] However this view is now challenged, since the cognitive deficits found in senile dementia are different from those of normal ageing.[37] Moreover, personality is preserved, unlike the process of dementia, where there is no semblance of previous personality or functioning in the terminal stages.

The features of Alzheimer's disease in the over-65 age group are similar to those found in the younger age group.

Multi-infarct Dementia

This is also known as atherosclerotic dementia and although it can occur in those under 65, it is more common in the elderly population, accounting for about 10 per cent of cases of dementia.

Pathology

The post-mortem brain will show discrete areas of softening due to narrowing of the arteries or haemorrhaging.

Clinical Features

The prevalence is higher in males than females and will often be associated with other forms of atherosclerosis such as angina or peripheral vascular disease, etc. The onset is sudden and deterioration is step-wise rather than gradual. Often the patient will

---

[36] See above, p. 277.

[37] An important point when considering a case such as *In the Estate of Helena Agnes Blackall, dec'd* (Supreme Court, Unreported Judgment, 1 April 1998, affirming (Barron J *diss*) High Court, Unreported Judgment, McCracken J, 28 June 1996).

present with a cerebro-vascular accident (stroke), thereafter failing to fully regain memory. The patient's condition will remain static for a time or may even improve slightly until the next sudden deterioration occurs.[38] Since insight is often preserved, patients become frustrated and depressed. Emotional control is poor and results in sudden, brief outbursts of tearfulness which resolve in a few seconds. This is known as emotional incontinence. Catastrophic reactions similar to those seen in Alzheimer's disease are common. Depression is most commonly associated with lesions in specific sites of the brain such as the right posterior cortex.

Investigations

The EEG may be normal in some patients. CAT or MRI scan of the brain will show areas of abnormality corresponding to the site of the infarct. Unlike Alzheimer's disease, the degree of dementia is related to the extent of brain tissue damage.

Differential Diagnosis

Other forms of dementia must be excluded.

Treatment

There is no effective treatment, although control of hypertension, when present, will reduce the risk of further strokes. Depression when present responds particularly well to antidepressants. Symptomatic treatment of restlessness and agitation may be necessary.

Prognosis

Death is usually from some related vascular disorder such as myocardial infarct (heart attack) or cerebrovascular accident (stroke).

---

[38] Although there may be an apparent "lucid interval" — albeit not one of complete pre-illness clarity.

OTHER FORMS OF SENILE DEMENTIA

Normal Pressure Hydrocephalus

Normal pressure hydrocephalus, first described in 1965 by Adams,[39] is the only treatable form of senile dementia. It presents with memory impairment and slowness of movement, particularly disturbances in walking. It may resemble depressive illness. Diagnosis is confirmed by CAT scan, and the insertion of a shunt to allow for the drainage of cerebrospinal fluid results in amelioration of symptoms in most patients.

Lewy Body Disease

Lewy body disease is a form of senile dementia, associated with acute or sub-acute confusional states, depression and symptoms of stiffness and tremor similar to that found in Parkinson's disease. It is difficult to distinguish clinically from other forms of senile dementia and the exact diagnosis is usually made at post-mortem. The Parkinsonian symptoms respond to treatment with anti-Parkinsonian drugs. It may represent up to 20 per cent of those with dementia over the age of 70.[40]

HEAD INJURY

Brain damage following an accident can influence testamentary capacity in some patients and the site of injury as well as the severity will determine this. Since recovery from head injury proceeds slowly, no attempt should be made to assess this for at least 6 months and ideally 12 months in order to maximise the potential for change. The site of the injury as well as its severity can be determined by CAT scans and by psychological testing.

---

[39] R.D. Adams, C.M. Fisher, S. Hakim, R.G. Ojemann and W.H. Sweet (1965), "Symptomatic Occult Hydrocephalus with 'Normal' Cerebrospinal Fluid Pressure: a Treatable Syndrome", *New England Journal of Medicine*, Vol. 273, pp. 117–26.

[40] R.H. Perry, D. Irving, G. Blessed, A. Fairbairn and E.K. Perry (1990), "Senile Dementia of Lewy Body Type", *Journal of Neurological Science*, Vol. 95, pp. 119–39.

Head injury affects intelligence, memory, language and personality.[41] Impaired judgement and planning may distort the patient's ability to make a will. Impulsivity or lack of initiative may
also have a similar effect. These traits develop following frontal
lobe damage. Memory impairment may also affect testamentary
capacity, since the patient may be unable to recall recently made
decisions and ultimately changes may lead to difficulty in understanding the nature and extent of the estate to be disposed of.[42]

Radiological investigations, particularly CAT or MRI scan of
the brain, will confirm the site of injury. In addition, specific
neuropsychological tests will assist in making a thorough assessment. The Weschler Adult Intelligence Scale[43] is helpful in assessing memory deficits and comprehension. A detailed interview
with relatives will also reveal aspects of behaviour relating to
judgement and initiative, which can supplement the radiological
and psychological data to hand.

SUMMARY

Testamentary capacity is most likely to be affected by the dementias and assessment should be made over several interviews.
There is no known treatment for these. They must be distinguished from acute confusional states, which respond to treatment of their cause, most commonly infections. Dementia can also
resemble depressive illness and the accompanying confusion may
lead to a mistaken diagnosis.

---

[41] The effect of head injury, in context of a subsequent nullity application by a
child, is alluded to in *W(K)* v *W(M)* (High Court, Unreported Judgment,
Lynch J, 19 July 1994).

[42] However, it is worth noting that it seems that such traits, in the absence of
proof of underlying pathology, will not of themselves invalidate a will; see
Sefton v *Hopwood* 1 Fos&F 578. A similar theme is found in *Bird* v *Luckie*
(1850) 8 Hare 301.

[43] See Chapter 4, p. 58.

Chapter 13

OTHER DISORDERS AFFECTING TESTAMENTARY CAPACITY

While testamentary capacity is most commonly affected by the dementias, other disorders considered in this chapter may in certain circumstances affect testamentary capacity.

SCHIZOPHRENIA[1]

In relation to testamentary capacity, problems may arise due to the auditory hallucinations and paranoid delusions which persist in some patients in spite of treatment.[2] Some patients will experience auditory hallucinations giving instructions to carry out a particular action. Somewhat more common are persistent delusions of variable content. A patient making a will may thus be acting in response to these hallucinations or delusions. For example, experiencing a voice instructing the patient to leave property to a particular person or deciding to do so on the basis that the next of kin is plotting against him, have obvious implications for testamentary capacity.[3]

Provided the psychiatrist is confident that adequate treatment has been given, then decisions can be made about the capacity of

---

[1] This disorder is described in detail in Chapter 15, pp. 332–45.

[2] This issue is considered at length — although not in situations necessarily attracting the exact diagnosis of schizophrenia — in Chapter 14, pp. 307–15.

[3] See, for example, the *locus classicus* of testamentary capacity, *Banks* v *Goodfellow* [1870] LR 5, QB 549; *Dew* v *Clark* (1826) 3 Add 79, 5 Russ 166; and *Hope* v *Campbell* [1899] AC 1.

the patient to dispose of property.[4] It must be remembered that some schizophrenic patients have persistent symptoms. However, the effect on disposing capacity is not related to having a chronic illness but to the content of the hallucinations and delusions.[5]

PARANOID PSYCHOSIS[6]

Although the prevalence of this disorder is unknown, it is associated with several risk factors. Immigrants, the elderly, those who are deaf, those who abuse alcohol and those who have sensitive or even suspicious pre-morbid personalities are at particular risk. In addition, many of those who suffer from paranoid psychosis are single, separated or divorced. This is believed to be related to the previous personality of the sufferer, which leads to isolation and in turn to paranoid psychosis.

This disorder is difficult to diagnose and, particularly if the patient is unmarried, may go unnoticed for many years, since the day-to-day functioning of the patient is often not affected by the illness, unlike those who suffer from schizophrenia. The core symptoms of the disorder are delusions of a persecution.[7] For example, a patient may complain that the CIA are spying on him and have a video installed in his home. These symptoms may be concealed, while the patient gathers "evidence" for the police. It is only when he requests police assistance to deal with his persecutors that the bizarreness of the claims becomes apparent.

Treatment is generally not accepted due to lack of insight and, even with treatment, symptoms sometimes continue, although in an attenuated form. Frequently treatment is refused until the delusions have become so intrusive as to impinge upon others so

---

[4] In the absence of evidence of marked thought disorder; see Chapter 14, pp. 321–2.

[5] This does not amount to a clinical justification for judicial severance of dispositions. See *In the Estate of Bohrmann* [1938] 1 All ER 271.

[6] See Chapter 10, p. 226, and Chapter 15, p. 346.

[7] As in *In the Estate of Bohrmann* [1938] 1 All ER 271.

that compulsory treatment becomes necessary.[8] If the focus of symptoms is a close relative or the next of kin, then decisions relating to wills can be impaired by the delusions.[9] Moreover, if alcohol is considered to be the cause of the psychosis in a particular case, then every attempt must be made to encourage abstinence, since this will lead to improvement. Attempts to persuade the patient of the falsity of his beliefs will always be met with hostility and rebuke and must be avoided. Overall, it is difficult for the patient to maintain trust in authority figures such as doctors and solicitors, a factor making this condition difficult to treat.

PERSONALITY DISORDER[10]

Personality disorder of itself has no impact on testamentary capacity, since the patient retains an understanding of the issues involved in making and changing wills.[11] However, in rare circumstances, a patient with personality disorder may come under undue pressure to make a will in a particular manner, although most will be able to withstand these pressures.[12] Those with dependent personality disorder may, however, be unable to assert themselves in these circumstances. The hallmark of dependent personality disorder is the sufferer's constant need for reassurance of their worth, persistent fears of being abandoned and objective evidence that they have been taken advantage of at work and in social situations. By definition, these traits are present throughout adult life and the patient is unable to alter his behaviour despite being made aware of the negative effect it is having on his life.

---

[8] See Chapter 18.

[9] The "insane delusion" of the testator to his daughter in *Dew* v *Clark* (1826) 3 Add 79, 5 Russ 166 appears to have been such a case.

[10] See Chapter 9.

[11] However, in the context of the presumptions as to a state of affairs that arises, it is not without its significance; see discussion in Chapter 14, p. 321.

[12] This phenomenon of duress or undue influence is more likely to arise in the case of elderly testators. However, in such cases, the vulnerability is age-related rather than attributable to a personality disorder.

The patient may come to attention because of obvious excessive dependence on family members or low self-esteem, but more usually in association with decompensation at a time of crisis (e.g. bereavement resulting in a depressive illness or a stress reaction).[13]

Personality disorder of this severity is uncommon,[14] but is included here for completeness. In the context of testamentary capacity, the patient is unlikely to admit coercion directly. Rather, the possibility must be kept in mind when making such assessments in those with personality disorder. There is no effective treatment for personality disorder of this severity.

OBSESSIVE-COMPULSIVE DISORDER[15]

This is an uncommon disorder, affecting less than 0.5 per cent of the population. It is more common in men than in women and usually begins in late adolescence. The cause is unknown, although there is increasingly a recognition that availability of 5-hydroxy-tryptamine, a brain chemical, plays an important part in causation. Freudian theories, which linked it to abnormalities in personality development, have been rejected by the body of mainstream psychiatry. Although some patients have obsessional personality disorder,[16] the two are distinct and must be assessed on separate axes.[17]

Two symptom clusters are found — obsessional rituals and obsessional compulsions. Sometimes, but not always, a compulsion precedes the execution of the ritual (e.g. thoughts (ruminations) of contamination leading to ritualistic hand-washing). The format of

---

[13] Wills made in such circumstances, it could be argued, should also be regarded with suspicion; see Chapter 14, p. 320.

[14] This author has only on two occasions seen dependent personality disorder of this magnitude.

[15] This rare disorder arose in a nullity context (*T(S)* v *J(B) (orse T(B))* High Court, Unreported Judgment, O'Hanlon J, 11 February 1993). However, it has not so far arisen in reported probate cases.

[16] See Chapter 9, p. 206.

[17] See Chapter 3.

the rituals vary from patient to patient, but the most common are repeated hand-washing (up to 60 times per day) or checking doors, windows, taps, etc., repeatedly even though the patient knows there is no need to. Compulsions, also known as ruminations, consist of thoughts — usually of a blasphemous, violent or mathematical nature — constantly running through the patient's mind (e.g. repeated thoughts of kidnapping a baby or continually adding the numbers on car number plates). Ruminations of contamination are also common, as is obsessional doubting. Ruminations are very distressing, since the patient often feels they augur insanity. Both the ruminations and rituals are initially resisted but this diminishes with time. The constellation of symptoms found in the individual patient rarely changes over time and is generally limited to one or two discrete features. Thus a patient presenting with obsessional checking will exhibit this feature for the duration of the illness.

Obsessional doubting in particular may have an impact on the person's ability to make a will. The feature of this symptom is the patient's uncertainty about the correctness of the decision he has made. He will vacillate and retract decisions previously reached.[18]

Treatment is with a combination of behaviour therapy and anti-obsessional drugs. The latter consist of the newer serotonin re-uptake inhibitors, largely used as antidepressants, but recently shown to have anti-obsessional properties. Treatment will be required for life. Follow-up studies show that between 30 and 60 per cent of patients improve. Obsessive-compulsive disorder is so incapacitating that it is one of the few disorders in which psychosurgery is sometimes necessary, although this is now rare with the wide availability of modern treatments.

---

[18] However, that is the freedom of testation that the law allows. That said, this is more likely to cause problems of interpretation if there have been a number of testamentary instruments and repeated but incomplete revocations or interlineations.

Differential Diagnosis

a) Obsessional symptoms occur in depressive illness but other features of depression will also be to the fore. Treatment is with antidepressants. The symptoms improve as the depressive symptoms improve.

b) Obsessional symptoms may be confused with delusions or they may occur in some psychotic disorders such as schizophrenia.

MENTAL RETARDATION

Much effort has been directed at finding an all-embracing but non-pejorative definition — hence the proliferation of terms such as "learning disability", "mental handicap", "mental deficiency", "mental retardation" and "mental subnormality".[19] The WHO has adopted the term "mental retardation" as being the most appropriate. Most of those with significant learning difficulties who possess estates will have been made Wards of Court as adolescents.

Two main aspects of mental retardation require consideration. Firstly, the learning disability, usually measured by the intelligence of the patient, leads to disabilities such as difficulties in reading, doing arithmetic and in comprehending matters generally. Although the intelligence quotient (IQ) is used as an indicator of the severity of the retardation, it also has its critics. An IQ above 70 is regarded as within the normal range, between 50 and 70 indicating mild retardation, between 35 and 50 indicating moderate retardation, between 20 and 25 indicating severe retardation and below 20 profound retardation. Those with an IQ lower than 50, i.e. moderately retarded, are unlikely to understand issues relating to property and money and testamentary capacity is likely to be compromised in such patients.[20]

---

[19] For older pejorative classification, see Chapter 14, p. 309–10.

[20] The wills of such persons are probably void.

Secondly, the social handicaps which result from mental retardation are likely to impinge upon the areas of occupation and relationships. The sufferer may be easily influenced and thus open to coercion, much as the patient with personality disorder is.[21] Even those with "mild" handicap (i.e. an IQ greater than 50), although capable of understanding the concept of possession and disposal of property, may be unduly influenced by peers and family members. It is thus important to extend the assessment for testamentary capacity beyond mathematical measures such as IQ to the more nebulous but difficult areas of social disability and possible peer or family coercion.

Practical Considerations

The assessment of mental retardation in relation to testamentary capacity will be assisted by the knowledge that other workers have of the patient, since he/she will invariably have come to the attention of health care workers in this field at a young age, thus providing a valuable source of ancillary information. However, those with mild handicap (i.e. IQ above 50) may not have been detected and may be holding down a simple job and may only come to attention when some associated problem presents (e.g. loss of a parent). However, a collateral history from a relative will indicated that the child was a slow learner and may have had transient behavioural problems due to increasing demands as adolescence approached. Such a person will have acquired basic literacy and numeracy skills.

Psychiatric Illness and Mental Retardation

Those with mental retardation also suffer from the range of psychiatric disorders, including schizophrenia, depressive illness and eating disorders. However, the presentation is likely to be atypical and there is a danger of ascribing the behavioural disturbance with which they frequently present as indicative of some stress or frustration, rather than of a definitive psychiatric illness. In

---

[21] See p. 293 above.

particular, depressive illness presents in this group with agitation and with acting out-behaviour such as wrist-cutting.[22]

SUMMARY

Testamentary capacity is affected by a range of psychiatric disorders, of which schizophrenia is the most common. Other rarer disorders affecting testamentary capacity are paranoid psychosis and obsessive-compulsive disorder. Adults who are mentally retarded will generally have been wards of court, although those with mild retardation may be functioning in the community. Such people may be subject to undue pressure from peers and family, particularly when disposing of property or money. Any assessment relating to testamentary capacity must be cognisant of the intelligence of the patient.

---

[22] Since detailed discussion of mental retardation is beyond the scope of this book, being largely a problem presenting in childhood, the interested reader is referred to established texts in the field; for example, A.M. Clarke and A.D.B. Clarke (eds.) (1965), *Mental Deficiency: the Changing Outlook*, 2nd edition, London: Methuen.

Chapter 14

TESTAMENTARY CAPACITY

INTRODUCTION

Unlike the law in relation to "nervous shock"[1] and criminal "insanity",[2] the law in relation to wills[3] is less concerned with defining whether or not a person who purports to make a will is suffering from a "recognisable psychiatric illness", or "nervous shock" or from "a defect of reason caused by a disease of the mind" respectively. Rather reassuringly, and in contrast with those other areas of law, it is concerned more with functional outcome, irrespective of the definition of a psychiatric disability or whether or not the disability under which the person is labouring amounts

---

[1] Chapter 8.

[2] Chapter 16.

[3] The Wills Act, 1837, was repealed in Ireland upon the statutory consolidation of the law of succession by the Succession Act, 1965, but remains in force in England, subject to certain amendments which are beyond the scope of this text. Similarly, the English exceptions in relation to noncupative wills in the Navy and Marines (Wills) Act, 1914 (which was amended by Acts in 1930, 1939 and 1953), and the Wills (Soldiers and Sailors) Act, 1918, were repealed by the Act of 1965 but are still in force in England. Wills are executed by only a relatively small percentage of the population and the reported cases, inevitably, represent a certain social bias in that only those endowed with property, and substantial property at that, are inclined to make wills at all. Most people, apparently through laziness, make no attempt to execute wills. Or, perhaps, laziness is an inappropriate attribution. Intestacy (i.e. dying without making a will) may be cynically referred to as a "lazy-man's will" and, in the event that it is likely that there might be a dispute about any bequests, or in relation to the will specifically or generally, failure, or refusal to make a will at all simply leaves it to the law to apportion the estate in accordance with statutory rules about which there can be no complaint.

to a disease of the mind, which in its turn produces a defect of reason. Although the law is drawn, largely, from the same well of Victorian jurisprudence, the relative clarity of the approach, from a clinical perspective, is quite remarkable.

That said, statutory regulation of testamentary dispositions (e.g. in relation to the rights of spouses *inter se* prohibiting the disinheriting of one by the other by the creation of a surviving spouse's legal right to a share in the other's estate)[4] has removed a common cause of complaint from this area of the law.

Briefly, certain formal requirements must be satisfied for a disposition of property by will to be valid and effective. Thus, the document effecting the disposition must be in writing, signed by the person disposing of the property, who must be over the age of 18 years,[5] or have been married,[6] and the signature must be witnessed. Furthermore, it is essential that the testator be of sound disposing mind and have *animus testandi*.[7]

---

[4] See Succession Act, 1965, ss. 111 to 115.

[5] Formerly, at common law, males of 14 and females of 12 years of age were competent to dispose of personal property by will which was valid, although the testator or testatrix later lived to their majority without confirming it. In some instances, apparently, infants of a definite and reasonable age were enabled by custom to dispose of real estate by will. However, all wills of minors were rendered invalid by the provisions of the Wills Act, 1837, s. 7. See Jarman (1951), op. cit., at page 49 and the footnotes thereto. The age of majority specified at 21 years in s. 7 was reduced by the Family Law Reform Act, 1969, s. 3(1)(a) to 18 years in the case of wills made after 1 January 1970. And, as observed by O'Flaherty and Lynch JJ in *In the Estate of Helena Agnes Blackall, dec'd* (Supreme Court, Unreported Judgment, 1 April 1998, affirming (Barron J *diss*) High Court, Unreported Judgment, McCracken J, 28 June 1996), there is no upper age limit to the making of a will.

[6] Nullity of Marriage Act, 1971, s. 1, consolidated as the Matrimonial Causes Act, 1973, s. 11, reproduced as amended by the Marriage Act, 1983, s. 2(4), sets the age at 16 years. However, in Ireland, the age below which one can marry without the consent of the President of the High Court was raised from 16 to 18 years by Family Law Act, 1995, s. 31.

[7] The intention of making a will; i.e., he must intend the wishes expressed to take effect only on his death as a will is construed to speak and take effect as if it had been executed immediately before the death of the testator, unless a contrary intention appears from the will, see Succession Act, 1965, ss. 77 and 89, and the Wills Act, 1837, s. 24. *Ex hypothesi*, this must depend on the putative testator's being of sound disposing mind.

TESTAMENTARY CAPACITY[8]

The requisite capacity for making a valid will, in addition to majority or marital status (now effectively the same in Ireland) is not defined. However, as in the law on criminal "insanity",[9] a person is presumed to be sane and of sound testamentary capacity[10] (or sound disposing mind)[11] until the contrary is shown.[12] Although in England, the Court of Protection is empowered to order the execution of a will for an adult, but mentally disordered, person, where it has reason to believe that he is incapable of making a valid will for himself,[13] there are no equivalent statutory provisions in Ireland.

---

[8] See, generally, J.B. Clark and J.G. Ross Martin (1993), *Theobald on Wills* 15th edition, London: Sweet & Maxwell, Chapter 3.1; C.H. Sherrin, R.F.D. Barlow, R.A. Wallington and S.L. Meadway (1995), *Williams on Wills*, 7th edition, London: Butterworths, Volume I, pp. 33–43; J.C. Brady (1995), *Succession Law in Ireland*, 2nd Edition, Dublin: Butterworths, Chapter 2; T. Jarman (1951), *A Treatise on Wills*, R. Jennings and J.C. Harper (eds.), 8th edition, London: Sweet & Maxwell, Vol. 1; T.H. Maxwell (1900), *Miller's Probate Practice*, Abingdon, Oxford: Professional Books Ltd., 1980 reprint; P. Coughlan (1998) *Property Law*, 2nd Edition, Dublin: Gill & Macmillan, pp. 393–4.

[9] See Chapter 16.

[10] Although the formal validity of a will is determined by statute (Succession Act, 1965, Part VIII and the Wills Act, 1963, which contain near identical provisions), both under domestic and private international law rules, under the latter, the question of testamentary capacity is determined by the law of the domicile of the testator *at the time of the making of the will*. See W. Binchy (1988), *Irish Conflicts of Laws*, Dublin: Butterworths (Ireland) Ltd., Chapter 23; and, for example, *In the Estate of Fuld (No. 3), Hartley* v *Fuld* [1965] 3 All ER 776. The law in Ireland and England is, for all practical purposes, identical in this regard.

[11] Although "testamentary capacity", strictly speaking, refers not alone to being of sound disposing mind, but includes having reached one's majority or having been married, in this text, it is used interchangeably with the former. "To constitute testamentary capacity, soundness of mind is indispensably necessary" *Banks* v *Goodfellow* [1870] LR 5, QB 549 at 559 *per* Cockburn CJ.

[12] See, for example, *Steed* v *Calley* 1 Keen 620, cited in Maxwell (1980), op. cit., p. 103; *In re Glynn dec'd* [1990] 2 IR 326; and below.

[13] Mental Health Act, 1983, ss. 96 and 97, which consolidated and re-enacted the previous law. Section 97 specifies the formalities which must be complied with. See *Theobald on Wills* (1993), op. cit., pp. 33–34 and the footnotes thereto.

Displaying a sensitivity not untypical of his class and time, but pithily identifying the potential range of the problems to be encountered, Cranworth LJ stated:

> There is no difficulty in the case of a raving madman, or a drivelling idiot, in saying that he is not a person capable of disposing of property; but between such an extreme case, and that of a man of perfectly vigorous understanding, there is every shade of intellect, every degree of mental capacity. There is no possibility of mistaking midnight for noon, but at what precise moment twilight becomes darkness is hard to determine.[14]

Reflecting a dated classification of psychiatric disability (including mental handicap) as late as 1951, it was asserted:

> The will of an idiot is of course void. Mental imbecility arising from advanced age, or produced permanently or temporarily by excessive drinking or any other cause, may destroy testamentary power.[15]

However, the essential issue of functional impairment rather than clinical or legal definition is preserved.

Time

Insofar as being of sound disposing mind is concerned, the relevant date is the date of the making of a will or codicil,[16] not the date of the testator's death (when the will or codicil becomes effective).[17] Thus, it is settled law[18] that, if having made a will or codicil

---

[14] *Boyse* v *Rossborough* 6 HLC 1, at 45.

[15] Jarman (1951), op. cit., p. 50 and the footnotes thereto.

[16] A codicil — an instrument executed by a testator which adds to, alters, explains or confirms a previously made will — is a will for the purposes of the Succession Act, 1965, such that, in order to be valid, it must be executed with the same formalities as a will. See also Wills Act, 1837, ss. 1 and 9.

[17] *Arthur* v *Bokenham* (1708) 11 Mod Rep 148; *Banks* v *Goodfellow* [1870] LR 5, QB 549.

[18] *Warn* v *Swift* (1832) 1 LJ Ch 203; *In the goods of Crandon* (1901) 84 LT 330.

while of sound disposing mind, a testator subsequently becomes
incompetent and dies, the testament is still valid. As a corollary, a
will, executed by a testator of sound disposing mind, will be valid
whereas a codicil thereto, subsequently executed during a period of
incompetency, will be invalid.[19] The converse also holds true, such
that if a testator makes a will or codicil while he is not of sound
disposing mind, subsequent recovery of sufficient testamentary capacity before death is insufficient to validate the instrument.[20]

As to what constitutes the time of the making of the will or
codicil, it is generally necessary that the testator should be of
sound disposing mind both at the time instructions are given for
the drawing up of the will and the time of its execution.[21] However, despite the logic and coherence of this approach, there is
authority which supports the validity of a will drawn up in accordance with instructions given when the proposed testator was
competent, even though, at the time of execution, whereas he appreciated that he was being requested to execute as his will a
document drawn up in accordance with those instructions, he was
unable to follow all of its provisions. Also, he was unable to remember the instructions he gave in relation thereto.[22]

---

[19] *Brouncker* v *Brouncker* (1812) 2 Phillim. 57.

[20] e.g. *Public Trustee* v *Prisk* [1896] 14 NZLR 306. *Williams on Wills* (1995),
op. cit., p. 35 notes that supervening loss of capacity (referred to as "insanity") *ex hypothesi* prevents a variation of any will made while of sound disposing mind. And, since the same disposing mind is required for the
revocation of a will, its absence also prevents any revocation of a will made
when of sound capacity.

[21] There may be some interval between the two events, up to the execution in
accordance with the provisions of the Succession Act, 1965, s. 78, or the Wills
Act, 1837, s. 9, and the Wills Act Amendment Act, 1852, s. 1.

[22] See, for example, *Perera* v *Perera* [1901] AC 354; *Thomas* v *Jones* [1928] P.
162; *Battan Singh* v *Amirchand* [1948] AC 161 [1948] 1 All ER 152; and
Parker v *Felgate* [1883] 8 PD 171 (where, extraordinarily, and in addition,
the testatrix was roused from a "partial" coma to execute the will). One would
have considered that, given the antiquity of some of these cases, their precedental value would have been rendered negligible. However, an analogous
approach was taken *In re Glynn dec'd* [1990] 2 IR 236, where the testator had
suffered a major cerebrovascular accident and was dysphasic; medical evidence of lack of competence at the time of execution was rejected in favour of
that of the attesting witnesses (approving *In re Wallace: Solicitor for the*

In addition to understanding that he is signing a will, a testator's physical act of execution should also be voluntary and intentional.[23] As to whether or not a putative testator who cannot follow
the provisions of a will in respect of which he had previously given
instructions when competent can then be truly said to understand
that those provisions will only take effect upon his death — and,
thus, to have the requisite *animus testandi*, and to have voluntarily and intentionally signed a will — although providing a convenient rule of law, seems highly questionable from a clinical
perspective, given the conditions affecting cognitive capacity[24]
which result in such a situation.

What Constitutes a Sound Disposing Mind in Law?

An old dictum which captures the essence of requisite testamentary capacity, inclusively and exclusively, asserts:

> It is not sufficient, in order to make a will, that a man
> should be able to maintain an ordinary conversation, and
> answer familiar and easy questions; he must have more
> mind than suffices for that. He must have what lawyers call
> a disposing mind; he must be able to dispose of his property
> with understanding and reason. That does not mean that
> he should make what other people think a sensible will, or
> a reasonable will, or a kind will; because by the law of this
> country he has absolute dominion over his own property,
> and if he, being in possession of his faculties, thinks fit to
> make a capricious will, a harsh will, or a cruel will, you have

---

Duchy of Cornwall v *Batten* (1952) 2 TLR 925 at 930 *per* Devlin J). *In the
Estate of Helena Agnes Blackall, dec'd* (see fn 5, p. 300 above), there was no
difference in the testatrix's condition between the giving of the instructions
and the execution of the will.

[23] *Langalis* v *Langley* (1952) 1 SCR 28. There is a presumption of knowledge
and approval of the testament arising from proof of due execution and a prior
reading over of the will before execution. However, the testator must be competent. See *In re Begley: Begley* v *McHugh* [1939] IR 479; and the dissenting
judgment of Barron J in *In the Estate of Helena Agnes Blackall, dec'd* (see fn
5, p. 300 above).

[24] See Chapters 12 and 13.

not right to set it aside on that ground, for that would be interfering with the liberty the law gives him — that would be
to make his will for him, and not to allow him to make his
will. But he must be able to understand his position; he must
be able to appreciate his property, to form a judgement with
respect to the parties whom he chooses to benefit by it after
his death, and if he has capacity for that, it suffices.[25]

In the context of "want of intelligence occasioned by defective organisation,[26] or by supervening physical infirmity or the decay of
advancing age,[27] as distinguished from mental derangement" in
the classic case of *Banks* v *Goodfellow*,[28] it was held:

> . . . though the mental power may be reduced below the or-
> dinary standard, yet if there be sufficient intelligence to
> understand and appreciate the testamentary act in its dif-
> ferent bearings, the power to make a will remains. It is
> enough if . . . "the mental faculties retain sufficient
> strength fully to comprehend the testamentary act about to
> be done".[29]

---

[25] *Sefton* v *Hopwood* 1 Fos&F 578. A similar theme is found in *Bird* v *Luckie* (1850) 8 Hare 301. The extent to which a modern testator can be capricious or irrational in his will towards his spouse and children has been modified substantially by statute; see Succession Act, 1965, Part IX.

[26] One can only speculate that this equates with mental retardation in modern nosology; see Chapter 13, p. 296.

[27] See Chapter 12, pp. 276–89.

[28] [1870] LR 5 (1870) QB 549.

[29] *Banks* v *Goodfellow* [1870] LR 5, QB 549 at 566 *per* Cockburn CJ, approved in *In the estate of Bellis: Polson* v *Parrott* (1929) 45 TLR 452. Later, he continued:

> "By the terms a sound and disposing mind and memory it has not been under-
> stood that a testator must possess these qualities of the mind in the highest de-
> gree; neither has it been understood that he must possess them in as great a
> degree as he may formerly have done: the mind may have been in some degree
> debilitated, the memory may have become in some degree enfeebled, and yet
> there may be enough left clearly to discern and discreetly to judge of all those
> things and all those circumstances which enter into the nature of a rational,
> fair and just testament."

That said, however, notwithstanding similar presumptions in the areas of marriage and criminal liability[30] in relation to capacity, testamentary capacity has been held to require the highest degree of "mental soundness".[31]

Although from the perspective of functional outcome, it is abundantly clear what a sound disposing mind should be capable of, the law has not seemed satisfied to assess the end point but has delved further. Displaying a prescience that is still largely valid today, although he arguably overstated the conclusions, Cockburn CJ asserted:

> [T]he mind, though it has various faculties, is one and indivisible. If it is disordered in any one of these faculties, if it labours under any delusion arising from any such disorder, though its other faculties and functions may remain undisturbed, it cannot be said to be sound. Such a mind is unsound, and testamentary incapacity is the necessary consequence.[32]

In considering elements of cognitive function, however, the court in *In the Estate of Bellis, Polson* v *Parrott*[33] perhaps made overly fine distinctions in separating "mind, memory, understanding, thought, judgment and reflection".[34]

> When the law uses the[se] terms . . . it must not be supposed that they are quite synonymous, that each means precisely the same thing. By no means: they are separate faculties, though nearly connected with and graduating into

---

[30] See Chapters 11, 15 and 16.

[31] See *Boughton* v *Knight* [1873] LR 3 P&D 64 *per* Hannen J: "Because it involves a larger and wider survey of facts and things than any one of those matters [criminal responsibility, capacity to marry, contractual capacity and capacity to give evidence as a witness]." See also *Re Park* [1954] P 112 at 136, where, although it was held that the deceased lacked testamentary capacity, he nevertheless had sufficient capacity to consent to marriage a few hours earlier.

[32] *Banks* v *Goodfellow* [1870] LR 5, QB 549 at 559.

[33] 45 TLR 452.

[34] See Chapter 2, pp. 31–5.

each other; and one or more of these faculties may be defective in a greater or lesser degree, while the others remain perfect in the same individual.[35]

Rather, these are elements of cognitive functioning, impairment of any one or any combination of which may, on the facts, result in testamentary incapacity.[36]

It is undoubtedly the case that many psychiatric disorders (including organic disorders with psychiatric presentations) are global in nature, although they manifest themselves selectively or preferentially in certain symptoms and signs.[37] This alone, as Cockburn CJ appears to assert, in all cases, is sufficient to render a putative testator incompetent in all circumstances. Although understandable, given the time of assertion, even then the causative role of delusions[38] (in causing testamentary incapacity) appears to have been of central importance.[39]

However, that said, in characterising the conditions that will cause a failure of testamentary capacity, Cockburn CJ articulated

---

[35] From *Ingram v Wyatt* 1 Hag ECC 384 at 401, per Nicholl J.

[36] Barron J, in *In the Estate of Helena Agnes Blackall, dec'd* (see fn 5, p. 300 above) applied these distinctions in a considered and persuasively argued dissenting judgment that highlights the different elements in the evidence.

[37] See Chapter 2.

[38] It is worth noting that the authorities appear to regard delusions as including hallucinations. See *Miller's Probate Practice* (1900), p. 118 and the (ancient) footnotes thereto. Although both are symptoms of psychotic illness, they are not, in modern classifications, interchangeable. That this judicial notion is perpetuated in more modern writings is evidenced by the judicial definition of a delusion, while generally accurate, provided by J.C. Brady (1995), op. cit., p. 74 and *Williams on Wills* (1995), op. cit., Volume I, p. 39, citing *inter alia Dew v Clark* (1826) 3 Add 79, 5 Russ 166.

[39] See Chapter 12. The analogous authority of *Waring v Waring* [1848] 6 Moo PCC 341, which effectively held that unsoundness of mind on one subject equated with unsoundness of mind on any subject, including that of testamentary capacity, irrespective of the relevance of the other "unsoundness" thereto, has long been overruled (See *Williams on Wills* (1995), op. cit., Volume I, p. 36 at fn. 3).

his proposition in a manner more reminiscent of the M'Naghten Rules[40] some 20 years previously. Thus, he stated:

> If the human instincts and affections, or the moral sense, become perverted by mental disease; if insane suspicion, or aversion, take the place of natural affection; if reason and judgment are lost, and the mind becomes a prey to insane delusions calculated to interfere with and disturb its functions and to lead to a testamentary disposition, due only to their baneful influence — in such a case it is obvious that the condition of the testamentary power fails and that a will made under such circumstances ought not to stand.[41]

Although elements of this dictum pithily describe the loss of cognitive function which, it seems, is essential to a loss of testamentary capacity, the apparent emphasis on the causative role of "insane delusions" which appears cumulative, seems unfortunate. Thus, the court went on to hold:

> It is essential to the exercise of such a power [of testation] that a testator shall understand the nature of the act and its effects; shall understand the extent of the property of which he is disposing; shall be able to comprehend and appreciate the claims to which he ought to give effect; and with a view to the latter object, that no disorder of the mind shall poison his affections, pervert his sense of right, or prevent the exercise of his natural faculties — that no insane delusion shall influence his will in disposing of his property and bring about a disposal of it which, if the mind has been sound, would not have been made.[42]

Notwithstanding what had been held generally, the testator was nevertheless found to have been of sound disposing mind, despite his hallucinations involving evil spirits and a man who was already dead and his delusional beliefs that they were pursuing

---

[40] See Chapter 16.

[41] [1870] LR 5, QB 549 at 565.

[42] [1870] LR 5, QB 549 at 565.

him. The court was nonetheless apparently satisfied that this obviously psychotic state, which must have been associated with significant thought disorder, even if it did not present as overt cognitive impairment, was incapable of exerting effect on the "testator's ability to comprehend and appreciate the claims to which he ought to give effect"; in other words, his moral duty.[43]

But it does not appear that the determination of testamentary incapacity is to be confined to the issue of moral duty. However, given that, from the authorities, understanding that one is making a will, having the requisite *animus testandi* and understanding the extent of the property being disposed of are also important, incapacity in any of these areas is fatal to the validity of a will. If the degree of psychiatric disorder is sufficient to impair capacity in any of these areas, there is, it seems, a failure of testamentary capacity. There is no evidence that psychiatric disorder can selectively or disproportionately affect an appreciation of moral duty, above the other elements[44] — although severe global disorders may perhaps manifest themselves selectively.[45]

This is illustrative of the problems inherent in attempting to assimilate dicta of the older cases, at this remove, into a modern understanding of psychiatric disorder, and the conceptual basis of its disease classification, and what, under that classification, might be held to affect testamentary capacity.[46] A significant part of the problem arises from the older approach to "insanity", which term is used almost synonymously with failure of testamentary capacity. Thus, formerly, insanity was classified as either moral or intellectual. Moral "insanity" was regarded as manifesting itself by a perverted or disordered state of feelings, passions, and emotions, without any apparent intellectual dysfunction. Such a state,

---

[43] This issue of appreciation of moral duty appears to have been determinative, the other matters being of lesser importance in the instant case.

[44] Unless one categorises sociopathic personality disorder with psychiatric disorder; see Chapters 3 and 9.

[45] See Chapter 2.

[46] See Chapters 3, 12 and 13.

in modern classifications, would generally be characterised as sociopathic personality disorder which, depending on the classification adopted, may amount to a psychiatric disorder properly so-called. A value judgment might simply assert that it was a definition of "badness". Although it may have once been considered that it could not exist independently of some disturbance of intellectual or psychological function, and it may co-exist with some other psychiatric disorder, not infrequently it exists as a single condition.[47]

Broadly, it could be asserted that mere moral "insanity" was insufficient to impeach testamentary capacity. Reflecting a recurring theme in testamentary law, it was held that:

> Because a man does not duly appreciate the acts or feelings which generally influence mankind, that therefore he is to be considered mad, and unfit to make a disposition of his property, is not the law of this country.[48]

However, even the old law recognised that what might amount, in one case, to mere caprice, in another would constitute intellectual "insanity" or psychiatric disorder masquerading as mere caprice. Thus, in the area of family relations in particular, a testator's harsh and critical view of his children and relations, as manifested in his testamentary dispositions, could be regarded as only resulting from psychiatric disorder (although clearly this was not invariably so).[49] Statutory redress, insofar as spouses and children are concerned, nowadays, makes the necessity for this distinction less relevant.[50]

---

[47] See Chapter 9, p. 205.

[48] *Frere* v *Peacocke* 1 Rob 442 at 456 *per* Fust J. See also *Banks* v *Goodfellow* [1870] LR 5, QB 549, above. See also provisions in relation to capricious or eccentric wills, pp. 323–6 below.

[49] See, for example, *Boughton* v *Knight* [1873] LR 3 P&D 64, and still applicable in England; see *Re Ford Estate, Royal Trust Co.* v *Ford* [1970] 72 WWR 646.

[50] See Succession Act, 1965, Part IX. A point highlighted in Brady (1995), op. cit., p. 75. The distinction remains of importance, however, in England.

On the other hand, the old category of intellectual "insanity", which appears to be the predominant class of "insanity" in the reported cases, included lunatics, idiots and, perhaps, the "feeble-minded", best described as those suffering from psychiatric disorder and mental handicap, including subnormality (congenital and acquired), in modern classifications.[51]

A further problem arises because of the emphasis, in the category of intellectual "insanity", on "insane" delusions, the definition of which appeared also to include hallucinations.[52] Whereas the effects of delusional beliefs on testamentary dispositions might be readily inferred and appreciated, the same is not automatically true in respect of hallucinations (except, perhaps, auditory hallucinations).[53] Insofar as both are symptoms of serious psychiatric disorder, and are often associated with cognitive impairment, the failure to distinguish between them in the authorities might be regarded as academic. However, although the law appears content to separate out the effects of psychotic symptoms from their association with cognitive dysfunction (and sometimes effects on normal cognitive function), given that modern clinicians have well-constructed conceptual models of delusions and hallucinations, and the differences between them,[54] the perpetuation of the constructs in the older cases is a recipe for confusion.

Thus, adopting a model that is no longer of relevance, the existence of "insane" delusions was regarded as the settled criterion of insanity.[55] The condition of "persistent delusions" was regarded as "mania"[56] whereas partial "insanity" was "monomania",[57] or what

---

[51] See Chapter 13.

[52] *Miller's Probate Practice* (1900), op. cit., p. 118.

[53] See Chapter 13.

[54] See Chapter 15, pp. 348–54.

[55] See, for example, *Wheeler and Barsford* v *Alderson* (1831) 3 Hag Ecc 574; *Fulleck* v *Allinson* 3 Hag 537. Although "fluctuation of mind" was also, sometimes, considered to be a symptom.

[56] See Chapter 15.

[57] For example, *Dew* v *Clark* (1826) 3 Add 79, 5 Russ 166.

might now be called a monosymptomatic delusional complex. Although the older judicial and working definitions of delusions have a resonance and relevance even today, and are thus referable to modern clinical practice, it is clear, as noted, that they are also capable of referring to hallucinations. Thus, a delusion was regarded as "a belief in facts which no rational person would have believed".[58] This was expanded to encompass

> the existence of such a false image in the mind as subsists in spite of reason and the evidence of the senses, and which cannot be removed by any exercise of judgment or faculties, thus amounting to a disease of the mind.[59]

And to something that is

> . . . so indelibly fixed on the mind of the deceased that no reasoning, no demonstration, no remonstrance of friends, could convince him that it was devoid of foundation.[60]

Raising a suspicion as to the general competence of a person suffering from persisting psychotic symptoms, which appears justifiable in the modern understanding of psychiatric disorder, Brougham LJ considered that "if the mind is unsound on one subject, and that unsoundness is always existing, such a mind is not sound on all subjects".[61] Although entirely consistent with the valid assertion that a person might be generally "unsound" even though any unsoundness was manifested only, or principally, with reference to one particular question or one particular person,[62]

---

[58] *Dew* v *Clark* (1826) 3 Add 79, 5 Russ 166 *per* Nichol J. This is the classic exposition referred to in even the modern academic texts.

[59] *Miller's Probate Practice* (1900), op. cit., p. 118.

[60] *Chambers and Yatman* v *Queen's Proctor* (1840) 2 Curt 415 *per* Fust J.

[61] *Waring* v *Waring* [1848] 6 Moo PC 341; although a similar suspicion might be raised even in the presence of a history of past psychotic illness, since resolved.

[62] e.g. *Dew* v *Clark* (1826) 3 Add 79, 5 Russ 166, where the testator was described as having an "insane" aversion to his only daughter, as a consequence of which he left her a fairly meagre legacy from an otherwise large estate.

however, and despite the validity of such suspicion, this approach was overruled and disapproved of in subsequent cases.[63]

Therefore, although the presence of delusions is deemed to raise a presumption against testamentary capacity,[64] delusions *per se*[65] were (and are) not regarded as sufficient to impugn it.[66] Thus, if a testator's delusions are regarded as not having affected, or as being associated with impairment of, his cognitive function (described as "the general faculties of his mind")[67] and therefore, it is supposed, cannot have influenced him in any particular disposition of his property, a court will uphold the validity of a will made despite the presence of the delusions. The essential (though perhaps artificial) question for the court appears to reduce to this: did the delusion affect, or was the delusion capable of affecting, the making of the will? In this question, the judicial focus appears more on the influence, or potential influence, of "delusions" on particular testamentary dispositions, as a test of testamentary capacity,[68] rather than on the functional cognitive capacity of what may be a clearly psychotic testator.[69] This is reflected also in

---

[63] *Creagh* v *Blood* [1845] 8 Ir Eq R 434; *Walcot* v *Alleyn* Milw Rep 72; and *A-G* v *Parnther* 3 Br CC 171; *Dew* v *Clark* (1826) 3 Add 79, 5 Russ 166.

[64] See p. 319 below.

[65] This may apply, surprisingly, even in the case of extreme religious delusions where a testator believes himself to be, or to be commanded to do certain things by, for example, the Saviour; see, e.g., *Hope* v *Campbell* [1899] AC 1.

[66] That is not to say either that there must be global cognitive impairment or that the presence of psychotic symptoms may not, in certain cases, be sufficient to establish unsoundness of disposing mind, even if it appears that in all other respects a testator conducted himself with apparent propriety; see below.

[67] *Miller's Probate Practice* (1900), p. 116, and *Williams on Wills* (1997), Volume I, p. 39.

[68] The presence of delusions is not a test of cognitive function, although disordered cognitive function is frequently associated with psychotic symptoms.

[69] This culminated in the absurd proposition that a testamentary disposition purportedly affected by a "delusion" could be severed from a will, without affecting the validity of the will as a whole; see below. The role of judicial value judgment has already been noted. By contrast, "superstitious terrors" have been found to render a will invalid if they interfere with the free exercise of judgment by a testator; see *Sherburne* v *Middleton* (1842)

consideration of psychiatric disorder, regarded as "latent" and leaving a testator "free from the consciousness and influence of the delusion".[70] In such circumstances, the presence of psychiatric disorder, in the absence of a connection between the delusion and the will, would not be sufficient to impugn its validity.[71] However, where it is considered that the nature of a delusion is such as could influence a testator in the making of a particular disposition, a conclusion that the delusion, if still existing, was latent at the time, so as to leave the testator free from any influence arising from it, is regarded as unjustified.[72] Although, in a fuller articulation of the issue, it is considered that a testator's mind must not be so dominated by an "insane" delusion[73] as to overpower his judgment, such that he is incapable of understanding what the law requires him to understand[74] in the execution of his will,[75] this represents no more than an acknowledgement of an observable association of psychotic symptoms with severe cognitive impairment in extreme cases. As such, and given that even an apparent relationship between the subject matter of a delusion and a disposition is regarded as not inevitably resulting in a finding, in law, that the delusion causally affected the making of a particular, or

---

9 Cl&Fin 72. As to whether or not this merely amounts to a species of a category of "delusion" sufficient to deprive a testator of testamentary capacity within the law, as stated, is unclear.

[70] Presumably, in the context of remission of disease, whether spontaneous or induced. This difficult concept of disease latency also arose in the nullity case of *C(S) v D(P) (orse C(P)* (High Court, Unreported Judgment, McCracken J, 14 March 1996). See Chapter 11, p. 263.

[71] See, for example, *Banks v Goodfellow* [1870] LR 5, QB 549.

[72] *Waring v Waring* [1848] 6 Moo PC 341.

[73] Even a delusion which, though not apparent at the time of execution, but is nevertheless proved to have existed at that time, can result in the invalidity of a will. *Bagot v Bagot* 1 LR Ir 308. This appears to differ from cases involving presumptions of the continuance of a state of things; see p. 320 below.

[74] See pp. 319–20 below.

[75] For example, *Banks v Goodfellow* [1870] LR 5, QB 549; *Hope v Campbell* [1899] AC 1; *In the Estate of Walker, Watson v Treasury Solicitor* (1912) 28 TLR 466.

any, disposition,[76] it seems quite inadequate as a comprehensive articulation of the proper approach to less obvious cognitive impairment in the presence of such symptoms.

What Effect does a "Partial Delusion" Have on the Validity of a Will?

The law also seeks to remedy the effects of "partial delusions" through a process of severance, as if the effects of psychotic disease on cognitive processes were so divisible. In this regard, it might amount to no more than a specific application of the principle in relation to delusions in general. Thus, in *In the Estate of Bohrmann*[77] it was held that, because of a delusion under which he laboured, the testator was competent to make all but one part of his will. In that he was deluded that London County Council was persecuting him, the clause of a codicil which substituted American for English charities, was held to be void and the remainder valid.[78]

What is the Effect of a "Lucid Interval" in a Period of Incompetence on Testamentary Capacity?

As the relevant time for the determination of testamentary incapacity is (subject to what has already been said) the date of execution of a will or codicil, logically, if a putative testator is suffering from a (testamentary) incapacitating illness, during which he experiences temporary recovery,[79] that recovery, known as a "lucid

---

[76] For example, *Banks* v *Goodfellow* [1870] LR 5, QB 549; *Smee* v *Smee* [1879] 5 PD 84; *Murfett* v *Smith* [1887] 12 PD 116.

[77] [1938] 1 All ER 271.

[78] The analogy for severance was based on the practice of the courts to exclude from a will matters of which the testator did not know or approve, and the exception itself to the general rule on testamentary capacity, have been criticised. See *Theobald on Wills* (1993), op. cit., p. 34 and the footnotes thereto, and Brady (1995), op. cit., p. 74.

[79] See Chapters 12 and 13. It is not unusual for psychiatric disorders (including organic disorders with psychiatric manifestations) which affect testamentary capacity to remit and relapse, either spontaneously or in response to some external factor.

interval", may be sufficient for testamentary purposes. Thus, in the classic, if quaintly expressed, statement of the principle, it was held that:

> If you can establish that the party afflicted habitually by a malady of the mind has intermissions, and if there was an intermission of the disorder at the time of the act, that being proved, is sufficient, and the general habitual insanity will not affect it. . . .[80]

Acknowledging, with some validity, that unless evidence of delusional thinking is actively sought, it may be missed,[81] in general, absence of delusions, where they previously existed, has been regarded as the test of recovery. However, in such circumstances, failure to show the absence of delusions may well result in a will being found invalid, even where the testator appeared to be of sound disposing mind.[82]

Development of "insight"[83] by a patient into his psychotic symptoms, whether hallucinations or delusions, is often evidence of (frequently temporary) recovery from psychotic illness and thus of a "lucid interval". This has also been accepted judicially, with some precision, in an old, but nevertheless useful, dictum whereby it was held that:

> The most satisfactory proof of recovery of the person from an unsound state of mind is the conviction by him of the non-reality of the delusions which arose from the disease. . . .[84]

However, the conclusion that:

---

[80] *Cartwright* v *Cartwright* (1793) 1 Phillim 100 *per* Wynn J. This is a special application of the general principle in relation to testamentary capacity. Thus, execution of a will under the "influence of a delusion", subject to what has already been set out, is void, although it may precede or follow execution without affecting its validity; see *Jones* v *Godrich* 5 Moo PC 30.

[81] *Nichols* v *Binns* 1 S&T 239 at 244 *per* Cresswell J.

[82] *Smee* v *Smee* [1879] 5 PD 84.

[83] See Chapter 2, pp. 31–5.

[84] *In re Dyce Sombre* 1 M'N&G 116 at 133, *per* Cottenham LJ.

> . . . a denial that the [delusions of hallucinations] exist or
> an attempt to explain them by accounting for them, unless
> the explanation be most satisfactory, does not lead to the
> conclusion of recovery, but only shows the ingenuity of the
> person in concealing the infirmity[85]

seems misplaced and arguably merely represents failure of recovery. The common clinical experience is that, whereas the origin of a delusion may originally have had some basis in objective reality, its continuance has none. As for hallucinations, by definition, they can have no such basis. That an attempt to explain them away can amount to satisfactory evidence of recovery seems clinically untenable. To characterise such explanations or attempted explanations as evidence of ingenuity attributes rather too much rationality to very severely disturbed thought processes as manifested by the psychotic symptoms and the explanations thereof in the first instance.

In this regard, it is noted that there is at least one instance of what were referred to as feigned delusions.[86] The will was not invalidated on that account.

PROOF OF TESTAMENTARY CAPACITY

Presumption of Sound Disposing Mind

The law presumes that a testator is of sound disposing mind[87] when making his will, and that his will is valid.[88] However, such

---

[85] *In re Dyce Sombre* 1 M'N&G 116 at 133, *per* Cottenham LJ. In this case, the "medical men" were convinced of the testator's recovery, although he later affirmed his delusional beliefs and the will was found invalid as a result. It is unclear at this remove as to whether or not this represented a true "lucid interval" followed by relapse or a deliberate ruse by the patient. It would be most unusual for the degree of thought disorder associated with psychotic states for a sufferer to sustain a coherent explanation of the symptoms such that it indicated (feigned) recovery — except, perhaps, in the early phases of a paranoid psychosis; see Chapter 12.

[86] *Ditchburn* v *Fearn* (1842) 6 Jur 201.

[87] As averred to above, this is sometimes expressed, reflecting the law's preoccupation with the clinically irrelevant concept of "sanity", as the testator's being sane.

presumptions are rebuttable by the evidence of the person seeking to challenge a will.[89] Once testamentary capacity is challenged, or the circumstances are such that his capacity may have been affected,[90] the onus of proof is on the person who propounds[91] the will that the testator was competent.[92]

The law also presumes that a state of things shown to exist continues to exist unless and until the contrary is established. Thus, a putative testator in respect of whom there is no evidence that he lacked testamentary capacity, before the execution of his will is presumed to continue to have the requisite testamentary capacity unless and until the contrary is shown. However, as an exception to the general rule of competence, the corollary is also held to be true. Thus, once proved, unsoundness of mind is presumed to exist even if it is not always apparent; and if proved to have existed prior to, and subsequent to a certain time, it is presumed to have existed at that time also, unless there is adequate evidence of a "lucid interval".

The burden of proof that a will was made in a "lucid interval" is upon the person so alleging.[93] In such circumstances, it is sufficient that the testator fulfils the conditions laid down in relation

---

[88] *Wellesley* v *Vere* (1841) 2 Curt 917, *Re Brocklebank's Will* (1856) 4 Nfld LR 88.

[89] See, for example, *In re Glynn dec'd* [1990] 2 IR 326.

[90] Possibly including advanced age and a previous minor cerebrovascular accident. See *In the Estate of Helena Agnes Blackall, dec'd* (see fn 5, p. 300 above), *per* Barron J. *A fortiori*, this would apply in multi-infarct dementia; see *In re Glynn dec'd* [1990] 2 IR 326 and Chapter 13.

[91] The person who institutes an action to obtain probate in solemn form of law.

[92] See, for example, *Barry* v *Butlin* (1838) 2 Moo PC 480; *Sutton* v *Sadler* (1857) 3 CB (ns) 87; *Smee* v *Smee* [1879] 5 PD 84; *Fulton* v *Andrew* [1875] LR 7 HL 448; *Parker* v *Felgate* [1883] 8 PD 171; *Re Begley: Begley* v *McHugh* [1939] IR 479; *In re Wallace: Solicitor for the Duchy of Cornwall* v *Batten* (1952) 2 TLR 925; *In re Glynn dec'd* [1990] 2 IR 326.

[93] See, for example, *Cartwright* v *Cartwright* (1793) 1 Phillim 100; *Bannatyne* v *Bannatyne* (1852) 2 Rob Eccl 472; *White* v *Driver* (1809) 1 Phillim 84.

to testamentary capacity generally and proof of "complete mental recovery" is not essential.[94]

Evidential Burden of Proof

What must be proved in order to establish testamentary capacity is well settled. Thus, it has been held:

> [A testator] must be able to appreciate his position; he must be able to appreciate his property, to form a judgment with respect to the parties whom he chooses to benefit by it after his death, and if he has capacity for that, it suffices.[95]

This can be summarised as a requirement to establish that a testator understood three essential factors at the same time:

1. The effect of his wishes being carried out on his death, i.e. that he was giving property to certain persons upon his death, and

2. The extent of the property of which he purports to dispose, and

3. The extent and nature of the claims which others might have on him such that he could decide whether to provide for them from his property or to exclude them.[96]

Thus, subject to doubtful authority in respect of "partial delusions",[97] failure on any one ground should cause a failure of the whole testament.

---

[94] See, for example, *Creagh* v *Blood* (1845) 8 Ir Eq R 434; *Chambers and Yatman* v *Queen's Proctor* (1840) 2 Curt 415; and, generally, *Williams on Wills* (1995), op. cit., Volume I, p. 38 and the footnotes thereto.

[95] *Sefton* v *Hopwood* 1 Fos & F 578 *per* Cresswell J.

[96] See *Williams on Wills* (1995), op. cit., Volume I, p. 35, quoted with approval in *In the Estate of Helena Agnes Blackall, dec'd* (see fn 5, p. 300 above); *Harwood* v *Baker* (1840) 3 Moo PC 282; *Banks* v *Goodfellow* [1870] LR 5, QB 549, "It is essential to the exercise of such a power [of testation] that a testator shall understand the nature of the act and its effects; shall understand the extent of the property of which he is disposing; shall be able to comprehend and appreciate the claims to which he ought to give effect. . . ."; and *Boughton* v *Knight* [1873] LR 3 P&D 64; *Battan Singh* v *Amirchand* [1948] AC 161 [1948] 1 All ER 152.

[97] See p. 315 above.

Evidence of Statements and Conduct of Testator

Both oral and documentary evidence in relation to the testator's
being of sound disposing mind is admissible.[98] Thus, to establish
that he knew that he was making a will, evidence of statements
made, or acts performed, by the testator, both before, and at the
time of, execution of his will may be relevant,[99] as is evidence of
the circumstances in which the will was made. This applies *a fortiori* to proof of a "lucid interval".[100] Thus, evidence of the testator's
conduct before and after execution is admissible, although its importance seems to vary with the nature of the condition impugn-
ing testamentary capacity and from which the testator was
suffering.[101] Similarly, evidence that the terms of a will conform
with expressions of intention, whether prior or subsequent to execution, is also admissible as to testamentary capacity.[102]

Evidence of Prior Psychiatric Disability

However, that a person was generally regarded as suffering from
"unsoundness of mind" (by which it is presumed is meant a
serious psychiatric disorder) is not admissible as evidence of
testamentary incapacity, nor it appears, is a family history

---

[98] For a comprehensive and staccato-like treatment of the evidential issues
from which the following is drawn, see *Williams on Wills* (1995), op. cit., Volume I, pp. 42–3.

[99] For example, see *Butlin v Barry* (1837) 1 Curt 614; *In the Goods of Nora
Breen, dec'd* (High Court, Unreported Judgment, Barr J, 5 May 1995); *Duffy
v Duffy* (High Court, Unreported Judgment, O'Hanlon J, 10 August 1994).
On the basis of old authority, which, with the passage of time, must surely
assume progressively less relevance, a hand-written will strongly favours
testamentary capacity. See *Cartwright v Cartwright* (1793) 1 Phillim 100,
which involved a will made in a "lucid interval".

[100] *Marsh v Tyrell* 2 Hag 122, even though there may be evidential difficulties
in ascertaining the total absence of all delusions in a lucid interval; see
Wheeler and Barsford v Alderson (1831) 3 Hag Ecc 574; *Brogden v Brown* 2
Add 445.

[101] See *Beavan v M'Donnell* (1854) 10 Exch 184; *Mudway v Croft* (1843) 3
Curt 671; *Boughton v Knight* [1873] LR 3 P&D 64.

[102] *Boughton v Knight* [1873] LR 3 P&D 64; *Brouncker v Brouncker* (1812) 2
Phillim 57.

thereof.[103] Given the antiquity of the authorities, it is difficult to define what conditions in the modern classifications[104] amount to "unsoundness of mind" as envisaged by the courts. Nevertheless, as a general proposition, given the fluctuating manifestations of many conditions[105] affecting testamentary capacity and the observable fact that, while family history may be relevant in terms of pre-disposing other family members to developing psychiatric disorder, a positive family history can have no probative value as to causation, either clinically or legally.[106]

Evidence of Medical Witnesses and Medical Experts

A medical witness who attended a testator may give evidence as a witness of fact, but, in accordance with general principles, unless expert, cannot give evidence as to the existence of facts which he has not personally observed.[107] However, also in accordance with general principles, an expert witness who did not see or examine the testator may express an opinion on facts otherwise proved in evidence.[108] Notwithstanding the evidence of expert medical witnesses, the evidence of other eyewitnesses[109] who observed and knew the putative testator has been preferred.[110]

---

[103] *M'Adam* v *Walker* (1813) 1 Dow 148; *Greenslade* v *Dare* (1855) 20 Beav 284.

[104] See Chapters 12 and 13.

[105] See Chapters 12 and 13.

[106] See Chapter 3.

[107] See *Martin* v *Johnston* (1858) 1 F&F 122; *In the Estate of Helena Agnes Blackall, dec'd* (see fn 5, p. 300 above), although there was no real dispute between the various witnesses, including the family doctor of the 99-year-old testatrix, as to her testamentary capacity either generally, or at the time of execution of her will, the subject matter of the action.

[108] As in *Duffy* v *Duffy* (High Court, Unreported Judgment, O'Hanlon J, 10 August 1994).

[109] Only their evidence, as distinct from their opinions, as to testamentary capacity is relevant. The inferences as to testamentary capacity are to be drawn by the court. See *In re Glynn dec'd* [1990] 2 IR 236, *per* McCarthy J (Hederman J concurring).

[110] *Boughton* v *Knight* [1873] LR 3 P&D 64; *In re Glynn dec'd* [1990] 2 IR 236.

Thus, in *In re Glynn dec'd*,[111] a will executed by a testator who had sustained a major cerebrovascular accident and who, the medical evidence by the doctor caring for him indicated, was unfit to make a will, because, it appears from the report, he was dysphasic, was held to be valid. The evidence of a priest, who had drawn up the will on the instructions of the testator given before his illness, and another witness, that the testator appreciated that he was executing a will and that it represented his testamentary wishes, was preferred.[112]

Then, in *Duffy* v *Duffy*,[113] the evidence of an expert in clinical pharmacology as to the effects of benzodiazepines and opiates on the testamentary capacity of a testator, who was suffering "cerebral hypoxia" (caused by anaemia secondary to a gastric carcinoma) was not, in the opinion of the court, sufficient to dislodge the evidence given by the solicitor who drew up the will and the other witnesses (including the testator's principal physician) who visited and conversed with the testator on the date he executed his will, and the period immediately preceding that date.

As in the case of incapacitating physical illness, it has been held that

> ... nothing less than firm medical evidence by a doctor in a position to assess the testator's mental capacity could suffice to discharge the onus of proving him to have been a capable testator.[114]

Arguably, a stringent approach applies *a fortiori* to instances where the disability is, or is alleged to be, primarily psychiatric in origin.

---

[111] [1990] 2 IR 236.

[112] See also, *Parker* v *Felgate* [1883] 8 PD 171.

[113] High Court, Unreported Judgment, O'Hanlon J, 10 August 1994, where the testator, who was terminally ill, died four days after executing his will in hospital.

[114] *In re Corboy: Leahy* v *Corboy* [1969] IR 148 at 167 *per* Budd J.

Evidence on the Face of the Will

The rules of evidence in relation to the rationality of a will on its face, formerly of such importance, are now of little practical concern, given statutory provisions that create a surviving spouse's legal right in the estate of the deceased spouse. Protection is also afforded the children of testators by the entitlement of any child, where the court is of the opinion that the testator failed in his moral duty to make proper provision for the child in accordance with his means, whether by will or otherwise, to apply for an order for such provision, as the court thinks just, to be made out of the testator's estate.[115]

In the absence of concerns about whether or not a testator had due regard to those who had a moral claim on his estate, evidence on the face of the will, of its being perfectly rational, proper and natural in its provisions, may provide compelling evidence of a "lucid interval", especially if it is drawn up without assistance from anyone else in the testator's own handwriting (or, by extension, by a person without any interest therein), irrespective of how short the interval was. Evidence of the circumstances of execution is also important in such cases. Thus, in a fairly extreme case, *Walcot* v *Alleyn*[116] the will of a barrister was held valid, notwithstanding that he had been deluded for a number of days prior to its execution and committed suicide the following day.[117]

---

[115] Succession Act, 1965, Part IX, generally, and s. 117 in particular. The court must consider the application from the point of view of a prudent and just parent, taking into account the position of each of the children of the testator and any other circumstances which the court considers of assistance in deciding that will be as fair as possible to the child to whom the application relates and to the other children, s. 117(2). These statutory provisions are based on a clear policy of ensuring that the wills of spiteful, vindictive or, even, simply thoughtless parents, do not result in clear injustice to their children. Although, as with the common law rules, it involves significant value judgements, it is a considerably more honest approach to implicitly acknowledge the policy basis rather that to dress it up as a rule of evidence.

[116] Milw. 72. See also *Cartwright* v *Cartwright* 1 Phillim 100; *Nichols* v *Binns* 1 S&T 239.

[117] As to whether or not such a conclusion would be reached on the evidence today must be questionable.

However, a will, on its face, may appear extravagant or foolish or provide clear evidence of eccentricities. Such evidence of eccentricities may raise an inference of lack of testamentary capacity. Thus, reflecting a common perception that may have some basis, but reaching a conclusion that has none, it has been held:

> As persons actually insane in some particulars are commonly highly eccentric in many or most, so persons highly eccentric in many or most particulars are, at least not infrequently, actually insane in some. People who dwell on the confines of two empires are likely enough to be found in sometimes the one and sometimes the other.[118]

For example, capturing the essence of the distinction between what might properly be called traits and disease, but by no means exhaustively (presuming that "deranged in a legal sense" is synonymous with testamentary capacity), it was held:

> A man may, in his ordinary habits, affect singularity, and to believe what he does not; he may talk idly and dress absurdly, and from solitary habits may be shy and suspicious; he may have prejudices or fancies, but he may not be deranged in a legal sense.[119]

Thus, evidence of eccentricity *per se* as a personality trait, short of its being classified as a personality disorder,[120] is properly regarded simply as a species of the normal human condition. However, if a will reflects non-compliance with, or disregard of, normative values, and examination of the life and habits of the testator indicates more than a simple personality trait or traits, but rather evidence of a (or many) personality disorder(s), the situation is less clear-cut. As personality disorders are not associated, generally, with cognitive impairment, there is no reason to

---

[118] *Dew* v *Clark* (1826) 3 Add 79, 5 Russ 166 *per* Nichol J, although given the antiquity of the dictum, the conclusion might be indulged.

[119] *Walcot* v *Alleyn* Milw Rep 72.

[120] Although even then, it may be difficult to impugn testamentary capacity; see Chapter 13.

infer that a will, even a capricious, foolish or extravagant will, executed by a testator with a personality disorder, should raise any inference of lack of testamentary capacity, unless there is evidence that such personality disorder is associated with some other major psychiatric disorder. Nor does it appear that evidence of such personality disorder, upon examination of the life and habits of a testator, would necessarily be capable, of itself, of establishing a lack of testamentary capacity.[121] The notion that:

> It is the prolonged departure without an adequate external cause from the state of feeling and modes of thinking usual to the individual when in health, that is the true feature of disorder in mind[122]

although superficially appealing, is neither definitionally nor conceptually correct. Nor does it appear to be directly applicable to a testator with personality disorder.

Given the presumption of law against the validity of a will of a person who was previously "insane", and which presumption is affected by the provisions of the will itself,[123] a presumption against validity could well arise in the case of a testator suffering from a personality disorder. If such a testator makes a capricious will, having previously sought and received advice from a psychiatrist (and perhaps having received inpatient treatment), he could, for the purposes of testamentary capacity, come within the category of "insane".[124]

However, none of this is to deny that the converse is also possible: a testator may suffer from a (or many) personality disorder(s), without ever having sought or received any specialist advice or treatment, make a will that is entirely rational and proper on its face. In such a situation, no presumptions or inferences may be

---

[121] See also Chapter 13.

[122] *Mudway v Croft* (1843) 3 Curt 671 at 678.

[123] See p. 323 above.

[124] Similar considerations also apply to the presumption of law in relation to previous "insanity" *simpliciter*; see above.

raised — notwithstanding the presence of a potentially serious underlying personality disorder.

Evidence of Other Conditions

Evidence of alcohol intoxication at the time of executing a will is sufficient, on principle, to establish lack of testamentary capacity,[125] whereas chronic alcohol abuse *per se*, in the absence of evidence of actual intoxication, is not.[126] However, for example, chronic alcohol abuse associated with the development of Korsakoff's psychosis or alcoholic dementia or alcohol-induced or associated organic brain damage[127] could clearly well do so. Similar considerations would logically apply to any intoxicant, whether acutely or chronically ingested. Furthermore, execution of a will while suffering from *delirium tremens*,[128] or any other acute withdrawal state,[129] must result in a finding of invalidity on the basis of lack of testamentary capacity.[130]

Evidence of old age, frailty (including emotional or psychological frailty) or physical incapacity of a testator, or the fact that the will was made *in extremis*, without more, is not sufficient, of itself, to establish testamentary incapacity, although the circumstances may well raise a suspicion of duress or undue influence.[131] Accordingly, there must be some evidence of cognitive failure or an inability to understand what the law requires to make a will

---

[125] See *Legeyt* v *O'Brien* Milw 337.

[126] See *Ayrey* v *Hill* (1824) 2 Add 206; *Handley* v *Stacey* (1858) 1 F&F 574; *Wheeler and Barsford* v *Alderson* (1831) 3 Hag Ecc 574, as if made, by analogy, in a "lucid interval".

[127] See Chapter 12, pp. 281–2.

[128] A state of acute alcohol withdrawal; see Chapters 10 and 13.

[129] See Chapter 10 for a description of drugs of dependence.

[130] See *Brunt* v *Brunt* (1873) LR 3 P&D 37, where the putative revocation by destruction of a will by a testator suffering from *delirium tremens* was held not to amount to a revocation at all. The same considerations, on principle, *a fortiori* must also apply to execution.

[131] See Chapter 13 for a description of a dependent personality disorder.

valid.[132] Thus, even the wills of dysphasic testators have been found valid.[133] Arguably, similar considerations should also arise where it is established that the putative testator was suffering from a severe grief reaction, even in the absence of a depressive illness and cognitive impairment.[134]

Evidence of a deficient memory in a testator is not sufficient *per se* to render a will invalid.[135] Thus, the fact that a testator is not aware of, and cannot fully recollect, the actual full extent of what is to be given away may not destroy testamentary capacity, provided that he can recollect the major portion of it, is nevertheless aware that such property as is his is being disposed of, and that he is executing a will for that purpose.[136] A total failure of memory, on the other hand, would be sufficient to establish testamentary incapacity, as such a testator could not then be said to understand all that is involved in making a will.[137]

In such cases of old age, frailty, poor memory, severe physical incapacity[138] or grief,[139] and especially where there is any reason to anticipate that a will about to be executed will be challenged in

---

[132] See *Emes v Emes* (1865) 11 Gr 325; *In the Estate of Helena Agnes Blackall, dec'd* (see fn 5, p. 300 above).

[133] For example, *Goods of Field* (1834) 3 Curt. 752, 163 All ER 890; *In the Estate of Holtam, Gillett v Rogers* (1913) 108 LT 732; and *In re Glynn dec'd* [1990] 2 IR 236.

[134] See Chapter 6, p. 104.

[135] As, for example, may occur in the dementias; see Chapter 12.

[136] *In the Estate of Helena Agnes Blackall, dec'd* (see fn 5, p. 300 above). This certainly applies where a testator has a great many assets. However, the fact that a testator of very few means is unable to recollect what he has to dispose of may be sufficient to raise a question as to capacity on the face of the will. In *In re Glynn dec'd* [1990] 2 IR 236, a mistake of the testator as to providing for his sister did not invalidate the will.

[137] See, for example, *Murphy v Lamphier* (1914) 32 OLR 19. Total failure of memory in the dementias will be associated with other gross cognitive deficits also; see Chapter 12.

[138] As in *Duffy v Duffy* (High Court, Unreported Judgment, O'Hanlon J, 10 August 1994).

[139] And in cases of remitting and relapsing conditions, e.g. as the dementias may initially appear.

the future on the grounds of lack of testamentary capacity, it is generally considered desirable to have the proposed testator medically examined. In *In the Estate of Helena Agnes Blackall, dec'd*[140] Barron J (who dissented) stated:

> The authorities show that the mental faculties including memory and understanding are something which must be investigated. Of course, in the usual case it would probably be obvious that they are not impaired. The level of investigation in each case must depend upon the apparent condition of the testator. . . . It may be that in an appropriate case, nothing less than firm medical evidence by a doctor in a position to assess the testator's mental capacity could suffice to discharge the onus of proving him to have been a capable testator.

Such an examination should be carried out by an experienced medical practitioner to ascertain whether or not the testator is competent to make a will, with due consideration of the matters which he must understand.[141] Assessment of the level of alertness or the state of consciousness of the testator, and the effect on his understanding of the presence or absence of psychotic symptoms or cognitive impairment is necessary. The medical practitioner should record the results of his examination and findings and, if satisfied as to the testator's testamentary capacity, attest the will as a witness.[142]

---

[140] See fn 5, p. 300 above. In this case, Barron J was of the view that such medical examination as there had been was insufficient for these purposes. See also *In re Corboy: Leahy* v *Corboy* [1969] IR 148 at 167 *per* Budd J (above).

[141] See Chapter 12.

[142] *Kenward* v *Adams* [1975] CLY 3591; *Re Simpson* (1977) 121 SJ 224. See pp. 321–2 above.

Part Five

CRIMINAL RESPONSIBILITY

Chapter 15

PSYCHIATRIC DISORDERS AND CRIME

Most patients with psychiatric disorders do not commit crime and conversely most crime is not committed by those who are psychiatrically ill. In spite of these facts, there is a common perception among the public that the two are inextricably linked, particularly in relation to violent offences.

The most serious offence, that of murder, is occasionally perpetrated by a sufferer with psychiatric disorder. In those circumstances, the defence that the person was "insane" at the time of the crime is often entered to effect a particular type of sentence. This plea, based on the M'Naghten Rules,[1] states that the crime must have been committed by somebody who had a disease of the mind, rather than of the brain, or by somebody who was unaware of the nature of the crime he was committing. Recourse to the "insanity" defence is viewed by the public as a soft option for the party who wishes to avoid a prison sentence. A finding of guilty but insane carries with it a mandatory committal to the Central Mental Hospital at the government's pleasure. Prior to 1991, the term was at the pleasure of the court. This change means that all requests for discharge are now handled by the Minister for Justice.

While addressing the disorders to which the insanity defence may be applied, a number of other related disorders will also be considered here.

---

[1] See Chapter 16.

SCHIZOPHRENIA

Schizophrenia[2] is the disorder which is at the nub of psychiatry and which created the necessity to build institutions to house the sufferers. Moreover, it is the disease which has led to the stigmatisation of psychiatry, and to the erroneous association between mental illness and violence. An erroneous but popular myth is that it is a split personality.[3] Affecting 1 per cent of the population, the number of new cases is of the order of 15/100,000. It begins in adolescence or early adulthood, although more benign forms also occur among the older age groups. It is slightly more common in men than in women and there is no association with the social class of the parents, although downward socio-economic drift is a consequence of the disease in sufferers.[4] The onset in women is a few years later than in men, probably accounting for the somewhat better prognosis in women. Immigration has long been believed to be associated with an increased risk of developing schizophrenia, leading to speculation that the most unstable in a population migrate. This has not been verified by research, but data based on hospital admission data, as distinct from outpatient data, do confirm the dramatically higher admission rate for immigrants,[5] a finding that has become politically sensitive in Britain.

Aetiology

A number of appealing and fashionable theories were postulated in the 1950s which placed the blame on family interactions and dynamics and included the "double bind" theory of Bateson, the

---

[2] See, for example, *R* v *Arnold* (1724) St Tr 695; *R* v *Hadfield* (1800) 27 St Tr 1281; *People (AG)* v *Fennell* (No. 1) [1940] IR 445.

[3] Split personality is controversial and is best conceptualised as a variant of hysteria (Chapter 6, p. 96) or multiple personality disorder (Chapter 5, pp. 73–4).

[4] E.M. Goldberg and S.L. Morrison (1963), "Schizophrenia and Social Class", *British Journal of Psychiatry*, Vol. 109, pp. 785–802.

[5] G. Harrison, D. Owens, A. Holton, D. Neilson and D. Boot (1988), "A Prospective Study of Severe Mental Disorder in Afro-Caribbean Patients", *Psychological Medicine*, Vol. 18, pp. 643–57.

"schism and skew" hypothesis of Lidz and the social generation theory of Faris and Dunham. These have now been disproved and psychiatrists today look to genetics and neurobiology to explain the cause.

Predisposing Factors

Twin studies, family studies and adoption studies indicate that children of schizophrenic parents who are adopted do have a higher risk of developing the disorder than do the adopted children of non-schizophrenic parents. Monozygotic twins with one affected person are also at increased risk when compared to dizygotic twins. Although the mode of inheritance is uncertain, the lifetime expectancy of developing the disorder is of the order of 8–15 per cent for children, siblings and non-identical twins. For identical twins or for the children of two schizophrenic parents, the risk is over 40 per cent. The second-degree relatives of patients such as nephews, nieces or first cousins run a risk of 2–4 per cent. The risk in an unrelated person, such as an adopted sibling, is 0.8 per cent. The earlier the age of onset, the higher the risk to other family members. Genetic marker studies have so far been equivocal and the mode of inheritance is likely to be polygenic rather than by a single abnormal gene. Moreover, the question of whether environmental or genetic influences predominate in the causation of this disease has been the subject of investigation and it has been suggested that environmental factors play a greater role in men and genetic influences in women.[6]

The fact that some patients develop schizophrenia without any family history suggests that environmental influences are also important. The exact nature of these is uncertain, but some pointers exist. For example, studies of identical twins discordant for the disease suggest that these influences lead to damage to and enlargement of certain areas of the brain known respectively as the hippocampus and the ventricles. The observation that there is

---

[6] D. Castle and R.M. Murray (1991), "The Neurodevelopmental Basis of Sex Differences in Schizophrenia", *Psychological Medicine*, Vol. 21, pp. 565–75.

an excess of winter/spring births among schizophrenics points to an infection *in utero* or in the early post-natal period. The influenza virus has been extensively investigated.[7] Birth trauma has also been implicated, possibly as a result of anoxia (lack of oxygen) to the brain during delivery.

Neuropathological changes have been described in the cerebral cortex of some patients and specific studies examining areas rich in neurotransmitters associated with schizophrenia are currently the focus of investigation using modern imaging techniques.[8] The abnormalities include diminution in the temporal areas and in the hippocampus and deficiencies in the grey and white matter of the temporal lobes. Attempts to relate these changes to symptoms are currently under investigation.

Precipitating Factors

Life-events have been implicated in the precipitation of the first episode of illness in about 60 per cent of patients.[9] However, life stresses are involved in precipitating all acute psychiatric disorders and are not specific to schizophrenia. The events include childbirth, surgery,[10] bereavement, etc., and are prominent in the three weeks prior to the onset, even when those factors that are a consequence of the illness are controlled for (e.g. losing a job due to prodromal illness). The distinction between a schizophrenic episode precipitated by childbirth (puerperal psychosis) and by other events is probably spurious, although both have a better prognosis than an illness of insidious onset. In general, the more sudden the onset, whether there is a precipitant or not, the better the prognosis.

---

[7] P.C. Sham, E. O'Callaghan and N. Takei (1992), "Schizophrenia Following Pre-natal Exposure to Influenza Epidemics between 1939 and 1960", *British Journal of Psychiatry*, Vol. 160, pp. 461–6.

[8] See Chapter 2.

[9] G.W. Brown and J.L.T. Birley (1968), "Crisis and Life Changes and the Onset of Schizophrenia", *Journal of Health and Social Behaviour*, Vol. 9, pp. 203–14.

[10] See *R* v *Hadfield* (1800) 27 St Tr 1281 (head injury).

Perpetuating Factors

Family dynamics have been identified as maintaining the disease but not predisposing or precipitating it. The constellation of abnormalities dubbed "high expressed emotion" or "high EE" include criticism by the family, emotional over-involvement or hostility to the patient.[11] Moreover, the greater the amount of time spent with such a family, the greater the risk of relapse. However, the factor most likely to provoke relapse or maintain the illness is poor compliance with treatment.

Mechanism of Schizophrenia

In view of the mechanism of action of the antipsychotic drugs in blocking dopamine receptors in the brain, there is a widely held view that a hyperdopaminergic state or supersensitivity of the dopaminergic receptors is the underlying abnormality in schizophrenia. It is uncertain if there are other more fundamental abnormalities.

Many schizophrenic patients, particularly those with negative symptoms,[12] have enlarged ventricles, abnormal EEGs and soft neurological signs such as abnormal eye movements. The significance of these is uncertain, but they point to a neuro-developmental abnormality.

Categories of Schizophrenia

The onset of schizophrenia may be acute, developing over a few weeks or even days, or insidious. ICD-10 recognises seven categories: paranoid, hebephrenic, catatonic, simple, undifferentiated, residual and post-schizophrenic depression. In clinical practice, the tradition of diagnosis on the basis of the original four groups (i.e. paranoid, catatonic, hebephrenic and simple) is still largely

---

[11] C.E. Vaughn and J.P. Leff (1976), "Influence of Family and Social Factors on the Course of Psychiatric Illness", *British Journal of Psychiatry*, Vol. 129, pp. 125–37.

[12] See p. 341 below.

adhered to and for this reason most attention will be directed to these categories.

Paranoid Schizophrenia[13]

Paranoid schizophrenia is the most common subtype and is among the least disabling, at least in terms of personality deterioration. Personality remains intact, although the symptoms are florid. The common symptoms include delusions, with variable content, but especially of persecution,[14] and hallucinations. The prognosis is regarded as better than in other forms of schizophrenia, due to preservation of volition and personality.

Hebephrenic Schizophrenia

Hebephrenic schizophrenia is best documented in literature in the character of Ophelia in Hamlet. In its presentation, it is the most bizarre, with hallucinations, delusions, inappropriate mannerisms, laughing and giggling, rambling speech and self-absorption. Negative symptoms develop rapidly and prognosis is generally regarded as poor.

Catatonic Schizophrenia

Catatonic schizophrenia has the best prognosis and the symptoms are predominantly motor (related to movement) in nature with posturing, mutism interspersed with excitement and negativism (e.g. withdrawing a hand when a handshake is invited) or automatic obedience. Delusions and hallucination may occur and the onset is usually acute. Catatonia is rare now in the developed world, although common in the third world.[15]

---

[13] See also Chapters 10, 11 and 13.

[14] See *R* v *M'Naghten* (1843) 10 Cl. & F. 200 and *R* v *Arnold* (1724) St Tr 695, who appear to have fallen into this category.

[15] This author has only ever seen one case.

Simple Schizophrenia

This is a diagnosis made on the basis of negative symptoms only and consists of an insidious but progressive decline in functioning, oddities of conduct and emotional flattening. Psychotic symptoms are fleeting and rare. Vagrancy may ensue, as the sufferer becomes increasingly aimless and self-absorbed. It is a diagnosis that is uncommonly made and is difficult to make due to the lack of prior positive symptoms.

These descriptive categories have in recent years been undermined by the knowledge that the patients may present with a different syndrome at each admission. DSM-IV has largely abandoned these categories although they are retained in ICD-10.[16] Some clinicians still use these categories also.

Paraphrenia

Paraphrenia is a term sometimes used to describe schizophrenia of late onset (i.e. in the elderly). The symptom pattern resembles that of paranoid schizophrenia and personality is preserved. Historically, it was believed that this disorder was distinct from schizophrenia of earlier onset. At present, the clinical practice of subsuming this category under the more general heading of schizophrenia is at variance with ICD-10, which includes it under the category known as persistent delusional disorder.[17] Irrespective of which practice is adhered to, there is now a belief that it is not a disorder specific to the elderly; hence the abandonment of the term paraphrenia.

Chronic or Residual Schizophrenia

This is the descriptive term used for the protracted and usually irreversible state of negative symptoms[18] found in some patients following an acute episode. Many patients with residual schizophrenia also have chronic hallucinations and delusions. Residual

---

[16] See Chapter 3, p. 45.

[17] See p. 345–6 below.

[18] See p. 341 below.

schizophrenia may be punctuated by acute episodes requiring extra medication and at times hospitalisation.

Symptoms of Schizophrenia

These are divided into two groups: positive and negative.

Positive Symptoms

Since psychotic symptoms can be found in several psychiatric disorders, and the distinction between manic-depressive psychosis and schizophrenia was often blurred, leading to misdiagnosis, Kurt Schneider identified a group of symptoms called *the first rank symptoms of schizophrenia*. He contended that the presence of even one of these symptoms, in the absence of an organic disorder such as dementia, was diagnostic of schizophrenia. The Schneiderian approach is now generally accepted by clinicians and also by ICD-10 and DSM-IV. However, the absence of these symptoms still does not definitively exclude schizophrenia and some disagree with this procrustean approach pointing to the occasional occurrence of these symptoms in the manic patient also. Nevertheless, much weight is attached to them and they are as follows.

1. First Rank Symptoms of Schneider[19]

- *Third person auditory hallucinations* — commenting on the patient's actions/thoughts or discussing the subject in the third person, e.g. "he's going out now"; "he should be given a medal".

- *Echoes de la pensée* — voices repeat the patient's thoughts a few seconds after the thought has occurred.

- *Primary delusion* — this belief arises *de novo* and is not based on any prior hallucinations or other delusions; e.g. the patient looks at a spoon and suddenly knows that the KGB are pursuing him. (The delusion arises on the basis of a genuine perception which others would regard as commonplace. If the

---

[19] See examples in the cases cites in Chapter 16.

patient had an auditory hallucination telling him that the KGB are in pursuit, this would be a secondary delusion and not a first rank symptom.)

- *Thought insertion* — the experience of thoughts being put into his mind which are not his own. (This must be distinguished from obsessional ruminations,[20] in which irrational thoughts intrude into thinking but are felt to be the patient's own.)

- *Thought withdrawal* — the experience of thoughts being removed as if by some external force. (This must be distinguished from inattentiveness.)

- *Thought broadcasting* — the experience of one's exact thoughts being known to others, even those not in the vicinity. (This excludes a belief that thoughts can be inferred from behaviour.)

- *Passivity experiences* — the belief that his actions, emotions or sensations are "made" or caused by a force outside himself; e.g. when he writes, his hand is forcibly moved by an alien force. (This must be distinguished from a general feeling of being under the influence of God, parents, etc.)

- *Somatic passivity* — the experience of being the passive recipient of bodily sensations imposed by some external agency.

2. Other Positive Symptoms, Not of the First Rank

- *Formal thought disorder* — impairment of connection between thoughts, leading to incoherent or irrelevant speech, known as "word salad". Some patients develop their own words or neologisms, making comprehension difficult. Formal thought disorder is difficult to distinguish from flight of ideas found in mania although the connection between thoughts is maintained in the latter.[21]

---

[20] See Chapter 13, p. 295.

[21] See pp. 348–54 below.

- *Delusional mood* — the feeling that something strange is afoot. This is often a precursor to fully crystallised delusional beliefs.

- *Secondary delusions* — the content can vary and include delusions of persecution, of reference, of being an alien, of being part of a good–evil battle, etc. These secondary delusions are consequent upon other delusions or hallucinations.

- *Catatonic behaviour* — bizarre posturing or extreme underactivity with *flexibilitas cerea* (waxy flexibility). This is the ability to place a limb in a contorted position and maintain it for long periods.

- *Incongruity of affect* — inappropriate emotions, e.g. laughing when discussing sad events.

- *Other hallucinations* — of smell, taste, sight, touch.

- *Lack of insight* — that an illness is present or if accepted, it is explained in terms of delusions.

Prominent persecutory delusions can lead to violence, although most paranoid schizophrenics are not violent. Examples of paranoid delusions include the belief that the KGB are bugging the patient's home. By definition, these beliefs are held with conviction and are unshakeable; arguing with the patient can increase the conviction of their veracity or lead to aggressive outbursts. These persecutory delusions are often associated with the belief that his name was mentioned on radio/television (delusions of reference) and may also be associated with delusions of grandeur. For example, the delusion that the KGB are following the patient may be explained by his possessing valuable scientific data. Hallucinations may occur and may further convince the patient of the reality of the delusions. Thus, he may say that he can taste poison in his soup (gustatory hallucination) or smell gaseous emissions (olfactory hallucination). The weaving of these delusions into a story is known as systematisation and is associated with long-standing disease. These are difficult to treat or eliminate.

Negative Symptoms

These are the most disabling and insidious features of the disease. Indeed, it is largely due to these symptoms that the social prognosis is so poor, leading not just to difficulties with employment but also to problems in making permanent relationships[22] and marital breakdown among many sufferers. The common negative symptoms include apathy, social withdrawal, poverty of thought, blunting or flattening of affect, mannerisms and stereotypies.

Blunting of affect is the term used to describe the reduced range of emotional responses found in patients. Mannerisms are repetitive movements suggesting a prior purpose (e.g. flicking dust from the table) whilst stereotypies have no purpose (e.g. rocking, grimacing).

The apathy and lack of motivation may be mistaken for laziness, whilst the flattening of personality makes emotional involvement and rapport extremely difficult. These features are often present in vestigial form prior to the initial acute episode and parents often describe increasing withdrawal, lack of interest in school, friends, etc., as well as difficulty communicating in a previously outgoing teenager.

Surprisingly, the development of negative symptoms is not related to the speed of initial diagnosis or to aggressive treatment. The presence of negative symptoms is related to the disease process itself, with CAT scan of the brain showing enlarged ventricles in this group of patients.

Treatment

This is often provided in an acute inpatient psychiatric unit with outpatient follow-up during remission or partial remission. This will be determined by the floridity of the symptoms and by any associated dangerousness. Sometimes compulsory admission to hospital may be essential for the protection of the patient or of

---

[22] However, the negative symptoms of schizophrenia do not appear to have been prominent in nullity cases involving schizophrenia as a cause of relational incapacity; see Chapter 11.

others.[23] Major tranquillisers are the mainstay of treatment both during the acute phase and for prophylaxis. These include drugs such as chlorpromazine, haloperidol and thioridazine. The newer products such as resperidone and olanzepine are used increasingly in the acute phase of the illness. In many patients, once discharged from hospital, if compliance is a problem, drugs of this therapeutic class may then be administered every few weeks in depot injection form, depending on individual needs. Compulsory outpatient treatment is not available under the present Mental Treatment Act and thus repeated admission may occur due to lack of insight and the associated poor compliance.[24] Following a first episode of schizophrenia, medication is continued for two years. If relapse occurs during that period or after it has been discontinued, treatment is re-instituted for life.

Negative symptoms are untouched by the present array of drug treatments, although some recent medications are showing benefit in these symptoms. These include clozapine, olanzepine and respiridone. Serious side effects are uncommon with these new drugs, with the exception of clozapine, which can cause a blood disorder.[25] Because of the potentially serious side effects, this very potent drug is reserved for those who are unresponsive to conventional antipsychotic medication.

Do Major Tranquillisers have Side Effects?

Major tranquillisers must not be confused with minor tranquillisers such as diazepam or lorazepam, which have addictive potential.[26] The former are used for the treatment of acute and chronic schizophrenia as well as for relief of agitation. This group of drugs is also used in treating acute mania or hypomania. The commonest side effect is that of sedation, particularly when prescribed in

---

[23] See Chapter 18.

[24] See Chapter 18.

[25] See below, p. 343.

[26] See Chapter 10, p. 232.

excessive doses. This is in fact a useful yardstick by which to titrate the required dose against response.

A common side effect, but one which is remediable by reducing the dose or by adding antidotes, is that of Parkinsonism, a cluster of symptoms resembling Parkinson's disease, but reversible. This is not dose-related and is not a universal phenomenon. Earlier clinicians recommended the routine use of anti-Parkinsonian drugs, but this has been superseded by the view that they should only be added when symptoms develop. Another side effect is akathisia or "restless leg syndrome". The predominant feature is of an uncontrollable urge to pace. At its most serious, the patient may be in constant motion, even when standing in one spot. Treatment is with benzodiazepines or by dosage reduction. The disorder, as with Parkinsonism, is reversible.

The most serious side effect of major tranquillisers is tardive dyskinesia and occurs in about 15 per cent of those on long-term antipsychotic drugs. The risk is lower with the newer range of drugs. It is probably dose-related and can occur at any time during treatment but particularly after the first year on treatment. The symptoms include regular tongue movements, writhing movements of the limbs or sideways motions of the lower jaw. This condition can occur in the elderly, unrelated to major tranquillisers. It is a disorder that should be prevented, since it is relatively untreatable and also in view of its visibility and stigmatising effect. The risk of developing tardive dyskinesia can be reduced significantly by using minimal doses of major tranquillisers and by avoiding the routine use of anti-Parkinsonian drugs.

Other side effects are less common but include skin rashes, particularly when exposed to sunlight, drowsiness, weight gain, galactorrhoea (secretion of breast milk), gynaecomastia (breast enlargement) and amenorrhoea (discontinuation of menstruation). Jaundice can occur in some and rarely blood disorders, except with clozapine, which can lead to a low white cell count (leucopenia) and death. Close monitoring is therefore essential and for the first 18 weeks of treatment, weekly blood checks are mandatory. The drug is only available at prescribed centres that have proper monitoring in place. A rare and potentially fatal side effect of the older major tranquillisers is the neuroleptic malignant syndrome characterised by fever, muscle rigidity and lowered consciousness. It can be confirmed by measuring muscle enzymes. Treatment in medical intensive care with the drug bromocryptine is essential.

What about Psychotherapy?

Intensive psychodynamic therapy is dangerous in patients with schizophrenia, since it can provoke a relapse. However, talking therapies do have a role in reducing EE[27] in relatives who are over-involved or hostile to the patient. Social skill training is also helpful as part of the rehabilitation of those with long-term illness. Some patients do return to open employment. Those who continue to be incapacitated by symptoms or by negative symptoms can be cared for as outpatients but need some stimulation by day, such as sheltered workshops or day centre activities, depending on the extent of incapacity. The degree of stimulation is also a consideration, since over-stimulation can provoke relapse and under-stimulation reinforces negative symptoms. The number of hours spent in the company of relatives must also be controlled if high EE is a feature and less than 40 hours per week is recommended.

Prognosis

Predicting the outcome for an individual patient should be done with extreme caution. Good prognostic factors include acute onset, late age of onset, good pre-morbid personality, no negative symptoms and the presence of depressive symptoms. Those schizophrenic patients with a concomitant axis two disorder[28] especially of the antisocial type, have a very poor prognosis and are often found in prison rather than in hospital, due to their aberrant behaviour overshadowing the psychotic symptoms. Long-term follow-up studies indicate that 25 per cent of all sufferers achieve

---

[27] See p. 335 above.

[28] See Chapter 3, p. 45.

full social and symptomatic recovery; a further 25 per cent have minor problems; 25 per cent have episodic relapses and significant social and work-related problems with only a limited capacity for independent living; and 25 per cent have poor prognosis, remaining chronically psychotic with either positive or negative symptoms, severe social impairment and independent living unlikely.

Schizophrenia and the Law

The insanity defence is usually used when a patient commits a crime in response to delusions or hallucinations. The link between the content of the delusion/hallucination is usually clear. In some instances, however, the person may at the time of the crime be free from obvious delusions and exhibit only hostility or impulsivity,[29] i.e. sub-clinical disorder. It is possible that this poor impulse control could lead to a crime in the absence of psychotic symptoms that, with more medication, could be controlled. If the patient remained untreated, then overt psychotic phenomena would later become prominent. The requirement for a successful insanity defence — that the patient should suffer a disease of the mind rather than of the brain — is now inappropriate and a historical anachronism in view of the advances in understanding the neuro-pathological basis for the disease.

At an earlier phase of the proceedings, a patient may be unfit to plead, especially if grossly thought-disordered or if the delusions are all encompassing.

SYNDROMES RELATED TO SCHIZOPHRENIA

Persistent Delusional Disorder[30]

In this group of disorders, the patient has encapsulated delusions but hallucinations are absent and personality is preserved.

---

[29] See Chapter 16, pp. 380–4, on irresistible impulse.

[30] On the basis of the content of delusions, specific syndromes of schizophrenia have been described; e.g. delusions of love or De Clerambaults syndrome, delusions of jealousy or Othello syndrome (see Chapter 10) and delusions of a shrinking penis or Koro.

Paranoid Psychosis[31]

This is characterised by paranoid delusions. These patients frequently do not come to attention for some time and are viewed as being just querulous. Frequently it is their constant haranguing of the police or solicitors, in order to report or redress the wrong they believe is being done to them, which leads their family to recognise the gravity of the problem. Insight is absent and treatment is unlikely to be sought voluntarily. They are usually referred for treatment when their behaviour begins to impinge upon others, leading to fear that a violent crime will be committed. A variant is pathological jealousy, in which delusions that the spouse is having an affair are evident.[32] Other variants, referred to as mono-symptomatic delusional psychosis, include the delusion that the body emits an odour, that a part of the body is deformed, diseased or misshapen. As with paranoid psychosis, the disorder is often unrecognised until, say, the patient visits a plastic surgeon and fails to be satisfied by the operation which has been carried out. In this group of disorders, hallucinations and other symptoms of the first rank[33] are absent. Moreover, personality is preserved so that the negative features found in schizophrenia are not in evidence.

Treatment is with major tranquillisers, usually indefinitely. If compliance is a problem, these may be required in depot form.

Folie à Deux or Symbiotic Psychosis

This is an exotic but rare disorder shared by two or more people in close emotional proximity. They are often isolated from the general community by language, choice or culture. One person — usually the dominant one — is the psychotic one, whilst the other person(s) take(s) on the patient's delusions as his/their own. Initially the couple must be separated temporarily, in order to treat the ill partner. The non-ill partner then recovers spontaneously.

---

[31] See Chapter 10.

[32] See Chapter 10.

[33] See p. 338 above.

Treatment of the ill person is of the primary underlying disorder, usually but not always schizophrenia.

Schizotypal Disorder

This is classified as a personality disorder in DSM-IV and as a variant of schizophrenia in ICD-10.[34] It is a disorder characterised by eccentric behaviour and anomalies of thinking and affect which do not meet the criteria for schizophrenia. Onset is insidious and it runs a chronic course. It may at times evolve into full-blown schizophrenia. Treatment is with major tranquillisers.

Schizo-affective Psychosis

This is a controversial disorder and has only just been recognised by the ICD system of classification. Even among clinicians, there is still scepticism about its validity. Since it is included in ICD-10 and may be used in the court setting by some clinicians, it is appropriate that it be considered.[35]

The diagnosis is made when both schizophrenic and affective symptoms occur simultaneously or within a few days of each other in an episode of illness. The affective symptoms may be depressive or manic in type. The diagnosis should not be made when a depressive illness follows a schizophrenic episode — this common occurrence is diagnosed and treated as post-schizophrenic depression with antidepressants and/or ECT if required. There is doubt as to the relationship between schizo-affective psychosis and either manic-depression or schizophrenia. Different schools believe that schizo-affective psychosis is a variant of one or the other illness. The prognosis is better than for schizophrenia, since negative symptoms do not develop and treatment of the acute symptoms is symptomatic, either with antidepressants or major tranquillisers. Maintenance treatment to prevent relapse is with lithium.

---

[34] See Chapters 3 and 9.

[35] As, for example, in *S* v *K* (High Court, 2 July 1992) reported at [1993] 1 Fam LJ 18.

DRUG INDUCED PSYCHOSIS

Since abuse of drugs such as cocaine, LSD and amphetamines can lead to psychotic symptoms,[36] the possibility exists that murder committed during such an episode may lead to the use of the insanity defence. Although crimes committed while voluntarily intoxicated are excluded from this defence, the psychotic symptoms can sometimes persist and resemble schizophrenia in every respect. Indeed, it is possible that the exogenous substance triggered the illness in a chemically/genetically vulnerable subject.

The acute episode is treated with major tranquillisers as well as a longer-term approach directed to overcome the substance misuse. If symptoms persist, as they can particularly following amphetamine misuse, long-term medication either orally or by depot injection is necessary. In its chronic form, there is nothing to distinguish amphetamine psychosis from residual schizophrenia except that the former will have had an exogenous precipitant.

MANIA

Mania and its milder form hypomania are part of the condition known as manic-depressive illness/psychosis, also called bipolar affective disorder. It is characterised by recurrent episodes, either of depressive illness or mania/hypomania or by a combination of both simultaneously, known as a mixed affective state. The presentation is usually with a depressive illness,[37] so the diagnosis will not then be made until the patient suffers a manic episode.

Epidemiology

Manic depression affects less than 1 per cent of the population and is slightly more common in women than men.

---

[36] See also Chapter 10, pp. 233–6.

[37] See Chapter 6, pp. 99–104.

Aetiology

Unlike schizophrenia, around which many novel theories developed, no such interest has focused on manic-depression, except for suggestions of a link to genius. This remains to be proven.

Predisposing Factors

There is strong evidence for a genetic contribution to manic-depressive illness, particularly from twin studies with monozygotic (identical) pairs showing a higher concordance for the disorder (68 per cent) than dizygotic (non-identical) pairs (25 per cent). Adoption studies demonstrate that the rate of manic-depressive illness is higher among the biological relatives of adoptees with the disorder than in the adoptive parents. The mode of inheritance is uncertain but may be sex-linked.

It is generally agreed that adverse early circumstances, such as loss or separation from a parent, contribute to the development of depressive illness. However, the contribution to manic-depressive illness is questionable and the degree and specificity of the contribution to the depressive illness is unknown and is a minefield of methodological problems for researchers.

Some researchers suggest that particular personality attributes may render the person vulnerable to depressive illness or manic depression. In particular, those with obsessional traits[38] were considered to be at increased risk of depressive illness, as were those who have learnt throughout their lives that their efforts end in failure (learned helplessness). More recent theories have focused on the negative thought patterns, termed a "negative cognitive set", that some are prone to exhibiting in the face of stress. However, the evidence to support these theories is limited and they are still under investigation.

Precipitating Factors

There is little doubt that both depressive illness and manic-depression can be precipitated by events or stressors such as

---

[38] See Chapter 9, p. 206.

childbirth, road accidents, death, moving house, or effectively any life event that involves the perception of loss or threat by the victim. Physical illness, including brucellosis, cancer and multiple sclerosis, can also lead to depressive illness. The mechanisms of this are unclear and are not just related to insight about the illness, since some cancers can present with depressive illness, especially cancer of the lung or pancreas, in advance of physical symptoms being apparent. In spite of the relationship between events and illness, many, if not most, develop the illness without any obvious precipitant or predisposing factor.

Perpetuating Factors

One of the most common reasons for the maintenance of depressive or manic-depressive illness is inadequate treatment or no treatment at all. Depressive illness is commonly misdiagnosed as being an anxiety disorder or due to circumstances (adjustment disorders) for which counselling is required. Indeed, the distinction can at times be difficult, but once depressive illness is diagnosed it should be treated with antidepressants — the choice is not between counselling and antidepressants, but a combination of both. However, many are reluctant to comply with chemical treatment due to misinformation and to family pressure to seek alternative non-medical help.

Even with treatment, some patients do not show a response to antidepressants prescribed and others must be tried. It is essential to prescribe in therapeutic doses, a problem particularly pertinent to general practice where traditionally lower doses of antidepressants have been used than those recommended by the pharmacological data sheets. The duration of the treatment trial is also important, and a minimum of six weeks before regarding the antidepressant as ineffective is recommended. Similarly, with manic-depression about 30 per cent of those treated with lithium for prevention of relapse do not achieve a full response. Alternatives are then recommended, either alone or in combination with lithium.

Social factors can maintain depressive illness, especially isolation or lack of personal supports. Personality disorder in the presence of depressive illness or manic-depression also prolongs the illness, although the mechanisms are unclear. Unlike the depressive phase, mania or hypomania seldom escapes treatment, due to its intrusiveness in the lives of family members.

Mechanism of Affective Disorders

Biochemical abnormalities underlie the symptoms in this group of disorders. Those with depressive illness exhibit abnormalities of the neurotransmitters serotonin and nor-adrenaline or of the receptors concerned with their uptake in the brain. Indeed, the rationale for prescribing antidepressants is to re-establish the metabolism of these transmitters. The biochemical abnormalities underlying mania and manic-depression are less well established but believed to be related to the movement of sodium and potassium across cell membranes — lithium normalises this process. Other theories have examined the role of hormones such as cortisol, and melatonin has received attention in relation to seasonal affective disorder, a disorder of depression that has its onset in the autumn months. There is no link, however, between hormone release and post-natal depression.

Symptoms

The hypomanic patient presents with over-activity, irritability and pressure of speech. Mood may be elated, but a sizeable number of patients are hostile. Behaviour is disinhibited and may be associated with increased risk-taking, leading to experimentation with drugs, sexual promiscuity or excessive spending. Hyperactivity is marked. A more severe form of the disorder is mania, in which these symptoms are present, but delusions and to a lesser extent hallucinations are also prominent. The delusions are classically grandiose in content. The patient may feel that he is related to somebody famous (e.g. a film star), he may be convinced that he has special abilities such as the power to invent electricity and may claim a special relationship with God or some religious figure. Persecutory delusions may arise from the grandiose beliefs (e.g. the patient may feel that the KGB are trying to kidnap him because of his special genius). Auditory hallucinations may occur but are less prominent than in schizophrenia.

Because judgement is impaired, pregnancy may occur, traffic accidents are possible and large debts may be incurred. Insight is lacking, co-operation with treatment is often refused and compulsory detention may be the only option.[39]

Manic episodes are often followed by a depressive swing, which needs treatment as for a depressive illness.[40]

Treatment

Acute Phase Treatment

This is divided into two phases: treatment of the acute episode and prevention of relapse. The manic patient usually requires in-patient treatment but the person with hypomania can at times be treated at home. The manic and hypomanic patient generally shows a rapid response to major tranquillisers such as chlorpromazine or haloperidol. A very small number of patients fail to respond to safe doses of these drugs, in which case electroconvulsive treatment may be necessary. Along with severe depressive illness, intractable mania is one of the indications for this treatment.

Prevention of Relapse

Once the patient's mood has normalised, described as normothymia or euthymia, the further management depends on the prior history. If the patient has no previous history of mania or hypomania, then medication can be gradually discontinued on an outpatient basis. Some patients may swing into a depressive phase rapidly after the manic episode. At that point, major tranquillisers are discontinued and antidepressants instituted. If the patient has a history of three or more episodes of either depression or mania/hypomania in the previous two years, lithium is added as a

---

[39] See Chapter 18.

[40] See Chapter 6, p. 103.

prophylactic against relapse. Although this treatment is usually commenced whilst an inpatient, it is likely that full stabilisation may not occur for several months. During this period, the patient can be treated as an outpatient.

Lithium is not a drug that is given lightly, since it requires regular assessment of the blood levels, initially fortnightly but three-monthly when adequate blood levels have been reached — the level recommended for therapeutic response is between 0.6 and 1.2 mmols/litre. At higher levels, toxic effects occur, whilst at lower levels it is ineffective. Moreover, teratogenic effects have been described in the foetus and women of childbearing age must be advised of this risk so that pregnancies can be planned. Recent research suggests that lithium may be less teratogenic than was previously believed. Annual checks of thyroid and renal function are also necessary.

If a full response to lithium is not achieved, then the addition of carbamazepine or sodium valproate (both anti-epileptic drugs finding increasing usage as mood-stabilisers), either alone or in combination with lithium, can achieve this. Blood levels of these drugs should also be monitored in order to achieve therapeutic levels and the therapeutic level required is higher than that for epilepsy. These may be used in preference to lithium from the outset; those who have episodes in rapid succession every few weeks are particularly helped by these compounds. These are known as rapid cyclers.

Prognosis

Treatment with lithium and the other prophylactic agents is life-long and the effects, if successful, are to attenuate episodes or to bring about a total cessation of episodes of depression and elation. About 30 per cent of those treated with lithium require additional or alternative treatment with the compounds described above. The natural history of the disease is for the time period between the episodes to shorten initially and, from the 50s onwards, to decrease in frequency. The natural history is rarely apparent now with the successful prevention of episodes.

Mania and the Law

Since crime can occur as a result of delusions, but more commonly as a result of impaired judgement and risk-taking, the insanity defence could in some patients be entered.

Since mania is treatable, the patient is unlikely to be permanently unfit to plead, although he may be so found before treatment is initiated, especially if flight of ideas is present, making communication impossible.

DEPRESSIVE ILLNESS[41]

In the context of the insanity defence, it is most likely to be posed when a patient under the influence of delusions or hallucinations, of a negative and hopeless variety, murders or attempts to murder another. The postpartum mother who kills her child in the mistaken belief that it harbours the devil, or the person convinced that the world is about to end and murders his family are common examples of this. Although depressive psychosis is uncommon, and criminal acts such as murder even more uncommon, the role of depressive psychosis must not be forgotten. In recognition of the importance of postpartum psychosis in the causation of infant murder, the crime of infanticide was formulated. However, murder associated with depressive psychosis can occur at any time of life. On occasion, the party may attempt to kill himself, or indeed successfully kill himself, as part of the delusional process.[42] Such patients when in custody are especially demanding in view of their continuing delusions, and if insight returns after treatment are at further risk of suicide.

Depressive Illness and Suicide Pacts

Suicide pacts are rare. They occur in the context of a severe depressive illness in one partner, usually the dominant one, and a

---

[41] See Chapter 6, pp. 99–104.

[42] So-called dyadic murders. See M. Bolster, F. O'Garabhan and J. Harbison, (1995), "Dyadic Deaths in Ireland", *Medico-Legal Journal of Ireland*, Vol. 1, No. 3, pp. 91–4.

partner who is not psychiatrically ill but who has had a close and dependent relationship with the other. The driving force behind the pact is the ill partner and if the pact fails with one person dying and the other surviving, then the insanity defence may be raised.[43]

OTHER PSYCHIATRIC DISORDERS AND CRIMINAL LAW

Depressive Illness and Shoplifting

Some patients, when depressed, shoplift and their illness comes to attention when they are apprehended and prosecuted. Those involved in the legal system should be especially alert to an underlying depressive illness when the offender is a woman of previously good repute, although there have been cases of men offending in this way also. The goods taken are usually inexpensive. In some patients, the offence has occurred as a result of a lapse in concentration, whilst in others the patient is aware of his/her actions and may commit the offence in a public manner but is unable to explain the rationale.[44] Theories of a "cry for help" are invoked to explain such overt offending. When treated, recidivism is uncommon.

Other Disorders and Shoplifting

Less commonly than in association with depressive illness, shoplifting may also occur in association with organic brain syndromes such as dementia or in mania when the patient is disinhibited. A group of patients who tend to indulge in many crimes including shoplifting are drug abusers. The items are then sold to sustain the habit and, unless the patient is stabilised on prescribed drugs or detoxified, recidivism is common.

---

[43] See Criminal Law (Suicide) Act, 1993. The explanatory memorandum issued by the Department of Justice indicated that the suicide pacts constituted the mischief sought to be addressed by section 2.

[44] See however, *R v Clarke* [1972] 1 All ER 219, 56 Cr App R 225, CA.

Dementia[45]

Patients with dementia may become deluded in a manner similar to the schizophrenia patient. The delusions are usually of a persecutory nature and may also be associated with hallucinations. The possibility of serious crime therefore exists, although it is small since the demented patient lacks the capacity to plan. Given the nature of the condition, it may arise early in criminal proceedings when assessing the fitness of the subject to plead.

Other Offences

Traffic offences such as speeding may occur in mania. The manic patient is both overactive and lacking in judgement. He is unlikely therefore to have any insight into the risk he poses and indeed his grandiosity may further impair judgement. Manic patients may also incur debts that they are unable to meet. Treatment of the manic episode is essential and recidivism is uncommon, provided the patient remains well.

SEXUAL OFFENCES

A number of offences are included in this group. However, little is known about the causes of such sexual deviations (paraphilias), and most theories are speculative. Others have focused specifically on possible causes of rape and child sexual abuse.

General Theories of Causation

The importance of understanding the causes of sexual deviation lies in applying these models to assessment and treatment. The earliest theories were developed by psychoanalysts Ellis and Freud. In particular Freud held that these behaviours were related to developmental abnormalities that continued into adult life. He invoked Oedipal conflicts, castration anxiety and a host of other psycho-dynamic factors, which have largely been relegated to history due to their untestability. Interestingly, the legacy of

---

[45] See Chapter 12.

Freud in this area has been his use of the term "perversion" to indicate that either the aim or the object of the sexual desire was distorted.

Behavioural theorists point out that it is the behaviour itself which is abnormal and that it is not symptomatic of any underlying abnormality. The problem is viewed as an inappropriate frequency of behaviour, thoughts or feelings, which is reinforced and maintained by the antecedents or consequences of the action. A variant of this model is provided by Wolf[46] who postulates three variables that interact to lead to and reinforce the deviant behaviour. The first is an abnormal developmental history, probably amounting to severe personality disorder. The second is a set of situational factors which overcome the social controls against sexual deviance; and the third is a deviant and extensive fantasy life.

The idea that deviant sexual behaviour has biological roots offers a degree of comfort, since it allows for the possibility of a physical treatment. Flor-Henry[47] has been a vociferous exponent of the theory that sexual deviations are a consequence of the male pattern of cerebral (brain) organisation. However, this view does not provide any support for the use of anti-androgen drugs to control deviant sexual behaviour, since elevated levels of testosterone, the male sex hormone, are found in only a few of the most aggressive of offenders.

A global theory has also been presented[48] which suggests that males have a biological tendency towards sexual aggression, which is countered by the socialisation process. Risk factors for development of the paraphilias include poor parenting, cultural attitudes including tolerance of pornography and situational

---

[46] S.C. Wolf (1985), "A Multi-factor Model of Deviant Sexuality", *Victimology: An International Journal*, Vol. 10, pp. 359–74.

[47] P. Flor-Henry (1987), "Cerebral Aspects of Sexual Deviation", in G.D. Wilson (ed.), *Variant Sexuality: Research and Theory*, Baltimore: John's Hopkins University Press.

[48] D.R. Laws and W.L. Marshall (1990), "A Conditioning Theory of Aetiology and Maintenance of Deviant Sexual Preference and Behaviour" in W.L. Marshall, D.R. Laws and H.E. Barbaree (eds.), *Handbook of Sexual Assault: Issues, Theories and Treatment of the Offender*, New York: Plenum.

factors that serve as disinhibitors, such as alcohol. This model thus tries to encapsulate developmental, biological, socio-cultural and situational factors in the aetiology of sexual deviations.

Theories of Rape

The debate about whether rape is essentially aggressive, sexual or sadistic has concerned theorists for many years.[49] With an aggressive aim, the motivation is to humiliate and defile the victim and the woman is the object of the offender's destructive wishes. Psychodynamic theorists postulate that the victim is viewed as a substitute for the object of the offender's original hatred (i.e. the mother). The sexual aim of rape, on the other hand, is to serve the sexual fantasies of the offender, which involve great sexual skill on his part and intense pleasure by the woman. Unacknowledged homosexual feelings are believed to underpin these fantasies and the failure of the act to fulfil these leads to its repetition. The sadistic motive combines both elements so that violence must be present for sexual arousal to occur. This group of offenders also demonstrate other forms of psychopathic behaviour. A variant of this model construes rape as expressing power or anger. Although having much intuitive appeal, the psychodynamic theories have not led to any major advances in treatment.

Behavioural theories have contributed little to understanding the causes of rape, with the exception of sadistic rapists who demonstrate increased sexual arousal from depictions of forceful sex when compared to mutually consensual sex. However, this constitutes a small group. Biological explanations have also been invoked. Brain dysfunction, when assessed neuropsychologically and neurologically, have been demonstrated in some rapists, although the findings were subtle and provide only a limited

---

[49] M.L. Cohen, R. Garofolo, R. Boucher and T. Steghorn (1971), *The Psychology of Rapists, Seminars in Psychiatry*, Vol. 3, pp. 307–27, New York: Grune and Stratton.

explanation.[50] The role of testosterone levels in the genesis of rape and a genetic propensity to violence is relevant only to a subgroup of rapists. Recent years have seen a coalescence of theoretical approaches, including social learning theory. Thus, the cause of rape is not seen as unitary but multifactorial including hostility to women, attitudes facilitating violence, antisocial personality characteristics and prior sexual experience.

Theories of Child Sexual Abuse

Psychodynamic theories at their simplest have suggested that child sexual abuse is not motivated by sexual needs, but is an expression of non-sexual needs, with the exception of those who threaten violence. This theory states that the motivations include coping with feelings of powerlessness, attempting to process their own abusive childhoods and seeking affection. Two types of paedophile are recognised in this scheme: the regressed abuser who has developed an age-appropriate sexual orientation but who under certain circumstances regresses; and the fixated paedophile whose primary sexual interest is in children. Family systems theory has also been used in understanding incest (sexual abuse within the family). In particular, an interplay between a father with a personality disorder or from a subculture with a tolerance of incest, a mother who has withdrawn from the marital role, who may be passive and/or masochistic, and a daughter who is manipulated into the role of mother, including the sexual role, sets the scene for such behaviour.

Neither behavioural nor physiological theories provide any further understanding of paedophilia. A theoretical framework incorporating a number of approaches has been conceptualised by Finkelhor.[51] Firstly, the abuser needs appropriate motivation (for example, the abuse satisfies a need, the child is a source of

---

[50] S. Hucker, R. Langevin, R. Dickey, L. Handy, J. Chambers and S. Wright (1988), "Cerebral Damage and Dysfunction in Sexually Aggressive Men", *Annals of Sex Research*, Vol. 1, pp. 33–47.

[51] D. Finkelhor (1984), *Child Sexual Abuse: New Theory and Research*, New York: Free Press.

arousal, alternative sources of gratification are blocked). Secondly, the internal inhibitions against abuse need to be overcome (e.g. alcohol abuse, cultural tolerance of abuse, weak sanctions against abusers). Thirdly, the external inhibitions need to be overcome (e.g. sleeping arrangements). And fourthly, the child's resistance must be overcome (e.g. coercion or a situation of unusual trust). Potentially the most interesting area of development, carrying with it the potential for treatment, has been the exploration of the cognitive or thought processes of paedophiles. The theory[52] is that those who find themselves attracted to children may respond by changing their view of the world so as to support their behaviour. Thus, sentiments like "the child enjoyed it", "it is a good way to teach children about sex", "children have a right to have sex", etc., are utilised to overcome the internal inhibitions as described in Finkelhor's model.

Assessment of Sexual Offenders

The abuser is generally male and often has difficulty establishing relationships with adults and may have a history of having been abused himself in childhood, although this is not inevitable. The sexual motive is apparent in some who have an increased level of erotic attraction to children or adolescents. In others, particularly involving very young children, the abuse may be a variant of physical abuse motivated by the need to humiliate and to inflict pain. Some studies suggest that sexual abuse of boys is more common than of girls, although the latter are more likely to disclose the abuse. Abusers also tend to have other sexual deviations, such as voyeurism, exhibitionism, etc. Occasionally, females abuse a male child or adolescent. Although most studies point to this

---

[52] G.G. Abel, J.V. Becker and J. Cunningham-Rathner (1984), "Complications, Consent and Cognitions in Sex between Children and Adults", *International Journal of Law and Psychiatry*, Vol. 7, pp. 89–103.

occurring in the context of a psychotic illness, recent studies suggest that this is not always the case.[53]

Most research has been conducted on the assessment of paedophiles and rapists. Two general approaches are utilised, one being physiological, the other by structured interview. The physiological approach is based on the theory that the paraphilias are due to deviant sexual arousal. Since it is a physiological response, it can be assessed by measuring the penile response to sexually explicit stimuli. Penile tumescence is measured either by recording, on a sensor or transducer, changes in penile circumference or total penile size in response to exposure to a variety of sexual materials. The sexual material is presented in three possible modalities, i.e. videotape, audiotape or slide. When presented with the material which is the most sexually provocative, penile tumescence increases and this change is registered on a graph.

Caution must be exercised in using this physiological approach, since some can have false responses in spite of having a deviant pattern of arousal. The results of these tests should not be used as evidence that a sexual offence has been committed or that a particular person fits the profile of the offence. Their main role is to determine and monitor treatment.[54]

A number of self-report questionnaires are also available, although they are of somewhat limited value since their accuracy depends on truthful responses by the subject. One such measure,[55] consisting of 225 items, assesses sexual interest through

---

[53] R.S. Krug (1989), "Adult Male Report of Childhood Sexual Abuse by Mothers: Case Descriptions, Motivations and Long-Term Consequences", *Child Abuse and Neglect*, Vol. 13, pp. 111–19.

[54] For discussion of the merits of the respective systems and of the interpretation of the results, the reader is referred to other sources: see W.D. Murphy, M.R. Haynes and P.J. Worley (1991), "Assessment of Adult Sexual Interest" in C.R. Hollin and K. Howells (eds.), *Clinical Approaches to Sex Offenders and their Victims*, Chichester: John Wiley and Sons.

[55] R. Langevin, L. Handy, D. Paitich and A. Russon (1983), "A New Version of the Clarke Sex History Questionnaire for Males" in R. Langevin (ed.), *Erotic Preference, Gender Identity and Aggression*, Hillsdale, NJ: Lawrence Erlbaum.

questions about deviant and non-deviant sexual responses as well as fantasies. As with physiological measures, these scales should never be used to prove that an offence has occurred. The most frequently used assessment measure is the clinical interview, which also has obvious limitations. Questions focus on the number and type of sexual partner, the frequency of deviant and non-deviant sexual behaviour and, in particular, the content of masturbatory fantasies.

Attempts have been made to use psychological tests to prove or disprove allegations. In particular, personality tests such as the Minnesota Multi-phasic Personality Inventory[56] have been administered to those already convicted of such offences in an attempt to profile the abusers. The test is then administered to the person charged with the offence and the more closely he/she resembles the profile obtained for the generality of abusers, the greater is the corroborative power of the test, so the argument goes. This approach, however, is extremely dangerous and should be viewed with extreme caution, since tests such as these were developed for the purpose of obtaining personality profiles from the general healthy population and have not been validated as tools for identifying sexual abusers. In the context of court, the legal team should seek advice from a psychiatrist or psychologist who has an interest in psychometrics (the science of developing measurement instruments in psychiatry/psychology). Unless a tool has been developed specifically for the purpose for which it has been used, has adequate sensitivity, specificity, predictive validity and reliability, the results provided by it will be not only meaningless but dangerous.

Treatment

Although recidivism rates remain high following treatment, the use of cognitive techniques has resulted in some improvement. In particular, dealing with denial, rationalisation and minimisation is one of the first steps. This can occur in group or individual

---

[56] See Chapter 9, p. 217.

treatment. Other group approaches may be more psychodynamic, exploring family relationships or using victim role-play to achieve empathy.

Social skills training, in a group setting or individually, is one element of intervention designed to address the problems many such offenders have in dealing with adult relationships. This is done by role-play, rehearsal and modelling. Whilst improvement can be demonstrated in an institutional setting, maintaining these changes following release is difficult. Sex education is also one of the themes addressed during treatment with sex offenders, since a lack of accurate sexual knowledge has been found among sexual offenders.

Aversion therapy, in which material associated with deviant imagery is paired with unpleasant consequences (e.g. electric shock or unpleasant smell), resulting in extinction of the deviant behaviour, has also been used. A variant of this, known as orgasmic or masturbatory reconditioning, in which the non-deviant replace deviant fantasies, has been used in some centres.

The use of surgical or chemical castration in treatment has been reported over the years to reduce the recidivism rates dramatically. The main problem with surgical procedures, including the use of oestrogen implants, is an ethical one, since the treatment is irreversible and there is an increased risk of thrombosis and breast enlargement. Other medications, such as the anti-androgen drug cyproterone acetate or the tranquilliser benperidol, have fewer side effects but research on their long-term usage is not available. The usefulness of such treatments is limited by the fact that some offenders commit their crimes for motives other than sexual gratification and reducing libido may not be sufficient to control their offending.

Prognosis

Recidivism is common and up to 40 per cent re-offend, doing so up to ten years after the index event. Attempts to identify potential re-offenders have proven difficult and the only consistent predictor is a past history of offending. Various approaches to prediction have been reviewed and criticised by Grubin.[57]

OTHER SEXUAL OFFENCES

Exhibitionism

This is the behaviour which is associated with the most common sexual offence, i.e. indecent exposure. It is defined as the exposure of the genitals to unprepared members (usually) of the opposite sex, usually strangers, for gratification. The perpetrator rarely tries to engage the victim in further sexual activity. It is almost entirely confined to men, although there have been rare accounts of female exhibitionism, usually of the breasts. Perpetrators fall into two main categories. The first are shy, inhibited men who struggle against the impulse and derive little pleasure from the activity. Indeed, they feel humiliated and guilty about their behaviour. The penis is flaccid and masturbation does not occur during the exposure. The second category of exhibitionist is sociopathic and derives pleasure from the act. There is no guilt and he exposes in an aroused state. In both groups, the exposure is preceded by increasing tension and is only relieved by a strong emotional reaction from the victim. Some may make obscene telephone calls also. Recidivism is common.

Voyeurism

The voyeur derives sexual pleasure from observing the sexual behaviour of others or from watching others undress. Confined to men, it is often accompanied by masturbation. The perpetrators are shy and have difficulty establishing relationships with women.

Fetishism

This is defined as the deriving of pleasure from inanimate objects, usually items of clothing. Most commonly, these include under-

---

[57] D. Grubin (1997), "Predictors of Risk in Serious Sex Offenders", *British Journal of Psychiatry*, Vol. 170 (supplement 32), pp. 17–21.

clothes, shoes or rubber clothing. Rarely, the object of pleasure may be a deformity or disability not usually regarded as attractive, such as a scar or lameness. Fetishism rarely comes to attention unless the partner seeks help. In the context of the law it may come to attention when the perpetrator, almost exclusively male, is discovered stealing from a neighbour's clothesline.

SUMMARY

Many psychiatric disorders can be associated with serious crime, although this association is rare. The insanity defence can be invoked in some cases of murder associated with psychotic disorders, except those due to drugs. The distinction between diseases of the mind and the brain is now extinct due to greater understanding of the neurobiological basis of these disorders. The aetiology of sexual offences is not understood and debate about the sexual as distinct from the aggressive underpinning of these crimes is still active.

Chapter 16

INSANITY

INTRODUCTION

Just as schizophrenia is the condition at the nub of psychiatry, so "insanity", going to the issue of criminal responsibility, is at the nub of the interface between psychiatry and the criminal law.[1] That said, the characterisation of any condition as "insanity" is an unhappy one. A relic of an old and now outdated forensic and clinical nosology, it has long since passed out of the medical lexicon,[2] and is manifestly out of place in a society that seeks to avoid language with any pejorative connotation.[3] In *People (DPP)* v

---

[1] See, generally, Glanville Williams (1961), *Criminal Law: The General Part*, 2nd edition, London: Stevens & Sons Ltd., pp. 441–551; P.J. Richardson (ed.) (1997), *Archbold, Criminal Pleadings, Evidence and Procedure*, London: Sweet & Maxwell, sections 17-74 to 17-101; J.C. Smith and B. Hogan (1988), *Criminal Law*, 6th edition, London: Butterworths, pp. 185–98; F. McAuley (1993), *Insanity, Psychiatry and Criminal Responsibility*, Dublin: Round Hall Press, Chapters 2–6; R. Card (1988), *Cross Jones and Card: Introduction to Criminal Law*, 11th edition, London: Butterworths, pp. 149–60; D.N. Robinson (1996), *Wild Beasts and Idle Humours: the Insanity Defence from Antiquity to the Present*, Cambridge, MA: Harvard University Press.

[2] See, however, *Doyle* v *Wicklow County Council* [1974] IR 55 at 71 *per* Griffin J (SC) (quoting with approval *People (A-G)* v *Hayes* (Court of Criminal Appeal, Unreported Judgment, 30 November 1967) *per* Henchy J).

[3] See, for example, the discussion of "immaturity" in the context of personality disorder (Chapter 8) in the High Court (High Court, Unreported Judgment, Kinlen J, 5 May 1994) (a finding not upset on appeal; see *O'M(M)* v *O'C(B)* [1996] IR 208).

Neilan,[4] Keane J, in agreeing with O'Hanlon J in *People (DPP)* v *Ellis*,[5] stated:

> . . . our law in this entire area is archaic and in urgent need of statutory reform. I am comforted, however, by the reflection that the conclusions I have reached on this topic, if they are upheld, will result in a legal framework for dealing with mentally ill persons who have been charged with criminal offences which bears at least some limited relationship to the requirements of society today. (See the Third Report of the Henchy Committee on *The Treatment and Care of Persons Suffering from Mental Disorder who appear before the Courts on Criminal Charges* (Prl. 8275)). That, of course, of itself is no reason for deferring the reform of the existing law, disfigured as it is not merely by out-of-date conceptions of insanity but also by offensive descriptions of those suffering from mental illness which have long since passed out of the vocabulary of civilised people.[6]

Keane J's aspirations, alas, remain unfulfilled.[7] Literally meaning "not healthy", "insanity" is best regarded as legal shorthand for certain psychiatric disorders that excuse criminal responsibility in the sufferers for acts that, if carried out by persons not so afflicted, would be punishable as crimes. It is a legal tag without any diagnostic or therapeutic value,[8] and its characterisation is a source of bewilderment to medical practitioners. Given the antiquity of most frequently applied dicta,[9] this should hardly be regarded as surprising. The issue is complicated further by the legal

---

[4] [1990] 2 IR 267, [1991] ILRM 184.

[5] [1990] 2 IR 291, [1991] ILRM 225.

[6] [1990] 2 IR 267 at 289–290.

[7] See *People (DPP)* v *Gallagher* [1991] ILRM 339, where a unanimous Supreme Court disagreed with Keane J's conclusions in *Neilan*. Meanwhile, statutory reform is still awaited.

[8] ". . . for it is legal insanity with which the courts are concerned, and not medical insanity." *Doyle* v *Wicklow County Council* [1974] IR 55 at 72 *per* Griffin J (SC).

[9] *R* v *M'Naghten* (1843) 10 Cl. & F. 200.

juxtaposition with "insanity" of other conditions that excuse criminal responsibility — those in relation to "non-insane" automatism. These conditions are quite different from an aetiological and pathophysiological point of view, and are generally neither of interest nor concern to psychiatrists.[10] Yet, the disposition of an accused is quite different if he is found to have acted as a "non-insane" automaton rather than as a result of his "insanity".[11] Devlin J, as he then was, in *R v Kemp*,[12] set out his understanding of the then relevant English law. Thus, he stated:

> Under the common law this question [i.e. whether or not the accused was suffering from a "disease of the mind"] would not have arisen. In the eyes of the common law, if a man is not responsible for his actions, he is entitled to be acquitted in the ordinary form of acquittal, and it matters not whether his lack of responsibility was due to insanity or to any other cause. That position in common law was altered by statute, the Trial of Lunatics Act of 1883, which introduces what I think is best called a qualified form of acquittal as distinguished from the absolute acquittal, which is all that is known in common law, an acquittal which is expressed in the verdict of guilty but insane, but which has been held to be a verdict of acquittal[13] and to mean in effect not guilty because insane. As a result of that qualified verdict the accused is detained in strict custody until Her Majesty's pleasure be known, and he is sent to some institution where his mental state can be assessed and considered; in the case of an absolute acquittal, the prisoner, of course, is entitled to be discharged. The object of the Act, no doubt, was that people who committed crimes of violence, even though they were not responsible for their actions, ought not to be allowed to go free because they might commit an act of violence again, and so they ought to be kept in

---

[10] See below, p. 392 *et seq.*

[11] See below, p. 413.

[12] [1957] 1 QB 399, [1956] 3 All ER 249, (1956) 40 Cr App R 121.

[13] See, for example, *People (DPP) v Gallagher* [1991] ILRM 339 (SC).

custody until their position should be determined. It is that Act which now governs the matter and which makes a dividing line, as it were, between those sorts of lack of responsibility which would give rise to a complete acquittal . . . and those other sorts that fall within the terms of the Act permitting only the qualified form of acquittal . . .[14]

However, the law is not simply concerned with identifying those psychiatric conditions that could give rise to further acts of violence in the sufferer, who, accordingly, ought to be kept in custody until his situation was determined. Antisocial behaviour arising from psychiatric disorder can manifest itself in other activities (e.g. exhibitionism)[15] that do not necessarily involve violence. Indeed, the object of prevention has been characterised as "recurrence of the dangerous conduct".[16] Thus, the law on "insanity" has been applied, among other activities, in relation to theft,[17] dangerous driving[18] and arson.[19] But, on principle, the application of a qualified form of acquittal on the basis of possible recurrence of a certain anti-social activity must be a questionable proposition. If the object of the law in relation to criminal "insanity" is to facilitate the management of offenders with psychiatric disability and to protect others, recourse to the mechanisms of civil committal, if necessary, seem more appropriate and humane.[20] Furthermore, risk prediction is not an exact science. A cynical view of detention under the provisions of the Act could seem directed more at blanket prevention rather than individuated evaluation. Whatever

---

[14] [1957] 1 QB 399 at 403. The Act of 1883 remains the law in Ireland, although not in England; see Criminal Procedure (Insanity) Act, 1964, s. 5 and Sch. 1.

[15] See Chapter 15, p. 364–5.

[16] *R* v *Sullivan* [1984] AC 156 at 172, Cr App R 176 at 182, *per* Lord Diplock.

[17] *R* v *Clarke* [1972] 1 All ER 219, 56 Cr App R 225, CA. However, the Court of Appeal held that M'Naghten's Rules did not apply.

[18] *R* v *Hennessy* (1989) 89 Cr App R 10, CA. Here, however, the primary condition was diabetes mellitus.

[19] *Doyle* v *Wicklow County Council* [1974] IR 55.

[20] See Chapters 17 and 18.

validity such an approach might have had in 1883, it seems less defensible with the passage of time. Although the Act remains the law in Ireland,[21] the Government have indicated their intention to address the definition of "criminal insanity" in future legislation.[22] Nevertheless, in the absence of the former practice of individuated judicial assessment of persons committed under the provisions of the Act, its application remains a current problem.[23]

As Devlin J noted, prior to 1883 a person found not to have been responsible for his actions at the time that he committed the act did not receive a technical acquittal. Rather, it was unqualified. In Coke's time (1552–1634), the disability had to be of such a nature that the accused resembled a beast more than a man. Hale was of the view that a person labouring under

> melancholy distempers hath yet ordinarily as great under-standing, as ordinarily a child of fourteen years hath, is such a person as may be guilty of treason or felony.[24]

The criterion was a total lack of reason, and competence at the age of fourteen was regarded as the best measure. In *R v Arnold*,[25] where, on a modern reading, the accused might be regarded as suffering from paranoid schizophrenia,[26] the jury was instructed that, to be exempt from punishment, the accused must be a man:

> . . . that is totally deprived of his understanding and memory, and doth not know what he is doing, no more than an

---

[21] This is discussed further below, see p. 413 *et seq.*

[22] See White Paper on a New Mental Health Act (1995), Department of Health, para. 7.26.

[23] See *Gallagher* v *Director of the Central Mental Hospital & Others* (High Court, Unreported Judgment, 9 July 1996); *Neilan* v *DPP* [1990] 2 IR 267 [1991] ILRM 184; *People (DPP)* v *Ellis* [1990] 2 IR 291, [1991] ILRM 225, [1991] ILRM 225; *People (DPP)* v *Gallagher* [1991] ILRM 339.

[24] 1 Hale PC 30. See also *Doyle* v *Wicklow County Council* [1974] IR 55 at 66; McAuley (1993), op. cit., pp. 18–22; Robinson (1996), op. cit. Robinson traces in detail the historico-political and legal-medical development of the defence.

[25] (1724) St Tr 695.

[26] See Chapter 15.

infant, than a brute, or a wild beast; such a one is never the object of punishment . . ."[27]

Not being so satisfied on the evidence, the jury convicted, as they also did in *R* v *Earl Ferrers*.[28] In *R* v *Hadfield*,[29] the accused had suffered severe head trauma and, almost certainly, brain damage, as a consequence of which he suffered sequelae now readily recognised as such.[30] In 1800, he had attempted to shoot George III and was tried for treason. He was characterised as a man who had become ". . . completely insane from violence to the brain, which permanently affects its structure. . ."[31] However, at times he had appeared relatively normal. The clinical evidence, even at the time, was to the effect that such a person could conduct himself rationally on some subjects, but reveal his "insanity" on a particular subject. Hadfield was subject to religious delusions. Indeed, he believed that heaven wanted him dead but he could not kill himself. Hence his treasonable attack on the king. However, notwithstanding that he had failed to meet the accepted criterion for "insanity" at the time, he was acquitted. And following his acquittal, the Criminal Lunatics Act, 1800, provided for the detention, at the pleasure of the executive, of persons charged with treason or felonies who:

> may have been or may be of unsound mind at the time of committing the offence wherewith they may have been or shall be charged, and by reason of such insanity may have

---

[27] (1724) 16 St Tr 695 at 754, reproduced in Robinson (1996), op. cit., p. 134.

[28] (1760) 19 St. Tr. 886.

[29] (1800) 27 St. Tr. 1281.

[30] See Chapter 6, p. 107, and Chapter 15, pp. 345–8. Hadfield, on the evidence adduced, was quite deluded and probably had schizophrenia.

[31] (1800) 27 St Tr 1281 at 1320–1321, reproduced in Robinson (1996), pp. 147–8.

been or may be found not guilty of such offence, and it may be dangerous to permit persons so acquitted to go at large.[32]

In *R* v *Oxford*,[33] the accused, who had entered the young Queen Victoria's carriage and discharged two pistols, was acquitted on the grounds of "insanity" caused by a "lesion of the will". This, briefly, was the background against which the formulation most used in the area of criminal "insanity", M'Naghten's Rules, is set. However, the elaboration of coherent principles from the Rules has been hindered, at least to some extent, by the different manner in which they are applied at different times, and in different jurisdictions. The failure of psychiatrists to approach the issues involved in a scientific manner, and consistently to accept appropriate standardised nomenclature and definitions,[34] can hinder rather than advance the legal appraisal of the problem and renders the elaboration of coherent principles of widespread applicability all the more difficult. For the clinician, the case law is problematic. Just as the early cases on so-called "nervous shock"[35] are replete with tales of Victorian ladies miscarrying because they experienced some calamity, so also the cases on "insanity" recount the most extraordinary (from a clinical point of view) tales of co-ordinated, purposive movement,[36] resulting in the most appalling of injuries to victims, under the guise of "automatism". The explanation is difficult. Perhaps, though, it is the case that clinically

---

[32] Criminal Lunatics Act, 1800, s. 1. A nearly identical provision is found in the Lunacy (Ireland) Act, 1821 (1&2 Geo IV c. 33), s. 16, which provided for the verdict of "not guilty on the ground of insanity" and detention at the pleasure of the executive; it also only applied to murder, high treason and felonies. The distinction between misdemeanours and felonies was abolished by the Criminal Law Act, 1997, s. 3.

[33] [1840] 4 St. Tr. (ns) 497, 9 C&P 526.

[34] See Chapters 2 and 3.

[35] See Chapter 9.

[36] See p. 399 below.

rare events naturally self-select as far as legal problems are concerned.[37]

M'NAGHTEN'S RULES

The starting point for discussion, and description, of the law in relation to "insanity" in common law jurisdictions is often conveniently taken from M'Naghten's case.[38] Despite the unsatisfactory circumstances of their articulation, these "Rules" have been fairly rigidly applied. And, indeed, in relation to "insanity" at the time of the commission of a criminal offence, they have been repeatedly accepted in English[39] and, subject to certain effective modifications, in Irish law.[40]

On 20 January 1843, Daniel M'Naghten, in the "insane" belief that he was being persecuted by the Tory Party and that, as a consequence, his life was in danger,[41] followed Edward Drummond, secretary to the Prime Minister Sir Robert Peel, whom he mistook for Peel, up Whitehall (to his bank) and shot him in the back. Drummond died five days later from his injuries and M'Naghten was tried for murder. His subsequent acquittal on the ground of insanity

> excited public opinion and gave rise to a debate in the House of Lords. In the course of the debate it was decided to take the opinion of the Judges on the law governing such

---

[37] Conditions recognised clinically also appear to frequently "self-select" the attention of the criminal law. See Chapter 15.

[38] *R* v *M'Naghten* (1843) 10 Cl. & F. 200.

[39] Richardson (1997), op. cit., p. 1532 and the cases cited. See also E.P. Trager (1998), "The Insanity Defence Revisited", *Medico-Legal Journal of Ireland*, Vol. 4, No. 1, pp. 15–19.

[40] See, for example, *People (A-G)* v *O'Brien* [1936] IR 263; *People (A-G)* v *Hayes* (Court of Criminal Appeal, Unreported Judgment, 30 November 1967); and *Doyle* v *Wicklow County Council* [1974] IR 55.

[41] See Chapter 15 for paranoid psychosis and schizophrenia. It is likely that M'Naghten was suffering from paranoid psychosis.

cases. This was accordingly done by summoning the Judges and submitting to them a series of five questions[42]

as follows:

Question 1

"What is the law respecting alleged crimes committed by persons afflicted with insane delusion in respect of one or more particular subjects or persons as to instance, where at the time of the commission of the alleged crime the accused knew he was acting contrary to law, but did the act complained of with a view, under the influence of insane delusion, of redressing or preventing some supposed grievance or injury, or of producing some public benefit?"

Answer

"Assuming that your lordships' inquiries are confined to those persons who labour under such partial delusions only, and are not in other respects insane, we are of the opinion, that, notwithstanding the party did the act complained of with a view, under the influence of insane delusion, of redressing or revenging some supposed grievance or injury, or of producing some public benefit, he is nevertheless punishable, according to the nature of the crime committed, *if he knew, at the time of committing such crime, that he was acting contrary to law*, by which expression we understand your lordships to mean the law of the land."

Question 2

"What are the proper questions to be submitted to the jury when a person alleged to be afflicted with insane delusion respecting one or more particular subjects or persons, is charge with the commission of a crime (murder, for example), and insanity is set up as a defence?"

---

[42] *People (A-G)* v *O'Brien* [1936] IR 263 at 268 *per* Kennedy CJ (CCA). See also, Robinson (1996), op. cit., pp. 163–70.

Question 3

"In what terms ought the question be left to the jury as to the prisoner's state of mind at the time when the act was committed?"

Answers 2 and 3

"That the jury ought to be told in all cases that *every man is presumed to be sane*, and to possess a sufficient degree of reason to be responsible for his crimes, *until the contrary be proved* to their satisfaction: and that, to establish a defence on the ground of insanity, it must be clearly proved that, *at the time of the committing of the act, the party accused was labouring under such a defect of reason, from disease of the mind, as not to know the nature and quality of the act he was doing, or, if he did know it that he did not know he was doing what was wrong*. The mode of putting the latter part of the question to the jury on these occasions had generally been, whether the accused, *at the time of doing the act, knew the difference between right and wrong*, which mode, though rarely, if ever, leading to any mistake with the jury, is not, as we conceive, so accurate when put generally, and in the abstract, as when put as to the party's knowledge of right and wrong in respect to the very act with which he is charged. If the question were to be put as to the knowledge of the accused, solely and exclusively with reference to the law of the land, it might tend to confound the jury, by inducing them to believe that an actual knowledge of the law of the land was essential in order to lead to a conviction, whereas the law is administered upon the principle that everyone must be taken conclusively to know it without proof that he does know it. If the accused was conscious that the act was one which he ought not to do, and if that act was at the same time contrary to the law to the land, he is punishable; and the usual course, therefore, has been to leave the question to the jury, whether the party accused had a sufficient degree of reason to know that he was doing an act that was wrong: and this course, we think, is correct, accompanied with such observations and explanations as the circumstances of each particular case may require."

Question 4

"If a person under an insane delusion as to the existing facts commits an offence in consequence thereof, is he thereby excused?"

Answer

"The answer must, of course, depend on the nature of the delusion; but making the same assumption as we did before, that he labours under such partial delusion only, and is not in other respects insane, we think he must be considered in the same situation as to responsibility as if the facts with respect to which the delusion exists were real. For example, if, under the influence of his delusion, he supposes another man to be in the act of attempting to take away his life, and he kills that man, as he supposes in self-defence, he would be exempted from punishment, if his delusion was that the deceased had inflicted a serious injury to his character and fortune, and he killed him in revenge for such supposed injury, he would be liable to punishment."

Question 5

"Can a medical man, conversant with the disease of insanity, who never saw the prisoner previously to the trial, but who was present during the whole trial, and the examination of all the witnesses, be asked his opinion as to the state of the prisoner's mind at the time of the commission of the alleged crime, or his opinion whether the prisoner was conscious, at the time of doing the act, that he was acting contrary to law, or whether he was labouring under any and what delusion at the time?"

Answer

"We think the medical man, under the circumstances supposed, cannot in strictness be asked his opinion in the

terms above stated, because each of those questions involves the determination of the truth of the facts deposed
to, which it is for the jury to decide: and the questions are
not mere questions upon a matter of science, in which case
such evidence is admissible. But where the facts are admitted or not disputed, and the question becomes substantially
one of science only, it may be convenient to allow the question to be put in that general form though the same cannot
be insisted on as a matter of right."[43]

In *People (AG)* v *O'Brien*,[44] having examined the language of the
questions and answers, and the context in which the Rules were
expressed, Kennedy CJ stated:

. . . the questions submitted to the Judges for opinion were
in express terms limited to crimes committed by "persons
afflicted with insane delusions in respect of one or more
particular subjects or persons". It follows . . . that the opinions given by the Judges must in every case be read with
the like specific limitation.[45]

The essential elements of the Rules are often summarised thus:

1. Every person is presumed to be sane and to possess a suffi-
    cient degree of reason to be responsible for his actions, unless
    and until the contrary is proven.

2. It is a defence to a criminal prosecution if it is established
    that, at the time of committing an offence, the accused was la-
    bouring under such a defect of reason, from disease of the
    mind, so as not to know the nature and quality of the act, or, if
    he did know it, he did not know that it was wrong.

3. An accused who commits a crime under a partial delusion, is
    judged as if the facts with respect to which the delusion exists
    were real.

---

[43] [1843] 4. St. Tr. (n.s.) 930.

[44] [1936] IR 263.

[45] [1936] IR 263 at 269.

The very language of the Rules, irrespective of whether they are expressed in long or short form, in construction, conceptualisation and rationalisation can most charitably be described as problematic. Any attempt to craft a coherent explanation of the rules within the framework provided by modern psychiatry is, to say the least, difficult. Noting the qualified nature of the questions asked of the Judges, robust dissatisfaction with the rules was expressed as far back as 1936. Thus, it was stated that the answers to the second and third questions (number 2 in the summary):

> . . . have been commonly read as applying to the whole field of insanity, which is, of course, of far wider area, and comprises a more extensive and varied range of cases of mental disease than those which can be conveniently summed up as affliction with insane delusion. Hence, the dissatisfaction expressed by many legal and medical persons with the opinions as so read with the wide and general interpretation wrongly given to them. The scientific exploration of mental diseases has in modern times been pursued with results to knowledge not contemplated at a time not very remote from the present. A vast area of research and discovery lies in the relatively short period of time between Hogarth's cartoon of Bedlam and current theories as to the upsetting of the glandular balance of the human body.[46]

Valid over 60 years ago, this criticism could be repeated with greater force in more modern times.[47] That different legal systems regard the same rules in a different manner does not assist an attempt to articulate a coherent approach.[48]

---

[46] *People (A-G)* v *O'Brien* [1936] IR 263 at 269–270 *per* Kennedy CJ. At p. 271, he continued: "It is not ours to make laws. We have only to ascertain and declare the law as it is, whether, when ascertained, it is found to be in the circumstances of our day deserving of approval or otherwise. If otherwise, we have a legislature competent to alter or adapt it in the light of the latest science and of the conditions of the time in which we live." The legislature has, thus far, not seen fit to so alter or adapt the law.

[47] See Chapters 1, 2 and 3.

[48] See pp. 380–6 below.

What is the Scope of the Rules in the Law on Criminal "Insanity"?

Of the four substantive questions asked of the judges, three expressly refer only to "insane" delusions.[49] The remaining question appears to be of a general propositional nature in relation to "insanity".[50] In England, the Court of Criminal Appeal has held that the Rules were not limited to cases in which the accused was suffering from delusions, but also applied in all cases of "insanity", whatever its nature or whatever disease of the mind from which the accused was suffering.[51] In *O'Brien*,[52] however, there is a clear suggestion that Irish criminal jurisprudence might not regard the Rules as exhaustive of the issue of criminal responsibility in an accused with a psychiatric disorder.[53] The matter was ultimately resolved by the Supreme Court in *Doyle* v *Wicklow County Council*,[54] where Griffin J stated:

---

[49] For a definition of a delusion, see Glossary. Given that a delusion, by definition, is symptomatic of a serious psychiatric disorder, the adjectival "insane", being unhelpful, pejorative and clinically meaningless, will be omitted in the remainder of the text.

[50] See *R* v *Windle* [1952] 2 QB 826, 36 Cr App R 85, CCA; *R* v *Sullivan* [1984] AC 156 HL.

[51] *R* v *Windle* [1952] 2 QB 826, 36 Cr App R 85, CCA. See also *R* v *Sullivan* [1984] AC 156 HL.

[52] See *People (A-G)* v *O'Brien* [1936] IR 263.

[53] On the facts, however, the accused's appeal against his death sentence failed. See also *People (A-G)* v *Boylan* [1937] IR 449.

[54] [1974] IR 55. Given that the Rules in M'Naghten's case effectively arose from a moot ("The Judges protested as to the inconvenience of being called upon to express their opinions in the abstract, not in relation to the facts of a particular case and without argument or debate of the matter." — *People (A-G)* v *O'Brien* [1936] IR 263 at 268 *per* Kennedy CJ), the Supreme Court noted (at p. 66) that "the answering of a question in a Case Stated which arises in the course of a claim for compensation for criminal injury is not the most appropriate circumstance in which to consider the application of rules which have been widely applied in criminal trials for upwards of 130 years". However, given the effective abolition of the death penalty upon the enactment of the Criminal Justice Act, 1964 (now further amended by the Criminal Justice Act, 1990), the court also considered that it was "less likely that this Court will be required to consider the M'Naghten rules in a criminal appeal" and pronounced accordingly.

In my opinion, the M'Naghten rules do not provide the sole or exclusive test for determining the sanity or insanity of an accused. The questions put to the judges were limited to the effect of insane delusions and I would agree with the opinion expressed by the Court of Criminal Appeal in *O'Brien* that the opinions given by the judges must be read with the like specific limitation.[55]

As to whether or not the Rules are otherwise exhaustive of the law on criminal "insanity", it has been roundly asserted that they:

do not provide for . . . volitional and emotional factors in mental disorder. They are concerned solely with effects of cognition or intelligence, and do not expressly consider defects of emotion, or of conation (or will). By implication, however, since they purport to state exhaustively the rules relating to insanity as a defence, they deny the relevance of insane impulse. This is in fact the position adopted by English courts and by most courts in the Commonwealth and the United States. Usually, judges make no effort to justify the exclusion of the defence; they simply affirm that it is not recognised by the law.[56]

Nevertheless, it had previously been held that although substantial grounds of objection in practice might be raised against admitting the defence of "irresistible impulse" (or "insane impulse"),[57]

. . . the English Court of Criminal Appeal[58] to the contrary notwithstanding, that is not sufficient to rule it out of

---

[55] [1974] IR 55 at 70.

[56] Williams (1961), op. cit., pp. 507–8. For "insane" impulse, see below. In fact, English law still regards the Rules as exhaustive.

[57] See Chapter 15 in relation to impulsivity in the context of psychiatric disorder.

[58] See, for example, *R* v *Kopsch* (1926) 19 Cr App Rep 50 (CCA). See also, *Sodeman* v *R* [1936] 2 All ER 1138 (PC); *A-G for South Australia* v *Brown* [1960] AC 432. However, proposals for reform and the incorporation of such a defence within the Rules were made as far back as 1923 by the Atkins

consideration, if it be shown to rest on any established principles of the criminal law.[59]

In *Doyle* v *Wicklow County Council*,[60] Griffin J, having noted that:

> it appears to be the general opinion of medical men that there are types of insanity outside the rules which deprive the insane man of choice or responsibility, just as much as the types covered by the rules.[61]

disposed of the matter. He adopted with approval Henchy J's statement of the law in the Court of Criminal Appeal in *People (AG)* v *Hayes*,[62] where he had said:

> In the normal case, tried in accordance with the M'Naghten rules, the test is solely one of knowledge: did he know the nature and quality of his act or did he know that the act was wrong? The rules do not take into account the capacity of a man on the basis of his knowledge to act or to refrain from acting, and I believe it to be correct psychiatric science to accept that certain serious mental diseases, such as paranoia or schizophrenia,[63] in certain cases enable a man to understand the morality or immorality of his act or the legality or illegality of it, or the nature and quality of it, but nevertheless prevent him from exercising a free volition as to whether he should or should not do that act. In the

---

Committee (Cmnd. 2005) and the Royal Commission on Capital Punishment (Cmnd. 8932), see Smith and Hogan (1988), op. cit., pp. 198–199. It falls, however, within the scope of the defence of diminished responsibility; see below.

[59] *People (A-G)* v *O'Brien* [1936] IR 263 at 271 *per* Kennedy CJ, having cited "Digest of the Criminal Law" by Sir James FitzJames Stephens, Article 29, which included defective "mental power" with "disease of the mind" in a M'Naghtenesque formulation that also provided for irresistible impulse as an excusing factor in criminal responsibility.

[60] [1974] IR 55.

[61] [1974] IR 55 at 69. See also Chapter 15.

[62] Central Criminal Court, 30 November 1967.

[63] See Chapter 15, pp. 332–45.

present case, the medical witnesses are unanimous in saying that the accused man was, in medical terms, insane at
the time of the act. However, legal insanity does not necessarily coincide with what medical men would call insanity,
but if it is open to the jury to say, as say they must, on the
evidence, that this man understood the nature and quality
of his act, and understood its wrongfulness, morally and
legally, but that nevertheless he was debarred from re-
fraining from assaulting his wife fatally because of a defect
of reason due to his mental illness, it seems to me that it
would be unjust, in the circumstances of this case, not to
allow the jury to consider the case on those grounds.[64]

Although in *O'Brien,* on the evidence, the defence of irresistible
impulse failed on appeal, it was accepted in *Doyle* v *Wicklow
County Council.*[65] And, in this regard, the Rules are still demon-
strative of the approach to be taken to the matter. Thus, in the
most recent case in which the issue arose in Irish law, *People
(DPP)* v *Courtney,*[66] the Court of Criminal Appeal approved the
trial judge's direction to the jury, where he stated:

There is a limited form of insanity recognised by our law,
commonly called irresistible impulse, that means in this
case an irresistible impulse caused by a defect of reason
due to mental illness. Merely because an impulse is not in
fact resisted does not mean that it is an irresistible impulse. If so, no one could ever be convicted of a crime —
they would only have to say, "I found the impulse irresistible". It must be an irresistible impulse, not an unresisted
impulse, to constitute that form of insanity. Diminished
self-control or weakened resistance to impulse is not necessarily the same as irresistible impulse. Diminished self-
control makes the resistance to an impulse more difficult

---

[64] [1974] IR 55 at 71. This was followed and applied in *People (DPP)* v
Courtney (Court of Criminal Appeal, Unreported Judgment, 21 July 1994)
per O'Flaherty J.

[65] [1974] IR 55. See reporter's note at p. 74.

[66] Court of Criminal Appeal, Unreported Judgment, 21 July 1994.

> but does not necessarily make it irresistible. This must
> arise from a defect of reason due to mental illness . . . Did
> the accused act because he did not resist the impulses
> rather than because he could not? That is for you to decide,
> bearing in mind all the evidence and the facts as found by
> you on the basis of such evidence.

Expert evidence adduced on behalf of the accused was to the effect
that he had a vulnerable personality[67] and that he was suffering
from a post-traumatic stress disorder[68] as a result of certain experiences he had while serving as a soldier with a contingent of the
Defence Forces with the United Nations Interim Force in Lebanon
over three years previously. It was also contended that the year
prior to the murder with which he was charged, he had suffered a
marked exacerbation of his symptoms and that his history of excessive drinking was a symptom of his post-traumatic stress disorder. This was the mental illness to which the disease of the
mind had to be referable. However, on the facts, the expert evidence was to the effect that the accused's self-control was significantly diminished, but not lost. Having considered the trial
judge's question, the jury returned a verdict of guilty, which was
not upset on appeal.

Thus, at least in Irish law, knowledge of the wrongfulness of
the act is not inconsistent with a successful defence.[69]

What does the Law on Criminal "Insanity" Seek to Achieve?

What the law on criminal "insanity" seeks to achieve is often regarded with great puzzlement by clinicians, especially by psychiatrists outside the forensic sphere. At the same time, lawyers, with

---

[67] See Chapter 9.

[68] See Chapter 6.

[69] See, in contrast, *R* v *Windle* [1952] 2 QB 826, 36 Cr App Rep 85 (CCA);
Stapleton v *R* (1952) 86 CLR 358, discussed in *Doyle* v *Wicklow County
Council* [1974] IR 55 at 70; and the commentary in Richardson (1997), op.
cit., pp. 1534–5.

their conceptions of psychiatric disability largely, it seems, fashioned by the case law on "insanity" (and so-called "nervous shock") may regard legal definitions as synonymous with clinical problems, such that neither group can necessarily see the conceptual (and practical) problems encountered by the other. This is notwithstanding repeated exposition in academic texts,[70] and the cases,[71] which highlight the very significant differences between the lawyer's and the doctor's primary concerns when it comes to a client, or a patient, as the case may be, with a psychiatric disability. Thus, as Devlin J (as he then was) succinctly put it:

> . . . the law . . . is not concerned with the origin of the disease or the cause of it but simply with the mental condition which has brought about the act. It does not matter, for the purposes of the law, whether the defect of reason is due to a degeneration of the brain or to some other form of mental derangement. That may be a matter of importance medically, but it is of no importance to the law, which merely has to consider the state of mind in which the accused is, not how he got there.[72]

Therefore, the law is directed at the issue of criminal responsibility for the actions of the accused, not at a clinical definition of psychiatric disability. Nevertheless, it is unfortunate that the Rules seem so couched in the language of psychiatry with scant obvious regard for their central relevance, i.e. to issues of moral culpability and excusal from punishment. Confusingly, psychiatric disability — characterised as a "mental derangement" or "unsoundness of mind"[73] — may be labelled as "insanity" when what is meant is simply a lack of legal responsibility because of that

---

[70] For a comprehensive discussion of the different conceptions of legal "insanity" and psychiatric disability, see McAuley (1993), op. cit., Chapter 1; and Williams (1961), op. cit., pp. 442–6.

[71] See, for example, *R* v *Kemp* [1957] 1 QB 399 at 407 *per* Devlin J; and *Doyle* v *Wicklow County Council* [1974] IR 55 at 72 *per* Griffin J (SC).

[72] *R* v *Kemp* [1957] 1 QB 399 at 407.

[73] See Chapter 14 in relation to testamentary incapacity.

disability. Furthermore, the "insanity" defence also, as interpreted and applied — and, arguably, arising from the Victorian political *milieu* that gave rise to both M'Naghten's Rules and the Trial of Lunatics Act, 1883 — is raised in situations where the problem of psychiatric disability is utterly irrelevant and the central issue is solely that of legal liability.[74] Nevertheless, the authorities persist in the application of the "insanity" test as formulated, with, from a clinical perspective, bizarre and clinically irrelevant and inconsistent results. It would be preferable if the law merely and solely focused on *mens rea* and omitted all fixed (and, it seems, frequently erroneous) notions of "diseases of the mind".[75] Once absence of *mens rea* has been established, it is surely not beyond the legislature to define — as a matter of policy and necessity — what the appropriate disposition should be in such cases.[76]

Notwithstanding such linguistic and conceptual confusion, it is apposite briefly to set out the state of the law, however clinically and intellectually unsatisfactory it might be, and to attempt to reconcile it with a modern framework of psychiatry.

GENERAL PRINCIPLES

The "Special Verdict"

"Insanity" at the time of the commission of an offence is effectively reducible to an example of the absence of *mens rea*, the necessary mental element for the commission of a crime. It is a matter of defence and the prosecution must still establish, beyond a reasonable doubt, that the accused did the act or omission with which he

---

[74] As, for example, in *R* v *Windle* [1952] 2 QB 826, 36 Cr App R 85, CCA; *R* v *Sullivan* [1984] AC 156 HL.

[75] Notwithstanding that it has been argued that if the Rules did not exist, it would, in any event, be necessary to invent something very like them as "there is a strong moral impulse to exempt those who . . . are manifestly incapable of acting rationally from criminal responsibility" to be so constrained by such an ancient formulation could be regarded as fundamentally unsatisfactory. However, see the able arguments in its support; McAuley (1993), op. cit., pp. 25 and 26.

[76] See pp. 413–16 below and Chapter 17, pp. 438–43.

is charged. Should they fail to do so, the accused is entitled to be acquitted, irrespective of whether or not he was "insane" at the relevant time.[77] Therefore, it is only if it is proven that he did the act that the issue arises.

However, if it is so proven and if it is established, and in jury trials, this is a matter for the jury to determine, that the person was:

> insane, so as not to be responsible, according to law, for his actions at the time when the act was done or the omission made . . . the jury shall return a special verdict to the effect that the accused was *guilty of the act* or omission charged against him, *but was insane* as aforesaid at the time . . .[78] (emphasis added).

Where such a special verdict, often shortened to "guilty but insane", is returned, the accused is kept in custody:

> as a criminal lunatic, in such place and in such manner as the court shall direct till the pleasure of the Lord Lieutenant shall be known.[79]

However, in England, since 1964, the verdict is one of "not guilty by reason of insanity",[80] whereupon the accused is ordered to be

---

[77] This would appear to be correct both at common law and on the reading of the Trial of Lunatics Act, 1883, s. 2(1), which introduces the special verdict; see below.

[78] Trial of Lunatics Act, 1883, s. 2(1), as extended to Ireland by s. 3. Unlike the earlier Acts of 1800 and 1821 (fn 32 above), the Act of 1883 also applied to misdemeanours. For an illuminating insight into the political thinking underpinning the change in the law, see McAuley (1993), op. cit., pp. 110–11 and the references therein; and Robinson (1996), op. cit., Chapter 5.

[79] Trial of Lunatics Act, 1883, s. 2(2), as applied by s. 3, a point of significant importance; see *People (DPP) v Ellis* [1990] 2 IR 291 (SC), [1991] ILRM 225; *People (DPP) v Gallagher* [1991] ILRM 339 (SC); *Gallagher v Director of the Central Mental Hospital & Others* (High Court, Unreported Judgment, 9 July 1996). This should be contrasted with the situation in Britain (see below) and the provisions in respect of a person found "guilty but insane" by court-martial; see Defence Act, 1954, s. 203, as amended by the Courts-Martial Appeals Act, 1983, s. 6.

[80] Criminal Procedure (Insanity) Act, 1964, s. 5 and Sch. 1.

detained in a hospital selected by the Home Secretary, usually a secure hospital such as Broadmoor.[81]

However, the provisions relating to the special verdict do not apply to summary trials[82] (whether in the District Court or in a Magistrates' Court). Here, if "insanity" is established in an offence that requires *mens rea* to be established, at common law, the court must give an ordinary acquittal whereupon the accused is unconditionally discharged.[83] Should the interests of either the accused or of the public require protection in such a situation, then recourse must be had to the relevant civil commitment procedures.[84]

DEFECT OF REASON

"A defect of reason is by itself enough to make the act irrational and therefore normally to exclude responsibility in law."[85] "Defect of reason", it has been held, means the deprivation of reasoning power and requires more than momentary confusion or absent-mindedness in someone who otherwise retains their reasoning power but fails to use it fully.[86]

---

[81] As a consequence, an accused is indefinitely detained until the Home Secretary or a Mental Health Review Tribunal is satisfied that the accused's detention is not longer required for the protection of the public.

[82] Although the provisions relating to the requirement that the prosecution prove the act or omission charged beyond a reasonable doubt clearly do, as in the case of jury trials.

[83] As in the common law before 1800; see pp. 313–14 above. See also *State (C)* v *Minister for Justice* [1967] IR 106 at 121 *per* Walsh J.

[84] In Ireland, under the Mental Treatment Act, 1945; see Chapter 17. However, in Britain, the Mental Health Act, 1983, s. 37(3) empowers a magistrate to make a hospital or guardianship order without registering a conviction if satisfied that an accused is suffering from mental illness or severe mental impairment and did the act charged. The granting of a somewhat similar power to a court to remand an accused or convicted person in custody for treatment is also contemplated by the White Paper on a New Mental Health Act (1995), Department of Health, para. 7.20. This should be contrasted with the proposed procedure in respect of fitness to plead; see Chapter 16. Such a procedure, as Williams (1961, op. cit., p. 475) has maintained, would be "superior".

[85] See *R* v *Kemp* [1957] 1 QB 399 at 408, (1956) 40 Cr App R 121 at 127, Assizes, *per* Devlin J.

[86] See *R* v *Clarke* [1972] 1 All ER 219, 56 Cr App R 225, CA.

However, as to where the line is to be drawn between momentary confusion and absent-mindedness (which could be symptomatic of early, and undiagnosed, psychiatric disability, e.g. dementia)[87] and a more profound interference with reasoning generally, is unclear.[88] The pathophysiology, or perhaps the phenomenology, at least in such cases, appears to be of importance. Taken to its logical conclusion, the nature of this critical element of the defence is less one of law than one of medical evidence and the risk of recurrence into the future — again also based on medical evidence. The only issue of law, therefore, is whether the evidence is sufficient to fulfil the legal criteria. In this, it does not differ from any other area of law. However, where irresistible impulse[89] is accepted as a defence, as noted, the non-deprivation of powers of reason may not be fatal to its being successfully raised.

DISEASE OF THE MIND

It has been asserted that

> [T]he Rule was not intended to apply to defects of reason caused simply by brutish stupidity without rational power. . . . The words ensure that unless the defect is due to a diseased mind and not simply to an untrained one there is insanity within the meaning of the Rule.[90]

Therefore, it is only where the deprivation of reasoning powers is caused by a "disease of the mind" that the "insanity" defence may be raised with any success. Similarly, an irresistible impulse must be caused by defect of reason caused by a "mental illness".[91]

---

[87] See Chapter 12, pp. 276–89.

[88] As, for example, in a symptomatic psychotic illness, or depression. See Chapter 15, pp. 332–55.

[89] See above, pp. 380–4.

[90] *R v Kemp* [1957] 1 QB 399 at 408, [1956] 3 All ER 249, (1956) 40 Cr App R 121 at 127, Assizes, *per* Devlin J.

[91] *People (A-G)* v *Hayes* (Court of Criminal Appeal, Unreported Judgment, 30 November 1967); and *People (DPP)* v *Courtney* (Court of Criminal Appeal,

Although clinically, the concept of "mind" may be difficult to appreciate, because, as a construct, it has no particular relevance to practice, lawyers have no such difficulty. Thus, it has been held that:

> [T]he law is not concerned with the brain but with the mind,
> in the sense that "mind" is ordinarily used, the mental facul-
> ties of reason, memory and understanding. If one reads for
> "disease of the mind" "disease of the brain", it would follow
> that in many cases pleas of insanity would not be established
> because it could not be proved that the brain had been af-
> fected in any way, either by degeneration of the cells or in
> any other way. . . . The condition of the brain is irrelevant.[92]

However, the relevance of this proposition — given advances in the search for objectively discernible indicia of some abnormality of central nervous system structure or function in many psychiatric disorders is concerned — must now be called into question.[93] Thus, the stress is on functional outcome,[94] and, as yet, it seems objective evidence of physical "damage" to the central nervous system is not necessary. That said, its presence does not operate to exclude the application of the test of "insanity" in the Rules. Thus:

> If the effect of a disease is to impair these faculties . . . it
> matters not whether the aetiology of the impairment is or-
> ganic, as in epilepsy [or arteriosclerosis], or functional, or
> whether the impairment itself is permanent or is transient
> and intermittent, provided it subsisted at the time of the
> commission of the act.[95]

Unreported Judgment, 21 July 1994). In this context, "mental illness" appears to accord with a clinical assessment and diagnosis.

[92] *R* v *Kemp* [1957] 1 QB 399 at 407, [1956] 3 All ER 249 at 253, (1956) 40 Cr App R 121, *per* Devlin J.

[93] See Chapter 15, p. 345.

[94] See p. 385 above.

[95] *R* v *Sullivan* [1983] 3 All ER 673, *per* Lord Diplock at 677. See also *R* v *Kemp* [1957] 1 QB 399, [1956] 3 All ER 249, (1956) 40 Cr App R 121, *per* Devlin J.

Accordingly, "physical" conditions with significant non-physical sequelae could result in a finding of "insanity".[96] Although the curability or otherwise of the condition is irrelevant:[97]

> A malfunctioning of the mind of transitory effect caused by the application to the body of some external factor such as violence, drugs, including anaesthetics, alcohol and hypnotic influences cannot fairly be said to be due to disease.[98]

This introduces the concept of an "external" as distinct from an "internal" factor in the assessment of the applicability of the law on criminal "insanity". And, in effect, it reduces clinically to a functional impairment of reasoning and understanding (for which

---

[96] For example, depressive illness associated with physical disease, thyroid hormone deficiency, etc; see Chapter 15.

[97] See *R v Kemp* [1957] 1 QB 399, [1956] 3 All ER 249, (1956) 40 Cr App R 121 per Devlin J; and *Bratty v A-G for Northern Ireland* [1963] AC 386, [1961] 3 All ER 523, HL.

[98] See *R v Quick* [1973] QB 910, [1973] 3 All ER 347, CA, 57 Cr App R 722 at 734. However, it may ground an acquittal on automatism, see *R v Sullivan* [1983] 3 All ER 673, [1983] 3 WLR 123 HL. Although the effects of the administration of sedative or hypnotic agents or anaesthetics do not constitute a "disease" in the sense generally understood (see Chapter 3), there is no reason in logic or principle why their disinhibitive and other effects — which if manifested in a psychotic patient would relieve him of criminal responsibility — should not also relieve the person so affected of responsibility, provided the intoxication was not self-induced. That said, it remains to be determined whether or not this means that a psychotic illness, induced by — or related to — prior exposure to drugs of abuse (see Chapters 10 and 15) is sufficient to avoid criminal responsibility for an act committed while in that psychotic state. Both *Kemp* and *Sullivan* suggest that the aetiology is irrelevant from a legal perspective. As to whether such a state might be considered to be an "illness" or a "condition", see Chapter 3. This dictum seems more directed at the transitory effects of acute intoxicants. However, there is no reason in logic or principle why the transitoriness of a condition should be determinative of the outcome (see below at p. 405). Indeed, *Sullivan* indicates that transitory conditions may be excused if not self-induced. Nevertheless, if "transitory and intermittent" are to be taken as cumulative, then a once-off, non-automatous event may not excuse responsibility for a criminal act. For instance, a post-drug abuse induced psychosis may be permanent — although the symptoms, if properly controlled, may only be transitory. However, there are dicta in the context of alcohol-induced states. In this regard, see *R v Davis* (1881) 14 Cox CC 563 and *A-G for Northern Ireland v Gallagher* [1963] AC 349, [1961] 3 All ER 299, HL.

can be substituted cognitive functioning) and memory, from certain organic and functional causes other than "physical" causes such as trauma and ingested or applied substances. As to why such a distinction is deemed necessary appears from the judgment of Devlin J in *Kemp*.[99] This was amplified in *Hill* v *Baxter*,[100] where he stated:

> For the purposes of the criminal law there are two categories of mental irresponsibility, one where the disorder is due to disease and the other where it is not. The distinction is not an arbitrary one. If disease is not the cause, if there is some temporary loss of consciousness arising accidentally, it is reasonable to hope that it will not be repeated and that it is safe to let an acquitted man go entirely free. But if disease is present, the same thing may happen again, and therefore, since 1800, the law has provided that persons acquitted on this ground should be subject to restraint.[101]

As to whether or not this now remains a defensible proposition must be highly questionable. However, it inevitably underpins, and adds some coherence to, the categorisation of some conditions within the law on "automatism".[102]

Automatism

The law on automatism seems designed to "mop-up" the residual category of instances where the "mind" is disordered, but the cause lies elsewhere than in "insanity" as defined. Thus, on the authorities, *mens rea* may be lacking because of "automatism", elegantly though unfathomably described as a "failure of the mind *not* due to disease" (emphasis in the original).[103] However, some-

---

[99] See p. 385 above.

[100] [1958] 1 QB 277, 42 Cr App R 51.

[101] [1958] 1 QB 277 at 285, 42 Cr App R 51 at 60.

[102] See below.

[103] See Richardson (1997), op. cit., p. 1535 and the cases cited therein.

what confusingly, automatism is also taken to involve involuntary movements of the body or limbs of a person, where the act is "beyond the control of that person's mind",[104] although even this phrase is extraordinarily opaque. The critical relevance in the distinction between "automatism" and "insanity" is in the resultant verdict and disposition. If "automatism" is successfully pleaded, the accused is entitled to an unconditional discharge.[105] However, once raised, it may be open to the jury to find that "insanity" is the appropriate defence, whereupon the special verdict[106] and indefinite detention at the pleasure of the executive automatically follow.

Although it has been baldly stated that there are genuine cases of "automatism",

> the layman can[not] ably attempt without the help of some medical or scientific evidence to distinguish the genuine from the fraudulent.[107]

The law further appears to distinguish between "insane automatism" and "non-insane automatism".[108] At its crudest, the distinction is reducible to the "cause" of the "automatism", i.e. whether it is caused by a "disease of the mind" or by a "failure of the mind *not* due to disease". Thus "insane automatism" is merely "automatism" as a symptom of "insanity" and is therefore a synonym for "insanity".

Although not a particular concern of psychiatrists, rather lying within the remit of neurologists, epilepsy is the condition most frequently noted in the case law on "non-insane" automatism. However, whereas an assault committed during the tonic-clonic

---

[104] Cross, Jones and Card (1988), op. cit., p. 166. As to the evidential burden, see Richardson (1997), op. cit., p. 1535 and the cases cited therein.

[105] As was also the situation that applied in relation to "insanity" prior to 1800, above.

[106] See pp. 386–8 above.

[107] *Hill* v *Baxter* [1958] 1 QB 277, 42 Cr App R 51, DC, *per* Devlin J.

[108] For a historically interesting treatment of the subject, see Williams (1961), op. cit., pp. 487–8 and the references cited therein.

phase of an epileptic attack, or during a (neurally mediated) reflex or spasmodic movement, clearly constitutes an automatous attack, for which no criminal (or civil) liability should lie, it is difficult to envisage a situation whereby other than relatively minor injuries are sustained by a victim — unless, for example, the sufferer is armed with an automatic firearm or driving a vehicle at the time of the epileptic attack. Although such instances are capable of being avoided through proper licensing and supervision procedures, without recourse to finding such persons "insane" merely because of the risk of recurrence,[109] however, the case law on "automatism" generally does not confine itself to anything as limiting as this and the leading authorities are appropriately instructive in that regard.

Part of the problem of forensic nosology appears to arise from the description in the legal texts of acts being carried out while there is a loss of consciousness on the part of the accused. From a clinical perspective, loss of consciousness means literally that; the person is unresponsive and usually flaccid and immobile. Any muscular action that does occur is mediated through neural reflexes or spontaneous motor activity, perhaps initiated by the agent that induced the unconsciousness in the first instance. Thus, it appears that what the cases are describing are, in all instances, episodes of clouding or impairment of consciousness where cognitive function and memory are both impaired. Such situations may arise *inter alia* during episodes of metabolic

---

[109] An anomaly in this regard is identified in McAuley (1993), op. cit., p. 84. A somewhat related assertion by Lord Denning to the effect that a disorder which manifested itself in violence and was prone to recur is a disease of the mind for which a person should be detained in hospital rather than be given an unqualified acquittal in *Bratty* v *A-G for Northern Ireland* [1963] AC 386 at 410–412, [1961] 3 All ER 523 at 533–534 HL, is criticised in Smith and Hogan (1988), p. 188. See also the not dissimilar issues raised in *R* v *Quick* [1973] QB 910, [1973] 3 All ER 347, CA, 57 Cr App R 722, CA, involving hypoglycaemia, where a different view was taken. Nevertheless, this seems to have shifted following *R* v *Hennessy* (1989) 89 Cr App R 10, CA, and *R* v *Burgess* (1991) 93 Cr App R 41, CA and considered at p. 349 below.

disorder,[110] including hypo- and hyper-glycaemia[111] but it is incorrect to characterise these as episodes of loss of consciousness. As such, they are not unlike episodes of clouding of consciousness following a head injury. None of these conditions falls naturally within the remit of psychiatrists. Somnambulism presents a particularly difficult issue in this regard and is discussed later.[112]

Cerebral Ischaemia

Thus, in *R v Kemp*,[113] the accused assaulted his wife with a hammer in a motiveless and irrational attack and was charged with causing grievous bodily harm with intent to murder. At the time he was suffering from cerebral arteriosclerosis (*sic*),[114] and it was common case that he lacked the requisite *mens rea* and that he did not know what he was doing. The broad submission on behalf of the accused was that he was suffering from a physical disease and not a "disease of the mind". Accordingly, on the facts, the principles of "automatism" should apply with an ordinary acquittal. It was argued that if a physical disease caused actual

---

[110] See Chapter 6.

[111] *R v Quick* [1973] QB 910, [1973] 3 All ER 347, CA, 57 Cr App R 722, CA and *R v Hennessy* (1989) 89 Cr App R 10, CA, respectively. See pp. 400–1 below.

[112] pp. 404–5.

[113] [1957] 1 QB 399, (1956) 40 Cr App R 121, Assizes.

[114] Precisely what was involved is unclear. One doctor gave evidence that the cerebral arteriosclerosis induced "melancholia" as a result of which the accused committed the act. Two other doctors were of the view that it led to a "congestion of blood in the brain and that this is a well-recognised consequence of hardening of the arteries" (at p. 405 of the report). On this latter evidence, it was suggested that the accused had suffered a temporary "lapse of consciousness, either a complete loss or a clouding of it, which made him act irrationally and irresponsibly". Although the explanation is opaque at this remove, the accused seems to have suffered acute cerebral anoxia secondary to a cerebrovascular accident or a transient ischaemic attack, which caused a temporary lapse of consciousness. Or, it may have been a step in a multi-infarct dementia process (see Chapter 12, p. 287), although this appears less likely from the judgment. He was also suffering a depressive type illness. "not an irrational depression, produced by his poor state of health" (at p. 407 of the report); see Chapter 6.

"degeneration of the brain", then it would be a disease of the mind but, until it did so, a temporary interference with cerebral function caused by the disease was akin to a concussion. Devlin J rejected this argument, stating:

> I am invited to say that this disease at this stage is purely physical; when it interferes with the brain cells so that they degenerate, it then becomes a disease of the mind. This would be a very difficult test to apply for the purposes of the law. I should think it would be a matter of great difficulty medically to determine precisely at what point degeneration of the brain sets in, and it would mean that the verdict depended upon a doubtful medical borderline.[115]

As to how such an argument could even be grounded on any coherent conceptualisation of automatism[116] is far from clear, unless it is rooted in the medical evidence and the accepted absence of *mens rea*.

Holding that, as a matter of law, the accused was suffering a "disease of the mind", Devlin J, having noted a distinction (which from a modern perspective, has little relevance or foundation) that it was possible to distinguish "between diseases which have a mental origin and diseases which have a physical origin",[117] went on to say that the words "disease of the mind" were to limit the effect of "defect of reason" and that:

---

[115] [1957] 1 QB 399 at 407. See Chapters 2 and 12, and especially pp. 22–7 and p. 289, which illustrate that the concerns of Devlin J are still real, insofar as radiological assessment of brain degeneration — at least in the dementias — does not necessarily correlate sensitively with the clinical state of the patient and his/her functional abilities. The reliability of radiological assessment varies for different conditions. The argument made presumed, firstly, that subclinical cerebral injury can always, or nearly always, be detected. Secondly, it also appeared to presume that a disorder of function may only be accompanied, or caused, by physical damage — in the sense of being objectively ascertainable — and not by other forms of temporary, functional embarrassment, e.g. transient loss of blood supply and oxygenation. Neither then, nor now, would such argument be sustainable.

[116] pp. 392–3 above.

[117] See Chapter 2.

Hardening of the arteries [*sic*] is a disease which is shown on the evidence to be capable of affecting the mind in such a way as to cause a defect, temporarily or permanently, of its reasoning, understanding and so on, and so is . . . a disease of the mind . . . within the meaning of the Rules.[118]

There is no real inconsistency between this conclusion and a comparable medical construct. There is, however, a circularity in the manner by which it is achieved and a lack of coherence as to its dramatic consequences — in terms of disposition.[119]

Cerebral Tumour

By contrast, in the earlier case of *R* v *Charlson*,[120] the accused was charged with causing grievous bodily harm to his young son by striking him with a mallet and throwing him out of a window in an outburst of impulsive violence. The evidence was to the effect that he was suffering a cerebral tumour as a result of which he was "acting as an automaton without any real knowledge of what he was doing", being liable to not being able to control his outbursts of temper. By direction of the trial judge, who accepted the medical evidence that the accused was not suffering from a "disease of the mind", he was given an unconditional acquittal.[121] This case has been roundly criticised and is not followed in English law,[122] and, indeed, fails to accord with what must be the clinical

---

[118] *R* v *Kemp* [1957] 1 QB 399 at 408, (1956) 40 Cr App R 121 at 127, Assizes, *per* Devlin J, which was further reflected in *R* v *Sullivan* [1983] 3 All ER 673, [1983] 3 WLR 123 HL, *per* Lord Diplock at 677, above. However, the argument is circular. On this basis, many conditions that might otherwise seem excluded could, given sufficient evidence, fulfil the criteria for a "disease of the mind".

[119] See pp. 413–16 below.

[120] [1955] 1 WLR 317, [1955] 1 All ER 859, 39 Cr App R 37.

[121] As he did not have the necessary guilty intent.

[122] It was not followed in *R* v *Kemp* (above) although here Devlin J noted that the doctors were not so agreed. *Kemp* is regarded in England as being correct in law. See Williams (1961), op. cit., p. 489 (somewhat unconvincingly in part because of the reliance on "loss of consciousness" criticised above); Smith and Hogan (1988), op. cit., p. 188; and Cross (1988), op. cit., p. 169.

reality of such a condition. However, notwithstanding any medical evidence that might be accepted in such a case in the future, the concept of failure of volitional control could still be problematic.[123]

Epilepsy

Epilepsy is not an issue of central concern to psychiatrists. However, previously, it fell within the definition of mental disorder[124] and, before the availability of the effective anti-epileptic medications of the last 40 years, many persons suffering from epilepsy were detained in psychiatric facilities. Its causes are legion, but a structural abnormality of the brain may not always be detectable. That there is a disorder of nervous tissue, however, is not disputed. However, in *Bratty* v *A-G for Northern Ireland*,[125] the accused was charged with the murder of a girl whom he had strangled with one of her stockings. Defence evidence was to the effect that he suffered from psychomotor epilepsy[126] at the time of the attack and accordingly was unaware of what he was doing and lacked the requisite *mens rea*, thus raising the defence of automatism. However, the House of Lords affirmed the trial judge's ruling that there was no evidence to support automatism as a result of some cause other than a "disease of the mind" and that the defence was one of "insanity".[127]

---

[123] Although cerebral insults may well affect rational capacity, the defences of acting as an automaton and not being able to control an outburst of temper (irresistible impulse) may be inconsistent. See, for example, *People (A-G)* v *O'Brien* [1936] IR 263.

[124] See the English Mental Health Act, 1959. It was also a ground for avoiding a marriage; see Chapter 11.

[125] [1963] AC 386, [1961] 3 All ER 523, HL.

[126] Complex partial seizures, a category of epilepsy that includes most types of attacks that do not conform to the classic criteria of grand mal, Jacksonian seizures or petit mal. Automatisms, patterned movements, apparently purposeful movements, incoherent speech, turning of head and eyes, smacking of the lips, twisting and writing movements of the extremities, clouding of consciousness and amnesia commonly occur. See M.A. Krupp and M.J. Chatton (eds.) (1984), *Current Medical Diagnosis and Treatment*, Los Altos, CA: Lange Medical Publications, p. 589.

[127] The jury had already rejected that defence.

Bratty, where all the doctors were agreed that epilepsy was a "disease of the mind" was followed in *R* v *Sullivan*,[128] notwithstanding that, in the latter case, the doctors argued that the condition could not be so regarded. However, given the irrelevance of the aetiology of the "mental condition which has brought about the act",[129] considerations of clinical nomenclature or assignation could not be determinative of the issue.

However, from a clinical perspective, it is difficult to envisage how such complex and purposive movements could be attendant upon an epileptic seizure. That said, much as the law of "nervous shock" is replete with bizarre examples of clinically suspect consequences of non-physical injury, so the law on "insanity" is peppered with examples of "insane automatism". Thus, cases have been determined where the sufferer of a psychomotor attack continues "in a muddled form, the action in which he happened to be engaged at the moment of the epileptic seizure". Such an instance is reportedly illustrated by a woman, "having a vertiginous attack" (*sic*) while cutting bread with a knife, who continued her action during the "automatic" phase and cut off her child's arm. Or by the assertion that killing during an epileptiform seizure may be caused by a homicidal impulse, possibly the result of some angry emotion before the fit.[130] Or by "furor" induced by petit mal epilepsy, allegedly caused by a head injury sustained as a baby, was such that the sufferer did not know that he was repeatedly stabbing his victim.[131] Although it may be possible that an epileptiform seizure may involve actions of some considerable complexity, however, given the antiquity of some of these determinations and reports, it would, ordinarily, be suspect to afford them any precedental value at this stage.

---

[128] [1984] AC 156 HL.

[129] *R* v *Kemp* [1957] 1 QB 399 at 407 *per* Devlin J, above at p. 395.

[130] Williams (1961), op. cit., pp. 477–8 and the references cited therein, including *R* v *Perry* (1919) 14 Crim App R 48 at 51, 55, *R* v *Kumalo* (1956) (3) S.A. 238 (Natal).

[131] *People (A-G)* v *Hopkins* (1953) 1 Frewen 142.

The "Diabetic" Cases

In *R* v *Quick*,[132] the accused, who was diabetic, was charged with
assault on a patient under his care, and raised the defence of
"automatism" on the grounds of hypoglycaemia caused by an inappropriate dose of insulin, which the trial judge determined
amounted to "insanity". But, the Court of Appeal concluded thus:

> . . . [the] mental condition, if it ever existed, was not caused
> by his diabetes, but by his use of the insulin prescribed by
> his doctor. Such malfunctioning of his mind as there was
> was caused by an external factor and not by a bodily disor-
> der in the nature of a disease which disturbed the working
> of his mind. It follows . . . that [he] was entitled to have his
> defence of automatism left to the jury . . . [133]

Although this conclusion accords more fully with the notion of
automatism as a "failure of the mind *not* due to disease"[134] at least
insofar as, clinically, hypoglycaemia is consistent with a disorder
of cognitive functioning, it only accords insofar as the disease referred to is not a psychiatric disease.

But, this seems to be what is contemplated. Thus, in *R* v *Hennessy*,[135] the accused, who was an insulin-dependent diabetic of
long standing, failed to eat or to take his insulin for several days
such that at the time he committed the offences charged, he was
hyperglycaemic.[136] In addition, he was suffering from some anxiety
and depression, as a consequence of personal and marital difficulties, and the evidence suggested that this could also raise his
blood sugar further. Arguing that he was in a state of automatism, the trial judge held (and the Court of Appeal agreed) that as

---

[132] [1973] QB 910, (1973) 57 Cr App R 722, CA.

[133] *R* v *Quick* [1973] QB 910 at 922, 57 Cr App R 722 at 735, CA, *per* Lawton
LJ.

[134] See pp. 392–5 above.

[135] (1989) 89 Cr App R 10, CA.

[136] That is, his blood sugar was abnormally high. Although he was clearly not
in a keto-acidotic coma, severe hyperglycaemia is capable of interfering with
cognitive function, and the evidence given was to that effect.

he had put his state of mind in issue, the preliminary question to be answered was whether this was a case of automatism of "insanity". The trial judge, having concluded that it was "insanity", the accused changed his plea, was convicted and then appealed. The Court of Appeal rejected the argument that the accused's depression and marital troubles were a sufficiently potent external factor in his condition, over-riding his lack of insulin. In the court's view, stress, anxiety and depression could be the result of the operation of "external" factors but they were not, in themselves, separately or together of the kind capable in law of causing or contributing to a state of automatism. They constituted a state of mind that was prone to recur, and lacked the feature of novelty or accident[137] and did not come within the exception of "some external physical factor".[138] Accordingly, the issue was properly one of "insanity".[139]

In any event, the "diabetic" cases are hardly illustrative of those involving the involuntary movements of the body or limbs of a person that can clearly occur in tonic-clonic seizures and other epileptiform manifestations. Accordingly, it seems far from helpful to characterise such states as automatous. In a hypoglycaemic state, depending on the evidence adduced, the answer as to whether or not *mens rea* was present may well be, if it is not always, in the negative.[140] In a hyperglycaemic state, the same result should, in logic, ensue.[141]

---

[137] See *R* v *Sullivan* [1984] AC 156, 77 Cr App R 176, *per* Lord Diplock.

[138] See *R* v *Quick* [1973] QB 910, [1973] 3 All ER 347, CA, 57 Cr App R 722 at 734.

[139] The duration of a failure of cognitive functioning and memory is irrelevant (see *R* v *Sullivan* [1984] AC 156, HL), although the risk of recurrence might be (see below at p. 405).

[140] Unless there had been a negligent or reckless failure to follow the appropriate medical advice. In *Quick*, the accused had been drinking on the day of the incident, and had only had a small amount to eat after taking his morning insulin, clearly contrary to medical advice. He had had twelve previous hypoglycaemic episodes, and must have known of the risks involved in not eating or ensuring that he took some carbohydrate.

[141] The distinction made between *Hennessy* and *Quick*, at least in relation to diabetes mellitus, seems conceptually overly fine from a clinical perspective

Alcohol

An illustration of an instance where both "internal" and "external" factors appeared to be at work and where the issue of causation between the "defect of reason" and a "disease of the mind" arose, is *R v Burns*.[142] Here, evidence was given that the accused, who was charged with indecent assault, had a history of clinical alcoholism[143] and periods of amnesia.[144] The amnesia was characterised as amnesia "in the ordinary sense of not remembering and 'in the sense that the thing does not register at the time because the brain function is impaired at the time'".[145] At the time of the offence, it was probable that the accused had consumed not alone alcohol but also opiates and a benzodiazepine. Evidence was adduced to the effect that he had brain damage[146] which required, in addition, drink or drugs, to cause him to act as he did — in the words of the doctor who gave evidence on his behalf, at a "virtually non-sentient level of physical functioning amounting to the condition implicit in the term of automatism". The Court of Appeal noted that the trial judge, in his summing up of the medical evidence, had effectively equated "insanity" with automatism. Nevertheless, the appellate court was satisfied that there was some evidence of other factors operating upon a disease of the accused's mind and of the possibility that he did not appreciate the

---

in that diabetes is a disease in the classical sense (see Chapter 3); and if it manifests itself as an impairment of cognitive function, that an intervention was material in producing that impairment in one case, but an omission in the other, seems a less than convincing reason for the different outcomes, notwithstanding the distinction between acts and omissions insofar as the criminal law is concerned. If it is considered that both Quick and Hennessy were aware, or ought to have been aware, of the risks they were running, the difference in approach arguably becomes less tenable. See also *R v Bailey* (1983) 77 Cr App R 76.

[142] (1974) 58 Cr App R 364, CA.

[143] See Chapters 10 and 15.

[144] Probably alcohol-induced.

[145] (1974) 58 Cr App R 364 at 368, CA.

[146] Presumably alcohol-induced brain damage. See Chapter 10.

effect they might have.[147] In such circumstances, the jury had not been properly directed on the matter.

An old case also dealing with the long-term effects of intoxication, and which, on one level, reveals an unusual prescience in this area, is *R* v *Davis*.[148] Here, the accused, who had been charged with wounding with intent, raised the defence of "insanity", with evidence that he was suffering *delirium tremens*[149] at the relevant time. The jury was instructed that "drunkenness is one thing and the diseases to which drunkenness leads are different things".[150] Accordingly, if he was suffering a "defect of reason" (even if temporary) because of a "disease of the mind" caused by drinking, but differing from drunkenness (such that he did not know that his act was wrong) he was guilty but insane at the time. Once *delirium tremens* is characterised as a "disease of the mind", as it must post-*Sullivan*,[151] the result advocated in *Davis* will apply. The same result should follow, even if it is confused, as it may have been, with alcoholic dementia or any other form of alcohol-induced brain damage[152] either of which could clearly qualify, on a modern formulation, as a "disease of the mind".[153]

---

[147] In the absence of negligence, recklessness or failure to follow medical advice; see *R* v *Bailey* (1983) 77 Cr App R 76. Nevertheless, the appeal was dismissed on the grounds that if the jury had rejected the evidence on the issue of "insanity", they would equally have rejected it on the issue of "automatism", if it had been left to them. For a cogent criticism of this conclusion, see Richardson (1997), op. cit., p. 1538. But see *A-G for Northern Ireland* v *Gallagher* [1963] AC 349, [1961] 3 All ER 299, HL. *infra*.

[148] (1881) 14 Cox CC 563.

[149] See Chapter 10, pp. 223–30.

[150] *R* v *Davis* (1881) 14 Cox CC 563 at 564, per Stephen J., followed in *People (DPP)* v *Beard* [1920] AC 489 HL, and *A-G for Northern Ireland* v *Gallagher* [1963] AC 349, [1961] 3 All ER 299, HL.

[151] See above, p. 399.

[152] See Chapter 12, p. 289.

[153] Cross (1988), op. cit., p. 184.

Somnambulism

Clouding of consciousness can also occur in relation to sleep, including the phases during which one enters and leaves sleep.[154] Although not a problem of particular clinical concern, "sleepwalking" is a not insignificant issue in the legal texts and presents its own peculiar difficulties. Thus, in older cases, in which persons killed others either while sleepwalking or immediately upon rousing from sleep,[155] criminal responsibility did not attach. An example, based on a real-life case, is illustrative of the problems:

> A mother while dreaming that her daughter was being seduced by a soldier, got up in her sleep, took an axe and killed her daughter, presumably thinking that she was killing the supposed soldier. Even though assuming the dream "facts" to be accurate, the sleepwalker was killing another person, which in law would not constitute a defence, nevertheless, no crime was committed, because "dream knowledge" is not knowledge for legal purposes.[156]

In a modern Canadian decision, *R* v *Parks*[157], the accused had driven 23 kilometres to his wife's parents' house where he killed his mother-in-law and severely injured his father-in-law. Defence witnesses gave evidence to the effect that sleepwalking was not regarded as a disease of the mind, mental illness or mental disorder. He was acquitted on the grounds of non-insane automatism.

---

[154] The so-called hypnogogic and hypnapompic phases.

[155] And presumably in that clouded state of consciousness called the hypnapompic state.

[156] Williams (1961), op. cit., pp. 482–3 and the references cited therein. This has parallels in M'Naghten's Rules (Question 4) in relation to the bizarre proposition that persons labouring under delusions should be judged according to what the law would be if the facts of the delusions were real. (This is also found in the earlier case of *R* v *Hadfield*, above). See also *Doyle* v *Wicklow County Council* [1974] IR 55 at 70–71, in relation to "knowledge" for the purposes of the rules on "insanity". In this regard, it is worth noting that an accused who fails to appreciate that what he was doing was wrong because of some reason other than a defect of reason from disease of the mind generally has no valid defence, see *R* v *Hennessy* (1989) 89 Cr App R 10 at 14.

[157] 56 CCC (3d) 449.

An appeal by the Crown was rejected by the Ontario Court of Appeal, which concluded that sleep is a normal condition and that "the impairment of the [accused's] faculties of reason, memory and understanding was caused not by any disorder or abnormal condition but by a natural normal condition — sleep". Later, however, in *R* v *Burgess*[158] the accused, who was charged with assault, which he claimed was committed while he was sleepwalking, was found not guilty by reason of insanity. Having reviewed the expert evidence in the case (some of which suggested that he was suffering from a hysterical dissociative state),[159] the English Court of Appeal was satisfied that whatever the accused was suffering from, it was caused by an "internal" as distinct from an "external" factor.[160] Thus,

> . . . this was an abnormality or disorder, albeit transitory, due to an internal factor, whether functional or organic, which had manifested itself in violence. It was a disorder or abnormality which might recur . . .[161]

In a modification of earlier assertions,[162] the Court went on to state that a risk of recurrence of a condition could be an added reason for its categorisation as a "disease of the mind", although the absence of such a risk would not necessarily exclude it.[163]

---

[158] (1991) 93 Cr App R 41, CA.

[159] See p. 406 below.

[160] See *R* v *Sullivan* [1984] 1 AC 156, 77 Cr App R 176, p. 399 above.

[161] (1991) 93 Cr App R 41 at 48.

[162] See, generally: *Bratty* v *A-G for Northern Ireland* [1963] AC 386, [1961] 3 All ER 523, HL, and the criticisms thereto at footnote 109 above; *R* v *Quick* [1973] QB 910, [1973] 3 All ER 347, CA, 57 Cr App R 722, CA; *R* v *Sullivan* [1984] AC 156, HL; and *R* v *Hennessy* (1989) 89 Cr App R 10, CA, above. In *Bratty*, Denning LJ stated: " . . . any mental disorder which has manifested itself in violence and is prone to recur is a disease of the mind. At any rate it is the sort of disease for which a person should be detained in hospital rather than be given an unqualified acquittal."

[163] (1991) 93 Cr App R 41 at 46. The reasoning here is opaque.

Dissociative States

A further issue that arises out of consideration of "automatism" is that of "automatism" induced by a "dissociative state". *Rabey* v *R*[164] is illustrative.[165] Here, the accused was charged with causing bodily harm with intent to wound a fellow geology student with whom he had become infatuated and who did not reciprocate his feelings. He had hit her on the head with a rock he had taken from the geology laboratory and tried to choke her. The defence of "automatism" was successful in the trial court. Evidence was accepted that he was in a "dissociative state"[166] as a result of the "psychological blow" of having been rejected by the girl and which was held to be an "external" factor, akin to the kinds of other (physical) "external" factors contemplated in previous cases.[167] The Ontario Court of Appeal ordered a new trial, which finding was upheld by (a four to three majority of) the Supreme Court of Canada where, clearly confining themselves to the nature of an "external" factor within the authorities, the majority were of the view that:

> . . . the ordinary stresses and disappointments of life which are the common lot of mankind do not constitute an external cause constituting an explanation for a malfunctioning of the mind which takes it out of the category of a "disease of the mind"[168] . . . [T]he dissociative state must be considered as having its source primarily in the respondent's psychological or emotional make-up.

Accordingly, the defence was one of "insanity" and not "automatism". However, the case was decided on its own facts and the

---

[164] (1977) 37 CCC (2d) 461 affirming (1980) SCR 513, 54 CCC (2d) 1. See the thorough discussion in McAuley (1993), op. cit., pp. 75–81.

[165] See also *R* v *Burgess* (1991) 93 Crim App R 41, which is very similar in its facts. Here a hysterical dissociative state was suggested by one psychiatrist as an explanation for the accused's assault.

[166] A dissociation between the accused's mind and behaviour. See Chapter 6.

[167] See *R* v *Sullivan* [1984] 1 AC 156, (1983) 77 Crim App R 176, p. 343 above.

[168] *Rabey* v *R* (1980) 2 SCR 513 at 519, approved in *R* v *Burgess* (1991) 93 Cr App R 41 at 45.

possibility of "automatism" caused by a "dissociative state" as a result of "emotional shock without physical injury" was not wholly excluded. The Court left to another case to decide whether or not such a state resulting from

> being involved in a serious accident although no injury has resulted; being the victim of a murderous attack with an uplifted knife, notwithstanding the victim has managed to escape serious injury; seeing a loved one murdered or seriously assaulted and the like situations

would suffice with the presumption that

> [S]uch extraordinary external events might . . . affect the average normal person without reference to the subjective make-up of the person exposed . . .[169]

Thus, the "nature" of the accused is determinative of the outcome, except where any reasonable person might also be similarly affected by the "external" factor.[170]

PROOF

Standard of Proof

When an accused puts his state of mind in issue, the question of whether he has raised the defence of insanity is one of law for the judge.[171] If it has been raised, what is then required is that "insanity" be proved to the satisfaction of the jury. This has been taken to indicate a standard of proof on the balance of probabili-

---

[169] *Rabey* v *R* (1977) 37 CCC (2d) 461 affirmed (1980) 2 SCR 513, 54 CCC (2d) 1. For a compelling legal criticism of the decision, see McAuley (1993), op. cit., pp. 76–80 and the references cited therein, especially that in relation to *R* v *Falconer* (1989) 46 A Crim R 83.

[170] Although this has superficial resemblance to *People (DPP)* v *Courtney* (Court of Criminal Appeal, Unreported Judgment, 21 July 1994) it should be noted that automatism and irresistible impulse are probably inconsistent defences, see *People (A-G)* v *O'Brien* [1936] IR 263 at 272 *per* Kennedy CJ.

[171] Smith and Hogan (1988), op. cit., at p. 186, expressly approved in *R* v *Hennessy* (1989) 89 Cr App R 10 at 14.

ties: i.e. that it was more likely than not that the accused was "insane" at the time of the act alleged.[172] At least insofar as the accused's knowledge of the nature and quality of his act is concerned, however, it has been asserted that

> [W]hat is required is that the jury must be so convinced
> that there was no insanity as to be able to conclude beyond
> a reasonable doubt that the requisite *mens rea* was
> present.[173]

and that this may not necessarily amount to a jury's being "satisfied" (let alone, as may be suggested, being "clearly satisfied") as to the consequences of the defect under which the accused was labouring, but rather to conceding to a doubt that he may have been.

As it is presumed that everyone knows the law, where it is accepted that the accused did, in fact, know the nature and the quality of his act but he maintains that he did not know that it was wrong, it has been held that the burden of persuasive proof is on the accused.[174]

However, where automatism is raised as a defence, it is not for the defence to prove it. Rather, it is for the prosecution to negative

---

[172] *Sodeman* v *R* [1936] 2 All ER 1138. However, in *People* v *Fennell (No. 1)* [1940] IR 445, the Court of Criminal Appeal stated, in respect of the trial judge's charge to the jury: "If the onus, according to the authorities, is to be established 'clearly' or 'specifically' or 'to the reasonable satisfaction of the jury', it is, in the opinion of the court, only 'chopping logic' to say that in this case the use of the words 'beyond reasonable doubt' adds any greater burden to the onus on the accused." However, as to whether or not this indicates that the required standard is beyond a reasonable doubt, as may be suggested, is less certain.

[173] Williams (1961), op. cit., p. 517. See also *People (A-G)* v *Boylan* [1937] IR 449, where the Court of Criminal Appeal rejected the contention that the charge to the jury on the standard of proof should have been in broadly similar terms.

[174] *Sodeman* v *R* [1936] 2 All ER 1138; *R* v *Carr-Briant* [1943] KB 607, [1943] 2 All ER 156.

it, beyond a reasonable doubt, once the defence lays a foundation for it.[175]

Thus, if, having heard all the evidence, a jury is unsure as to whether the accused was "insane" or that he simply intended to commit the offence with which he is charged, they cannot be satisfied beyond a reasonable doubt that he had the requisite *mens rea* and an acquittal must result.[176]

What Proof?

Determination of the issue is solely a matter for a jury properly directed on the law, on the basis of the evidence adduced,[177] including expert medical evidence.[178] Although such expert evidence is invariably adduced,[179] and is admissible, it has been held, in a case of provocation, that:

> Jurors do not need psychiatrists to tell them how ordinary folk who are not suffering from any mental illness are likely to react to the stresses and strains of life. It follows that the proposed evidence [of the psychiatrist] was not admissible to establish that the defendant was likely to have been provoked. The same reasoning applies to its suggested

---

[175] *R* v *Burns* (1974) 58 Cr App R 364 at 374. However, see *Bratty* v *A-G for Northern Ireland* [1963] AC 386, [1961] 3 All ER 523, HL, above.

[176] As to the verdict where the jury is satisfied as to the existence of such a delusion, see below.

[177] *R* v *Rivett* (1950) 34 Cr App R 87; *R* v *Latham* (1965) Crim LR 424. Evidence in relation to the surrounding circumstances of the offence may be clearly relevant, e.g. *R* v *Layton* 14 Cox 149, where the absence of motive was deemed to be corroborative. However, at this remove, such an authority must be of dubious precedental value.

[178] Although this would also include a detailed personal history of the accused, in particular with regard to his past psychiatric history, a family history of psychiatric disease, while a factor to be considered when assessing or diagnosing the condition under which the accused is labouring, is not determinative or otherwise particularly relevant of itself. *R* v *Tucket (Tuchet)* (1844) 1 Cox 103, is so ancient as to only be capable of being regarded as irrelevant in this respect. See Chapter 2.

[179] Although it does not appear on the face of the judgment in *People (A-G)* v *O'Brien* [1936] IR 263.

admissibility on the issue of credibility. The jury had to decide what reliance they could put on the defendant's evidence. . . . The jury in this case did not need and should not have been offered the evidence of a psychiatrist to help them decide whether the defendant's evidence was truthful.[180]

Thus, the admissibility of such expert evidence is confined to:

establish[ing] a defence of insanity, or any form of mental illness or any form of derangement that might have occurred by [an] accused's use of drugs and alcohol in regard to which . . . he had become dependent. [It is] admissible in such circumstances, as it will be if the defence of diminished responsibility or such is given recognition in our law. . . .[181]

In Britain, adducing expert evidence is now a prerequisite to an acquittal on the ground of "insanity".[182] In the absence of statutory guidance as to the nature of the evidence that must be adduced, it has been suggested that a jury may probably not find an accused "insane" in the absence of some medical evidence to that effect.[183]

---

[180] *R* v *Turner* [1975] QB 834 at 841, 60 Cr App R 80 (CA) *per* Lawton LJ, approved and followed in *People (DPP)* v *Kehoe* [1992] ILRM 481 (CCA). See also *R* v *Weightman* [1991] Crim LR 204, 92 Cr App R 291.

[181] *People (DPP)* v *Kehoe* [1992] ILRM 481 at 484 (CCA) *per* O'Flaherty J. A similar approach in respect of identification evidence was followed in *R* v *Stockwell* (1993) 97 Cr App R 260 (CA).

[182] Criminal Procedure (Insanity and Unfitness to Plead) Act, 1991, s. 1(1). As in the case of unfitness to plead, the Act stipulates that the evidence of two registered medical practitioners is necessary, at least one of whom must be "duly approved" by the Secretary of State for Health, pursuant to the provisions of the Mental Health Act, 1983. There is no such statutory procedure in Ireland, although a similar practice is almost invariably followed. Although not a criminal case, in *Doyle* v *Wicklow County Council* [1974] IR 55, the evidence suggested that the youth who set fire to the plaintiff's abattoir was suffering from a mental disorder which prompted him to set fire to the premises as a means of protest against the slaughter of animals in the belief that he was justified in so doing. As to whether or not such an act would now be regarded as evidence of a mental disorder or "disturbed values" must be questionable.

[183] Smith and Hogan (1988), op. cit., p. 198, citing *R* v *Dix* (1982) 74 Cr App R 306 in relation to the defence of diminished responsibility.

In this regard, the opinion of an expert that the accused was probably "insane" at the relevant time is sufficient to allow the issue to go to the jury.[184] However, the evidence of an expert who has not examined the accused may be inadmissible on the fifth of M'Naghten's Rules.[185]

An appellate court may find that the accused was "insane" notwithstanding the finding of the jury to the contrary, if satisfied that no reasonable jury could thereby have found the accused guilty.[186] In both *People (AG)* v *Fennell (No. 1)*[187] and *People (A-G)* v *Hopkins*,[188] the Court of Criminal Appeal held that the evidence of insanity of the accused adduced at their trials was not so convincing or coercive as to compel a jury of reasonable men to accept it. The court left open the question as to whether or not, if there was a statutory duty[189] on the court to form its own view on the matter, the onus of proof of insanity was discharged.

---

[184] *R* v *Perry* (1919) 14 Cr App R 48.

[185] See above and Robinson (1996), op. cit., Chapter 5, which considers the rise of medical jurisprudence in this area (in particular, his reference at p. 166 to Dr Isaac Ray, M'Naghten's expert *in absentia*). He further notes that Maule LJ's reply to this question was a simple "yes" (at p. 174).

[186] See *R* v *Rivett* (1950) 34 Cr App R 87; although in this case the Court of Criminal Appeal upheld the jury's verdict notwithstanding the practically unanimous evidence of the "insanity" of the accused. In England, the Court of Criminal Appeal has also previously refused to admit fresh expert evidence not available at the trial because of the poverty of the accused (an outcome less likely either in England or in Ireland given the provisions for legal aid and, for example, the miscarriage of justice provisions of the Criminal Procedure Act, 1993). See, however, the criticism of this (now antiquated) approach in Williams (1961), op. cit., p. 454, n. 11–12.

[187] [1940] IR 445, where the diagnoses on offer varied between dementia praecox (schizophrenia) superimposed upon congenital mental deficiency and "moral imbecility". In regard to the latter, see Chapter 14. The appeal was refused.

[188] (1953) 1 Frewen 142, where the suggested "insanity" alleged (described as "highly disputable and speculative matters arising out of evidence of a theoretical nature") was "furor" induced by "petit mal" epilepsy, possibly as a result of a head injury as a child. See Chapter 6, pp. 107–8. Here, a re-trial was ordered on the grounds that the trial judge's summing up of the medical evidence had been unsatisfactory.

[189] Pursuant to the provisions of the Courts of Justice Act, 1924, s. 35, applied to the Court of Criminal Appeal by the Courts (Supplemental Provisions) Act,

It has been asserted that a jury hardly seems an appropriate or satisfactory body to decide between the evidence of conflicting experts,[190] still less to reject their unanimous opinion.[191] It has also been suggested that, as:

> [I]n many scientific questions a jury may perhaps safely be left to follow expert evidence; but in the affairs of the mind there is a tendency for some laymen to assume that they are as well qualified to judge as the specialist

the issue of determining the "insanity" of an accused should be remitted to a medical tribunal which would report to the court.[192] However, the fact that psychiatrists may seem inconsistent and unscientific in their approach to the legal issue of "insanity" is perhaps more a reflection on that profession than on the vagaries of certain lay members of a jury in reaching their conclusions.

NATURE OF THE VERDICT

Pursuant to the Trial of Lunatics Act, 1883, which extended the previous law on "insanity" to include misdemeanours,[193] the

---

1961, and, in respect of the Special Criminal Court, by the Offences Against the State Act, 1939, s. 44(2), which essentially empowers the Court of Criminal Appeal to substitute the special verdict for a guilty verdict, and to make the usual consequential order; see pp. 413–16.

[190] The fear has been raised that where there is disagreement between prosecution and defence experts, there is a risk that a jury, directed as to the burden of proof lying on the accused, will disregard the whole evidence and return a verdict of guilty. This outcome is difficult to comprehend with any great particularity at this remove and suggests rather, in the absence of consideration and application of the principles set out above, the need for particularly careful charging of the jury. See Williams (1961), op. cit., section 165. The context of the criticism and the role of a jury in determining the issue of "insanity" is probably more instructive as to the raising of this concern.

[191] See Smith and Hogan (1988), op. cit., p. 198; and Williams (1961), op. cit., p. 453, who notes that "they sometimes make a mess of it, even when the medical evidence is unanimous".

[192] Williams (1961), op. cit., p. 453.

[193] The distinction was abolished by the Criminal Law Act, 1997, s. 3.

appropriate verdict, where the accused is found to have been "insane", is a special verdict that he was:

> guilty of the act or omission charged but insane, so as not to
> be responsible, according to law, for his actions at the time
> when the act was done or the omission made.[194]

Despite the manner of its expression, this did not alter the essence of the previous law, and technically constitutes an acquittal. This remains the form of verdict in Ireland, and it retains that character, thus ". . . the special verdict is a verdict of acquittal; the trial is concluded; the court does not pronounce a sentence. . . ."[195]

However, in England, the form of verdict is now in the nature of an express acquittal to the effect that the accused "is not guilty by reason of insanity".[196]

DISPOSITION OF THE ACCUSED

Once the special verdict is returned, the trial court must make an order detaining the accused in custody:

> as a criminal lunatic, in such place and in such manner as
> the court shall direct till [the executive's] pleasure be
> known; and it shall be lawful for [the executive] thereupon,
> and from time to time, to give such order for the safe cus-
> tody of the said person during such pleasure, in such place
> and in such manner as to [the executive] may seem fit.[197]

---

[194] Trial of Lunatics Act, 1883, s. 2(1).

[195] See *People (DPP)* v *Gallagher* [1991] ILRM 339 at 344 (SC) *per* McCarthy J for a unanimous Supreme Court. For a comprehensive discussion of the linguistic elements and their rationality, see McAuley (1993), op. cit., p. 110–12. The Act of 1883 had the effect of making it clear that the jury must first find that the accused did the (physical) act with which he was charged. See Williams (1961), op. cit., p. 455.

[196] Pursuant to the provisions of the Criminal Procedure (Insanity) Act, 1964, s. 1. Even before the law was changed, it was still regarded as an acquittal, see *Feistead* v *R* [1914] AC 534.

[197] Trial of Lunatics Act, 1883, s. 2(2), as modified by s. 3, the powers of which were saved by the Mental Treatment Act, 1945, s. 284.

In *People (DPP)* v *O'Mahony*[198] it was stated:

> Under our law a person found not guilty by reason of in-
> sanity can only be detained so long as the court is satisfied
> that his mental condition persists in a form and to the ex-
> tent that his detention in an appropriate institution is nec-
> essary for the protection of himself or of others.[199]

In Ireland, up until 1990,[200] the usual order made where the jury
returned the special verdict was that the accused be detained "until further order of the court".[201] In *People (DPP)* v *Ellis*,[202]
O'Hanlon J held that he had no jurisdiction to make any order
directing the release of the accused and ordered that he be detained at the pleasure of the executive, to whom an application for
release should be made in the first instance. In *People (DPP)* v
Neilan[203] Keane J was of the view that the release of an accused
was a judicial function and that the provisions of the Act of 1883
that purported to vest that function in the executive were constitutionally vulnerable.[204] However, a unanimous Supreme Court
held otherwise. In *People (DPP)* v *Gallagher*,[205] it was held that:

> the role of the court is to order the detention of the person,
> the former accused, until the executive, armed with both
> the knowledge and resources to deal with the problem, de-
> cides on the future disposition of the person. At that stage

---

[198] [1986] ILRM 244 (SC), which also rejected diminished responsibility as a
defence in Irish law; see p. 416.

[199] [1986] ILRM 244 at 249 *per* Finlay CJ (SC).

[200] From approximately 1973 and the decision of the Supreme Court in *State
(O)* v *O'Brien* [1973] IR 50.

[201] A fact reflected in the wording of the Defence Act, 1954, s. 203, as
amended by the Courts-Martial Appeals Act, 1983, s. 6.

[202] [1990] 2 IR 291, [1991] ILRM 225.

[203] [1990] 2 IR 267 [1991] ILRM 184.

[204] Neilan had been suffering from an acute paranoid psychosis at the time of
the murder with which he was charged. He was, for all intents and purposes,
well by the time of his actual trial.

[205] [1991] ILRM 339.

also, the Director of Public Prosecutions ceases to have his ordinary statutory role. The result of the prosecution has been an acquittal but the statute which permits the special verdict requires that the former accused be detained at least for some minimum time.[206]

The role of the court is to order that the accused be kept in custody. It is then up to the executive to determine where that should be, and for how long. In Ireland, such persons are kept in custody in the Central Mental Hospital[207] and, in Britain, in a "special hospital" designated by statute for that purpose, e.g. Broadmoor or Rampton Hospitals.[208]

However, problems can arise when the clinical staff in such institutions form the view that a person committed to their care there is no longer suffering from a psychiatric disability requiring treatment — or even that he never required such treatment.[209] In *Gallagher*, it was held that:

> If and when a person detained pursuant to . . . the Act of 1883 seeks to secure release from detention . . . he may apply to the executive . . . for his release on the grounds that he is not suffering from any mental disorder warranting his continued detention in the public and private interests, then the executive, in the person of the Minister for Justice . . . must inquire into all of the relevant circumstances. In doing so, it must use fair and constitutional procedures. Such an inquiry and its consequences may be the subject of judicial review so as to ensure compliance with such procedures.[210]

---

[206] [1991] ILRM 339 at 344 (SC) *per* McCarthy J.

[207] Established pursuant to the provisions of the Central Criminal Lunatic Asylum (Ireland) Act, 1845 (8 & 9 Vict c. 107), which effectively provides for the prompt transfer to the Central Mental Hospital of a person in respect of whom a special verdict is found, on the order of the executive.

[208] Pursuant to the provisions of the Mental Health Act, 1983.

[209] As in *Neilan* and *Gallagher*.

[210] [1991] ILRM 339 at 345.

In the absence of statutory reform, the difficulties of this approach are illustrated by the *habeas corpus* proceedings in *Gallagher* v *Director of the Central Mental Hospital & Others*.[211] In Britain, persons so detained may have their detention reviewed by a Mental Health Review Tribunal.

DIMINISHED RESPONSIBILITY[212]

Under the proposals contained in the White Paper for a New Mental Health Act,[213] it is proposed to introduce the verdict of "guilty, but with diminished responsibility" in cases of murder. As the proposals have not, as yet, been published, it is unclear whether or not they will follow the model of the English Homicide Act, 1957, section 2(1), which provides that:

> Where a person kills, or is a party to the killing of another, he shall not be convicted of murder if he was suffering from such abnormality of mind (whether arising from a condition of arrested or retarded development of mind or any inherent causes or induced by disease or injury) as substantially impaired his mental responsibility for his acts and omissions in doing or being a party to the killing.

The definition implicit in this approach seems wider than the proposed definition of "mental disorder" as suggested under the same proposals[214] and appears sufficiently wide[215] to encompass

---

[211] High Court, Unreported Judgment, 9 June 1996 (Divisional High Court, Geoghegan, Laffoy and Kelly JJ). Particular difficulties involved in an executive approach are noted in Keane J's judgment in *People (DPP)* v *Neilan* [1990] 2 IR 267 [1991] ILRM 184. In *Gallagher*, the psychiatrists in the Central Mental Hospital were of the view that the accused was never "insane" in the legal sense, notwithstanding the verdict of the jury.

[212] For an insightful analysis of the Criminal Justice (Mental Disorder) Bill, 1996, introduced by the Opposition before the fall of the "Rainbow Coalition" Government, see F. Boland (1997) 4 Web JCCI, in association with Blackstone Press Ltd.

[213] Paras. 7.26 and 7.27.

[214] White Paper on a New Mental Health Act, para. 2.13.

psycopathic disorder,[216] intoxication,[217] addiction[218] and the sequelae therefrom. Alternatively, a definition embracing the concept of "mental disorder", as defined in mental health legislation, may be adopted.

A successful plea of "guilty, with diminished responsibility", in England, results in a range of possible sentences: from absolute discharge, a hospital or guardianship order, to life imprisonment. Presumably, similar provisions will apply under new Irish legislation.

---

[215] See, generally, Smith and Hogan (1988), op. cit., pp. 201–6; Cross (1988), op. cit., pp. 160–4; and Richardson (1997), op. cit., pp. 1594–7.

[216] *R* v *Byrne* [1960] 2 QB 396, [1960] 3 All ER 1, CCA, 44 Crim App R 246. Under the new proposals, involuntary hospitalisation will not be available for personality disorders.

[217] However, in *R* v *Fenton* (1975) 61 Cr App R 261, CA, intoxication was outside the defence.

[218] For which, under the new proposals, involuntary hospitalisation will not lie; see Chapter 18.

Chapter 17

FITNESS TO PLEAD

INTRODUCTION[1]

Whereas the law on criminal "insanity" is essentially concerned with whether or not a person accused of committing a criminal offence had the requisite *mens rea* for the offence at the time of its commission because, effectively, he was then suffering from a psychiatric disorder,[2] the issue of his fitness to plead is concerned with a later stage in the process, i.e. his capacity at the time of the actual trial.[3] Special provision is made for those accused who are found incapable or to be suffering from a disability at or during trial. However, the issue is addressed differently by the different levels of courts[4] and throws into particularly sharp relief an anomalous treatment of those suffering psychiatric disability when they encounter the criminal justice system. This interface appears still firmly rooted in an ancient and increasingly irrelevant historical tradition. In England, statutory reforms have, on two occasions over the last 35 years, at least sought to update the

---

[1] See, generally, Williams (1961), op. cit., pp. 433–8; Richardson (1997), op. cit., sections 4-164–4-184; Smith and Hogan (1988), op. cit., pp. 182–5; McAuley (1993), op. cit., Chapter 7; Card (1988), op. cit., pp. 145–9.

[2] See Chapter 16.

[3] Although it must be acknowledged that evidence of severe psychiatric disorder before and after the commission of the offence may be compelling evidence that the accused was also suffering from that condition at the time of the alleged offence.

[4] See pp. 438–43 and 446–54 below.

law. However, in Ireland, a late Georgian statute,[5] which has particular political and cultural roots,[6] and common law precedent is the only "regulation" — apart from invoking constitutional protections, which has not yet occurred.[7]

At first blush, it seems that the matters to be decided upon in a determination of whether or not an accused person is "fit to plead" are matters of function — largely cognitive function. However, the essential procedural elements were set out in the Criminal Lunatics Act, 1800,[8] which provided that:

> . . . if any person indicted for any offence shall be insane, and shall upon arraignment be found so to be by a jury lawfully empanelled[9] for that purpose, so that such person cannot be tried upon such indictment, or if upon the trial of any person so indicted such person shall appear to the jury charged with such indictment to be insane, it shall be lawful for the court before whom any such person shall be brought to be arraigned or tried . . . to direct such finding to be recorded, and thereupon to order such person to be kept in strict custody until [his Majesty's pleasure] shall be known; and if any person charged with any offence shall be brought before any court to be discharged for want of prosecution, and such person shall appear to be insane, it shall be lawful for such court to order a jury to be empanelled to try the sanity of such person; and if the jury so empanelled shall find such person to be insane, it shall be lawful for such court to order such person to be kept in strict custody,

---

[5] Lunacy (Ireland) Act, 1821, s. 17, (1&2 Geo IV), the provisions of which were saved by the Mental Treatment Act, 1945, s. 284.

[6] See Chapter 16, pp. 371–4.

[7] The issues raised in *State (C)* v *Minister for Justice* [1967] IR 106 and *O'Connor* v *The Judges of the Dublin Metropolitan District* [1992] 1 IR 387 deal with essentially procedural issues.

[8] Enacted in the wake of the acquittal in *R* v *Hadfield* (1800) 27 St Tr 1281 (Chapter 16, p. 372) "An Act for the safe custody of insane persons charged with offences".

[9] The Juries Act, 1976, s. 19(2), and the British Juries Act, 1974, s. 11(5), specifically provide for the empanelling of juries to decide such issues.

in such place and in such manner as to such court shall seem fit [until his Majesty's pleasure] shall be known; and in all cases of insanity so found, it shall be lawful for [his Majesty] to give such order for the safe custody of such person so found to be insane, [during this pleasure, in such place and in such manner as his Majesty shall seem fit].[10]

Thus, the provisions effectively apply only in respect of persons charged with indictable offences who are "insane, at the time of arraignment"; and, to invoke the disposal elements of the section, they must be so found by a jury specially empanelled for the purpose of ascertaining the accused person's "sanity".[11] Reliance on legislation and the associated jurisprudence of this vintage[12]

---

[10] Criminal Lunatics Act, 1800, s. 2. Identical provisions applied in Ireland, this provision having been effectively adopted by the Lunacy Ireland Act, 1821 (1&2 Geo IV c 33), s. 17, whereby "the (pleasure) of the Lord Lieutenant, or other Chief Governor or Governors of Ireland for the time being" was substituted for "his Majesty's (pleasure)". The legislation relevant to Ireland also requires that a person so ordered to be kept in custody was also to be taken care of. The provisions of s. 16, which provided that where a person charged with treason, murder or other offence was acquitted by reason of his "insanity", the trial court could, if it was thought proper or necessary, order the person to be kept in custody at the executive's pleasure, was extended to s. 17. Although the provisions of s. 16 were superseded by the Trial of Lunatics Act, 1883, s. 2, the disposition elements remained the same. Thus, once an order had been made, the executive was then empowered to make such order as it saw fit as to the manner and place of custody and care. The Central Criminal Lunatic Asylum (Ireland) Act, 1845 (8&9 Vict c. 107), s. 8, provided for the transfer of all such "insane" persons to the Criminal Lunatic Asylum (its name was changed to the Central Mental Hospital by the Mental Treatment Act, 1961, s. 39, and it is now administered by the Eastern Health Board pursuant to the provisions of the Health Act, 1970, s. 44). The Defence Act, 1954, s. 202, as amended by the Courts-Martial Appeals Act, 1983, s. 5, provides that a court-martial which finds a person unfit to plead "shall order that such person be kept in custody in an institution suitable for the detention of such person until such time as he is fit to take his trial or until his release is sooner ordered by the Minister or the High Court". The logic of this approach seems also to have informed the provisions in relation to those found "insane" by a court-martial in terms of the then understanding of the appropriate disposition; see Chapter 15, p. 358 and *People (DPP)* v *Ellis* [1990] 2 IR 291 (SC).

[11] However, the issue of unfitness to plead before a court of summary jurisdiction is also problematic; see pp. 446–54 below.

[12] *Hadfield* was 43 years before *R* v *M'Naghten* (1843) 10 Cl. & F. 200; see Chapter 16, pp. 372–3.

invokes criticism similar to that levelled at use of the labels "sanity" and "insanity" in general.[13] Irrespective of the label, however, it is clear that whatever condition the accused is labouring under, it must be such that he "cannot be tried upon such indictment", thus importing a functional element which it is left to the jury to ascertain. Although the powers and procedures of the court were reformed over a century and a half later in England, the concept of "insanity" was effectively restated in statute as "any disability [of an accused] such that apart from this Act[14] it would constitute a bar to his being tried".[15]

What Amounts to a Finding that an Accused is Unfit to Plead in Law?

As in the law on "criminal insanity" the issue to be determined is a legal and not a medical matter. Thus, it has been held:

> A decision as to whether a person is "unfit to plead" is a judicial decision founded on medical evidence and is not a medical decision.[16] The determination of that issue is a judicial function which should be performed in a judicial manner upon proper notice to the [person accused] with proper opportunity for him, if required, to be adequately represented and should not be postponed indefinitely at the instance initially of the [executive] and thereafter by medical [practitioners]. . . . This [cannot be] done in the absence of the [person accused] nor without giving him due notice thereof and affording him, or someone competent to

---

[13] See Chapter 16, p. 368.

[14] Criminal Procedure (Insanity) Act, 1964, s. 4, as amended by the Criminal Procedure (Insanity and Unfitness to Plead) Act, 1991, which applies to arraignments on or after 1 January 1992.

[15] See *R v Robertson* [1968] 3 All ER 557, 1 WLR 1767 (CA), 52 Cr App R 690.

[16] This echoes the determination of Ó Dálaigh CJ in *State (C) v Minister for Justice* [1967] IR 106 at 116, where he stated: ". . . it is for the court that has seisin of a criminal matter to determine whether or not the accused is suffering from insanity of such a character as renders him unfit to stand his trial." (See also pp. 121 and 126, *per* Walsh J). See also *R v Peacock* 12 Cox CC 21.

represent his interests, an opportunity of hearing the evidence thereon.[17]

The issue of fitness to plead is not dependent solely on a medical assessment of a person's state of consciousness or mental alertness.[18] Nor is it concerned with "insanity in its broad medical connotation, nor as a defence to a criminal charge".[19] Rather it is concerned with his ability to reach the level of function required of an accused, in the interests of justice,[20] to participate in his trial on a criminal charge.[21] Thus, it appears, even before arraignment,

---

[17] *State (Caseley)* v *Daly and another* (High Court, Unreported Judgment, Gannon J, 19 February 1979). Although expressed in the context of District Court proceedings (see pp. 447–53 below) it is a principle applicable to all levels where the matter falls to be determined. Therefore, although an accused may not understand the nature of the proceedings against him, that is not a sufficient warrant for his not being brought before the court that is properly seised of the matter. Notwithstanding that the giving of notice to a person who is incompetent may be problematic, it is not beyond the limits of a properly functioning administrative system to ensure that someone competent may be found to represent his interests. Depending on the level of court involved, such arrangements may ultimately depend on there being next of kin. The adequacy of the system has yet to be tested. See also, *State (C)* v *Minister for Justice* [1967] IR 106.

[18] See for comparison the law in relation to testamentary capacity (Chapter 14) and "criminal insanity" (Chapter 16).

[19] *State (C)* v *Minister for Justice* [1967] IR 106 at 114 *per* Ó Dálaigh CJ. Later, at p. 115, he notes: ". . . the range of insanity entitling an accused to avoid trial is quite limited" or, in the words of Walsh J (at p. 121) "It is . . . possible for a person who is suffering from a disease of the mind to be tried and convicted . . . because the exemption from trial for insanity is limited to the cases where the disease is such that the person is 'unfit to plead'".

[20] "The issue is not merely that it would be unfair to the defendant to continue with the trial once he has been found unfit to plead, or that it would be unsafe to convict someone who cannot plead to the indictment, but rather that it is in the nature of a criminal trial that the defendant is capable of playing a rational part in the proceedings"; McAuley, op. cit., p. 136.

[21] Here, the focus is on functional disability caused by psychiatric disorder (see Chapter 15) rather than by physical illness or disability *per se* unaccompanied by any cognitive impairment, or states of temporary impairment, e.g. caused by acute intoxication by pharmacologically active substances, including alcohol. However, in trials by court-martial, in addition, the trial court must be satisfied that an accused is fit to stand trial and requires a certificate of a medical practitioner, or medical officer, to that effect; see Rules of Procedure (Defence Forces), 1954 (SI 243 of 1954), r. 97(6).

it is essential, in the first instance, that he is able to understand the charges put to him on the indictment, in order to decide whether to plead guilty or not guilty. As a corollary, he must also be capable of seeking, and consulting with, legal advisers, and understand the importance of so doing, such that he is be able to understand the advice and opinions offered (although he is never actually bound by them) and able to instruct them in accordance with his understanding. If he cannot understand the charges or is incapable of understanding and taking the necessary corollary steps, such that he is deprived of understanding how he should plead, he is, in effect, unfit to plead in law.[22]

This is articulated in the leading case, and classic exposition, of what constitutes "insanity" to render an accused unfit to plead. The unfortunate accused was both deaf and dumb and "appeared to be of non-sane mind".[23] Notwithstanding that the disabilities under which he laboured were essentially physical,[24] what the jury was directed to enquire into is still essentially relevant:

> First, whether the prisoner is mute of malice or not; secondly, whether he can plead to the indictment or not; thirdly, whether he is of sufficient intellect to comprehend the course of proceedings on the trial, so as to make a proper defence — to know that he might challenge any of you to whom he might object — and to comprehend the details of the evidence, which in a case of this nature must constitute a minute investigation. Upon this issue, therefore, if you think there is no certain mode of communicating

---

[22] "Unfitness to be tried", which is a more coherent expression of the disability, is the expression used in the English Criminal Procedure (Insanity) Act, 1964, as amended by the Criminal Procedure (Insanity and Unfitness to Plead) Act, 1991. "It is the ability to participate to the requisite extent in any necessary trial process that is important . . .", Archbold (1997), op. cit., Sections 4–169.

[23] *R* v *Pritchard* (1836) 7 C&P 303. Such a person would probably also be regarded as "insane" for testamentary purposes also; see Chapter 14.

[24] And, accordingly, that in relation to physical disabilities, the case is of dubious precedental value.

the details of the trial to the prisoner, so that he can clearly understand them, and be able properly to make his defence to the charge; you ought to find that he is not of sane mind. It is not enough that he may have a general capacity of communicating on ordinary matters.[25]

The first two issues put to the jury are not matters which properly arise in assessing whether or not an accused nowadays is fit to plead. The first proposition solely, and properly, seeks to establish whether the accused's silence in reply to the indictment being read to him amounts to a deliberate refusal to plead or arises from an inability to plead orally or by sign.[26] If the accused's silence is attributed to a deliberate refusal to answer the charges — hence the quaintly phrased "standing mute of malice" — a plea of not guilty is entered on his behalf.[27] It is only if the enquiry reveals a physical impairment — "muteness by visitation of God" — that consideration of the second issue arises, i.e. whether or not a mode

---

[25] (1836) 7 C&P 303 at 304 *per* Alderson B. Here, and in the earlier case which the direction followed, *R v Dyson* (1831) 7 C&P 305, the nature of the charges (bestiality and beheading of a non-marital child respectively) undoubtedly complicated the assessment. This direction was subsequently approved in *R v Berry* [1876] 1 QBD 447; *R v Governor of Stafford Prison, ex parte Emery* [1909] 2 KB 81 (see p. 370 below) (all relied on in *State (C) v Minister for Justice* [1967] IR 106 at 115 *per* Ó Dálaigh CJ) and *R v Robertson* [1968] 3 All ER 557, 1 WLR 1767 (CA), 52 Cr App R 690. See, generally, Archbold (1997), op. cit., Sections 4–161. The final limb has a resonance with what is required to have sound disposing mind; see *Sefton v Hopwood* 1 Fos&F 578, above.

[26] If, when called upon to plead, an accused person "stands mute" or fails or refuses to plead, the court must then enquire whether he stands "mute of malice" or "by visitation of God". For the history of the origins, and nature, of the problem, see McAuley (1993), op. cit., p. 136 at fn 20.

[27] In Ireland, determination of this issue, which still uses the expression "mute of malice", is a matter for the judge alone; Juries Act, 1976, s. 28, and Criminal Justice Act, 1928, s. 80. In England, a jury must be sworn to decide this issue and a finding that the accused is "mute of malice" requires that a plea of "not guilty" be entered; see Criminal Law Act, 1967, s. 6(1). The burden of proof is on the prosecution and it must be established beyond a reasonable doubt. See *R v Sharp* [1958] 1 All ER 62, 122 JP 51, (1957) 41 Cr App R 197.

of communication[28] can be worked out to enable the accused to understand the matters required of him in the third proposition and to plead according to his understanding. Thus, it has been held that the issue of whether a person is "capable of pleading to and of taking his trial on indictment" is one issue only and that if a person is unable to communicate with his legal advisers he is unfit to plead.[29] Given the advances in the education of persons suffering from (physically based) communication disorders and in the management of physical disability, the relevance of "muteness by visitation of God" *per se* has significantly receded and it seems quite inappropriate, in a modern context, to regard such persons as "insane", even if certain communication difficulties persist despite education and management. However, one such case is still cited as authority supporting this notion of "insanity". Thus, in *R v Governor of Stafford Prison, ex parte Emery*[30] the accused was not alone deaf, but also illiterate, and, not surprisingly, stood mute when arraigned. The jury found, in accordance with the evidence, that he was incapable of pleading and following and understanding the trial because of his communication difficulties and it was held that this amounted to a finding of "insanity" within the meaning of the Act of 1800.[31]

---

[28] Originally, it seems, this second issue of an accused's fitness to plead was understood in the sense of his being able to plead by sign or in writing, following which his understanding of the proceedings was considered. However, the central issue is really whether or not he can understand the proceedings as a whole, of which an ability to communicate must be a necessary part. See Williams (1961), op. cit., para. 143.

[29] *R v Sharp* [1958] 1 All ER 62, 122 JP 51, (1957) 41 Cr App R 197. Where a person is found "mute by visitation of God", the jury must then be re-sworn to decide whether or not he is "fit to plead", in which case the evidence in relation to the first issue must be repeated as far as necessary; however, there would appear to be no particular objection to presenting both issues to the jury at the same time. In *R v Halton* (1824) Ry & M 78, the accused was so deaf that he could not hear the reading of the indictment and deemed to be mute by visitation.

[30] [1909] 2 KB 81.

[31] It is worth noting again that it is also capable of amounting to a disability within the meaning of the Act of 1964, s. 4, in England and still represents

Although the third proposition may arise with or without the first two questions having to be addressed, an accused suffering from a serious psychiatric disorder might well be regarded, on this formulation, as "standing mute by visitation of God". However, the underlying patho-physiology is radically different from that producing communication disorders.[32] Perpetuation of the problem of communication disorder as "insanity" is only apt to confuse, and to conspire to retard the development of a coherent approach to the issue of unfitness to stand trial. Rather, the issue of intellectual competence, defined functionally, should be adopted and the issue of isolated inability to communicate left to another remedy. In *R v Harris*,[33] the illiterate accused was unable to speak because of an unhealed throat wound caused by his failed attempted suicide. His fitness to plead, in being tried by a jury, is an example of an instance where the coherence of the underlying proposition of "muteness by visitation of God" was tested. Not unsurprisingly, he was found fit to plead, and pleaded not guilty; however, because he was unable at that time to instruct counsel as to his defence, the trial was adjourned. Although the jury found that his inability to communicate was caused by a self-inflicted act, and therefore, by definition, not by "visitation of God", there appears to have been a Cartesian-like separation of this consequence from the underlying condition which precipitated the attempted suicide in the first instance. Thus, it is reducible to an instance of communication difficulty *simpliciter* with little relevance to what might be properly called fitness to plead; nevertheless it lies, somewhat unsatisfactorily, in the armoury of precedent on the subject.[34]

As a matter of policy, it seems, rather than of clinical empiricism, an inability to recollect the events giving rise to the offence with which an accused is charged, is not sufficient to establish

---

the law in Ireland today, such that the pre-1964 cases still determine what the law is, even in England.

[32] As, for example, in a rare case of hysteria, see Chapter 6, p. 96.

[33] (1897) 61 JP 792.

[34] As does *R v Roberts* [1954] 2 QB 329, where a deaf and dumb accused was found unfit to plead because he could not be communicated with.

that he is unfit to plead, or to stand trial.[35] Thus, in *Russell v HM Advocate*,[36] a claim by the accused that she was suffering from (the quaintly Freudian) hysterical amnesia[37] in relation to the offences with which she had been charged was rejected as supporting the contention that she was unfit to plead. Although consistent with a properly rigorous approach to the making of such a diagnosis,[38] it is further consonant with the approach of the law, in general, in relation to criminal offences committed while an accused is suffering from self-induced intoxication, with or without subsequent amnesia for the events of the offence alleged to have occurred during some period coinciding with the period of intoxication.[39] The underlying policy consideration appears to be that, whatever unfairness might arise because of an accused's inability to account for his whereabouts, or to maintain an alibi, arising from his amnesia, from whatever cause, it is preferable to the practical difficulties which would be encountered in the prosecution of offences where the amnesia was attributable directly to the offence charged (e.g. amnesia of a driver caused by intoxication or a head injury resulting from dangerous or drunken driving). Whether or not such considerations make the approach properly applicable to an instance of significant memory impairment, if not actually total memory loss, caused by a dementing

---

[35] However, it may be invoked as evidence of "insanity"; see, for example, *People (AG) v O'Brien* [1936] IR 263 (CCA) (unsuccessfully); and *R v Clarke* [1972] 1 All ER 219, 56 Cr App R 225 (CA); see Chapter 16, pp. 380–4.

[36] (1946) SC (J) 37 followed in *R v Podola* [1960] 1 QB 325, [1959] 3 All ER 418, 43 Cr App R 220 CCA, which approved *Emery*, above. In *Podola*, the jury had found that the accused was not suffering from hysterical amnesia and the issue in the Court of Appeal concerned the onus of proof (below). However, it was held that the issue could only arise if the alleged amnesia could bring Podola within the scope of the Act of 1800 (then in force), which it held it could not.

[37] See Chapter 6, p. 96 in relation to the rarity of this condition.

[38] See Chapter 6, p. 96.

[39] See Smith and Hogan (1988), op. cit., p. 183.

process or other psychiatric disorder,[40] subsequent to, but not at,[41] the time of the alleged offence, must be questionable.[42] Provided, of course, it is assumed that any residue would not be sufficient to render the accused unfit to plead at the arraignment, and thus would not actually interfere with an accused's ability to understand the matters which the law requires him to understand, the outcome is probably unexceptional.[43] With advanced understanding of the patho-physiology of psychiatric disorder and memory impairment, a more sophisticated approach might be warranted.[44] On principle, it also appears that the value judgements implicit in the policy approach are inapplicable to those suffering psychiatric disorder and who risk being treated somewhat unjustly as a consequence. However, without significant reform of the law on disposition,[45] such a proposition is meaningless.

In summary, therefore, in the absence of physical communication difficulties, the jury's concern is limited to being satisfied that the accused is "sane"[46] i.e. of sufficient intellect or with sufficient cognitive function to comprehend the course of the proceedings of the trial so as to:

1. Make a proper defence, i.e. to instruct counsel; and

2. Challenge a juror to whom he might wish to object;[47] and

---

[40] See Chapter 12, pp. 276–88. Or, for example, a significant head injury with marked anterograde amnesia; see Chapter 6, pp. 107–9.

[41] This would risk the "insanity" defence being invoked, perhaps by the trial judge; see *People (AG)* v *O'Brien* [1936] IR 263 (CCA); and, more appositely, *R* v *Clarke* [1972] 1 All ER 219, (1972) 56 Cr App R 225 (CA).

[42] See also Smith and Hogan (1988), op. cit., p. 184.

[43] See *People (AG)* v *O'Brien* [1936] IR 263 (CCA) where the jury convicted, notwithstanding the accused's assertion that he had no awareness of the events in question.

[44] See below, pp. 443–6.

[45] See below, pp. 443–6.

[46] An expression still retained in the Juries Act, 1976, s. 19(2).

[47] An unlimited number of challenges for cause shown, Juries Act, 1974, s. 12, and Juries Act, 1976, s. 20. Although, in Ireland, each side is also entitled to seven peremptory challenges (i.e. without cause shown), in England, the

3. Understand the details of the evidence.[48]

Lack of rigorous application by courts of this functional analysis of
the accused's intellectual comprehension of the issues raised —
coherently and persuasively articulated in the older cases — has
been criticised, as has the *de facto* assumption that the issues are
merely species of the underlying impairment and are thus interchangeable (failure in relation to one amounting to a failure in
relation to all) rather than cumulative.[49] However, rather than
regarding the criteria set out as cumulatively exhaustive, a more
coherent response might be to regard them as non-exhaustive examples of factors the jury must take into account in assessing an
accused's intellectual comprehension of his participation in the
criminal process. Thus, evidence that the accused was suffering
from a psychiatric disorder should not *per se* be sufficient to

---

right of peremptory challenge was abolished by the Criminal Justice Act,
1988, s. 118(1). Unlike in the United States where jury empanelling may
take several days and jurors are questioned on a large number of issues, and,
thus, challenges for cause shown are relatively easy to sustain, in the Irish
and British legal traditions, and given the instructions given to jurors at jury
selection, challenges for cause shown are practically unknown. How an accused could effectively challenge a juror, when one of the issues to be established by the jury then being empanelled is whether or not he is competent to
do so, does not appear to have greatly engaged the parliamentary drafters or
the Oireachtas. In England, where the issue of whether or not an accused
stands "mute of malice" is determined by a jury (in Ireland, it is a function
reserved to the judge; Juries Act, 1976, s. 28, and Criminal Justice Act, 1928,
s. 80; see p. 425 above), it has been held that an accused has no right of
challenge, a not unsurprising finding given the concept in the first instance,
but somewhat unconvincingly; see *R* v *Paling* (1978) 67 Cr App R 299 CA. In
both Ireland and England, the Juries Acts are silent on the issue of challenge
on the actual fitness to plead issue.

[48] Although intellectual comprehension appears to be treated as a separate
issue to the issue of being "mute", in all the unhappy connotations of that
expression, or pleading to the indictment, as noted, it must surely be a necessary corollary thereof.

[49] See McAuley (1993), op. cit., p. 139, citing Grubin (1991), "Unfit to Plead in
England and Wales 1976–86: A Survey", *British Journal of Psychiatry*, Vol.
158, p. 277, Mackay (1991), "The Decline of Disability in Relation to the
Trial", *Criminal Law Review*, p. 87.

establish unfitness to plead,[50] unless the jury was also satisfied that the intellectual or cognitive impairment, either primarily or as a consequence of, or associated with, psychotic symptoms was sufficient to impair that participation. In reality, given the circumstances in which the issue falls to be determined, the presence of severe psychotic disease, as distinct from paranoid delusions[51] in relation to one issue, or one person only,[52] and where the rest of the personality is generally quite well preserved, is almost invariably associated with such severe cognitive impairment that the diagnosis of one necessarily implies the other.

Such an approach to functional ability (involving not alone assessment of intellectual capacity but also integrity of cognitive functioning) could further avoid the scenario of a person's exposing himself to being unjustly found guilty — where, on account of psychiatric disorder, he is unwilling to defend himself or he falsely confesses to a criminal offence and where he is not, strictly speaking and on that ground alone, unfit to plead, if he otherwise falls outside the criteria of unfitness to plead. Although superficially appealing as an approach, it nevertheless hardly seems consistent to simply leave the issue to be weighed as a factor in assessing the prosecution evidence, or in relation to responsibility and punishment.[53]

---

[50] As appears often to be the case. See the cogent criticisms in McAuley (1993), op. cit., pp. 139–42.

[51] However, in McAuley (1993), op. cit., pp. 139 and 142, two specific unreported cases are cited: *People (DPP)* v *Murray* (*Irish Times*, 28 June 1991); *People (AG)* v *Hayes* (see Chapter 16, pp. 382–3 — this was one of the defining cases on irresistible impulse) which correctly indicate the potential effects of paranoid delusions on an accused's fitness to plead in the first instance. But *Murray*, on the facts described, appears to have had a disorder where an inability to participate in the whole process could also legitimately be argued.

[52] See, for example, Chapter 10, pp. 236–9.

[53] As suggested in Williams (1961), op. cit., para. 143. However, unless there was clear evidence of psychiatric disability manifesting itself in the unwillingness of an accused to defend himself or an indication that his confession was false, the logistical implications of having to positively assert every accused's fitness to plead could be oppressive and unmanageable.

TRIAL OF THE ISSUE OF FITNESS TO PLEAD

In Ireland, when the matter arises, which is, generally, before arraignment, a special jury is empanelled to determine the issue at that time.[54] When the issue arises during a trial, however, the trial jury may determine the matter.[55] As a trial judge is under a duty to consider the issue of an accused's fitness to be tried throughout the criminal proceedings, where there appears to be doubt in that regard the trial must not proceed unless and until that doubt has been resolved.[56] In either case, therefore, the issue is determined as soon as it arises, consonant with the thrust of the legislation. The issue for the jury when the issue to be tried is "whether an accused is or is not competent to plead" is to inquire whether he "be insane or not" for that purpose.[57]

Although the situation in England, prior to statutory reform, was effectively the same, judicial procedure adapted itself in an attempt to address the most draconian consequences of a finding of unfitness to plead.[58] Thus, in *R v Roberts*[59] the trial jury heard

---

[54] In accordance with the Lunacy (Ireland) Act, 1821, s. 17.

[55] *R v Podola* [1960] 1 QB 325, [1959] 3 All ER 418, 43 Cr App R 220, i.e. based on dicta in cases decided in the English superior courts before 1964 (these provisions were incorporated into statute in England in 1964). In a non-jury criminal court (Special Criminal Court), the court itself may decide the issue; see, however, in McAuley (1993), op. cit., pp. 142–4, referring to *People (DPP) v Murray (Irish Times*, 28 June 1991). The Juries Act, 1976, s. 19, provides for different forms of oaths to be taken by jurors depending on whether or not the issue to be tried is a criminal or civil one, or an issue of "fitness to be tried". As to whether or not this necessitates the swearing of a different jury, or the re-swearing of the trial jury, is unclear.

[56] *R v Southey* (1865) 4 F&F 864, 176 ER 825; *R v Berry* [1876] 1 QBD 447; *State (Coughlan) v Minister for Justice and another* (1968) ILTR 177. It is suggested that a trial judge may resolve his doubts by reading the medical reports but that it is undesirable for him to hear medical evidence; and that it is only if the judge has doubts (or either party raise the issue) that a jury should be empanelled to determine the issue; see Smith and Hogan (1988), op. cit., p. 183.

[57] Juries Act, 1976, s. 19(2).

[58] See p. 438 below.

[59] [1954] 2 QB 329, [1953] 2 All ER 340 *per* Devlin J, followed in *R v Pickstone* [1954] Crim LR 565, although the trial judge expressly refused to follow this arrangement in *R v Benyon* [1957] 2 QB 111, 2 All ER 513,

the evidence and decided both the general issue (i.e. of guilt or innocence) and the issue of fitness to be tried. Thus, if the jury were
not satisfied that the accused was guilty of the act or omission
charged as the offence laid, a finding of not guilty was appropriate. However, if, on the evidence, they were satisfied as to his
guilt, they were then to consider his fitness to be tried. A finding
of unfitness indicating that he had been disadvantaged in his defence, the accused would thereupon be disposed of in the usual
manner for persons found unfit to be tried on arraignment. A
finding of fitness to be tried was to result in conviction of the accused. Although arising in the context of the preliminary investigation of an indictable offence in the District Court,[60] argument
that the constitutional rights of an accused could only be properly
vindicated by grafting such provisions onto present procedure was
rejected by the Supreme Court.[61]

In England, however, substantive statutory modification[62] refers to "disability"[63] and "fitness to be tried", rather than "insanity" and provides that, although the issue is to be determined as
soon as it arises,[64]

> [I]f, having regard to the nature of the supposed disability,
> the court are of opinion that it is expedient to do so and in

---

because he considered it unsupported by authority. Devlin J's approach was
modified and incorporated into statutory reform; see above.

[60] See p. 446 below.

[61] *O'Connor* v *The Judges of the Dublin Metropolitan District and another*
[1994] 3 IR 246 (SC) *per* Finlay CJ for the court, affirming the High Court
(O'Hanlon J), reported at [1992] 1 IR 387. While superficially appealing as a
solution, as an approach it is internally incoherent and represents, at best,
no more than a clever pragmatic ruse to ameliorate the effects of the worst
excesses of outdated legislation which, in Britain, was subsequently amended
significantly. Tinkering at the margins is not a justifiable substitute for
coherent and principled statutory reform.

[62] Criminal Procedure (Insanity) Act, 1964, ss. 4 and 4A, as substituted by
the Criminal Procedure (Insanity and Fitness to Plead) Act, 1991, s. 2.

[63] See p. 422 above.

[64] Criminal Procedure (Insanity) Act, 1964, s. 4(4), as amended by the Criminal Procedure (Insanity and Fitness to Plead) Act,1991, s. 2.

the interests of the accused, they may postpone consideration of the question of fitness to be tried until any time up
to the opening of the case for the defence.[65]

Thus, it is determined by a jury either before or during the trial,
as in Ireland. However, in the exercise of this discretion of postponement, it has been held the court should not decide the issue of
fitness to be tried at arraignment, but postpone it until some time
before the opening of the case for the defence, if there is a reasonable chance of the prosecution evidence being successfully challenged such that the defence does not have to go into evidence.
Thus, the apparent strength or weakness of the prosecution case
as disclosed on the depositions or statements should be assessed,
followed by consideration of the nature and degree of the suggested disability from the medical reports before the court and
what was expedient in the interest of the accused. Postponement
of the trial of the issue of fitness to be tried would, accordingly, be
inexpedient where the prosecution case appeared very strong and
the suggested condition of the accused very disabling. However,
where the prosecution case was so thin that, whatever the degree
of the accused's disability, it would be inexpedient not to postpone
determination of the issue, the chances of a successful defence
were good.[66]

Furthermore, it is provided that if, before the question of fitness for trial is determined, the jury return a verdict of acquittal

---

[65] Criminal Procedure (Insanity) Act, 1964, s. 4(2), as amended by the Criminal Procedure (Insanity and Fitness to Plead) Act, 1991, s. 2.

[66] These arguments were advanced in the High Court in *O'Connor* v *The
Judges of the Dublin Metropolitan District & another* [1994] 3 IR 246 (SC) *per*
Finlay CJ for the court, affirming the High Court (O'Hanlon J) reported at
[1992] 1 IR 387, in reliance on *R* v *Webb* [1969] 2 QB 278, [1969] 2 All ER
626, 53 Cr App R 360 CA; *R* v *Burles* [1970] 2 QB 191, 1 All ER 642, 54 Cr
App R 196 CA, where there was a certainty of the prosecution not proving the
case (as admitted by counsel for the prosecution when the case was called for
trial).

of the charges upon which the accused is being tried, the question of fitness for trial is not to be determined.[67]

PROOF

Standard of Proof

Although legislation implicitly allows either the prosecution or the defence or the trial judge to raise the issue, it is silent as to where the burden of proof lies or as to what the standard is.[68] A court may refuse to put the issue of fitness to be tried to a jury if it is not satisfied that there is sufficient evidence to support it.[69]

---

[67] Criminal Procedure (Insanity) Act, 1964, s. 4(3), as amended by the Criminal Procedure (Insanity and Fitness to Plead) Act, 1991, s. 2.

[68] Unlike in the case of "criminal insanity"; see Chapter 16, pp. 407–9. It has been held that if the allegation is raised by the defence, and is contested by the prosecution, the onus of proof is on the defence who must satisfy the jury on the balance of probabilities that the accused is unfit to be tried: *R* v *Podola* [1960] 1 QB 325, [1959] 3 All ER 418, 43 Cr App R 220. If the prosecution raises the allegation, and it is contested by the defence, the onus rests on the prosecution who must satisfy the jury beyond a reasonable doubt that the accused is unfit to be tried: *R* v *Sharp* [1958] 1 All ER 62, 122 JP 51, (1957) 41 Cr App R 197; *R* v *Robertson* [1968] 3 All ER 557, 1 WLR 1767 (CA), 52 Cr App R 690. The burden of proof relates to unfitness to stand trial, not to fitness. Although it has been asserted that if the evidence is not contested by either side, there is no issue as to where the burden of proof lies and the jury must simply be satisfied that the accused is unfit to be tried, the preferable position must be that the onus still should lie on the party maintaining the allegation; see McAuley (1993), op. cit., p. 133. That said, what the prosecution is alleging in such a situation is not that the accused committed a criminal offence, but rather that he is unfit to stand trial; to require that the same standard apply has been criticised as inappropriate; see Williams (1961), op. cit., para. 143. Where the issue is raised by a trial judge, the onus of proof appears to lie on the prosecution (see *R* v *Sharp* [1958] 1 All ER 62, 122 JP 51, (1957) 41 Cr App R 197), irrespective of whether or not it is challenged by the defence. Although the standard of the balance of probabilities seems to be most consonant with general principle, if the onus is deemed to be on the prosecution, then, in accordance with practice, it must be established beyond a reasonable doubt. This is consistent with the general notion that an accused is not obliged to establish anything in a criminal trial. The onus rests entirely upon the prosecution. See Smith and Hogan (1988), op. cit., p. 184.

[69] See, for comparison, *R* v *Vent* (1935) Cr App R 55; *Russell* v *HM Advocate* (1946) SC (J) 37; and *State (C)* v *Minister for Justice* [1967] IR 106, also cited as *State (Coughlan)* v *Minister for Justice and another* (1968) ILTR 177.

There must be a proper direction to the jury on the evidence,[70] and it is for the trial judge to explain the principles upon which the issue is to be decided.[71] If the jury disagree, a fresh jury must be sworn.[72] As the verdict is the verdict of a jury in criminal proceedings, the provisions in respect of majority verdicts apply.[73]

Evidence, with regard to the criteria enunciated, may be led in the usual manner and the jury, as arbiters of fact, are bound by the evidence. However, they are not entitled to substitute their own view such that if they think that the accused is not capable of acting in his own best interest, this, of itself, is insufficient to ground their finding him unfit to plead.[74] Similarly, that an accused is quite abnormal is not sufficient, of itself, to find him unfit to plead.[75] However, where an accused has been certified as "insane", it raises a presumption of "insanity" that holds good in respect of his fitness unless displaced by the evidence.[76]

Even where the issue has not been raised at the trial stage, it has been held that an appellate court can nevertheless quash the conviction of an accused on the ground that he was incapable of participating in his trial, because of psychiatric disorder.[77]

---

[70] *R* v *Levionnois* (1956) 23 Cr App R 230 (CA).

[71] *R* v *Berry* (1978) 66 Cr App R 156.

[72] *R* v *Darkhu* [1956] 1 WLR 989, 3 ALL ER 428, 40 Cr App R 130.

[73] Juries Act, 1976, s. 17, and the Criminal Justice Act, 1984, s. 25.

[74] *R* v *Robertson* [1968] 3 All ER 557, 1 WLR 1767 (CA), (1968) 52 Cr App R 690.

[75] *R* v *Berry* (1978) 66 Cr App R 156.

[76] See *R* v *Green-Emmott* (1932) 22 Cr App R 183, 29 Cox CC 280, in the context of entering a recognisance. That said, "insanity" is not a synonym for unfitness to plead; see Chapters 16 and 18 and *State (C)* v *Minister for Justice* [1967] IR 106 at 115, *per* Ó Dálaigh CJ and at 121 *per* Walsh J.

[77] *R* v *Kolacz* (1950) VLR 200 (Supreme Court of Victoria), cited in Williams (1961), op. cit., p.438. In Britain, it appears that an appeal lies from a jury's finding that an accused is fit to be tried, see *R* v *Podola* [1960] 1 QB 325, [1959] 3 All ER 418, 43 Cr App R 220 CCA. Given that the issue involves the accused's competence to instruct counsel as to his defence, as with the raising of the issue by the defence in the first instance, this must involve a certain professional paternalism to be exercised by his lawyers. As noted, a judge must be satisfied that there is sufficient evidence of an accused's unfitness to

What Proof?

Although an accused must have sufficient intellectual function to enable him to participate in all stages of the trial process,[78] in Ireland, it has been suggested that the evidence of the prison medical authorities that an accused is a danger to himself or to others, or is suffering from such psychiatric disorder as requires treatment and is refusing such treatment, is sometimes sufficient to establish unfitness to plead.[79] On the basis of the older authorities,[80] not even this "modern approach" was required, and a jury might act on its impressions of the accused's behaviour.[81] Nothing more specific is required evidentially by statute. Thus, in England, before statutory reform[82] it was pointed out that a person could theoretically be subject to indeterminate committal in a

---

plead to put the matter to the jury in the first instance (see *State (C) v Minister for Justice* [1967] IR 106 at 120 *per* Walsh J, in the context of summary proceedings) and it appears that an appeal lies from a refusal to do so. Should the appeal against a judge's refusal to put the issue to a jury be successful, a new trial could be ordered, as the original would have been a nullity. See *R v Crane* [1921] 2 AC 299, referred to in *R v Podola* [1960] 1 QB 325, [1959] 3 All ER 418, 43 Cr App R 220 CCA. See also *State (C) v Minister for Justice* [1967] IR 106 at 120 *per* Walsh J. However, in *People (A-G) v Fennell* (No. 2) [1940] IR 453, the former Supreme Court held that no appeal lay against a jury's finding in the Central Criminal Court that an accused was not unfit to plead, as it did not amount to a "decision" within the meaning of Article 34.4.3 of the Constitution. But see Kelly (1994), op. cit., pp. 515–16.

[78] See p. 429 above. It is the issue of "fitness to be tried", as in the Act of 1964, rather than "fitness to plead", that is important.

[79] i.e. that the accused is "certifiably insane"; effectively that he fulfils the criteria for civil commitment, see McAuley (1993), op. cit., p. 140, referring to information provided by the Director of Public Prosecutions. He also states that the trial of persons found unfit to plead, in practice, only takes place if there is a suspicion that an accused is feigning disability (p. 142).

[80] *R v Goode* (1837) 7 Ad&E 536, 112 ER 572; *R v Davis* (1853) 6 Cox CC 326.

[81] The fact that the determination of the issue is left to a jury, without any particular scientific competence in the area, thus classified as "amateurs", has been criticised; see Williams (1961), op. cit., para. 143. However, the practical realities of the practice in Ireland, which does not effectively differ from that required by statutory reform in England, now render this criticism otiose.

[82] And, theoretically still in Ireland, although the procedure, in practice, as noted makes this unlikely.

secure psychiatric facility ("criminal lunatic asylum") on the evidence of a single prison officer, although he could not be subject to committal to an ordinary psychiatric facility without the agreement of two registered medical practitioners.[83] Now, however, legislation in England (and *de facto* practice in Ireland) has anchored assessment of the issue in a medical, or more specifically, a psychiatric disorder, model. Thus, British legislation provides that the issue may not be determined except on the written or oral evidence of two or more registered medical practitioners, at least one of whom is duly approved.[84] Nevertheless, it appears that if a court is satisfied that there is insufficient evidence to support an allegation of unfitness to be tried, it may refuse to put the matter to a jury.[85]

DISPOSITION OF THE ACCUSED

Where a jury finds that an accused is fit to be tried, the trial proceeds in the normal manner, with resultant conviction or acquittal. However, notwithstanding that he has been found fit to be tried, it has been suggested that an accused may still rely on

---

[83] Minute of Evidence (1950) of the British Medical Association to the Royal Commission on Capital Punishment (Cmnd 8932 of 1953). This appears to follow logically from the application of the older authorities on the issue; see Williams (1961), op. cit., p. 435 and the footnotes thereto.

[84] Criminal Procedure (Insanity) Act, 1964, s. 4(6), as amended by the Criminal Procedure (Insanity and Fitness to Plead) Act, 1991, s. 2. Section 8 of the Act of 1964, as amended, provides that "registered medical practitioner" means a person fully registered within the meaning of the Medical Act, 1983, and is the equivalent of a registered medical practitioner within the meaning of the Irish Medical Practitioners Act, 1978; and "duly approved" means approved for the purposes of section 12 of the Mental Health Act, 1983, by the Secretary of State as having special experience in the diagnosis of treatment of mental disorder — in effect, a consultant psychiatrist, although one approved as having an expertise in forensic psychiatry, a recommendation effectively made by the Atkin Committee and endorsed by the Royal Commission on Capital Punishment (Cmd. 8932 of 1953); Williams (1961), op. cit., p. 435, fn 5.

[85] *Russell* v *HM Advocate* (1946) SC (J) 37. There does not appear to be any onus on the court to ensure that the prosecution has enquired into the reliability of the evidence adduced on behalf of the defence, either in statute or on the authorities. See McAuley (1993), op. cit., pp. 97–107.

evidence of his "unfitness" in order to argue that he is disadvantaged in his defence and thus there is a reasonable doubt as to his guilt, e.g. the accused's amnesia for the circumstances of the crime alleged could properly be put before a trial court as a matter for consideration when weighing the evidence.[86]

In Ireland, in accordance with the Lunacy (Ireland) Act, 1821,[87] once a jury has found an accused is found "insane . . . so that [he] cannot be tried upon . . . indictment" the finding is recorded and, in practice, the accused is ordered to be kept in strict custody, in the Central Mental Hospital (formerly the Central Asylum for the "Criminally Insane") at the pleasure of the executive. However, the statutory provisions suggest that this is discretionary rather than mandatory, indicating merely that "it shall be lawful for the court . . . to order such person to be kept in strict custody".[88] Thus, a situation arises whereby persons who have only been accused of having committed indictable offences, but who have never been tried for them, let alone found guilty, are exposed to indeterminate custody in a secure psychiatric facility because they were unfit to be tried. The issue of whether or not the accused is liable otherwise to involuntary civil commitment does not arise for consideration.[89] That the question of whether or not the Act of 1821

---

[86] Williams (1961), op. cit., para. 143, an approach which tempers the extreme possible consequences of "amnesia" cases, above, and the approach in *Russell* v *HM Advocate* (1946) SC (J) 37, followed in *R* v *Podola* [1960] 1 QB 325, [1959] 3 All ER 418, 43 Cr App R 220 CCA.

[87] See p. 420 above.

[88] A point highlighted in McAuley (1993), op. cit., pp. 140, 144.

[89] See Chapter 18. However, such detention is mainly therapeutic, rather than simply custodial, in intent and is without taint or suggestion of criminality. Furthermore, an accused who is unfit to be tried, in common with all other accused persons, carries with him a presumption of innocence unless and until he is found guilty in accordance with law. It seems, therefore, as a matter of principle, that unless such a person is a candidate for involuntary civil commitment for treatment purposes (whether active or preventative), there is no sound reason, consonant with criminal policy, why he should be detained at all, least of all where there has been no finding of guilt and therapy is neither necessary nor the primary aim of (indefinite) detention. For a comprehensive and detailed treatment of the situation in Ireland, and the "medical activism" involved, see McAuley (1993), op. cit., pp. 144–50.

survived the enactment of the Constitution in 1937 has not arisen is, perhaps, partly explained by the relatively small number of fitness to plead cases which come before the courts on an annual basis. That said, the disposition elements of the Trial of Lunatics Act 1883, which are identical to those in the Act of 1821 were found not to be constitutionally vulnerable in *People (DPP)* v *Gallagher*.[90] In this regard, the observations of the former Supreme Court in *In re Philip Clarke*,[91] cited with approval by the Supreme Court in *SC* v *Smith*[92] and noted in *Gallagher* are apposite and could sustain an argument in support of its constitutional validity. However, unlike the accused in *Gallagher*,[93] or the applicants in *Clarke* or *SC*,[94] a person detained under the provisions of the Act of 1821 might pose no risk at all and be suffering from a relatively benign[95] and perhaps non-recurring condition.[96] In *RT* v *Director of the Central Mental Hospital & another*[97] Costello J, as he then was, found that the provisions of the Mental Treatment Act, 1945, in relation to a person suffering a psychiatric disability who was found unfit to plead in the District Court to be constitutionally invalid.[98] The disposition in such cases is identical. Although the provisions of the Act of 1821 are excluded from the provisions of the Mental Treatment Act, 1945,[99] it remains to be determined whether or not the same constitutional frailty might

---

[90] [1991] ILRM 339 (SC).

[91] [1950] IR 235; see Chapter 18.

[92] Supreme Court, Unreported Judgment, Hamilton CJ, O'Flaherty, Blayney, Denham, Barrington JJ, 31 July 1996 (272/1995).

[93] Personality disorder, see Chapter 9.

[94] Schizophrenia, see Chapter 15.

[95] A dementia, see Chapter 12, pp. 277–89.

[96] See, for example, Chapter 15, pp. 348–55.

[97] [1995] 2 ILRM 354.

[98] Section 207.

[99] By virtue of the provisions of section 284.

attach. However, pending statutory reform,[100] exercise of the apparent residual discretion in the Act of 1821 could arguably not alone save its constitutionality but also preserve the constitutional rights of the psychiatrically disordered sought to be detained under its provisions.

In England,[101] where a jury decides that the accused is, in fact, under a "disability", whether before or during the trial, the trial must not proceed, or proceed further, as the case might be. It must then be determined, either by a different jury to that which found the accused unfit to be tried or the trial jury, respectively,[102] whether the accused did the act or made the omission charged against him as the offence on the basis of the evidence (if any) already given in the trial and on such evidence as may be adduced or further adduced by the prosecution, or by a person appointed by the court to put the case for the defence.[103] If the jury is not satisfied, in respect of any offence with which the accused is charged, that the accused did the act or made the omission charged, they must return a verdict of acquittal in respect thereof as if the trial had proceeded to a conclusion in the normal manner.[104]

---

[100] As promised in the White Paper on a New Mental Health Act (1995) (Department of Health, Dublin), Chapter 7, and see pp. 443–6 below.

[101] Prior to the enactment of the Criminal Procedure (Insanity and Fitness to Plead) Act, 1991, the procedure for disposition of persons found unfit to plead was not significantly different to that which persists in Ireland, i.e. indeterminate detention at the pleasure of the executive. Thus, a person found unfit to plead was ordered to be admitted to a hospital specified by the Home Secretary under the provisions of the Criminal Procedure (Insanity) Act, 1964, s. 5 (1)(c) and Schedule 1, where the accused was detained without limitation as to time, the power of discharge being exercisable only with the consent of the Home Secretary; Mental Health Act, 1983, ss. 23 and 41.

[102] Criminal Procedure (Insanity) Act, 1964, s. 4A(5), as substituted by the Criminal Procedure (Insanity and Fitness to Plead) Act, 1991, s. 2.

[103] Criminal Procedure (Insanity) Act, 1964, s. 4A(2), as substituted by the Criminal Procedure (Insanity and Fitness to Plead) Act, 1991, s. 2.

[104] Criminal Procedure (Insanity) Act, 1964, s. 4A(4), as substituted by the Criminal Procedure (Insanity and Fitness to Plead) Act, 1991, s. 2. Thus, notwithstanding a finding of "unfitness to be tried" within that limitation, inconsistent though it may appear, an accused may still benefit from an acquittal and thus avoid completely the risk of detention, whether the indeterminate detention of the older legislation, or at all. However, notwithstanding

Where the jury, having found that the accused was under a disability, proceeds and is satisfied, and makes a finding, on the evidence, that the accused did the act or made the omission charged against him as the offence[105] the court must either

1. Make an order that the accused be admitted to a hospital as may be specified by the Secretary of State,[106] or

2. Where the offence is not one for which the sentence is fixed by law,[107] make:

    a) a guardianship order within the meaning of the Mental Health Act, 1983;

    b) a supervision and treatment order;[108] and

    c) an order for the absolute discharge of the accused

    as is considered most suitable in all of the circumstances of the case.[109]

In such situations, a finding that amounts to guilt of a criminal offence must be made before the other powers of the court may be

---

the practical advantage to the accused, the principle that allows a person who is unfit to be tried nevertheless to be tried where he cannot instruct counsel as to his defence or understand the evidence, is unclear. Given the nature of the criminal process, and the nature of psychiatric disability, it appears more pragmatic policy than coherent principle.

[105] Criminal Procedure (Insanity) Act, 1964, s. 4A(3), as substituted by the Criminal Procedure (Insanity and Fitness to Plead) Act, 1991, s. 2.

[106] In accordance with the procedure set out in the Criminal Procedure (Insanity and Unfitness to Plead) Act, 1991, Schedule 1.

[107] Criminal Procedure (Insanity) Act, 1964, s. 5(3), as substituted by the Criminal Procedure (Insanity and Fitness to Plead) Act, 1991, s. 3; effectively the crime of murder.

[108] In accordance with the provisions of the Criminal Procedure (Insanity and Unfitness to Plead) Act, 1991, Schedule 2.

[109] Criminal Procedure (Insanity) Act, 1964, s. 5(2), as substituted by the Criminal Procedure (Insanity and Fitness to Plead) Act, 1991, s. 3.

invoked, notwithstanding the disability of the accused in the first instance.[110]

SUGGESTED REFORM IN THE WHITE PAPER ON A NEW MENTAL HEALTH ACT

The White Paper on a New Mental Health Act[111] acknowledges that more options than are at present available to the courts for arranging for the treatment of persons found unfit to plead because of "mental disorder"[112] should be provided. In this regard, the administrative provisions proposed are the same as those where the issue of "mental disorder" arises either during the trial or after conviction but prior to sentencing, which is dealt with separately from the issue of unfitness to plead or criminal "insanity".[113] Although in each case, the trial judge is empowered to order a medical report from a consultant psychiatrist, authorised for that purpose by his or her employer and attached to, or employed

---

[110] The graduated options permitted, from committal to a secure unit, through to absolute discharge, all of which are functions reserved to the judge, and appears more just, in all of the circumstances — especially supervision and treatment orders (which require that the person's mental condition is such as requires, and may be susceptible to, treatment but is not such as to warrant the making of an admission order or a guardianship order). However, from the perspective of the accused under a disability, a fundamental and irreconcilable incoherence remains even with this approach.

[111] Department of Health (1995), Dublin. The funding implications and the requirements for the provision of secure units are beyond the scope of the present discussion.

[112] As defined in the White Paper, paras. 2.8–2.20. This implicitly recognises the necessity for updating the law and confining it to issues of lack of capacity caused by psychological disability.

[113] This disjunctive treatment of what is essentially one issue arguably arises more from the application of precedent than logic. As to why the issue of fitness to plead as currently understood could not be simply "rolled-up" in this procedure, rather than dealing with it separately, is unclear — except that philosophically one appears directed more at a paternalistic treatment of psychiatrically disordered person who come into contact with the criminal justice system, whereas the other appears more concerned with the integrity of that system insofar as capacity to participate as an accused person is concerned. However, there is no coherent reason as to why they should be treated, in practice or principle, as mutually, or even partially, exclusive.

in a service in the area in which the person ordinarily, or currently, resides, it must be recommended by the Probation and
Welfare Service in the case of "mental disorder" *simpliciter*. For
the preparation of the medical report, the person could be remanded either on bail or, in the case of those who are not permitted bail,[114] in custody.[115]

The purpose of the medical report is primarily to establish
whether or not the person is suffering from a "mental disorder",
its seriousness and the authorised consultant's recommendations
as to the most appropriate form of treatment. If the medical report
indicates a need for treatment, depending on the severity of the
underlying disorder, treatment on an outpatient basis, or in-
patient treatment, either on a voluntary or involuntary basis or
treatment in a secure special psychiatric centre, may be recommended. Thus, where the "mental disorder" is not severe and the
person is willing to accept either outpatient treatment or in-
patient treatment on a voluntary basis, it is proposed that he will
enter into a recognisance that he will undergo treatment;[116] the
case is adjourned until treatment[117] is completed, whereupon the
criminal proceedings resume.[118] It is further envisaged that treatment will be provided in the service in which the consultant psychiatrist who made the medical report is employed.

---

[114] However, if the incapacity is so severe as to render an accused unfit to
plead, the possibility arises that he will also be incapable of entering into a
recognisance; see pp. 447–8.

[115] Similar provisions would also apply to children (i.e. those under 18 years);
however, the parents or guardians would have to be informed and allowed a
reasonable opportunity to appeal the decision.

[116] Presuming that he has sufficient capacity to enter into a recognisance; see
pp. 447–8.

[117] Whether this is for primarily therapeutic purposes or for the purposes of
establishing fitness to plead seems irrelevant insofar as the completion of
"treatment" in one will invariably constitute completion of "treatment" and
"recovery" for the other.

[118] Whether trial or sentencing. Logically, there is no reason why it should
not also apply to arraignment.

However, if the medical report discloses that the person fulfils the criteria for involuntary[119] committal, and he is not willing to accept treatment on a voluntary basis, the consultant psychiatrist will be empowered to decide to detain the person for treatment in the same manner as a person who was not before the courts. The psychiatrist will then be required to inform the court of the detention order, whereupon the case will be adjourned until treatment is completed and there is sufficient recovery for proceedings to continue. It is proposed that detention will take place in an approved centre in which the consultant psychiatrist who made the medical report was attached, initially for 28 days, extendable to three months, by a further period of six months and by periods of one year thereafter, the psychiatrist informing the court of any extension, which would be reviewed by the proposed Mental Health Review Board.

In cases where the medical report indicates that the person fulfils the criteria for involuntary admission, is unwilling to accept treatment on a voluntary basis and that his behaviour is so disturbed that he requires care in the secure environment of a special psychiatric centre, and where the latter is confirmed by the clinical director of the special centre, the consultant psychiatrist will be empowered to detain the person and arrange for his transfer. Again, it is proposed that detention will be for the periods specified for detention in an approved centre, and the criminal proceedings will be adjourned pending completion of treatment and recovery.

Where a person is not granted bail, it is envisaged that recommended treatment may be provided in prison or, in severe cases, on transfer from prison to a special psychiatric centre.[120]

Although it is expressly provided that, should a person found unfit to plead recover sufficiently, then the trial would proceed in

---

[119] See Chapter 18.

[120] However, this does not appear to amount to a power to "remand . . . to custody for treatment" as articulated in the White Paper on a New Mental Health Act (1995), op. cit., para. 7.20.

the normal manner, if sufficient recovery does not take place to allow the trial to proceed and ongoing treatment is required in an approved or other centre, it is the function of the court, on the basis of the advice of the consultant psychiatrist responsible for the person, to decide where that treatment should be received.[121]

UNFITNESS TO PLEAD IN A COURT OF SUMMARY JURISDICTION — GENERAL

The Act of 1800 and the statutory reforms in England[122] apply only to trials on indictment[123] and not to proceedings before the District Court or a Magistrates' Court and there is no equivalent procedure laid down in statute.[124] However, given that, in relation to indictable offences, a number of accused are found to be unfit to plead at arraignment, the possibility arises that at least some may have been in that condition for some time before, including the time they were before the lower court which returned them for trial on indictment.[125]

Thus, if a court of summary jurisdiction is dealing with an offence that is capable only of being tried summarily, there is no statutory power to commit the accused to the Circuit Criminal Court or the Crown Court for a jury to determine his fitness to plead.[126] Thus, the matter falls to be decided solely by the District

---

[121] White Paper on a New Mental Health Act (1995), op. cit., paras. 7.14–7.22.

[122] Criminal Procedure (Insanity) Act, 1964, as amended by the Criminal Procedure (Insanity and Unfitness to Plead) Act, 1991, s. 4.

[123] See *Metropolitan Stipendiary Magistrate, ex parte Aniifowosi* (1985) 149 JP 748, DC. However, the Butler Committee on Mentally Abnormal Offenders (above) had recommended that they should apply to magistrates' courts also.

[124] Nor is there any procedure where the Circuit Court or Crown Court is hearing criminal appeals from the District or Magistrates' Court respectively. See, for example, *State (C) v Minister for Justice* [1967] IR 106 at 120 *per* Walsh J.

[125] A point raised by Walsh J in *State (C) v Minister for Justice* [1967] IR 106 at 120.

[126] *Metropolitan Stipendiary Magistrate, ex parte Aniifowosi* (1985) 149 JP 748, DC.

Judge or Magistrates, as the case may be. Similarly, the matter may arise to be determined in the lower court during the process by which the accused is returned for trial by jury. Consequently, a person accused of serious offences, in respect of whom the issue of his unfitness to plead is raised at an earlier stage in the proceedings (i.e. at the stage which determines whether or not he should be returned for trial), is dealt with in a manifestly different manner to that which pertains if the same issue were to be raised at arraignment or at the trial of the general issue.[127]

District Court

The test applicable to the issue of fitness to be tried in trials on indictment[128] applies also in the case of District Court proceedings, whether upon a summary trial or by way of preliminary investigation.[129] Thus, it was held that

> Th[e] test [in respect of indictable offences], *mutatis mutandis*, is applicable in the case of District Court proceedings, whether on summary trial or by way of preliminary investigation. There can be little doubt that a District [Judge] must stop short if he is satisfied that the accused is insane in the sense already explained and this no less in a preliminary investigation than in a summary trial. On a preliminary investigation an accused person has important rights, which he must be in a position to exercise if the preliminary investigation is to be a valid basis for his return for trial [on indictment].[130]

---

[127] Although in England, there has been some harmonisation of the disposition of such an accused at the different court levels, in Ireland, there is no such coherence; see p. 453 below.

[128] As set out in *R v Pritchard* (1836) 7 C&P 303; see pp. 424–5 above.

[129] Pursuant to the provisions of the Criminal Procedure Act, 1967.

[130] *State (C) v Minister for Justice* [1967] IR 106 at 115 *per* Ó'Dálaigh CJ (and see also, at page 120, *per* Walsh J), followed in *O'Connor v The Judges of the Dublin Metropolitan District & another* [1994] 3 IR 246 (SC) *per* Finlay CJ for the court, affirming the High Court (O'Hanlon J) reported at [1992] 1 IR 387.

Furthermore, once so satisfied, then an accused is not in a condition to consent either to the continuation of the proceedings or to the summary trial of an indictable offence,[131] and it raises the question as to whether or not the accused is in a condition to enter into a recognisance for the purposes of being admitted to bail, such that he would otherwise require to be remanded in custody if the matter were not being dealt with there and then.[132] Thus, an inquiry as to an accused's fitness to plead is a matter for the District Judge, upon the summary trial of a summary offence, a summary trial of an indictable offence triable summarily and upon the preliminary investigation in relation to an offence triable only on indictment.

As to the appropriate disposition in such cases, the authorities are clear. A District Judge can remand an accused in custody, without requiring him to be brought before the court on each remand date, if he is satisfied that through illness, he is unable to attend.[133] However, at the making of such a remand, the court — where the illness is of psychiatric nature going to the issue of fitness to plead — would have to be "judicially satisfied of the continued 'unfitness to plead' of the accused".[134]

In *State (Caseley)* v *Daly & another*[135] the prosecutor who had been charged with arson, was remanded in custody by the District Judge for further examination with consent to bail if forthcoming.

---

[131] Under the provisions of the Criminal Justice Act, 1951. See *State (C)* v *Minister for Justice* [1967] IR 106 at 120–121 *per* Walsh J. However, it has been suggested that, in the English context, the fact that an accused cannot exercise his election for jury trial does not affect the jurisdiction of the lower court to proceed to deal with the matter summarily. Where the election of the accused is essential, it is difficult to contemplate the legitimacy of such an approach. See Williams (1961), op. cit., para. 154.

[132] *State (C)* v *Minister for Justice* [1967] IR 106 *per* Walsh J at 126, followed in *O'Connor* v *The Judges of the Dublin Metropolitan District* [1992] 1 IR 387. See also *Green-Emmott* (1932) 22 Cr App R 183, 29 Cox CC 280 where the accused had been "certified".

[133] See, for example, District Court Rules, 1948, and the Criminal Procedure Act, 1967, s. 24(4).

[134] *State (C)* v *Minister for Justice* [1967] IR 106 at 124 *per* Walsh J.

[135] High Court, Unreported Judgment, Gannon J, 19 February 1979.

While in custody, he was transferred to the Central Mental Hospital by order of the Minister for Justice under the provisions of the Lunatic Asylums (Ireland) Act, 1875.[136] On the next remand date, he did not attend court and medical evidence was given in his absence of his inability to attend because of illness. Accordingly, the District Judge made a series of further orders for remand until the prosecutor was well enough to attend court.[137] As the High Court noted, at this stage, the District Court:

> did not hold an enquiry as to whether or not the prosecutor was "unfit to plead", and his order of further remand was not an adjudication of a judicial nature but was administrative only. [The court] was then dealing with an ill man with the benefit of the presumption of innocence in relation to a criminal charge not as yet supported by the evidence. . . . At most the [District Court] had evidence to indicate that if the prosecutor were to be released he might not, by reason of his illness, attend court when required to answer the charge and hear the evidence thereon.

Although a person remanded for further examination may legitimately be transferred to a psychiatric facility, for the duration of the original remand, unless so extended, Gannon J pointed out:

> An order made pursuant to section 24(4) of the Criminal Procedure Act, 1967, could . . . [be] a proper order . . . for the period therein specified if on the evidence it could reasonably . . . [be] expected that the [person accused] might sufficiently recover from his illness to permit the matter pending before the court to proceed. But if the evidence offered . . . suggest[s] a continuing incapacity of indefinite duration the District [Judge] should . . . [take] steps to deal with the matter . . . pending under the provisions of the Mental Treatment Act, 1945.

---

[136] Section 13; see Chapter 18, p. 499.

[137] Pursuant to the provisions of the Criminal Procedure Act, 1967, s. 24(4).

In *State (C)* v *Minister for Justice*,[138] it was suggested that the alternative to further remands is to withdraw the charges or to offer
no further evidence so that the proceedings would be discontinued, but leaving the way open for a renewal of charges at a later
date, if the accused's condition was sufficiently recovered.[139] In
such circumstances, the accused is released and is then in a position to seek appropriate treatment.

    Given that charges remain extant, it was argued in *O'Connor* v
Judges of the Dublin Metropolitan District[140] that the approach
adopted by Devlin J (as he then was) in *R* v *Roberts*[141] was necessary to vindicate the constitutional rights of an accused who was
"unfit to plead" in the District Court at the preliminary examination stage. However, the Supreme Court declined to put the "very
major gloss" on the decision in *C* that was contended for, holding
that, given the nature of the preliminary examination, it would be
unconstitutional to do so. It held that if the District Court found
an accused unfit to plead, the court

> . . . must decline to enter upon the preliminary examination
> and should make no order of any description with regard to
> the further attendance of the accused or with regard to his
> custody.

Thus, an accused found unfit to plead, pending statutory reform,
will have no order made against him in the District Court, even if
the prosecution authorities do not elect to discontinue proceedings. Although unlikely, it may be that the condition giving rise to
an accused's unfitness to plead may not be sufficient to fulfil the
criteria for involuntary detention under the provisions of the

---

[138] [1967] IR 106.

[139] [1967] IR 106 at 116 *per* Ó Dálaigh CJ and at 124 *per* Walsh J.

[140] [1994] 3 IR 246 *per* Finlay CJ for the court, affirming the High Court
(O'Hanlon J) reported at [1992] 1 IR 387.

[141] [1954] 2 QB 329, see pp. 432–3 above.

Mental Treatment Act, 1945.[142] Also, the District Court has no power to order or direct committal to a psychiatric facility or that he undergo the requisite treatment. This was succinctly stated by Gannon J thus:

> No person can be committed by court order to detention in a place or institution designated for mental health treatment (or lunatic asylum as it might have been called) without a proper investigation by trial of the grounds for doing so. . . . [E]ven section 207 of the Mental Treatment Act, 1945, which extends this type of enquiry to the stage of preliminary investigation before a District [Judge], does not enable a District [Judge] to commit the person before him to detention in a mental treatment institution. . . . The power conferred on the Minister by section 13 of the 1875 Act does not authorise the admission to, or detention in, the Central Mental Hospital of a person other than a person in respect of whom a District [Judge] has made an order of remand in proceedings pending before him for the purpose of further examination, and then only for the period of the specified period of remand. Section 8 of the Criminal Justice Act 1960 does not purport to confer on the Minister power to commit to detention in the Central Mental Hospital a person who has not properly been committed to detention in prison by court order.[143]

Thus, in the absence of statutory guidance, it appears that there may be a significant issue as to the custodial disposition of an accused who meets the criteria for unfitness to be tried by reason of psychiatric disorder, short of fulfilling the criteria for involuntary civil committal, in the District Court. However, the decision of

---

[142] See Chapter 18 and *State (C) v Minister for Justice* [1967] IR 106 at 115, *per* Ó Dálaigh CJ, and at 121 *per* Walsh J.

[143] *State (Caseley) v Daly & another* (High Court, Unreported Judgment, Gannon J, 19 February 1979). To which list might be added the provisions of the Criminal Lunatics (Ireland) Act, 1838 (1 Vict c. 27), ss. 2 and 3, as saved by the Mental Treatment Act, 1945, s. 284; and the Lunatic Asylums (Ireland) Act, 1845 (8&9 Vict c. 107), s. 12, as saved by the Mental Treatment Act, 1945, s. 284.

Gannon J in *State (Caseley)* v *Daly & another*[144] suggests an alternative approach, whereby a person removed to a psychiatric facility by virtue of an order of the Minister for Justice under section 13 of the Lunatic Asylums (Ireland) Act, 1875,[145] might be dealt with under the provisions of section 207 of the Mental Treatment Act, 1945. This provides that a patient detained in a state-run psychiatric facility who is charged with an indictable offence may be dealt with by a District Judge sitting in that psychiatric facility. If the District Judge is of the opinion that the evidence given constitutes *prima facie* evidence that the patient has committed the offence and that he would, if placed on trial, be unfit to plead, he must by order certify that the patient is suitable for transfer to the Central Mental Hospital (copies of this order are sent to the Minister and to the person in charge of the relevant psychiatric facility). Where such an order is made, the patient must be retained in the relevant psychiatric facility and his detention continued. The Minister must also require the Inspector of Mental Hospitals to visit the patient and to report on his mental condition. Having considered the report, the Minister may, if he thinks fit, then by order direct and authorise the patient's transfer to the Central Mental Hospital.[146] Given that in *RT* v *Director of the*

---

[144] High Court, Unreported Judgment, Gannon J, 19 February 1979.

[145] 8&9 Vict c. 67, as saved by the Mental Treatment Act, 1945, s. 284, and as restricted by the Supreme Court in *State (C)* v *Minister for Justice* [1967] IR 106. This would also apply to the Criminal Lunatics (Ireland) Act, 1838 (1 Vict c. 27), ss 2 and 3, as saved by the Mental Treatment Act, 1945, s. 284. However, the Act of 1838 refers to "insanity" and the Act of 1875 refers to the person's being of "unsound mind", which are not synonymous with "unfitness to plead". See *State (C)* v *Minister for Justice* [1967] IR 106 at 115, *per* Ó Dálaigh CJ; and at 121 *per* Walsh J. See also Chapter 18, pp. 498–9.

[146] Whereupon the patient may be transferred at any time to the district mental hospital for the district in which he is ordinarily resident, if he is not already detained there; Mental Treatment Act, 1945, s. 207(2)(f), as inserted by the Mental Treatment Act, 1961, s. 25(1). His detention, whether continued in the original facility or in the district mental hospital for the district in which he is ordinarily resident, is regarded as detention under a chargeable (or private, as appropriate) patient reception order, effectively as a person of unsound mind (see above); Mental Treatment Act, 1945, s. 207(2)(g), as inserted by the Mental Treatment Act, 1961, s. 25(1). It is proposed that this section will be replaced by the proposals for the implementation of a new

Central Mental Hospital & others,[147] Costello J (as he then was) found that the provisions of section 207 were unconstitutional, such an approach must be considered as constitutionally impermissible.

Magistrates' Court

In England, magistrates who are satisfied as to the guilt of an accused, may make a hospital order[148] without proceeding to trial or conviction of an accused who appears unfit to plead on account of mental illness or severe mental impairment. However, the consent of persons acting on behalf of the accused is normally required. As there is no trial involved, a hospital order can be made where the offence charged is triable either summarily, or on indictment, at the election of the accused, and the accused's disability is sufficient to preclude the giving of the requisite consent to a summary trial,[149] or even where the accused elects for jury trial.[150] Where the offence is capable of being tried only on indictment, it is unclear as to whether or not such an order may be made.[151]

Thus, in the Magistrates' Court, as in the case of trials on indictment, notwithstanding that an accused is unfit to plead, proceedings effectively continue to consideration of the accused's guilt before the issue is disposed of. In Ireland, by contrast, consideration of whether or not the accused is guilty, or ought, on the information to hand, be returned for trial in a higher criminal court, or of his capacity to elect for a summary trial of an indictable

---

Mental Health Act, as suggested by the White Paper on a New Mental Health Act, para. 7.34. See also Chapter 18, pp. 491–4.

[147] [1995] 2 ILRM 354.

[148] In accordance with the provisions of the Mental Health Act, 1983, s. 37(3), replacing the previous provisions of the Mental Health Act, 1959, s. 60(2).

[149] *Lincolnshire (Kesteven) Justices, ex parte O'Connor* [1983] 1 All ER 901, [1983] 1 WLR 335, DC.

[150] *Ramsgate Justices, ex parte Kazmarek* (1984) 80 Cr App R 366, DC.

[151] See Card (1988), op. cit., para. 9.9, referring to *Ramsgate Justices, ex parte Kazmarek* (1984) 80 Cr App R 366, DC.

offence is postponed until his fitness to be tried has been determined. Such an approach is constitutionally predicated.[152]

---

[152] See above, *State (C)* v *Minister for Justice* [1967] IR 106 *per* Ó'Dálaigh CJ at 115, followed in *O'Connor* v *The Judges of the Dublin Metropolitan District* [1994] 3 IR 246 (SC) *per* Finlay CJ for the court, affirming the High Court (O'Hanlon J) reported at [1992] 1 IR 387.

Part Six

CONTROL OF THE PSYCHIATRICALLY DISORDERED

Chapter 18

CIVIL COMMITTAL

In certain circumstances, a person suffering from a psychiatric disability may be detained and treated for that disability against his will. This involves not alone depriving the patient of his liberty, but it also effectively dispenses with the patient's consent to treatment that is normally required in medical practice.[1] As it affects a constitutionally protected right,[2] any such deprivation of liberty must be in accordance with law. In Ireland, the powers and procedures for "civil"[3] committal are currently contained in the Mental Treatment Acts, 1945 and 1961,[4] and in Britain in the Mental Health Act, 1983.[5] The Act also restricts the institution of

---

[1] See T. Cooney and O. O'Neill (1996), *Psychiatric Detention and Civil Commitment in Ireland*, Delgany: Baikonur. This point has been taken up by the White Paper on a New Mental Health Act (Department of Health, 1995), Chapter 6. See also Chapter 19 below.

[2] Article 40.4 of the Constitution states: "No person shall be deprived of his liberty save in accordance with law." See, generally, Kelly (1994), op. cit.

[3] As distinct from the procedures invoked in the criminal process in relation to persons suffering a psychiatric disability charged with a criminal offence (see Chapters 16 and 17 above and pp. 498–9 below) and matters relating to wards of court (see Mental Treatment Act, 1945, s. 283). In relation to the latter, the White Paper on a New Mental Health Act, para. 10.16, proposes that wards of court should be subject to the same procedures governing admission, either as voluntary or involuntary patients, as other persons.

[4] As amended and adapted by the Health Act, 1970, and the Mental Treatment Acts (Adaptation) Order, 1971 (SI 108 of 1971). The Health (Mental Services) Act, 1981, significantly altered the provisions in relation to civil committal, but the Act was never commenced. There are proposals to amend the law significantly in relation to civil committal under the proposals for the implementation of a new Mental Health Act, as suggested by the White Paper on a New Mental Health Act.

[5] Detailed discussion of British legislation is beyond the scope of this chapter.

civil proceedings in respect of acts purporting to have been done in pursuance of the Act without the prior leave of the High Court.[6]

Whereas previously, "civil" committal was a judicial process, involving the arrest and conveying of a patient to appear before two magistrates (subsequently peace commissioners) who then ordered — or refused to order — the patient's committal[7] on foot of a doctor's certificate, the Act of 1945 relegated the issue solely to a matter of clinical decision-making.[8]

The legislation specifies the classes of patients who may be admitted for psychiatric treatment and to whom the Acts apply: voluntary patients, temporary patients and persons of "unsound mind". Somewhat different procedural approaches are applied to "chargeable patients"[9] and patients admitted to private institutions or as private patients in a state-run institution. The description

---

[6] Mental Treatment Act, 1945, s. 260, when the court must be satisfied that "there are substantial grounds for contending that the person against whom the proceedings are to be brought acted in bad faith or without reasonable care". See, for example, *Murphy v Greene* [1990] 2 IR 566 (SC); *O'Reilly v Moroney & another* [1992] 2 IR 145 (HC) (Murphy J) affirmed *O'Reilly v Moroney & another* (Supreme Court, Unreported Judgment, 16 November 1993) (Blayney diss); and *Bailey v Gallagher* (Supreme Court, Unreported Judgment, 23 May 1996) The same standard applies to the substantive proceedings, if leave is granted. The White Paper on a New Mental Health Act (Department of Health, July 1995), para 10.29, proposes a similar restriction, with substitution of "reasonable" for "substantial". See: J. Spellman (1998), "Section 260 of the Mental Treatment Act 1945 Reviewed", *Medico-Legal Journal of Ireland*, Vol. 4, No. 1, pp. 20–4.

[7] See, for example, *The State (at the prosecution of Kitty Power) v William Jones and Patrick J Murray, Peace Commissioners for the City and County of Waterford* [1944] IR 68, where the prosecutrix sought an order of certiorari to quash a finding by two peace commissioners that she was a dangerous lunatic, and the consequential committal warrant, pursuant to the provisions of the Lunacy (Ireland) Act, 1867, s. 10, now repealed.

[8] The history is reviewed in *SC v Smith & others* (High Court, Unreported Judgment, Budd J, 27 and 31 July 1995). See also M. Finnane (1981), *Insanity and the Insane in Post-famine Ireland*, London: Croom Helm.

[9] Originally, a patient who was receiving mental hospital assistance and who was unable to provide the whole of the cost of such assistance, Mental Treatment Act, 1945, s. 3. Now classified as an "eligible" patient, meaning a person with full or limited eligibility within the meaning of the Health Act, 1970, ss. 45 and 46; see Mental Health Act, 1945, s. 3, as amended by the Health Act, 1970, s. 81.

that follows sets out the procedures in relation to chargeable patients only, with references to the different procedural approach in respect of private patients where they apply. It is also worth noting that there are defined geographical limits within which the powers of recommendation, reception and detention may be exercised.

VOLUNTARY PATIENTS

Application

In order to have a person admitted to a psychiatric hospital[10] as a "voluntary patient" and as a chargeable patient,[11] an application is made[12] to the person in charge of the psychiatric institution[13] to have the patient received in the hospital as a voluntary and chargeable patient.[14] Such an application may only be made by the parents or guardian of a patient, where the patient is aged less than 16 years, or the patient himself.[15] Where the patient is less than 16 years, the application must be accompanied by the

---

[10] In an approved institution maintained by the local mental hospital authority, the Health Board or in an approved institution in which voluntary patients are received pursuant to an arrangement made between the local mental hospital authority and another authority pursuant to the provisions of the Health Act, 1970, s. 26. Generally, it is the "district mental hospital" for the mental hospital district in which the patient ordinarily resides.

[11] As distinct from a private patient; see fn 9 above.

[12] In the prescribed form, known colloquially as the "blue form" — as distinct from the "white form" (person of unsound mind — see p. 469 below) and the "pink form" (temporary patients — see p. 462 below). It is proposed that such provisions will no longer apply upon the implementation of a new Mental Health Act, as suggested by the White Paper on a New Mental Health Act, para. 3.32.

[13] Such powers are also exercisable by any other medical officer authorised in that capacity by the authority maintaining the institution, now the local health board. See Mental Treatment Act, 1953, s. 3.

[14] Mental Treatment Act, 1945, s. 190(1) as adapted by the Mental Treatment Acts (Adaptation) Order, 1971 (SI 108 of 1971). An application may similarly be made for a patient to be received in an approved institution as a voluntary private patient; see Mental Treatment Act, 1945, s. 191(1).

[15] Mental Treatment Act, 1945, ss. 190(2) and 191(2) (private patients). See also the provisions of the Non-Fatal Offences Against the Person Act, 1997, s. 23.

recommendation of a medical practitioner[16] stating that he has examined the patient on a specified date not earlier than seven days before the date of the application and is of the opinion that he will benefit by the proposed reception.[17]

Reception and Treatment

Upon the making of the application, the patient — whether a private or a non-private patient — may be received into the hospital as a voluntary patient (if there is accommodation for him in the hospital that is not required for a person of unsound mind).[18] He may be treated there and, on his recovery, discharged.[19]

---

[16] Not being one who is disqualified in relation to the patient, i.e. where he is interested in the payments (if any) to be made on account of the taking care of the person, or if he is the spouse, parent, step-parent or parent-in-law, child, step-child or child-in-law, sibling, step-sibling or sibling-in-law, or guardian or trustee of the patient, or if he is a medical officer of a district mental hospital (Mental Treatment Act, 1945, s. 190(5), as inserted by the Mental Treatment Act, 1961, s. 19(2)). Although restrictions are specified in relation to the medical practitioners who may recommend or certify in respect of a non-private patient and certify in respect of a private patient (see below), unusually, no restrictions as to who may make a recommendation for reception as a voluntary patient are set out in relation to private patients.

[17] Mental Treatment Act, 1945, s. 190(3) as amended by the Mental Treatment Act, 1961, s. 19(1), and s. 191 as amended by the Mental Treatment Act, 1961, s. 20 (private patients). Where a request for a recommendation is made to the authorised medical officer (which provision has no relevance to private patients), essentially, the medical officer of the patient's dispensary district, or of the nearest district, the Act requires that he *shall* examine the patient and give the recommendation if he is of the opinion that the patient will benefit by the proposed reception (Mental Treatment Act, 1945, s. 190(4), as inserted by the Mental Treatment Act, 1961, s. 19(2)). However, the Health Act, 1970, s. 81, repealed all references to an "authorised medical officer". Presuming that this role was taken over by a medical practitioner for whose services the patient is eligible, this requirement is now imposed upon such medical practitioners. See fn 74 below.

[18] See p. 469 below.

[19] Mental Treatment Act, 1945, s. 192, as adapted by the Mental Treatment Acts (Adaptation) Order, 1971 (SI 108 of 1971). The patient having been received as a voluntary chargeable patient, the reception is valid (as is the application upon which it was based), notwithstanding that it is ascertained that the patient was not ordinarily resident in the relevant area that the institution served, as required by the Mental Treatment Act, 1945, s. 192, as

Discharge[20]

A patient (not less than 16 years of age) who is being treated in an approved institution as a voluntary patient must give written notice to the person in charge of the institution[21] that he wishes to leave the institution not earlier than 72 hours from the giving of the notice. He is then entitled, and must be allowed, to leave on or at any time after the expiration of that period.[22]

Where a voluntary patient becomes mentally incapable of expressing himself as willing or not willing to remain in the approved institution, he must be discharged, within 28 days of becoming incapable, into the custody of such person as the person in charge of the institution approves of — unless, however, within that period, he becomes capable of expressing himself or a reception[23] order relating to him is obtained.[24]

---

amended by the Mental Treatment Act, 1961, s. 21. This amended provision has no relevance to private patients.

[20] These provisions apply to both private and non-private patients.

[21] Usually the consultant psychiatrist in charge, but see also fn 13 above.

[22] It is proposed that this provision will be abolished upon the implementation of a New Mental Health Act, as suggested by the White Paper on a New Mental Health Act (Department of Health, 1995), para. 3.32.

[23] For, example, to have him received as a temporary patient or as a patient of unsound mind; see pp. 462–90 below.

[24] Mental Treatment Act, 1945, s. 195. The provisions, whereby notice of all receptions, discharges and deaths of voluntary patients had to be given to the Minister within three clear days after the occurrence of the relevant event, and whereby the Minister had to keep a register of all voluntary patients in approved institutions, including the particulars in relation to each such patient pursuant to the provisions of the Mental Treatment Act, 1945, ss. 197 and 198, were repealed by the Mental Treatment Act, 1961, s. 42. It is proposed that nurses will have legal authority to hold a voluntary patient for up to six hours within which time the patient must be examined by a medical practitioner and that a consultant psychiatrist may hold such a patient for a period of 48 hours, within which the procedures for detention must be completed upon the implementation of a new Mental Health Act, as suggested by the White Paper on a New Mental Health Act, para. 3.34.

TEMPORARY PATIENTS

Application

In order to have a person admitted to a psychiatric hospital[25] and detained there as a "temporary patient" and as a chargeable patient,[26] an application is made[27] to the person in charge of the psychiatric institution[28] to have the patient received and detained in the hospital as a temporary and chargeable patient.[29]

The applicant may be the patient's spouse[30] or relative[31] (or the appropriate community welfare officer[32] at the request of the

---

[25] In an approved institution maintained by the local mental hospital authority, or in an approved institution in which temporary patients are received pursuant to an arrangement made between the local mental hospital authority and another authority. Generally, it is the "district mental hospital" for the relevant health board area in which the patient ordinarily resides. Mental Treatment Act, 1945, s. 184(1), as adapted by the Mental Treatment Acts (Adaptation) Order, 1971 (SI 108 of 1971). However, in cases of urgency and where a patient is living in a different area, or if his usual place of abode cannot be readily ascertained, the provisions of that Act nevertheless apply by virtue of the Mental Treatment Act, 1953, s. 4, as adapted by the Mental Treatment Acts (Adaptation) Order, 1971 (SI 108 of 1971).

[26] As distinct from a private patient; see above at fn 9.

[27] In the prescribed form, known colloquially as the "pink form" — as distinct from the "white form" (person of unsound mind — see p. 469 below) and the "blue form" (voluntary patients — see 459 above).

[28] See fn 13 above.

[29] Mental Treatment Act, 1945, s. 184(1) as adapted by the Mental Treatment Acts (Adaptation) Order, 1971 (SI 108 of 1971) (a temporary chargeable patient reception order). An application may similarly be made for a patient to be detained and received in an approved institution as a temporary private patient (Mental Treatment Act, 1945, s. 185(1)) (a temporary private patient reception order).

[30] The White Paper on a New Mental Health Act, para. 3.13, proposes that spouses in dispute will be disqualified from making an application in respect of each other. In this regard, *Murphy* v *Greene* [1990] 2 IR 566 (SC); *O'Reilly* v *Moroney & another* [1992] 2 IR 145 (HC) (Murphy J) affirmed *O'Reilly* v *Moroney & another* (Supreme Court, Unreported Judgment, 16 November 1993) (Blayney *diss*), and *Bailey* v *Gallagher* (Supreme Court, Unreported Judgment, 23 May 1996) (all section 260 applications) are instructive.

[31] A relative is a lineal ancestor or a lineal descendant or a lineal descendant of an ancestor not more remote than a great-grandparent (Mental Treatment Act, 1945, s. 3).

spouse or relative)[33] and must in all cases be at least 21 years of age.[34] Where any other such person applies for a recommendation, the application must contain a statement of the reasons why it was not made by the spouse or relative (or community welfare officer at the request of the spouse or relative), of the connection of the applicant with the patient, and of the circumstances in which the application is made.[35]

Examination

The application must be accompanied by a certificate of a medical practitioner[36] certifying that he has examined[37] the patient on a

---

[32] Of the local health board. Formerly the "assistance officer"; see Mental Treatment Act, 1945, s. 3, as amended by the Health Act, 1970, s. 81, and as adapted by the Mental Treatment Acts (Adaptation) Order, 1971 (SI 108 of 1971).

[33] Mental Treatment Act, 1945, s. 184(2). The community welfare officer has no role in respect of private patients (see s. 185(2)). Otherwise, the provisions are identical. These categories will be extended upon implementation of a new Mental Health Act, as suggested by the White Paper on a New Mental Health Act, para. 3.10, to include authorised officers of a health board and, in certain circumstances, members of the Garda Síochána.

[34] Mental Treatment Act, 1945, ss. 184(3A), as inserted by the Mental Treatment Act, 1961, s. 16(1), and 185(3A) as inserted by the Mental Treatment Act, 1961, s. 17(1) (private patients). Unlike in the case of applications to have a person received and detained as a person of unsound mind (see below), there is no requirement that the applicant must have seen the patient within 14 days before the making of the application. However, the White Paper on a New Mental Health Act, para. 3.11 proposes that the applicant must be at least 18 years of age and must have had contact with the person within the previous two days before the application is made.

[35] Mental Treatment Act, 1945, ss. 184(3) and 185(3) (private patients).

[36] Not being one who is disqualified in relation to the patient, i.e. where he is interested in the payments (if any) to be made on account of the taking care of the person, or if he is the spouse, parent, step-parent or parent-in-law, child, step-child or child-in-law, sibling, step-sibling or sibling-in-law, or guardian or trustee of the patient, or if he is a medical officer of a district mental hospital (Mental Treatment Act, 1945, s. 184(7), as inserted by the Mental Treatment Act, 1961, s. 16(3)). Restrictions also apply in relation to the medical practitioners who may certify in respect of a private patient. Thus, a certificate may not be given in respect of a private patient by a medical practitioner who is in charge of the approved institution into which the patient is to be received, or who is the employee of such a person, or who has an interest in the institution (Mental Treatment Act, 1945, s. 185(5)).

specified date not earlier than seven days[38] before the date of the application and that he is of the opinion either that the patient:

- Is suffering from mental illness, and requires for his recovery not more than six months suitable treatment, and is unfit on account of his mental state for treatment as a voluntary patient, or

- Is an addict, and requires for his recovery at least six months' preventive and curative treatment.[39]

The Making of the Order

The person to whom the application is made, having considered the application and the accompanying certificate of the medical

---

[37] As to what constitutes an examination for the purposes of committal, see *O'Reilly* v *Moroney* (Supreme Court, Unreported Judgment, 16 November 1993), affirming the High Court's refusal (Murphy J) (reported at [1992] 2 IR 145) to grant leave to initiate proceedings pursuant to s. 260 of the Act. However, see the vigorous dissent of Blayney J. It is proposed that this will remain a matter of clinical discretion upon the implementation of a new Mental Health Act, as suggested by the White Paper on a New Mental Health Act (Department of Health, 1995), para. 3.19.

[38] To be reduced to two days upon the implementation of a new Mental Health Act, as suggested by the White Paper on a New Mental Health Act (Department of Health, 1995), para. 3.19.

[39] Mental Treatment Act, 1945, s. 184(4), as amended by the Mental Treatment Act, 1961, s. 16(2). Where a request for a certificate is made, the Act requires that he *shall* examine the patient and give the certificate if he is of the opinion specified (Mental Treatment Act, 1945, s. 184(6), as inserted by the Mental Treatment Act, 1961, s. 16(3)). See also the Health Act, 1970, s. 81, deleting references to the "authorised medical officer". Where the patient is a private patient, the certificate must be signed by two medical practitioners certifying that each of them has examined separately the patient and that each is of the specified opinion (Mental Treatment Act, 1945, s. 185(4)). Otherwise, the provisions in respect of chargeable and private patients are identical. Upon the implementation of a new Mental Health Act, as suggested by the White Paper on a New Mental Health Act, para. 3.17, the recommendation of only one medical practitioner will be required. Furthermore, addiction *per se* will no longer be a ground for involuntary committal, para. 2.20. Personality disorder and social deviance will also be excluded (paras. 2.18 and 2.19) and other definitional changes implemented in relation to mental illness, significant mental handicap and severe dementia (para. 2.13).

practitioner, may, if he so thinks proper, make an order[40] to have the patient received and detained[41] as a temporary patient in his institution.[42]

The Conveyance to Hospital

Once the order has been made (whether in respect of a private patient or not), the applicant, or any person authorised by him may, not later than seven days after the date on which the order was made, take the patient and convey him to the institution named in the order.[43] In this regard, the hospital authority[44] may co-operate

---

[40] The order having been made is valid (as is the application upon which it was based) notwithstanding that it is ascertained that the patient was not ordinarily resident in the area that the relevant institution serves, as required by the Mental Treatment Act, 1945, s. 184(8), as inserted by the Mental Treatment Act, 1961, s. 16(3), as adapted by the Mental Treatment Acts (Adaptation) Order, 1971 (SI 108 of 1971). This provision has no relevance to private patients. The authority of a medical practitioner to detain a patient must be granted by the relevant authority under the provisions of the Mental Treatment Act, 1953, s.3 (see fn 13 above).

[41] The powers will only be exercisable by a consultant psychiatrist, specially approved for that purpose by his employing authority, under the proposals for the implementation of a new Mental Health Act, as suggested by the White Paper on a New Mental Health Act, para. 3.25.

[42] Mental Treatment Act, 1945, s. 184(5). Where the patient is a private patient, the order is made by the person in charge of the approved institution if he is a medical practitioner; in any other case, it is made by the chief medical officer of the approved institution or the patient's medical attendant, where the approved institution is for the reception of one person only (Mental Treatment Act, 1945, s. 185(6), as amended by the Mental Treatment Act, 1961, s. 17(2)). See also Mental Treatment Act, 1953, s. 3.

[43] Mental Treatment Act, 1945, s. 186 (1)(a). The issue of a "spent" certificate arose in an application under s. 260 of the Act (see below), in *Bailey* v *Gallagher* (Supreme Court, Unreported Judgment, 23 May 1996) (leave granted to institute proceedings). However, there is no provision in the Act for the course of action undertaken by the Gardaí in *Bailey*, although it may not have been an uncommon procedure in some parts of the country. The decision of the Supreme Court does not dwell on the point. Nor is it considered in *Murphy* v *Greene* [1990] 2 IR 566.

[44] Effectively the consultant psychiatrist in charge of the hospital.

with the applicant, or with any relative or guardian of the patient, in making arrangements for his removal to hospital.[45]

However, where, on foot of an application, a medical certificate has been given (whether in respect of a private patient or not), the applicant, or any person authorised by him may, not later than seven days after the date on which the patient was examined,[46] take the patient and convey him to the institution in which it is proposed to have him received and detained. Thereupon, the person in charge of the institution (his staff, or any other medical officer of the institution) may receive and take charge of the patient and detain him for a period of 12 hours, during which time the order must either be made or refused.[47] Thus, in practice, the patient frequently accompanies the applicant to the psychiatric institution where he or she may be detained and examined before the reception order is made. However, before the patient may be taken and conveyed to hospital, the applicant must inform the patient of the nature of the medical certificate and of the fact that a second medical opinion may be requested. If a second opinion is requested, the patient may not be conveyed to hospital unless the second opinion, in writing, agrees with that expressed in the medical certificate.[48]

---

[45] Mental Treatment Act, 1945, s. 188. Note that this particular provision does not apply to private patients. New provisions will also be implemented in respect of such arrangements, including, where necessary, the obtaining of a District Court order under the proposals for the implementation of a new Mental Health Act, as suggested by the White Paper on a New Mental Health Act, paras. 3.23 and 3.24.

[46] Where, in the case of a private patient, two examinations were carried out, the relevant date is the date of the earlier examination (if different). In all other cases, it is the date as recited on the certificate (Mental Treatment Act, 1953, s. 5(2)).

[47] Mental Treatment Act, 1953, s. 5. In such circumstances, the provisions in relation to taking a patient to hospital upon the making of an order do not apply. The White Paper on a New Mental Health Act para. 3.27 proposes that such provisions should continue.

[48] Mental Treatment Act, 1953, s. 5(3). A medical practitioner who gives the second opinion must not be within the degrees of relationship to the patient prohibited in regard to any patient in respect of whom a certificate is sought (see fn 16 above).

Reception and Detention

Upon the making of the order, the patient may be received, taken charge of, detained "until the expiration of a period of six months[49] from the date on which the order is made or his earlier removal[50] or discharge by proper authority[51] or death", and retaken, in the event of his escape, within 28 days — but not after the expiration of the six-month period from the date of the making of the order — and again detained for that period by:

- The person in charge of the approved institution mentioned in the relevant reception order,

- The officers, assistants and servants of that person, and

- Any medical officer of the approved institution.[52]

Extension of Detention[53]

Where the chief medical officer[54] of an approved institution is of the opinion that a person detained as a temporary patient will not

---

[49] It is proposed that this period will be limited to 28 days under the proposals for implementation of a new Mental Health Act, as suggested by the White Paper on a New Mental Health Act, para. 4.9.

[50] See below, pp. 490–8.

[51] While there is no definition of "proper authority" contained in the Act, the persons vested by the Act with the power to discharge a person, who is the subject of a chargeable patient reception order, are the resident medical superintendent of the institution in which he/she is detained and the Minister (in the circumstances considered in ss. 221 and 222 of the Act). See pp. 496–8 below.

[52] Mental Treatment Act, 1945, s. 186. This applies to both private and non-private patients. These provisions will remain essentially unchanged upon the implementation of a new Mental Health Act, as suggested by the White Paper on a New Mental Health Act, para. 3. 39.

[53] All of these provisions apply to both private and non-private patients. These provisions will be significantly amended, and be subject to review by a Mental Health Review Board under the proposals for the implementation of a new Mental Health Act, as suggested by the White Paper on a New Mental Health Act, para. 4.9.

[54] See Mental Treatment Act, 1953, s. 3. Where the relevant approved institution consists of premises for the reception of one person only, the powers

have recovered on the expiration of the six months period for which the patient may be detained, that period may be extended. Thus, a series of endorsements on the order may extend the original period by periods, none of which must exceed six months and the aggregate of which must not exceed 18 months.[55]

Upon the endorsement of the order, the chief medical officer must give the patient, and the applicant for the reception order, a notice stating the particulars of the endorsement and that the patient or the applicant may send an objection to the extension to the Inspector of Mental Hospitals.[56] On receipt of such an objection, the Inspector of Mental Hospitals must require of the chief medical officer to give him a full report on the patient, and the chief medical officer must forthwith comply. Having considered that report, the Inspector of Mental Hospitals must then take such steps as he considers necessary for ascertaining whether or not the impugned detention should be continued.[57]

---

and duties fall on the patient's medical attendant (Mental Treatment Act, 1945, s. 189(2)).

[55] Mental Treatment Act, 1945, s. 189(1), as amended by the Mental Treatment Act, 1961, s. 18. However, where the patient is an addict, each extension must be for less than six months and the aggregate period is limited to six months. See, for example, the difficulties that arose, the patient having been transferred (see below), in *SC* v *Smith & others* (Supreme Court, Unreported Judgment, 14 July 1994) *per* Blayney J for the unanimous court.

[56] In this regard, the comments of Budd J in *SC* v *Smith & others* (High Court, Unreported Judgment, 27 and 31 July 1995) (below) in the context of considering the constitutionality of the Mental Treatment Act, 1945, s. 172 (detention of a person of unsound mind), and how review procedures might operate, seem apposite. Thus, he stated:

> "Bearing in mind that the applicant was diagnosed prior to his present treatment as being subject to mental illness, one might wonder, even if there was provision in the Mental Treatment Act, 1945, as amended, for ensuring that the safeguards provided by the Act are brought to the attention of the patient (which there is not), whether the patient would have the literacy or competency to activate any of the safeguarding procedures; and whether any of his kith or kin would have the desire or the capacity to initiate such a process on the patient's behalf."

[57] Mental Treatment Act, 1945, s. 189(1), as amended by the Mental Treatment Act, 1961, s. 18.

PERSONS OF UNSOUND MIND[58]

Application[59]

In order to have a person admitted to a psychiatric hospital[60] and detained there as a "person of unsound mind" (PUM) and as a chargeable patient,[61] an application, which must be accompanied by a statement of particulars in relation to the patient,[62] is made[63] to a registered medical practitioner[64] for a recommendation[65] that the patient be received and detained in the hospital as a person of unsound mind.[66]

---

[58] This category of involuntary patient will be abolished by the implementation of the proposals for a new Mental Health Act, as suggested by the White Paper on a New Mental Health Act (Department of Health, 1995).

[59] Provision is also made for application by members of the Garda Síochána (s. 165), and the local community welfare officer (s. 166) (see fn 32 above).

[60] Generally, it is the "district mental hospital" for the relevant health board area in which the patient ordinarily resides. Mental Treatment Act, 1945, s. 162(1), as adapted by the Mental Treatment Acts (Adaptation) Order, 1971 (SI 108 of 1971).

[61] A different procedure is prescribed where the patient is to be received and detained in a private institution, an authorised institution (under the Act) or a private charitable institution or as a private patient in a district mental hospital. See Mental Treatment Act, 1945, Part XIV, Chapter II, s. 177(1) and (2). Essentially, it provides for a one-step rather than a two-step admission process (see below).

[62] Mental Treatment Act, 1945, ss. 162(5) and 177(6) (private patients).

[63] In the prescribed form, known colloquially as the "white form" — as distinct from the "pink form" (temporary patients — see p. 462 above) and the "blue form" (voluntary patients — see p. 459 above).

[64] Not being one who is disqualified in relation to the patient, i.e. where he is interested in the payments (if any) to be made on account of the taking care of the person, or if he is the spouse, parent, step-parent or parent-in-law, child, step-child or child-in-law, sibling, step-sibling or sibling-in-law, or guardian or trustee of the patient, or if he is a medical officer of a district mental hospital (Mental Treatment Act, 1945, s. 162(6), as inserted by the Mental Treatment Act, 1961, s. 6(1)). Similar restrictions apply in respect of the medical practitioners who may sign a private patient reception order (see below).

[65] In the case of private patients, the application is for a reception order — as distinct from a recommendation (Mental Treatment Act, 1945, s. 177(1) and (2)).

[66] Pursuant to the provisions of the Mental Treatment Act, 1945, s. 162(1), as amended by the Mental Treatment Act, 1961, s. 6.

As in the case of an application for a temporary order, the applicant may be the patient's spouse[67] or relative[68] (or the appropriate community welfare officer at the request of the spouse or relative)[69] and must in all cases be at least 21 years of age. Furthermore, the applicant must have seen the patient within 14 days before making the application.[70] Where any other such person applies for a recommendation, the application must contain a statement of the reasons why it was not made by the spouse or relative (or community welfare officer at the request of the spouse or relative), of the connection of the applicant with the patient, and of the circumstances in which the application is made.[71]

Examination

Before a medical practitioner may make a recommendation that a patient be received in a psychiatric hospital and detained there as a person of unsound mind, he must first have examined[72] him.[73] If

---

[67] See fn 30 above in respect of changes proposed in this regard by the White Paper on a New Mental Health Act (Department of Health, 1995).

[68] A relative is a lineal ancestor or a lineal descendant or a lineal descendant of an ancestor not more remote than a great-grandparent (Mental Treatment Act, 1945, s. 3).

[69] Mental Treatment Act, 1945, s. 162(2). The community welfare officer (see fn 32, above) has no role in respect of private patients; see s. 177(3). Otherwise, the provisions are identical.

[70] Mental Treatment Act, 1945, ss. 162(4) and 177(5) (private patients). See fn 38 above in relation to the changes proposed in this regard by the White Paper on a New Mental Health Act.

[71] Mental Treatment Act, 1945, ss. 162(3) and 177(4).

[72] As to what constitutes an examination for the purposes of committal, see *O'Reilly* v *Moroney* (Supreme Court, Unreported Judgment, 16 November 1993) affirming the High Court's refusal (Murphy J) (reported at [1992] 2 IR 145) to grant leave to initiate proceedings pursuant to s. 260 of the Act. However, see the vigorous dissent of Blayney J. The White Paper on a New Mental Health Act (Department of Health, 1995), para. 3.19, proposes that what constitutes an "examination" should be left as a matter of professional discretion.

[73] Where the application is in respect of a private patient, a different procedure applies. Thus, the medical practitioner to whom the application is made must arrange with another medical practitioner for two separate examinations of the patient, one by each of them. If they are each separately satisfied that it is proper to make the order — a private patient reception order —

he has not already seen the patient within the previous 24 hours, the medical practitioner may, within 24 hours after receipt of the application, visit and examine him before making such a recommendation.[74] In any case, however, where he is not satisfied that it is proper to make the recommendation, he must refuse the application.[75] Where such an application is refused, the applicant, in any further application in respect of that patient, must disclose the circumstances of the refusal, insofar as he is aware of them, to the medical practitioner to whom the application is made.[76]

Special Applications[77]

By Gardaí

Where a member of the Garda Síochána is of the opinion that it is necessary that a person believed to be of unsound mind should, for the public safety or the safety of the person himself, be placed forthwith under care and control, he may take him into custody

---

they must make it forthwith in the prescribed form. In all other cases, they must refuse to make the order (Mental Treatment Act, 1945, s. 178(1)).

[74] With the deletion of references to the "authorised medical officer" (Mental Treatment Act, 1945, s. 3, as amended by the Health Act, 1970, s. 81) it is unclear if these provisions have mandatory force. However, given the seriousness of the nature of the application, a failure to examine a patient could be regarded as acting without reasonable care for the purposes of a section 260 application (see fn 6 above). The White Paper on a New Mental Health Act (Department of Health, 1995), para. 3.19 proposes that the time within which the medical practitioner must have seen the patient prior to the making of the application will be two days (see fn 38 above). As to examination, see fn 72 above.

[75] Mental Treatment Act, 1945, s. 163(1), as amended by the Mental Treatment Act, 1961, s. 7.

[76] Mental Treatment Act, 1945, s. 164(1), as amended by the Mental Treatment Act, 1961, s. 8. Failure to comply is an offence for which, on summary conviction thereof, a fine is prescribed (s. 164(2)). Similar provisions apply in respect of a refusal in respect of private patients (s. 180).

[77] These provisions have no relevance in relation to private patients. A similar procedure is contemplated for involuntary admission in certain circumstances by the White Paper on a New Mental Health Act (Department of Health, 1995), para. 3.12.

and remove him to a Garda station.[78] If the garda has reasonable grounds for believing the patient is in any house or premises, he may enter that house or premises to take him into custody.[79] Once the patient has been removed, the garda must apply to a medical practitioner[80] for a recommendation for the patient's reception and detention as a person of unsound mind in a psychiatric hospital.[81] Upon application being made, the medical practitioner may forthwith examine the patient.[82] If he is satisfied that it is proper to make the recommendation, he may so make it in the prescribed form.[83] In all other cases, he must refuse the application.[84]

In *In re Philip Clarke*,[85] an order of *habeas corpus* was sought by the prosecutor who had been detained under this provision. In essence, his claim was that he had been unlawfully detained since there had been no judicial determination of his case between the time of his arrest and the time of his detention in the psychiatric hospital. In the Divisional High Court, Gavan Duffy P (Davitt and Dixon JJ agreeing) stated:

---

[78] However, the section only refers to persons who are not already under care and control. It was held to have been improperly invoked in *State (C) v Minister for Justice* [1967] IR 106 at 124–125 *per* Walsh J, where he stated: "[It] does not contemplate . . . interference with the process of the court; nor does it contemplate that it should be used in respect of persons who are in fact under care and control."

[79] Mental Treatment Act, 1945, s. 165(1), as amended by the Mental Treatment Act, 1961, s. 9(1).

[80] Not being a medical practitioner disqualified in relation to the patient; see above (Mental Treatment Act, 1945, s. 165(5), as inserted by the Mental Treatment Act, 1961, s. 9(4)).

[81] Mental Treatment Act, 1945, s. 165(2), as adapted by the Mental Treatment Acts (Adaptation) Order, 1971 (SI 108 of 1971).

[82] Where he is the authorised medical officer; essentially, the medical officer of the patient's dispensary district, or of the nearest district, the Act requires that he *shall* forthwith examine the patient. However, see fn 74 above.

[83] Whereupon, the appropriate community welfare officer (see fn 32, above) is deemed to be the applicant for the recommendation (Mental Treatment Act, 1945, s. 165(4)).

[84] Mental Treatment Act, 1945, s. 165, as amended by the Mental Treatment Act, 1961, s. 9.

[85] [1950] IR 235.

Section 165 of the Act of 1945 empowers a Garda Síochána, as a first step, to be followed by two separate medical examinations, to arrest a person believed to be of unsound mind, if he thinks it necessary for the public safety or the safety of the person himself. That seems to be a necessary and proper power for an emergency and the dual medical examination constitutes a reasonable safeguard. The attack here is really an attack on the method of procedure, replacing that under the former law, which, though a district justice or a peace commissioner intervened, was necessarily summary, where a dangerous lunatic or idiot was concerned; and I think the new procedure is an improvement.[86]

In the Supreme Court, O'Byrne J for the court said:

It was conceded that the Constitution does not prohibit all interference, by legislation, with the right of the individual to personal liberty. The main argument, on behalf of the appellant, against the validity of the section, was based upon the absence of any judicial intervention or determination between the arrest of the person alleged to be of unsound mind and his subsequent detention under a reception order.

The impugned legislation is of a paternal character, clearly intended for the care and custody of persons suspected to be suffering from mental infirmity and for the safety and well being of the public generally. The existence of mental infirmity is too widespread to be overlooked, and was, no doubt, present to the minds of the draughtsmen when it was proclaimed in Article 40.1 of the Constitution that, though all citizens, as human beings, are to be held equal before the law, the State may, nevertheless, in its enactments, have due regard to differences of capacity, physical and moral, and of social function. We do not see how the common good would be promoted or the dignity and freedom of the individual assured by allowing persons, alleged

---

[86] [1950] IR 235 at 237.

to be suffering from such infirmity, to remain at large to the possible danger of themselves and others.

The section is carefully drafted so as to ensure that the person, alleged to be of unsound mind, shall be brought before, and examined by, responsible medical officers with the least possible delay. This seems to us to satisfy every reasonable requirement, and we have not been satisfied, and do not consider that the Constitution requires, that there should be a judicial enquiry or determination before such a person can be placed and detained in a mental hospital.

The section cannot, in our opinion, be construed as an attack upon the personal rights of the citizen. On the contrary, it seems to us to be designed for the protection of the citizen and for the promotion of the common good.

In our opinion, the section in question is not repugnant to either the letter or spirit of the Constitution and, accordingly, we are of opinion that this ground of appeal fails.[87]

By Community Welfare Officers

Similar provisions apply where the appropriate community welfare officer is informed or knows that a patient believed to be of unsound mind is not being properly cared for. Thus, where the patient

1. Is not under proper care or control, or

2. Is neglected or cruelly treated by any relative or other person in whose care or charge he is,

---

[87] [1950] IR 235 at 247. Although the Mental Treatment Act, 1945, s. 165, was subsequently amended by the Mental Treatment Act, 1961, s. 9, the amendments were largely procedural and of no relevance to the point argued on the issue of a lack of a judicial determination prior to detention. Thus, the decision in *Clarke* stands. There are only the vaguest similarities with the provisions of the Lunacy Ireland Act, 1867, s. 10, above. *Clarke* was referred to in *People (DPP)* v *Gallagher* [1991] ILRM 339 (SC), by way of analogy with the power of the executive under the Trial of Lunatics Act, 1883, s. 2 (see Chapter 16), and effectively approved in *SC* v *Smith & others* (Supreme Court, Unreported Judgment, 31 July 1996).

the community welfare officer must apply to a medical practitioner for a recommendation for the reception and detention of the patient, as a person of unsound mind, in a psychiatric hospital.[88] Where the patient is of no fixed abode, upon the matter being reported to the Gardaí, the patient may be taken into custody by the Gardaí and removed to a Garda station for the purpose of his examination by the medical practitioner.[89]

The Recommendation

The recommendation[90] of the medical practitioner must:

1. State the date of his examination of the patient and be signed,[91] either on the date of the receipt of the application (where the examination took place before the date of the application) or, in any other case, on the date of the examination;[92]

2. Contain a certificate that the patient is of unsound mind, is a proper person to be taken charge of and detained under care and treatment, and is unlikely to recover within six months from the date of the examination;

---

[88] Mental Treatment Act, 1945, s. 166(1), as adapted by the Mental Treatment Acts (Adaptation) Order, 1971 (SI 108 of 1971).

[89] Obstruction of either the medical practitioner or the community welfare officer in the execution of their duties is an offence for which, on summary conviction, a fine is prescribed (Mental Treatment Act, 1945, s. 166, as amended by the Mental Treatment Act, 1961, s. 10).

[90] In the case of private patients it is an actual reception order which is made (see p. 477 below).

[91] In the case of private patients, the reception order must not be signed by the applicant or any of the specified relatives of the applicant or patient, his guardian, trustee, partner or assistant (Mental Treatment Act, 1945, s. 178(2)) and neither of the medical practitioners signing the order may be within the specified degrees of relationship, or guardian, trustee, partner or assistant of the other (Mental Treatment Act, 1945, s. 178 (2)(aa), as inserted by the Mental Treatment Act, 1961, s. 15. Otherwise the provisions in respect of private patients apply *mutatis mutandi* to those in respect of a recommendation for chargeable patients.

[92] A private patient reception order may not be made after the seventh day after the day on which it is applied for (Mental Treatment Act, 1945, s. 178(2)(e)).

3. Contain a statement of the facts upon which the medical prac-
    titioner has formed his opinion that the person is a person of
    unsound mind, distinguishing facts observed by himself and
    facts communicated by others.[93]

In this regard, given the advances in the understanding of the
aetiology and pathophysiology of psychiatric disorder since 1945,
and given the treatment advances represented by modern psycho-
pharmacotherapy, it must be questionable as to whether a recommendation could ever *bona fide* be given by a medical
practitioner in respect of any patient, on an initial application, for
him/her to be detained as a person of unsound mind. Given that
patients detained as temporary patients only occasionally have
their periods of detention extended, it hardly seems justifiable
that provision still remains for the indefinite detention of a patient outside of the setting of a psychiatric facility.[94]

The Conveyance to Hospital

When the recommendation for reception has been made, the applicant, or any person authorised by him, may take the patient
and convey him to the hospital mentioned in the recommendation.[95] In this regard, the hospital authority may co-operate with
the applicant, or with any relative or guardian of the patient, in
making arrangements for his removal to hospital.[96]

In cases where the medical practitioner making the recommendation certifies that the case is one in which an escort is required to ensure the safe conveyance of the patient to hospital, the

---

[93] Mental Treatment Act, 1945, s. 163(2), as amended by the Mental Treatment Act, 1961, s. 7.

[94] See White Paper on a New Mental Health Act, para. 4.3.

[95] Mental Treatment Act, 1945, s. 167(1). Where a private patient reception
order has been made, the provisions apply *mutatis mutandi* (Mental Treatment Act, 1945, s. 181(1)). Where the recommendation has been made under
section 165, any member of the Garda Síochána may do so.

[96] Mental Treatment Act, 1945, s. 168. This has no relevance for private patients.

person to whom the certificate is given may present it to the member in charge of any Garda Station.[97] The garda thereupon must either request the resident medical superintendent of the relevant psychiatric hospital to arrange for an escort or himself arrange for such escort as, in his opinion, is necessary. Upon request, the resident medical superintendent of the relevant psychiatric hospital may, at his discretion, either arrange for such escort as, in his opinion, is necessary, or indicate that he does not intend to make such arrangements. In the event of the resident medical superintendent's refusal, the garda must then, himself, arrange for the necessary escort.[98]

However, where the patient is not conveyed to hospital within seven clear days after the day upon which it was made, the recommendation ceases to have effect. If during this period the medical practitioner certifies that the patient will not be fit to be removed until after the expiration of the seven clear day period, the recommendation does not cease to have effect upon the expiration of that period, but it does lapse after a further seven clear days.[99]

Reception and Detention

Where a person is removed to a psychiatric hospital on foot of a recommendation for reception,[100] the resident medical superinten-

---

[97] See fn 45 above in respect of the proposals of the White Paper on a New Mental Health Act in this regard.

[98] Mental Treatment Act, 1945, s. 169, as amended by the Mental Treatment Act, 1961, s. 12. Similar provisions apply in respect of private patient reception orders, with the proviso that in such cases, the Gardaí must, upon presentation of the certificate in relation to the necessity for an escort, "thereupon . . . arrange for such escort as may be necessary" (Mental Treatment Act 1945 s. 183 (1)).

[99] Mental Treatment Act, 1945, s. 167, as amended by the Mental Treatment Act, 1961, s. 11. Where a private patient reception order has been made (see above), these provisions effectively apply *mutatis mutandi* (Mental Treatment Act, 1945, s. 181(3) and (4)).

[100] Where the person is a private patient, the reception order has already been made (see fn 65 above). The next provisions, accordingly, have no application thereto.

dent[101] of the hospital or another medical officer of the hospital acting on his behalf, upon the patient's arrival and the presentation of the recommendation, must examine[102] the patient. If the hospital medical practitioner is satisfied that the patient is a person of unsound mind and is a proper person to be taken charge of and detained under care and treatment, he forthwith makes an order[103] for the reception[104] and detention of the patient as a person of unsound mind in the hospital. In all other cases, he must refuse to make such an order.[105]

---

[101] A person whom the health board is obliged to appoint in respect of each psychiatric hospital under its functional control (see also Mental Treatment Act, 1953, s. 3). It is proposed to replace the post of resident medical superintendent with the post of clinical director under the proposals for the implementation of a new Mental Health Act, as suggested by the White Paper on a New Mental Health Act, para. 11.8.

[102] This is invariably a complete psychiatric and physical evaluation, often carried out initially by a member of the hospital staff and later (within 24 hours of admission) reviewed by a consultant psychiatrist (see Chapter 2, pp. 31–5).

[103] In the prescribed form — a chargeable patient reception order.

[104] No person may be received under a private patient reception order if the order was made by or on the application of a member of the governing body (not including a member of a mental hospital authority) of, or the person carrying on, or in charge of, the institution, any person interested in the payments (if any) to be made on account of taking care of the patient, any medical practitioner who is a regular medical attendant at the institution, or the specified relatives, guardian, trustee, partner or assistant of any such person (Mental Treatment Act, 1945, s. 179).

[105] Mental Treatment Act, 1945, s. 171, whereupon the applicant for reception, for the purposes of the Act, is regarded as the applicant for the order. The order and the recommendation for reception on which it was based and, upon refusal of the making of the order, the recommendation for reception are valid notwithstanding that it later transpires that the patient was not ordinarily resident in the area that the hospital serves as required by the Act (Mental Treatment Act, 1945, s. 171(3), as inserted by the Mental Treatment Act, 1961, s. 13, as adapted by the Mental Treatment Acts (Adaptation) Order, 1971 (SI 108 of 1971)). However, in cases of urgency, a patient may be received and detained in a hospital serving the area in which he is for the time being, even where this is not his place of ordinary residence (or where it cannot be readily ascertained) (Mental Treatment Act, 1945, s. 176, as amended by the Mental Treatment Act, 1961, s. 14, and adapted by the Mental Treatment Acts (Adaptation) Order, 1971 (SI 108 of 1971)). See also fn 25 above in respect of "temporary" patients.

Upon the making of the order, the patient may be received, taken charge of, detained "until his removal or discharge by proper authority or his death",[106] and retaken, in the event of his escape, within 28 days and again detained by:

1. The mental hospital authority maintaining the district mental hospital mentioned in the chargeable patient reception order,

2. The resident medical superintendent of that hospital, and

3. The other officers and the servants of that hospital.[107]

In *SC* v *Smith & others*[108] the applicant was detained as a person of unsound mind in the Central Mental Hospital.[109] In a *habeas corpus* application, it was argued that those provisions of the Mental Treatment Act, 1945 (as amended), that relate to the making of a recommendation for reception of a patient as a person of unsound mind,[110] the making of a reception order on foot of such a recommendation,[111] and the powers of detention, and consequential powers, given to the staff of the facility where the patient is detained as a result of the reception order,[112] are repugnant to the Constitution. It was also argued that the effect of the making of a chargeable patient reception order is so far-reaching that it involved a judicial function; that there is lack of a proper and fair procedure before the making of such an order; and that the making of a judicial order before detention or access to an independent

---

[106] See above, p. 467.

[107] Mental Treatment Act, 1945, s. 172. In relation to a private patient reception order, the person carrying on the relevant institution and his officers, assistants and servants and any medical officer of the institution have identical powers (Mental Treatment Act, 1945, s. 181(2)).

[108] Unreported Judgment, High Court, 27 and 31 July 1995, Budd J.

[109] See pp.494–6 below.

[110] Mental Treatment Act, 1945, s. 163, as amended by the Mental Treatment Act, 1961, s. 7.

[111] Mental Treatment Act, 1945, s. 171, as amended by the Mental Treatment Act, 1961, s. 13.

[112] Mental Treatment Act, 1945, s. 172.

judicial authority within a reasonable time after the making of such a reception order is necessary. In this regard, it was noted that the provisions in relation to the application for, and the making of a reception order do not require an opinion to be held that it is necessary for the public safety, or the safety of the patient himself, that he be placed forthwith under care and control.[113] Also, it was conceded that, in cases of urgency and danger, the need for judicial intervention at the outset of any detention should be taken as meaning that a judicial ruling should take place as soon as reasonably practicable.

Having noted the statutory provisions under which the applicant was held, Budd J distinguished *Clarke's* case.[114] He stated:

> The guiding principle when dealing with applications concerning personal freedom is that a statute restrictive of a person's liberty should be very strictly and narrowly construed. . . . *Clarke's* case was dealing with detention under section 165 of the Mental Treatment Act, 1945, which involves a member of the Garda Síochána detaining a person believed to be of unsound mind where the Garda is of opinion that it is necessary for the public safety or that of the person concerned that the person be placed under care and control. Safety aspects were involved and to the fore. In my view, neither the High Court nor the Supreme Court had indefinite detention without any automatic review in their contemplation. In *Clarke's* case, the Supreme Court were concentrating on section 165 which provides for the making of a recommendation, whereas section 172 deals with the effect of a chargeable patient reception order being made, namely, the reception and taking charge of the patient to whom the order relates and his detention until removal or discharge by proper authority or death, i.e. detention of an

---

[113] See Mental Treatment Act, 1945, ss. 162 and 163, as amended by the Mental Treatment Act, 1961, ss. 6 and 7 respectively, contrasted with the Mental Treatment Act, 1945, s. 165, as amended by the Mental Treatment Act, 1961, s. 9, above.

[114] See pp. 472–4 above.

infinite duration without automatic independent review. The Health (Mental Services) Act, 1981, provided, *inter alia*, for an appeal against detention and an automatic review of long-term detention by a specialised tribunal. While the 1981 Act was enacted, it has never been brought into force and I respectfully echo Costello P's comment about this.[115] While Clarke's case may govern the position with regard to section 165, it does not cover sections allowing for indefinite detention. I agree with Costello P that the purpose of the Mental Treatment Act, 1945, as amended, was to provide for the care and treatment of patients for their own safety and for the safety of others. The State has to be particularly solicitous and vigilant in the protection of the citizen's rights, particularly the right to liberty, when dealing with a person who is vulnerable and disadvantaged, such as a patient suffering from mental disorder. The Oireachtas has to be careful when framing statutes which deprive such a person of liberty; it is essential that the legislative framework should contain proper safeguards to lessen the risk of error or abuse in the care and treatment of such patients.

While the Minister for Health and the Inspector of Mental Hospitals[116] may be presumed to act properly and to observe constitutional proprieties in carrying out their functions under the Mental Treatment Act, 1945, as amended, their roles fall far short of being an automatic independent review. . . .

In applying the touchstone of the Constitution . . . I have come to the conclusion that the effect of a chargeable patient reception order under sections 163, 171 and particularly section 172, which allows for detention until removal or discharge by proper authority or death, without any automatic independent review, falls below the norms

---

[115] In *RT* v *The Director of the Central Mental Hospital and the Attorney General (notice party)* [1995] 2 ILRM 354.

[116] A person appointed by the Minister for Health pursuant to the provisions of the Mental Treatment Act, 1945, s. 12.

required by the constitutional guarantee of personal liberty.
The State accordingly has failed to respect, and as far as
practicable by its laws, to defend and vindicate the personal
rights of the citizen, particularly the right to personal liberty. There are no adequate safeguards to protect the applicant against an error in the operation of section 172. There
is no formal review procedure in respect of the opinion of
the resident medical superintendent and of the Inspector of
Mental Hospitals. In the absence of an independent review
of the decision to detain and the lack of an automatic review of long-term detention of a "white card patient", such
as the applicant, the provisions of section 172 of the Mental
Treatment Act, 1945, as amended, are repugnant to the
Constitution.[117]

Having concluded that the applicant was being detained in accordance with the law, but that the law, specifically the Mental
Treatment Act, 1945, section 172, was invalid having regard to
the provisions of the Constitution, the matter was referred to the
Supreme Court by way of case stated.

The Supreme Court[118] indicated that it would confine itself to
the issue referred, but nevertheless expressed *obiter* views in relation to the other provisions that the applicant had sought to impugn. Thus, Hamilton CJ stated:

Section 172 of the Act cannot be construed solely in relation
to the facts of one particular case: it must be construed in the
light of its own language within the framework of the Act in
its entirety and within a constitutional framework . . .

---

[117] Having thus decided the issue of the constitutionality of the Mental
Treatment Act, 1945, on this ground, Budd J declined to express any view on
the other grounds put forward, i.e. that the other sections are unconstitutional because of the lack of judicial or quasi-judicial intervention prior to the
reception and detention of a patient.

[118] Supreme Court, Unreported Judgment, 31 July 1996 (272/1995), Hamilton
CJ, O'Flaherty, Blayney, Denham, Barrington JJ. The court confined itself to
the issue referred, i.e the constitutionality of the Mental Treatment Act,
1945, s. 172.

Though the decision made by the registered medical practitioner to make a recommendation for a reception order may, and the decision of the medical superintendent to make a chargeable patient reception order will, result in the deprivation of the liberty of the person to whom they relate, such decisions cannot be regarded as part of the administration of justice but are decisions entrusted to them by the Oireachtas in its role of providing treatment for those in need, caring for society and its citizens, particularly those suffering from disability, and the protection of the common good. These decisions can only be made when it is established that the person to whom they relate is a person of unsound mind and is a proper person to be taken in charge of and detained under care and treatment. These decisions can be set aside in the appropriate circumstances by the court upon an application for judicial review or upon complaint made to the High Court in accordance with Article 40.4.2 of the Constitution but this does not mean that the decisions are part of the administration of justice. . . .

In an echo of the earlier decision of the Supreme Court in *People (DPP)* v *Gallagher*,[119] on the critical point of whether or not a judicial inquiry of some description into a person's continuing detention was necessary, the Supreme Court was satisfied:

. . . that the original detention of a person . . . pursuant to a chargeable patient reception order made in accordance with the provisions of . . . the Act is not part of the administration of justice and does not require a judicial inquiry or determination and that the sections which permit of such detention do not constitute an attack upon the personal rights of the citizen but rather vindicate and protect the rights of the citizens concerned by providing for their care and treatment and are not repugnant to the Constitution on this ground. . . .

---

[119] [1991] ILRM 339.

Before a "chargeable patient reception order" can be made
in respect of any person, two doctors . . . must be satisfied
that the person is a person of unsound mind and is a proper
person to be taken charge of and detained under care and
treatment.

The court is satisfied that the sections of the Act which
permit the detention of a citizen, who is of unsound mind
and requiring care and treatment and who has been so certified, after examination, by two separate medical practitioners, satisfy every reasonable requirement and do not
constitute an attack upon the personal rights of the citizen.

In relation to the power to detain a patient until discharge by
"proper authority"[120] the court, although not distinguishing
Clarke's case stated:

It must be presumed . . . that the Oireachtas intended, when
giving to the resident medical superintendent the power of
detention, and to him and the Minister the power of discharge, that the permitted discretions and adjudications
given to them are to be exercised in accordance with the
principles of constitutional justice and that any departure
therefrom would be restrained and corrected by the courts.

In the exercise of the powers conferred and obligations imposed by the Act, the resident medical superintendent and
the Minister are obliged to act in accordance with the principles of constitutional justice, are not entitled to act in an
unlawful manner, are not entitled to act arbitrarily, capriciously, or unreasonably and must have regard to the personal rights of the patient, including the right to liberty,
which can be denied only if the patient is a person of unsound mind and in need of care and treatment who has not
recovered and must be particularly astute when depriving
or continuing to deprive a citizen suffering from mental disorder of his/her liberty.

---

[120] See pp. 496–8 below.

It is important that any person exercising any power or discretion under the Act, which touches on the rights of a patient, should be conscious, not only of the wording of the power or discretion which the statute appears to confer upon him or her but also of the constitutional rights of the patient which the statute presumes that he or she will respect when purporting to exercise that power or discretion.

Having considered the provisions in relation to discharge and complaints[121], the court was satisfied:

... that in exercising the powers conferred on them by the Act that the resident medical superintendent and the Minister are not engaged in the administration of justice and that no judicial intervention is necessary or required unless they or either of them fail to comply with the requirements of fair procedures and constitutional justice or fail to have regard to the constitutional right to liberty of the patient.

On the central point of the determination of the High Court — in the absence of an independent review procedure — the Supreme Court considered that:

While it may be desirable that the necessity for the continued detention of the person, in respect of whom a changeable patient reception order has been made, be subject to automatic review by an independent review board as provided for in the Mental Treatment Act, 1981, which has not, unfortunately, after 15 years, been brought into force by the Minister, the failure to provide for such review in the Act has not been shown to render the provisions of the Act, and in particular section 172 thereof, constitutionally flawed because of the safeguards contained in the Act. . . . If, however, it were to be shown in some future case, that there had been a systematic failure in the existing safeguards, and that the absence of such a system of automatic review

---

[121] See Mental Treatment Act, 1945, the provisions of Part XVIII and s. 266, as amended by the Mental Treatment Act, 1961, s. 36, and the Health Act, 1970, s. 81.

was a factor in such failure, that might cause this court to hold that a person affected by such failure was being deprived of his constitutional rights.

Having considered what recourse a person might have in such circumstances, the Supreme Court went on to say, in fairly unequivocal terms:

> . . . that the detention of a patient does not require automatic review by an independent tribunal because of the obligation placed on a person in charge of a district mental hospital to discharge a patient who has recovered.

It was noted that:

> Inherent in [the Act] is the obligation placed on the resident medical superintendent to regularly and constantly review a patient in order to ensure that he/she has not recovered and is still a person of unsound mind and is a proper person to be detained under care and treatment. If such review is not regularly carried out, in accordance with fair procedures and rendering justice to the patient, then the intervention of the court can be sought because of the obligation placed on the resident medical superintendent to exercise the powers conferred on him by the Act in accordance with the principles of constitutional justice. There is no suggestion that such a review is not carried out.

Acknowledging that the State is obliged by virtue of the provisions of Article 40.3.1, in its laws, to respect, and as far as practicable to defend and vindicate the personal rights of the citizen — and its entitlement to have due regard to differences of capacity and the particular requirements of particular citizens, particularly those suffering from incapacity, including mental disorders — the court asked:

> . . . do the provisions of section 172 of the Act, having regard to the citizen to whom it is applicable, constitute a failure by the Oireachtas to respect and, as far as practicable, defend and vindicate the personal rights of such citizens?

Answering the question in the negative, the court concluded:

> In view of the requirements set forth in sections 163 and
> 171,[122] which do not of themselves constitute an attack upon
> the personal rights of the citizen affected thereby or a fail-
> ure to defend and vindicate such rights, the court is satis-
> fied that it has not been established that the provisions of
> section 172 constitutes a failure by the Oireachtas to re-
> spect and, as far as practicable, defend and vindicate the
> right of such citizens affected thereby.
>
> In being so satisfied, the court has had regard to the pre-
> sumption of constitutionality which the Act is entitled to
> enjoy and in particular the presumption that the Oireach-
> tas intended that the proceedings, procedures, discretions
> and adjudications by the resident medical superintendent,
> the Inspector of Mental Hospitals and the Minister permit-
> ted by the . . . Act are to be conducted in accordance with the
> principles of constitutional justice and in particular with re-
> gard to the principle thereof that no person should be unnec-
> essarily deprived of his liberty, even for a short period.

That said, however, the warning of the Supreme Court to those
concerned with the administration of the statutory provisions is
apposite:

> This . . . places a heavy responsibility on [resident medical
> superintendents, the Inspector of Mental Hospitals and the
> Minister] to ensure that no person detained pursuant to the
> provisions of section 172 of the Act is detained *for any pe-*
> *riod longer than is absolutely necessary for his proper care*
> *and treatment and that the safeguards provided for in the*
> *Act be stringently enforced.* The necessity for the continued
> detention of a patient, to whom section 172 of the Act ap-
> plies, must be regularly reviewed to ensure that he/she is
> not being unnecessarily detained. [*emphasis added*]

---

[122] See pp. 469–78 above.

In Britain, the Mental Health Act, 1983, provides for automatic review of all detentions by a Mental Health Review Tribunal. The Health (Mental Services) Act, 1981, which was never brought into force, also contemplated a formalised review of involuntary detention.[123]

Refusal to Order Reception and Detention[124]

Where a resident medical superintendent or other medical officer of a psychiatric hospital refuses to make a reception order, he must give the applicant a written statement of the reasons for the refusal, sending a copy to the Minister. He must also give the Minister such additional information as the Minister may require as to the circumstances of the refusal. The Minister, in turn, may communicate such facts as he thinks proper in relation to the refusal to the patient in relation to whom the order was sought or to any other *bona fide* inquirer.[125]

---

[123] The White Paper on a New Mental Health Act (Department of Health, 1995), para. 1.14, notes that the Act was overtaken by "developments in international law which require different safeguards against improper detention than those provided" in that Act (i.e. the Council of Europe Recommendations for the Legal Protection of Persons Suffering from Mental Disorders Placed as Involuntary Patients (1983) and the United Nations Principles for the Protection of Persons with Mental Illness and for the Improvement of Mental Health Care (General Assembly, December 1991) — both reproduced in the White Paper); and by the thrust of the development of the psychiatric services, following publication of the report *Planning for the Future* in 1984. Notwithstanding that it is accepted that the Act of 1945 does not comply fully with the state's obligations under the European Convention for the Protection of Human Rights and Fundamental Freedoms, statutory reform has yet to take place. As Costello J (as he then was) noted in *RT* v *Director of the Central Mental Hospital & others* [1995] 2 ILRM 354 at 368: "The best is the enemy of the good. The 1981 reforms which would have remedied the defects were not brought into force because more thorough reforms were being considered. . . . The prolonged search for excellence extending now for over 14 years has had most serious consequences for the applicant herein." This view was approved by Budd J in the High Court in *SC*. Although the decision of the Supreme Court in *SC* has provided some leeway, the administrative problem remains as to how its injunctions are to be enforced.

[124] Because of the different procedure in respect of private patients, these provisions have no relevance thereto.

[125] Mental Treatment Act, 1945, s. 173.

Defects in the Recommendation or Reception Order[126]

Where, within 21 days after the reception of a patient into a psychiatric hospital, the recommendation for reception is found in any respect to be defective or incorrect, the resident medical superintendent of the relevant hospital may refer the recommendation for amendment to the person who made it. That person may, with the consent of the Minister, amend the recommendation within that 21-day period. Similarly, where a reception order is found to be defective or incorrect within the same period, the person who made the order may, with the consent of the Minister, amend the order within that 21-day period.[127] An amended recommendation or reception order is effective as if the amendment had been contained in it when it was signed.

Where, within that 21-day period, the Minister is satisfied that a recommendation or a reception order in respect of a patient is defective, he may require by notice in writing to the resident medical superintendent[128] of the relevant psychiatric hospital that the incorrect or defective recommendation or reception order be amended. If the relevant document is not so amended to the satisfaction of the Minister within the 21-day period after the reception of the patient into the psychiatric hospital, the Minister may, if he so thinks fit, direct that the patient be discharged from hospital. If the Minister so directs, the patient must be discharged accordingly. However, notwithstanding any defect discovered in the recommendation or reception order, the patient may be received, taken charge of, detained, and retaken (in the event of his

---

[126] These provisions were not considered in *SC* v *Smith & others*, pp. 479–87 above.

[127] Where the defect is in a private patient reception order, the order may be amended by the medical practitioners who made it, with the consent of the Minister (Mental Treatment Act, 1945, s. 182 (1)).

[128] In the case of a private patient reception order, the person in charge of the relevant institution (Mental Treatment Act, 1945, s. 182(2)).

escape)[129] during the 21-day period after his reception into a psychiatric hospital, as if the order had been properly made.[130]

TREATMENT AND MANAGEMENT OF PATIENTS IN PSYCHIATRIC HOSPITALS

General

The patient, once received and detained, is usually kept in the hospital named in the reception order[131] until treatment has been completed and he is considered fit for discharge. However, as part of his overall management, whether physical or psychiatric, treatment elsewhere may be required.[132]

Transfer to Another Psychiatric Facility Maintained by the Same Authority

Thus, the mental hospital authority,[133] acting on the advice of the resident medical superintendent of their district mental hospital, may transfer a patient detained in a district mental hospital or any psychiatric institution maintained by them to a district mental hospital or any other institution maintained by them.[134]

---

[129] In pursuance of the powers exercisable, by the persons specified, in the Mental Treatment Act, 1945, ss. 172 and 181 (private patients), above.

[130] Mental Treatment Act, 1945, s. 174. With the exception of the minor procedural differences (see above), the remainder of these provisions apply *mutatis mutandi* in relation to patients received on foot of private patient reception orders (Mental Treatment Act, 1945, s. 182).

[131] Thus, these provisions have no application to patients received into psychiatric hospitals as voluntary patients (see above). Nor do they apply to patients detained in private psychiatric facilities.

[132] Similar provisions apply in respect of non-state run institutions (see Mental Treatment Act, 1945, s. 213). The applicant for a reception order (see fn 65 above) may also request such a transfer (see s. 214), subject to the consent of the Minister.

[133] The health board; see Mental Treatment Act, 1945, as adapted by the Mental Treatment Acts (Adaptation) Order, 1971 (SI 108 of 1971).

[134] Mental Treatment Act, 1945, s. 205, as adapted by the Mental Treatment Acts (Adaptation) Order, 1971 (SI 108 of 1971).

Transfer to Another Psychiatric Facility Maintained by Another Authority

Similarly, a patient may be transferred temporarily to another district mental hospital (maintained by a different authority) if the mental hospital authority, acting on the advice of the resident medical superintendent, are of the opinion that:

1. It would be for the benefit of the health of a patient detained in a psychiatric institution maintained by them, or

2. It is necessary for the purpose of obtaining special treatment for him.

In such cases, however, application for the transfer must first be made to the Minister who, if he thinks fit, may make an order directing and authorising the transfer. At the request of the transferring authority, the Minister may, at any time, by order direct and authorise the return of the patient to the place whence he came.[135]

Transfer to the Central Mental Hospital[136]

Transfer of a detained patient to the Central Mental Hospital in Dundrum may also be effected in certain circumstances. Thus, a patient detained in a state-run psychiatric facility may be charged with an indictable offence before a District Judge sitting in that psychiatric facility.[137] If the District Judge is of the opinion that the evidence given constitutes *prima facie* evidence that the patient has committed the offence and that he would, if placed on

---

[135] Mental Treatment Act, 1945, s. 206, as adapted by the Mental Treatment Acts (Adaptation) Order, 1971 (SI 108 of 1971), which permits two mental health authorities to make and carry out such an arrangement for the specified purposes.

[136] Originally the "Central Criminal Lunatic Asylum", established by the Central Criminal Lunatic Asylum (Ireland) Act, 1845 (8&9 Vict. c. 107), its name was changed by the Mental Treatment Act, 1961, s. 39, and it is now administered by the Eastern Health Board pursuant to the provisions of the Health Act, 1970, s. 44.

[137] The provisions do not apply to patients detained in private institutions.

trial, be unfit to plead, he must by order certify that the patient is suitable for transfer to the Central Mental Hospital (copies of which are sent to the Minister and to the person in charge of the relevant psychiatric facility). Where such an order is made, the patient must be retained in the relevant psychiatric facility and his detention continued. The Minister must also require the Inspector of Mental Hospitals to visit the patient and to report on his mental condition. Having considered the report, the Minister may, if he thinks fit, then by order direct and authorise the patient's transfer to the Central Mental Hospital. However, should the Minister decide not to make such an order, he must give notice to that effect to the person in charge of the psychiatric facility.[138]

If transferred, the patient may be detained[139] in the Central Mental Hospital until sent to another psychiatric facility, or until he is discharged or dies.[140] Thus, the Minister may, by order, direct and authorise the sending back of a patient transferred to the Central Mental Hospital to the facility whence he came, or, if he is ordinarily resident in a different area, he may be transferred to the relevant district mental hospital.[141] The transferred patient

---

[138] Whereupon the patient may be transferred at any time to the district mental hospital for the area in which he is ordinarily resident, if he is not already detained there (Mental Treatment Act, 1945, s. 207(2)(f), as inserted by the Mental Treatment Act, 1961, s. 25(1), as adapted by the Mental Treatment Acts (Adaptation) Order, 1971 (SI 108 of 1971)). His detention, whether continued in the original facility or in the district mental hospital for the area in which he is ordinarily resident, is regarded as detention under a chargeable (or private, as appropriate) patient reception order, effectively as a person of unsound mind (see above); Mental Treatment Act, 1945, s. 207(2)(g), as inserted by the Mental Treatment Act, 1961, s. 25(1), as adapted by the Mental Treatment Acts (Adaptation) Order, 1971 (SI 108 of 1971).

[139] Notwithstanding any other provision of the Acts.

[140] Mental Treatment Act, 1945, s. 207(1) and (2), as amended by the Mental Treatment Act, 1961, s. 25(1), as adapted by the Mental Treatment Acts (Adaptation) Order, 1971 (SI 108 of 1971).

[141] Mental Treatment Act, 1945, s. 207(3), as amended by the Mental Treatment Act, 1961, s. 25(2), as adapted by the Mental Treatment Acts (Adaptation) Order, 1971 (SI 108 of 1971). A patient's detention, upon such a transfer, is deemed to be a detention under a chargeable (or private, as appropriate) patient reception order, effectively as a person of unsound mind, see fn 138 above.

must be discharged from the Central Mental Hospital if the director of that hospital and the Inspector of Mental Hospitals agree and certify that he has ceased to be of unsound mind.[142]

These statutory provisions were found to be unconstitutional in *RT* v *Director of the Central Mental Hospital & others*.[143] Here, a patient initially detained in a Health Board hospital on foot of a temporary certificate was, upon his transfer, pursuant to these provisions, detained in the Central Mental Hospital for some 16 years. Costello J (as he then was) noted that the section had:

> . . . serious legal consequences as they directly impinge on the constitutional right to liberty of temporary patients. Such patients have a right to their liberty, at most, 18 months after the reception order, which restricted their liberty, was made. If transferred under the section, then they may be detained there lawfully after the expiration of that period for an unlimited time which . . . may extend over many years. The defects in the section are such that there are no adequate safeguards against abuse or error both in the making of the transfer order, and in the continuance of the indefinite detention which is permitted by the section. These defects, not only mean that the section falls far short of internationally accepted standards but, in my opinion, render the section unconstitutional, because they mean that the State has failed adequately to protect the right to liberty of temporary patients.[144]

---

[142] Mental Treatment Act, 1945, s. 207(4). The statutory lacunae are obvious, as is the absence of any formalised review procedure. For a review of the practical operation of the section (and s. 208), see M. Crosby, L. Hutchinson, M. O'Malley and A. O'Connor (1995), "Section 207 of the Mental Treatment Act 1945: A Critical Review of its use, 1955–1994", *Medico-Legal Journal of Ireland*, Vol. 1, No. 1, pp. 11–12. See also: *State (H)* v *Daly* [1977] IR 90.

[143] [1995] 2 ILRM 354.

[144] [1995] 2 ILRM 354 at 368. See also Chapter 17.

Transfer to Another Facility for Special Treatment[145]

If a mental hospital authority, acting on the advice of the resident medical superintendent of their district mental hospital, are of the opinion that a patient detained in any psychiatric facility maintained by them requires treatment (including surgical treatment) not available there, it may direct and authorise the removal of the patient to any hospital or other place where the treatment is obtainable.[146] Similar provisions exist in respect of patients detained in mental institutions not maintained by a mental hospital authority.[147]

When a patient has been so removed for treatment, he may be kept there as long as is necessary for the purpose of his treatment whereupon he must then be taken back to the place from which he was removed, unless it is certified by a medical practitioner that his detention is no longer necessary.[148]

In *SC* v *Smith & others*[149] the applicant had been transferred to the Central Mental Hospital and detained there on foot of such a transfer, although the original temporary certificate on foot of which he had originally been detained had expired and had not been renewed. The hospital authority argued that the extension of the original certificate was unnecessary and that they were empowered to detain the applicant in the Central Mental Hospital

---

[145] In *SC* v *Smith & others* (see pp. 479–87 above), the Supreme Court was of the view that these provisions, far from infringing the personal rights of the detained patient, amounted to a vindication of his rights by making provision for such treatment, when necessary.

[146] Mental Treatment Act, 1945, s. 208(1), as adapted by the Mental Treatment Acts (Adaptation) Order, 1971 (SI 108 of 1971), in a place in which he may be received on foot of an arrangement pursuant to statute; thus ". . . a mental hospital authority and the controlling authority of any hospital or other place where treatment is obtainable may make and carry out an arrangement for the[se] purposes . . ." (s. 208(2)).

[147] Mental Treatment Act, 1945, s. 208(3), in which case the authorisation and arrangements are made by the patient's medical attendant. Section 208(4) was repealed by the Mental Treatment Act, 1961, s. 42.

[148] Mental Treatment Act, 1945, s. 208(5).

[149] Supreme Court, Unreported Judgment, 14 July 1994.

simply for the length of time for which he required treatment. On his application for *habeas corpus*, a unanimous Supreme Court rejected this contention as unsatisfactory. In directing the release of the applicant, Blayney J stated:

> If a patient's period of detention, or any extension of it, were to expire while he was receiving treatment in a hospital to which he had been removed, and if subsequently his treatment were to determine, and he were moved back to the mental hospital to which he had been committed, it would not be possible lawfully to detain him there. There would be no extension under [the Act] in being, and [the transfer section] would have ceased to be applicable, since the patient would no longer be being kept under that subsection. Such a result to my mind demonstrates clearly that [this] contention could not be correct.
>
> There is a further consideration that leads to the same conclusion. While in the instant case the hospital to which the applicant was removed was also a psychiatric hospital, so that the doctors treating him there would be competent to form an opinion as to whether or not he had recovered, in the case of the more usual removal under [the section] the patient would be being transferred to a general hospital for treatment by a surgeon or a physician. So if, for example, one were to take the case of a patient transferred to a general hospital for the purpose of obtaining treatment for some liver or blood complaint, the situation would be that he would be entirely dependent on the view of his medical advisors in that hospital as to the period of time in which he could be involuntarily detained there, and all they could take into account would be the length of time for which he required treatment. It could be that during this time the patient would have recovered from his mental illness but, if the [respondents] are correct, he could nonetheless be involuntarily detained in the hospital as long as he required treatment for the physical complaints for which he had been sent there.

Th[at] construction would also deprive a patient of the safeguards contained in section 189.[150] . . . It is to be noted that the power given . . . is not to "detain" but to "keep". The phrase used is that a person removed to a hospital or other place "may be kept there". And this is to be contrasted with the latter art of the subsection where "detention" is referred to. The person is to be kept for as long as is necessary for the purpose of his treatment and "shall then be taken back to the place from which he was removed unless it is certified by a registered medical practitioner that his detention is no longer necessary". This provision clearly proceeds on the basis that there is still a valid detention order in being pursuant to which the patient was being kept, but gives the right to a registered medical practitioner to terminate the detention if he certifies that it is no longer necessary. If no doctor does so certify, the patient must be returned to the mental hospital from which he came, and for this to be lawfully done there must still be in being a valid order detaining him, which could only be an [original] order . . . or an extension [there]of . . .

DISCHARGE OF PATIENTS

When treatment has been completed, the patient must be discharged by "proper authority". A patient, the subject of a chargeable patient reception order, must be released on his recovery.[151] Any relative or friend of a person detained as a chargeable patient may apply to the person in charge of the institution in which he is detained, to allow him to take care of that person. If he is satisfied

---

[150] See p. 468 above.

[151] Mental Treatment Act, 1945, ss. 218 and 219, as amended by the Mental Treatment Act, 1961, ss. 28 and 29 respectively. See also s. 208, above. A similar provision applies in respect of private patients (Mental Treatment Act, 1945, s. 217, as amended by the Mental Treatment Act, 1961, s. 27).

that the person detained will properly be taken care of, the resident medical superintendent may order the discharge.[152]

While there is no definition of "proper authority" contained in the Act, the persons vested with the power to discharge a person detained in a psychiatric facility are, effectively, the resident medical superintendent or the person in charge of the institution in which he is detained,[153] or the resident medical superintendent or the chief medical officer of the institution *and* the hospital authority.[154]

Notwithstanding this power of discharge, the person in charge of the facility, if he certifies in writing that the person is dangerous or otherwise unfit for discharge, may refuse the patient's release. Thereupon, notice in writing of objection to the certificate may be given to the Minister by or on behalf of the person to whom the certificate relates. On receipt of the notice, the Minister may require the person in charge of the relevant mental institution to give a copy of the certificate to him and then require the Inspector of Mental Hospitals[155] to examine the person in question. Having considered the Inspector's report, the Minister, if he so thinks fit, and within 14 days of receipt of the certificate, may

---

[152] Mental Treatment Act, s. 220, as amended by the Mental Treatment Act, 1961, s. 30. Where a patient is detained as a private patient in an institution, his discharge may be directed by the person paying the necessary account, or by his next of kin (with, where appropriate, the approval of the resident medical superintendent); see Mental Treatment Act, 1945, s. 215, as amended by the Mental Treatment Act, 1961, s. 26, and the Mental Treatment Act, 1953, s. 3.

[153] Mental Treatment Act, 1945, ss. 217, 218, 219 and 220, as amended by the Mental Treatment Act, 1961, ss. 27, 28, 29 and 30 respectively. See also Mental Treatment Act, 1953, s. 3. In the case of a private patient, the person paying the account may direct the discharge (s. 215 as amended by the Mental Treatment Act, 1961, s. 26).

[154] The chief executive officer of the health board; Mental Treatment Act, 1945, s. 216 (in the case of a person detained under a reception order who wishes to become a voluntary patient), as amended by the Mental Treatment Act, 1961, s. 42, and adapted by the Mental Treatment Acts (Adaptation) Order, 1971 (SI 108 of 1971). See also the Mental Treatment Act, 1953, s. 3.

[155] A person appointed by the Minister pursuant to the provisions of the Mental Treatment Act, 1945, s. 12.

by order direct the discharge of the person.[156] The Minister may also direct the discharge of a patient upon receipt of a recommendation by two independent medical practitioners who have examined the patient, on foot of an application to the Minister, that the person could be discharged without risk of injury to himself or to others.[157]

MANAGEMENT OF MENTALLY DISORDERED OFFENDERS[158]

Remand for Further Examination

Originally, where, in summary proceedings, a person remanded in custody for further examination was found to be of "unsound mind" by two medical practitioners, the Minister for Justice was empowered to remove and detain him in a psychiatric facility.[159] The Minister was also empowered to keep him there until it was certified to him that the person was of sound mind, whereupon he was to be remitted to the place whence he came to be brought before the court again. This provision, insofar as it purported to allow executive interference in judicial proceedings,[160] was found to be unconstitutional in *State (C) v Minister for Justice*.[161] Thus, where such a person is removed to a psychiatric facility, he may only be detained there until his next remand date before the District Court.[162]

---

[156] Mental Treatment Act, 1945, s. 221.

[157] Mental Treatment Act, 1945, s. 222.

[158] The White Paper on a New Mental Health Act, paras. 7.28–7.31, set out the proposed procedural reforms in this area. However, they represent only minor variations on the current statutory theme.

[159] Lunatic Asylums (Ireland) Act, 1875 (38&39 Vict c. 67), s. 13. This provision is limited to those who are in custody, whether on foot of summary proceedings in the District Court or during the course of a preliminary examination. It is inapplicable if an accused is released on bail. See *State (C) v Minister for Justice* [1967] IR 106 at 119 *per* Walsh J.

[160] In that it operated to prevent an accused person from appearing before the District Court on the return date of his remand.

[161] [1967] IR 106. See also Chapter 17 above.

[162] See also *State (Caseley) v Daly & another* (High Court, Unreported Judgment, Gannon J, 19 February 1979). However, a similar provision persists in

Remand for Trial

Where two medical practitioners certify that a person returned for trial in custody by the District Court "is or has become insane, or is an idiot", the Minister for Justice is empowered to transfer him to a psychiatric facility. He may then be detained there until the sitting of the court of trial to which he had been sent forward,[163] whereupon the appropriate judicial interventions then take place.[164]

Sentenced to Imprisonment

Where a person has been sentenced and committed to prison, and where it is certified by two medical practitioners that he is or has become "insane" he may be transferred by order of the Minister for Justice to a psychiatric facility[165] or the Central Mental Hospital.[166] He may then be detained there until he becomes of "sound mind" whereupon he must be transferred back to the institution whence he came, or discharged, as the case might be.[167]

English legislation; see Mental Health Act, 1983, ss. 47 and 48, replacing a corresponding power under the Criminal Lunatics Act, 1884, repealed in Ireland by the Statute Law Revision Act, 1983.

[163] Criminal Lunatics (Ireland) Act, 1838 (1 Vict c. 27), s. 3, saved by the Mental Treatment Act, 1945, s. 284.

[164] See Chapters 16 and 17.

[165] Criminal Lunatics (Ireland) Act, 1838 (1 Vict c. 27), s. 2, saved by the Mental Treatment Act, 1945, s. 284.

[166] Lunatic Asylums (Ireland) Act, 1845 (8&9 Vict c. 107), s. 12, saved by the Mental Treatment Act, 1945, s. 284.

[167] In practice, most are transferred directly to the Central Mental Hospital, although they may be transferred indirectly, having been sent initially to a local psychiatric facility under the Act of 1838, s. 2.

Chapter 19

CONSENT TO TREATMENT AND RESEARCH

CONSENT AND PSYCHIATRIC DISORDER

In Ireland and Britain, there is only minimal specific legislative provision governing the issue of consent to medical or surgical treatment.[1] Thus, the Non-Fatal Offences Against the Person Act, 1997, section 23, provides (in terms identical to the provisions of the English Family Law Reform Act, 1969, section 8):

> The consent of a minor who has attained the age of 16 years to any surgical, medical or dental treatment which, in the absence of consent, would constitute a trespass to his or her person, shall be as effective as it would be if he or she were of full age; and where a minor has by virtue of this section given an effective consent to any treatment, it shall not be necessary to obtain any consent for it from his or her parent or guardian.

The section further provides that "surgical, medical or dental treatment" includes any procedure undertaken for the purposes of diagnosis and to any procedure, including the administration of an anaesthetic, which is ancillary to any such treatment. Psychiatric treatment — involving drug therapy — clearly falls within the category of "medical treatment". However, the Mental Treatment Act, 1945, as amended, contains no provision in relation to a requirement to obtain personal or proxy consent to treatment —

---

[1] Although there are broadly similar provisions in respect of the control of infectious diseases (see Health Act, 1947, and Public Health (Control of Diseases) Act, 1984), there appear to be lacunae in respect of treatment without consent.

unlike the English Mental Health Act, 1983, which requires patient consent *inter alia* for psychosurgery and electroconvulsive therapy (ECT).[2] A patient admitted as a voluntary patient, given that he requests and agrees to admission for treatment, it seems, is capable of giving a legally effective consent to treatment. There is nothing in the Act, or indeed, at common law, to suggest that such a consent to treatment may be dispensed with.

However, for a person admitted as a temporary patient, the criteria for admission to a psychiatric facility include unfitness, on account of the mental state of the patient, for treatment of his mental illness as a voluntary patient.[3] Thus, an effective inability to consent to necessary hospital treatment, being a factor to be considered in involuntary detention in the first instance, it logically follows that treatment for mental illness might also be lawfully instituted and, indeed, continued without his consent, once admitted. It is less clear, however, if similar considerations apply in relation to a person admitted as a temporary patient on account of his being an addict.[4] Such a person is one who by reason of his addiction to drugs or intoxicants is either dangerous to himself or others or incapable of managing himself or his affairs or of ordinary proper conduct.[5] The Act admits his involuntary detention, but is silent as to his treatment without consent. Whereas, in many instances, an addict may not, on account of his addiction, be in a position to give a legally effective consent, he might well be able to do so. That said, within the context of the statutory framework, to sanction detention without consent, without

---

[2] See sections 57 and 58, as expanded by the Mental Health (Hospital, Guardianship and Consent to Treatment) Regulations, 1983. These issues are discussed in the White Paper on a New Mental Health Act (Department of Health, 1995), Chapter 6, wherein it is proposed that provisions similar to those in the English legislation be adopted (para. 6.12).

[3] See Chapter 18, pp. 459–61.

[4] Under the provisions recommended by the White Paper on a New Mental Health Act, this, alone, will no longer be a ground for involuntary detention (para. 2.20).

[5] Mental Treatment Act, 1945, s. 3.

conferring a power to treat without consent, appears illogical to the point of being self-defeating.[6] What is clear, however, is that in the case of mental illness (and probably addiction), the power to treat without consent seems primarily confined to management of that condition[7] — and not to the management of other inter-current conditions. Thus, for example, where an acute surgical emergency arises in a patient detained as a temporary patient, consent is required for its treatment. Should the patient be inca-pable of giving an effective consent, then the convention has been to have recourse to the consent of a proxy consent giver.[8] That said, there is no statutory guidance as to this approach, reliance being placed upon the accepted practice in respect of those inca-pable of giving effective consent, e.g. minor children under the age of 16 and chronically incapacitated adults. Necessity, of course, would be sufficient to permit proceeding without proxy consent.[9]

For the purposes of involuntary detention, there is no statutory definition of what constitutes unsoundness of mind — although it appears to connote mental illness, with an inability to care prop-erly for oneself or to deal with one's property.[10] In this regard, its being distinguished from the category of mental illness that war-rants detention as a temporary patient, is a distinction of degree rather than of kind. A *fortiori*, therefore, it seems that treatment — for the underlying mental illness — may be instituted and

---

[6] This opaqueness of legislation seems a feature of the time of enactment — similar criticisms having been levelled at the English Mental Health Act, 1959, and the National Assistance Act, 1947; see I. Kennedy and A. Grubb (1994), *Medical Law*, Second Edition, London: Butterworths, p. 330.

[7] This is the effect of the Mental Health Act, 1983, s. 63; "The consent of a patient shall not be required for any medical treatment given to him for the mental disorder from which he is suffering, not being [ECT or psycho-surgery], if the treatment is given by or under the direction of the responsible medical officer."

[8] However, there is no statutory basis for this convention.

[9] See *Re F* [1990] 2 AC 1. This issue is given statutory expression in the Men-tal Health Act, 1983, s. 62, in respect of those treatments (e.g. ECT and psy-chosurgery) that would normally require patient consent.

[10] See RSC 1986 Order 67.

continued without first obtaining a legally effective consent from the person so detained as a person of unsound mind. Detention being pursuant to statute (the statutory conditions having been complied with) and thus lawful, it is arguable that treatment may also be lawfully given, without the necessity for the intervention of a proxy consent giver.[11]

Given the unfortunate absence of express statutory provisions in relation to consent, however, this approach is, at best, intuitive, and one must fall back upon a consideration of the relevant common law and constitutional issues.

THE CONSTITUTIONAL DIMENSION

In *In re Philip Clarke*[12] the Supreme Court considered the nature of the Mental Treatment Act, 1945. O'Byrne J, in delivering the judgment of the court, stated:

> [This Act] as shown in the title, was primarily intended to provide for the prevention and treatment of mental disorders and the care of persons suffering therefrom and is of a paternal character, clearly intended for the care and custody of persons suspected to be suffering from mental infirmity and for the safety and well-being of the public generally . . . We do not see how the common good would be promoted or the dignity and freedom of the individual assured by allowing persons, alleged to be suffering from such infirmity, to remain at large to the possible danger of themselves and others.[13]

---

[11] Unlike in the case of minors under the age of 16 years; see Mental Treatment Act, 1945, s. 190, where it is at least implied that parental or guardian consent is required even for voluntary admission. In any event, in respect of minors, the provisions of Articles 41 and 42 of the Constitution would probably necessarily require such consent.

[12] [1950] IR 235, considering the constitutionality of the Mental Treatment Act, 1945, s. 165.

[13] A view cited with approval by the Supreme Court in *SC* v *Smith & others* (Supreme Court, Unreported Judgment, 31 July 1996 (272/1995), Hamilton CJ, O'Flaherty, Blayney, Denham, Barrington JJ).

Although directed at the issue of detention, it is arguable, from the language of the finding, that the same paternalistic approach is implied in respect of treatment upon detention.

Both the voluntariness of the consent and the capacity to give effective consent arise. Determination of voluntariness ultimately falls to be determined on the facts. However, the concept appears academic in a situation of involuntary detention. Although, in the ordinary course of events, capacity is to be presumed, in the case of psychiatric disability, presumption of lack of capacity is probably the norm. And, depending on the primary psychiatric disorder from which the patient is suffering, the degree of impairment of cognitive functioning and the degree of thought disorder will vary quite widely.[14] A paternalistic view would hold that it is sufficient to say that where the clinician is satisfied that there is sufficient capacity to give an effective consent it should be sought. However, to adopt such a subjective approach runs the risk of exposing patients who actually have sufficient capacity to consent, to being treated without such consent having been sought or obtained. Common law remedies after the event may be poor consolation. An objective approach to the assessment of capacity is required.[15]

Where capacity is impaired — and even where it is apparently normal — the degree of disclosure that is required in order to ensure that the consent given is effective, is particularly problematic. Although a difficult issue in the general area of treatment, in the management of psychiatric disability, the issues are thrown into an even more problematic milieu.

Although not directed specifically at the issue of psychiatric disability — but rather chronic and untreatable severe organic brain damage — the observations of the Supreme Court in *In the matter of A Ward of Court (withholding medical treatment) (No.*

---

[14] See Chapters 12 and 15.

[15] Independent assessment is proposed by the White Paper on a New Mental Health Act, para. 6.12.

2)[16] are apposite. Hamilton CJ cited, with approval, an extra-
judicial comment of Costello J, as he then was, that stated:[17]

> . . . there are very powerful arguments to suggest that the
> dignity and autonomy of the human person (as constitu-
> tionally predicated) require the State to recognise that de-
> cisions relating to life and death are, generally speaking,
> ones which a competent adult should be free to make with-
> out outside restraint, and that this freedom should be re-
> garded as an aspect of the right to privacy which should be
> protected as a "personal" right by Article 40.3.1. But like
> other "personal" rights identified by the Courts, the right is
> not an absolute one, and its exercise could in certain cir-
> cumstances be validly restricted. For example, in the case
> of contagious diseases, the claims of the common good
> might well justify restrictions on the exercise of a constitu-
> tionally protected right to refuse medical treatment. But in
> the case of the terminally ill, it is very difficult to see what
> circumstances would justify the interference with a decision
> by a competent adult of the right to forego or discontinue
> life saving treatment.[18]

In the course of his judgment, the Chief Justice also averred to
the unenumerated constitutional rights to bodily integrity and
privacy, but without firm comment in relation to the issue of consent. Denham J went on to consider the matter further. In an
echo of what Costello J had written, she stated:

> Medical treatment may not be given to an adult person of
> full capacity without his or her consent. There are a few
> rare exceptions to this; e.g., in regard to contagious dis-
> eases or in a medical emergency where the patient is
> unable to communicate. This right arises out of civil, crimi-
> nal and constitutional law. If medical treatment is given

---

[16] [1996] 2 IR 100 (Supreme Court, Hamilton CJ, O'Flaherty, Egan, Blayney, Denham JJ).

[17] [1996] 2 IR 100 at 125.

[18] "The Terminally Ill: The Law's Concern" (1986) XXI Ir. Jur. (n.s.) 35.

without consent it may be trespass against the person in civil law, a battery in criminal law, and a breach of the individual's constitutional rights. The consent which is given by an adult of full capacity is a matter of choice. It is not necessarily a decision based on medical considerations. Thus, medical treatment may be refused for other than medical reasons, or reasons most citizens would regard as rational, but the person of *full age and capacity* may make the decision for their own reasons.[19] [*emphasis added*]

Insofar as constitutional rights were concerned, she asserted:

The requirement of consent to medical treatment is an aspect of a person's right to bodily integrity under Article 40, s. 3 of the Constitution, which right was first recognised by Kenny J in *Ryan* v *Attorney General* [1965] IR 294 . . .[20]

Having considered the law in relation to the unenumerated constitutional right to privacy, she went on to hold that part of the right to privacy is the giving or refusing of consent to medical treatment, although a component in the decision may relate to personal dignity. Furthermore, as part and parcel of their constitutional rights, a patient has a right to choose whether or not to accept medical treatment. Characterised as a "right to choose",

---

[19] [1996] 2 IR 100 at 156. This is remarkably resonant of J.S. Mills (1859), *On Liberty* (1980 reprint, Oxford: Clarendon Press), where he states:

[T]he only purpose for which power can be rightfully exercised over any member of a civilised community, against his will, is to prevent harm to others. His own good, either physical or moral, is not a sufficient warrant. He cannot rightfully be compelled to do or to forebear because it will be better for him to do so, because it will make him happier, because, in the opinion of others, to do so would be wise, or even right. These are good reasons for remonstrating with him, or reasoning with him or persuading him, or entreating him, but not for compelling him, or visiting him with any reason in case he do otherwise. . . . The only part of the conduct of any one, for which he is amenable to society, is that which concerns others. In the part which merely concerns himself, his independence is, of right, absolute. Over himself, over his own body and mind, the individual is sovereign.

[20] [1996] 2 IR 100 at 156.

Denham J considered that "this concept is the requirement of consent to medical treatment seen from another aspect".[21]

What is clear from the judgments of the Supreme Court is that ordinarily consent to treatment must be obtained prior to the institution of treatment, and that this requirement is predicated upon an individual's constitutional rights. Whether the right is to be characterised as a right to bodily integrity, privacy or a right to choose — or whether it arises from the dignity of the individual that the constitution seeks to assure — is largely academic. That there is an undoubted requirement for consent prior to treatment seems beyond reasonable challenge. Whether the law — either through its criminal or civil code or in particular in the law in relation to civil committal — adequately respects and vindicates that right is a matter of some debate.

In *SC* v *Smith & others*,[22] although the issue raised was solely in relation to the constitutionality of the provisions of the Mental Treatment Act, 1945, that permit near indeterminate detention of a "person of unsound mind", the comments of the Supreme Court are of general relevance to the question of treatment of patients in psychiatric facilities without consent. The Chief Justice noted:

> Though the decision made by the registered medical practitioner to make a recommendation for a reception order may, and the decision of the medical superintendent to make a chargeable patient reception order will, result in the deprivation of the liberty of the person to whom they relate, such decisions . . . are decisions entrusted to them by the Oireachtas in its role of providing treatment for those in need, caring for society and its citizens, particularly those suffering from disability, and the protection of the common good. These decisions can only be made when

---

[21] [1996] 2 IR 100 at 164.

[22] Supreme Court, Unreported Judgment, 31 July 1996 (272/1995), Hamilton CJ, O'Flaherty, Blayney, Denham, Barrington JJ. The court confined itself to the issue referred, i.e the constitutionality of the Mental Treatment Act, 1945, s. 172 (Case stated from the High Court — Unreported Judgment, 27–31 July 1995, Budd J.).

it is established that the person to whom they relate is a person of unsound mind and is a proper person to be taken in charge of and *detained under care and treatment*. These decisions can be set aside in the appropriate circumstances by the court upon an application for judicial review or upon complaint made to the High Court in accordance with Article 40.4.2 of the Constitution. . . . [*emphasis added*]

While referring only to the making of a chargeable patient reception order, nevertheless, the same considerations arguably apply to temporary orders also.[23] The Chief Justice continued:

. . . the sections which permit of such detention do not constitute an attack upon the personal rights of the citizen but rather vindicate and protect the rights of the citizens concerned by *providing for their care and treatment* and are not repugnant to the Constitution. . . . [*emphasis added*]

The court is satisfied that the sections of the Act which permit the detention of a citizen, who is of unsound mind and requiring care and treatment and who has been so certified, after examination, by two separate medical practitioners, satisfy every reasonable requirement and do not constitute an attack upon the personal rights of the citizen.

However, the court went on to sound a warning note in relation to such detention and treatment. Thus;

In the exercise of the powers conferred and obligations imposed by the Act, the resident medical superintendent and the Minister are obliged to act in accordance with the principles of constitutional justice, are not entitled to act in an unlawful manner, are not entitled to act arbitrarily, capriciously, or unreasonably and must have regard to the personal rights of the patient, including the right to liberty which can be denied only if the patient is a person of unsound mind and in need *of care and treatment* who has not recovered and must be particularly astute when depriving

---

[23] See Chapter 18, pp. 462–9.

or continuing to deprive a citizen, suffering from mental disorder, of his/her liberty.

It is important that any person exercising any power or discretion under the Act, which touches on the rights of a patient, should be conscious, not only of the wording of the power or discretion which the statute appears to confer upon him or her but also of the constitutional rights of the patient which the statute presumes that he or she will respect when purporting to exercise that power or discretion. [*emphasis added*]

Finally, the court reminded practitioners:

[The Act] . . . places a heavy responsibility on [resident medical superintendents, the Inspector of Mental Hospitals and the Minister] to ensure that no person detained pursuant to the provisions of section 172 of the Act is detained *for any period longer than is absolutely necessary for his proper care and treatment and that the safeguards provided for in the Act be stringently enforced.* The necessity for the continued detention of a patient, to whom section 172 of the Act applies, must be regularly reviewed to ensure that he/she is not being unnecessarily detained. [*emphasis added*]

The best that might be surmised, therefore, in the absence of express statutory provision — or judicial decision — dealing with the matter of the requirement to obtain consent from a patient who is the subject of a committal order is that the legislation is deemed to be paternalistic in nature. It seeks to take account of the differences in capacity of individuals and is directed at the treatment and care of individuals who cannot care for themselves. But — and most importantly — because of effective impact of the legislation on the patient's constitutional rights, due regard must be had to those constitutional rights at all times, especially with regard to length of treatment.[24] To this might be added, also, with

---

[24] See Chapter 18, p. 479. However, it remains unclear as to what administrative provisions are necessary in this regard.

regard to the necessity for treatment or the permissibility of proceeding without effective consent.

If it is accepted that the lawfulness of proceeding without effective consent is confined to the management of the psychiatric illness where there is no, or impaired, capacity to consent, the question then arises as to who may consent to the treatment of a person committed to a psychiatric facility for an intercurrent physical condition. Again, Denham J addressed the issue in the context of a patient with severe permanent organic brain damage. In this regard, she stated that no matter what the condition of an individual, "(s)he has a right of equality within the Constitution".[25] She continued:

> [A]ll citizens as human persons are equal before the law. This is not a restricted concept, it does not mean solely that legislation should not be discriminatory. It is a positive proposition.
>
> The right to equality arises in recognition that citizens are human persons. . . . Due regard may be had to differences. It may be that in certain instances a person may not be able to exercise a right. But the right exists. The State has due regard to the difference of capacity and may envisage a different process to protect the rights of the incapacitated. It is the duty of the Court to uphold equality before the law. It is thus appropriate to consider if a method exists to give to the insentient person, the ward, equal rights with those who are sentient.[26]

Although Denham J's remarks are directed at how the rights of an individual deemed to be insentient might best be vindicated, they are relevant also to how problems arising from any lack of

---

[25] *In the matter of A Ward of Court (withholding medical treatment) (No. 2)* [1996] 2 IR 100 at 159 (Supreme Court, Hamilton CJ, O'Flaherty, Egan, Blayney, Denham JJ).

[26] [1996] 2 IR 100 at 159.

capacity might be addressed. Nor are they inconsistent with the approach in *SC* v *Smith*.[27]

Where one cannot make the necessary decision as to the medical treatment that one requires, Denham J notes that

> an easy way to deal with the matter would be to say that no decision can then be made. . . [However] That would be to refuse . . . the rights given to other persons. That would be to say effectively that by [an] incapacity to make a decision (s)he has lost that right.[28]

Such an approach is clearly inconsistent, not alone with the beneficent nature of clinical undertakings, but also with the constitutional requirement to vindicate the personal rights of the citizen and the promotion of the common good. It also ignores the express reservation in Article 40.1 that permits the state to have regard to differences of physical capacity. Although the section refers to the enactments of the state, to so confine such a reservation without regard to permitted practices and conventions hardly seems protective of the personal rights of the citizen.

Although, in that case, it was held that, in taking a decision, it must be made so as to preserve, defend and vindicate the life of the ward, identical considerations must also apply to matters of treatment not involving matters of life and death. Similarly, and substituting personal rights in general for the right to life, it can be argued from the judgment that because of the constitutional presumptions and the constitutional requirement that personal rights be respected, be protected as best they may from unjust attack and that they be defended and vindicated as far as practicable, it falls to be established on the balance of probabilities they are best respected, protected and vindicated by the approach sought to be adopted.

---

[27] Supreme Court, Unreported Judgment, 31 July 1996 (272/1995), Hamilton CJ, O'Flaherty, Blayney, Denham, Barrington JJ.

[28] [1996] 2 IR 100 at 160.

Insofar as the criminal law is concerned, the provisions of the Non-Fatal Offences against the Person Act, 1997,[29] are clear. Insofar as the common law is concerned, there is no particular guidance as to tests of capacity, or indeed as to the duty of disclosure.

THE COMMON LAW DIMENSION

As late as 1953, the former Supreme Court, in a case involving non-disclosure of a mishap in previous treatment, articulated the difficulties arising in the therapeutic setting as follows:

> It is clear that there are some matters which a doctor must disclose in order to afford his patient an opportunity of deciding whether [he or] she accepts his view or wishes to consult another doctor and an opportunity to make a choice between alternative courses. An example would be where a dangerous operation was contemplated.

> On the other hand, there are matters which the doctor must decide for himself having accepted the responsibility of treating his patient and having regard to his professional skill and knowledge upon which the patient relies. A clear example would be where in the course of an operation an unexpected complication appears.[30]

That said, however, insofar as a general proposition was concerned, Kingsmill-Moore J, in a classic exposition of social and judicial paternalism, stated:

> I cannot admit any abstract duty to tell patients what is the matter with them, or, in particular, to say that a needle has been left in their tissue. All depends on the circumstances — the character of the patient, her health, her social position, her intelligence, the nature of the tissue in which the needle is embedded, the possibility of subsequent

---

[29] See, for example, ss. 2 and 3.

[30] *Daniels* v *Heskin* [1954] IR 73 at 81 *per* Lavery J.

infection, the arrangements made for future observation and care and innumerable other considerations.[31]

The current Supreme Court has determined that the duty of disclosure regarding the risks of a procedure or intervention, in the therapeutic setting, is an antecedent duty of care, similar to the duty of care in diagnosis and treatment. Thus, as to whether or not treatment without adequate disclosure amounted to a trespass or negligence, it was held that claims of trespass should be confined to cases where there was no consent to the particular procedure and where it was feasible to seek such consent. Thus,

> If there had been such a failure to give a warning as to possible future risks that would not involve the artificial concept of an assault, but, rather, a possible breach of duty of care giving rise to a claim in negligence.[32]

A decision of the Chief Justice of Canada was relied upon, thus:

> I can appreciate the temptation to say that the genuineness of consent to medical treatment depends on proper disclosure of the risks which it entails, but in my view, unless there has been misrepresentation or fraud to secure consent to the treatment, a failure to disclose the attendant risks, however serious, should go to negligence rather than to battery. Although such a failure relates to an informed choice of submitting to or refusing recommended and appropriate treatment, it arises as the breach of an anterior duty of care, comparable in legal obligation to the duty of due care in carrying out the particular treatment to which the patient has consented. It is not a test of the validity of the consent.[33]

---

[31] [1954] IR 73 at 87.

[32] *Walsh* v *Family Planning Services & others* [1992] IR 496 at 531, *per* O'Flaherty J.

[33] *Reibl* v *Hughes* (1980) 114 DLR (3d) 1 at 10 (Sup Ct Canada) *per* Laskin CJ.

As to how the standard of care, however, is to be determined, the Court was divided. In Britain, since *Bolam* v *Friern Hospital Management Committee*[34] the test for the standard of care required of a medical practitioner — in diagnosis and treatment — has been that of the ordinary skilled person exercising and professing to have that special skill. As McNair J in his direction to the jury stated:

> . . . a doctor is not guilty of negligence if he has acted in accordance with a practice accepted as proper by a responsible body of medical men skilled in that particular art. . . . Putting it the other way round, a doctor is not negligent if he is acting in accordance with such a practice, merely because there is a body of opinion that takes a contrary view.[35]

Characterised as the *Bolam* test, this, in effect, is no more than judicial recognition of what is generally referred to as adherence to different "schools of thought". Thus, it is a recognised fact of clinical life that medical practitioners may disagree as to the most appropriate approach to be taken in any given condition. The traditional legal view had been that where more than one school of thought was adhered, or subscribed, to by a respectable[36] body of professional opinion, adherence to one rather than to the other did not establish breach of the appropriate standard of care or negligence. As to whether or not a particular practice is one that is general and approved is a matter of fact to be determined as any

---

[34] [1957] 2 All ER 118, [1957] 1 WLR 583.

[35] [1957] 2 All ER 118 at 122, [1957] 1 WLR 583 at 587.

[36] Sometimes characterised as "a *responsible* body of medical men" or "a competent *reasonable* body of opinion" (see *Bolam* v *Friern Hospital Management Committee* [1957] 2 All ER 118 at 122, [1957] 1 WLR 583 at 587–588), or a "*respectable* body of professional opinion" (see *Maynard* v *West Midlands Regional Health Authority* [1985] 1 All ER 635 at 639, [1984] 1 WLR 634 at 639, *per* Scarman LJ) or "approved of and adhered to by a substantial number of *reputable* practitioners" (see *Dunne* v *National Maternity Hospital & others* [1989] IR 91, [1989] ILRM 735).

other.[37] In the earlier case of *Marshall* v *Lindsey County Council*[38]
Maugham LJ had stated:

> . . . in this matter, as in so many others, the doctors differ,
> and in the presence of this undoubted honest difference of
> opinion it is not open in my opinion to a jury to hold that it
> is negligence to accept one view rather than the other.

This was quoted with approval in *Daniels* v *Heskin*[39] where
Kingsmill Moore J went on to say:

> I should like to say with emphasis that an honest difference
> of opinion between eminent doctors, as to which is the bet-
> ter of two ways of treating a patient, does not provide any
> ground for leaving a question to the jury as to whether a
> person who has followed one course rather than the other
> has been guilty of negligence. It would be different if a doc-
> tor had expressed the opinion that the course adopted was
> definitely erroneous.[40]

In effect, it is not for the court (whether judge or jury) to decide
which of the two alternative courses is, in its opinion, preferable.
The sole function of the court is merely to decide whether the
course followed, on the evidence, complied with the careful conduct of a medical practitioner of like specialisation and skill to
that professed by a defendant doctor. In *Bolitho* v *City and Hack-
ney Health Authority*,[41] however, a unanimous House of Lords effectively restated the test of the standard of care required of a
medical practitioner to defeat liability in negligence. Browne-
Wilkinson LJ noted that the decided cases:

---

[37] See for example, *O'Donovan* v *Cork County Council* [1967] IR 173; *Dunne* v
National Maternity Hospital & Others [1989] IR 91, [1989] ILRM 735.

[38] [1935] 1 KB 516.

[39] [1954] IR 73 (Supreme Court).

[40] [1954] IR 73 at 85 (Supreme Court).

[41] [1997] 4 All ER 771 (13 November 1997).

show[ed] that the court has to be satisfied that the exponents of the body of opinion relied on can demonstrate that such opinion has a logical basis. In particular, in cases involving, as they so often do, the weighing of risks against benefits, the judge before accepting a body of opinion as being responsible, reasonable or respectable, will need to be satisfied that, in forming their views, the experts have directed their minds to the question of comparative risks and benefits and have reached a defensible conclusion on the matter.[42]

In a dictum of Sachs LJ in *Hucks* v *Cole*,[43] on which Browne-Wilkinson LJ relied in *Bolitho*,[44] it had been held:

When the evidence shows that a lacuna in professional practice exists by which risks of grave danger are knowingly taken, then, however small the risks, the court must anxiously examine that lacuna — particularly if the risks can be easily and inexpensively avoided. If the court finds, on an analysis of the reasons given for not taking those precautions that, in the light of current professional knowledge, there is no proper basis for the lacuna, and that it is definitely not reasonable that those risks should have been taken, its function is to state that fact and where necessary to state that it constitutes negligence.[45]

However troublesome this dictum is — on several levels — it nevertheless anticipates that the court ought to reserve to itself the right to have the final say on the issue of determining the standard of care in deciding the question of the liability of medical practitioners in negligence. In *Bolitho*, Browne-Wilkinson LJ went on to hold:

---

[42] [1997] 4 All ER 771 at 778.

[43] (1968) reported as (1993) 4 Med LR 393.

[44] [1997] 4 All ER 771 at 778.

[45] (1968) (1993) 4 Med LR 393 at 397. This has echoes of the earlier Scottish decision of *Hunter* v *Hanley* (1955) SLT 213 (1st division).

. . . in cases of diagnosis and treatment there are cases where, despite a body of professional opinion sanctioning the defendant's conduct, the defendant can properly be held liable for negligence (I am not here considering questions of disclosure of risk). In my judgment, that is because, in some cases, it cannot be demonstrated to the judge's satisfaction that the body of opinion relied on is reasonable or responsible. In the vast majority of cases, the fact that distinguished experts in the field are of a particular opinion will demonstrate the reasonableness of that opinion. In particular, where there are questions of assessment of the relative risks and benefits of adopting a particular medical practice, a reasonable view necessarily presupposes that the relative risks and benefits have been weighed by the experts in forming their opinions. But if, in a rare case, it can be demonstrated that the professional opinion is not capable of withstanding logical analysis, the judge is entitled to hold that the body of opinion is not reasonable or responsible.

I emphasise that, in my view, it will very seldom be right for a judge to reach the conclusion that views genuinely held by a competent medical expert are unreasonable. The assessment of medical risks and benefits is a matter of clinical judgment which a judge would not normally be able to make without expert evidence. . . . it would be wrong to allow such assessment to deteriorate into seeking to persuade the judge to prefer one of two views, both of which are capable of being logically supported. It is only where a judge can be satisfied that the body of expert opinion cannot be logically supported at all that such opinion will not provide the bench mark by reference to which the defendant's conduct falls to be assessed.[46]

This appears to suggest an assessment on the basis of consideration of the probability, gravity and cost of prevention of the damage, and the social utility of the doctor's conduct as in cases of

---

[46] [1997] 4 All ER 771 at 779.

"ordinary" negligence — albeit with an expert gloss. This restatement of *Bolam* is an echo of Walsh J in *O'Donovan* v *Cork County
Council*[47] where he expressed the following view:

> A medical practitioner cannot be held negligent if he hon-
> ours general and approved practice in the situation with
> which he is faced . . . That proposition is not, however,
> without qualification. If there is a common practice which
> has inherent defects, which ought to be obvious to any per-
> son giving the matter due consideration, the fact that it is
> shown to have been widely and generally adopted over a
> period of time does not make the practice any the less neg-
> ligent. Neglect of duty does not cease by repetition to be ne-
> glect of duty.[48]

This was restated and affirmed in *Dunne* v *National Maternity
Hospital & others*.[49] Here, as in *Bolitho*, the appropriate standard
to be applied in cases of disclosure was not considered. However,
in *Walsh* v *Family Planning Services & others*[50] Finlay CJ (with
whom McCarthy J agreed), applied the "test" laid down in *Dunne*
v *National Maternity Hospital & others*[51] to the issue of disclosure
prior to treatment. Thus, the disclosure of the risks of treatment
was considered to be a matter of professional judgment (the
Bolam test[52]), except where the disclosure of a particular risk was
so obviously necessary to an informed choice on the part of the
patient that no reasonably prudent medical man would fail to
make it (modified by *Donovan*).[53] The Chief Justice stated that he
was:

---

[47] [1967] IR 173 (Supreme Court).

[48] [1967] IR 173 at 193 (Supreme Court).

[49] [1989] IR 91, [1989] ILRM 735.

[50] [1992] IR 496.

[51] [1989] IR 91, [1989] ILRM 735.

[52] *Bolam* v *Friern Hospital* [1957] 2 All ER 118, [1957] 1 WLR 583.

[53] *Donovan* v *Cork County Council* [1967] IR 173 (SC).

. . . satisfied that there is, of course, where it is possible to do so, a clear obligation on a medical practitioner carrying out or arranging for the carrying out of an operation, to inform the patient of any possible harmful consequence arising from the operation, so as to permit the patient to give an informed consent to subjecting himself to the operation concerned. I am also satisfied that the extent of this obligation must, as a matter of common sense, vary with what might be described as the elective nature of the surgery concerned.[54]

However, other members of the Court were of the view that the Court should determine not alone the existence of the duty of care, but also the standard of care. Thus O'Flaherty J (with whom Hederman J agreed) held that:

[Disclosure is] a matter for the trial judge, in the first instance, to find whether there has been a breach of duty of care owed by the defendants to a person such as the plaintiff. This has to be resolved on the established principles of negligence. This was the approach of the Supreme Court of Canada in *Reibl* v *Hughes*.[55] . . . [in the case of elective surgery] if there is a risk — however exceptional or remote — of grave consequences involving severe pain stretching for an appreciable time into the future and involving the possibility of further operative procedures, the exercise of the duty of care owed by the defendants requires that such possible consequences should be explained in the clearest language to the plaintiff.[56]

In England, the resolution of the appropriate standard of care in disclosure has been equally problematic. Thus, in the leading

---

[54] [1992] IR 496 at 510, *per* Finlay CJ. Although Egan J agreed with Finlay CJ and McCarthy J in terms of allowing the appeal, his judgment is not clear as to which approach he favoured in addressing the issue of the standard of care in disclosure.

[55] (1980) 114 DLR (3d) 1 (Sup Ct Canada).

[56] [1992] IR 496 at 535, *per* O'Flaherty J.

decision of the House of Lords on the issue, *Sidaway* v *Governors of Bethlem Royal Hospital*,[57] the Law Lords were also divided on the correct approach. Lord Diplock favoured the application of the *Bolam* test, i.e. what to tell a patient is a matter of clinical decision making, the standard of disclosure to be determined by the profession itself as in matters of diagnosis and treatment. Lord Scarman favoured full disclosure of all material risks incident to the proposed treatment so that the patient, rather than the medical practitioner, could make the real decision as to whether or not to undergo treatment.[58] This approach has obvious practical difficulties. Lord Bridge and Lord Keith, on the other hand, while favouring the application of the *Bolam* test, considered where disclosure of a particular risk "as so obviously necessary to an informed choice on the part of the patient that no reasonably prudent medical man would fail to make it".[59] This latter approach is effectively a preview of *Bolitho*.[60] Lord Templeman, for his part, took the view that the duty of the doctor — who must have regard to the best interests of the patient — is to "provide the patient with information which will enable the patient to make a balanced judgment if the patient chooses to make a balanced judgment".[61]

That said, however, in the later case of *Farrell* v *Varian*,[62] O'Hanlon J relied on *Sidaway* and, in particular, the judgments of Bridge and Lord Keith — essentially a *Dunne/Bolitho* approach.

---

[57] [1985] AC 871.

[58] O'Flaherty's view, in *Walsh* v *Family Planning Services & others* [1992] IR 496, effectively reflects this view.

[59] [1985] AC 871 at 900 *per* Lord Bridge. This was the approach favoured by Finlay CJ and McCarthy J in *Walsh* v *Family Planning Services & others* [1992] IR 496. See also R.F.V. Heuston and R.A. Buckley (1992), *Salmond & Heuston on the Law of Torts*, 20th Edition, London: Sweet & Maxwell, pp. 236–7; and B. McMahon and W. Binchy (1990), *Irish Law of Torts*, 2nd Edition, Dublin: Butterworth (Ireland) Ltd., p. 269.

[60] See above at p. 516.

[61] [1985] AC 871 at 905.

[62] High Court, Unreported Judgment, O'Hanlon J, 19 September 1994.

As a matter of practicality, his approach is worth noting. He stated:

> With regard to the nature and extent of the warning which should be given to a patient contemplating an operation, I am of the opinion that the doctor's obligation does not extend to enumerating all the possible risks, however remote, which are involved. Such a procedure could only subject many patients to unnecessary fears and worries, and possibly have the effect of deterring many patients from submitting to treatment which it was obviously in their best interests to undergo.

In *Bolton* v *Blackrock Clinic & others*,[63] the High Court appeared to accept that the standard of care in relation to disclosure was to be determined on ordinary negligence principles. However, on appeal, and without reference to the basis of the decision in the High Court, the Supreme Court decided that the matter ought to be determined on the *Dunne* principles.[64] In summary, therefore, the definitive determination in Ireland of the standard of care in disclosure must await another day.

However, in Britain, notwithstanding that *Bolitho* (just as *Dunne*) expressly excluded consideration of disclosure, to the extent that *Bolam* is now modified by *Bolitho*, so *Sidaway* — and the duty of disclosure — must now be taken to be also decided on *Bolitho* principles. If so, the decision of the Court of Appeal in *Gold* v *Haringey Health Authority*[65] — in which leave to appeal to the House of Lords was refused — as to the interpretation of *Sidaway* must also be regarded as suspect.[66] In Ireland, in

---

[63] High Court, Unreported Judgment, Geoghegan J, 20 December 1994.

[64] *Bolton* v *Blackrock Clinic & others* (Supreme Court, Unreported Judgment, 23 January 1997, Hamilton CJ, Barrington and Murphy JJ). See W. Binchy and C. Craven (1998), "Doctors in the Dock", *Gazette Law Society of Ireland*, Vol. 92, No. 5, pp. 18–21. This also appears to have been the approach adopted by the High Court in *Reid* v *Beaumont Hospital Board & another* (High Court, Unreported Judgment, Johnson J, 18 July 1997).

[65] [1987] 2 All ER 888, [1988] QB 481.

[66] See also the views expressed in Kennedy and Grubb (1994), op. cit., p. 187.

contrast to *Gold* v *Haringey* — which involved an elective procedure — there is an apparently greater readiness on the part of the
court to interfere in such cases. As Finlay CJ noted in *Walsh*, the
obligation or duty to disclose risks:

> . . . must, as a matter of common sense, vary with what
> might be described as the elective nature of the surgery
> concerned . . . the obligation to give a warning of the possi-
> ble harmful consequences of a surgical procedure which
> could be said to be . . . elective . . . may be more stringent
> and onerous . . . [I]t may be, certainly in relation to very
> clearly elective surgery, that the court might more readily
> reach a conclusion that the extent of warning given or omit-
> ted contained inherent defects which ought to have been
> obvious to any person giving the matter due consideration
> than it could do in a case of complicated medical or surgical
> procedures, and an allegation that, although generally
> adopted, they were inherently unsafe.[67]

Given *Bolitho* — and the inevitable effect it must have on the interpretation of the majority opinions in *Sidaway* — and considering the approach taken by the Irish courts on the issue, the final
say as to the determination of the standard of care in disclosure
prior to interventions must be regarded as being in the hands of
the courts, and not the medical profession. In psychiatry, however, where many agents have not insignificant side-effects, and
capacity to consent may be impaired, the problems presented in
relation to non-disclosure of risks has yet to be specifically addressed by our courts. That a relatively benign approach might be
taken is suggested by McCarthy J's approach in *Murphy* v
Greene[68] where he stated:

---

[67] *Walsh* v *Family Planning Services & others* [1992] IR 496 at 510–511, *per*
Finlay CJ (with whom McCarthy J agreed).

[68] [1990] 2 IR 566.

The standard of reasonable care under the Act may be quite different from such standard in ordinary medical practice.[69]

In addition, irrespective of the approach actually taken, the conclusions of the courts also recognise (either implicitly or explicitly), the existence of the *therapeutic privilege*, i.e. a *privilege*, if not an actual obligation, in some instances, to keep from a patient certain information about proposed treatment where disclosure would be likely to be positively injurious. Although some information may be withheld for this reason, the nature and the extent of what may be withheld remains undefined. Nevertheless, given the thrust of the written decisions, there can be little doubt but that, although the exercise of such a privilege is a matter for clinical decision-making, it remains subject to the overriding control of the court. Although the extent of judicial benediction for the exercise of this privilege in the context of treatment of psychiatric disorder remains to be determined, dicta as to the paternalistic nature of the legislation on involuntary detention and the application of a different standard of care[70] suggest a relatively benign approach. With the advent of Mental Health Review Boards,[71] the scope for definition should increase.

RESEARCH

Advances in psychiatry are research dependent, just like advances in any other branch of medicine. The thrust of modern practice is directed at diagnosis and treatment that is evidence-based. Thus, research is also central to the justification of procedures and treatments currently employed. In Britain, research in

---

[69] [1990] 2 IR 566 at 581 (albeit expressed in a section 260 application (see Chapter 18, p. 418, fn 6), the approach suggests judicial benediction that might not otherwise be forthcoming). This dictum was applied in *Melly* v *Moran* (High Court, Unreported Judgment, McGuinness J, 19 June 1997), although the decision was overturned on appeal (Supreme Court, Unreported Judgment, 28 May 1998).

[70] Above, pp. 505–9.

[71] White Paper on a New Mental Health Act (Department of Health, 1995) para. 6.12.

humans — unlike research on animals — has never been regulated by statute, although since 1991, the Department of Health has issued guidelines on local research ethics committees. In Ireland, pharmacological trials are subject to the provisions of the Control of Drugs and Clinical Trials Acts, 1987 and 1990. However, the legislation has no application to research involving radiation exposure,[72] in which circumstances, common law provisions must be relied upon and the provisions of the Declaration of Helsinki (1989) adhered to.

Insofar as the disclosure of risks of research prior to participation in such research is concerned, the dictum in *Halushka* v *University of Saskatchewan*[73] is apposite:

> There can be no exceptions to the ordinary requirements of disclosure in the case of research as there may well be in ordinary medical practice. The researcher does not have to balance the probable effect of lack of treatment against the risk involved in the treatment itself. The example of risks being properly hidden from a patient where it is important that he should not worry can have no application in the field of research.
>
> The subject of medical experimentation is entitled to a full and frank disclosure of all the facts, probabilities and opinions which a reasonable man might be expected to consider before giving his consent.[74]

Thus, there is no role for the exception provided by the therapeutic privilege. Insofar as research involving radiation exposure (which the Medical Exposures Directive expressly contemplates)

---

[72] The studies referred to throughout this text that indicate findings on CT or MRI scanning clearly fall within this category. This has assumed a particular importance because of the Medical Exposures Directive (97-43 Euratom of 30 June 1997) — which is required to be introduced into the domestic legislation of all member states by 13 May 2000).

[73] 53 DLR (2d) 436 at 442–443 (Sask. CA 1965).

[74] See McMahon and Binchy (1990), op. cit., pp. 269–70, and the footnotes thereto and Kennedy and Grubb (1994), op. cit., pp. 1059–60, wherein they consider that the "reasonable" standard does not go far enough.

is concerned, Article 3(1)(c) provides that medical exposure for biomedical and medical research must be examined by an ethics committee, set up in accordance with national procedures and/or by the competent authorities. In both Britain and Ireland, this, in the absence of statutory requirements, would be in accordance with NHS guidelines and local customs, respectively. Article 4(2)(b) goes on to provide that for each biomedical and medical research project *inter alia* it must be ensured that:

1. The individuals concerned participate voluntarily,

2. These individuals are informed about the risks of the exposure,

3. In the case of patients who voluntarily accept to undergo an experimental diagnostic or therapeutic practice and who are expected to receive a diagnostic or therapeutic benefit from this practice, the target levels of doses are planned on an individual basis.

Thus, a ceiling must be established in respect of exposure whether the research is potentially therapeutic or purely non-therapeutic. Insofar as the issues of voluntariness and risk disclosure are concerned, these must be determined in accordance with domestic law. Although the law in both Britain and Ireland in respect of liability for non-disclosure in the therapeutic setting is unhappy[75] and somewhat unclear, *Halushka* should be considered the appropriate touchstone. Irish legislation in respect of pharmacological trials provides a useful model of disclosure. Furthermore, it provides a model in respect of the voluntariness of consent to participate in research.[76]

---

[75] See above, pp. 503–24.

[76] See below, pp. 532–4.

Statutory Control of Clinical Research in Ireland

In the context of clinical research involving pharmacological agents, the Control of Clinical Trials Act, 1987,[77] has given full expression to the requirement for full and informed consent. It serves to vindicate the right of the citizen to privacy and bodily integrity and it addresses, directly, the vexed question as to whether or not proxy consent can be given on behalf of a person under a disability to participate in research which is not to his benefit. It provides as follows.

When May a Clinical Trial be Conducted?

A person may not conduct a clinical trial unless

1. He is a registered medical practitioner or a registered dentist, and

2. The Minister has granted permission in respect of that trial, and

3. Ethics committee approval has been granted.[78]

"Conducting a clinical trial", for the purposes of the Act, means:

the conducting of a systematic investigation or series of investigations for the purpose of ascertaining the effects

---

[77] As amended by the Control of Clinical Trials and Drugs Act, 1990 (Number 17 of 1990), and the Irish Medicines Board Act, 1995 (Number 29 of 1995). Introduced in the Seanad in April 1986 following the expression of public concern after the death of a participant in a clinical trial being carried out by a private research company in 1984, where it appeared from the subsequent inquiry and inquest that the young man in question had died as a result of the interaction of the trial drug with another prescribed pharmacologically active agent being taken by him unknown to those conducting the clinical trial. Concern also arose over the manner in which it was alleged that those participating in clinical trials were recruited and the terms under which they participated. The legislation, as initiated, was the object of strong criticisms on wide-ranging grounds by a number of medical bodies, especially the Royal College of Physicians of Ireland, and some 61 amendments were incorporated before it was passed into law on the 22 December 1987. See R. Pearce, *Annotation* [1987] ICLSA.

[78] Control of Clinical Trials Act, 1987, s. 6(1).

(including kinetic effects) of the administration of one or more substances or preparations on persons where such administration may have a pharmacological or harmful effect, *but does not include* the conducting of such a systematic investigation or series of investigations. . . .

(i) where the administration of one or more substances or preparations . . . is on a patient in the ordinary course of medical practice . . . or of dental practice and the principal purpose of that administration is to prevent disease in, or to save the life, restore the health, alleviate the condition or relieve the suffering, of the patient, or

(ii) where the substance or preparation concerned is to be administered to persons undergoing a course of training leading to a qualification which will entitle such a person to be registered as a registered medical practitioner or as a registered dentist or as a registered pharmaceutical chemist and

(iii) where it is to be administered as part of such a course of training, or for the purpose of examining the nutritional effect of the substance or preparation concerned where that substance or preparation is a normal dietary constituent.[79]

"Administration" in this context, means either directly or indirectly to a person by introduction into the body (whether orally, by injection or in any other way) or by external application (whether by direct contact with the body or not).[80] Ordinary therapeutic and training applications are thus excluded from the ambit of the legislation.

---

[79] Control of Clinical Trials Act, 1987, s. 6, as amended by the Control of Clinical Trials and Drugs Act, 1990, s. 2. Thus, trials involving physical agents such as heat, light, manipulations and ultrasound are also excluded from the ambit of the legislation. However, radiopharmaceuticals (for isotope scanning) could be included.

[80] Control of Clinical Trials Act, 1987, s. 1.

Permission to Conduct a Clinical Trial Must be Sought

A person who proposes to arrange for the conducting of a clinical trial must apply to the Irish Medicines Board for permission to make such arrangements *before* the trial is undertaken. The application must set out:

1. The name, address and description of the applicant,

2. Sufficient information to enable a scientific evaluation of the proposed trial and the substance or preparation proposed to be used,

3. The identity (including qualifications) of members of the ethics committee,

4. The name, address and qualifications of each person who is to conduct the trial,

5. The criteria used for the recruitment and selection of participants,

6. Details of any inducements or rewards to be made to prospective participants,

7. Such further information, evidence, documents, samples and other materials as may be necessary to indicate the nature of the trial,

8. The appropriate fee,

9. The Irish Medicines Board may request such further information as may, in their opinion, assist them in their decision.[81]

Permission to Conduct a Clinical Trial

The Irish Medicines Board must within 12 weeks either:

1. Grant permission for the proposed clinical trial to be undertaken in accordance with the application, or

---

[81] Control of Clinical Trials Act, 1987, s. 3, as amended by the Irish Medicines Board Act, 1995, s. 35.

2. Grant such permission subject to such modifications or conditions as they may specify, or

3. Refuse to grant permission (with reasons).

Furthermore, a clinical trial may not be conducted until the ethics committee for the trial has given its approval.[82]

Amendment of Application

Where it is proposed to conduct the clinical trial other than in accordance with the permission granted, application must be made to the Irish Medicines Board which, within six weeks, may either agree, or refuse to agree, to the proposed amendment of the permission. Where there is such agreement, it must not be acted upon until the ethics committee has given its approval to the amendment. In addition, in the case of a trial already approved by the ethics committee, the amendment must not be acted upon until the participants in the trial have been made aware of such matters as the committee considers they should be aware of, having regard to the amendment.[83]

Revocation of Permission

The Irish Medicines Board may, at any time, and giving reasons therefor, revoke a permission to conduct a clinical trial if they are of the opinion that the trial (or any part thereof) is being conducted in a manner not in accordance with the permission, or, for any other reason the trial should not continue.[84]

---

[82] Control of Clinical Trials Act, 1987, s. 4, as amended by the Irish Medicines Board Act, 1995, s. 35.

[83] Control of Clinical Trials Act, 1987, s. 5, as amended by the Irish Medicines Board Act, 1995, s. 35.

[84] Control of Clinical Trials Act, 1987, s. 7, as amended by the Irish Medicines Board Act, 1995, s. 35.

The Ethics Committee

The Irish Medicines Board must be satisfied that the ethics committee proposed for the clinical trial is competent to consider the justification for conducting the proposed clinical trial and the circumstances under which it is to be conducted. If so satisfied, approval of the ethics committee is granted. The composition of an ethics committee may, at any time, be changed with the approval of the Board.

The ethics committee must firstly consider the justification for conducting the proposed clinical trial. In this regard, the ethics committee must be satisfied that the risks to participants would be commensurate with the objectives of the trial. The ethics committee must also consider the circumstances under which the clinical trial is to be conducted, having regard *inter alia* to:

1. The objectives of the proposed trial and its planning and organisational structure;

2. The qualifications and competence of each person who is to conduct the trial and the resources available to him;

3. The criteria for the recruitment and selection of participants;

4. The procedures for compliance with participant consent;

5. The extent and nature of the medical examination that persons selected as participants are to undergo before participation;

6. The extent to which the health of participants is proposed to be monitored during and after the clinical trial;

7. Whether or not the persons selected as participants are to undergo independent medical examination before, during or after the clinical trial;

8. Details of the proposed methods of recruitment;

9. Details of any proposed inducements or rewards to be made for becoming or being a participant;

10. Any payments to be made to a person for conducting the clinical trial or any part thereof;

11. The criteria to be used to ensure that the identity of each participant remains confidential;

12. Any payments to be made to any person for facilities used for the purposes of the clinical trial;

13. Such other matters as may be prescribed by regulations under the Act.

If the ethics committee is satisfied that the proposed trial is justified, and with the circumstances under which it is proposed to be conducted, approval is given to the person who is arranging to conduct the proposed trial who must, in turn, communicate that approval, in writing, to the Board.[85]

Consent to Participation

Consent to participation must be given in accordance with the Act and is not valid unless:

1. It is given in writing, signed by the person participating; and

2. The person consenting is capable of comprehending the nature, significance and scope of his consent; and

3. It is obtained by, or on behalf of, the person conducting the clinical trial.

Consent to participation may be withdrawn at any time without incurring any contractual liability and no inducement or reward, other than that provided for in the permission to undertake the clinical trial, may be offered to any person for becoming or being a participant.

The person conducting the clinical trial must ensure that every participant, *before* giving his consent, is made aware of:

---

[85] Control of Clinical Trials Act, 1987, s. 8, as amended by the Irish Medicines Board Act, 1995, s. 35.

1. The objectives of the trial; and

2. The manner in which the substance or preparation is to be administered; and

3. The risks of any discomfort involved in, and the possible side-effects of, the trial; and

4. Whether or not a pharmacologically inactive substance or preparation [a placebo] is to be administered to some consenting participants; and

5. Such other matters as may be prescribed by regulations under the Act or specified in the permission to conduct the clinical trial.

Furthermore, a clinical trial must not be conducted on any person within the period of six days after disclosure has been made to the participant (unless the permission, or any amendment thereto, specifies otherwise). Therefore, full disclosure is mandatory and written consent is required.

However, if it is proposed to conduct a clinical trial on any person suffering from an illness, the remedy or alleviation of which constitutes an objective of the trial and where the substance or preparation under trial is to be administered for the purpose of saving the life of the person, restoring his health, alleviating his condition or relieving his suffering:

1. Where the person is capable of comprehending the nature, significance and scope of a consent to be given but is physically unable to give such consent in writing, his consent clearly given in any other manner is sufficient if given in the presence of two witnesses present at the same time, to a registered medical practitioner who is treating him for that illness and if the consent is expressed in writing and is attested by the signatures of both witnesses;

2. Where the person is incapable of comprehending the nature, significance and scope of a consent to be given, he may be a participant only if a written and signed consent is given by a

person or persons, independent of the person who applied to undertake or is conducting the trial, who, in the opinion of the ethics committee, is or are competent to give a decision on such participation.[86]

It is questionable as to whether persons suffering from psychiatric disability can fulfil the statutory criteria so as to be in a position to give a proper personal consent. If that is so, proxy consent may only be invoked for therapeutic research. Research, which is not therapeutic and not directed at the wellbeing of the subject thereof, is prohibited. That said, the limits of the legislation and the validity of any proxy consent purported to have been given in pursuance of its provisions, remain to be tested in the courts. As security for compensation is required to be provided under the Act,[87] such a determination of the limits of proxy consent may be some way off.

---

[86] Control of Clinical Trials Act, 1987, s. 9, as amended by the Irish Medicines Board Act, 1995, s. 35.

[87] See Control of Clinical Trials Act, 1987, s. 10, as amended by the Control of Clinical Trials and Drugs Act, 1990, s. 3, as amended by the Irish Medicines Board Act, 1995, s. 35. The furnishing of information to the Minister is required by s. 11, as amended by the Irish Medicines Board Act, 1995, s. 35, and offences, punishments and defences are prescribed in ss. 12 and 13, as amended by the Control of Clinical Trials and Drugs Act, 1990, ss. 4 and 14.

Chapter 20

CONFIDENTIALITY[1]

A duty of confidence has been said to arise:

> . . . when confidential information comes to the knowledge
> of a person . . . in circumstances where he has notice, or is
> held to have agreed, that the information is confidential,
> with the effect that it would be just in all the circumstances
> that he should be precluded form disclosing the information
> to others.[2]

Codes of professional ethics in both Britain[3] and Ireland[4] regard
confidentiality as fundamental to the doctor/patient relationship
and as a time-honoured principle of medical ethics. According to
Hippocrates:

---

[1] See, generally, A-M O'Neill (1995), "Matters of Discretion: the Parameters
of Doctor–Patient Confidentiality", *Medico-Legal Journal of Ireland*, Vol. 1,
No. 3, pp. 94–104; K. Doran (1996), "The Doctrine of Confidentiality: the Le-
gal Protection of Medical Records", *Medico-Legal Journal of Ireland*, Vol. 2,
No. 3, pp. 86–91; K. Doran (1997) "Medical Confidentiality: the Role of the
Doctrine of Confidentiality in the Doctor–Patient Relationship", *Medico-
Legal Journal of Ireland*, Vol. 3, No. 1, pp. 21–6; K. Doran (1997), "The Legal
Position Governing Access to Medical Records", *Medico-Legal Journal of Ire-
land*, Vol. 3, No. 2, pp. 50–6. This chapter is not concerned with the provi-
sions of the Data Protection Act, 1988, or the Data Protection (Access
Modification) (Health) Regulations, 1989, which limits personal access to
medical records. See D. Tomkin and P. Hanafin (1993), *Irish Medical Law*,
Dublin: The Round Hall Press, pp. 52–4.

[2] *A-G* v *Guardian Newspapers Ltd. (No. 2)* [1988] 3 All ER 545 at 658–659,
[1988] 3 WLR 776 at 805 *per* Lord Goff (the *Spycatcher* case).

[3] General Medical Council (1993), *Professional Conduct and Discipline: Fitness to Practise* (the "Blue Book"), London: General Medical Council.

[4] The Medical Council (1993), *A Guide to Ethical Conduct and Behaviour and
to Fitness to Practise*, 4th Edition, Dublin: The Medical Council.

> Whatsoever things I see or hear concerning the life of men,
> in my attendance on the sick or even apart therefrom,
> which ought not to be noised abroad, I will keep silence
> thereon, counting such things to be as sacred secrets.

Patient information, especially in the area of psychiatric disability, may be particularly sensitive. A duty of confidentiality is basic to the therapeutic relationship in that it facilitates proper management based on full disclosure — in a setting of confidence without fear of unauthorised access to the information by a third party to the patient's detriment. Thus, the preservation of confidentiality has been characterised as being in the public interest.[5] In *X* v *Y*[6] Rose J captured the essence of the interest:

> In the long run, preservation of confidentiality is the only
> way of securing public health; otherwise, doctors will be
> discredited as a source of education, for future individual
> patients "will not come forward if doctors are going to
> squeal on them". Consequently, confidentiality is vital to
> secure public as well as private health, for unless those in-
> fected come forward they cannot be counselled and self-
> treatment does not provide the best care.[7]

It is not determined by the patient's death and continues thereafter.[8] Information received by a clinician about a patient in a professional respect must not be disclosed to any person without the patient's consent. The situation with respect to confidential information about a patient obtained in a professional capacity from a third party is not expressly dealt with. However, it seems that similar considerations apply.[9] In this regard, the clinician is

---

[5] *X* v *Y* [1988] 2 All ER 648.

[6] [1988] 2 All ER 648.

[7] [1988] 2 All ER 648 at 653.

[8] "Blue Book", para. 91. However, see Kennedy, Grubb (1993), op. cit., p. 643.

[9] There are no reported cases on this point, although newspaper reports of February 1997 indicated that an inquiry had been carried out into the disclosure by a consultant of certain information he had received in respect of a patient from a third party — who was not his patient — after that third

effectively regarded as being in a fiduciary relationship with the patient. That said, the breadth of the duty is dependent on the circumstances. As Bingham LJ stated in *W* v *Edgell*:[10]

> Where a prison doctor examines a remand prisoner to determine his fitness to plead or a proposer for life insurance is examined by a doctor nominated by the insurance company or a personal injury plaintiff attends on the defendant's medical adviser . . . the professional man's duty of confidence towards the subject of his examination plainly does does not bar disclosure of his findings to the party at whose instance he was appointed to make his examination.[11]

Furthermore, certain situations arise whereby it is regarded as ethically permissible to disclose confidential information without the patient's prior consent. They are characterised under two broad headings — in the private and in the public interest. The private interest issue[12] is self-explanatory. However, although the basis of the law's protection of confidence is that there is a public interest that confidences (as defined) should be protected and protected by the law, nevertheless

> . . . that public interest may be outweighed by some other countervailing public interest which favours disclosure.[13]

---

party's death. It was reported that the practitioner had been censured by the Medical Council. Being a censure, it was not a determination of a type capable of being appealed to the High Court.

[10] [1990] 1 All ER 835 (CA).

[11] [1990] 1 All ER 835 at 848 (CA). However, the important point here is in relation to "findings". The better view is that prior to such an examination, it is recommended that the doctor should explain the nature, context and reporting implications of the examination, and then only the *significance* of the medical findings, rather than the precise details, should be disclosed — except with the consent of the person examined. However, in cases of unfitness to plead, both explanation and consent may be difficult, by virtue of the condition from which the person is suffering. See Chapter 17.

[12] See below, p. 538.

[13] *A-G* v *Guardian Newspapers Ltd (No. 2)* [1988] 3 All ER 545 at 659, [1988] 3 WLR 776 at 807 *per* Lord Goff (the *Spycatcher* case).

To regard the duty of confidentiality as an expression of the protection of an individual's constitutional right to privacy[14] is also capable of admitting similar exceptions.

IN THE PRIVATE INTEREST

When Necessary to Protect the Interests of the Patient

Clinicians are rarely, if ever, solely responsible for the patients under their care. This applies across clinical specialities, and especially in psychiatry, where the consultant is usually the leader of a multidisciplinary team comprising psychiatric nurses, community psychiatric nurses, psychologists, social workers, occupational therapists and workshop managers. The obligation is probably best expressed in the "Blue Book" which states:

> Most doctors in hospital and general practice are working in health care teams, some of whose members may need access to information, given or obtained in confidence about individuals, in order to perform their duties. It is for doctors who lead such teams to judge when it is appropriate for information to be disclosed for that purpose. They must leave those whom they authorise to receive such information in no doubt that it is given to them in professional confidence . . .[15]

Therefore, notwithstanding that the other members of the team may not be members of a profession, properly so called, with ethical canons in respect of confidentiality, the duty nevertheless is imposed with the passing of the information and the circumstances in which it is passed. However, although it is also considered that there is a responsibility to ensure that arrangements exist to inform patients of the circumstances in which information about them is likely to be shared and to give patients the opportunity to state any objection to this,[16] the view has been expressed

---

[14] See *McGee* v *Attorney General* [1974] IR 284 (SC); and *Kennedy* v *Ireland* [1987] IR 587, [1988] ILRM 472 (HC); and below, p. 540.

[15] Blue Book, para. 79.

[16] Blue Book, para. 79.

that the law may not go this far. Thus, implied consent to the transfer of such information may be permitted whenever the circumstances justify it.[17] It might be anticipated that in the management of those with psychiatric disorder in particular, that necessity — absent express consent — would be sufficient justification.

IN THE PUBLIC INTEREST

On Foot of an Order for Discovery

Either during the course of litigation, or during the course of an inquiry pursuant to the provisions of the Tribunal of Inquiries (Evidence) Acts, 1921 and 1979, discovery of medical records may be ordered, either against an individual who is a proper party to the proceedings, or against the institution or persons who hold the individual's records. Thus, where a litigant refuses to disclose his clinical records, which the other party or parties claim to be relevant to the determination of the proceedings, an order for discovery may be made if the court is satisfied that the documents sought to be disclosed are relevant. A similar order may be obtained against an institution or other individual (e.g. general practitioner), where necessary. Rarely, the records of a person who is not a party to the litigation may be discovered. Thus, it has been reported that the Tribunal of Inquiry into the Blood Transfusion Service Board[18] ordered discovery of the clinical and laboratory records of certain patients who had been treated with the Board's products, where those records were considered to be central to the issues the Tribunal had to determine. Similar orders were made in the High Court in related litigation. In such circumstances, a masking order — such that the identity of the person to whom the records relate cannot be identified — may also be made. Although it might have been considered not to have been required, notwithstanding the making of such orders, however, an

---

[17] Kennedy and Grubb (1993), op. cit., pp. 644–5, which also discusses the defence of discretionary disclosure on "a need-to-know basis".

[18] The "Finlay Inquiry", March 1997.

institution or individual served with such an order might consider it prudent to notify the patient whose records are the subject matter of the order. But any practice of not notifying the party whose records are sought must be considered questionable.[19] If the patient had not been a notice party to the application, this then permits such appeal or objections as he might consider appropriate to be considered. The justification for the making of such orders lies in the public interest in the proper prosecution of litigation — having all appropriate matters before a court — and, accordingly, the proper administration of justice or the proper carrying out of a judicial inquiry into matters of public concern. These are considered to outweigh the private interest of an individual in insisting on maintaining confidentiality in respect of his medical history. Nevertheless, only discovery of that which is necessary and relevant will be ordered; hence the use of a masking order in appropriate circumstances.

When Necessary to Protect the Welfare of Society

Statutory provisions require the notification to public health authorities of persons known or suspected to be suffering from certain infectious diseases.[20] Although expressed in terms of treatment, in this regard, the extra-judicial observation of Costello J (as he then was) is apposite as justification:

> . . . in the case of contagious diseases, the claims of the common good might well justify restrictions on the exercise of a constitutionally protected right to refuse medical treatment.[21]

---

[19] See *Haughey* v *Moriarty* (Supreme Court, Unreported Judgment, 28 July 1998, Hamilton CJ, Denham, Barrington, Keane, Murphy JJ).

[20] Health Act, 1947, and the Infectious Disease Regulations, Public Health (Control of Disease) Act, 1984. In Britain, provision is also made under the National Health Service (Venereal Diseases) Regulations, 1974 (SI 29 of 1974), for contact tracing.

[21] "The Terminally Ill: The Law's Concern" (1986) XXI Ir. Jur. (n.s.) 35, quoted with approval in *In the matter of A Ward of Court (withholding medical treatment) (No. 2)* [1996] 2 IR 100 at 125 *per* Hamilton CJ.

Such consideration could also be used to justify both notification of contagious disease and, accordingly, a restriction on a constitutional right to privacy. In *Kennedy v Ireland*,[22] Hamilton P (as he then was), in dealing with the extent of the right to privacy, noted:

> It is not an unqualified right. Its exercise may be restricted by the constitutional rights of others, or by the requirements of the common good . . . in certain circumstances the exigencies of the common good may require and justify . . . intrusion and interference . . . [with one's communications of a private nature].[23]

The statutory provisions are clear as to the categories of conditions in respect of which reporting is required. The mischief that is sought to be addressed is also clear. Psychiatric conditions do not fall into a similar category. In respect of individuals who indicate — in the context of a psychiatric consultation — that they have been, or are, engaged in the sexual abuse of others, or are the victims of such abuse, in the absence of mandatory reporting, there is no absolute requirement or, it might be argued, justification, for breaching a patient's confidentiality, without consent, on that ground alone. This arises, not least because of the therapeutic nature of the relationship. That said, breach in the interest of the protection of another might be justifiable.

In other situations, confidential information may be collated for research purposes, or for clinical audit. In those circumstances, the professional canons require that patient anonymity be protected.[24]

---

[22] [1987] IR 587, [1988] ILRM 472 (HC). See also, generally, *National Irish Bank v RTE*, High Court, Unreported Judgment, Shanley J, 6 March 1998; D. Donnelly and T. O'Sullivan (1998), "A Question of Balance: Private Rights of Confidentiality against the Public Interest", *Bar Review*, Vol. 3, No. 9, pp. 431–8.

[23] [1987] IR 587 at 592, [1988] ILRM 472 at 476 (HC).

[24] In this regard, it might be noted that a negligent failure to do so ought to be judged on ordinary rather than on professional negligence principles.

When Necessary to Safeguard the Welfare of Another Individual or Patient

Ethically, this is one of the most difficult issues to resolve. The judicial *locus classicus* is *Tarasoff* v *Regents of the University of California*.[25] Here the family of the deceased, Tatiana Tarasoff, claimed that her death had been caused by the failure of a psychologist, and his superior, both employees of the defendant university, to warn her that a patient had confided his intention to kill her some weeks before he actually did. The Supreme Court of California was cognisant of the competing interests:

> We recognise the public interest in supporting effective treatment of mental illness and in protecting the rights of patients to privacy, and the consequent public importance of safeguarding the confidential nature of psychotherapeutic communication. As against this interest, however, we must weigh the public interest in safety from violent assault . . .

As a practical matter, the court noted:

> . . . that the open and confidential character of psychotherapeutic dialogue encourages patients to express threats of violence, few of which are ever executed. Certainly a therapist should not be encouraged routinely to reveal such threats. . . . [his] obligations to his patient require that he not disclose a confidence unless such disclosure is necessary to avert danger to others, and even then that he do so discreetly, and in a fashion that would preserve the privacy of his patient to the fullest extent compatible with the prevention of the threatened danger.

The conclusion, which recites the universality of the ethical principle, is apposite:

> The revelation of a communication under [these] circumstances is not a breach of trust or a violation of professional ethics; as stated in the Principles of Medical Ethics of the

---

[25] (1976) 131 Cal Rptr 14 (Supreme Court of California).

American Medical Association (1957), section 9: "A physician may not reveal the confidence entrusted to him in the course of medical attendance . . . *unless he is required to do so by law or unless it becomes necessary in order to protect the welfare of the individual or of the community.*" [*emphasis added*] We conclude that the public policy favouring protection of the confidential character of patient–psychotherapist communications must yield to the extent to which disclosure is essential to avert danger to others. The protective privilege[26] ends where the public peril begins. . . . we see no sufficient societal interest that would protect and justify concealment. The containment of such risks lies in the public interest.

That said, however, the principle has been applied differently in different jurisdictions in the United States. Thus, some courts have held that it applies whenever it is foreseeable that persons will be endangered by a patient. Others have required that not only a victim, but a readily identifiable victim, be foreseeable.[27] And therein lies the problem — as an ability to warn a third party about the dangerous propensities of a patient may, as a matter of practicality, be well nigh impossible on the facts. The analogy of infectious disease may be illustrative of the problem. In respect of communicable diseases (e.g. HIV), the identification of the party likely to be at risk may well be considerably easier. If, however, an infected patient was merely promiscuous with an identifiable class of persons, no one member of which could be actually identified, then the ability to warn — notwithstanding professional canons — may not be possible.[28]

In the later case of *W* v *Edgell*[29] there was no readily identifiable victim, other than the public at large. Here, *W*, who was

---

[26] Under the California Evidence Code, such communications would ordinarily be privileged. Such legal privilege is not part of Irish or British law.

[27] See Kennedy and Grubb (1993), op. cit., p. 669 and the cases cited therein.

[28] It should be noted that HIV is not a notifiable disease for the purpose of the Infectious Disease Regulations.

[29] [1990] 1 All ER 835.

suffering from schizophrenia,[30] had been detained as a patient in a secure hospital without limit as to time[31] after he shot and killed five people and wounded two others. Ten years later he applied to a mental health review tribunal[32] to be discharged or transferred to a secure regional unit with a view to his eventual discharge. Although the hospital psychiatrist supported the application, it was opposed by the Secretary of State, and Dr Edgell was instructed by W's solicitors to examine W and to report on his condition with a view to using the report in support of the application. Dr Edgell, having examined W, opposed the application and drew attention to W's longstanding interest in firearms and explosives. In the circumstances, the solicitors elected to withdraw the application. When Dr Edgell learned that his report had not been put either to the tribunal or to the hospital who were looking after W, he contacted the medical director of the hospital who, having discussed the case, agreed that the hospital should receive a copy of the report in the interests of W's further treatment. Also, at Dr Edgell's prompting, the hospital sent a copy of the report to the Secretary of State who, in turn, forwarded it to the tribunal when referring the case to them for consideration. W subsequently sought an injunction restraining use or disclosure of the report and damages. Having failed in the High Court,[33] his appeal was dismissed by a unanimous Court of Appeal. Sir Stephen Brown P, having considered the nature of the competing interests and the relevant law (including the guidelines of the General Medical Council),[34] was of the view that what was involved was a balancing of two public interests and that:

---

[30] See Chapter 15.

[31] See Chapter 16.

[32] See Chapter 18 on civil committal. There are no equivalent legislative provisions in Ireland, although they are recommended by the White Paper on a New Mental Health Act (Department of Health, 1995). In fact, persons so detained are excluded from the provisions of the Mental Treatment Act, 1945, by the provisions of s. 284.

[33] [1980] 1 All ER 1089, [1989] 2 WLR 689.

[34] See fn 3 above.

The balance of public interest clearly lay in the restricted disclosure of vital information to the director of the hospital and to the Secretary of State who had the onerous duty of safeguarding the public safety. . . . It is clear that Dr Edgell did have highly relevant information about W's condition which reflected on his dangerousness. . . . The suppression of the material contained in [the] report would have deprived both the hospital and the Secretary of State of vital information, directly relevant to questions of public safety.[35]

The conclusion of Bingham LJ contains an echo of *Tarasoff*:

Where a man has committed multiple killings under the disability of serious mental illness, decisions which may lead directly or indirectly to his release from hospital should not be made unless a responsible authority is properly able to make an informed judgment that the risk of repetition is so small as to be acceptable. A consultant psychiatrist who becomes aware, even in the course of a confidential relationship, of information which leads him in the exercise of what the court considers a sound professional judgment, to fear that such decisions may be made on the basis of inadequate information and with a real risk of consequent danger to the public, is entitled to take such steps as are reasonable in all of the circumstances to communicate the grounds of his concern to the responsible authorities.[36]

On the facts of *Edgell*, the feasibility of disclosure was readily apparent. However, the problems of a more general propositional nature raised by *Tarasoff* remain. The issue has yet to arise in an Irish context.

---

[35] [1990] 1 All ER 835 at 846.

[36] [1990] 1 All ER 835 at 852 to 853.

Furthermore, the practical impact of the extension of the Freedom of Information Act, 1997, to health authorities, general practitioners and voluntary hospitals, has yet to be assessed.[37]

---

[37] See, generally, K. Doran and D. Cusack (1997), "Access to Medical Records: the Effect of the Freedom of Information Act 1997", *Medico-Legal Journal of Ireland*, Vol. 3, No. 3, pp. 107–8.

BIBLIOGRAPHY

Abel, G.G., J.V. Becker and J. Cunningham-Rathner (1984), "Complications, Consent and Cognitions in Sex between Children and Adults", *International Journal of Law and Psychiatry*, Vol. 7.

Achte, K.A., E. Hillbom and V. Aalberg (1967), *Post-Traumatic Psychosis Following War Brain Injuries*, Report from The Rehabilitation Institute for Brain-Injured Veterans in Finland, Vol. 1, Helsinki.

Adams, R.D., C.M. Fisher, S. Hakim, R.G. Ojemann and W.H. Sweet (1965), "Symptomatic Occult Hydrocephalus with 'Normal' Cerebrospinal Fluid Pressure: a Treatable Syndrome", *New England Journal of Medicine*, Vol. 273, pp. 117–26.

American Psychiatric Association (1994), *Diagnostic and Statistical Manual*, Fourth edition, Washington, DC: American Psychiatric Association.

Andrews, B., J. Morton, D. Bekerian et al. (1995), "The Recovery of Memories in Clinical Practice", *The Psychologist*, Vol. 8, pp. 209–14.

Balla, J.L. and S. Moraitis (1970), "Knights in Shining Armour — a Follow-up Study of Injuries after Legal Settlement", *Medical Journal of Australia*, Vol. 2, pp. 355–61.

Barbach, L.G. and M. Flaherty (1980), "Group Therapy in Situationally Orgasmic Women", *Journal of Sex and Marital Therapy*, Vol. 6, pp. 19–29.

Bard, M. and D. Sangrey (1986), *The Crime Victim's Book*, 2nd edition, New York: Brunner Mazel.

Barlow, D.H. (1988), *Anxiety and its Disorders: The Nature and Treatment of Panic*, New York: Guildford Press.

Beck, A.T. (1962), "Reliability of Psychiatric Diagnoses: A Critique of Systematic Studies", *American Journal of Psychiatry*, Vol. 119, pp. 210–16.

Beck, A.T., A. Freeman et al. (1992), *Cognitive Therapy for Personality Disorders*, New York: Guildford Press.

Beck, A.T., C.H. Ward, M. Mendelson, J. Mock and J. Erbaugh (1961), "An Inventory for Measuring Depression", *Archives of General Psychiatry*, Vol. 4, pp. 561–71.

Bell, P., M. Kee, G.C. Loughrey, P.S. Curran and R.J. Roddy (1988), "Post-Traumatic Stress in Northern Ireland", *Acta Psychiatrica Scandinavica*, Vol. 77, pp. 166–9.

Bench, C.J., R.J. Dolan, K.J. Friston and R.S.J. Frackowiak (1990), "Positron Emission Tomography in the Study of Brain Metabolism in Psychiatric and Neuropsychiatric Disorders", *British Journal of Psychiatry*, Vol. 157 (suppl. 9), pp. 82–95.

Binchy, W. (1984), *A Casebook on Irish Family Law*, Dublin: Professional Books.

Binchy, W. (1988), *Irish Conflicts of Laws*, Dublin: Butterworths (Ireland) Ltd.

Binchy, W. and C. Craven (1998), "Doctors in the Dock", *Gazette Law Society of Ireland*, Vol. 92, No. 5, pp. 18–21.

Bisson, J.I. and M.P. Deahl (1994), "Psychological Debriefing and Prevention of Post-Traumatic Stress Disorder: More Research is Needed", *British Journal of Psychiatry*, Vol. 165, pp. 717–20.

Boehnlein, J.K. (1989), "The Process of Research in Post Traumatic Stress Disorder", *Perspectives in Biological Medicine*, Vol. 32, pp. 455–65.

Bolster, M., F. O'Garabhan and J. Harbison (1995), "Dyadic Deaths in Ireland", *Medico-Legal Journal of Ireland*, Vol. 1, No. 3, pp. 91–4.

Bowlby, J. (1984), *Attachment and Loss, Vol. 1: Attachment*, 2nd edition, Harmondsworth: Penguin.

Brady, J.C. (1995), *Succession Law in Ireland*, 2nd Edition, Dublin: Butterworths.

Bramley, P.M. and N.V. Lowe (1992), *Bromley's Family Law*, 8th edition, Butterworths.

Brandon, S., J. Boakes, D. Glaser and R. Green (1998), "Recovered Memories of Childhood Sexual Abuse", *Implications for Clinical Practice*, Vol. 172, pp. 296–307.

Breslau, N., G.C. Davis, P. Andreski and E. Peterson (1991), "Traumatic Events and Post-Traumatic Stress Disorder in an Urban Population of Young Adults", *Archives of General Psychiatry*, Vol. 48, pp. 216–22.

Brown, G.R. and B. Anderson (1991), "Psychiatric Morbidity in Adult Inpatients with Childhood Histories of Sexual and Physical Abuse", *American Journal of Psychiatry*, Vol. 148, pp. 55–61.

Brown, G.W. and J.L.T. Birley (1968), "Crisis and Life Changes and the Onset of Schizophrenia", *Journal of Health and Social Behaviour*, Vol. 9, pp. 203–14.

Brown, G.W. and T. Harris (1978), *Social Origins of Depression*, London: Tavistock Publications.

Brown, S.A. and M.A. Schuckit (1988), "Changes in Depression among Abstinent Alcoholics", *Journal of Studies in Alcohol*, Vol. 49, pp. 412–17.

Burnstein, A., P.E. Ciccone, R.A. Greenstein, N. Daniels, K. Olsen, A. Malarek and N. Johnson (1988), "Chronic Vietnam PTSD and Acute Civilian PTSD: A Comparison Of Treatment Experiences", *General Hospital Psychiatry*, Vol. 10, pp. 245–9.

Byrne, R. and W. Binchy (1997), *Annual Review of Irish Law 1996*, Dublin: Round Hall Sweet & Maxwell.

Calhoun, K.S., B.M. Atkeson and P.A. Resick (1982), "A Longitudinal Examination of Fear Reactions in Victims of Rape", *Journal of Counselling Psychology*, Vol. 29, pp. 655–61.

Campbell, E.J.M., J.G. Scadding and R.S. Roberts (1979), "The Concept of Disease", *British Medical Journal*, Vol. 2, pp. 757–62.

Canino, G., M. Bravo, M. Rubio-Stipec and M. Woodbury (1990), "The Impact of Disasters on Mental Health: Prospective and Retrospective Analyses", *International Journal of Mental Health*, Vol. 19, pp. 51–69.

Card, R. (1988), *Cross Jones and Card: Introduction to Criminal Law*, 11th edition, London: Butterworths.

Casey, P. (1994), "Panic Disorder", *Irish Medical Journal*, Vol. 4, No. 9.

Casey, P. (1996), "Litigation and the Toxicity of Psychotropic Drugs", (Reply), *Irish Journal of Psychological Medicine*, Vol. 13, No. 3, pp. 89–90.

Casey, P.R. (1997), "Clinical Assessment of Personality", *Advances in Psychiatric Treatment*, Vol. 3, pp. 182–7.

Castle, D. and R.M. Murray (1991), "The Neurodevelopmental Basis of Sex Differences in Schizophrenia", *Psychological Medicine*, Vol. 21, pp. 565–75.

Charney, D.S., A.Y. Deutch, J.H. Krystal, S.M. Southwick and M. Davis (1993), "Psychobiological Mechanisms of Post-Traumatic Stress Disorder", *Archives of General Psychiatry*, Vol. 50, pp. 294–305.

Chui, H.C., E.L. Teng and V.W. Henderson (1985), "Clinical Subtypes of Dementia of Alzheimer Type", *Neurology*, Vol. 35, pp. 1544–50.

Clark, J.B. and J.G. Ross Martin (1993), *Theobald on Wills*, 15th edition, London: Sweet & Maxwell.

Clarke, A.M. and A.D.B. Clarke (eds.) (1965), *Mental Deficiency: the Changing Outlook*, 2nd edition, London: Methuen.

Cohen, M.L., R. Garofolo, R. Boucher and T. Steghorn (1971), *The Psychology of Rapists, Seminars in Psychiatry*, Vol. 3, pp. 307–27, New York: Grune and Stratton.

Cooney, T. and O. O'Neill (1996), *Psychiatric Detention and Civil Commitment in Ireland*, Delgany: Baikonur.

Coughlan, P. (1998), *Property Law*, 2nd Edition, Dublin: Gill & Macmillan.

Cretney, S.M. and J.M. Masson (1997), *Principles of Family Law*, 6th edition, London: Sweet & Maxwell.

Crosby, M., L. Hutchinson, M. O'Malley and A. O'Connor (1995), "Section 207 of the Mental Treatment Act 1945: A Critical Review of its use, 1955–1994", *Medico-Legal Journal of Ireland*, Vol. 1, No. 1, pp. 11–12.

Crowe, M. and C. Dare (1998), "Survivors of Childhood Sexual Abuse: Approaches to Therapy", *Advances in Psychiatric Treatment*, Vol. 4, No. 2, pp. 96–100.

Crowe, R.R., R. Noyes, D.L. Paul and D. Slymen (1983), "A Family Study of Panic Disorders", *Archives of General Psychiatry*, Vol. 40, pp. 1065–9.

Davidson, J. (1992), "Pharmacological Treatments in PTSD", *British Journal of Psychiatry*, Vol. 160, pp. 309–14.

Davison, K., and C.R. Bagley (1969), "Schizophrenia-like Psychosis Associated with Organic Disorders of the Central Nervous System: a Review of the Literature" in R.N. Herrington (ed.), *Current Problems in Neuropsychiatry*, *British Journal of Psychiatry Special Publication No. 4*, Ashford, Kent: Headley Brothers.

De Paulo, B., J. Stone and G. Lassiter (1985), "Deceiving and Detecting Deceit" in B. Schlenker (ed.), *The Self and Social Life*, New York: McGraw-Hill.

Department of Health (1984), *The Psychiatric Services: Planning for the Future*, Dublin: Government Publications.

Department of Health (1995), White Paper on a New Mental Health Act, July, Dublin: Department of Health.

Derogatis, L.R. (1986), "The Psychosocial Adjustment to Illness Scale (PAIS)", *Journal of Psychosomatic Research*, Vol. 30, pp. 77–91.

Deutsch, L. (1992), "Bias, Confusion, Emotion Led to Verdict, Responses Show", *Champaign-Urbana News Gazette*, May.

Dodson, C. and D. Reisberg (1991), "Indirect Testing of Eyewitness Memory: the (Non-) Effect of Misinformation", *Bulletin of the Psychonomic Society*, Vol. 29, pp. 333–6.

Donnelly, D. and T. O'Sullivan (1998), "A Question of Balance: Private Rights of Confidentiality against the Public Interest", *Bar Review*, Vol. 3, No. 9, pp. 431–8.

Doran, K. (1996), "The Doctrine of Confidentiality: the Legal Protection of Medical Records", *Medico-Legal Journal of Ireland*, Vol. 2, No. 3, pp. 86–91.

Doran, K. (1997) "Medical Confidentiality: the Role of the Doctrine of Confidentiality in the Doctor–Patient Relationship", *Medico-Legal Journal of Ireland*, Vol. 3, No. 1, pp. 21–6.

Doran, K. (1997), "The Legal Position Governing Access to Medical Records", *Medico-Legal Journal of Ireland*, Vol. 3, No. 2, pp. 50–6.

Doran, K. and D. Cusack (1997), "Access to Medical Records: the Effect of the Freedom of Information Act 1997", *Medico-Legal Journal of Ireland*, Vol. 3, No. 3, pp. 107–8.

Duncan, W.R. and P.E. Scully (1990), *Marriage Breakdown in Ireland*, Dublin: Butterworths (Ireland) Ltd.

Durkheim, E. (1951), *Suicide: a Study in Sociology*, Translated by J. Spaulding and G. Simpson, New York: Free Press.

Encel, S. and C.E. Johnson (1978), *Compensation and Rehabilitation: A Survey of Worker's Compensation Involving Back Injuries and Lump Sum Payments*, Sydney: New South Wales University Press.

Endicott, J. and R.L. Spitzer (1978), "A Diagnostic Review: the Schedule for Affective Disorders and Schizophrenia", *Archives of General Psychiatry*, Vol. 35, pp. 837–44.

Ersland, S., L. Weisaeth and A. Sund (1989), "The Stress upon Rescuers Involved in an Oil Rig Disaster, 'Alexander L. Kielland', 1980", *Acta Psychiatrica Scandinavica* (supplement 355), Vol. 80, pp. 131–7.

Eysenck, H.J. and S.B.G. Eysenck (1964), *Manual of the Eysenck Personality Inventory*, London: University of London Press.

Femina, D.D., C.A. Yeager and D.O. Lewis (1990), "Child Abuse: Adolescent Records vs. Adult Recall", *Child Abuse and Neglect*, Vol. 145, pp. 227–31.

Fennell, C. (1992), *The Law of Evidence in Ireland*, Dublin, Butterworths (Ireland) Ltd.

Fenwick, P. (1993), "Brain, Mind and Behaviour: Some Medico-Legal Aspects", *British Journal of Psychiatry*, Vol. 163, pp. 565–73.

Finkelhor, D. (1984), *Child Sexual Abuse: New Theory and Research*, New York: Free Press.

Finkelhor, D. (1994), "The International Epidemiology of Child Sexual Abuse", *Child Abuse and Neglect*, Vol. 18, pp. 409–17.

Finnane, M. (1981), *Insanity and the Insane in Post-Famine Ireland*, London: Croom Helm.

Fleming, J.G. (1987), *The Law of Torts*, 7th Edition, Sydney: The Law Book Company.

Flor-Henry, P. (1987), "Cerebral Aspects of Sexual Deviation", in G.D. Wilson (ed.), *Variant Sexuality: Research and Theory*, Baltimore: John's Hopkins University Press.

Folstein, M.F., S.E. Folstein and P.R. McHugh (1975), "'Mini-Mental State': a Practical Method for Grading the Cognitive State of Patients for the Clinician", *Journal of Psychiatric Research*, Vol. 12, pp. 189–98.

Frank, J.B., T.R. Kosten, E.L. Giller et al. (1988), "A Randomised Clinical Trial of Phenelzine and Imipramine for Post-Traumatic Stress Disorder", *American Journal of Psychiatry*, Vol. 145, pp. 1289–91.

Fullerton, C., J. McCarroll, R.J. Ursano and K. Wright (1992), "Psychological Responses of Rescue Workers: Fire-fighters and Trauma", *Journal of Orthopsychiatry*, Vol. 62, pp. 371–8.

Garner, D.M. and P.E. Garfinkel (1979), "The Eating Attitudes Test: an Index of Symptoms of Anorexia Nervosa", *Psychological Medicine*, Vol. 9, pp. 273–9.

Garry, M., C.G. Manning, E.L. Loftus and S.J. Sherman (1996), "Imagination Inflation: Imagining a Childhood Event Inflates Confidence that it Occurred", *Psychonomic Bulletin Review*, Vol. 3, pp. 208–14.

General Medical Council (1993), *Professional Conduct and Discipline: Fitness to Practise* (the "Blue Book"), London: General Medical Council.

Ginsberg, D., I. Marks and H. Waters (1984), "Cost-Benefit Analysis of a Controlled Trial of Nurse Therapy for Neurosis in Primary Care", *Psychological Medicine*, Vol. 14.

Gittleson, N.L., S.E. Eacott and B.M. Metha (1978), "Victims of Indecent Sexual Exposure", *British Journal of Psychiatry*, Vol. 132, pp. 61–5.

Goldberg, D.P. (1972), *The Detection of Psychiatric Illness by Questionnaire*, Oxford: Oxford University Press.

Goldberg, E.M. and S.L. Morrison (1963), "Schizophrenia and Social Class", *British Journal of Psychiatry*, Vol. 109, pp. 785–802.

Goldfield, A.E., R.F. Mollica, B.H. Pesavento and S.V. Farone (1988), "The Physical and Psychological Sequelae of Torture: Symptomatology and Diagnosis", *Journal of the American Medical Association*, Vol. 259, pp. 2725–9.

Goodrich, "Emotional Disturbance as Legal Damage" (1922), 20 Mich. L. Rev. 497.

Green, B.L., J.D. Lindy, M.C. Grace, G.C. Glesser, A.C. Leonard, M. Korol and C. Winget (1990), "Buffalo-Creek Survivors in the Second Decade: Stability of Stress Symptoms", *American Journal of Orthopsychiatry*, Vol. 60, pp. 43–54.

Green, B.L., M.C. Grace, J.D. Lindy, G.C. Gleser and A. Leonard (1990), "Risk Factors for PTSD and Other Diagnoses in a General Sample of Vietnam Veterans", *American Journal of Psychiatry*, Vol. 147, No. 6, pp. 729–33.

Grubin (1991), "Unfit to Plead in England and Wales 1976–86: A Survey", *British Journal of Psychiatry*, Vol. 158, p. 277.

Grubin, D. (1997), "Predictors of Risk in Serious Sex Offenders", *British Journal of Psychiatry*, Vol. 170 (supplement 32).

Gull, W.W. (1868), "The Address in Medicine to the Annual Meeting of the British Medical Association at Oxford", *Lancet*, 8 August, pp. 171–6.

Hamilton, L. (Chief Justice) "The Terminally Ill: The Law's Concern" (1986) XXI Ir. Jur. (n.s.) 35.

Hamilton, M. (1967), "Development of a Rating Scale for Primary Depressive Illness", *British Journal of Social and Clinical Psychology*, Vol. 6, pp. 278–96.

Harrison, G., D. Owens, A. Holton, D. Neilson and D. Boot (1988), "A Prospective Study of Severe Mental Disorder in Afro-Caribbean Patients", *Psychological Medicine*, Vol. 18, pp. 643–57.

Hathaway, S.R. and J.C. McKinley (1940), "A Multiphasic Personality Schedule (Minnesota): 1. Construction of the Schedule", *Journal of Psychology*, Vol. 10, pp. 249–54.

Havard (1956), *Reasonable Foresight of Nervous Shock*, 19 Mod L Rev, p. 478.

Hawton, K. and J. Catalan (1990), "Sex Therapy for Vaginismus: Characteristics of Couples and Treatment Outcome", *Sexual and Marital Therapy*, Vol. 5, pp. 39–48.

Herman, J.L. (1992), "Complex PTSD: a Syndrome in Survivors of Prolonged and Repeated Trauma", *Journal of Traumatic Stress*, Vol. 5, pp. 377–91.

Heuston, R.F.V. and R.A. Buckley (1992), *Salmond & Heuston on the Law of Torts*, 20th Edition, London: Sweet & Maxwell.

Howells, J.G. (1975), *World History of Psychiatry*, New York: Brunner Mazel.

Hucker, S., R. Langevin, R. Dickey, L. Handy, J. Chambers and S. Wright (1988), "Cerebral Damage and Dysfunction in Sexually Aggressive Men", *Annals of Sex Research*, Vol. 1.

Jarman, T. *A Treatise on Wills* by R. Jennings and J.C. Harper (1951), 8th edition, London: Sweet & Maxwell, Vol. 1.

Kassin, S.M., S. Rigby and S. Castillo (1991), "The Accuracy–Confidence Correlation in Eyewitness Testimony: Limits and Extensions of the Retrospective Self-awareness Effect", *Journal of Personality and Social Psychology*, Vol. 61, pp. 698–707.

Keane, T.M., J.M. Caddell and K.L. Taylor (1988), "Mississippi Scale for Combat-Related Post-Traumatic Stress Disorder: Three Studies in Reliability and Validity", *Journal of Consulting and Clinical Psychology*, Vol. 56, pp. 85–90.

Keeton, W.P., D.B. Dobbs, R.E. Keeton and D.G. Owen (1984), *Prosser and Keeton on the Law of Torts*, 5th edition, St Paul, MN: West Publishing Company.

Kelleher, M. (1994), "The Prediction of Suicide and the Law on Abortion", *Irish Journal of Psychological Medicine*, Vol. 11, No. 2., pp. 55–6.

Kelly, J.M. (1994), *The Irish Constitution,* 3rd Edition, G. Hogan and G. Whyte (eds.), Dublin: Butterworths.

Kelly, R. and B.N. Smith (1981), "Post-Traumatic Syndrome: Another Myth Discredited", *Journal of Royal Society of Medicine*, Vol. 74, pp. 274–7.

Kendell, R.E. (1975), *The Role of Diagnosis in Psychiatry*, Oxford: Blackwell Scientific Publications.

Kendell, R.E. and W.J. DiScipio (1968), Eysenck "Personality Inventory Scores of Patients with Depressive Illness", *British Journal of Psychiatry*, Vol. 114, pp. 767–70.

Kennedy, I. and A: Grubb (1994), *Medical Law*, Second Edition, London: Butterworths.

Krug, R.S. (1989), "Adult Male Report of Childhood Sexual Abuse by Mothers: Case Descriptions, Motivations and Long-Term Consequences", Vol. 13.

Lancet (1989), "Psychiatric Intervention after Disaster", Editorial, *Lancet*, Vol. ii, p. 138.

Langevin, R., L. Handy, D. Paitich and A. Russon (1983), "A New Version of the Clarke Sex History Questionnaire for Males" in R. Langevin (ed.), *Erotic Preference, Gender Identity and Aggression*, Hillsdale, NJ: Lawrence Erlbaum.

Lasegue, E.C. (1873), "On Hysterical Anorexia", *Medical Times Gazette*, Vol. 2, pp. 265–9

Laws, D.R. and W.L. Marshall (1990), "A Conditioning Theory of Aetiology and Maintenance of Deviant Sexual Preference and Behaviour" in W.L. Marshall, D.R. Laws and H.E. Barbaree (eds.), *Handbook of Sexual Assault: Issues, Theories and Treatment of the Offender*, New York: Plenum.

Leonard, B. (1996), "Litigation and the Toxicity of Psychotropic Drugs", *Irish Journal of Psychological Medicine*, Vol. 13, No. 3, pp. 89–90.

Levin, S.M. and L. Stava (1987), "Personality Characteristics of Sex Offenders: a Review", *Archives of Sexual Behaviour*, Vol. 16, No. 1, pp. 57–79.

Lindemann, E. (1944), "Symptomatology and Management of Acute Grief", *American Journal of Psychiatry*, Vol. 101, pp. 141–8.

Linder, R. (1965), "Diagnosis: Description or Prescription? A Case Study in the Psychology of Diagnosis", *Perceptual and Motor Skill*, Vol. 20, pp. 1081–92.

Lishman, W.A. (1968), "Brain Damage in Relation to Psychiatric Disability after Head Injury", *British Journal of Psychiatry*, Vol. 114, pp. 373–410.

Lishman, W.A. (1987), *Organic Psychiatry: The Psychological Consequences of Cerebral Disorder*, Oxford: Blackwell Scientific Publications.

Litz, B.T., S.M. Orsillo, M. Freidman, P. Ehlict and A. Batres (1997), "Post-Traumatic Stress Disorder Associated with Peace Keeping Duty in Somalia for US Military Personnel", *American Journal of Psychiatry*, Vol. 154, No. 2, pp. 178–84.

Loughrey, G.C., P. Bell, M. Kee, R.J. Roddy and P.S. Curran (1988), "Post-Traumatic Stress Disorder and Civil Violence in Northern Ireland", *British Journal of Psychiatry*, Vol. 153, pp. 544–60.

Luntz, B.K. (1994), "Antisocial Personality Disorder in Abused and Neglected Children Grown Up", *American Journal of Psychiatry*, Vol. 151, pp. 670–4.

MacFarlane, A. (1992), "Commentary: PTSD among Injured Survivors of a Terrorist Attack", *Journal of Nervous and Mental Diseases*, Vol. 180, pp. 505–9.

Mackay (1991), "The Decline of Disability in Relation to the Trial", *Criminal Law Report*, Vol. 87.

Martin, J.B. and J.F. Gusella (1986), "Huntington's Disease: Pathogenesis and Management", *New England Journal of Medicine*, Vol. 315, pp. 1267–76.

Masters, W.H. and V.E. Johnson (1970), *Human Sexual Inadequacy*, Boston: Little Brown.

Maxwell, T.H. (1900), *Miller's Probate Practice*, Abingdon, Oxford: Professional Books Ltd., 1980 reprint.

Mayou, R., B. Bryant and R. Duthie (1993), "Psychiatric Consequences of Road Traffic Accidents", *British Medical Journal*, Vol. 307, pp. 647–51.

McAuley, F. (1993), *Insanity, Psychiatry and Criminal Responsibility*, Dublin: Round Hall Press.

McElroy, S.L. and P.E. Keck Jr. (1995), "Recovered Memory Therapy: False Memory Syndrome and Other Complications", *Psychiatric Annual*, Vol. 25, pp. 731–5.

McFarlane, A.C. (1988), "The Aetiology of Post Traumatic Stress Disorders Following a Natural Disaster", *British Journal of Psychiatry*, Vol. 152, pp. 116–21.

McFarlane, A.C. (1988), "The Phenomenology of Post-Traumatic Stress Disorder Following a Natural Disaster", *Journal of Nervous and Mental Diseases*, Vol. 176, pp. 22–9.

McMahon, B. and W. Binchy (1990), *Irish Law of Torts* (2nd edition), Dublin: Butterworths (Ireland).

Medical Council, The (1993), *A Guide to Ethical Conduct and Behaviour and to Fitness to Practise*, 4th Edition, Dublin: The Medical Council.

Mendelson, G. (1984), "Follow-up Studies of Personal Injury Litigants", *International Journal of Law and Psychiatry*, Vol. 7, pp. 179–88.

Merskey, H. (1996), "Ethical Issues in Search of Repressed Memories", *American Journal of Psychotherapy*, Vol. 50, pp. 323–35.

Mikkelson, E., T. Gutheil and M. Emens (1992), "Sexual Abuse Allegations by Children and Adolescents: Contextual Factors and Clinical Subtypes", *American Journal of Psychotherapy*, Vol. 46, pp. 556–70.

Mill, J.S. (1859), *On Liberty*, 1980 reprint, Oxford: Clarendon Press.

Miller, H. (1961), "Accident Neurosis", *British Medical Journal*, Vol. 1, pp. 992–8.

Millon, T. (1993), "Borderline Personality Disorder: A Psychosocial Epidemic", in J. Paris (ed.), *Borderline Personality Disorder*, Washington, DC: American Psychiatric Press.

Moran, R. and D. Walsh (1992), *Activities of Irish Psychiatric Hospitals and Units 1991*, Dublin: Health Research Board.

Morgan, J.N., M. Snider and M.G. Sobol (1984), "Lump Sum Redemption Settlements and Rehabilitation" in G. Mendelson, "Follow-up Studies of Personal Injury Litigants", *International Journal of Law and Psychiatry*, Vol. 7, pp. 179–88.

Mullen, P.E., J. Martin, J.C. Anderson, S.E. Romans and G.P. Herbison (1994), "The Effects of Child Sexual Abuse on Social, Interpersonal and Sexual Function in Adult Life", *British Journal of Psychiatry*, Vol. 165, pp. 35–47.

Murphy, W.D., M.R. Haynes and P.J. Worley (1991), "Assessment of Adult Sexual Interest" in C.R. Hollin and K. Howells (eds.), *Clinical Approaches to Sex Offenders and their Victims*, Chichester: John Wiley and Sons.

Nadelson, C.C., M.T. Notman, H. Zackson and J. Gornick (1982), "A Follow-up Study of Rape Victims", *American Journal of Psychiatry*, Vol. 139, pp. 1266–70.

Nash, M.R., T.L. Hulsey, M.C. Sexton, T.L. Harralson and W. Lambert (1993), "Long-term Sequelae of Childhood Sexual Abuse: Perceived Family Environment, Psychopathology and Dissociation", *Journal of Consulting and Clinical Psychology*, Vol. 61, pp. 276–83.

Office of the Attorney General (1976) *The Law of Nullity in Ireland*, Discussion Paper, Dublin: Office of the Attorney General.

Oliver, H.E. (1993), "Intergenerational Transmission of Child Abuse: Rates, Research and Clinical Implications", *American Journal of Psychiatry*, Vol. 150, pp. 1315–24.

O'Neill, A-M (1995), "Matters of Discretion: the Parameters of Doctor–Patient Confidentiality", *Medico-Legal Journal of Ireland*, Vol. 1, No. 3, pp. 94–104.

Overall, J.E. and D.R. Gorsham (1962), "The Brief Psychological Rating Scale", *Psychological Reports*, Vol. 10, pp. 799–812.

Palmer, R.L., L. Coleman, R. Chaloner, R. Oppenhimer and J. Smith (1993), "Childhood Sexual Experiences with Adults: a Comparison of Reports by Women Psychiatric Patients and General Practice Attenders", _British Journal of Psychiatry_, Vol. 163, pp. 499–504.

Paris, J. (1993), "Personality Disorders: A Biopsychosocial Model", _Journal of Personality Disorders_, Vol. 7, No. 3, pp. 255–64.

Pathe, M. and P.E. Mullen (1997), "The Impact of Stalkers on their Victims", _British Journal of Psychiatry_, Vol. 170, pp. 12–17.

Pattie, A.H. and C.J. Gilleard (1976), "The Clifton Assessment Schedule: Further Validation of a Psychiatric Assessment Schedule", _British Journal of Psychiatry_, Vol. 129, pp. 68–72.

Pearce, R., _Annotation_ [1987] ICLSA.

Peck, D.F. and C.M. Shapiro (1990), _Measuring Human Problems: A Practical Guide_, Chichester: John Wiley and Sons.

Perry, E.K., B.E. Tomlinson, G. Blessed, K. Begmann, P.H. Gibson and R.H. Perry (1978), "Correlation of Cholinergic Abnormalities with Senile Plaques and Mental Test Scores in Senile Dementia", _British Medical Journal_, Vol. ii, pp. 1457–9.

Perry, R.H., D. Irving, G. Blessed, A. Fairbairn and E.K. Perry (1990), "Senile Dementia of Lewy Body Type", _Journal of Neurological Science_, Vol. 95, pp. 119–39.

Pokorny, A.D. (1983), "Prediction of Suicide in Psychiatric Patients: Report of a Prospective Study", _Archives of General Psychiatry_, Vol. 40, pp. 249–57.

Pope, H.G., Jr. and J.I. Hudson (1995), "Can Memories of Childhood Sexual Abuse be Repressed?", _Psychological Medicine_, Vol. 25, pp. 121–6.

Pope, H.G., Jr. and J.I. Hudson (1996), "'Recovered Memory' Therapy for Eating Disorders: Implications of the Ramona Verdict", _International Journal of Eating Disorders_, Vol. 19, pp. 139–45.

Quinn, K.M. (1985), "Meet the Malingerer: Clinical Presentation and Detection", _Audio-Digest Psychiatry_, Vol. 14, p. 24.

Richardson, P.J. (ed.) (1997), _Archbold: Criminal Pleadings, Evidence and Procedure_, London: Sweet & Maxwell.

Robertson, E.E., A. Le Roux and J.H. Brown (1958), "The Classical Differentiation of Pick's Disease", *Journal of Mental Science*, Vol. 104, pp. 1000–24.

Robins, L.N., J.E. Helzer, J. Croughan and K.S. Ratcliff (1981), "National Institute of Mental Health Diagnostic Interview Schedule", *Archives of General Psychiatry*, Vol. 38: pp. 381–9.

Robinson, D.N. (1996), *Wild Beasts and Idle Humours: the Insanity Defence from Antiquity to the Present*, Cambridge, MA: Harvard University Press.

Robinson, R.A. (1975), "The Assessment Centre" in G. Howells (ed.), *Modern Perspectives in the Psychiatry of Old Age*, Edinburgh: Churchill Livingstone.

Romans, S.E., J.L. Martin, J.C. Anderson, M.L. O'Shea and P.E. Mullen (1995), "Factors that Mediate between Child Sexual Abuse and Adult Psychological Outcome", *Psychological Medicine*, Vol. 25, pp. 127–42.

Roth, M., E. Tym and C.Q. Mountjoy (1986), "CAMDEX: a Standardised Instrument for the Diagnosis of Mental Disorders in the Elderly with Special Reference to Early Detection of Dementia", *British Journal of Psychiatry*, Vol. 149, pp. 698–709.

Russell, G.F.M. (1979), "Bulimia Nervosa: an Ominous Variant of Anorexia Nervosa", *Psychological Medicine*, Vol. 9, p. 429.

Ryan, R.H. and R.E. Geiselman (1991), "Effects of Biased Information on the Relationship between Eyewitness Confidence and Accuracy", *Bulletin of the Psychonomic Society*, Vol. 29, pp. 7–9.

Scadding, J.G. (1967), "Diagnosis: The Clinician and the Computer", *Lancet*, pp. 877–82.

Sham, P.C., E. O'Callaghan and N. Takei (1992), "Schizophrenia Following Pre-natal Exposure to Influenza Epidemics between 1939 and 1960", *British Journal of Psychiatry*, Vol. 160, pp. 461–6.

Shatter, A. (1997), *Shatter's Family Law*, 4th Edition, Dublin: Butterworths.

Sheldrick, C. (1991), "Adult Sequelae of Child Sexual Abuse", *British Journal of Psychiatry*, Vol. 158 (suppl. 10), pp. 55–62.

Sherrin, C.H., R.F.D. Barlow, R.A. Wallington and S.L. Meadway (1995), *Williams on Wills*, 7th edition, London: Butterworths, Volume I.

Shutt, C.H. and F.C. Dohan (1968), "Neck Injuries to Women in Auto Accidents: a Metropolitan Plague", *Journal of the American Medical Association*, Vol. 206, pp. 2689–92.

Sierles, F.S., Jang-June Chen, R.E. McFarland and M.A. Taylor (1983), "Post-Traumatic Stress Disorder and Concurrent Psychiatric Illness: a Preliminary Report", *American Journal of Psychiatry*, Vol. 140, pp. 1177–9.

Skinner, B.F. (1963), "Behaviourism at Fifty", *Science*, Vol. 140.

Smith, J.C. and B. Hogan (1988), *Criminal Law*, 6th edition, London: Butterworths.

Solomon, S.D. and G.J. Canino (1990), "Appropriateness of DSM-III-R Criteria for Post-Traumatic Stress Disorder", *Contemporary Psychiatry*, Vol. 31, 227–37.

Solomon, Z., M. Mikulincer and E. Avitzur (1988), "Coping, Locus of Control, Social Support and Combat-Related Post-Traumatic Stress Disorder: a Prospective Study", *Journal of Personality and Social Psychology*, Vol. 55, pp. 279–85.

Southwick, S.M., C.A. Morgan, A.L. Nicolaou and D.S. Charney (1997), "Consistency of Memory for Combat Related Traumatic Events in Operation Desert Storm", *American Journal of Psychiatry*, Vol. 154, No. 2, pp. 173–7.

Spellman, J. (1998), "Section 260 of the Mental Treatment Act 1945 Reviewed", *Medico-Legal Journal of Ireland*, Vol. 4, No. 1, pp. 20–4.

Stefano, F. and The Centres for Disease Control, Vietnam Experience Study (1988), "Health Status of Vietnam Veterans — 1: Psychosocial Characteristics", *Journal of the American Medical Association*, Vol. 259, pp. 2701–7.

Steketee, G. and E.B. Foa (1987), "Rape Victims: Post-Traumatic Stress Responses and their Treatment — a Review of the Literature", *Journal of Anxiety Disorders*, Vol. 1, pp. 69–86.

Steller, M. and G. Koenken (1989), "Criteria-based Statement Analysis" in Raskin, D.C. (ed.), *Psychological Methods in Criminal Investigation and Evidence*, New York: Springer, pp. 217–45.

Szasz, T. (1960), "The Myth of Mental Illness", *American Psychologist*, Vol. 15, pp. 113–18.

Tarsh, M.J. and C. Royston (1985), "A Follow-up Study of Accident Neurosis", *British Journal of Psychiatry*, Vol. 146, pp. 18–25.

Taylor, K. (1979), *The Concept of Illness, Disease and Morbus*, Cambridge: Cambridge University Press.

Thompson, D.J. and D. Goldberg (1987), "Hysterical Personality Disorder: the Process of Diagnosis in Clinical and Experimental Settings", *British Journal of Psychiatry*, Vol. 150, pp. 241–5.

Thompson, G.N. (1965), "Post-Traumatic Psychoneurosis — a Statistical Survey", *American Journal of Psychiatry*, Vol. 121, pp. 1043–8.

Tomkin, D. and P. Hanafin (1993), *Irish Medical Law*, Dublin: The Round Hall Press.

Torgersen, S. (1980), "The Oral, Obsessive and Hysterical Personality Syndromes: a Study of Heredity and Environmental Factors by Means of the Twin Method", *Archives of General Psychiatry*, Vol. 37, pp. 1272–7.

Trager, E.P. (1998), "The Insanity Defence Revisited", *Medico-Legal Journal of Ireland*, Vol. 4, No. 1, pp. 15–19.

Tyrer, P. (1989), "Choice of Treatment in Anxiety" in P. Tyrer (ed.), *Psychopharmacology of Anxiety*, pp. 255–82, Oxford: Oxford University Press.

Tyrer, P. and J. Alexander (1979), "Classification of Personality Disorders", *British Journal of Psychiatry*, Vol. 135, pp. 163–7.

Vaughn, C.E. and J.P. Leff (1976), "Influence of Family and Social Factors on the Course of Psychiatric Illness", *British Journal of Psychiatry*, Vol. 129, pp. 125–37.

Veitch, E. (1972), "Solatium — A Debt Repaid?", *Irish Jurist*, Vol. V11, pp. 77–95.

Wechsler, D. (1958), *The Measurement and Appraisal of Adult Intelligence*, Baltimore, MD: Williams and Wilkins.

Welch, S.L. and C.G. Fairburn (1994), "Sexual Abuse and Bulimia Nervosa: Three Integrated Case Control Comparisons", *American Journal of Psychiatry*, Vol. 151, pp. 402–7.

White, J.P. (1989), *Irish Law of Damages for Personal Injuries and Death*, Dublin: Butterworths, Part III.

Widom, C.S. (1984), "Child Abuse, Neglect and Adult Behaviour: Research Design and Findings on Criminality, Violence and Child Abuse", *American Journal of Orthopsychiatry*, Vol. 59, pp. 355–67.

Williams, Glanville (1961), *Criminal Law: The General Part*, 2nd edition, London: Stevens & Sons Ltd.

Williams, L.M. (1994), "Recall of Childhood Trauma: a Prospective Study of Women's Memories of Child Sexual Abuse", *Journal of Consulting and Clinical Psychology*, Vol. 62, pp. 1167–76.

Wing, J.K., J.E. Cooper and N. Sartorius (1974), *The Measurement and Classification of Psychiatric Symptoms*, London: Cambridge University Press.

Wolf, S.C. (1985), "A Multi-factor Model of Deviant Sexuality", *Victimology: An International Journal*, Vol. 10.

World Health Organisation (1992), *International Classification of Diseases*, Tenth Edition, Geneva: World Health Organisation.

Younstrom, N. (1991), "Legal Terms may Elude Jurors in Capital Cases". *American Psychological Association Monitor*, October.

Zahn, T.P., R. Moraga and W.J. Ray (1996), "Psycho-physiological Assessment of Dissociative Disorders" in L.K. Michelson and W.J. Ray (eds.), *Handbook of Dissociation: Theoretical, Empirical and Clinical Perspectives*, New York: Plenum, pp. 269–87.

Zaragoza, M.S. and K.L. Mitchell (1996), "Repeated Exposure to Suggestion in the Creation of False Memories", *Psychological Science*, Vol. 7, pp. 294–305.

INDEX